IN A
DARK
WOOD

Playing God in Yellowstone

Group Memory:
A Guide to College and Student
Survival in the 1980s

IN A
DARK
WOOD

The Fight over Forests
and the Rising Tyranny
of Ecology

ALSTON CHASE

A RICHARD TODD BOOK

Houghton Mifflin Company

BOSTON   NEW YORK   1995

Library of Congress Cataloging-in-Publication Data

Chase, Alston.
In a dark wood : the fight over forests and
the rising tyranny of ecology / Alston Chase.
p.   cm.
"A Richard Todd book."
Includes index.
ISBN 0-395-60837-6
1. Old growth forests — Northwest, Pacific.   2. Forest
conservation — Northwest, Pacific.   3. Nature conservation —
Northwest, Pacific.   4. Forest ecology — Northwest, Pacific.
5. Logging — Northwest, Pacific.   I. Title.
SD387.O43C48   1995
333.75'17'09795 — dc20   95-22128   CIP

Book design by Anne Chalmers
Map on page xxiv by Jacques Chazaud
Text type: Trump Medieval (Adobe)
Ornament: Rococo Two (Monotype)

Printed in the United States of America

MP 10 9 8 7 6 5 4 3 2 1

For information about this and other Houghton Mifflin
trade and reference books and multimedia products, visit
The Bookstore at Houghton Mifflin on the World Wide Web
at http://www.hmco.com/trade/.

To the memory of my mother,

who loved nature,
pursued art,
and
relished the life of the mind

What force moves nations? . . . The movement of peoples is not produced by the exercise of power; nor by intellectual activity, nor even by a combination of the two, as historians have supposed; but by the activity of *all* men taking part in the event.

Leo Tolstoy

Ideas shape the course of history.

John Maynard Keynes

CONTENTS

PREFACE

MOST ENVIRONMENTAL — and antienvironmental — stories are moral tracts that depict life as a struggle between the forces of good and evil. But *In a Dark Wood* does not fit this form. It is a tale without heroes or villains, in which the bad guy isn't a person at all but an idea.

Yet, as often happens to authors, I came upon the idea in question almost by accident, and after a long odyssey. Every book is, in a sense, a voyage of discovery. A reader opens the cover with hopes of traveling to strange and wonderful places, or meeting interesting people, or discovering truths that will enhance or even transform his or her life. So, too, writing a book is a journey. The author goes in search of unknown lands and often reaches destinations quite different from those expected. And along the way he or she is profoundly changed by the journey.

In a Dark Wood represents the culmination of such wandering, which began in April 1973. I was a burned-out college professor then, outraged by the war in Vietnam and depressed by student and faculty assaults on the liberal arts. Seeking renewal, my wife and I did what many of my students had done: returned to nature. We purchased an old homestead in the remote mountains of Montana and moved there in 1975, after I gave up my academic tenure. But before leaving academe, in January 1974, I took an entire college class to the ranch for winter term. The course I offered was called "A Retreat Seminar on Environmental Ethics."

At the time I thought of myself as an environmentalist, as I still do. But I wondered: What was the connection between the political revolution I was witnessing on campus and the sudden concern for nature? Was environmentalism, a political movement, successfully achieving its aims, which were supposedly defined by the science of ecology?

My effort to answer these questions prompted me to write *Playing God in Yellowstone*, which appeared in 1986. At the time (and, indeed, even today), that park was governed by a principle known as "ecosystems management." Until beginning work on *Playing God*, I had never heard of this policy; but, knowing that it was supported by the environmental community, I fully expected to find that it did indeed preserve natural values. Instead I discovered that Yellowstone was losing critical vegetation and wildlife, and that the cause of this decline was precisely the "environmental" philosophy itself.

This conclusion shocked many people, including me. But even more surprising was the public response to it. As expected, the Reagan administration hated *Playing God*, even banning sale of the book in Yellowstone. By contrast, I was pleased that the work was warmly received by most scholars, including many in the National Park Service. The most disturbing reaction came from environmentalists, who either ignored the book or, alternatively, portrayed its author as both curmudgeonly and conniving. Despite my efforts, I failed to stimulate debate on ecosystem management within the conservation community. Environmentalists simply would not discuss the issue. Even when I pleaded with George Frampton, then director of the Wilderness Society and at this writing assistant secretary of the interior, to look at the evidence I had collected, he refused.

This was my epiphany. By writing *Playing God*, I had unwittingly violated an unspoken taboo. Belief in the mysterious ecosystem was deemed an absolute requirement for those who called themselves environmentalists. The subject was simply not open to discussion. To these faithful, the concept retained political appeal despite its failures. But what was the source of this allure?

Rather than pursue this question directly, I decided to leave the subject and write a different kind of book, which would become *In a Dark Wood*. I set out to explore the anatomy of the fight over old-growth forests and threatened species in the Pacific Northwest — the biggest preservation conflict in history in terms of area size, economic cost, and number of human lives affected. I would interview all sides of the dispute — mainstream environmentalists, radicals of all persuasions, loggers, millworkers and their bosses, forest rangers, federal and university scientists — to discover what had driven them to this collision.

Yet, while researching this book, I found to my surprise that these fights over owls and old trees also concerned the ecosystem. Like the archvillain Moriarty in the Sherlock Holmes mysteries, this evanescent and elusive idea kept cropping up in the most surprising places. I had to know: Where did it come from, how did it grow, and where would it lead?

These are the questions I ultimately sought to answer in *In a Dark Wood*. And the conclusions were far more disturbing than I had anticipated. An ancient political and philosophical notion, ecosystems ecology masquerades as a modern scientific theory. Embraced by a generation of college students during the campus revolutions of the 1960s, it had become a cultural icon by the 1980s. Today, not only does it infuse all environmental law and policy, but its influence is also quietly changing the very character of government. Yet, as I shall show, it is false, and its implementation has been a calamity for nature and society.

Here, then, was the real villain — an idea that society had embraced but did not understand. I therefore realized that *In a Dark Wood* was not about good and evil people. Like the narrator of *The Divine Comedy*, who found himself lost in wilderness, the contending armies of environmental wars are victims, driven not merely by competing interests but also by intellectual traditions they do not comprehend. And indeed, as I interviewed people for the book, I found myself liking many on all sides of the conflict. I became friendly with folks who disliked — even hated — one another. I found myself admiring scientists who despised one another's work, activists and corporate chieftains who regularly contested in courtrooms, radical "monkeywrenchers" and conservative loggers who sought to destroy their opponents' way of life.

Each side has its share of saints and sinners. But the extreme polarization that characterizes preservation fights derives not from the virtue or turpitude of individuals but from the polarity of the ideas they believe in. Environmental battles are not between good guys and bad guys but between beliefs. And the real villain is ignorance.

In a Dark Wood, therefore, is written in an ecumenical spirit. I am indebted to many people, from all sides of the dispute, who generously devoted their time and efforts to help me write, and improve, this book.

For suggesting corrections to all or parts of the manuscript, I especially thank Joseph P. Kalt of Harvard University's John F. Kennedy School of Government; W. Arthur McKee of Oregon State University; Chadwick D. Oliver of the University of Washington; Douglas W. MacCleery of the National Forest Service; and others who wish to remain anonymous.

For their help in fact-checking parts of the story, I am indebted to Robert Sutherland of the Garberville, California, environmental group EPIC; Eric Forsman of Oregon State University; Daniel Gasman of the City University of New York; Jack Ward Thomas, chief of the National Forest Service; and Ralph Saperstein, vice president of the Northwest Forestry Association.

Many other university, industry, and government scholars and officials helped to educate me about scientific and management issues and often supplied hard-to-find data and journal articles. In this regard I am especially grateful to Jerry F. Franklin and Robert Lee of the University of Washington; Lee M. Talbot, former senior scientist with the President's Council on Environmental Quality; Daniel Botkin of the Center for the Study of the Environment; Dale Thornburgh of the University of California at Arcata; Charles Meslow, Norm Johnson, and Tom Spies at Oregon State University; Jay Rasmussen of the Oregon Coastal Zone Management Association; Earl Baysinger of the U.S. Fish and Wildlife Service; Ray C. Erickson, former scientist with the Fish and Wildlife Service; Frank Ferguson, supervisor of the Plumas National Forest; and Ron Mastrogiuseppe, former forest ecologist at Redwood National Park.

I also acknowledge the advice and information generously supplied by Stephen Rosenzweig of the University of Arizona; James Lindquist, retired California state silviculturalist; Randal O'Toole, director of the Thoreau Institute; Stephen Boyce of Duke University; Charles Harris at the University of Idaho; James Kennedy at Utah State University; Harold K. Steen, director of the Forest History Society; Glen Juday at the University of Alaska Fairbanks; Robert Taylor of the California Forestry Association; Larry Irwin of the National Council on Air and Stream; and the relatives, friends, and associates of "Mr. Redwood," Emanuel Fritz, including Barbara Fritz, Fred Landesberger, Robert Grundman, and Henry Trobitz.

For earlier instruction in the mysteries of deep ecology, I thank Bill Devall and George Sessions. For the long hours they gave, often over the interval of years, to interviews — and often to fact-checking — I owe a special debt to the environmentalists Judi Bari, Mike Roselle, Howie Wolke, Dave Foreman, Karen Pickett, Kelpie Willsin, Gary and Betty Ball, and Greg King of the environmental movement Earth First!; Alex Pacheco and Ingrid Newkirk of People for the Ethical Treatment of Animals; Dana Beal of the New York Greens; James Monteith, formerly with the Oregon Wilderness Coalition; Andy Kerr of the Oregon Natural Resources Council; Terry Thatcher, formerly with Oregon's Environmental Law Center, and Max Axline, now with the center; Chuck

Powell, Ruthann Cecil, and Cecelia Lanman of EPIC; Andy Stahl and Vic Sher, formerly with the Seattle office of the Sierra Club Legal Defense Fund; Tim McKay of the Northcoast Environmental Center; Kenneth Margolis of Ecotrust; Lewis Regenstein, with the Interfaith Council for the Protection of Animals and Nature; Paul Watson of the Sea Shepherds Conservation Society; Klaus Sheerer of Robin Wood; Edward Goldsmith, editor of *The Ecologist*; Joachim and Annalise Vielhauer of the German Greens; Jeff DeBonis of the American Forest Service Employees for Environmental Ethics; Dennis Martinez of the Sinkyone Intertribal Council; Steve and Eric Beckwith of Lake Tahoe, California; and Marc Gaede of Los Angeles.

Loggers, millworkers, lumber company executives, their families, and other North Coast residents graciously endured my repeated visits and phone calls, and liberally supplied, without complaint, information I sought. For this I especially thank lumberman Mark Silvernagel and his wife, Toni, along with "gyppo" logger Tom Hirons, all of Mill City, Oregon; Valley Crisis Center staffer Cherie Girod of Mill City; her brother, cutter Larry Robertson of Scio, Oregon; *Evergreen Magazine* editor Jim Peterson of Grants Pass, Oregon; Northwest Forest Council staffer Chris West of Portland; former director of the Association of O&C Counties Ray E. Doerner of Roseburg, Oregon; retired millworker Bob Gaines of Sweet Home, Oregon, and his wife, Jeane; dairyman Gordon Ross of Coos Bay, Oregon; lumber industry statistician Paul F. Ehinger, of Portland; Oregon Lands Coalition staffers and organizers Jackie Lang of Salem, Valerie Johnson of Tigard, Rita Kaley of Eugene, and Evelyn Badger of Roseburg; former Mendocino County supervisor John Shemolino of Fort Bragg, California; millworker George Alexander of Ukiah, California; former Arcata Lumber Company executive Lloyd Hecathorn and attorney Bill Bertain, both of Eureka, California; Pacific Lumber Company president John Campbell of Scotia, California; and past and present Pacific Lumber Company employees Kelly Bettiga, Peter Kayes, Woody Murphy, Gene Kennedy, and Doug Coleman, of Scotia, Fortuna, and Eureka, California.

This book never would have been completed without the help, faith, and patience of many people. I am obliged to John W. Sommer of the University of North Carolina at Charlotte, who faithfully supported my work over the years and who quietly encouraged me to continue scholarly pursuits long after I had given up my academic tenure. I am indebted to my agent, Bob Dattila, and my first editor, John Herman, for acquiring the book when it was just a newborn idea. And I am deeply grateful to my present editor, Richard Todd, for his patience in waiting for a work that seemed to take forever to write, his thoughtful suggestions for improving it, and his steadfast confidence in the appeal of its message, even during times when its author had doubts.

Writing a book of this kind is a great undertaking, consuming the years and energies not merely of the author but of his entire family. Spouse and children are unseen foot soldiers, and sometimes unheralded casualties. They provide the most important sustenance of all, and they suffer the stress of the campaign in silence. Our sons, David and Sidney Godolphin, were always there when this old, scarred veteran of intellectual combat needed emotional support.

And what can I say to Diana — my wife, friend, and companion of thirty-one years — for putting up with this compulsive workaholic? As John Stuart Mill said of his wife, Harriet Taylor, her exalted sense of truth and right is my strongest incitement, and her approbation my chief reward. Such gifts can never be repaid.

In the final analysis, *In a Dark Wood* is my book alone. I have tried to make it as flawless as possible. But I know that perfection can only be approximated, and that whatever mistakes it contains are my fault, and only mine.

PROLOGUE

Dramatis Personae

IN CHRONOLOGICAL ORDER

EMANUEL FRITZ, 1967. Fritz was like his beloved redwood trees — straight, thin, and unbending. His career as forest ranger, professor of forestry, and editor of the *Journal of Forestry* spanned almost the entire history of redwood logging. Known as "Mr. Redwood," he had a vision: that forestry is a science, which would ensure that redwood logging was sustainable. Yet this seemingly simple idea evaporated every time he reached for it.

MARC GAEDE, 1970. By monkeywrenching, Gaede had returned to his roots. Back in 1959, when Gaede was eleven, Bill Breed, a curator at the Museum of Northern Arizona, had introduced him to a game he called "billboarding." Taking axe and saw, he drove Gaede and Gaede's friend Ted Danson — later star of the television show *Cheers* — along Route 180 from Flagstaff to the Grand Canyon, where they cut down outdoor advertising signs. Eventually they cleaned the route out, notching more than five hundred kills. It was their way of beautifying America.

TOM HIRONS, 1971. As usual, Hirons was worrying about money, and the future of logging, which was almost the same thing. By mortgaging everything he owned, Hirons had raised $225,000 to buy all the old logging equipment he needed — yarder, log loader, D-6 cat, crummy, pickup, fire truck, and miscellaneous rigging and tools. He decided to call his new venture Mad Creek Logging, which, under the circumstances, seemed appropriate.

LEW REGENSTEIN, 1972. Regenstein worked for the Fund for Animals out of a cramped one-room office near Pennsylvania Avenue. One day a tall man in a big cowboy hat strode into his office. "Hi," the man said, "My name's Tom Garrett, from Garrett, Wyoming. I'm here to save the whales." Son of a fourth-generation rancher, Garrett had come east to join the gunfight over endangered species at the Beltway Corral.

BILL BERTAIN, 1972. Bertain was in the laundry wrapping bundles of clean sheets and clothes when his father, George, came in. Tears streamed from the old man's eyes. "Stan Murphy just died," George said. "Dropped dead of a heart attack at Rhonerville Airport, returning from San Francisco. It's the worst thing that's happened to Humboldt County in forty years." The winds of change had reached this tiny town built and run by the Pacific Lumber Company. For the redwood region it was the end of an era.

EARL BAYSINGER, 1972. Much to Baysinger's bemusement, the Nixon administration liked his comments on its new bill, provisionally titled the Endangered and Threatened Species Act of 1972. The acronym for this legislation, EATS, gave Baysinger sleepless nights as he fretted over what political enemies might make of it. But luckily no one noticed.

JAMES D. WILLIAMS, 1974. An ichthyologist working in the Washington Office of Endangered Species in 1974, Williams got a call from David Etnier, a former colleague at the University of Tennessee. While tramping along the banks of the Little Tennessee River, Etnier had found a minnow he had never seen before. Apparently the creature lived nowhere else, and Etnier thought it ought to be listed as an endangered species. But it didn't have a name yet. A few months later Williams proposed listing the fish as endangered in the *Federal Register*. As it still didn't have a name, the announcement referred to it by genus only, *Percina sp.* This was in effect a promissory note meaning "a minnow to be named later." But soon the world would know its name: snail darter.

JAMES MONTEITH, 1974. As the Oregon Wilderness Coalition's second full-time staffer, James Monteith embodied the ideals and ferment that were swirling through the Oregon campuses. Corvallis was buzzing with debates over trees and forest creatures. The university had started a Coniferous Forest Biome Project, developing an inventory of life forms in virgin forests. Meanwhile, disturbing rumors circulated — that fishers were disappearing, that streams produced less water after surrounding forests were clear-cut, and that the spotted owl was in trouble.

ERIC FORSMAN, 1975. Forsman walked quickly up the forest path. He couldn't believe his bad luck. The owl was the first he had radio-collared, and already it was lost. Then abruptly his radio emitted a faint squeak, before lapsing into silence again. What was wrong? Finally, as Forsman reached the ridgetop overlooking Mill Creek, the owl's signal came in loud and clear. The bird was fully three miles from where he had collared it. Spotted owls, he suddenly realized, had an extraordinarily large home range.

BILL DEVALL, 1975. Devall sought an alternative philosophy, an intellectual compass that would give direction to his unease. Then, as he was walking through the library one day in 1975, he recalls, "this article sort of fell into my lap." Written by a Norwegian philosopher named Arne Naess, the paper was titled "The Shallow and the Deep: Long-Range Ecology Movements." Things suddenly fell into place. Devall would become the apostle of deep ecology!

GLEN JUDAY, 1977. The researchers assembled around the table at their retreat in the Gifford Pinchot National Forest in south central Washington. Each took his turn, saying what he was finding and what he thought important. The experience hit Juday with the force of a hammer blow. Not only did they find their ideas converging, but put together, he believed, their collective insights indicated a major crisis.

WOODY MURPHY, 1979. Stanwood A. Murphy, Jr. — whom everyone called "Woody" — knew that by choosing to work in the woods rather than at company headquarters in San Francisco, he had put his chances for advancement at risk. The new managers of the Pacific Lumber Company were coat-and-tie people who never rolled their sleeves up. A team of blueblooded Stanford graduates and members of the Bohemian Club, they seldom ventured among workers. None had worked his way up through the ranks. They were out of touch.

JERRY FRANKLIN, 1980. Franklin and his colleagues debarked from the helicopter, high on slopes of Mount St. Helens. The landscape, covered with volcanic dust, looked like the surface of the moon. Just two weeks earlier, on May 18, 1980, the long-dormant volcano had erupted with a ferocity not witnessed in the lower forty-eight in recorded times. The devastation was so complete, they theorized, that nothing could have survived. But that day they found a cornucopia of living creatures. The mountain was already being reborn.

ROBERT SUTHERLAND, 1980. The "man who walks in the woods" was the man of the hour. Robert Sutherland had adopted that title for himself because he believed that all names once had a meaning which had been lost, and because he thought that everyone is entitled to choose his or her own, conveying the person's essence. So instead of Robert, which he'd had no role in choosing, he opted for the moniker "the man who walks in the woods" — or "woods" for short — because it best described him. And now, to stop a logging juggernaut, he was being asked to live up to his name.

ERIC BECKWITH, 1986. Living in a remote homestead high in the Sierras and self-taught since he was eleven, Beckwith was intensely interested in saving the forests. When a government scientist told him the best strategy was to "get the Endangered Species Act involved," he sat down and wrote Secretary of the Interior Donald Hodel a letter asking that the northern spotted owl be listed as an endangered species. Signed by both Eric, nineteen, and his brother Willow, fifteen, it amounted to saying, "Hey, guys, this is wrong."

ANDY STAHL, 1986. Stahl had just settled into his new office at the Sierra Club Legal Defense Fund in Seattle, where he was perfectly placed to lead the fight to save old growth. But a phone message suggested that events were overtaking him. The caller was his contact within the U.S. Fish and Wildlife Service. "Somebody's petitioned to list the owl — again," the official said, adding, "and this time it's serious."

GEORGE ALEXANDER, 1987. The morning of May 8, 1987, Alexander felt especially uneasy. His band saw was in bad shape. As he made a center cut through a long, thin "pecker pole," the blade hit an eleven-inch nail, and the saw exploded like a bomb, throwing him nearly thirty feet. A twelve-foot section broke off its track, sending shrapnel through Alexander's mask, hitting him in the throat and face, breaking his jaw in five places, knocking out a dozen teeth, and nearly severing his jugular vein. He fell to the floor, the blade wrapped around him. As other workers used a blowtorch to remove the blade from his face, Alexander's friend Rick Phillips held his artery together until the ambulance arrived.

GREG KING, 1987. It had been a helluva year. Just eighteen months earlier King had been a quiet, mild-mannered Bruce Wayne sort of guy writing for *The Paper*, a Sonoma County journal. Now he was miraculously transformed into the scourge of the Pacific Lumber Company — a nemesis who, in the eyes of loggers, was not so much Batman as the Joker.

JOHN CAMPBELL, 1987. As president of the Pacific Lumber Company, Campbell tried to understand how logging had become so controversial. Why, he wondered, didn't someone remind people that redwoods are a renewable resource that grows like crabgrass! A single acre of eighty-year-old trees adds enough wood in five years to build a good-sized house. But mature trees don't grow; they shrink. The only way to rejuvenate the woods is to harvest them. And Pacific Lumber, he mused, had been such a good citizen!

JIM PETERSON, 1988. Returning from Montana, Peterson, editor of the forest products journal *Evergreen*, conceived the idea for the Silver Fire Roundup. Setting the date for August 27, 1988, at the Josephine County Fairgrounds, he and the other planners asked all loggers to come wearing yellow ribbons like the strips people had tied outside their homes when American embassy personnel in Tehran were being held prisoner by Iranian militants. Feeling themselves captives of hostile foreign forces, they saw the ribbons as a symbol of their solidarity, too.

CHERIE GIROD, 1989. Girod put down the phone and looked at her watch. Eleven o'clock, and this was already the third phone call about suicide this morning. Like the others, the caller was an unemployed logger. He asked Cherie if life insurance policies paid benefits to families when the policyholder commits suicide. He didn't say he was thinking of killing himself. But Cherie knew.

JUDI BARI, 1990. Bari remained in Highland Hospital, drifting in and out of consciousness. The bomb had broken her pelvis in ten places, pulverized her tailbone and two lower vertebrae, perforated her colon like a piece of Swiss cheese, and cut off all feeling in her left leg. But she had to live for her daughters' sake, she told herself. She tried to picture their faces — Jessica, four, and Lisa, nine. But hard as she tried, she couldn't. She was about to die, Bari thought. But first she had to know: Who had planted the bomb, and why?

JACK WARD THOMAS, 1990. Thomas sat behind the desk of his Le Grande, Oregon, Forest Service office. Having just returned from testifying before Congress, the scientist was tired. He wondered if this spotted owl–old-growth business would ever end. He was just a good 'ol boy from Texas, and had never laid eyes on a spotted owl until he was asked to head up a team to study the little troublemaker. The fight over owls and old growth, he realized, meant that America's values were changing. It was a mirror in which we could see ourselves, and a test of our stewardship over ecosystems.

CHADWICK OLIVER, 1993. Preserving old growth, Oliver argued, increased "the risk of a very large disturbance destroying a forest." Because of what he called the misguided "steady-state" theory of ecosystem stability, preservationist policies would ultimately produce the "timber famine" and loss of biodiversity which everyone sought to avert.

LARRY ROBERTSON, 1994. Robertson sat at home, wondering when he would work again. After several years of finding only occasional jobs felling small trees, he now had to contemplate an entirely new career. But who would hire him, he wondered? If he had noticed the dead alder, things might have been different. Instead, when the mature myrtlewood he was cutting fell, it dislodged the smaller tree. Rain-soaked and heavy, it smashed his shoulder, dislocating the socket and stretching nerves. His arm had become a dangling, useless appendage that was mending only slowly.

IN A
DARK
WOOD

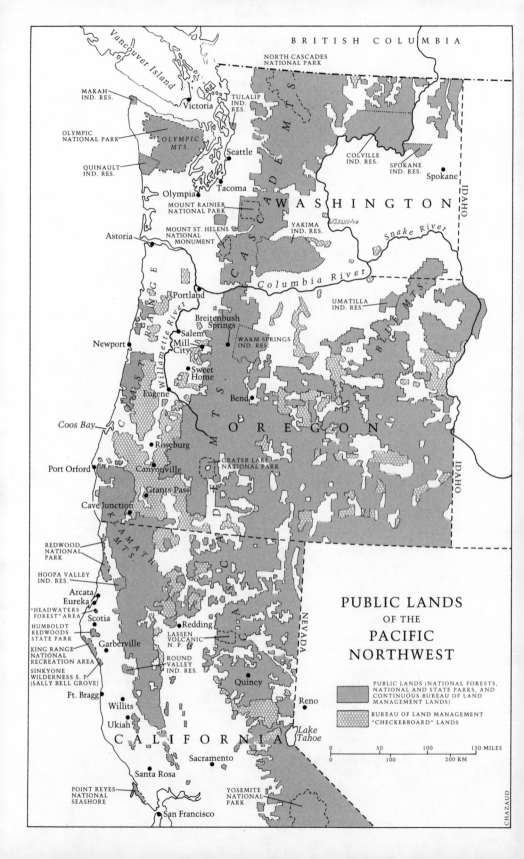

BRITISH COLUMBIA

NORTH CASCADES
NATIONAL PARK

Vancouver Island

MAKAH
IND. RES.

TULALIP
IND. RES.

Victoria

OLYMPIC
NATIONAL PARK

*OLYMPIC
MTS.*

COLVILLE
IND. RES.

SPOKANE
IND. RES.

Spokane

QUINAULT
IND. RES.

Seattle

C A S C A D E   M T S.

WASHINGTON

IDAHO

Olympia   Tacoma

MOUNT RAINIER
NATIONAL PARK

Astoria

MOUNT ST. HELENS
NATIONAL
MONUMENT

YAKIMA
IND. RES.

Snake River

Columbia River

Portland

UMATILLA
IND. RES.

C O A S T   R A N G E

Willamette River

Breitenbush
Springs

Salem

B L U E   M T S.

Newport

Mill
City

WARM SPRINGS
IND. RES.

Sweet
Home

O R E G O N

Eugene

Bend

Coos Bay

Roseburg

C A S C A D E   M T S.

Port Orford

Canyonville

CRATER LAKE
NATIONAL PARK

Grants Pass

IDAHO

Cave Junction

K L A M A T H   M T S.

REDWOOD
NATIONAL
PARK

HOOPA VALLEY
IND. RES.

Arcata
Eureka

"HEADWATERS
FOREST" AREA

Scotia

PUBLIC LANDS

OF THE

HUMBOLDT
REDWOODS
STATE PARK

Garberville

Redding

LASSEN
VOLCANIC
N. P.

C A S C A D E

NEVADA

PACIFIC
NORTHWEST

KING RANGE
NATIONAL
RECREATION AREA

SINKYONE
WILDERNESS S. P.
(SALLY BELL GROVE)

ROUND
VALLEY
IND. RES.

Ft. Bragg

Quincy

Reno

Willits

PUBLIC LANDS (NATIONAL FORESTS,
NATIONAL AND STATE PARKS, AND
CONTINUOUS BUREAU OF LAND
MANAGEMENT LANDS)

Ukiah

*Lake
Tahoe*

BUREAU OF LAND MANAGEMENT
"CHECKERBOARD" LANDS

C A L I F O R N I A

50   100   150 MILES

0   100   200 KM

Sacramento

Santa Rosa

POINT REYES
NATIONAL
SEASHORE

YOSEMITE
NATIONAL
PARK

San Francisco

CHAZAUD

1

THE SEARCH FOR NATURE

"WE POISON THE CADDIS FLIES in a stream and the salmon runs dwindle and die. We poison the gnats in a lake and the poison travels from link to link of the food chain and soon the birds of the lake margins become its victims," wrote Rachel Carson in her 1962 bestseller, *Silent Spring*. "These are matters of record, observable, part of the world around us. They reflect the web of life — or death — that scientists call ecology."[1]

This passage was probably the first place where most Americans encountered ecology. The book launched the modern environmental movement, which changed the values and politics of the nation. Carson's warnings about the risks of pesticides opened the floodgates of concern about a host of other issues as well, from diminishing wilderness to air pollution. She had aroused the fear, already growing in the hearts and minds of many, that unbridled consumption and technological growth were spreading blight and death across the landscape.[2]

The country quickly mobilized to confront these threats. Formerly staid conservation groups grew into professional lobbying organizations with tremendous clout in Washington. Groups of radical reformers, demanding immediate change, multiplied. Concern for the earth infused the curricula of schools and colleges. And government reacted. Within little more than a decade, Congress had passed a plethora of laws designed to protect the environment.[3]

These efforts seemed tremendously successful. Air quality improved, water pollution diminished, and wildlife sanctuaries proliferated. The National Wilderness Preservation System grew from 9.1 million acres to 96 million between 1964 and 1993, while the amount of federal land subject to conservation restrictions grew from 51 million acres to 271 million during the same period. The national park system covered 76 million acres, an area more than fourteen times the size of Massachusetts.[4]

Yet, despite these achievements, more than thirty years since this awakening there is today a growing sense, shared by many, that the crusade in which they placed their hopes has not lived up to its promise.[5]

Something is amiss. Environmental organizations occupy expensive office buildings in Washington and New York, but many face declining memberships and budget deficits. The nation is gripped by pessimism and distrust, and opinion seems badly polarized. An antienvironmental campaign, called the Wise Use Movement, is gaining strength. Followers of this latter-day reaction perceive environmentalism not as liberating nature but as enslaving society. National parks and wilderness are losing many of the plant and wildlife species they were established to protect. The list of creatures feared at risk of extinction is growing exponentially. Environmental regulations add staggering costs to the economies of some regions, causing hardship. Rather than giving us reason to hope, the movement seems to have lost its way.[6]

What went wrong? Why does a movement that seemed to succeed so spectacularly at first raise so many doubts today? And how can it be put back on track?

Perceptions of nature form the framework of our lives. Shared beliefs about it are the deep structure of society. Since the dawn of civilization people have embraced the axiom that their social institutions must be in harmony with the earth. They have viewed nature as the objective reservoir of value, and have turned to this protean and fungible source to shape and justify their law, economy, art, religion, educational system, and family mores.[7]

Views of nature form the bedrock assumptions of politics in particular. The millennia-long tradition of natural law expressed this insight. So did Enlightenment theories which were based on fictional stories about the "state of nature." The views of Aristotle, the ancient Stoics, medieval German jurists, Saint Thomas Aquinas, Thomas Hobbes, John Locke, Baron de Montesquieu, Jean-Jacques Rousseau, and even Karl Marx, whose ideas infuse the political arrangements with which we live, all reflect the view that politics derives from nature.[8]

Yet, while virtually all cultures confer special status on nature, the word is systematically ambiguous. In one sense it refers to the physical laws that govern the behavior of phenomena. But in a political context "nature" and its cognates serve as metaphors for moral or religious truth. Saying that something is "natural" is to assert both that it is desirable and that its virtues have foundation in reality.[9]

Thus, while nature may appear to be an absolute standard, views about it are inevitably subjective. Nature, like beauty, is in the eye of the beholder. Over the ages the idea has been used to justify every conceivable political system, from anarchy to absolutism. Plato invoked nature to argue for benevolent despotism; Aristotle to justify Athenian democracy; Thomas Hobbes to argue for the restoration of the Stuart monarchy; John Locke to authenticate the "Glorious Revolution" of 1688, which restored a Protestant monarch to the English throne; Jean-Jacques Rousseau to argue for ideas that would inspire the French Revolution; and Mussolini and Hitler to authenticate totalitarianism.[10]

This ambiguity in turn means that every political system rests on presuppositions, often tacit and unexamined, which represent a consensus of beliefs about the nature of nature, but which themselves are vulnerable because they cannot be rationally defended. So long as consensus remains, the public continues to acknowledge the moral authority of its laws and institutions. But when it breaks down — when, that is, significant numbers of people come to question whether governmental edicts are consistent with nature — a political crisis ensues.[11]

The character of this crisis, however, often remains concealed from those who are gripped by it. At the time people are merely aware that something is wrong, that society has failed to "work." Only gradually, as reformers begin to realize that tinkering with the machinery of government is insufficient and that more radical prescriptions are necessary, does it begin to dawn that the problems lie at the culture's taproot, its relations with nature itself.[12]

That happened in America in the 1960s. The country experienced a cultural crisis that touched every area of public life. Many were gripped by an overpowering sense that something was profoundly wrong. Federal laws and policies were losing their legitimacy. College students in particular rejected beliefs that had served as the rationale for political institutions since the Revolution. The reason, members of this cohort believed, was that society was ignoring or flouting the laws of nature. And although this insight was often tacit or unspoken, it sustained their sense of righteousness as they fought to save the earth.[13]

In this way, the search for political legitimacy led many to a new environmentalism. Up until the 1960s, the conservation movement had consisted of two groups, both of which were focused narrowly on wildlife and wilderness. The first were conservationists — mostly hunters — like Theodore Roosevelt, who campaigned for the establishment of forest preserves and game sanctuaries. The second were pure preservationists, like John Muir, a co-founder of the Sierra Club, who, worshiping nature and representing a spiritualism descending from the Puritans, fought for the establishment of national parks and wilderness.[14] But the movement that evolved following the publication of *Silent Spring* would be quite different. To be sure, it continued to fight for wilderness and was concerned about a lengthening list of other environmental issues. Yet rather than merely "environmental," it was, like classical political philosophies, also the outline of a complete theory of morality and politics.[15]

The political doctrine which this cohort of Americans rejected was that conceived more than 270 years earlier by John Locke. The influence of this seventeenth-century English philosopher — who wrote the constitution of the Carolina Colony and whose ideas were incorporated into the Declaration of Independence — was so profound that in 1955 the historian Louis Hartz would write, "Locke dominates American political thought, as no thinker anywhere dominates the political thought of a nation."[16]

Locke's philosophy was a form of humanism. People, he believed, are good and nature is benign. The "state of nature" (i.e., life without government) was, he wrote in 1691, "a state of liberty, yet . . . not a state of license . . . which willeth the peace and preservation of all mankind." Individuals are therefore born with inalienable rights of "life, liberty and property." As rational agents they can understand and follow this natural law (which is a law of reason) and therefore have a right to govern themselves. And, being moderately altruistic, they require minimal government to oversee their affairs.[17]

But in the 1960s the Lockean consensus, which had been eroding for centuries, finally collapsed, igniting a spiritual and political crisis. During that fateful decade a competing intellectual tradition known as positivism reached the zenith of its influence within the universities, undermining the last vestiges of natural law and driving the final nail into the coffin of the Lockean consensus. Indeed, this transformation had been under way even during Locke's own lifetime. By the seventeenth century, physicists had discovered that by analyzing the objects of experience mathematically, they could explain and predict the behavior of phenomena. And since nature could be depicted in purely quantitative terms, it had no ethical dimension. This, in turn, meant that the claims of Locke and other natural law theorists — namely, the belief that moral laws can be found in nature — were false. This newer view, eventually known as positivism, therefore concluded that science — the study of nature — must be "objective."[18]

Positivism was the engine that drove the scientific and industrial revolutions. It liberated science from theology and politics, making the impartial pursuit of truth possible. And just such "disinterested intellectual curiosity," as the historian George M. Trevelyan put it, was "the lifeblood of real civilization." When the search for truth is confused with political advocacy, the pursuit of knowledge is reduced to the quest for power. But positivism also had a darker side. Its very call for "morally neutral" inquiry seemed to imply ethical nihilism. If moral laws cannot be derived from the study of nature, then how can our most cherished values be rationally defended? This is exactly what many of the 1960s college generation wondered.[19]

Although at that time many educators continued to believe in teaching the values of the "Judeo-Christian tradition," they were becoming a distinct minority. The positivist ideal of "scholarly objectivity" now defined the culture of America's colleges and universities. And this had happened just as the country was being convulsed by issues of value that touched the very soul of democracy. Civil rights, the war in Vietnam, Watergate, political assassinations, feminism, and the cold war raised questions about the Constitution, political obligation, and the legitimate limits of governmental power for which the positivist tradition of the professoriate had no answers.[20]

The scholarly prohibitions against making "value judgments" therefore collided with the ethical issues of the day to destroy the prevailing political consensus. Since professors taught that values cannot be rationally defended, students inferred that the values of our economy, government, and educational institutions could not be rationally defended either. So many did what countless generations before had done when faced with similar crises: they went back to the land in search of new spiritual and political foundations. And that path took them into the forest.[21]

"From the earliest times," writes Sir James George Frazer in *The Golden Bough*, "the worship of trees has played an important part in the religious life of European peoples." Indeed, all journeys to the heart of nature eventually reach a forest. The word *wilderness*, originally meaning "the place of wild beasts," is virtually synonymous with forests. Of Nordic origin, it "once had specific reference to the woods," the historian Roderick Nash observes. And there is, he adds, "the possibility that wild is in part related to 'weald' or 'woeld,' the Old English terms for forest."[22]

Yet forests are not simple symbols. Dark and mysterious, they conjure a complex of conflicting images — of nature and the supernatural, of sanctuaries and unseen enemies, of virginity and defilement, of good and evil. Throughout history, humans have vacillated in their attitudes toward them. On the one hand, notes J. E. Cirot in *A Dictionary of Symbols*, the forest is a "symbol of the earth, [a] place where vegetable life thrives and luxuriates, free from any control or cultivation." Yet on the other it embodies "the sylvan terrors that figure so prominently in children's tales . . . the perilous aspects of the unconscious, that is, its tendency to devour or obscure the reason. . . . The forest harbors all kinds of dangers and demons, enemies and diseases. That is why forests were among the first places in nature to be dedicated to the cult of the gods, and why propitiatory offerings were suspended from trees."[23]

This ambivalence persisted throughout history. Ancient Greek mythology, notes the historian Michael Williams, supposed forests to be home to both virtuous dryads and evil satyrs and centaurs. To Christian monks in medieval times, writes Clarence Glacken, forests represented both wild nature which needed to be civilized and a sanctuary from worldly enemies. By moving into and clearing the forests, monks saw themselves "bringing back to civilization the lands that had been abandoned." Yet, says Glacken, "there was often a deep feeling among the monks that in their forest retreats, their clearings, their tillage, they were duplicating conditions like those of Paradise before the Fall."[24]

Early American settlers shared the same contradictory views. To them "wild nature was sublime," notes Williams, yet "clearing the forests was a form of redemption." This inconsistency persists to modern times. From the 1600s on, the cutting of forests has alternately been characterized as propitiatory or sinful, patriotic or subversive, promoting progress or despoiling paradise, harvesting a resource or raping nature.[25]

Thus, a generation's search for a new vision of nature would lead to deep green places which reflected more than five thousand years of human equivocation. But for most this was not a coordinated quest, or even a conscious one. Rather, the discovery of a new ethic seemed to occur almost by accident. Unobserved, countless individuals, each unaware of the others, each following his or her own star or driven by his or her own demon, not even aware that he or she was engaged in a search, slowly labored at a wheel until, quite suddenly, each separately found the answer to a question hitherto only partly articulated.[26]

Along the way, some of this cohort joined mainstream organizations such as the Wilderness Society and the Sierra Club and began lobbying and litigating for a new political order. Others founded radical brigades, which, employing tactics honed during years of campus protest, sought change through "direct action." Collectively they formed a multifarious movement representing every hue of the activist rainbow. But gradually, despite their differences, their ideas would coalesce around a uniform philosophy — a new metaphor of nature — which would energize and direct their actions, stir discord, and eventually inseminate the entire body politic.[27]

As a first step these pilgrims discovered ecology, which seemed to incarnate the virtues positivism lacked. Instead of being reductionist, it was holistic; and rather than being morally neutral, it appeared to carry an important ethical message. Based on the notion that nature was organized into networks of interconnected parts called ecosystems, the new science seemed to say that conditions were good so long as ecosystems kept all their parts and remained in balance.[28]

Combining the ecosystem idea with the nature worship they had inherited from early preservationists, the more radical activists conceived a unique ideology, eventually called biocentrism. If everything is dependent on everything else, they reasoned, then all living things are of equal worth, and the health of the whole — the ecosystem — takes precedence over the needs and interests of individuals.[29] This was the idea a generation was looking for. The metaphor of the ecosystem revived the notion of nature as purposive and as the foundation of value. Since an ecosystem's "health" — that is, its stability — was the highest good, then any human activity that upset this balance was not merely mistaken but immoral. The ecosystem would thus serve as scaffolding for the construction of a new, misanthropic ethic of nature to replace the older, humanistic one.

For biocentrists the task was to rearrange society to fit the new ideal. And the path to reform led straight to nature's seemingly perfect ecosystems — forests. For, more than other parts of nature, the woods appeared to embody the supreme ecosystem virtues of stability, interconnectedness, and longevity. And loggers, by disturbing these places, seemed not merely mistaken but morally wrong.

By the late 1980s concern about vanishing trees had reached every corner of the continent. Controversy, often mingled with concerns about threatened or endangered species, erupted over the "Northern Lands" of New England; Tongass National Forest in Alaska; the vast pine plantations of the Southeastern states and their residents the red-cockaded woodpecker and Louisiana black bear; the subalpine fir stands of Montana and Idaho and their grizzly bear populations; the high ponderosa of Arizona and New Mexico and its inhabitant the Mexican spotted owl; the lush Douglas fir stands of the southern Sierra Nevada and their controversial native the California spotted owl.[30]

But these skirmishes paled in comparison with the titanic struggle that erupted over the "ancient forests" of the Pacific Northwest and their now famous occupant, the northern spotted owl. There, activists, eager to stop the cutting, ignited a conflict whose implications would reverberate across the continent, changing the course of federal policy and affecting the lives of millions.[31] The alpha and omega of environmental controversies, this issue would convulse two great areas: the Douglas fir stands of Oregon, Washington, and Northern California, and the giant redwoods of the Golden State's coast range. The fight over Douglas fir would affect private landowners throughout the region and would concern the future of 24 million acres of public lands in Oregon and Washington alone — an area greater than Massachusetts, Connecticut, New Hampshire, Vermont, and Rhode Island combined — in addition to five California national forests comprising nearly another 6 million acres.[32]

The battle for the redwoods would determine the fate of the last significant old-growth groves of this species still remaining in private hands, thus provoking a collision between radical activists and free marketeers that would reverberate all the way to Wall Street. Along the way the contest would exceed others in nearly every dimension — in duration; scope of forest planning; spending on threatened species; environmental and anti-environmental litigation; and social, economic, and political impact — and its outcome would determine the future of preservationism itself.[33]

Beginning almost imperceptibly in the early 1970s and continuing today, this conflict would consume the time and resources of environmentalists, Congress, the courts, five presidential administrations, investors in New York and Texas, multinational wood products corporations, loggers, scientists, and radicals of all persuasions. It would generate over twenty major lawsuits and culminate in the most ambitious conservation plan ever conceived. It would provoke cries that the federal government was destroying logging as a way of life. It would precipitate more spending than ever before on creatures at risk (more than $152.4 million for northern spotted owls and Chinook and sockeye salmon in 1992 alone), and would put hitherto sacrosanct environmental laws, such as the Endangered Species Act, in political jeopardy for the first time ever.[34]

·   ·   ·

So began a galvanizing battle over the fate of the Northwest forests, a proxy war between the forces of humanism and biocentrism engulfing nearly everyone living in the area — loggers and their families, forest rangers, university professors, and environmentalists of all stripes. But it was also a war fought by outsiders, including Wall Street speculators, federal officials, and corporate and environmental lobbyists, all determined to see their respective ideologies emerge victorious.[35]

As with all great social transformations, the fight was multidimensional. It was at once a battle over the future of great trees, a social revolution propelled by demographic changes, and a scientific controversy over the relative importance of stability and change in nature. To loggers, mature forests were simply stands of decaying trees that had to be cut before they rotted away. To environmentalists, they were "ancient forests" embodying the permanence and constancy of nature. To many foresters, old-growth forests were "biological deserts" containing few animals, such as elk and grouse, which they thought desirable. To environmentalists, they represented the biocentric ideal that confers equal importance on all living things, from elk to boring beetles.

But most fundamentally the struggle was a conflict of visions pitting established ideas about nature against new ones. Thus, it was fought over an ambiguous word that no one understood. Yet, however obscure the issue, the combatants, as in all historic upheavals, viewed it as simple — indeed, as hanging on the fate of a single symbol. Just as the Greeks and the Trojans saw their war as a fight over a woman, so this many-layered contest over old-growth forests, logging culture, science, and humanism focused on the fate of that appealing little woodland creature, the northern spotted owl.

The survival of this life form, environmentalists argued, required preservation of ancient forests. The bird, they insisted, was an "indicator species," a canary in the mine, whose decline was a barometer of the failing health of the planet. To loggers, it was a Trojan horse, deliberately constructed to breach the walls and bring ruin to their culture. So both sides viewed the Endangered Species Act — the law that gave these creatures their special status — as the foundation document of the new age, to be preserved or revoked at all costs.

This law, established in 1973, provided stiff penalties for harming the critical habitat of threatened or endangered species. Its powerful enforcement provisions stopped mega-projects in their tracks. An intellectual product of emerging national values, it was also the foundation law of biocentrism. Environmentalists battled state and federal government and private businesses over snail darters in Tennessee, cave bats in Indiana, grizzly bears in Montana, red squirrels in Arizona, red-cockaded woodpeckers in Georgia, black bears in Louisiana, squawfish in Colorado, smelt in California, panthers in Florida. As these fights multiplied, so did the bitterness. Environmental debate became increasingly angry, divisive, and ultimately destructive, not just to people but to wildlife as well.[36]

But, however bitter and ineffective, the fight over the spotted owls and old growth was destined to dwarf these earlier skirmishes in acrimony and social upheaval. As the fight escalated, ecosystems ecology became a politically influential science; and biocentrism, once considered the subversive religion of a few radicals, would infuse popular culture and become a dominant influence in the application of federal law and policy. As the conflict spread, it sparked an antienvironmental backlash, thereby polarizing politics until the entire country was caught between the Scylla and Charybdis of uncompromising — and mutually uncomprehending — political forces.

Thus, the awakening inspired by Rachel Carson would evolve into something far more than increased concern about wilderness and pesticides. Ecosystems ecology emerged as a new kind of discipline challenging the very canons of traditional scientific method. Biocentrism was not merely an environmental idea but a new vision of the universe. The effects of this science and this philosophy would touch the lives of every American. And the Northwest conflict over forests and threatened species, which still continues, would become a zero-sum game, ending in tragedy for society and nature, and raising questions about the future of environmentalism itself.

I

CRISIS:
WHAT IS
NATURE?
1960–1972

What is, is without beginning, indestructible, entire, single, unshakable, endless, neither has it been nor shall it be. . . . Becoming is out of the question, and destruction is inconceivable.

Parmenides

Nothing endures but change.

Heraclitus

2

CORK BOOT
FEVER

IN THE BEGINNING loggers believed they were stewards of the earth who had found their Eden. Standing on the mountainside near Mod Creek in the Sweet Home district of Willamette National Forest in the spring of 1971, Tom Hirons watched the yarder, a machine that looked like a mammoth fishing rod, pull logs up the steep hillside to the loading dock.[1]

"God," Hirons thought, "I love this life."

Thin, bespectacled, and only thirty-two, he was already his own boss. Just the week before, Hirons had formed the North Fork Logging Company, thus becoming a "gyppo logger" — an independent contractor who took logs from the forests, where the cutters had felled them, to the mills, where they would be sawed into lumber. Now all he had to do was make a living for himself without getting his crew killed.

Hirons stood in the sunlight inhaling the cool, damp air. The view was spectacular. Row upon row of forested mountains stretched to the horizon. Freedom and fresh air, Hirons thought. What more could a man want?

Not that this was a particularly exciting job. He wasn't cutting the big old "yellow fir," the valuable old trees, some more than eight feet in diameter, which turned yellow when they passed their two hundred fiftieth birthday. Instead he was "yumyarding" — removing slash left from a previous logging operation. His assignment was to take everything more than eight inches in diameter and ten feet long. Most of this material, Hirons noted — hemlock and spruce — was just a little bit thicker than dog hair. Usually the Forest Service burned it to reduce the risk that, if left, it might fuel a forest fire. But these intentional burns had come under public criticism lately, so the agency had decided to remove it instead.

Nevertheless, it had been a busy week. Hirons's loggers had come in right after the cutters had gone, leaving the trees lying like corpses after a battle, neatly arranged side by side, perpendicular to the slope of the mountain. To prevent soil erosion the Forest Service required Hirons to do aerial logging, also called full suspension, which meant that rather than drag the logs uphill with steam-driven winches known as "donkeys," the loggers had to haul them up by a "skyline" so that they would not drag on the ground. One end of the skyline was attached to a tall tree, called a tail spar, limbed and left standing, guyed with cable or wire rope. The other end was suspended from the yarder, a steel tower with a pulley on top and a powered winch at the bottom, controlled by the crew chief, or siderod.[2]

It had taken Hirons and his crew three full days to rig the skyline. Using a bulldozer, they leveled a platform for the 125-ton yarder and loading dock, carefully bracing the mammoth machine and its 110-foot steel spar, or tower, with guy wires. Then a rigging slinger limbed and topped the 150-foot tree Hirons had chosen as the tail spar, spending the better part of a day swaying in the wind, affixing guy wires. When the skywire was in place, they suspended a two-ton trolley, or skycar, from it so that, hauled by the yarder, it could ride up and down the skyline. With its own diesel-operated hoist the skycar could lift and lower logs as it rode up and down the mountain.

Finally the tramway was assembled. Two teams of two men, a rigging slinger and a choker setter, started at the bottom of the unit, wrapping wire rope, or chokers, around bunches of logs, called turns, and attaching them to a cable dropped from the skycar. Using a "bug" — a two-way radio — to talk with the hook tender, who controls the skycar, the rigging slinger gave the command to start hauling. The skycar lifted the turn into the air, then hauled it uphill to the loading dock. There the loader operator stacked the logs carefully into two piles, separating the valuable Douglas fir from the less costly hemlock and pine.

Despite the difficulties, everything went all right. No one got hurt. The first logging trucks pulled up, were loaded, and left.

And, for the first time, Hirons relaxed.

In the same forest a year later Larry Robertson put down his chain saw and wiped his brow. It was his first day on the job, and he was scared to death. Limbs were flying, logs rolling, huge trees falling. At last he had found his niche.[3] Robertson, twenty-five years old, had finally become a cutter. His job was to fell the big trees that defined the forests of the Pacific Northwest. And the danger of this work produced in him an adrenaline rush he had never felt before.

Moving into the virgin forest before dawn, Robertson and his three companions began felling trees, which the loggers would later haul away. They worked in pairs. As one team downed the trees the other bucked them, cutting the fallen giants into forty-foot lengths and removing the limbs.

Robertson was on the cutting team. He carefully walked around a snag — a standing dead tree — and stood at the base of a Douglas wide as a car. Notching his saw as Gene Calkins, his partner, had told him, Robertson sighted the tree. Together they planned the fall path down to the smallest detail, clearing a landing bed so the tree would not disintegrate when it hit the ground.

After facing the tree at just the right angle, Robertson made the final cut. As the tree began to fall, time seemed reduced to slow motion. The tree leaned, imperceptibly at first, then steeply. A cracking explosion erupted. The tree crashed downward, its heavy limbs snapping like twigs as they collided with those of neighboring trees, sending splinters raining to the ground like shrapnel. On impact the huge tree bounced like rubber as seismic waves shook the ground beneath Robertson's feet, and limbs, crushed by the fall, sprayed into the air like spears.

The tree landed just where Robertson and Calkins had planned.

"You hit your shot," Calkins said.

"Right," said Robertson, feeling the way he imagined Dick Butkus, the Chicago Bears linebacker, did after sacking the Green Bay quarterback.

"Cork boot fever" is what they call the love of logging. And Hirons and Robertson had bad cases of the disease. Like most in the business both men — Hirons the logger and Robertson the cutter — loved their work.

For Hirons it was an unlikely career. He had grown up in Salem, where both his parents were bureaucrats. After graduating from high school, serving in the navy as a machinist's mate, and getting married, Hirons couldn't decide what he wanted to do. He tried various jobs — driving a beer truck, selling insurance — then went to college. Working as a logger during summer vacations, he started studying forestry. But the war in Vietnam was heating up at the time, and Hirons, the veteran, got so mad at Nixon that he decided he had to figure out how America had got into this mess. He switched his major to history.

A year after he graduated in 1970, a friend grubstaked Hirons's start as a gyppo. He bought a bulldozer, a yarder, and a loader, and was on his way.

Robertson, by contrast, like most in the business, was born to it. His father and grandfather were loggers. Yet after being discharged from the air force and marrying his childhood sweetheart, Robertson had tried logging and didn't like it. Then some friends started their own timber-felling company and offered Robertson a job. After just one day Robertson knew he was born to be a cutter.

Cutting, Robertson found, was very different from logging. It was like the contrast between playing offense and defense in football. Loggers are like offensive guards and tackles. Just as these linemen work in teams, leading sweeps, protecting the quarterback, so logging requires teamwork and close coordination. Like defensive linemen, cutters are the hot dogs. They work in pairs, a faller and a bucker, making their own decisions. Their satisfaction is in surviving and creating their own kind of art.

Yet for cutters and other loggers this is hard work, as hard as work can be. It means getting up at 3:00 A.M. six days a week, taking the crummy, or crew bus, out to the unit while it is still dark, and working all day, often in rain or snow, on hillsides so steep you can't stand up. For gyppos like Hirons it means owing your wife, soul, house, and family dog to the local banker while making payments of $20,000 a month for the yarders, skycars, crummy, loader, caterpillar tractors, and pickups you need to do the job. It means climbing hundred-foot skypoles to wrestle with ten-ton cables. It means "high-balling" — working at a double pace — to get logs out fast.

For choker setters and rigging slingers it means scrambling over teetering logs tall as a fence on ground that is almost perpendicular and dodging ten-ton turns as they swing perilously overhead. For cutters it means wrestling five-foot chain saws that sometimes jump out at you, while glancing over your shoulder to see if some snag is about to mash your body like a grape. And it means bucking logs as big as freight cars that threaten to roll over you without warning. Sudden death is a way of life. A tree might fall the wrong way when you cut it. A log might roll on you as you buck it. A snag might topple as you stand next to it. A turn of logs, swinging from the skyline, might knock a tree against you. Or a cable might break.[4]

Through this danger, the men formed a culture. Risk was addictive, the narcotic that kept them coming back to the woods. Like skiers and stock car racers, cutters and loggers lived for the high that comes from narrow escape, and they shared an intensity few outsiders ever knew. As in war, the threat of imminent death brought families together, cementing close friendships and fusing tight communities.

They developed a machismo, a romantic self-image that sustained them through hard times. Living next to nature loggers learned — or thought they learned — about loss and rebirth. They hurt when comrades died in accidents. They killed trees, but they also saw the forests grow back and watched as sons replaced their fathers on skypoles and yarders. Their own mortality generated a strong belief, driven by fatalism and faith, in the eternal powers of nature.

For more than three centuries sons had followed their fathers' spiked and cork-booted footsteps into the woods to prove their manhood and live in freedom. In the seventeenth century, ancestors of these Northwest loggers cut tall pines in New England to make masts for the Royal Navy. In 1623 America's first sawmill was established near York, Maine, and in 1691 the British government promulgated its "broad arrow" policy, reserving all trees more than twenty-five inches in diameter growing on unoccupied lands outside declared townships for the use of the navy. By 1800 loggers, having given nautical names to the tools of their trade — yarder, rigging slinger, hook tender, butt rigging, tail spar, cold deck — used big Maine rivers such as the Kennebec and Penobscot as freight ways, floating logs to the mills.[5]

Employing oxen and later steam-powered Lombard tractors, they dragged logs to the rivers, where lumberjacks used dynamite and long poles known as peaveys to unpile logjams and keep the wood moving. They built splash dams across rivers, then opened their sluices to create artificial freshets — momentary floods — to drive logs downstream. They developed "cruising" methods for estimating the amount of timber in a forest, and they borrowed technology from Europe, such as water-powered up-and-down saws and, by 1821, circular saws, to provide lumber to a growing nation.[6]

By 1850 the forests of New England had been extensively cleared, and as settlers moved west, loggers went with them, following their market. Lumbermen cut their way into the white pine stands of Saginaw Basin in Michigan, moving on to the Chippewa, Elk, Flambeau, Kittle, and Cauderray rivers of Wisconsin and Minnesota. Erecting nearly one hundred sawmills on Lake Huron alone, they made huge rafts to haul logs across the lake from Canada.[7]

By the 1890s these migrating lumbermen had stripped Midwest forests bare. Some then moved south to the longleaf, shortleaf, and loblolly pine forests stretching along the Appalachians from North Carolina to Georgia, or to the hardwood stands of Arkansas. Others continued their pilgrimage westward, to the Northwest. When they arrived, they found an already flourishing local industry. The Hudson's Bay Company built the first sawmill in Oregon Territory in 1828 on Mill

Plain on the north bank of the Columbia River. During the 1830s, 1840s, and 1850s, loggers had colonized the entire region. Some went north into what is now the state of Washington, setting up their saws at Mossyrock, South Bend, Hunt's Mill Point, and Wauna in Puget Sound.[8]

Loggers also sailed south from the mouth of the Columbia, along the coast to Astoria, Clifton, Gardiner, Coos Bay, Myrtle Creek, Coquille, Port Orford, Gold Beach, and Brookings Harbor. Others moved down the Willamette Valley to Mill City, Lebanon, Sweet Home, Harrisburg, Springfield, Mapleton, Oakridge, Myrtle Creek, Riddle, Canyonville, Butte Falls, and Cave Junction. From these towns they entered more remote country, using waterways for splash damming. Other loggers went east of the Cascades, building mills on the John Day and Minam rivers, in the Blue and Wallowa mountains of eastern Oregon.[9]

Meanwhile, some Maine lumbermen, skipping the Midwest entirely, sailed by ship around the horn of South America to San Francisco, Portland, and Seattle. These new arrivals spread northward from the Bay area and inland from the coastal cities of the Northwest. Plying coastal waters, ships brought loggers into, and wood out of, the ports of Fort Bragg, Eureka, Coos Bay, and Newport.[10]

Fate, it seemed, had made this region logging country, and the instruments of this fate were railroads. Finding a place blessed with deep topsoil and endless rain, a place where forests grew in profusion but where steep mountains and big trees discouraged farming and ranching, these companies became inadvertent instruments of a historical inevitability that fixed the region's future.[11]

In 1897 Alaska's Klondike gold rush fueled a housing boom in Seattle, driving timber prices skyward and attracting a new wave of logger immigration. Railroads, having received mammoth federal land grants, competed to capture the trade. In Oregon and California the Southern Pacific Railroad and lesser lines raced to connect San Francisco with Portland. They crisscrossed the Willamette Valley, as mills appeared in Yamhill and Luckiamute, Newberg, Oregon City, and Roseburg. Meanwhile, Washington's largest landowner, the Northern Pacific Railway Company, while keeping more than 1.6 million acres for itself, sold vast tracts to other firms, including that Great Lakes giant the Weyerhaeuser Timber Company. By 1913 sixty-four owners controlled more than 56 percent of the region's timber.[12]

But while three quarters of Washington's forests remained in private hands, something unprecedented happened in Oregon, transforming federal government into the state's largest logger and changing the politics of the region forever. The instruments of this transformation were the Oregon and California Railroad Revested Lands and Coos Bay Wagon Road Reconveyed Lands, otherwise known as the O&C lands, or the "Billion-Dollar Checkerboard."[13]

Like other railroad holdings, the O&C lands were land grants. In 1866 Congress gave the Central Oregon Railroad 3.7 million acres to build a line from Portland to the California border. Consisting of every other section of land twenty miles on either side of the right of way, this "checkerboard" property amounted to 12,800 acres for each mile of track laid. In 1869 the federal government awarded 105,000 acres — the odd-numbered sections three miles on either side of the right of way — to the state of Oregon for construction of the Coos Bay Wagon Road, which crossed the Willamette Valley, linking Roseburg with the sea.

Later the state transferred these lands to the Southern Oregon Company. Meanwhile, the Central Pacific created the California and Oregon Railroad Company, building a track from Sacramento to the Oregon border, eventually linking with Central Oregon's tracks coming down from Portland. By 1887 the Southern Oregon Company, renamed the Oregon and California (O&C) Railroad, completed the Oregon portion of this route, hooking up with the Northern Pacific's transcontinental track into Portland. Having acquired 2.9 million acres in federal land grants, it became a subsidiary of the Southern Pacific.

When the Klondike-inspired logging boom began, the O&C, like the other railroads, started selling its patented lands, but it did so illegally, violating the "settlers' clause" of its federal land grant agreement. Congress, which had given the land away to encourage settlement in Oregon, required the company to sell quarter-sections to each qualifying homesteader for no more than $2.50 an acre. But instead the O&C either logged the land before selling it or charged up to $40 for each acre. It sometimes held land back from the market, waiting for the price to go higher. It also sold parcels to "dummy entrymen" — stand-ins bribed by lumber companies to pose as homesteaders. In 1906 the Theodore Roosevelt administration exposed this scandal. The public cried foul, and the federal government investigated.

Two years later the Justice Department brought suit against the railroad, demanding forfeiture or forced sale of the O&C lands. The suit was joined by settlers who had applied for quarter-sections of the grant lands under the terms of the act of 1869. In 1915 the Supreme Court ruled that the law was an enforceable contract and the railroad's failure to sell at $2.50 an acre justified forfeiture. So in 1916 Congress passed the Revestment Act, which authorized the General Land Office of the

Interior Department to buy back these lands from the Southern Pacific at $2.50 an acre, then resell them to homesteaders at the same price.[14]

Altogether the government bought back more than 2.5 million acres from the railroad. But it had trouble finding homesteaders to buy these parcels. The terrain was too steep and the trees were too big for farming. Most lands remained in the public domain. To hasten privatization, Congress authorized the Land Office to log them, believing that removing forest would attract farmers. But still there were few takers. In the meantime, to compensate local governments for lost railroad property taxes, it decreed that a percentage of revenues from the sale of timber be disbursed to the eight counties where these lands were located, as payments in lieu of taxes.

So these O&C counties and the Interior Department found themselves in the timber business whether they wanted to be or not. They struck up a partnership that endured. The department began logging these former railroad lands for the purpose of serving and sustaining the local population. This commitment to supporting Oregon's communities was formalized by the 1937 O&C Sustained Yield Act, which stipulated that the O&C lands "shall be managed . . . for permanent forest production and the timber thereon shall be sold, cut and removed in conformity with the principle of sustained yield for the purpose of providing a permanent source of timber supply, protecting watersheds, regulating stream flow, and contributing to the economic stability of localities and industries, and providing recreational facilities."[15]

In 1946 the General Land Office merged with the National Grazing Service to form the Bureau of Land Management (BLM), but the 1937 act's unique mandate to serve local communities remained. To this end, the county governments' share of O&C revenues was set at 75 percent of logging revenues, of which, by 1952, a third was placed in a BLM "plowback fund" to support sustainable forest management.[16]

The O&C lands quickly became a money tree. They gave the bureau income that was independent of normal congressional appropriations and provided logging counties with a steady and lucrative source of funds. The money seemed to grow without limit. Appraised at $25 million in 1916, by 1969 the O&C lands had produced nearly $313 million for the counties. In 1970 alone these communities would receive more than $29 million. O&C counties produced 77 percent of Oregon's timber harvest and accounted for 85 percent of the sawmills, 87 percent of the state's lumber and wood products employment, and most of its pulp and paper. Eleven of the twenty-five largest lumber companies in the United States had mills in the O&C counties.[17]

Oregon's loggers had found the promised land. Only one other region could match it — the redwood country just south of the Oregon border.

No one is sure who cut the first redwood, but a French writer in 1827 reported seeing Russians at Fort Ross in Mendocino County cut a tree twenty feet in diameter. By the 1830s logging had begun in earnest around Big Sur, Sausalito, and Mill Valley.[18]

After James Marshall discovered gold in John Sutter's millrace in 1848, loggers were right behind the miners, seeking their own red gold of giant coastal trees. By 1850 they had blazed a trail from the Russian River into Mendocino and Humboldt counties. The next year a man named Jerome Ford built a mill at the mouth of the Big River in Mendocino County. Soon other mills appeared along the coast, shipping their lumber to San Francisco by boat, while others followed the railroads as they laid tracks northward, toward Oregon.[19]

In 1869 three loggers purchased six thousand acres in the Eel River valley near the town of Forestville, and founded the Pacific Lumber Company. As the company grew, more loggers arrived in Forestville, settling into unpainted shacks or double-decker bunkhouses and drinking themselves silly at the company saloon. Rootless and unmarried drifters, they never stayed long. Turnover was 300 percent a year. Then, in the 1880s, a new wave of immigrants arrived from Canada's Maritime Provinces — Nova Scotia, New Brunswick, and Prince Edward Island — bringing wives and children with them. Changing the town's name to Scotia, they stayed.[20]

In 1882, at Fort Bragg on the Mendocino coast, a logger from Wisconsin named Charles Russell Johnson, grandson of a Yankee sea captain, built a sawmill that would become the Union Lumber Company. Cutting these giants by hand, dragging them out of the woods by ox team, and shipping its wood south on schooners to San Francisco, Union Lumber would become the other great redwood player along the northern coast. Eventually it would be bought out by the multinational giant Georgia-Pacific.[21]

But the northern counties remained isolated. Getting to Humboldt and Del Norte required long trips by horse over dirt paths, corduroy log roads. It was here, in these narrow, dark, damp, and isolated valleys, that lumbermen built their homes, settling towns like Yamhill and Mill City, Scotia and Garberville. Some, like Scotia, were company towns, complete with commissaries, churches, hospitals, schools, hotels, even their own printed money. Others grew spontaneously. But wherever the lumbermen lived, they knew they had found timber heaven.[22]

Comprising the largest and fastest-growing contiguous timberland in North America, the Pacific Northwest, by 1970, was producing a quarter of all softwood lumber in the United States.[23] The dominant trees of this region — the Douglas fir and the coastal redwood — are a lumberman's dream. Sometimes more than three hundred years old, 220 feet high, and eight feet in diameter, Douglas fir is perfect for home construction. Growing straight with few limbs, the older trees are virtually knotless.[24] Redwoods are even bigger. Some, over two thousand years old, are up to 350 feet high. Their heartwood's beauty and near-absence of knots, combined with a resistance to decay (owing to an abundance of tannin and other rot-resistant chemicals called extractives), make these trees highly desirable for every building use from paneling to shingles.[25]

Both trees are exceptionally fast-growing. A Douglas fir can reach three feet in diameter in only eighty years, and a twenty-year-old redwood stands more than fifty feet tall. Redwoods, loggers have found, are nearly immortal. They drop seeds every year, and their roots continue to live even after the tree is felled. Cutting them, loggers liked to say, is like mowing your lawn. As soon as a tree is felled, it starts growing again, sending suckers out from the old roots.[26]

Yet this utopia consisted of two forests. The northern one, dominated by Douglas fir and western hemlock, covered 28 million acres, spanning five hundred miles from British Columbia to California. It straddled two mountain systems — the coastal range and the Cascades — and ended where these two backbones converged, in the Klamath Mountains of southern Oregon. Covering several climate zones, from western-slope rainforests to the dry upland east of the Cascades, these forests were a cornucopia of conifers: sugar pine, incense cedar, western red cedar, western hemlock, Pacific silver fir, Engleman spruce, western larch, ponderosa pine, Pacific yew, grand fir, noble fir, western white pine, Alaska cedar, lodgepole pine, subalpine fir, mountain hemlock, whitebark pine.[27]

Encompassing environmental conditions that ranged from marine to montane, dry prairie to temperate rain forest, these Northwest forests were rich in plant, animal, and insect life. The tall trees contribute to what biologists call "vertical" biodiversity, providing niches for species that inhabit different elevations, like people living on different floors of a skyscraper. The broken canopy that results when old trees lose their tops in storms or fire increases the abundance of birds. Snags allow sunlight in and provide habitat for burrowing beetles (up to 168 different kinds have been identified here), which serve as the food base for insectivorous birds. They provide perching sites for raptors and habitat for cavity-nesting birds (all seven species of woodpecker that live in the Northwest excavate holes only in deadwood). A single Douglas fir may support thirty pounds of lichens, which are food for northern flying squirrels, Columbia black-tailed deer, Roosevelt elk, and other mammals. Truffles grow among the tree roots, feeding still other creatures, such as the California red-backed vole.[28]

The southern forest was the habitat of the coastal redwoods, *Sequoia sempervirens*. Covering more than 2 million acres along a coastal strip five to thirty-five miles wide and 450 miles long, stretching from the Klamath Mountains to Big Sur, this was to the settlers the world's most special rain forest. "The largest, highest and straightest tree" he had ever seen was what the Spaniard who first encountered one, in 1769, called the redwood. When the first American settlers arrived, redwoods were growing on the hills of Oakland and covered San Mateo, Santa Cruz, and Marin counties. Shallow-rooted and unable to withstand freezing temperatures, they thrived on the steep, moist, fog-shrouded hillsides of the coastal range, where, densely packed, they protected one another from the wind.[29]

"The Titan race," Donald Culross Peattie called them in *A Natural History of Western Trees*. And indeed, having survived for 160 million years, they are remnants of the age of dinosaurs. Like their cousins the giant sequoia — *Sequoiadendron giganteum*, the biggest tree of all, living as long as 3,500 years and growing to a diameter of thirty-five feet — which survives in small numbers in the Sierra Nevada, and the deciduous dawn redwood, *Metasequoia glyptostroboides*, remnants of which still exist in China, the coastal redwoods are built on a prehistoric scale. They were the megaflora of the megafauna, the forest home for sabertoothed tigers, woolly mammoths, and giant beavers.[30]

Their size is almost too great for human comprehension. Inspiring pantheistic awe, they grow up to twenty feet in diameter. The lowest limbs are one hundred feet above ground, spanning the sky like Gothic arches, shutting out the sunlight. Beneath the closed canopy in eternal twilight is a seemingly enchanted forest where other vegetation grows in profusion: Douglas fir, tan oak, madrone and ferns, redwood sorrel vines, salal, salmonberry, huckleberry, rhododendrons, and azaleas.[31]

Loggers in these forests were not immune to their enchantment. Living in damp valleys, enduring hardships, hunting elk, and catching salmon, they found their lives shaped by the trees. The forest was to them what the sea is to fishermen and the earth to miners: a stern father and a giving mother. It was dangerous and fecund. It killed and it gave life. It gave meaning to their lives and identity to their culture. Having strong ties to place, they believed in God and went to church on Sunday. They loved the woods and cared for wildlife. But more than anything else, they believed in what they did for a living.

Loggers became what sociologists call an "occupational community": their jobs became their reason for being. Logging, says Robert G. Lee, natural resource sociologist at the University of Washington, "is distinguished by an unusual commitment to individualism, hard work, inventiveness, and entrepreneurial spirit. . . . These circumstances give rise to a very strong sense of personal identity as a logger. People form attachments to working in the woods and develop deep respect for both the natural world and the dangerous challenges of their work. . . . Identification as a logger is so firmly embedded in the self that people often cannot imagine doing anything else."[32]

The loggers thought they were the good guys, occupying the moral high ground. They brought the great trees out of the forests so people could build factories and homes. Like farmers, they were stewards of the earth, harvesting a renewable resource, benefiting both man and nature.

They had good reasons for thinking this: the experts told them so. The science of forestry, known as silviculture, taught that proper logging is good for forests. Likewise, federal forest policy was dedicated to the twin goals of sustainable forestry and community stability. Cutting trees no faster than they could grow, according to this philosophy, helped forests while providing an inexhaustible source of income for loggers. Sustainable logging thus enriched both man and nature. This was the Holy Grail of forestry, and they had found it.

Or so they believed.

3

MR. REDWOOD

EMANUEL FRITZ, the grand old man of redwood forestry, had a vision: that forestry is a science that would ensure that logging was sustainable. Yet this seemingly simple idea seemed to evaporate every time he reached for it. In 1972 he would confess to interviewers, "Nature is still against us."[1]

Known as "Mr. Redwood," Fritz, born in 1886, would live to be 102. His career — as ranger, professor at the University of California, consultant to the redwood industry, and editor of the *Journal of Forestry* — spanned almost the entire history of redwood logging. And his lifelong quest for sustainability embodied the hopes, victories, and defeats of a century of American forestry.

Born in Baltimore, the son of German immigrants, Fritz took forestry degrees at Cornell and Yale, then began teaching at Berkeley in 1919. Shortly after arriving in California he began visiting redwood companies to gather data for his courses on wood technology and lumber manufacturing. During these visits he became increasingly curious about how redwoods grew and were cut. He would take long hikes in the woods. At the rate at which redwoods were being harvested, Fritz soon realized, virgin stands would be gone within fifty years. The industry had to embrace the science of sustainable logging. But he faced one great obstacle: experts could not agree what sustainable forestry was.[2]

Silviculture, as the field is called, takes its name from the Latin word *silva*, meaning "forest." This science dates back to Roman times, and flourished in western Europe during the Middle Ages. But the modern discipline originated during the English Restoration, in the reign of Charles II. Following a period of brutal civil war, devastating plagues, and the wholesale stripping of forests for farms and fuel, the British navy was concerned that it would run out of trees with which to build ships.[3]

In response, the Royal Society commissioned one of its founding members, Sir John Evelyn, to study the king's forest reserves. His work, published in 1664 and titled *Silva: A Discourse of Forest Trees and the Propagation of Timber in His Majesty's Dominions*, was among the first to recommend raising trees according to scientific principles. In 1669 the French government, fearing it too was running out of trees, published the *French Forest Ordinance*, codifying management strategies for the preservation of forests.[4]

With the publication of *Silva* and the *Forest Ordinance*, England and France began to manage their woods scientifically, to ensure the preservation of forests in perpetuity. The realization that trees are a finite resource marked a turning point in European attitudes toward the environment. No longer did men take nature for granted. They realized that it needed human help.

Nor could forests be preserved simply by locking them up. This passive approach, Evelyn noted, would take "entire ages." Instead, he recommended active husbandry: "Truly, the waste and destruction of our woods has been so universal, that I conceive nothing less than an universal plantation of all the sorts of trees will supply." Humans, to whom God gave the earth, must be active stewards of the land. And silviculture would be their tool.[5]

The science flourished. By the early nineteenth century most European countries were practicing silviculture. Germany and France, in particular, had highly developed forestry programs dedicated to scientific management of forests.[6]

In the 1860s the idea crossed the Atlantic. To New England intellectuals who had studied in Europe and knew the science, forestry was an idea whose time had come. Like the English and French two centuries earlier, they feared that America was running out of trees. In 1864 George Perkins Marsh's book *Man and Nature* appeared, warning that by damaging nature, man destroyed himself.

Left alone, Marsh argued, nature remained orderly and unchanging: "In countries untrodden by man, the proportions and relative position of land and water, the atmospheric precipitation and evaporation, the thermometric mean, and the distribution of vegetable and animal life, are subject to change only from geological influences so slow in their operation that the geographical conditions may be regarded as constant and immutable." But humans disrupted this balance of nature. They were so badly scarring the face of the earth, Marsh wrote, that the planet was "fast becoming an unfit home for its noblest inhabitant."[7]

The book was widely influential. For the first time Americans began to realize that nature was finite. By 1893 the historian Frederick Jackson Turner had put this epiphany into words. The West, Turner suggested, was settled in a series of waves. Fur trappers came first, blazing the trails, followed by soldiers, who removed the Indians, then loggers, who by clearing the forests made way for farmers. Each group faced its own frontier, and now these frontiers were closing. America was reaching the next evolutionary step, which would require a profound realignment in thinking about nature.[8]

This fear of advancing civilization converged with its opposite, faith in progress, to stimulate interest in forestry. Charles Darwin's *Origin of Species* appeared in 1859, introducing the idea of evolution and turning the intellectual world on its head. Soon after, the English philosopher Herbert Spencer coined the expression "survival of the fittest," and the concept of evolution began to infuse every idea from biology to politics. Evolution meant progress, a biological success story culminating in human civilization. As man was thought more advanced than other creatures, he controlled the destiny of the planet. Just as Africa was then deemed the white man's burden, so was nature seen as his responsibility as well.[9]

Manipulating the earth for human benefit, an idea embryonic in Evelyn's time, reached full flower. Man would improve upon nature! Humanizing the earth became a moral imperative. Throughout the United States, towns and cities hired landscape architects to build or improve parks. In the late 1850s Frederick Law Olmsted built Central Park in Manhattan, then moved on to plan parks in Brooklyn, Montreal, Buffalo, and Boston. Governments, loggers, and farmers planted exotic trees, from Norway pines to Australian eucalyptus, to decorate roadways, attract rain, provide commercial timber, and serve as windbreaks. Fisheries introduced trout from Scotland and Germany to streams and lakes from Maine to California.[10]

Foresters, too, would toil in America's garden. Wilderness, they thought, was dreary and unproductive. Virgin timberland was an uncultivated, weedy pasture needing tender loving care. Like Evelyn, they believed that trees could not survive without human aid. And this help, they were convinced, would come from Germany and France, the Mecca and Medina of science.[11]

Two contradictory streams, therefore, sustained the impetus toward managing America's forests — faith in progress and fear of it, love of wilderness and contempt for it. Somehow silviculture would transcend these contradictions, applying Old World ideas to New World conditions, permitting America to use its wilderness and keep it, and preserving both forests and society. Thus, the country rushed to embrace forestry. In 1873 Congress passed the Timber Culture Act, encouraging settlers to plant trees in the Great Plains. Foresting this region, the government hoped, would encourage rainfall, irrigating dry-land farms. In 1878 Congress passed the Timber and Stone Act, permitting the sale of public timber for private use.[12]

In 1881 a Boston physician and amateur forester, Franklin B. Hough, profoundly influenced by Marsh and convinced that a timber famine lay just ahead, successfully lobbied Congress to establish a Division of Forestry within the Agriculture Department. Hough was made the country's first chief forester.[13]

Following Hough, two leaders of the Division of Forestry led this crusade for silviculture: Bernhard Eduard Fernow, the agency's third chief, who ran the division from 1886 to 1898, and Gifford Pinchot, who succeeded Fernow and stayed until he was fired by President Taft in 1910. Fernow, a dour Prussian and holder of a professional forestry license, came to the United States to attend a meeting of the American Forestry Association and stayed after marrying an American. Pinchot, a blue-blooded Philadelphian and friend of Theodore Roosevelt, was trained in France. Both were apostles of European silviculture, which would teach the barbarian Americans how to care for their forests.[14]

The closing of the "lumberman's frontier," Fernow and Pinchot argued, threatened a timber famine unless the country embraced scientific forestry. America must use what it had wisely. Wilderness destruction caused economic dislocation and human misery. Marsh's prediction — that by destroying nature man would ruin himself — seemed to be coming true already, as cut-and-run logging turned Midwestern communities into ghost towns. Boom and bust forestry was a viciously cruel cycle, manufacturing unemployment. But scientific forestry, they claimed, could end this. Sustainable logging would protect both forests and the lumberjack.[15]

Owing in part to Fernow's efforts, in 1891 Congress passed the Forest Reserve Act, authorizing the president to create national forests. Within a year President Benjamin Harrison created fifteen reserves covering over 13 million acres. By 1900 forestry schools had been established at Yale, Cornell, and Asheville, North Carolina. In 1906, Theodore Roosevelt greatly expanded the forest reserves, increasing the six forests in Oregon to 13 million acres. And in 1905 Congress established the U.S.

Forest Service within the Department of Agriculture, making Pinchot its first chief.[16]

Determined to show the nation what silviculture could do, Pinchot endowed the Forest Service with more functions than a Swiss army knife: it would promote community stability, avert timber famine, help lumberjacks, fight lumber monopolies, protect water supplies, provide grazing land, and furnish opportunities for public recreation. And it would achieve all these goals through the miracle of sustainable forestry. Cutting trees no faster than they grew would stabilize logging economies, end unemployment among lumberjacks, protect tree supplies, stem soil erosion, promote healthy grassland, fight private timber monopolies, and open forests to recreation.[17]

From the start, therefore, the Forest Service, just as the Bureau of Land Management did with O&C lands later, sought to save both culture and nature. To help local communities, national forests returned a portion of their timber revenues to the surrounding counties. The Agricultural Appropriations Act of 1906 gave local governments 10 percent of proceeds from timber sales. Two years later this was increased to 25 percent. In 1944 the Sustained Yield Forest Management Act authorized "community stability" as an official goal of the service.[18]

To promote preservation, the Forest Service championed scientific study. Hough and Fernow urged creation of experiment stations, similar to those in Europe, to test different logging techniques. And in 1902 Roosevelt opened two experimental forests in the Nebraska Sandhills. Planting ponderosa pine imported from the West, this facility tested the feasibility of "man-made forests." In 1908 the Forest Service established the Fort Valley Experiment Station in the San Francisco Mountains near Flagstaff, Arizona. In 1910 it founded the Forest Products Laboratory at Madison, Wisconsin. Eventually it had a vast network of experimental forests and laboratories, in every forest district throughout the country, dedicated to sustainable forestry.[19]

But, despite these efforts, and despite extravagant claims about the benefits of forestry Pinchot and his successors found Americans hard to convert. New World soil was not fertile ground in which to plant the seeds of the germinating science, and these early foresters faced problems that their European counterparts did not.

As chief forester Pinchot was responsible only for logging on public lands. But the most devastating logging, he believed, was that occurring on private property, where he had no authority. He could not order loggers to follow forestry practices. Instead, he had to convert them to his cause. And this he found hard to do.[20] Whereas European foresters maintained stands that had been altered from their natural state centuries earlier, American silviculturalists had to transform wild forests into cultivated ones and convince loggers of the monetary value of managing them for sustained use. Yet so long as vast expanses of virgin timber remained, log barons saw no reason to spend money on planting and re-seeding.[21]

When he arrived in California, Fritz quickly saw the problem: the European approach was unsentimental and scientific, whereas in America forests were an emotional issue. Pinchot's heavyhanded attempts to regulate private logging, Fritz thought, alienated the landowners, who owned most of the redwoods. Consequently, "the American foresters had no chance whatever in those days of managing a forest." Fritz tried to be more diplomatic. But tact, he soon discovered, would not be enough.[22]

In theory, conservation sounded simple. In practice, it was profoundly complicated. Each forest is unique, so what is sustainable in one may not be so in another. And American timberland was more diverse and complex than European-trained silviculturalists had anticipated. Fernow complained that unlike German foresters, who needed to know only six or eight species, Americans "must know the life history of at least one hundred tree species out of the 450 which are found native to the United States."[23]

In the redwood and Douglas fir forests of the Northwest, intellectual confusion reigned. Foresters could not agree which of two kinds of logging was better, selection cutting or clear-cutting. In selection cutting, trees are cut singly or in small groups, leaving the majority standing. In another variation of selection known as "high-grading," loggers periodically remove the biggest, most valuable trees and leave the rest. In effect, selection cutting thins the forests, allowing saplings to sprout or germinate from seeds between the trees that are left, thus creating un-even-aged stands.[24]

Early American foresters knew the virtues of selection cutting. It can open the canopy, letting in light so that remaining trees grow more quickly. It maintains forest cover, minimizing the danger of erosion and floods. It does little damage to wildlife habitat. It is more pleasing to the eye. And, because remaining trees are relatively close together, selection cutting makes it easier for some species to regenerate cut areas since they are not required to throw their seeds so far.[25]

But this harvest strategy, foresters discovered, also has disadvantages. Where it does open the canopy, it exposes remaining trees to wind, causing blowdown of shallow-rooted species. But by leaving much of the canopy intact, it permits shade-tolerant trees to outcompete less tolerant species. In redwood and Douglas fir country, where trees are huge and hills steep, selection cutting was technologically difficult. Until the 1930s timber companies practiced slackline logging, using steam "donkeys" to winch logs up slopes, often knocking down remaining trees en route. And the towed logs made deep ruts, intensifying soil erosion.[26]

But clear-cutting produced mixed results as well. By leveling an entire area, it avoided the problem of blowdown. It allowed shade-intolerant trees to flourish. By clearing the canopy, it aided those species that depend on strong winds to throw their seeds. And it made slackline logging easier. Yet it left ugly scars on the landscape and sometimes accelerated soil erosion. By leaving no seed trees, it discouraged regeneration of those species that could not throw seeds a sufficient distance. And in the redwood forests, once the giants were gone, there were no trees left to leach moisture out of the fog and provide water for the understory.[27]

Thus, deciding which harvest system was better depended on many local factors, including fire history, tree mortality, species composition, soil composition, and topography. By producing even-age stands, clear-cutting replicated historical conditions in those forests that were periodically consumed by catastrophic wildfires. By contrast, in producing uneven-age stands, selection cutting best mimicked the state of nature, in which fires were frequent and localized or insect infestations killed trees selectively. Clear-cutting was better for trees that sprout only when the understory, or duff, is removed; selection was better for species that grow only in duff. Clear-cutting favored trees that cannot reach full height unless the overstory is eliminated, and those shallow-rooted species on ridges where there is danger of blowdown. Selection was perhaps preferable for shade-tolerant species in sheltered sites.[28]

But most important to foresters, choosing which system was better depended on the kind of trees they wished to produce. If growing shade-tolerant species was the goal, then selection was desirable; for intolerant trees, clear-cutting was better.

These issues framed the intellectual debate surrounding forestry in the Douglas fir region. In 1903 the ranger and self-taught silviculturalist Edward T. Allen published a study titled *Red Fir*, in which he concluded that this tree is a shade-intolerant species that throws its seed up to a mile, and therefore is better harvested by clear-cutting. Since this species best seeds itself on clear ground, Allen also advocated burning slash after logging. Removing this debris also kills the sprouts of hemlock, a competitive, shade-tolerant, and less economically desirable tree which thrives in the humus of forest floors. After measuring thousands of trees, Allen, who was raised by his father, a retired Yale professor, in what is now Mount Rainier National Park, concluded that Douglas fir reaches its maximum annual growth when it is seventy-five years old, and therefore "the greatest production of wood can be secured by cutting every ninety years."[29]

In 1924 a German forester, J. V. Hofmann, reaffirmed Allen's findings. Realizing that Douglas fir regenerated after major forest fires had swept the region in 1902, he concluded that the fir stores its seeds in the dust of the forest floor, where they germinate after a fire. Believing, therefore, that Douglas fir could regenerate from seeds that had stayed dormant in the soil for a long time, he concluded that leaving seed trees was unnecessary. That meant large areas could be clear-cut at one time.[30]

But practice did not confirm these theories. By 1909 foresters in the Willamette National Forest had found that Douglas fir did not throw its seed far enough to propagate clear-cut areas. They recommended "leaving patches of strips of seed trees" in some areas and practicing selection cutting in others. Still other Oregon foresters recommended that Douglas fir be clear-cut then artificially reseeded.[31]

Gradually, however, advocates of clear-cutting began to win this debate, as their case was strengthened by the rising influence of a biological hypothesis known as succession. First conceived in 1784 by the naturalist Thomas Pownell, it posited that plants form communities which follow one another in a regular pattern over time. "The individual trees of those woods grow up," Pownell wrote, "have their youth, their old age, and a period to their life, and die as we men do. . . . By Succession of Vegetation the Wilderness is kept cloathed with Woods just as the human Species keeps the Earth peopled by its continuing Succession of Generations."[32]

In 1860 one of the founding fathers of American preservationism, Henry David Thoreau, in an essay that greatly influenced George Perkins Marsh and many subsequent biologists, used the same idea to explain why pines were the first to grow back in areas where logging had removed the hardwoods. Oaks deplete the soil for their own acorns, Thoreau theorized; therefore they cannot succeed themselves and are replaced by pine. And since pines, too, cannot supplant themselves, they are followed by oak. Yet since hardwoods are more advanced in the "order of development," Thoreau argued, pines must be viewed as "pioneers" for these deciduous trees. The end state of this seesaw evolution would be that, when left alone, the forests would exhibit "the greatest regularity and harmony . . . while in our ordinary woods man has often interfered and favored the growth of other kinds than are best fitted to grow there naturally."[33] For Thoreau, therefore, as for Marsh, forests evolved toward harmony and stability unless disturbed by people.

Then, in 1916, a plant ecologist at the University of Minnesota named Frederic E. Clements expanded on Thoreau's idea, developing a theory that took the community of foresters by storm and helped to persuade an entire generation to embrace clear-cutting Douglas fir. Just as humans pass from youth to adulthood, old age, and eventually death, argued Clements, biological communities are superorganisms that, like individuals, are born, grow, and die in predictable ways. At each stage of this process — what Clements called a "sere" — the dominant vegetation prepares conditions needed by the plants that will form the next successional community. Climate determines which plant communities will grow and where, directing a process that inexorably leads to an increase in stability.[34]

Seral succession begins, Clements said, with a "disturbance," such as a volcanic eruption or a cataclysmic forest fire, which removes all or most existing vegetation. Following a typical disturbance, "pioneer species" such as grasses, legumes, shrubs, and shade-intolerant trees colonize the area. By fixing the soil with nitrogen and providing cover for seedlings, they produce the conditions needed for shade-tolerant trees, which come next. By this process grassland gradually becomes forested and one tree community replaces another until a "climax" stage is reached, in which growth stops altogether. This mature phase persists until the forest suffers another disturbance, and the process begins again.[35]

Thus, said Clements, nature is always in motion toward a goal. Rejecting the Darwinian notion of nature as undergoing constant evolution, he supposed that when living communities are left alone, they inevitably advance in predictable ways. They move from disorder to order, from loose associations to close-knit communities, from growth to stability, and, ultimately, to decay. Only disturbances can halt or reverse this process. But after such interruptions, nature always renews its inexorable march toward balance and stability.

"Clements was working within a system that emphasized practical rather than pure research," the environmental historian Peter J. Bowler notes, "and saw science as a way of controlling the economy as a whole." Invoking the concept of the superorganism "allowed him to present ecology as a science that would show us how to manage the natural productivity of an entire region." The American prairies, the biologist believed, had not changed since the last ice age, and, with proper management, could recover from the Dust Bowl conditions which had been created by ill-advised sodbusting agriculture.[36]

In particular, seral succession seemed to explain the evolution of the Douglas fir forests of the Northwest. In early successional stages, these lands are dominated by herbs, shrubs, and small deciduous nitrogen-fixing plants such as red alder, ceanothus, and lupine. After twenty to eighty years, depending on the size of the disturbance, this deciduous vegetation gives way to shade-intolerant trees such as pine and Douglas fir. This second phase, a closed-canopy conifer forest lasting about sixty years, is a period of declining diversity.[37]

During the third, or "mature" stage, which occurs over eighty to two hundred years (but can last up to seven hundred years), shade-intolerant species such as Douglas fir predominate, and annual growth reaches its maximum. At the fourth and final, or climax, stage the most populous members of the community are shade-tolerant conifers such as spruce and hemlock. Aged trees succumb to parasites and insect infestation. The forest starts to die. Standing dead trees dry out, and litter accumulates on the forest floor, thus enlarging fuel loads and increasing the risk of forest fire. Eventually a conflagration — or volcanic eruption — does occur, destroying the forest and allowing succession to begin anew.

Seral succession was, therefore, a neat, simple hypothesis, and it quickly became conventional wisdom among foresters. It seemed to imply that nature had a goal, and in the Northwest this purpose was growing "climax" ancient spruce-hemlock forests. But since these trees were less commercially valuable than the subclimax Douglas fir, the most economical way to manage a forest was to introduce "disturbances" that would keep forests in a perpetual state of middle age by encouraging the quickest transition from early successional stages to the middle ones and removing decadent old growth. Clear-cutting, they thought, was the way to do this. It opened the forest canopy, aiding the rebirth of fir.[38]

Silviculturalists continued to debate the merits of clear-cutting in the years between the wars. Rather than the cut-and-run tactics practiced in New England and the Great Lakes, Northwest loggers knew that they had little choice but to practice sustainable forestry. In 1933 it was estimated that this region contained nearly two thirds of the country's entire timber resources. This was the nation's last and greatest timber frontier, but its trees were so big that loggers had little hope of selling cut-over lands to farmers, who could not remove the giant stumps. Timberlands were good for nothing else. This meant that foresters had to learn how to grow trees as well as cut them.[39]

But it was not until the 1950s that the need to settle the question of sustainability became acute. Until the Second World War national forests had remained virtually untouched, even as timber companies, following Hofmann's erroneous prescription, had been clear-cutting wide areas. Now the private companies were running short of trees just as the postwar housing boom was increasing the demand for lumber. To meet this demand, the National Forest Service accelerated timber harvests. Yet selection cutting was too slow a process to satisfy the market. Clear-cutting would be more efficient. But was it environmentally sound? The service had to know.[40]

The answer came in 1956 from Leo A. Isaac, a silviculturalist stationed at the forest experiment station in Portland. His seminal paper "The Place of Partial Cutting in Old-Growth Stands of the Douglas-Fir Region" became a landmark that would chart the course of Douglas fir logging for the next half century.

Douglas fir, Isaac concluded, was indeed a shade-intolerant species. But it could throw its seed no more than a quarter mile, and — contrary to Hofmann's claims — its seeds did not survive long periods of dormancy. Thus, he theorized, large clear-cuts were bad for Douglas fir, but small clear-cuts were good. "The results of this study," he wrote, "provide further proof of the accepted hypothesis that an intolerant tree like Douglas-fir is unsuited for a selection cutting that continuously harvests the oldest ripest trees in an all-aged forest."[41]

Selectively cutting Douglas fir, Isaac argued, permits tolerant species, such as western hemlock, to take over. And by shutting out the sunlight, hemlock prevents Douglas fir from growing back. In some stands Isaac studied selection cutting eliminated Douglas fir altogether. Also, he observed, it damaged the forest. Dragging trees across the ground destroyed tree roots and compacted soil. Opening the canopy caused premature blowdown of the remaining trees. So Isaac recommended what would become known as "dispersed patch" clear-cutting. Using this method, loggers clear patches ranging from ten to one hundred acres in a checkerboard fashion through a forest, allowing older trees at the border of the clear-cuts to reseed the harvested areas.

Isaac's answer was what loggers, foresters, politicians, and sportsmen wanted to hear. To silviculturalists influenced by Clements and others, he offered a prescription for forest health. Mature, virgin stands, they believed, are "biological deserts." No longer growing, old trees provide no new source of wood and offer poor wildlife habitat. Left untended, they lose their resistance to parasites and disease, and die. Once dead, they dry out, becoming tinder to fuel forest fires. By contrast, clear-cutting, like fire, is a "disturbance" that reverses seral succession and therefore keeps forests young and healthy. It also maximizes biological diversity — thanks to a phenomenon known as "edge effect." Biologists had long believed that the greatest variety of life occurs at the borders (known as "ecotones") between plant communities, such as between fields and forests. By drawing a checkerboard pattern on the landscape, they thought, dispersed patch clear-cutting lengthened these boundaries, increasing edge effect.

To loggers, Isaac's recommendations were a panacea. Clear-cutting was the cheapest, and the fastest, way to grow Douglas fir. By showing it to be both ecological and profitable, he proved that the politics of sustained yield and community stability were compatible. To politicians, his emphasis on cutting small patches meant that logging would avoid public complaints about denuding mountainsides. To hunters and the general public, it offered to expand the habitat of the game animals they wanted to see. Deer, elk, and upland game birds thrive in clear-cut areas and edges, where grass and browse species are plentiful.[42]

Hence, Isaac inspired the golden age of clear-cutting. Foresters everywhere heeded his Commandment: thou shalt always clear-cut Douglas fir. By clear-cutting, loggers did well for themselves by doing good to the earth. The moral high ground was theirs.[43]

In the Douglas fir region Forest Service experiment stations provided a pool of researchers, disciples of Fernow and Pinchot, who carried on the debate over sustainable forestry. By contrast, in redwood country foresters were rare, and loggers had little interest in science. As late as 1920 silviculture in the European tradition had not yet taken root.

This was the vacuum Emanuel Fritz sought to fill when he came to Berkeley in 1919. Virtually alone, Fritz badgered loggers to embrace science. This meant, he believed, persuading them to abandon clear-cutting in favor of selection. But how? They had little use even for virgin redwood, much less second growth.[44]

Redwood, early California loggers believed, was not good for much. Even the wood of ancient trees was too soft for construction. Apparently its only use was for shingles. Consequently, many companies cleared redwoods from the forests to make room for Douglas fir and white fir, deemed to be more valuable wood. Others felled forests simply to clear fields for farming. And still others sought to replace redwoods with exotic species such as eucalyptus and false nutmeg.

But all these efforts failed. Clear-cut land proved poor for crops and pastures. Only by repeated burning could farmers prevent redwoods from growing back from seeds and stumps. But burning accelerated erosion, leaving fields in poor condition. Eucalyptus was so hard that it snapped saws like rubber bands. And it couldn't compete with hickory, oak, and ash from the Southeast.

After these failures redwood companies, deeply in debt, became convinced that their future lay in learning how to regenerate redwood stands. To this end the Union Lumber Company opened a nursery at Fort Bragg, California, in 1920, and in 1922 the Pacific Lumber Company established the Scotia Nursery.[45]

When Fritz arrived in redwood country, therefore, these companies were ready to listen. They desperately needed to make their business sustainable but didn't know how. They wanted to reforest cut-over lands — but how, and with what species?

Replanting redwoods, they thought, was a bad idea. The tree regenerated not from seed, old-timers believed, but only by "suckering" off stumps. And second-growth redwood, they were convinced, was worthless because it disintegrated when dry. You have to raise a tree a thousand years to get good lumber from redwood, or so they thought. Old growth grows in the shade of a closed-canopy forest, and therefore very slowly. With razor-thin growth rings, it is relatively dense and full of the tannin which makes wood resistant to rotting. Only when a redwood is several hundred years old, they thought, does it develop the valuable knotless "heartwood" whose beauty and resistance to rotting gives it value. By contrast, redwoods that regenerate in the bright sunlight of a clear-cut grow too fast. This second growth is softer and more knotty. With widely spaced rings and little tannin, it is merely "commodity grade" lumber, worth far less than old growth.[46]

But Fritz suspected that the loggers' prejudice against second growth was unfounded. He knew that redwood could grow from seed, and thought that by selection cutting loggers could raise good-quality trees without needing to wait a millennium. If so, selection cutting would be the best way to make a profit.[47]

Persuading Union Lumber president C. R. Johnson to test the idea, in 1923 Fritz began measuring trees on an acre of the company's forest, on Big River near Fort Bragg. Eventually Fritz would make this patch famous among loggers, who would call it the "Emanuel Fritz Wonder Plot."[48]

The plot was a perfect place to test selection. Partially cut by river loggers in 1858, it contained a mixture of virgin and sixty-five-year-old second-growth timber. In 1933 he measured again and found his hunch was right. The rate of growth was astounding. In ten years the trees had increased by 50,000 board feet, and much of this new wood was high-grade. Fritz was convinced that he had proved the economic virtues of selective logging.[49]

The Wonder Plot demonstrated, Fritz believed, that although neither virgin forests nor clear-cuts produced sixty-five-year-old redwoods worth harvesting, selection cutting "would produce clear grades in considerable volume." Returning home, he typed up his results and sent copies to several lumber companies. Before long the press obtained a copy, and Fritz's revolutionary idea — selective logging — was the talk of the region.[50]

But Fritz had a hard time selling the idea. Lumber technology — using slacklines — made selective logging difficult and dangerous. Saving trees was expensive. And the Wonder Plot's second growth, although producing good lumber, was not equal in quality to old growth. So long as virgin timber remained, loggers had little interest in second growth, and Fritz had difficulty persuading them to think fifty years ahead, "when their old growth was used up and lumber would be still in demand." Yet gradually he won adherents. Besieged by the Save the Redwoods League and the Sierra Club, loggers wanted to show that they were good environmentalists. And a new technology, the bulldozer, replaced slacklines, making selective cutting easier.[51]

The breakthrough came in January 1935. At Fritz's urging the Hammond Lumber Company tried selective redwood logging on heavy timber along the Van Dusen River. Using bulldozers, company loggers avoided felling a single tree marked for retention. Later that year Pacific Lumber tried selective logging at Monument Creek, across the Eel River from Scotia. Again bulldozers did not accidentally bump a single tree marked for saving. Fritz's method seemed an unqualified success. The Pacific Lumber Company abandoned clear-cutting. In 1937 Union followed suit. By the Second World War many other companies had embraced selection as well.

Fritz had won the battle — or so it seemed. He succeeded where Fernow and Pinchot had failed, in persuading private loggers to embrace silviculture. But his victory was short-lived. During the housing boom that followed the war, one by one redwood companies abandoned selection cutting. The method was too slow to meet demand — and too costly and wasteful. At $75 per acre, reseeding was prohibitively expensive. And selectively cutting redwoods, they found, exposed these shallow-rooted, tall, and top-heavy goliaths to the wind. They blew down in prodigious numbers, shattering on impact. Some fell across highways or on buildings, requiring expensive salvage.[52]

Forsaking selection cutting and focusing on old growth, many loggers raced through the woods. Vast tracts of virgin redwoods disappeared like wheat under a thresher. Every year during the 1950s trees were cut at three times the rate of any prior year, reaching a peak unequaled before or since. The tractor, which made selective cuts possible, now became a tool for faster clear-cutting, permitting loggers to work on steeper slopes than they could manage with slacklines.[53]

Soil eroded at a biblical pace, bringing floods not seen since Noah's day. In the winter of 1954–55, and again in 1964–65, once-in-a-century floods raged down the Eel River, inundating Scotia. The second deluge, carrying logs like battering rams, sent torrents raging down Bull Creek, toppling 525 giant redwoods in Rockefeller Forest.[54]

By 1970 only Pacific Lumber remained committed to selection. The granddaddy of redwood loggers, this company stood as the shining star for environmentalists and foresters alike. It kept the flame of Fritz's idea — that redwood forestry could be both profitable and sustainable — alive. But privately even Fritz admitted that his hopes may have been too high. Looking back, he wistfully conceded that loggers' pessimism about selection "was better grounded than my optimism." In an interview he said: "Reforestation, even natural seeding in the case of selective cutting, is difficult almost anywhere in California. I wish that economic conditions were such that we dared spend seventy-five dollars per acre. That day may come; it isn't here yet."[55]

Was sustainable logging, then, an impossible ideal? Each time victory seemed near, someone moved the goal posts.

4

THE
ECO RAIDERS

IN THE FALL OF 1970 Marc Gaede, a Marine Corps veteran, was working as a photo curator at the Museum of Northern Arizona in Flagstaff. One Sunday morning, seething with anger over federal efforts to build a strip mine on Navaho and Hopi land near the Utah border, Gaede drove out to the rail line under construction between Lake Powell and Black Mesa. No one was there. Quite spontaneously he began pouring sand and sugar into fuel tanks and cutting hydraulic hoses on backhoes. His exploits would become known as the work of the "Arizona Phantom."[1]

In the meantime, he established his own three-person environmental organization, the Black Mesa Defense Fund, joining with the American Indian Movement to protest construction of the giant mine. His actions — one of which nearly cost Gaede his life — were the first confrontational protests by environmentalists in modern times.[2]

Sometimes desperation, not necessity, is the mother of invention. This is how ecotage was born. A contraction of "ecology" and "sabotage," the term refers to the tactic of damaging property in defense of the earth. Its innovation signaled the birth of radical environmentalism, a movement that would change the face of politics. But rather than being premeditated, it arose as the spontaneous reflex of ordinary individuals who, like Gaede, had watched forests and prairies disappear under bulldozers and asphalt until something inside them snapped.[3]

By sugaring the fuel tanks of bulldozers, ensuring that on combustion the cylinders would fill with a gooey mass of blackened carbon, Gaede sought to slow the relentless march of mechanization. Quite unintentionally he had reinvented a practice that four years later the writer Edward Abbey would call "monkeywrenching."[4]

· · ·

No one knows who first conceived the idea of damaging hardware to reverse the industrial revolution. Some credit a legendary Englishman named Ned Ludd, who, in 1811, supposedly led riots aimed at destroying machines that had replaced workers.[5]

Although the riots were real, Ludd probably was not. One of the earliest stories suggests that the real Ned Ludd was a retarded boy consistently teased by town rowdies. One day in 1779 Ludd, fed up with the razzing, retaliated, chased a heckler into a house where stockings were manufactured. Unable to catch his tormentor, he vented his rage on two weaving frames. Whether this story is apocryphal or not, before long, whenever a frame broke people would say, "Ned Ludd did it." So when riots, ignited by economic depression, erupted in Nottingham in the fall of 1811, its masked leader took the alias "General Ludd."

As Gaede haunted Black Mesa, environmentalists everywhere were reviving Luddism. In Kane County, Illinois, a man known as "the fox" began a one-person campaign against pollution, dumping stinking sewage onto the plush carpets of the executive offices of U.S. Steel, spreading dead fish in corporate lobbies, and capping smokestacks that needed but didn't have scrubbers.[6]

In Tucson another group calling itself "Eco Raiders" was exercising its creative capacity for chaos against real estate developers who were busy "Los Angelesizing" the Southwest. They shattered the windows of real estate offices with rocks, cut down hundreds of highway billboards, removed engineers' stakes from planned housing subdivisions, poured molten lead into locks at construction sites, ripped out electrical and plumbing fixtures in new but unoccupied homes, and sabotaged earthmoving equipment. And they seldom went off duty. Carrying a two-person saw with them wherever they went, they were always looking for targets of opportunity. Soon the Eco Raiders had Tucson lawmen foaming at the mouth. The sheriff's department assigned nine men full-time to a newly created Special Problems Task Force and finally caught a guy named Chris Morrison, who ratted on his comrades, putting them out of business.[7]

But others soon took their place. In Blaine County, Idaho, home of Sun Valley, ecoteurs took down virtually every billboard along Route 93, from Hailey to Ketchum. An undergraduate at the University of Vermont known as "Lobo" spread green terror in the hearts of outdoor advertisers up and down the East Coast, once even toppling a huge billboard by the Key Bridge in Washington, D.C. Another student, Sam Lovejoy of Montague, Massachusetts, felled a five-hundred-foot utility tower near his home. Then he turned himself in, issuing a press release to justify his act on ecological, legal, and human grounds.[8]

A new order was dawning. These young people, fired with the spirit of confrontation, were about to turn environmentalism on its head.

In retrospect the movement's evolution into radicalism might seem inevitable. Until the 1960s the conservation movement was a white, male, upper-middle-class philanthropy, a network of professional biologists, journalists, teachers, hunters, and businessmen. Starting quietly in the late nineteenth century, it had grown steadily. In the 1870s, notes the historian Stephen Fox, after President Ulysses S. Grant vetoed a congressional measure to protect buffalo, "scattered clubs of hunters and fishermen began to ponder the depletion of their quarry. . . . A group of professors and mountain lovers in Boston started the Appalachian Mountain Club, the first permanent organization of its kind in the United States."[9]

In 1883 three New Englanders established the American Ornithologists' Union, and in 1886 the journalist and naturalist George Bird Grinnell founded the Audubon Society. In 1935 a fervent hunter and editorial cartoonist with the *Des Moines Register*, Jay Norwood ("Ding") Darling, helped start the American Wildlife Institute (later renamed the National Wildlife Federation), dedicated to the propagation of game animals. And the same year the wealthy forester and avid hiker Robert Marshall, a fervent believer in public ownership of land, joined with other like-minded conservationists (including Aldo Leopold, author of *Sand County Almanac*) to start the Wilderness Society.[10]

Originally, *conservation* referred to the wise use of natural resources such as Gifford Pinchot preached, while *preservation* implied shielding nature from all human use. In the early years conservationism predominated. It was the Western environmentalist John Muir who first promoted the more purist philosophy. An avid hiker and amateur natural philosopher, Muir was, by the 1870s, deeply worried about the damage that logging and livestock were doing to the forests of the Sierra Nevada. Determined to stop this depredation, in 1892 he joined with a group of San Franciscans to found the Sierra Club, modeled after the Appalachian Mountain Club, and dedicated to preserving mountain forests. "The battle we have fought," he presciently declared to his fellow club members in 1895, "and are still fighting, for the forests is a part of the eternal conflict between right and wrong, and we cannot expect to see the end of it."[11]

Muir's and the club's reverence for forests and wilderness had deep roots in America's Puritan past. This attitude was what one of its early board members, Ansel Adams, would call, describing his own faith, "a vast, impersonal pantheism" — the belief that nature is God, and everything that exists is united by and infused with this holy spirit.[12]

Pantheism was one of the oldest of American spiritual doctrines. As early as the 1600s, as the great historian of Puritan ideas Perry Miller observed, the New England theologians were "obsessed" with nature and were drawn to pantheism and nature mysticism. What Miller calls the "inherent mysticism, the ingrained pantheism, of certain Yankees" would pass from the early New England theologians of the 1600s, to the prominent Congregational preacher Jonathan Edwards in the 1700s, to the Massachusetts philosophers of nature, Ralph Waldo Emerson and Henry David Thoreau, in the 1800s. "The God of Puritanism," Miller wrote, "was both sovereign and wise. His attributes were so balanced that He could be at one and the same time the object of worship and the source of knowledge. The same balance was therefore thought to be extended into the realm of nature, for God's works must reflect His perfections."[13]

According to Calvinist theology, God created the universe and sustained it but was not identical with it. Pantheism, therefore, was an official heresy. But the distinction between God as being *in* nature and as being identical *with* nature was a fine one which gradually eroded over time. Thus, in 1630 the German divine Johann Alsted, who strongly influenced the Puritans, would write, "A genuine reading of the book of nature is an ascension to the mind of God." Later, a Puritan textbook would declare nature to be the "ordinary power of God."[14]

By the 1730s Edwards had blurred the distinction further. Introducing the idea indirectly by using the metaphor of the sun, he explained how God infuses everything: "It is by a participation of this communication from the sun, that surrounding objects receive all their lustre, beauty and brightness. It is by this that all nature is quickened and receives life, comfort and joy."[15]

As Massachusetts society became increasingly liberal and tolerant, the notion that God was directly accessible through communion with nature was more openly expressed. Miller writes:

> From the time of Edwards to that of Emerson, the husks of Puritanism were being discarded, but the energies of many Puritans were not yet diverted — they could not be diverted — from a passionate search of the soul and of nature, from the quest to which Calvinism had devoted them. . . . These New Englanders . . . sought with renewed fervor for the accents of the Holy Ghost in their own hearts and in woods and mountains. But now that the restraining hand of

theology was withdrawn, there was nothing to prevent them, as there had been everything to prevent Edwards, from identifying their intuitions with the voice of God, or from fusing God and nature into the one substance of the transcendental imagination.[16]

Emerson and Thoreau would boldly embrace this apostasy, thus letting the pantheistic genie out of the bottle. On entering the woods Emerson declared, "I become a transparent eyeball; I am nothing, I see all; the currents of the Universal Being circulate through me; I am a part or particle of God." And Thoreau would cry, "In wildness is the preservation of the world." These pronouncements, echoing the Puritan longing for salvation through intimacy with God in nature, would quickly be joined by others. By 1849, when the Connecticut theologian Horace Bushnell announced that "God is the spiritual reality of which nature is the manifestation," these insights were already enlivening an emerging environmental consciousness.[17]

As a friend of Emerson's, whom he met in 1871, and a fan of Thoreau's writing, Muir would make the Sierra Club part of a pantheistic apostolic succession which eventually converted most modern environmental leaders, a line including Adams, Rachel Carson, Supreme Court Justice William O. Douglas, nature writer Sigurd Olson, Wilderness Society cofounder Aldo Leopold, conservationist and drama critic Joseph Wood Krutch, poet Robinson Jeffers, and Sierra Club president David Brower.[18]

The club prospered, and so did its philosophy. Ultimately its more militant preservationism would replace moderate conservationism as the dominant ideal of the national movement. The watershed would occur at a place called Hetch Hetchy. After President Woodrow Wilson, in 1913, approved the building of a dam at Hetch Hetchy in California's Yosemite National Park — a step opposed by Muir and urged by Pinchot — many environmentalists concluded that only pure preservation, not wise use, would protect the natural wonders they valued so highly. "These temple destroyers, devotees of ravaging commercialism," Muir wrote later, "seem to have a perfect contempt for Nature, and instead of lifting their eyes to the God of the mountain, lift them to the Almighty Dollar. Dam Hetch Hetchy! As well dam for water-tanks the people's cathedrals and churches for no holier temple has ever been consecrated by the heart of man."[19]

After Hetch Hetchy preservation became ascendant. Concern for the forests of the Sierra had led to a philosophy sanctifying nature which would become a national religion. All existence, these preservationists believed, was harmonious, stable, whole, and infused with the divine spirit. Salvation came from intuitive and direct communion with nature.[20]

"When he is symbolical in everything, then divinity is the highest goal of existence," wrote Olson. Endorsing a philosophy called organicism, conceived by the Russian mystic Peter Ouspensky, Leopold would assert, "Possibly, in our intuitive perceptions, which may be truer than our science . . . we realize the indivisibility of the earth — its soil, mountains, rivers, forests, climate, plants and animals, and respect it collectively not only as a useful servant but as a living being." Krutch embraced what he deemed "a kind of pantheism." Jeffers, preaching in his poems what he called "inhumanism," urged, "Organic unity — love that, not man apart," a phrase that would become the motto of another environmental group, Friends of the Earth.[21]

Together these new pantheists would also reflect another element of Calvinism: its belief that the universe of souls was divided into the elect and unelect — those predestined to salvation and those fated for eternal damnation. Possessing an indelible conviction in moral rectitude, sanctioned by the God of nature, these latter-day Puritans would become a formidable force.[22]

The Sierra Club did not first seek to save the redwoods. For many years its primary concern remained protecting the high mountains around Yosemite. It was another group, more patrician and motivated by very different ideas, which would first seek to rescue the big trees.[23]

In 1901 twenty-six wealthy San Franciscans formed the Sempervirens Club, dedicated to rescuing the redwoods. They lobbied to save Big Basin, a grove thirty-five miles south of San Francisco, as a preserve. And the following year they succeeded. The stand became California Redwood State Park, later dubbed Big Basin Redwood State Park. In 1908 an independently wealthy congressman, William Kent, purchased a grove north of San Francisco. Donated to the federal government, it would become known as Muir Woods National Monument. Then, in 1919, seven men met at San Francisco's Palace Hotel to formulate strategies for redwood preservation. Within a year they had enlisted twenty-six prominent conservationists to sign a charter creating the Save the Redwoods League.[24]

These founders — all men — were right out of the *Social Register*. They included Congressman Kent; Henry Fairfield Osborn, a professor of comparative anatomy at Columbia University and curator of the New York Museum of Natural History; Madison Grant, a New York lawyer and best-selling author; John Campbell Merriam, a professor of paleontology at Berkeley; and Stephen Mather, director of the newly created National Park Service and a tycoon who had made a fortune mining borax in Death Valley. Soon after, the group hired the advertising executive Newton Drury as director. Drury would himself one day become head of the National Park Service.[25]

Only a third of the league's founders were California natives, and only two were from Northern California. Their little universe rarely extended beyond the Commonwealth, Pacific Union, and Bohemian clubs of San Francisco and the Union, Boone, and Crockett clubs of New York. Businessmen and entrepreneurs, these early conservationists worshiped the great gods of free enterprise and progress. And in the West redwoods were their icons. This Brahmin class saw the big trees as symbols of their own superior breeding and ancient heritage.

Economic competition, these conservationists believed, created technology that benefited the world, just as nature's cutthroat Darwinian struggle for survival improved species, demonstrating that evolution was not random but represented an inexorable advance toward perfection. Among the biggest and oldest living things on earth, the redwoods were nature's own proof of this progress. The trees were to the natural world what modern civilization was to human history — a magnificent success story. By emerging victorious in the struggle for survival and dominating smaller trees, the redwoods proved that free competition, like natural evolution, led not only to progress but to inequality.[26]

Subscribing to an evolutionary theory called eugenics, several league founders believed that the white races were the most advanced on earth. Following Charles Darwin himself, the full title of whose major work was *On the Origin of Species by Means of Natural Selection; or, The Preservation of Favoured Races in the Struggle for Life*, at least eleven members, including Osborn, Grant, and Harold Bryant, who later led the naturalist division of the National Park Service, subscribed to eugenics, which its founder, Sir Francis Galton, defined as the science "which deals with all influences that improve the inborn qualities of a race." Madison Grant's bestseller, *The Passing of the Great Race*, predicted extinction of the "Nordic" race through interbreeding with what he saw as inferior stock.[27]

Many league leaders also embraced orthogenesis — the idea that evolution, far from being random, embodied purpose and progress. Like Frederic Clements, they saw change as constant and directional. Wilderness was not better than civilization; it merely represented an earlier stage of evolution. Man's intelligence freed him from the laws of organic evolution and gave him the power of "self-determined evolution." "Those natural elements that interfere with the highest development of man," Merriam argued, "should be eliminated." In 1927 he announced that eventually "the human race will have almost complete control of the biological world." Man had not lost the Garden of Eden. He was making a better one with technology: "The machine contributes to our opportunity."[28]

Hence, these Save the Redwoods League founders viewed themselves as redwoods among humans — the biggest and best, winners in evolution's free market struggle for survival. Their superiority proved that progress was real, that nature had a benign design, and that it was the class system, not equality, that was truly ecological.[29]

Such was the belief expressed by Walt Whitman in his 1855 poem "Song of the Redwood Tree":

> I see in you, certain to come, the promise of thousands of years,
>   till now deferr'd,
> Promis'd to be fulfill'd, our common kind, the race.
> The new society at last, proportionate to Nature. . . .
> I see the genius of the modern, child of the real and ideal,
> Clearing the way for broad humanity, the true America, heir
>   of the past so grand,
> To build a grander future.[30]

Driven by a conviction of evolutionary destiny, enchanted with redwoods as the master race of trees, these aristocrats led the charge to save the redwoods. Like Salvation Army soldiers seeking to save sinners one at a time, they would rescue redwoods grove by grove. And since they and the timber barons had grown up together and attended the same schools, they formed friendships with industry which allowed each to follow tactics of quiet persuasion.

Indeed, "quiet" was the word to describe this conservationism. Supported by wealthy and generous families such as the Rockefellers, the league members quietly negotiated with timber executives over brandy at the San Francisco Club or in the midst of high jinks at the Bohemian Grove. They quietly talked the companies into selling land to the league — or setting groves aside until the league could raise enough cash. They quietly lobbied at the state capitol in 1928, persuading legislators to create a state park system and float bonds to purchase groves for state parks.[31]

And the league was enormously successful. For five decades it would be the greatest force for conservation along the Pacific coast. By 1985 it had raised and spent $43 million to create 31 state parks in California, covering 250,000 acres.[32]

The vision of progress, spirit of compromise, and intimacy with industry which the league leaders embodied ebbed after the Second World War. Hitler's holocaust discredited their racist theories, while advances in genetics — revealing evolution to be random, not purposeful — disproved orthogenesis. After Hiroshima it was harder to believe in salvation by technology. Meanwhile, the postwar economic boom was transforming outdoor recreation. Redwood and Douglas fir groves were no longer the exclusive precincts of the rich. By the 1950s the entire nation was seeing the USA in its Chevrolets. Ordinary people, not merely the patricians, wanted to see and save the big trees.[33]

The league was out of step with these times. The Sierra Club, long the league's little sister, began to eclipse its bigger sibling. And the club harbored a decidedly less compromising attitude toward relations between man and nature. Rather than sharing a belief in tooth-and-claw evolution, the Sierra Club reflected a faith in what its cofounder John Muir called "an infinitely wise plan." And rather than worshiping progress, its ethic embraced a pantheistic love of the universe. In place of the conservationist ideal which the Save the Redwoods League leaders shared — that human beings are custodians of the earth — the club saw people as enemies of nature, which possessed a sacred value greater than humanity itself.[34]

Although it was not as well connected with the rich and powerful, under the aggressive leadership of its new director, David Brower, the Sierra Club would grow like red alder in a clear-cut. During the 1960s its membership increased over 20 percent a year. Unlike the league, which represented the rich, the club hitched its wagon to the star of rising middle-class professionals who worked for state and local governments, schools, and nonprofit organizations.

Soon the league's slide had turned into a free fall, precipitated by two nasty fights over national parks. In 1940 President Roosevelt appointed the league's Newton Drury director of the National Park Service. The next year logging companies, inventing the false story that the United States was running out of Sitka spruce with which to build warplanes, demanded the right to cut trees in Olympic National Park, which had just been established in 1938.[35]

Drury was suckered. Misled by false data from the field, he capitulated to these interests and, by 1941, began to allow logging in the park. These harvests continued after the war, cutting Douglas fir for the specious reason that these were "potential bug trees." Having infuriated environmentalists, Drury was forced to resign as director in 1950.[36]

His disgrace was a black mark for the league and traditional conservationism. But the worst was yet to come. A battle to establish a redwood national park was looming — a conflict that would signal the death of the old conservationism.

Strongly anti–New Deal, the Save the Redwoods League long remained lukewarm about the idea of a redwood national park, even though two of its leaders — Mather and Drury — had been Park Service directors. Ecological management, its members believed, was best when local. The state could run parks more effectively than the federal government could. As a nonprofit group, the league took tax law seriously and feared that lobbying for a park would jeopardize its tax-exempt status. Establishing a national park would also require expensive federal land purchases, and as late as 1959 Congress had never authorized money for this purpose.[37]

But after Drury died in 1959, the league's resistance waned. The accelerated cutting of the 1950s had taken its political toll. Many state parks the league had established were now threatened by road construction and erosion, underscoring the fact that bigger parks, protecting entire watersheds, were needed. Yet redwood forests had become too expensive for the league or even the state to buy. Meanwhile, serendipitously, the political climate for federal land purchases improved. In 1959 Congress appropriated funds to create Minute Man National Historic Monument in Massachusetts, making this park the first-ever created solely by public land acquisition. In 1961 it bought property to establish the Cape Cod National Seashore.[38]

Tentatively, the league began to support the idea of a redwood national park. In 1961 it proposed a modest federal preserve north of Orick, adjacent to the Jedediah Smith State Park, to protect the watershed of Mill Creek. By contrast, the Sierra Club, which had long pushed for a national park, wanted a big preserve, even though that would require large federal land purchases. In 1960 it launched a big media campaign for a park at Redwood Creek which would be large enough to protect the entire stream drainage. In 1963 *National Geographic* proclaimed its discovery of a redwood tree 367.8 feet tall, on lands belonging to the Arcata Redwood Lumber Company. Calling the tree the

"Mount Everest of All Living Things," the National Geographic Society tried to purchase the entire 140-acre grove from the company.[39]

Arcata's chief executive officer, C. David Weyerhaeuser, held a meeting of the board to discuss the offer. "Don't sell," Lloyd Hecathorn, then the company's vice president for marketing, remembers recommending. "Cut the tree. As long as it stands, the public will demand to make the grove a park." Instead, Weyerhaeuser turned the society down, explaining that, as the grove stood in the middle of Arcata lands, "it would be impossible to measure damage to the balance of the company's property by virtue of having a public park in the heart of our holdings."[40]

As Hecathorn predicted, the tall trees did rivet national attention. That same year the Sierra Club introduced a new tactic aimed at swaying public opinion, publishing a book, edited by David Brower, titled *The Last Redwoods*. It charged that the trees faced "apocalyptic devastation." Containing graphic photos, the book was, notes the historian Susan R. Schrepfer, "good propaganda." The media quickly joined the chase. In 1965 CBS television broadcast a special with Charles Kuralt, "Bulldozed America," which told the story of the destruction of the big trees. Simultaneously Raymond Dasmann's book *The Destruction of California* appeared, featuring a photo of redwoods on the cover. Using full-page advertisements in major newspapers, and lobbying hard without concern for jeopardizing its tax-exempt status, the Sierra Club took to the barricades.[41]

Such tactics enraged old-time conservationists. Emanuel Fritz, a league director, denounced *The Last Redwoods*, insisting that the book was misleading and unfair to timber companies. But the loggers made the league look bad. In 1966 the Miller Logging Company clear-cut right up to Jedediah Smith State Park's eastern boundary, breaking the continuous line of forest between the park and the league's projected national park. Later, Georgia-Pacific did the same along Redwood Creek, in effect, as the Sierra Club put it, defining the park boundaries "with chain saws."[42]

When Redwood National Park was finally established in 1968, the boundaries pleased no one. Trying to satisfy both the league and the club, Congress created a two-parcel park that included a little land at both Mill and Redwood creeks, but not enough to protect either. Almost immediately, nearly every environmentalist argued that neither was large enough. Park lines did not follow land contour, and logging continued upstream, threatening park groves with floods and siltation, or so environmentalists feared. Erosion from above the Redwood Creek corridor — a place known as "the worm" — posed a danger to the precious Tall Trees grove, which sat exposed on a horseshoe bend in the stream.[43]

The park acquired only 10,876 more acres of old-growth redwoods yet eventually cost $198 million, becoming the most expensive single land purchase ever made by the United States government. Nevertheless, the fight over it spelled the end of the old conservationism and the beginning of the new. The disappointing outcome exposed flaws in the league's tactics of compromise. Meanwhile, the Sierra Club continued to attract strong support from the upper-middle classes. In 1969 fully 80 percent of its members were professionals, and their numbers were increasing by 30 percent annually. The phenomenal success of *The Last Redwoods* introduced a new genre of activist propaganda. In 1968 another Sierra Club book, Paul Ehrlich's *Population Bomb*, appeared, becoming a bestseller.[44]

As the league's influence waned, the club's prospects soared. Consensus building gave way to mass media campaigns. Gone was the belief in volunteerism and quiet philanthropy. The league's ability to raise funds and political support from the superrich was no match for the club's genius for publicity. Now it would be the public, not the privileged few, who would determine environmental policy. As Sierra Club staffer Mike McCloskey prophesied in 1968, the redwoods were "a harbinger of more sophisticated campaigns ahead."[45]

Yet in the eyes of young activists the Redwood Park was not a victory for the Sierra Club. Having achieved success, the club joined the establishment. Staffs, previously small and unpaid, were replaced by cadres of salaried professionals. After firing the feisty Brower in 1969, the club lost some of its fervor for public protest and embraced instead the tactics of lobbying and litigation. It came to favor policies calling for federal action and to depend increasingly on public funds for its own financial support.[46]

The Redwood Park battle therefore exposed the Sierra Club's weaknesses too. Even as Brower invented confrontational politics, many activists began to think he hadn't gone far enough. Thus, in Newtonian fashion, each new action generated an equal and opposite reaction. Within the space of a decade, patrician conservationism had given way to middle-class environmentalism, which would soon be challenged by a still younger generation, neither upper nor middle class but hippie. Society was on a slippery slope to greater confrontation, but where would it lead?

5

REBELS
WITH A CAUSE

EARTH DAY, APRIL 22, 1970, signaled that America had entered a new era. Held the same spring that the Black Mesa strip mine first provoked Marc Gaede into action, it verified the radicalization of a generation. Indeed, it was the biggest environmental demonstration in history. More than 1,500 colleges and 10,000 schools held rallies. Congress recessed; 100,000 people paraded up New York's Fifth Avenue, and another 10,000 camped at the Washington Monument. Suddenly, *Audubon Magazine* remarked, "everybody is a conservationist."[1]

Or rather nearly everybody, it seemed, was a protester. Two months earlier the Chicago Seven had been convicted of inciting a riot at the Democratic National Convention. Less than two weeks after the environmental festivities, National Guardsmen shot and killed four students at an anti–Vietnam war protest at Kent State University. On campuses across the country during those angry times, the best and the brightest were consumed with fighting against the war in Vietnam, civil injustice, environmental decline, and collusion between the university and the military industrial complex.[2]

These were the playing fields where future environmental battles would be won. Many soon-to-be leaders of the movement had set out on a quest. And their goal was nothing less than to reinvent civilization.

The philosopher José Ortega y Gasset wrote that when one generation teaches its view of the world to the next, the succeeding generation will not accept this bundle of beliefs with the same conviction. Something — enthusiasm, understanding — will be lost in the process of transmission. The views of the next generation will be less sincere, less resolute, because the first generation would have arrived at its beliefs through *discovery*, whereas succeeding generations would have arrived at the same beliefs through *learning*. Later generations thus receive them on authority, and what is taken on authority is less secure than what is discovered spontaneously.[3]

As this process of transmission continues through centuries, commitment to the original ideas becomes increasingly tenuous. Eventually, according to Ortega, there is a crisis when a generation realizes that it no longer believes what it has been taught. The fundamental principles on which its view of the world is based are rejected, and people become filled with self-doubt and lack direction. They must begin to search for their beliefs all over again. The cycle begins anew when a society, having gone through a period of doubt, develops a new set of beliefs. That is, it discovers them and, having discovered them, holds to them with all the tenacity and enthusiasm of the newly converted.

This sequence — of growing doubt, rejection, crisis, and discovery — occurred with the birth of Christianity and again during the Renaissance. And in the Enlightenment a similar cycle started, which, in the 1960s, seemed to be reaching the crisis point again. For more than two centuries faith in man, reason, progress, and individualism had been on the wane. But not until now had an entire generation apparently rejected it entirely.

The campus was the crucible in which this transformation took place. These were the times of high scholasticism in the professoriate. University professors, even those who weren't suckling at the teat of federal research contracts, were seen by many of their students as narrow pedants preaching the scientific ideal of "value neutrality."[4] By the 1960s moral relativism, an idea whose influence had been growing for centuries, had come to define academic culture. The dominant scholarly ideologies of the day were logical and legal positivism — doctrines teaching that moral judgments are meaningless and that law rests on power alone. Adherents of a philosophy known as emotivism held that such "value judgments" are mere subjective expressions of opinion, and cannot be rationally defended.[5]

This idea precipitated the crisis. If one cannot say what people ought to learn or how they should behave, students inferred, then everything comes into question. Many students, born after the bombing of Dresden and Hiroshima, educated by My Lai and Kent State, suddenly came to the conclusion that reason and science were evil. Intellect created bombs and pesticides. But if reason was defective, then it could not be used to find truth or sanctify moral principles. An agonizing epiphany occurred: the protest generation lost faith not only in the prevailing political order but in the very nature of reason itself.[6]

This phenomenon — moral doubt and suspicion of reason — was not new. In ancient times the Greeks also feared intellect and sought an objective foundation for values. And they found an answer, a philosophy that endured for nearly two thousand years. But their theory rested on assumptions about nature that, by the 1960s, few still believed in.

From the moment that Adam and Eve first tasted the fruit of the tree of knowledge of good and evil, thinkers have suspected the damage that intellect can do. "Be not curious in unnecessary matters," cautions Ecclesiastes, "for more things are shown unto thee than men understand," adding, "He that increaseth knowledge increaseth sorrow."[7]

Early Greek mythology resonated with the same theme in the story of Prometheus, the Titan endowed with the gift of foreseeing the future, whom the goddess Athena had taught all the wisdom of the liberal arts. Prometheus' sin, according to the myth, was passing this knowledge on to humans. He taught them to walk on their hind feet, to use numbers and letters, to build ships and sail at sea, to cultivate the fields, and to tame beasts of burden. He gave them the secret of making fire.

Prometheus gave man, in short, all the knowledge of the gods, and for this Zeus punished them both. Prometheus was chained to a rock for a thousand years, and man, having received these stolen goods, was sent the first mortal woman, the lovely Pandora, with her dowry locked in a chest — a chest containing all the evils of the world. Although Pandora was forbidden to open it, her curiosity got the better of her. Wanting to know what it contained, she lifted the lid, unleashing on mankind an eternity of suffering.

The same theme of the dangers of knowledge was woven throughout classical Greek drama, in the plays of Aeschylus, Sophocles, and Euripides. These Greek mythmakers and dramatists feared *unlimited* knowledge because they were aware of the *limitations* of man. Rectitude, for them, lay in restraint. The cardinal virtues — wisdom, courage, temperance, and justice — were possible only through moderation. Yet the peculiar weakness of man was his ability to exceed limits. Our intelligence is nearly limitless, our curiosity boundless. And whatever we know how to do we eventually do. Whatever restriction is placed on us — not to eat the apple, not to open the chest — we ultimately violate. And it is in trespassing, in our capacity for excess, that we do so much damage.[8]

Thus, to the Greeks the worst crime of all — the sin of Prometheus — was what they called *hubris:* overweening pride or arrogance. The original meaning of the word *hubris* meant "unlimited appetite," and it was this sense — the refusal to recognize one's limitation, the temptation to put oneself above others — that constituted the greatest danger to the human soul. And the way that *hubris* showed itself was in intellectual pride.[9]

The way to prevent *hubris*, they believed, was to recognize the existence of something greater than oneself. The only limit to pride was humility inspired by reverence to the gods or to a higher good. The pursuit of knowledge, in particular, had to be guided by the concept of a limit, and this was done by requiring that knowledge accord with the rules of virtue. "The highest object of knowledge," wrote Plato, "is the essential nature of the Good. . . . Without that, knowledge to know everything else, however well, would be of no value to us."[10]

So, knowledge had to be permanently cemented to virtue. But what would be the glue in this union? How could we justify limiting knowledge to the pursuit of virtue? The key, suggested Aristotle, lay in the concept of *telos*, or proper end. The universe, Aristotle believed, was one system kept in motion by God, the Unmoved Mover.[11] Such a universe was *teleological* because everything had its own *telos*, its own proper end or function. To know a thing was to understand its role in the functioning of nature, and therefore to understand not only what a thing *was* but also what it *ought to be*. In this way, in the Aristotelian world, fact and value remained fused tightly together. When things behaved themselves, when they did what they were meant to do, they aimed at their proper end.[12]

And though to Aristotle man's function was the exercise of his reason, the *proper* exercise of reason required that it be done in moderation and in accordance with virtue. "The good of man," he said in the *Nicomachean Ethics*, "is the active exercise of his soul's faculties [i.e., reason] in conformity with excellence or virtue."[13]

This was also the vision of the early Catholic church fathers. All human law and morality, argued Saint Thomas Aquinas, rested on God's law — or natural law, as he called it — which defined our proper end. Human decrees derived their legitimacy from natural law. And natural law was accessible by either reason or revelation.[14]

Eventually, Enlightenment philosophers such as John Locke and Jean-Jacques Rousseau would invoke similar ideas to establish that the legitimacy of the state derived from the consent of the governed. As men were potentially rational and virtuous and thus could know the moral law, they had a right to govern themselves.[15]

But even before Locke's day science was already undermining this ancient rationale for morality and politics. By the sixteenth century the Aristotelian and early church vision of the unity of faith, virtue, and knowledge had begun to fall apart. Science was coming into its own, and the first idea it challenged was teleology. Scientists such as Francis Bacon, Galileo, and Kepler discovered, or thought they discovered, that they could understand the universe simply by observing the causes of things. Science, they came to believe, was the observation of quantifiable patterns in nature and the systematization of these patterns into "laws" or mathematical generalizations. Knowledge, therefore, was possible without knowing a thing's proper end, or *telos*.[16]

The philosophy of Aristotle, based on understanding things within a synergistic system, was abandoned because it did not lead to easy quantification of the objects of study. In place of the ancient view, scientists adopted a methodology of applying algebra, geometry, and calculus to nature. Aristotle's teleological view — that all things should be understood in terms of their proper ends — could be replaced with one that was strictly causal and value-neutral.[17] But if the world could be understood without knowing its purpose, then the pursuit of knowledge, no longer a search for the proper ends of things, was also no longer a search for the Good. Intellect apparently stood on its own. And if knowledge neither rested on faith nor needed to be guided by moral law, what would contain it?

By dropping teleology, Renaissance scientists had removed a major restriction to the pursuit of knowledge. The possibility of excess, of *hubris*, loomed larger. If the new science did not need religion, where would it lead? How would its pursuit be limited? For no matter how much we knew of a subject, we could always learn more. Would intellectual curiosity turn out to be insatiable?[18]

For the next two hundred years scholars fretted over the implications of the new science. Intellectual curiosity, they feared, had no limit. Laurence Sterne wrote in *Tristram Shandy* in 1760, "The desire for knowledge, like the thirst of riches, increases ever with the acquisition of it." Intellect was just another appetite. The Renaissance, in awakening the human mind and conceiving the possibility of finding truth without God, had found Pandora's box. But who would open it?[19] Would it, asked Bacon's contemporary Christopher Marlowe, be Doctor Faustus, the mysterious German alchemist who sold his soul to the devil in return for knowledge and magical power? Indeed, thanks to Marlowe and later the poet Goethe, both of whom wrote plays about him, Faust came to symbolize this darker side of the Enlightenment. He was the man who refused to accept limits. "I am the spirit," says Goethe's Faust, "that always desires." And Faust, Goethe knew, lurked within all of us.[20]

Indeed, Faust was alive and well in the West, and his influence was growing. The genie was out of the bottle. Science had a momentum of its own, and no one, it seemed, could stop it. Throughout the seventeenth and eighteenth centuries, philosophers such as Descartes, Leibnitz, Locke, Berkeley, and Kant, attempting to patch up the damage that Renaissance scientists had done, tried to show how morality rested on reason and how reason was not possible without faith.

"I have found it necessary to deny *knowledge* in order to make room for *faith*," wrote Kant in the preface to the 1787 edition of his *Critique of Pure Reason.* But few were persuaded. The claims of pure reason were too seductive to be so easily dismissed. Like Humpty Dumpty, the neat Aristotelian universe was easier to break apart than to put together again. Science went on its merry way and became increasingly secular. It did not need teleology or religion. Invention, intellectual curiosity, the empirical techniques of observation, and the manipulations of mathematics and analysis were sufficient to follow the twists and turns of nature. Western society thus became what the philosopher Oswald Spengler, in *The Decline and Fall of the West,* called the "Faustian culture." It was a civilization that knew no limits, and its greatest minds went in search of far horizons.[21]

Yet, as reason and faith flew farther apart, the reputation of each suffered. If knowledge and godliness were no longer inseparable, then, many supposed, it would be possible to discover truth without finding virtue. And if virtue was not knowable, it was opinion, not truth. Moral judgments, which no longer rested on anything objective — such as proper ends or moral law — came to be seen as entirely subjective. What was right or wrong was a matter of opinion. Morality was relative. Similarly, if knowledge was limited neither by God nor by natural law, then it was merely an instrument of the ego. No longer a handmaiden of theology, it came to be seen as the servant of the will.

A world dominated by egoism was not a pretty one, and modern novelists and dramatists in particular, no longer viewing reason as the steppingstone to virtue, came to see it as an instrument of destruction. The legend of Faust — the story of how too much knowledge leads to self-destruction — became a popular literary theme featuring the brilliant, cultured man who, out of a well-intentioned desire to make the world a better place, combined with a naive idea of how to go about it, invents or creates something — a machine, a chemical, a bomb, even a monster — that threatens to destroy the world and, in the end, always destroys its creator.

Such was the story of *Frankenstein*, written in 1816 by Mary Shelley, subtitled *The Modern Prometheus*. In it the brilliant Victor Frankenstein, constructing a creature out of parts of human cadavers stolen from graveyard vaults, gives life to a monster that later destroys him. Frankenstein, a man described by the writer as possessing "unbounded knowledge and piercing apprehension," and, like Faust, believing himself "destined for some great enterprise," is, in the end, destroyed for having created life, for usurping the role of God. "Are you mad, my friend," Frankenstein warns the reader at the end of the story, "or whither does your senseless curiosity lead you? Would you also create for yourself and the world a demoniacal enemy? . . . Learn from my miseries and do not seek to increase your own."[22]

As with Frankenstein, so with Kurtz, the avaricious, cruel, but — once again — brilliant character in Joseph Conrad's novella *Heart of Darkness*. Kurtz, who one critic describes as "a god-devil who has power, intelligence, and loyal followers — all but morality and responsible humanity," is, Conrad suggests, the model modern man. "All Europe contributed to the making of Kurtz," Conrad tells us. "His was a gifted creature. He was a universal genius. . . . No fool ever made a bargain for his soul with the devil."[23]

And what was Kurtz's sin? It was *hubris:* "The mind of man is capable of anything," Conrad writes. Kurtz "had no restraint. . . . He was an extremist." What Kurtz forgot, Conrad suggests, is that strength comes not through intelligence but through faith. "No," he writes, "you want deliberate belief. . . . Your strength comes in . . . your power of devotion, not to yourself, but to an obscure, backbreaking business."[24]

By the nineteenth century few could hide their disillusionment with the false hopes that the Renaissance had engendered. "Where there is the tree of knowledge," wrote Nietzsche, "there is always Paradise: so say the most ancient and the most modern of serpents."[25] If knowledge is the servant of the will, reason has no foundation. Rationality is irrational.

Just so, the nineteenth-century mind fell prey to a swarm of philosophies preaching versions of irrationality. God, said Freud, was merely a father figure representing our childish subconscious desires to see the world not as it is but as we want it to be. Knowledge, said Schopenhauer, was the servant of the will, and science our way of dominating nature. Life, said Nietzsche, was the Will to Power, and morality our way of exerting power over others.

This skeptical, anti-reason, anti-virtue vision in turn had dramatic consequences in politics and world events, for eventually it brought the legitimacy of *everything* into question, including the legitimacy of the state. If man was irrational, if reason was simply a tool of his will, if virtue was another name for his personal preferences, if God was merely a symbol of infantile desires, then there could be no natural law. What, then, justified and limited political power? On what did the authority of a government rest? The answer was quick in coming: on nothing at all.

Political power came to be seen by many intellectuals in particular as simply a bald fact, to be used — that is, exploited — by individuals or social classes. "Knowledge" and "virtue" were just words we use to give our exercise of power the patina of respectability. There was, according to Karl Marx, no objective truth. Our beliefs, far from being rational, merely reflected the interests of our economic class. God was an invention designed to keep the proletariat in its place: religion was "the opiate of the masses." Therefore the state, resting neither on God nor on reason, had no standing. It was merely the way one class suppressed another.[26] Similarly, apologists for fascism argued that government had no legitimate foundation in reason or in God. Knowledge and virtue were only means to power. The authority of the state rested on its power. Might made right.[27]

This was the condition of ideology at the outbreak of the Second World War. The rationale for democracy, many believed, was bankrupt. It rested on Lockean assumptions about the rationality of man and the existence of natural law which few thinkers credited. The choice, it was fashionable to hold then, was between fascism and communism.[28]

Indeed, these ideologies had enormous appeal. For, paradoxically, they incorporated notions that had once helped to fuel the popularity of Aristotelianism — elements the democratic, liberal, humanistic, scientific Western tradition had abandoned.

Like the earlier classical philosophies, both fascism and communism subjected the individual to a higher authority, fascists to the state or national culture and communists to the interests of the working class. Both adopted a vision of knowledge and history that was distinctly teleological: the fascists insisted that history was the inevitable unfolding of the destiny of the culture; the communists decreed that history was governed by immutable laws that would ultimately bring about the proletarian revolution. And both defined right and wrong in terms of their respective teleological visions: the fascists held that right actions were those that served the state; the communists supposed them to be those that brought about the destruction of the state and hastened the inevitable coming of the classless society.[29]

The popularity of both ideologies, in short, derived from those ideas — the appeal to collective rather than individual needs, to higher authority, and to a belief that history has a purpose and a direction — that many in liberal Western society had abandoned as superstition. So as hollow as they were, they filled a vacuum. They pretended to be complete and systematic theories that explained all the mysteries of human life. They allowed many people to believe that they could choose to be on the side of righteousness and destiny. They offered something to be for, not merely something to oppose.

This was the underlying crisis afflicting Western values, including democracy, in the twentieth century: although their justification appeared to rest on natural law, few still believed the classical doctrine. After World War I many philosophers had embraced emotivism — the view that value judgments have no "cognitive content." By the 1940s the influence of this ethical theory, which provided a simple rationale for the modern scientific ideal of "objective" and "morally neutral" scholarship, had spread beyond philosophy departments to the rest of academe.[30]

During the decade following Second World War, the idea that nature had a purpose had been thoroughly discredited in the eyes of most scholars in the physical sciences. Although a form of teleological explanation — carrying the technical-sounding name of functional analysis — was still popular among some biologists and social scientists, an increasing number of prominent philosophers and scientists regarded this as simply not scientific. Then, in 1959, a Princeton University professor, Carl Hempel, published a paper titled "The Logic of Functional Analysis," which appeared to drive the final nails into the coffin of teleology.[31]

"Functional analysis," notes Hempel, "is a modification of teleological explanation, i.e., of explanation not by reference to causes which 'bring about' the event in question, but by reference to ends which determine its course." His example is a claim made by the anthropologist Bronislaw Malinowski that "magic fulfills an indispensable function within culture [by reducing anxiety]. It satisfies a definite need which cannot be satisfied by any other factors of primitive civilization."

But such an explanation, Hempel argues, does not satisfy minimum scientific standards. It "no more enables us to predict than it enables us to explain." A rigorous theory must prove that there are no substitutes that could play the same role as the item at issue (i.e., magic). That is, it must show "that the specific item under analysis is . . . functionally indispensable." Malinowski's assertion, he notes, is "highly questionable on empirical grounds: in all concrete cases of application there do seem to exist alternatives" to magic. Anxiety, that is, sometimes manifests itself in ways other than in a belief in magic, and it could be reduced by ceremonies other than those that Malinowski observed. And since such a theory cannot rule out the possibility that functional equivalents exist, it cannot predict that an item such as magic will always be necessary to sustain the communities in question.

Rather than constituting science, Hempel says, functional theories are often invoked to justify ethical beliefs. Unavoidably they make tacit references to vague, nonempirical notions, such as the "proper working" or "normal functioning" of a system. Because of this vagueness there is a "danger of each investigator's projecting into those concepts . . . his own ethical standards of what would constitute a 'proper' or 'good' adjustment of a given system."

When a scientist says that something is necessary for the "survival of group or organism," these words may have "the deceptive appearance of clarity" but are in fact unavoidably value-laden. "For when we speak of biological needs or requirements . . . we construe these, not as conditions of just the barest survival but as conditions of persistence in, or return to, a 'normal' or 'healthy' state, or to a state in which the system is a 'properly functioning whole.'" Thus, "there is definite danger that different investigators will use the concept of functional prerequisite . . . in different ways, and with valuational overtones corresponding to their diverse conceptions of what are the most 'essential' characteristics of 'genuine' survival for a system of the kind under consideration."

Indeed, these same ethical overtones of functionalism may explain its popularity:

> Psychologically, the idea of function often remains closely associated with that of purpose. . . . [Yet] precisely this psychological association of the concept of function with that of purpose, though systematically unwarranted, accounts to a large extent for the appeal and the apparent plausibility of functional analysis as a mode of explanation; for it seems to enable us to "understand" self-regulatory phenomena of all kinds in terms of purposes or motives, in much the same way in which we "understand" our own purposive behavior and that of others.

Hempel's paper inadvertently highlighted a cultural crisis: it confirmed that modern scholarship viewed teleological explanations as unscientific. By implication this meant that they could not be invoked to justify natural law or the Lockean consensus. Yet many people still found teleology attractive, for it seemed to provide the only way to justify certain cherished values.

Modern science, therefore, was asking Americans to give up something they did not want to abandon: belief in a purposive universe. By 1960 universities had already rejected the Lockean consensus. Professors wedded to this notion of value-neutral scholarship felt uncomfortable with teleological notions such as natural law. And "value," as Harvard president Derek Bok would put it in 1978, "is an awkward subject which fits uneasily within our scholarly tradition of objective analysis."[32] By the end of the decade, the curricula of liberal arts colleges typically reflected the emergence of a scholarly tradition that preached the commandment: "Thou shalt not make value judgments."

Expounding this positivist orthodoxy, college faculties broke the last threads holding a new generation to the old order. By painting nature as random and without purpose or values, they prompted students to revolt. For while educators preached ethical neutrality, the issues facing the nation — civil rights, the draft, and the war in Vietnam — were moral ones, demanding commitment. Much of the liberal arts curriculum had become irrelevant to these concerns, and students knew it.[33] They realized that if values could not be rationally defended, then our country's economy, government, and educational institutions could not be rationally defended either. If humans were mere passing blips of DNA, they had no right to exercise dominion over nature. Humans, knowing no intellectual or technological limit, were committing *hubris!* The military-industrial juggernaut had to be stopped.

Students had inherited from modern science a decidedly inhospitable picture of the world. Far from being the triumphant end product of an evolutionary success story, as several Save the Redwoods League founders had thought, they were merely statistical anomalies. Humans were no longer the center of the universe. "We are all bloody accidents along the way," Sierra Club leader William Siri would proclaim. "We are the compilation of an enormous number of accidents."[34]

This bleak view captured the popular imagination. Humans were merely fellow passengers on spaceship earth. "Not man apart," a line from a poem by Robinson Jeffers, became the motto of David Brower's new group, Friends of the Earth, founded in 1969. And it was a constant theme in the works of the best-selling writer Loren Eiseley. There is no other world, no afterlife or any other transcendent existence — only randomness, a universe, as Eiseley wrote in his 1971 book *The Night Country*, "all of night, of outer cold and inner darkness."[35]

This nihilism pushed many smack into the state of crisis which Ortega described. No one can live without values, and few can survive without hope, no matter how tenuous, that nature is orderly and directional. But the hardheaded science that began in the Renaissance and culminated during the 1960s took away this hope for many college students of this time. They had to get it back. But how? If intelligence is evil, events random, natural law a fallacy, and value judgments irrational, students inferred, then they had to revisit nature to find a new worldview. Theirs was what Charles Reich, in his 1970 bestseller, *The Greening of America*, called "Consciousness III." At war with the "corporate state," they rediscovered what their parents had forgotten: that society must rest on some moral foundation, and morality comes from nature.[36]

Having "been exposed to some rather bad examples of reason, including the intellectual justifications of the Cold War and the Vietnam War," wrote Reich, "Consciousness III is deeply suspicious of logic, rationality, analysis, and of principles." It rejects the "Corporate State," mistrusts science, and longs for "freedom from the domination of technology." It places the highest values on experience, sincerity, commitment, and unspoiled nature. "Members of the new generation seek out the beach, the woods, and the mountains. They do not go to nature as a holiday from what is real. They go to nature as a source. . . . Nature is them."[37]

Dropping out, many young people sought these new values in the woods. Embracing the pantheism of Thoreau and Muir, they went to the wilderness as into a church. But, borrowing from campus political experiences, they rejected Sierra Club activism — conducting mail campaigns, filing lawsuits, lobbying — and turned to tactics that blended ecotage, media manipulation, and theater of the absurd. Recognizing that reason cannot resolve disagreements over values, they resorted to direct action to achieve their ends.[38]

As the first television generation, they understood intuitively that this industry is a medium not for ideas but for emotions. Attempting to persuade government to use its coercive powers to enforce their preferred political agenda, they embraced tactics designed to manipulate public attitudes by emotive techniques, becoming masters in the use of protest to sway public opinion.[39]

Thus, within a century the very notion of environmentalism had changed. In place of the conservationist ideals of Gifford Pinchot — the view that humans are custodians of the earth — this younger cohort embraced the doctrine that people are enemies of nature. Gone was the Save the Redwoods League's faith that evolution was guided by a benign, rational design. Gone was belief in quiet persuasion. Gone were tweedy league conservationists, and gone, too, were sweatered Sierra Clubbers like David Brower. In their place was a new generation espousing novel tactics that would change the world. Politics would involve less debate and more emotion. Victory would belong to those who captured the minds and hearts of the masses.

An activist diaspora began. In 1970 a group of American Quakers who had fled to Vancouver, British Columbia, to avoid the draft joined with an ex-seaman from New Brunswick named Paul Watson to found a small antiwar group, the Don't Make a Wave Committee. Attempting to stop nuclear testing at Amchitka Island in Alaska, they tried but failed to sail into the bomb drop zone.[40]

Moved by Isaac Asimov's novel *Foundations*, they saw themselves, like the characters in this story, attempting to start a new civilization after the collapse of the Inter-Galactic Empire. Soon changing their group's name to Greenpeace Foundations, eventually known as Greenpeace, they became an environmental giant, the largest and fastest-growing activist group ever. Their statement of purpose read: "Ecology teaches us that humankind is not the center of life on the planet. Ecology has taught us that the whole earth is part of our 'body' and that we must learn to respect it as we respect ourselves. . . . Life must be saved by non-violent confrontations and by what the Quakers call 'bearing witness.'"[41]

Later they would go to the northern seal-killing fields, where they took pictures, bringing the story to life for all of us, sometimes covering seal pups with their own bodies to save them from clubbing. They would follow whaling fleets in small boats, putting themselves between the whales and the harpoons, often at great risk to themselves, yet always within focus of a television camera. Soon Watson, expelled from Greenpeace for advocating ecotage, would found the more militant Sea Shepherds, who set sail in tiny trawlers to confront pirate whalers on the high seas.[42]

Farther down the coast, émigrés from Berkeley, Santa Cruz, Ohio State, and other universities carried activism into the valleys where loggers lived. Like Dust Bowl Okies, they hitched rides or drove north in their Volkswagen minibuses with marijuana seeds in their pockets, seeking truth in the woods. Building hippie shacks among the tall trees, they planted grass and waited for inspiration. Living bearded cheek to stubbled jowl with loggers, they were a new immigration wave which would transform the north woods once again.[43]

Settling in places such as Ukiah and Garberville, California, and Cave Junction, Oregon, these activists, campus-trained in the tactics of protest and guerrilla theater, built grassroots groups, including the Environmental Policy and Information Center in Garberville, the Oregon Wilderness Coalition in Eugene, the Phoenix Environment Center, and North Coast Rivers in Seattle.

Southern Oregon and Northern California became the marijuana capital of America, and redwood country — comprising Mendocino, Humboldt, and Del Norte counties — soon would be known as the "Emerald Triangle." Pot and other drugs emerged as the spiritual and economic base of the counterculture. Hallucinogenic experiences and sudden wealth made anything seem possible.

An upstairs-downstairs culture developed: the scrawny, long-haired grass tycoons lived in hippie shacks in the mountains but drove Mercedeses and kept hideaways in Central America. Their neighbors the mill hands lived in small frame houses in town, drove pickups, and sent their children to Sunday school. The region developed a unique character, partly radical-anarchist, partly blue-collar rural conservative. The rural hippies and other refugees from decaying urban centers felt that they had found a unique place entirely separate from America. It was — Ecotopia! Inspired by the 1975 novel of that name by Ernest Callenbach, they saw themselves as part of a seedling movement to establish an environmentally perfect society.[44]

But what would this society be like? They did not know. Having rejected old values, they had yet to formulate new ones. Unlike the Redwoods League leaders, they were not sustained by a belief in progress. They lacked John Muir's faith in a universe of "law, order, creative intelligence, and loving design."[45]

For them everything associated with past arrangements remained suspect: capitalism, communism, urban society, positivistic science, humanism, traditional politics. They were bent on finding an alternative to the corporate state, a formula for making human society ethically and ecologically sustainable. But they still needed an insight that would galvanize and focus their unease. They needed a philosophy to replace the evolutionary doctrines they had rejected. That is to say, they required a new metaphor for nature, an image to serve as the moral inspiration of a new world order.

Every ideology ever conceived has rested on a simple idea, a picture of reality so captivating, so convincing, that it could serve as a lens for viewing all of reality. But now there was a problem. Nature was so protean, so malleable, so fecund that it was bound to be distorted by any simple description. Over history, nature has been alternately likened to a sphere, a clock, a machine, a vegetable, a computer, a pyramid, and has been characterized as benign, hostile, rational, irrational, circular, conflicting, harmonious, in flux, unchanging, perpetually moving, motionless, unitary, and fragmented. Political philosophers have a limitless supply of cosmological buzzwords to justify everything from anarchy to absolutism.

In seeking a new view of nature, therefore, these activists had embarked on a journey to a vast and featureless land. Indeed, soon a novel vision would dawn, an idea so simple and powerful that it would seem to explain everything, unlock all mysteries, and provide a firm rationale for their ideals. And, just as earlier views of nature had led the Sierra Club and the Save the Redwoods League to focus on trees, this new vision would inspire a fight over forests. Springing from a source no one expected, it would catch the loggers completely by surprise.

6

LIFE IN
THE PEACE ZONE

BILL BERTAIN STOOD IN THE LAUNDRY wrapping bundles of clean clothes when his father, George, came in. Tears streamed from the old man's eyes. "Stan Murphy just died," George said. "Dropped dead of a heart attack at Rhonerville Airport, returning from San Francisco. It's the worst thing that's happened to Humboldt County in forty years."[1]

This August of 1972 the winds of change had reached this tiny town built and run by the Pacific Lumber Company. For the Bertains the death of the Pacific Lumber president, Stanwood A. Murphy — whom everyone called Stan — was a personal tragedy. For Scotia and the redwood region it was the end of an era.

The Murphys and the Bertains had been close friends for three generations. Bill, the youngest of ten siblings, grew up with Stan's children — Woody, Warren, and Suzanne — teaching the boys to serve Mass. After graduating with a degree in philosophy from Saint Mary's College in Moraga, California, in 1969, Bertain had enlisted in the U.S. Army, serving as an airborne infantryman. In May he had come home after his tour with the Eighty-second Airborne Division at Fort Bragg, North Carolina. He was just stopping by in Scotia, planning to work in the family laundry for a few months before heading south to enroll in the University of San Francisco Law School.

Three years before its president's death, the Pacific Lumber Company had celebrated its hundredth anniversary with a big party for workers at the Scotia Inn. Stan gave a speech, promising that "we will never, ever, sell Pacific Lumber." People jumped to their feet and cheered.[2] But the Murphy dynasty had come to an end. Stan had taken the reins of the company in April 1963, after his father, A. Stanwood Senior, died. But now the younger man was dead as well.[3]

· · ·

Palco, as Pacific Lumber is known, was the oldest redwood lumber company in America. Owning 197,000 acres of prime forest, it controlled the last remaining big stands of these trees not already in parks. Founded in 1869 and run by the Murphy family since 1905, the company was regarded as the most conservation-minded in the industry. Its management was paternalistic, public-spirited, and generous, making Scotia a workers' paradise.[4] "Half-necessity, half-dream, an entire town dependent on a single firm for its existence," wrote Hugh Wilkerson and John van der Zee in their 1971 book, *Life in the Peace Zone*. Tiny, almost miniature, Scotia was the paradigm of a company town. A 1951 *Saturday Evening Post* article, "Paradise with a Waiting List," called Scotia "the gem of the Redwood Empire."

Workers' bungalows lined the streets. Identically painted, with open front porches and unfenced yards and gardens, they exuded the pin-neat uniformity of a military base. The town had everything a family could desire — schools, churches, bank, post office, museum, shopping center, supermarket, pharmacy, variety store, gas station, and lunch counter. In its heyday Scotia also had a movie theater, skating rink, baseball diamond, even its own saloon and whorehouse, the Green Goose, later to become Bertain's laundry.[5]

Perks were generous. After ninety days on the job a logger or mill hand could rent a one-bedroom bungalow with garden and lawn for under $60 a month. Every five years the company would repaint his house, inside and out, for free. As his family grew, he could move into a larger house. He received a salary bonus each year, along with good accident and health insurance coverage and a choice between a pension plan or an investment program. If his son or daughter qualified for a four-year college, he or she received a scholarship of $1,000 per year from the company.[6]

It was, write Wilkerson and van der Zee, a place where time stood still: "In the town of Scotia there are streets and buildings existing so completely outside time that they have become vessels of the unconscious, provoking a sense of *déja vu* that is almost paralyzing in its intensity. There is the street you grew up on, the house, the lawn — not the way it is now, or even the way it was then — but the way it could have been if only the world had held still just a little. Nothing seems to have aged or changed. Nothing looks very old or very new."[7]

But times were changing. Something had gone terribly wrong.

Like most Scotia residents, both of Bertain's grandfathers had worked in the redwood industry, coming in with the first waves of logging families. Bertain's maternal grandfather began logging in 1882. His paternal grandfather, Louis, arrived from France in 1896 and tried logging before starting the laundry in Eureka in 1906. When in 1917 California enacted a law requiring logging companies to supply workers with one clean sheet a week, Palco contracted with Louis to provide the service. For a while Louis kept the laundry in Eureka, twenty miles from Scotia, carting the linen back and forth to the rail head in Eureka by horse cart. But in 1920 Palco moved the laundry, lock, stock, and washer, to the company town. George took over the business in 1928. After returning from the war in Vietnam in 1963, Bertain's brother Tom took over the reins from his father.[8]

The Bertains watched the company grow. In 1883 Pacific Lumber bought the land around Scotia and built its first sawmill on the site. In 1885 it constructed a rail link to Field's Landing on Humboldt Bay, securing a sea route for shipping lumber to San Francisco. The region's economy boomed. Cutting redwood for shingles, Palco almost single-handedly roofed California, running five machines, making fifty to sixty thousand shingles a day. In 1903 the Santa Fe railroad joined a group of Detroit financiers, led by Simon Jones Murphy, to buy the company, incorporating it in Maine on August 11, 1905, and immediately increasing its holdings from 20,000 to 37,000 acres.[9]

Murphy was another rolling-stone logger who had chopped his way west until he found timber's promised land. Raised on Prince Edward Island, he built his first sawmill on Maine's Penobscot River in 1848. When he ran out of wood, he and his sons moved to Michigan, then Wisconsin, and eventually Minnesota. Along the way he developed the Midas touch. Under the Minnesota forests that his loggers stripped Murphy found iron ore, which he soon turned into gold. From the Penobscot Building in Detroit he built a real estate empire, gobbling up everything from ranches in Arizona to citrus groves in Florida. Under Southwestern sagebrush he found copper, which he turned into another fortune.[10]

Eventually Murphy allied himself with the Santa Fe Railroad, which was in fierce competition with the Southern Pacific. Together with the Santa Fe he bought some of the short feeder tracks around Eureka, including Pacific Lumber's spur line from Scotia to Field's Landing. This move blocked the Southern Pacific's route north, forcing the larger company to buy him and the Santa Fe out. With the money from that sale Murphy purchased the real prize: Pacific Lumber.[11]

From then on the Murphy clan led Palco, shrewdly establishing it as the premier company along the redwood coast. Convinced that family men made the best employees, the company rebuilt Scotia from the ground up, adding cottages for workers, remodeling others, and constructing a bank, a hotel, a theater, and a hospital. In 1925 A. Stanwood Murphy, Simon's grandson, was made executive vice president, and in 1931 president.[12]

In 1910 Palco built Mill B, even today the biggest redwood sawmill in the world. To provide loggers with decent on-the-job housing in remote locations, the company mounted cabins on railroad flatcars, complete with plumbing and bathing facilities, hot and cold running water, and electric light plants. In 1919 Palco introduced the Continuous Service Compensation Plan, giving employees a bonus for every year they stayed with the company.[13]

And the company had good relations with environmentalists. A. Stanwood Murphy, in particular, was a close friend of Save the Redwoods director Newton Drury. In 1925, when "lady conservationists" tied themselves to trees to stop logging at Dyerville Flat along the east side of the Eel River, Murphy capitulated, agreeing to sell the league 3,000 acres of this prime forest, below cost. In 1931 he sold 9,400 acres to John D. Rockefeller, Jr., creating the Rockefeller Forest, and in 1939 the company sold 1,380 additional acres in the Dyerville area to the league.[14]

The company deferred logging along the south fork of the Eel River — a stupendous grove called "Avenue of the Giants" — for thirty-five years, until conservationists could raise enough money to buy it. In 1956 Palco sold 190 acres of the southern portion of Avenue of the Giants for expansion of Humboldt Redwoods State Park. In 1968 it conveyed 1,680 more acres to the league, and in 1969 another 1,240, all at below market value.[15]

Yet despite this generosity, Palco still owned more than half the virgin redwoods remaining in private hands. And even conservationists admitted that the company managed these groves, totaling more than 100,000 acres, wisely. Remaining faithful to Emanuel Fritz's ideal of selective logging, it cut trees far more slowly than they grew. Between 1957 and 1985 Palco's redwood timber volume would nearly double. And that would spell double trouble.[16]

The Bertains, like Larry Robertson and Tom Hirons, believed that they had found the secret of the good life, that they lived in paradise, where one could do well by doing good. They had proved that logging not only benefited people but was good for the earth as well. But, as it would turn out, they had succeeded too well.

By the end of the 1960s federal forests in the Northwest were supplying about 25 percent of the nation's supply of softwood saw timber. Productivity, owing to stimulation of new growth through clear-cuts, was rising substantially. Sales reached and remained at 9 to 10 billion board feet annually.[17]

While employment fluctuated with the market, logging towns remained healthy, thanks in part to the way federal timber sales contributed to community stability. Meanwhile, the redwood industry had found new markets for its trees. Consumers, discovering that redwood shrinks and warps less than other wood, naturally resists decay, and provides superior insulation, increasingly demanded it for siding, paneling, decking, and other decorative and outdoor uses.[18]

And there were still prodigious amounts of old growth.[19] Mature Douglas fir (trees 140 years and older) covered 37 percent of the forests of Oregon and Washington, not counting the 3.7 million acres in national parks and wilderness, and ancient redwood trees — not including the more than 85,000 acres already protected in national parks and state forests — covered another 100,000 acres in coastal California. The era when forests were cleared for cropland had come to an end, and the specter of a timber famine had evaporated. Between 1905 and 1970 per capita wood consumption dropped from 500 board feet to less than 200.

America's forests stopped shrinking and began to grow. Private timberlands that had been clear-cut earlier in the century were coming back, ensuring a continuing supply in the next century. As tree planting reached record levels, wildlife, benefiting from improving habitat conditions, flourished. The number of whitetail deer had multiplied forty times from 1930 to 1970, and elk and antelope increased fourfold during the same period.[20]

Eastern forests, denuded in the eighteenth and early nineteenth centuries, had grown back, becoming what the Appalachian Mountain Club would describe as "largely undeveloped forests" which "support vital and diverse ecosystems." In Vermont since 1850 the percentage of forested land had risen from under 40 percent to nearly 80 percent. Southern stands had increased in volume by one third between 1952 and 1970.[21]

Yet something was wrong. Loggers had become victims of their own success. The nation's values were changing, and with them the very meaning of "sustained yield." To some, achieving this goal required that timber volume removed by harvests should not exceed the rate of new growth. This was Palco's method, accomplished by selection cutting. But to others this system was penny wise and pound foolish. They aimed to convert virgin "biological deserts" into fast-growing, managed even-aged stands by eliminating old growth. And to do so rapidly required harvesting at a rate greater than current forest growth.[22]

The question was: Should foresters focus on a short-term goal of maintaining timber inventories or on a long-range plan of spurring forest growth? Protecting mature trees would maintain timber volumes for a brief period but might eventually lead to timber shortages, as old growth, already in decline biologically, was destroyed by fire, insects, wind, or disease. Preserving these trees would not provide for the future. Economically and ecologically, saving old growth was like investing in old people while ignoring the young. Its preservation, most foresters thought, could be justified only for aesthetic reasons.[23]

Optimizing forest growth, therefore, seemed to dictate cutting mature trees first. This would make room for faster-growing forests, which could be taken later, after stand growth had peaked and begun to decline. But there was a tradeoff: removing the bigger, mature trees unavoidably reduces forest timber volumes over the short run. Since old-growth stands contain more volume per acre, their removal can prompt public concern that forests are "running out of trees."[24]

Nevertheless, private companies in both Douglas fir and redwood forests followed the latter strategy, sometimes called maximum sustained yield. They sought to convert old, uneven-aged stands to younger, even-aged ones as rapidly as possible, thus accepting reductions in timber volume in return for increasing long-term productivity.[25]

This occasionally meant temporarily harvesting trees at a rate faster than could be sustained indefinitely in order to reach the point of maximum forest production — the so-called sustained yield capacity — as soon as possible. Once the virgin timber was gone, they intended to follow sustained yield strategies, harvesting no more timber than could be cut in perpetuity, and doing so by cutting stands when their biological or economic growth rates had reached their zenith.[26]

On public lands in the Douglas fir region, the Forest Service sought to follow a more conservative philosophy. For years it had endorsed a policy that in 1946 the Oregon-Washington regional forester H. J. Andrews defined as "the greatest even flow of forest products in perpetuity which the forest lands involved are capable of producing." But while preaching this, the Forest Service did not always practice it. When lumber demand exploded in the late 1950s, the agency, like private industry, raced to convert virgin stands to faster-growing younger ones. Only in 1969 did the service decide that this was a mistake. The government's *Douglas-*

Fir Supply Study, completed that year, found that ongoing harvest rates, if continued, would produce a 30 percent drop in timber supply once old growth was gone. To protect logging communities from such an economic hardship, in 1973 the service inaugurated a new policy of "nondeclining flow," which stipulated that no current planned harvest could be larger than any possible future one.[27]

Therefore, maximum sustained yield, practiced by many private firms throughout the Northwest, and nondeclining flow, ultimately followed by the Forest Service in Douglas fir country, both aimed at forest conversion, and both sought eventually to harvest forests at sustained yield capacity. The former merely sought to reach these goals more quickly — and therefore, many foresters believed, less wastefully as well.[28]

Following these strategies of forest conversion, loggers zealously cut their way through the woods. And they began to achieve their objectives. Even as harvests soared during the postwar building boom, trees grew faster than they were being cut. Growth rates ballooned, by 1970 exceeding cuts by more than 30 percent nationally. Between 1952 and 1987 timber volume per acre increased by 30 percent nationally, and by over 50 percent in the eastern United States.[29]

In the Douglas fir region net growth per acre (i.e., total growth less mortality) increased from under 50 cubic feet per year in 1952 to over 70 in 1970, and to 110 in 1987. As young trees replaced old ones, mortality dropped 60 percent. Growth rates in California fir forests would triple between 1964 and 1984. In redwood country between 1975 and 1985, net young forest growth would reach 2.9 percent a year. So, although old growth was indeed diminishing, these forests were not disappearing; they were simply becoming younger. Nearly 200,000 acres of old growth remained, covering almost the entire 2 million acres they had occupied a century earlier.[30]

To be sure, as productivity rose, timber volume shrank. The Northwest became the only region in the United States where inventories, measured in board feet, declined between 1950 and 1987. In Oregon and Washington softwood volume shrank 6.2 percent, while in California it declined 20 percent. Along California's North Coast, redwood volumes would shrink 5.9 percent between 1968 and 1985.[31]

Yet this drop was temporary. Growth, spurred by aggressive cutting, would eventually overtake harvests in the Northwest as they had elsewhere. The trouble was, although timber volumes would rise, the public would not wait.

By winning the battle for sustainability, loggers lost a larger war — the struggle to capture the hearts and minds of Americans. Silviculture was the science of managing forests for particular objectives. But the national goals for forestry were shifting.

A new era was dawning in which not sustainability but aesthetics and the desire to maintain forests in their "natural" state would be paramount, and increasing numbers of the public would perceive efficient forestry as an oxymoron. Forests would be seen by many as cathedrals in which to worship a new god. This would spell an end to the old silvicultural goal of maximizing wood production, at least in federal forests. The fundamental premise of forestry — that scientific management of wood production is good for both people and forests — was increasingly being challenged by those who shared an entirely different vision of nature.

Responding to a rising tide of hostility to human use of natural resources, Congress passed a host of legislation: the Wilderness Act of 1964, the Wild and Scenic Rivers Act of 1967, the Endangered Species Preservation Act of 1966, the Endangered Species Conservation Act of 1969, and the National Environmental Policy Act of 1969. These and other laws would have a profound effect on the Forest Service. The old-time ranger — white, male, educated in forestry, and reared in a rural area or small town — would be replaced by a new generation, educated in biology and coming from the cities or suburbs. A new forest science would replace the older one, challenging conventional biological assumptions that had guided logging for generations.[32]

Already public resistance to clear-cutting was increasing. The Forest Service, believing that this hostility was merely the result of an image problem, sought unsuccessfully to convince the public of its virtues. In 1970 the Montana School of Forestry issued a blistering report on federal clear-cutting in that state. Accusing the agency of timber mining, the report declared that "multiple use management, in fact, does not exist." The next year Senator Frank Church held highly visible hearings on clear-cutting, and rumors were rife that President Nixon might even ban the practice.[33]

Loggers were in the vortex of a hurricane but did not know it. The winds of change were sweeping north from Berkeley and east from the nation's capital, ready to blow their traditional culture off the map. Even as Bill Bertain stood in the laundry that day, Washington staffers of the Fish and Wildlife Service and the President's Council on Environmental Quality, together with environmental lobbyists and congressional staffers, were busy drafting a third Endangered Species Act, which would pass through Congress almost unnoticed, but which would eventually change the Northwest forever. Just a few miles from

Scotia a gigantic battle loomed. Like a reborn volcano, Redwood National Park, already the scene of one cataclysmic struggle between loggers and environmentalists, threatened to erupt again.[34]

A storm was approaching. But these dark clouds lay over the horizon, hidden by the forested hills, where loggers could not seem them. Living in their cocoon world, in little towns tucked into narrow valleys which hardly ever saw sunlight, deep in forests black with dampness, in this little land which was so much like early America and so unlike modern America, Bertain and people like him did not notice. Indeed, as the winds swirled violently around them, the loggers, in the eye of the storm, did not feel so much as a zephyr.

II

DISCOVERY:
NATURE IS AN
ANCIENT FOREST

1973–1981

The clearest way into the Universe is through
a forest wilderness.

John Muir

The sacred word "nature" is probably the most
equivocal in the vocabulary of the European
peoples.

Arthur O. Lovejoy and George Boas

7

BUILDING
AN ARK

IT HAD BEEN A LONG DAY. Now, the evening in the spring of 1973, it was dark outside and the Capitol building was almost empty. Three men sat at a corner table in the House of Representatives cafeteria, drinking coffee. Earl Baysinger, Frank M. Potter, Jr., and Clark Bavin hunched over a yellow legal pad, writing parts of what would become the Endangered Species Act of 1973.[1]

They were a good team, Baysinger thought. The chemistry was right. Baysinger was acting chief of the tiny three-man Office of Endangered Species and International Activities. Potter served as counsel to the Merchant Marine and Fisheries committee. And Bavin ran the U.S. Fish and Wildlife Service's law enforcement division. Potter called the meeting at the request of Congressman John Dingell of Michigan, chairman of the House Subcommittee on Fisheries and Wildlife Conservation. The congressman had submitted a version of the endangered species bill to the House in January, but he caught a lot of flak from hunters for doing so. The "hook and bullet crowd," as Baysinger called them, complained that the legislation treated hunters unfairly. The draft provided strict penalties for killing endangered species but no provisions for protecting habitat. Yet the real cause of extinctions, hunters argued, was habitat destruction.[2] Dingell, a member of the National Rifle Association and an avid hunter himself, took this criticism seriously. Sportsmen were his natural constituency. So he told Potter to put habitat protection into the law. Potter called the meeting with Baysinger and Bavin to help him do it.[3]

The need to save habitat struck a harmonious chord in Baysinger. Eighteen months earlier, as chief of the bird-banding laboratory at the Patuxent Wildlife Research Center in Laurel, Maryland, he had known many scientists who were putting leg bands or other markers on birds to track their movements and behavior. These researchers had warned Baysinger that wildlife habitat was shrinking dangerously, and that projects built or funded by government agencies such as the Bureau of Reclamation and the Army Corps of Engineers were major causes.

The government regularly squandered billions on pork barrel projects that destroyed wildlife habitat, then spent millions more trying to save the animals these projects had put in jeopardy. The Agriculture Department paid farmers to drain wetlands, then the Bureau of Sport Fisheries and Wildlife struggled to save the waterfowl. One hand of the government didn't know what the other was doing. It made no sense.

The three men had wordsmithed all afternoon, yet the right phrases eluded them. They faced a stumbling block in that all wildlife except migratory waterfowl were managed by the states. The federal government couldn't tell the states how to manage land for these creatures. Such an edict might be unconstitutional and would cause a political firestorm. After breaking for sandwiches and coffee, however, they hit on the key idea: though the law could not tell states or private interests how to manage habitat, it could regulate the activities of federal agencies. The act needed a paragraph that would force Washington to consider the ecological effects of projects.

Pulling the pad out of his briefcase, Baysinger wrote down: "All other federal departments and agencies shall . . . insure that actions authorized, funded, or carried out by them do not jeopardize the continued existence of such endangered species and threatened species or result in the destruction or modification of habitat . . . which . . . [the interior secretary] determines to be critical."[4]

With that single sentence they got the hunters off Dingell's back and put sharp new teeth into the act. These words, which would become known as section 7 of the law, were inserted into the revised Dingell bill, which passed the House in September 1973 by a vote of 390 to 12. In July the Senate had unanimously passed a similar bill, introduced by Oregon's Senator Mark Hatfield. Later in December, both houses overwhelmingly passed the conference bill, and on the twenty-eighth of that month President Richard M. Nixon signed the Endangered Species Act into law.[5]

That spring night in 1973 these men had created what one federal appeals court judge would call "the strongest piece of land use legislation in history." It would also become viewed by environmentalists as the most powerful conservation law in the world. But at the time they did not see its implications. They just wanted to save whales, wildcats, whooping cranes, and other creatures that were riding a runaway freight train to oblivion. They were knights-errant on a rescue mission. Americans, imbued with a new empathy for nature, were gripped by fear and loathing of the terrible butchery wrought by hunters, poachers, exotic pet importers, whalers, and fur companies.[6]

The victims of these bloody trades were furry and feathery creatures with great charisma. Humanity's first cousins in evolution, they were so close we could feel their pain. These three men, too, felt the hurt. Caught in the climate of urgency, they wanted to turn back the terrible red tide of carnage. And everyone, from outdoorsmen such as Dingell to the quintessential indoorsman Nixon, urged them on.

The momentum was overwhelming. They were responding to pressures beyond their control. They would build an ark to rescue the world. Yet like kayakers running scale six rapids, they could barely steer their vessel or keep it upright, much less stop the rushing forces that propelled it forward.

All great rivers begin as small streams, high in the mountains. Fed by glaciers and melting snows whose waters fell years and sometimes millennia ago, they reach back in time even as they represent the eternal, flowing, transfiguring present. Great torrents of social change also begin as small rivulets, deep in the wilderness, where they are fed by sources lying beyond the memory of man. History, as Leo Tolstoy insisted, is the product of countless small acts of ordinary people. So the decisions of numberless individuals, like small spring-fed rivulets, fed the endangered species cascade until it became a mighty current.

One of these ordinary people was Ray Erickson, biologist for the Bureau of Sport Fisheries and Wildlife, a branch of the Fish and Wildlife Service. Erickson was running the whooping crane breeding program at Patuxent when Baysinger met him. And it was Erickson who first fired Baysinger's concern about endangered species.[7]

A Minnesota native and a graduate of Gustavus Adolphus College in Saint Paul, Minnesota, Erickson came to Malheur National Wildlife Refuge in southeastern Oregon before World War II to study the nesting ecology of canvasback ducks. He fell in love with Oregon and vowed to return. So, after serving as a naval officer in the South Pacific, he came back to Malheur in 1946 to continue field research for his doctorate on the life history of the canvasback. Later at the refuge Erickson switched to studying sandhill cranes. And soon, because sandhills are very similar to whooping cranes, he found himself drawn to them as well. Moving to Washington, where in 1955 he was put in charge of habitat management in the Division of Wildlife Refuges, he started analyzing whooper population data from the Aransas National Wildlife Refuge in Texas — the crane's principal wintering ground — and quickly concluded that these birds seemed headed for extinction.

The tallest bird in North America, the whooping crane once ranged across the continent and from Alaska down to Mexico. A wading species that mates for life, it thrived in Pleistocene times, 500,000 years ago, when the continent was covered with vast marshes, inland seas, and great prairies. It continued to flourish after the last ice age, which ended 20,000 years ago. But as the continent dried over the next twenty millennia, the whooping crane's habitat shrank. Forests replaced marshes, and inland seas drained. Whoopers lost habitat to sandhill cranes, which adapted more readily to drier conditions. By the time Columbus arrived, the birds' numbers had already dwindled, some experts believe, to fewer than 1,500.[8]

With the coming of European settlers, the crane's numbers plummeted further. Colonists spread across the continent, destroying whooper habitat as they went. Virtually everything the white man did threatened these birds. Wintering grounds became rice plantations, oil fields, farm and rangeland. Summer nesting sites disappeared under sodbuster plows, wheat fields, and cattle ranches, as farmers and stockmen drained wetlands.

Hunting whoopers became a preferred sport and a business as well. In 1890 their skins sold for eighteen dollars each and eggs for two dollars. In the thirty years between 1870 and 1900, more than 90 percent of the whooping crane population disappeared. Only a small remnant population persisted, most wintering around the Blackjack Peninsula in Texas. Pushed by growing concern for the species, President Franklin Roosevelt purchased 74 square miles of Blackjack in 1937, establishing the Aransas National Wildlife Refuge.[8]

When Erickson started studying the bird, no more than fifty individuals survived. Aransas held only twenty-one adults; no young had survived the 1955 nesting season. The large white birds were easy targets for poachers and plinkers with a .22 or a shotgun, and they were being killed faster than they could reproduce.

But Erickson thought that he could save the whoopers. This species, he found, laid two eggs at a time but seldom raised more than one chick. If he could take one egg from each clutch found in the wild and hatch it in captivity, he could double crane reproduction. Eager to try his idea, he proposed experimenting with sandhills first, rearing them in captivity. If it worked, he would move on to whoopers.

But everyone seemed to be against it. The National Audubon Society opposed captive breeding because it interfered with nature and because it might jeopardize wild populations. Many of Erickson's colleagues had no interest in nongame species. The chief mission of the agency, as its name implied, was to serve fishermen and duck hunters. Its wildlife refuges were dedicated to what Erickson called "duck farming" — providing fowl as cannon fodder for hunters. Most treated his efforts to save whoopers, Erickson believed, with "mallards aforethought."[10]

Erickson's suggestion became an issue within the Fish and Wildlife Service. To settle it, agency director Daniel H. Janzen formed a whooping crane advisory group, composed of both staffers and representatives from environmental organizations. But this group made little progress. The Audubon Society and others continued in their strong opposition to captive breeding.[11]

Eventually the time for Erickson's idea came. In February 1961 the newly elected Kennedy administration sent letters to agency heads, urging them to listen to employees' suggestions for innovative ideas. Encouraged, Erickson sent another crane breeding proposal to his bosses. Luckily his memorandum circulated just before articles by another service biologist, Rachel Carson, appeared in the New Yorker, warning that insecticides were endangering bird populations around the world. Suddenly the political climate shifted in Erickson's favor. Enlisting the support of his former boss, J. Clark Sawyer, the head of wildlife refuges, in 1963 Erickson obtained $3,000 to establish a sandhill crane breeding facility at Monte Vista National Wildlife Refuge in Colorado.[12]

Two years later, in 1965, after the Monte Vista sandhill experiment proved successful, Senator Karl E. Mundt of South Dakota, ranking minority Republican member of the Senate Finance Committee, concerned by the dearth of whooping cranes in his state, put through appropriations of $350,000 to expand whooper breeding efforts and move them to the Patuxent facility in Laurel, Maryland.[13]

Meanwhile, public concern over other endangered species exploded. Conservationists and nature writers feared for the future of Puerto Rican parrots, Aleutian Canada geese, black-footed ferrets, California condors, peregrine falcons, sea otters, whales, Atlantic puffins, spotted cats, and a host of Hawaiian plants and animals. It was amazing, Erickson thought, how many people had become "foster parents" to one type of critter or another. The service was deluged with requests from individuals and special interest groups, eager to save their chosen species.

Erickson's successful efforts to attract public support and appropriations from Congress emboldened the agency to consider expanding rescue efforts to other species. In 1964 Janzen established the Committee on Rare and Endangered Wildlife Species, modeled after the Whooping Crane Advisory Committee, and put Erickson on the panel. Its job was to elicit information and opinions from the scientific and conservation communities.

The new committee sent letters to groups and a variety of individuals, from professors to lay people, asking for data. In July 1964 its findings were published in a volume called "The Redbook" — a compendium of what the committee knew about sixty-two endangered species. During the next two years subsequent editions of "The Redbook" appeared, each thicker than the last. The more closely Erickson and his colleagues looked, the more threatened creatures they found.[14]

At the suggestion of this committee, Interior Secretary Stewart Udall on June 5, 1965, sent a proposal to Congress to establish a "program to conserve, protect, restore, and where necessary to establish wild populations [and] propagate selected species of native fish and wildlife . . . that are found to be threatened with extinction." The bill sailed through Congress with little dissent. Known as the Endangered Species Preservation Act, it became law in 1966. Congressmen thought it a no-lose proposition. It was merely a symbolic law, they were assured, one that would cost society nothing. During hearings the Interior Department testified that only seventy-eight species would be listed as endangered. And these, everyone thought, were charismatic creatures such as whooping cranes and black-footed ferrets.[15]

Yet the law was virtually unprecedented. Until the late nineteenth century most efforts to protect wildlife came from private hunter groups such as the American Fisheries Society and National Rifle Association. Since 1892, when President Benjamin Harrison established the first U.S. wildlife refuge by setting aside Alaska's Afognak Island to protect "sea mammals, other animals, birds, timber, undergrowth, grass, moss and other growth in or about the island," the federal government had increasingly sought to protect wildlife, but almost all these efforts were directed at game animals and fish.[16]

The Lacey Act of 1900 prohibited interstate commerce in certain wildlife killed in violation of state law, and provided for the first real federal presence in the wildlife conservation movement. The federal government soon entered into treaties and passed laws that established a nationwide network of refuges for migratory birds and offered a firmer basis for its involvement in wildlife conservation. Some of these were the U.S.-U.K. (Canadian) Convention for Protection of Migratory Birds in 1916, the Migratory Bird Treaty Act in 1918, the Migratory Bird Conservation Act of 1929, the Fish and Wildlife Coordination Act of 1934, and the U.S.-Mexico Convention for the Protection of Migratory Birds and Game Mammals of 1936.[17]

But until the 1966 Endangered Species Act, nongame species received little attention. To be sure, following the creation of Yellowstone National Park in 1872, national parks were required to protect all wildlife. But they didn't. The U.S. Cavalry, which ran the parks from 1886 until 1916, favored game animals over other creatures. The National Park Service, established in 1916, assumed that tourists came to see big ungulates such as buffalo, elk, and antelope. In 1918 it launched an extermination program against predators it deemed a threat to park "animal shows."[18]

During this campaign rangers shot, trapped, and poisoned wolves, coyotes, mountain lions, lynx, bobcat, fisher, marten, porcupine, and otter. Park authorities sent rangers out to the Molly Islands in Yellowstone Lake to squash pelican eggs because they believed that pelicans ate trout. The campaign continued until 1938, when opposition from conservation groups forced the Park Service to end it. Similarly, state fish and game departments, which received their funds from the sale of hunting and fishing licenses, showed no interest in management of nongame species.[19]

The one exception to governmental disinterest in nongame species was a little-known treaty signed by President Roosevelt in 1940. Called the Convention on Nature Protection and Wildlife Preservation in the Western Hemisphere, it was virtually overlooked by legal scholars but would have profound implications in setting a precedent for the Endangered Species Act. Besides providing for protection of wildlife habitat and prohibiting the taking of certain protected species (identified in an "Annex"), it uniquely stipulated that other species, which it called "nature monuments," should also receive special attention. Just as historic buildings deserve protection, the convention averred, so should nature monuments — "living species of flora and fauna" — be kept "inviolate."[20]

The Convention on Nature Protection, however, was never seriously implemented and was quickly forgotten. Thus, the Endangered Species Conservation Act of 1966 represented a fresh start. Yet it was also more symbol than substance. It contained no restrictions on killing endangered species and authorized a paltry $15 million for habitat purchases. It applied only to certain animals and not to plants at all. And despite U.S. treaty obligations, it completely ignored foreign creatures.[21]

But it did prime the political pump. The 1966 act was the product of efforts by a comparatively small cadre of dedicated conservationists from government and old-line conservation groups. But its passage put endangered species on the political map, raising public consciousness and creating a political climate that made the next step toward species protection inevitable.

Conservationists quickly saw the act's flaws. The law, they noted, did not stop the slaughter of animals. By 1966 the "Redbook" list had grown to 202 species, including 42 mammals, 110 birds, 38 fishes, and 12 reptiles and amphibians. Yet the government still seemed intent on "speciecide."[22]

State agriculture officials continued to kill skunks, ground squirrels, coyotes, bears, mountain lions, bobcats, lynx, and countless other creatures they deemed threats to farmers and ranchers. Animal damage control agents of Erickson's own agency were liquidating predators at a prodigious rate. Using a persistent and dangerous poison known as "1080," these agents from 1966 to 1969 exterminated 1,887 bears; 42,190 bobcats; 296,610 coyotes; 652 mountain lions; and even 62 lobo wolves, even though this animal was already listed as an endangered species![23]

Meanwhile, public concern about the environment soared. In 1968 Paul R. Ehrlich's bestseller *The Population Bomb* appeared, warning that world population growth was "a race to oblivion," that by 1979 "killer smog" might wipe out 90,000 people in Los Angeles, that food and water rationing could be "standard" across America, and that pollution threatened wildlife as well as people. The insecticide Endrin, he said, had seeped into the Mississippi River, killing between 10 and 15 million fish; and by 1965 the city of Omaha was dumping 300,000 pounds of untreated manure and grease into the Missouri River.[24]

The Population Bomb thus embodied a growing genre. Promoting pessimism, it emphasized the fragility of nature. Yet its claims were seldom documented and often false. The robin, which Rachel Carson had declared on skimpy evidence to be on "the verge of extinction," is abundant today, and all forty of the bird species she said were in peril are still around, many of them thriving. Similarly, Ehrlich's book — like most environmental volumes from Fairfield Osborn's *Our Plundered Planet* in 1948 to Bill McKibbon's *End of Nature* in 1989 (neither of which had so much as one supporting citation) — was crammed with factual claims and prognostications but offered little in the way of scholarly evidence.[25]

The public, however, was ready to believe these claims, and therefore did not demand proof. So, true or not, they spurred worries of calamity. According to opinion polls, the numbers of people fearing water pollution rose from 35 percent of respondents in 1965 to 74 percent in 1970, while expressions of air pollution anxieties grew from 28 percent to 69 percent during the same period. A similar worry concerned endangered species. Particularly bothersome to environmentalists was that the 1966 act applied only to native American wildlife, and not even to subspecies living across the borders in Canada and Mexico. Magazines and newspapers fueled concern over the killing of foreign species for their skins, such as polar bears, crocodiles, elephants, leopards, and rhinos. The Johnson administration, besieged by antiwar protests, sought to placate environmentalists. It ordered the Fish and Wildlife Service to write legislation restricting importation of other nations' endangered animals.[26]

The agency sent a draft bill — regulating imports and, for the first time, applying to subspecies as well as species — to Dingell, who introduced it in the House. The bill failed to pass in 1968; but the following year the new president, Richard Nixon, equally eager to placate green voters, continued to push the legislation. The Endangered Species Conservation Act was signed into law in December 1969.[27]

The new law increased the authority of the interior secretary to acquire habitat. And rather than just applying to "native fish and wildlife," it potentially covered "any wild mammal, fish, wild bird, amphibian, reptile, mollusk, or crustacean on earth." But far from placating environmentalists, this legislation, with all its loopholes, merely prompted their anger. Because it contained no penalties for killing endangered domestic creatures, the carnage continued. In the name of predator control 200 to 250 Minnesota timber wolves were still being killed each year. In 1972 Louisiana opened a hunting season on alligators — permitting a take of 1,347 — although this species was also on the endangered list. The Interior Department continued to allow hunters to shoot Mexican ducks and Aleutian Canada geese, even though both subspecies were also on the list.[28]

And while recognizing the international dimension of wildlife protection, the 1969 law did almost nothing to stop killing in other countries. Two loopholes, inserted to pacify the wildlife and fur lobbies, rendered the act toothless. The first allowed importations to continue if it was determined that a ban would cause "economic hardships." The second prevented the secretary from listing a species until it was "threatened with worldwide extinction." So long as tigers thrived in one region of the world, for example, they could be exterminated everywhere else. These provisions accelerated the killing. Industries exploited economic hardship exemptions to stockpile animal parts in anticipation of greater restrictions in the future. Between 1968 and 1970 shipments of rare animal pelts soared as the industry imported 18,456 leopard skins; 31,105 jaguar pelts; 349,680 ocelot hides; and the fur of 3,100 cheetahs.[29]

By 1972 it was estimated that only two thousand cheetahs remained in all African preserves put together. And although great whales were listed in 1970, a loophole in the law — which declared that, since they were taken on the high seas, bringing their body parts into port was not considered "importation" — they continued to be hunted. One firm alone was permitted to import 12,092,000 pounds of sperm whale oil.[30]

These numbers fueled the engine of public outrage. Walt Disney movies and Marlin Perkins's television series *Wild Kingdom* drew attention to the plight of spotted cats. Concern for whales in particular reached fever pitch. Recordings of the sounds of whales became a big item on many people's Christmas lists. Farley Mowat's 1972 book *A Whale for the Killing* tugged at heartstrings throughout North America.[31] The same year the United Nations Conference on the Human Environment unanimously called for an immediate end to whaling, and just before Christmas the Canadian government announced that it would unilaterally outlaw the practice. Violence against animals in those dark times seemed a corollary to the terrible carnage in Vietnam, the genocide against Indians and cruel injustices to blacks that weighed on the American conscience after the 1968 assassination of Martin Luther King, the 1970 Kent State massacre, and the February 1973 Indian occupation of Wounded Knee. The military-industrial complex did not have a monopoly on villainy. The entire civilization was suspect.

In 1970 two bestsellers — the Club of Rome's *Limits to Growth* and Barry Commoner's book *The Closing Circle* — had both reflected and encouraged this agonizing national self-examination. Exponential human population growth, warned the Club of Rome, threatened to upset the entire ecosphere, increasing pollution and waste, depleting natural resources, and disrupting ecological processes that sustained life on earth. Nature, wrote Commoner, is an "ecosystem" in which everything is interdependent but which technology has upset, triggering a domino effect that would lead to ecological catastrophe.[32]

Propelled by rising public concern, Congress in the early 1970s enacted a series of environmental laws: the Clean Air Act Amendments of 1970, and the Federal Water Pollution Control Act Amendments, the Federal Environmental Pesticide Control Act, the Marine Mammal Protection Act, the Noise Control Act, and the Coastal Zone Management Act, all of 1972.[33]

The 1969 Endangered Species Conservation Act, in short, was part of an unstoppable flood of environmental legislation. One endangered species act set off demands for another. Not only did environmentalists object to the weakness of the act, but businesses did not like it either. By curtailing U.S. imports of endangered species, it put American companies at a disadvantage against foreign competitors. They demanded a level playing field. In response, the Nixon administration in March 1973 signed still another treaty, the Convention on International Trade in Endangered Species of Wild Fauna and Flora (CITES), which was intended to end international trade as a threat to the survival of endangered species.[34]

These currents swirled as Baysinger moved from Patuxent to the tiny Office of Endangered Species and International Activities. Sitting at his new Washington desk he thought: a flow chart of species politics would look like a bowl of spaghetti flung at the wall.[35]

No sooner had Baysinger arrived in Washington than conservationists began badgering him to list spotted cats — tigers, leopards, cheetahs, and jaguars — as endangered. But he could not satisfy their demands. The 1969 law prohibited listing a species unless it was threatened with worldwide extinction. So long as these animals still thrived somewhere, he could not legally put them on the list.

So activists held his feet to the fire. Driven by youthful zeal, they assailed him with phone calls and op-ed newspaper and magazine articles. They enlisted allies in the major media and even threatened lawsuits. Two men in particular never let Baysinger rest: a charming southern gentleman and ex–Central Intelligence Agency officer named Lewis Regenstein, and a tall cowboy from Wyoming named Tom Garrett.

Regenstein worked for the Fund for Animals out of a cramped one-room office near Pennsylvania Avenue. Garrett represented Friends of the Earth. Together the two played good cop–bad cop with Baysinger and other officials. Regenstein orchestrated angry phone calls and wrote critical newspaper pieces that provoked their ire. Garrett would drop by their offices, making reasonable suggestions.

Both men were unlikely activists. Regenstein grew up in Atlanta and studied political science at the University of Pennsylvania and Emory University before joining the CIA. Working at Langley, Virginia, in 1971, he happened on an article in the *U.S. Humane Society News* describing how Labrador fur hunters clubbed harp seal pups to death. Furious that the national media were ignoring this slaughter, Regenstein wrote an article about the seals' plight for the "Outlook" section of the

Washington Post. Shortly afterward he quit the agency to join the Fund for Animals. Renting an inexpensive office, he worked the phones, pestered officials, attended hearings, and befriended key newspaper writers.

Through his proselytizing he met Christine Stevens, head of the Society for Animal Protective Legislation, and wife of Roger Stevens, a director of the Kennedy Center. Frequently entertaining Washington's power elite, Christine peppered her parties with conservationists, including Regenstein, who often found himself sitting at a dinner table next to the wife of a Supreme Court justice or U.S. senator. And he used these opportunities to spread the gospel of wildlife preservation.

Then one day a tall man in a big cowboy hat strode into Regenstein's office. "Hi," the man said, "My name's Tom Garrett, from Garrett, Wyoming. I'm here to save the whales." Son of a fourth-generation rancher, Garrett had come east to join the gunfight over endangered species at the Beltway Corral.

The two formed a team. "We didn't know what we were doing," Regenstein recalls. "If we did, we probably wouldn't have gotten anything done."

They walked the halls of Congress and the departments, talking with Baysinger and Potter as well as Lee M. Talbot, a senior scientist at the President's Council on Environmental Quality; Talbot's deputy, Gerard Bertrand; Nathaniel Reed, assistant secretary of the interior for Fish, Wildlife, and Parks; and Reed's deputy, E. U. Curtis Bohlen.

Eventually their lobbying hit its mark. In 1971 Dingell proposed amendments to the 1969 act, calling for more habitat acquisition, more money for research and captive breeding, and the introduction of a new classification for creatures less than endangered but still at risk, which the bill termed "rare species." The bill was referred to the Interior Department for comment, and was one of the first tasks to land on Baysinger's desk.

Taking ideas from many people, including Erickson, Baysinger drafted comments on the Dingell bill. These included establishment of a "threatened species" classification that would allow for federal action before a species reached the brink of extinction; tightly restricting and regulating the conditions under which a threatened or endangered species could be killed or otherwise taken; expanding the definition of "species" to include what now are termed "populations" as well as distinct species and subspecies; extending coverage of the act to include all animals and plants; providing cooperative international wildlife conservation programs; and making it clear that the purpose of the act included preservation of "ecosystems" upon which threatened or endangered species depended.[36]

Much to Baysinger's surprise, these comments were forwarded to the White House with a recommendation that they serve as the department's response to Congressman Dingell's draft bill. After reading Baysinger's suggestions, the administration decided that, rather than relay them to the Democratic congressman, it would include them in Nixon's planned environmental message to Congress, and later put them into the president's own bill, the proposed Endangered and Threatened Species Act of 1972. The acronym for this bill, EATS, gave Baysinger many sleepless nights as he fretted over what political enemies might do with it. But luckily, no one noticed.

By the fall of 1972 Dingell, realizing that passing an entirely new law was better than revising the 1969 act, introduced the administration bill. But the congressional session ended before it could be enacted. The following January the Michigan congressman resubmitted the bill, now more felicitously titled the Endangered Species Conservation Act of 1973.[37]

But in drafting the legislation for Dingell and the White House, Baysinger ran into problems. One obstacle was the need for habitat protection, which he and his colleagues solved by composing section 7. The other impediment was the "taking" clause, which prescribed fines or imprisonment for those who "harass, harm, pursue, hunt, shoot, wound, kill, trap, capture, or collect" a threatened or endangered species. As with habitat protection, the problem was constitutional.

The federal government unquestionably had authority to regulate interstate or international commerce involving wildlife; to manage wildlife on federal lands; and to conserve species, such as migratory birds, covered by international treaties. But the mammals, fish, reptiles, amphibians, and multifarious plants and invertebrate creatures on nonfederal lands were seen as inviolable responsibilities of the states. Therefore, Baysinger feared that the "taking" clause might be struck down by the courts. Yet he also knew that most states ignored nongame species. Federal regulation in this sphere, he believed, was essential. But how could he make it legal?

Serendipity struck. Shortly after his late-night Capitol meeting with Potter and Bavin, custodians came to Baysinger's office to replace his file cabinets. As a former military intelligence officer, Baysinger had a deeply ingrained concern for the proper handling of official documents, and he made it a practice to check desks, file cabinets, and other document containers personally before they were released to the surplus property office. His check of one of these uncovered a large wad of paper jammed into the back of a drawer. It was a copy of the long-forgotten 1940 Convention on Nature Protection in the Western Hemisphere. Reading it, Baysinger discovered that the treaty stipulated "provisions for the taking of specimens of flora and fauna for scientific study." Eureka! This was just the precedent he needed to justify federal regulation of resident wildlife. Armed with these strong habitat and taking clauses, the new law sailed through Congress, passing the Senate on July 24, 1973, by a vote of 92 to 0. Two months later, on September 18, the House passed a similar version, 291 to 12.[38]

But then nothing happened. The bill sat in the White House untouched. By December Regenstein was worried. If the bill was not signed by the end of the year, it would be necessary to start from scratch in the next congressional session. All the carefully crafted language would be up for grabs. He called Talbot.

"Why hasn't Nixon signed the bill?" he asked.

The scientist checked. Somebody had forgotten to put the bill on Nixon's desk. It had fallen between the cracks. Urgently Talbot contacted the White House, which found the bill and rushed it to Nixon for signing. The act was signed into law on December 28, three days before it would have become null and void.[39]

The strong habitat and taking provisions aside, the 1973 law was still far more sweeping and powerful than its predecessors. It broadened the criteria for listing species as endangered, dropping the requirement that species must be in danger of "worldwide" extinction in favor of a new standard that they simply be at risk throughout "all or a significant portion of their range."[40]

It extended protection not merely to species and subspecies, but also to "lesser groups of the same species in common spatial arrangement that interbreed when mature." This permitted the interior secretary to declare a distinct population at risk even when the subspecies to which it belonged was not. It extended limited protection to plants as well as animals. It introduced the category of "threatened" species and gave the secretary broad discretion for deciding how these creatures should be protected.[41]

Yet, despite its unprecedented scope, outside the environmental community key aspects of the bill received little attention and raised little concern. The Endangered Species Act was on a fast track — so much so that congressmen and industry lobbyists virtually ignored some troubling provisions. Interest groups, says the political scientist Laura L.

Manning, "were asleep at the switch," owing to "successful agenda-setting by insider environmentalists backed by key congressmen." The law passed, writes the historian Steven L. Yaffee, because it had "ostensibly few associated costs. . . . It was not obvious who it would hurt."[42]

Many of the law's architects, including Baysinger, Regenstein, and Talbot, knew that they had crafted powerful landmark legislation that had the potential to apply to any creature on earth. They anticipated that it would cause controversy. But few others did. "None of our enemies really read the act," says Regenstein. "It was motherhood and apple pie. They just felt good saving whooping cranes and spotted cats. They didn't realize it applied to creepy-crawly things as well. Then, after the bill became law, they suddenly woke up, saying, 'Wait a minute. What does this mean?'"

8

A LAW
FOR ALL SEASONS

IN FACT, NO ONE KNEW what the new Endangered Species Act meant — not Baysinger, not Talbot, not Regenstein, nor anyone else. They set the ark adrift without knowing its final destination. To most congressmen the law had a simple mission: to save whales, big cats, ferrets, condors, puffins, cranes, and other higher-order fuzzy and feathered critters people found appealing. "Most animals are worth very little in terms of dollars and cents. However, their aesthetic value is great indeed," Senator Harrison Williams said during the hearings, expressing this sentiment.[1] The authors of the act, however, knew that it was meant to protect not merely charismatic creatures but almost all living things. But what was the reason for doing this?

According to the law itself, its goal was to save species for their "aesthetic, ecological, educational, historical, recreational, and scientific value." A law for all seasons, it offered a cornucopia of conservation goals: preserving ecological health, biodiversity, species and subspecies, ecosystems, habitat. But what did it mean to preserve these things? The authors of the act did not know. Unintentionally they had embraced a set of concepts that were not so much scientific as ethical, with implications far beyond what anyone envisaged.

"The purposes of this Act," the law read, "are to provide a means whereby the ecosystems upon which endangered species and threatened species depend may be conserved." To justify this goal, the Committee on Merchant Marine and Fisheries observed that "the events of the past few years have shown the critical nature of the interrelationships of plants and animals between themselves with their environment. Another word for the study of these inter-relationships is 'ecology.' The hearings proved (if proof is still necessary) that the ecologists' shorthand phrase, 'everything is connected to everything else' is nothing more than cold, hard fact."[2]

California Senator John Tunney concurred, observing:

> To allow the extinction of animal species is ecologically, economically, and ethically unsound. Each species provides a service to its environment; each species is a part of an immensely complicated ecological organization, the stability of which rests on the health of its components. . . . To permit the extinction of any species which contributes to the support of this structure without knowledge of the costs or benefits of such extinction is to carelessly tamper with the health of the structure itself.[3]

In speaking of the connectedness of things, of the role biological diversity plays in maintaining the health and stability of ecosystems, and of the chance that humans are upsetting this balance, the politicians were not merely rephrasing old beliefs once cherished by Thoreau and Marsh. They were also repeating what had become a common sentiment among the pop ecologists of the 1970s: Man is a threat to the balance of nature and thus to himself. This ancient doctrine had risen like a phoenix to become conventional wisdom. But this time it wore a new suit, known as "the ecosystem."[4]

The idea that nature is constant and harmonious is an ancient one, long predating the advent of Western civilization. It is a recurring theme in early Greek myth, and it served as the foundation of classical Hellenistic science. The Pythagoreans claimed to hear musical harmony in the universe, and Greek physicians believed in the balance of "humors" and emphasized the ability of nature to heal.

In the fifth century B.C. the historian Herodotus reported that Arabians believed "the whole world would swarm with these serpents" — snakes — were it not for the fact that "Divine Providence" was "a wise contriver." The Roman statesman and orator Cicero noted that "to secure the everlasting duration of the world-order, divine providence has made most careful provision to ensure the perpetuation of the families of animals and of trees and all the vegetable species."[5]

Despite its teleological character, the theme that Divine Providence ensured the harmony of nature continued to reverberate among naturalists during the Enlightenment. In the eighteenth century the Swedish scientist Carolus Linnaeus, whose work was a forerunner of modern ecology, elevated the notion that plants and animals interact for mutual benefit to the status of a scientific principle, which he called the "economy of nature."[6]

The same notions of the unity and harmony of nature, as we have seen, pervaded early American thought. A seventeenth-century Puritan physics text observed that "nature is order and the connection of causes with effects in the world, which is perfect, made by the perfect, best, and most wise." Likewise, wrote another early New Englander: "If we consider the *harmony* of the whole in all its parts, or the admirable suting [sic] of the things that are made one to another, so that there is nothing in vain, or useless, or incapable of being serviceable in its place, its nature being every way adapted to the place it bears; every wheel in this curious watch moving aright: and what less than Infinite wisdom, could so contrive and compose this?"[7]

The advent of evolutionary theories, however, complicated matters. If nature countenanced the "survival of the fittest," then how could it be harmonious? Yet standards of science itself seemed to demand the steady state hypothesis. Predictability is the essence of science. If random catastrophes were regular contributors to evolution, as the great geologist Sir Charles Lyell declared in 1833, that field "could never rise to the rank of an exact science." Empirical theories can explain only regular events, not random ones. So Lyell, and many geologists after him, favored "gradualism."[8]

Throughout the nineteenth century natural historians struggled to reconcile ideas of change and stability. And for the most part they tilted in favor of the latter. In 1801 Jean Baptiste Lamarck argued that the replacement of one species by another does not upset the balance of nature. His contemporary Alexander von Humboldt held similar views. Darwin was ambivalent. In his great work *On the Origin of Species*, notes the historian Joel B. Hagen, "nature was a battlefield on which individuals ceaselessly struggled in the 'war of nature,' but it was also a stable complex of interacting parts." Yet ultimately even Darwin tilted slightly in favor of stability, viewing natural selection, as Peter J. Bowler observes, as "a force that continued to operate and produce change even in a perfectly stable environment."[9]

It was in the context of this confusion that ecology was born. The term was coined in 1866 by the German evolutionist and zoologist Ernst Haeckel, forming a contraction of the Greek words, *oikos* (meaning "living relations") and *logos* (meaning "reason" or "study of"). Ecology is, according to Haeckel, "the whole science of the relations of the organism to the environment including, in the broad sense, all the 'conditions of existence.'" All things animate and inanimate, Haeckel suggested, are in effect part of a larger whole or community. "He intended his readers to visualize a kind of global organic economy in which all species played a part," notes Bowler. And all things, whether living or not, Haeckel additionally supposed, contain within them a spiritual element. "He argued that matter and spirit were manifestations of a single underlying substance," Bowler writes, "which meant that even the most primitive form of life had some spiritual qualities."[10]

Haeckel's positions, therefore, were more metaphysical than scientific. They encompassed two closely related doctrines, well known to philosophers, called *holism* and *monism*. Holism is the view that the whole is greater than the sum of its parts, that things can be understood only within the context of larger communities of which they are members. Monism holds that only one kind of substance exists. In contrast with the philosophy known as *dualism* — which supposes that the universe is composed of both spiritual and physical entities — monism posits that all things are infused by a single substance. Thus, physical monists are materialists, believing that everything is composed of matter. Spiritual monists are "idealists" because they believe that nature consists entirely of spiritual entities, or ideas. Haeckel began his career as a physical monist but ended, apparently, as an idealistic one.

The birth of ecology, therefore, signaled the marriage of two ancient notions: the balance and unity of nature. Along with Darwin's evolutionary theory, it helped to inspire the political views of Herbert Spencer, who maintained that society itself was a kind of biological organism in which the whole was greater than the sum of its parts, and it prompted preliminary studies in the concept of the biotic community, in which all members strive to sustain the balance of the whole.[11]

Until 1900, however, this science progressed little. During the late nineteenth century, according to the biological historian Ernst Mayr, "there was little contact among various groups that studied 'the conditions of life' or 'associations' of various kinds of organisms." Rather, biologists and natural historians seemed content to catalog species found in a measured area, and to describe wildlife observed in its natural environment.[12]

Then, at the turn of the century, ecology was suddenly energized by Frederic Clements, whose notion of the community as a complex organism incorporated both Haeckel's holism and monism. More than merely collections of plants and animals working for mutual betterment, he seemed to suggest, the community, infused with a spirit, could be understood only by knowledge of its own transcendent laws. Like Haeckel's, therefore, Clements's science seemed compromised by fuzzy thinking. Neither holism nor monism was scientific. Both men tacitly embraced the teleological doctrine of vitalism, the view that things are infused with a purposive spirit; yet spiritual objects cannot be studied empirically, and the supposed something extra that makes the whole "greater than the sum of its parts" can never be seen. Science studies particular observable events, not abstract superorganisms.[13]

Perhaps to extricate Clements from this philosophical dead end, in 1935 his friend the Oxford botanist A. G. Tansley introduced a new concept that he thought more acceptable, which he called the ecosystem. "Though the organisms may claim our primary interest," he wrote,

> when we are trying to think fundamentally we cannot separate them from their special environment, with which they form one physical system. It is the systems so formed which, from the point of view of the ecologist, are the basic units of nature on the face of the earth. Our natural human prejudices force us to consider the organisms . . . as the most important parts of these systems, but certainly the inorganic "factors" are also parts — there could be no systems without them, and there is constant interchange of the most various kinds within each system, not only between the organisms but between the organic and the inorganic. These *ecosystems*, as we may call them, are of the most various kinds and sizes.[14]

With the concept of the ecosystem, Tansley had rejected monism while retaining holism. Unlike Clements's complex organism, Tansley's ecosystems were entirely physical. But by calling them "the basic units of nature," Tansley still supposed them to be more fundamental than the individuals that formed their parts.

For this reason, as we shall see, in Germany following World War II biologists, reacting against failed holistic political doctrines, would become extremely hostile to ecosystem studies. But in the United States, where the pantheistic preservationism of Thoreau, John Muir, Rachel Carson, Joseph Wood Krutch, Aldo Leopold, and Ansel Adams already preached the unity of nature, the ecosystem would capture the imagination of a generation, inspiring the Endangered Species Act and changing American politics forever. The idea took off, almost literally, like a rocket.[15]

"One of the most frequently encountered criticisms of ecology throughout its early years," wrote the biologist Robert P. McIntosh in 1976, "was the extensive collection of data in the absence of organizing principles or theory." Now the discipline was swinging to the opposite extreme. The 1960s became "the decade in which theoretical-mathematical ecology burgeoned."[16]

Triggering this change was the development of a new mathematical field called cybernetics. Conceived by Massachusetts Institute of Technology mathematician Norbert Wiener during the Second World War and based on his work designing aiming devices for antiaircraft guns, cybernetics was the science for designing self-regulating machines such as guided missiles and thermostats. Such devices could exhibit "purposeful" behavior, such as taking aim at a target or maintaining a constant temperature, because they were governed by feedback loops that kept the machine in equilibrium. And cybernetics was the mathematics of such systems.[17]

Soon ecologists were applying cybernetics to their own field as well. Used with the ecosystem model, it seemed a powerful analytic tool. The ecosystem could be pictured as a feedback loop of energy flows operating like a thermostat to keep the community in balance, and this appeared to open the way for using the mathematics of physics to understand relations between living things and their environment.[18]

In a landmark 1946 paper G. Evelyn Hutchison, a British-trained zoologist teaching at Yale University, led the way. The ecosystem, he suggested, was a feedback loop of energy flows which operated to keep the system stable in the face of environmental disturbances. Urging that a new, more mathematical ecology be established, Hutchinson himself attempted to integrate ecology with evolution using new kinds of quantitative analysis. Examining the concept of "niche" — the habitat occupied by an organism — he and his students would reach a conclusion that soon became conventional wisdom throughout American culture: that biological diversity promotes ecosystem stability. "Communities of many diversified organisms," he would write in 1958, "are better able to persist than are communities of fewer less diversified organisms."[19]

Other ecologists raced to embrace this new theoretical approach. Searching nature for exemplars of self-contained ecosystems to which they could apply their tools of calculation, biologists branched off in three directions. Some constructed artificial communities for examination, establishing microorganisms in sealed microspheres. Others pursued "synecological" studies, focusing on groups of organisms associated as units on islands or in ponds and river drainages. A third contingent began to examine global phenomena such as weather systems and the atmosphere.[20]

Hutchinson's pupil, the Princeton biologist Robert H. MacArthur began using mathematical models to examine competition between species; next, in collaboration with Harvard's Edward O. Wilson, he turned his attention to the study of island biogeography, developing equations to explain species diversity and survival in island communities.[21]

A book by an early American physical chemist, Alfred Lotka, applying quantitative analysis to the study of various ecological problems, which had been ignored when it originally appeared in 1925 under the title *The Elements of Physical Biology,* was recognized as an ecological classic when it was reprinted in 1956 as *Elements in Mathematical Biology.*[22]

Others turned their attention to pure theory, examining ecosystems as closed thermodynamic systems that maintained themselves in equilibrium. Even before the war an early Hutchinson pupil, Raymond Lindemann, had written an influential paper that analyzed energy flow at Cedar Lake Bog, Minnesota. After the war two brothers, Eugene and Howard Odum, who also had studied with Hutchinson, would transform this modeling concept into a new specialty called systems ecology. Employing the tools of thermodynamics, systems ecology pictured ecosystems as complex wholes through which energy flowed in predictable ways to maintain equilibrium. "Succession," wrote Eugene Odum in 1969, is "an orderly process of community development that is reasonable, directional and, therefore, predictable," which "culminates in a stabilized ecosystem."[23]

Surprisingly, it was government that served as the godfather of this new theoretical science. Two years after its founding in 1946, the Atomic Energy Commission (AEC) established a Division of Biology and Medicine to study the effects of atomic fallout, inaugurating ambitious research programs at national laboratories and nuclear reservations in Oak Ridge, Tennessee; Brookhaven, New York; Hanford, Washington; and Savannah River in Georgia. At Savannah it contracted with Eugene Odum to conduct ecological studies of farmland abandoned after construction of the nuclear facility. Meanwhile, the Office of Naval Research was paying Howard Odum to study mineral springs in Florida. In 1954, at the request of the AEC, the Odum brothers traveled to Eniwetok, in the South Pacific, to study the effects of radiation "on whole populations and entire ecological systems in the field."[24]

Soon Uncle Sam was funding scores of ecologists. In the mid-1950s the discovery of the radioactive isotope strontium 90 in cow's milk deposited by airborne debris from atomic bomb testing caused a national outcry. In response, the AEC sponsored intensive studies to trace the movement of this substance in the food chain. In 1955 it hired an Ohio State University ecologist, John N. Wolfe, as its administrator of biology and medicine to direct this research.[25]

As federal ecosystem research continued, government agencies began to forge long-term associations with universities, establishing a permanent Savannah River laboratory with the University of Georgia and promoting joint appointments for its Oak Ridge ecologists at the University of Tennessee.[26]

With this infusion of funds, by the 1960s universities had expanded their ecological research. Many colleges had introduced courses in ecology; several foundations had inaugurated grants programs designed to promote the science; and some government agencies, including the National Park Service and the Fish and Wildlife Service, had adopted new policies designed to reflect an "ecological" perspective.[27]

Soon this interest spread to the National Aeronautics and Space Administration. In the late 1960s NASA's Viking lander program, intended to explore the possibility of life on Mars, brought together a variety of scientists, among them biologists, astronomers, geologists, and cyberneticists. Asked to determine whether life existed on Mars, this team had first to decide what the conditions were that produced and sustained life on earth. By attempting to answer these questions, they made many startling discoveries concerning the nature of the earth as an ecosystem.[28]

To many ecologists the model of the self-regulating ecosystem was a golden goose, laying platinum eggs. In 1963 the Ecological Society of America established a committee, headed by Eugene Odum, to make recommendations regarding possible U.S. participation in the International Biological Programme (IBP). The goal of this initiative was to create comprehensive models for understanding and managing ecosystems. One of its efforts would be the coniferous forest biome project, which would ignite the fight over old-growth forests. Legislation enabling the United States to participate was signed into law by President Nixon in October 1970. By the time the program ended in 1974, taxpayers had given participating ecologists around $50 million in support. And after the IBP ended in 1974, the National Science Foundation launched the Ecosystem Studies Program, thus continuing to funnel generous support to ecosystem studies.[29]

By 1970 ecology had become Big Science. Ironically, just as students across the country were protesting the university's intimacy with the "military-industrial complex," the very same ecologists whose field they worshiped were suckling at the teats of the AEC, the U.S. Navy, and other federal agencies. And because of this income flow the idea of the ecosystem reached its zenith of popularity in academe. Swayed by the mathematical elegance of their work, scholars continued to refine the notion of nature as composed of closed-circuit feedback systems, which, when operating properly, maintained their equilibrium.[30]

The apparent simplicity of this idea was seductive. It added an element of generality, promising to unite previously isolated fields by focusing attention on integrative concepts such as competition. Its use of mathematics, especially, gave the new science the patina of respectability, establishing, as Bowler observes, "a more 'scientific' image for ecology."[31]

And, indeed, if the study of ecosystems had been merely a multidisciplinary effort to avoid narrow specialization — if, in short, it had not embraced the holistic notion that the system was primary — then it would have represented a genuine and important scientific advance. Unfortunately, however, for the most part it did not.

Instead, at the heart of the new ecology lay the ancient teleological idea of the stability and unity of nature, and the same old monism and holism. As Bowler notes: "The concept of the feedback loop as a means by which a physical system could maintain itself in balance gained wide popularity in the post-war years. Vitalism was now unnecessary because machines could be made that would also exhibit purposeful behavior. The new science of cybernetics was founded by Norbert Wiener to exploit the idea of the construction of self-regulating machines. Hutchinson saw the same principles at work on a global scale." In other words, the modern ecosystem was merely Haeckel's and Clements's superorganism, only "energy" had replaced "spirit" as the driving force. "Drawing upon the long tradition of viewing communities as superorganisms," Bowler notes, "Hutchinson transformed this approach by replacing the organic metaphor with an economic one."[32]

As the 1960s drew to a close, many ecologists also rejected the ecosystem concept as mere recycled holism and teleology. Evolutionary ecologists in particular remained confirmed individualists, stressing that it is competition among creatures and not self-regulating, purposeful ecosystems that characterizes the dynamics of nature. Invoking the rigorous standards of modern science, they insisted that theories about purposeful evolution and complex wholes were not testable and therefore not scientific.[33]

But though such critics may have had science on their side, they failed to influence public opinion and policy. Hypotheses asserting that nature is random cannot justify political agendas. By contrast, ecosystems advocates, as Joel B. Hagen comments, "emphasized the important role that ecologists could play in shaping public policy." Government was picking up the tab, and it wanted scholars to develop new tools of management. As Peter J. Bowler summarizes the situation: "Where Clements had once justified government control of the environment by appealing to the image of society as a super-organism, the new systems theory offered the prospect of social control through the setting up of stable feedback loops of human interactions. In an atmosphere of post-war optimism, science seemed to offer the prospect of creating a new and more secure world."[34]

Ecosystems ecologists had a political agenda, and evolutionary biologists did not. It was natural, therefore, that the former and not the latter would inspire social change. The ecosystem concept also fit perfectly with the spiritual predilections of American environmentalists, systematizing the fuzzy, pantheistic, and animist notions of the unity and spirituality of nature shared by a long succession of religious and preservationist thinkers since the Puritans. All that the new science needed was a popularizer, someone to fire the public imagination.

Such a person was quick in coming. Fittingly it was the Sierra Club — the organization John Muir helped to create — that in 1971 would publish the book, *The Closing Circle* by the biologist Barry Commoner, which introduced the ecosystem model to popular culture. "Behind the ecological failure of modern technology," Commoner wrote, "lies a corresponding failure in its scientific base." Biology, he said, was "fragmented," overspecialized, and too preoccupied with abstract theorizing to consider the behavior of biological processes within their natural and social settings in the real world."[35]

The major flaw in biology up to this point, Commoner suggested, echoing Carson, was its penchant for "reductionism," which he described as "the view that effective understanding of a complex system can be achieved by investigating the properties of its isolated parts," a bias that promoted the creation of subspecialties and "tended to isolate scientific disciplines from the problems that affect the human condition."[36]

By contrast, cybernetics, which was "concerned with the cycles of events that steer, or govern, the behavior of a system," was the most fruitful way to study the environment. Although Wiener had developed cybernetics to build things such as guided missiles and antiaircraft guns, Commoner argued, this form of reasoning applied equally to nature, which consisted of closed-loop circuits called ecosystems. "The

First Law of Ecology," he said, is that "everything is connected to every-thing else." Hence, ecology resembled cybernetics because it was a mul-tidisciplinary study of "relationships and the processes linking each living thing to the physical and chemical environment."[37]

An ecosystem, Commoner wrote, "consists of multiple intercon-nected parts" that act together in a cyclical fashion to maintain stabil-ity. When undisturbed by outside forces, ecosystems undergo periodic fluctuations, but always return to a state of balance. But this natural harmony "is maintained only so long as there are no external intrusions on the system." For when outside forces "not controlled by the self-gov-erning cyclical relations" intervene, they are "a threat to the stability of the whole system" and the system can face total "ecological collapse." He went on: "The amount of stress which an ecosystem can absorb be-fore it is driven to collapse is also a result of its various interconnections and their relative speeds of response. The more complex the ecosystem, the more successfully it can resist a stress. . . . Like a net, in which each knot is connected to others by several strands, [a complex ecosystem] can resist collapse better than a simple, unbranched circle of threads." Hence, "all this results from a simple fact about ecosystems — [that] everything is connected to everything else: the system is stabilized by its dynamic self-compensating properties; these same properties, if over-stressed, can lead to a dramatic collapse; the complexity of the ecologi-cal network . . . determine[s] how much it can be stressed . . . without collapsing."[38]

How could such catastrophes be prevented? Commoner's answer was not to meddle in nature. The "Third Law of Ecology," he wrote, is "Na-ture knows best." Left alone, ecosystems remain stable. When people meddle, systems collapse. Preservation thus requires isolating ecosys-tems from humanity.[39]

The ideas nurtured by Haeckel, Clements, Tansley, Hutchinson, and the Odums had come of age. Here was the simple idea that moved Din-gell and his colleagues: since ecosystem instability threatened human-ity, biological diversity had to be protected by isolating threatened habitat from human interference. Few noticed there was little evidence for the doctrine. Ancient philosophical ideas, resurrected by govern-ment as a means of control and masquerading as science, had captured the public imagination, producing an Endangered Species Act whose consequences no one could anticipate.

9

A NEW METAPHOR
FOR NATURE

IN THE FIFTH CENTURY B.C., according to Plato, the philosopher Socrates walked the streets of Athens asking people he met questions such as, "What is justice?" and "What is virtue?" But the answers he received were invariably inadequate, and Socrates had no trouble exposing them. In almost every instance the attempted definition merely begged the question. For example, when Socrates asked the young Thessalian Meno to define virtue, his respondent suggested it meant "health" or "strength." When Socrates queried what these meant, Meno answered they were the "capacity to command justly," and when asked to explain this, the youth was ultimately reduced to saying that goodness is the capacity to obtain things by "righteous" or "honest" means.[1]

So with the purposes of the Endangered Species Act. When asked, "Why prevent species extinction?," its architects and supporters usually replied, "To protect ecosystem health." When asked to characterize this health further, they answered, "biodiversity." When queried about the reason for biodiversity, they replied that it was to ensure "ecosystem stability." And so they proceeded as in a Socratic dialogue, defining one nebulous term by another, equally vague and value-laden. Stability would be represented as necessary for "ecosystem integrity," preserving integrity as a means of maintaining "ecosystem resiliency," and so on and on.[2]

These questions were difficult to answer because they demanded ethical responses, not factual ones. Functional theories, as Hempel had shown, are not scientific. Science rests on observing properties of individual phenomena, but the supposed attributes of holistic entities such as ecosystems are not observable. Not a science, the new ecology was a theory of value, suggesting that nature *ought* to prefer stability, *ought* to be self-regulating, *ought* to prefer diversity.[3]

No sooner had society begun to reject one teleology than government, by promulgating the Endangered Species Act, embraced another. As the popularity of natural law waned, environmentalists and politicians rushed to endorse the ecosystem. The act made Hutchinson's model, nurtured by government and popularized by Commoner, the law of the land. Nature, this document said in effect, was a congregation of feedback machines which can be kept in equilibrium so long as they do not lose any parts. This was an appealing notion, reminiscent of Aldo Leopold's observation in his 1948 *Sand County Almanac* that in natural preservation, as in mechanics, "to keep every cog and wheel is the first precaution of intelligent tinkering."[4]

But what did it mean? Did the "balance of nature" really exist? What were ecosystems? Did they remain healthy only so long as they "kept all their parts"? What, for that matter, was "natural preservation"? Even as the act became law, evidence revealed it to rest on false assumptions.

IS THERE A BALANCE OF NATURE?

"One of the major criticisms of mathematical-theoretical approaches to ecology," writes Robert McIntosh, "is that they commonly rest on simplifying assumptions, often unstated, that make them tractable mathematically but nonsense biologically." So it was with the new ecologists' fascination with equilibrium. These scholars emphasized the ancient notion of the balance of nature, not because the evidence supported it but because their mathematics demanded it.[5]

Ecologists' increasing reliance "on the physical sciences and engineering for theory, mathematical approaches, concepts, models and metaphors," writes the biologist Daniel B. Botkin, "led to an increasingly sophisticated growth of mathematical theory (formal models) that required and led to exact equilibria, and to a world view of nature as the great machine. These foundations led to an untenable situation: the predominant, accepted ecological theories asserted that natural, undisturbed populations and ecological communities . . . would achieve constancy in abundance, an assertion that became inconsistent with new observations."[6]

The evolution of the earth is characterized not by stability but by constant environmental disturbances and extreme fluctuations in animal and plant populations. Ice ages, driven by little-understood climatic and solar cycles some 100,000 years in duration, constantly disrupted plant and animal communities. During the last glaciation, which ended 20,000 years ago, two huge ice sheets up to three miles thick covered North America as far south as Wyoming and Connecticut. Sea levels were four hundred feet lower than they are today. South of the ice was an eerie land of tundra and desert, raked by fierce, cold winds and sandstorms. In its spruce forests roamed huge mammals known as megafauna, such as woolly mammoths, short-faced bears, giant beavers, saber-toothed tigers, camels, and horses.[7]

Then temperatures warmed dramatically, triggering cataclysmic events. Fed by melting glaciers, huge reservoirs called proglacial lakes, some larger than our Great Lakes, abruptly appeared. When ice dams broke, many of these reservoirs emptied suddenly, flooding entire regions. One — 180-mile-long Lake Missoula in western Montana — emptied and refilled more than forty times over 1,500 years. Each time an ice dam broke, the entire lake drained within two weeks, sending a wall of water to inundate much of what is present-day Oregon and Washington, destroying most downstream life.[8]

Finding their watercourses periodically blocked by ice, major rivers changed course repeatedly. Rising seas submerged a thousand feet of coastline a year. New vegetation followed in the wake of retreating glaciers. Tundra sprouted in Pennsylvania and Connecticut, and trees spread rapidly northward, creating boreal forests. Douglas fir appeared in British Columbia, and hardwoods such as ash, elm, and oak also migrated into Canada. More than three hundred species of megafauna became extinct as new immigrants from Asia, such as bison, moose, elk, and deer, migrated southward.[9]

According to Daniel Botkin, a 1973 study of pollen evidence from the Lake of the Clouds in the Boundary Waters Canoe Area in Minnesota found that "the last glaciation was followed by a tundra period in which the ground was covered by low shrubs," which was then "replaced by a forest of spruce." Then 9,200 years ago the spruce "was replaced by a forest of jack pine and red pine . . . paper birch and alder immigrated into this forest about 8,300 years ago; white pine arrived about 7,000 years ago, and then there was a return to spruce, jack pine, and white pine." Botkin concludes: "Thus every thousand years a substantial change occurred in the vegetation of the forest, reflecting in part changes in the climate and in part the arrival of species that had been driven south during the ice age and were slowly returning."[10]

Nor did nature's wild swings happen only at a geologic pace. Dramatic changes regularly occur in a human lifetime. By the 1950s and 1960s, Botkin observes, "evidence indicated that . . . animal populations are not in a static equilibrium." A host of studies revealed that creatures of every kind, from insects to elephants, undergo extreme and often destructive fluctuations. Records of German coniferous forests show that the numbers of lasiocampid moths sometimes multiply by a factor of over ten thousand in two years. Chinch bug populations along the Mississippi rose and fell erratically and dramatically between 1823 and 1940.[11]

Moose and wolf populations also were found to vary wildly over time on Isle Royale National Park in Lake Superior. Trappers' records, Botkin reports, establish that Canadian lynx populations oscillated between eight hundred and eighty thousand over a 240-year period ending in the 1940s. Within ten years after Tsavo National Park was established in Kenya, offering protection to elephants from poachers, pachyderm numbers went through the roof. Elephants were destroying so much critical vegetation that Daphne Sheldrick, wife of the park superintendent, David Sheldrick, described it as a "lunar landscape." Catch records reveal that the supply of Peruvian anchovies rose to 8 million tons in the 1970s, then crashed, though numbers are now on the way back up. Atlantic menhaden, once abundant along the Maine coast, nearly disappeared by 1960 before starting to come back again.[12]

The evidence was clear: random disturbance, not permanence or order, governs nature. But curiously, supporters of the stability hypothesis interpreted these data as proof that they were correct. Evolution, like ice ages, they suggested, happens so slowly that it is imperceptible to humans. If extinctions occur frequently enough to be noticeable during our own lifetime, this means that humans have upset the ecological "balance" by accelerating change. And stopping this requires that we save all the cogs![13]

WHY SAVE SPECIES?

"It is in the best interest of mankind to minimize the losses of genetic variations," declared the House Committee on Merchant Marine and Fisheries. And this is surely true. Many life forms contain genetic material that could prove valuable to medicine or other human endeavors. But in saying this, the congressman was also referring to the role creatures play in maintaining the equilibria of ecosystems.[14]

Like stability, biological diversity was an attribute required not by nature but by mathematics. According to McIntosh: "The conventional wisdom of ecology held that diversity enhanced ecosystem stability by increasing the number of links in the ecological web. This idea became almost axiomatic to some biologists despite indications that diversity of trees in relatively stable or climax forests was less than that in seral or changing forests."[15]

In fact, as many biologists pointed out, diversity was often associated with unstable communities. And although environmentalists were quick to assert that "preserving biodiversity" was the main purpose of the Endangered Species Act, its architects were careful not to insert the term into the law because, as Baysinger put it, "biodiversity is a swamp." There are more concepts of biodiversity than cards in a canasta deck, and no objective way exists to decide which is "better." There is vertical diversity, horizontal diversity, species diversity, individual diversity. As the geneticist Anne E. Magurran writes, "Diversity is rather like an optical illusion."[16]

Here was a problem for the authors of the act. Directly confronting the impossibly complex issues of biodiversity would have shown the law's task to be impossible. Therefore, they ignored the problem and instead resurrected simpler language that geneticists had abandoned more than twenty years earlier, equating ecosystem health with rescuing "species, subspecies or distinct populations."

These expressions suggest that nature consists of different "kinds." But actually it is a continuum, and each plant or animal population contains individuals that differ genetically in billions of ways from one another. The cell of an ordinary house rat holds 100,000 genes, and one DNA molecule within such an animal contains enough genetic information to fill four thousand published volumes. To say that one species is more worth saving than another is like saying, "This bag of a trillion marbles is more important than that one."[17]

The supposition that nature is composed of kinds was the product of the field known as taxonomy. Maturing in the nineteenth century, before genetic testing existed, taxonomy based its classifications on the physical, or morphological, characteristics of a few specimens. If a red squirrel in one location was bigger and rosier than those found elsewhere, the taxonomist might give it a new name. Often this moniker would be the taxonomist's own, so that by this baptism he immortalized himself and ensured academic advancement.[18]

But the advent of genetic typing revealed this science to be flawed. Geneticists found that there is no necessary correlation between morphological and genetic characteristics. That one squirrel is redder or bigger than another does not mean that they differ genetically. This point is conclusively revealed by humans. People of different races look dissimilar but are genetically almost identical. Indeed, humans are so closely related that many geneticists believe that the species went through a "bottleneck" 100,000 years ago, and that everyone on earth has a common female ancestor![19]

Surprisingly, it was Paul R. Ehrlich — before he found his calling as an ecological prophet — who helped drive the last nails into the coffin of taxonomy. Species and subspecies are "arbitrary" categories, he wrote with coauthor Richard W. Holm in 1964. "Attempts to create a rigorous and objective definition of species based on genetic criteria have failed." It reveals more about the classifiers than the classified: "At any period taxonomy more or less reflects the prevailing world view of a somewhat earlier historical period." And they offered a devastating critique of the concept of subspecies: "So-called subspecies . . . are not evolutionary units. They are arbitrarily created to describe certain variation patterns in one or a few characteristics. They have no common genetic pattern nor may their genetic future be predicted. . . . Use of the subspecies concept may do only intellectual damage by creating a distorted view of nature."[20] They concluded: "As a tool for understanding biological processes, the subspecies has deservedly lost favor."

Yet Ehrlich and Holm spoke too soon. Although "subspecies" had already been tossed into the scientific dustbin, the act's authors resurrected it. And by portraying the world as composed of discrete categories of creatures, it made the impossibly complex chore of rescuing an infinite number of genetic combinations appear to be a simple and achievable goal of saving a few distinct "kinds." The impossible was made to seem possible.

HOW WOULD THE LAW WORK?

Nature, as it turned out, was not so much a web as a thicket. In addition to facing the challenge of defining biodiversity, those who would administer the law faced a host of methodological challenges:

- Since the ecosystem was merely a model to help scientists understand energy-flow dynamics, it did not correlate to anything on a map. In 1939 the plant geographer Richard Hartshorn observed: "The problem of establishing the boundaries of a geographic region . . . presents a problem for which we have no reason to even hope for an objective solution. . . . The regional entities which we construct on this basis are therefore in the full sense mental constructions." How, then, could administrators of the act identify the boundaries of ecosystems that needed protection?[21]

- Extinction is an integral part of evolution. Nearly all the creatures that ever lived are now extinct. As the biologists H. G. Andrewartha and L. C. Birch observed in 1954: "The vast majority of species are rare. . . . Nevertheless the misconception prevails that the extinction of a population is a very rare event." The act was intended to ignore natural extinctions and to rescue only those creatures put at risk by humans. But there was no way to tell the difference. The whooping crane dwindled for twenty thousand years before Erickson came to the rescue. How much of its decline was "natural"? How could one tell?[22]

- Likewise, the law would protect only "native" species. But how would we distinguish these from "exotic" creatures? If the wolves of Isle Royale National Park in Michigan — which walked across the ice of Lake Superior from Canada during the winter of 1948–49 to take up residence there — were for the purposes of the act deemed "natives" (as they were so declared in 1967), thus qualifying for protection, then why not include the feral horses of Assateague Island in Virginia (creatures later officially declared "exotic"), which were introduced by colonists in the early 1600s, and whose ancestor eohippus roamed the continent for a million years until going extinct ten thousand years ago?[23]

- Every grazing animal in North America except the pronghorn antelope immigrated to the continent after the last ice age ended fifteen thousand years ago. In evolutionary time, fifteen millennia is a mere eye blink. Were these relative newcomers — mammals such as white-tailed and mule deer, elk, moose, and bison — mere exotics which should therefore be ignored by the act?[24]

- And how could we gauge the extent of the crisis — if there was one? Despite growing public anxiety, the evidence about extinctions was equivocal at best. Biologists had no idea how many creatures went extinct each year.[25]

In the 1960s, scientists estimated, there were no more than 3 million plant and animal species on earth. And in 1973 Dingell's committee estimated that of these, 375 animal species were "threatened with extinction throughout the world." Yet no major North American grazing animal had disappeared in ten thousand years, and only five bird species are known to have become extinct in North America and Europe since 1600.[26]

If scholars could not locate ecosystems in the real world, if they could not distinguish human-caused extinctions from natural ones, if they did not know how many creatures were at risk, if they did not understand the meaning of the key words they used, if they knew next to nothing about the evolutionary requirements of earth's inhabitants, then how could they save creatures at risk?

The answer they gave was: by preserving the ecosystem.

WHAT ARE ECOSYSTEMS, AND HOW ARE THEY PRESERVED?

As endangered species legislation gestated between 1965 and 1973, a curious reversal occurred. Inspired by the promise of success of Erickson's whooper breeding, Interior Secretary Udall in 1965 suggested that more be done to "restore" and, where necessary, "propagate" selected species. The 1966 law provided virtually no money for protection of habitat. But, influenced by the idea of preserving ecosystems, the 1973 law put nearly all its emphasis on protection of habitat and virtually none on promoting active steps to rescue plants and animals.[27]

For nearly a century the dominant ideal guiding policy was that of stewardship, the vision that humans are responsible for sustaining nature. Embraced by early conservationists such as Theodore Roosevelt, Gifford Pinchot, and Aldo Leopold, it pictured the biosphere as a garden, which, given tender loving care, blooms indefinitely. Its advocates sought to nurture land for human benefit, actively maintaining conditions valued by society by breeding threatened creatures in captivity, culling overabundant game herds, and intentionally setting fires to revive vegetation.[28]

Leopold transformed this strategy into a new science. In 1934, as first director of the University of Wisconsin arboretum in Madison, he employed Civilian Conservation Corps workers to reconstruct the original tall-grass prairies. Eventually restoring around a third of the arboretum's 1,280 acres, Leopold founded what became known as restoration ecology — the science of returning land, plant, and animal communities to presettlement conditions. "Our idea," he wrote, "is to reconstruct . . . a sample of original Wisconsin — a sample of what Dane County looked like when our ancestors arrived here during the 1840s."[29]

But opposing stewardship was the countervailing preservationist view of mankind as nature's enemy, which advocated not managing land but keeping people off it. "Meddling in nature" was anathema. Rather than restoration, preservationists would practice benign neglect.

Once wilderness is defiled, they lamented, it is "gone forever." Humans, they believed, must be kept away from nature.[30]

Until the 1960s stewards were ascendant. But as the popularity of the ecosystem idea rose, so did the preservationist vision. Ironically it was Aldo Leopold's son Starker who helped this happen. In 1963 an Interior Department committee under his direction, in a document known as the *Leopold Report*, recommended that national parks be restored to their presettlement conditions. "As a primary goal," declared the Leopold Committee, "we would recommend that the biotic associations within each park be maintained, or where necessary recreated, as nearly as possible in the condition that prevailed when the area was first visited by the white man. A national park should represent a vignette of primitive America." Udall immediately endorsed the report, which became Park Service policy the next year.[31]

This sounded like restoration ecology — as though Starker wanted the federal government to do for national parks what his father had done for the arboretum — but it was not. Rather than being a call for stewardship, it was pure preservationism. In 1968 the Park Service with the younger Leopold serving as its chief scientist, issued its handbook of regulations, known as the "Greenbook," supposedly to implement the *Leopold Report*. But, claiming that parks were "comparatively self-contained ecosystems," the "Greenbook" recommended preservation, not restoration. Calling this recipe "ecosystem management," it stressed "the concept of preservation of a total environment, as compared with the protection of an individual feature or species."[32]

In short, the Park Service, borrowing ideas from the new ecology, supposed that since ecosystems were "self-regulating" — that is, were capable of maintaining themselves in "equilibrium" so long as they remained untouched — the best conservation strategy was to "let nature take its course." And this, as it turned out, was a recipe for disaster.

Far from "stabilizing," when left alone parks experienced dramatic fluctuations in plant and animal populations. Yellowstone's northern elk herd grew from 3,172 animals in 1968 to some 7,000 by 1971, and would reach 30,000 by 1988. Along the way these creatures would destroy critical browse species, such as willow and aspen, on which other animals depended. Similar eruptions of ungulate populations occurred at Rocky Mountain, Mount Rainier, and several other parks. If "sustaining biodiversity" meant protecting creatures such as beavers, grizzly bears, and white-tailed deer, then the federal policy was a flop.[33]

The national parks experience showed that "ecosystem management" was not enough. Creatures at risk, such as whooping cranes, needed active help. Passive protection, therefore, rather than being a strategy for endangered species recovery, was a prescription for extirpation. Since species were in trouble because their range was already insufficient, leaving them alone only ensured further decline. As the conservation biologist Jared Diamond ruefully remarked: "The twin goals of noninterference with nature and of preserving pristine natural habitats are incompatible. Both wildlife managers and conservation biologists are being forced to acknowledge that nature reserves can't be left to nature alone to manage."[34]

Thus, Park Service ecosystems management was a model for the recovery strategy of the Endangered Species Act, ensuring its failure. But although false, the idea of stable ecosystems remained compelling, not just because it was simple and coincided with ancient ideas of the balance of nature, but also because it seemed to justify so elegantly the most elusive goal of all: natural preservation itself.

What is this ideal? Saving nature cannot mean arresting change. As the historian Lynn White, Jr., put it in 1967, we cannot "deep-freeze an ecology as it was before the first Kleenex was dropped." Nor can we say it is preservation to permit *everything* to happen. Is it, then, an attempt to prevent human alteration of the landscape while permitting "natural change" to go unimpeded? But as humans are merely species like any other, anything they do is no less "natural" than anything else.[35]

Similarly, we cannot say that preservation means sustaining the "health" of the planet. As biological systems are inherently unstable and evolutionary change produces a constant stream of unique conditions, no single state of affairs can be either "healthy" or "unhealthy." The earth can be "healthy" for humans or "healthy" for dinosaurs, but it is never just plain healthy. Habitat can be good for deer or good for owls, but never merely good for wildlife. The earth was neither ill nor robust 4 billion years ago, before life began. Since then, distinctive conditions have favored different creatures, and the extinction of one species was often a boon to another. The same is true today. Protecting tropical wetlands helps mosquitoes but spreads malaria.[36]

Natural preservation, therefore, like art, lies in the eye of the beholder. When a society sets such goals, it designates those things it deems important, beautiful, ugly, or threatening. But the misleading concept of "stable" nature allowed activists to believe that their subjective goals were objective. If they could say that ecosystems functioned only when they were in balance, then they could also claim that only stable ecosystems were healthy. And if sustaining this condition required maximum biological diversity, then keeping all the parts was a matter of life and death for the planet.

Thus, the model of the steady-state ecosystem conferred legitimacy on the claims of those who sought to rescue wilderness, people who might otherwise be perceived as self-interested primitivists infatuated with the aesthetic features of climax communities. They were saving biodiversity to prevent the collapse of the ecosystem.

Not realizing, therefore, that there was no such thing as absolute preservation, that any policy inevitably hurt some creatures while helping others, Dingell and his colleagues believed that their law would be all things to all creatures. They could and should save everything! But in so believing, they unwittingly embraced a set of values that would have profound implications for the forests of the Northwest.

The law's bias in favor of stability entailed that the best states of nature were exemplified by late successional plant and animal communities, which were less chaotic than early successional ones. But whereas climax forests favor some creatures, such as spotted owls and flying squirrels, they are hostile to other, early successional species, such as Kirtland's warblers or silverspot butterflies. The heath hen — also known as the prairie chicken — a native of the Eastern states, went extinct in the 1920s when its environment, open grassland, was colonized by spreading forests. The endangered Kirtland's warbler needed young stands of jack pine. The Furbish lousewort, an endangered plant, preferred disturbed soils. If forests were allowed to grow old, owls might benefit, but other creatures would suffer.[37]

And what would this cost people? "Clearly," Dingell's committee noted, "it is beyond our capability to acquire all the habitat which is important to those species of plants and animals which are endangered today, without at the same time dismantling our own civilization."[38]

But, as Baysinger would lament later, "We assumed common sense would prevail."[39]

The Endangered Species Act did not reflect scientific opinion. It represented the confluence of ancient conceptual streams, one religious, the other philosophical. At the government's initiative, indigenous American beliefs in the sacredness of nature were combined with European theories of holism and monism to produce a new rationale for social engineering. Yet, in this unlikely collection of disparate ideas, preservationists would find their new metaphors for nature. Cybernetics, the science of machines developed to make antiaircraft guns, and ecology, a field advanced by the Atomic Energy Commission, combined to inspire a movement bent on the destruction of technology. The earth was a computer, a net, a machine! Preservation meant saving all the cogs!

The new ecology may have been a technocratic doctrine, but to environmentalists it was "the subversive science," providing poetical insights into the mysteries of nature. As the historian Theodore Roszak wrote in 1972:

> The science we now call ecology is the nearest approach that objective consciousness makes to the sacramental vision of nature which underlies the symbol of Oneness. . . . Its sensibility — wholistic, receptive, trustful, largely untampering, deeply grounded in aesthetic intuition — is a radical departure from traditional science. Ecology does not systematize by mathematical generalizations or materialist reductionism, but by the almost sensuous intuiting of natural harmonies on the largest scale. Its patterns are not those of numbers, but of unity in process.[40]

Throughout the 1960s and 1970s more and more conservationists hummed these melodies until they reached a roaring crescendo. "The net was tightening. All over the earth it was tightening," wrote Loren Eiseley in 1964. "Even the ice chinks at the poles were under man's surveillance. . . . Man has similarly defeated and diverted the entire web of life and dances, dimpling, over it."[41]

Philosophers sang a similar song, invoking the balance of nature to found a new ethics. "As a physical goal, we must seek to attain what I have called a steady state," observed Paul Sears in 1969. "We must learn that nature includes an intrinsic value system," wrote Ian L. McHarg in 1970. "The balance of nature provides an objective normative model which can be utilized as the ground of human value," said Thomas B. Colwell in 1969. "Other values must be consistent with it. The balance of Nature is, in other words, a kind of ultimate value. . . . The ends which we propose must be such as to be compatible with the ecosystems of Nature."[42]

Nature consists of "feedback loops," declared the Club of Rome's 1972 bestseller, *Limits to Growth*, echoing the cybernetic vision of Barry Commoner. And in 1976 the environmental writer Sigurd F. Olson would write: "A basic ecological truth which we still ignore, is the interdependence and interaction of all living things, including man. This is the guiding principle underlying human destiny, and we know unless we choose wisely in the few decades ahead, the fragile and intricate web of life could become a web of death."[43]

By replacing flux with stability, environmentalists had therefore taken sides in the ancient debate that began 2,500 years ago between Parmenides, who said nothing changed, and Heraclitus, who said everything did. They resurrected the idea of the eighteenth-century physicist Sir Isaac Newton that the universe is precise, machinelike, and orderly, and the views of Newton's contemporary, Carolus Linnaeus, who believed that plants and animals consisted of distinct and discrete kinds. But by doing so, they also supplanted optimism with pessimism.[44]

Early evolutionists viewed biological change as a linear progress toward perfection, and they thought that natural catastrophes, such as extinctions, were necessary steps, making room for new and better life forms. As "natural selection works solely by and for the good of each being, all corporeal and mental endowments will tend to progress towards perfection," Darwin wrote. "Thus from the war of nature, from famine and death, the most exalted object which we are capable of conceiving, namely the production of the higher animals, directly follows. . . . From so simple a beginning endless forms most beautiful and most wonderful have been, and are being evolved."[45]

But modern environmentalists, while welcoming cyclic events such as periodic forest fires — so long as conditions returned to their original state — abhorred unique occurrences such as extinctions. To them, every loss was absolute. The march of evolution was not a triumphant parade into the future but the rush of lemmings into the sea. The past was better than the present because it was less "disturbed." People might be living longer and eating better; the prices of raw commodities might be falling; timber volumes might be increasing; but starvation, resource depletion, and ecological collapse lay just around the corner.

With the full flowering of the ecosystem idea, therefore, extinctions assumed a new meaning. They represented leaks from a bucket that could never be refilled. The inventory of living creatures was finite, and human hubris was killing them off. Species disappearance signaled that critical parts of the great machine were gone forever. We were removing links in the web of life on which our own survival depended.

Environmentalists had resurrected teleology, the idea of an Aristotelian world following a deliberate design. Right conduct meant knowing one's proper place — one's end, or *telos*. All creatures should play a role in maintaining the stability of the great machine. The world is as it is because it is meant to be that way, and any change would be catastrophic. "You all know the argument from design," Bertrand Russell said. "Everything in the world is made just so that we can manage to live in the world, and if the world was ever so little different, we could not manage to live in it. This is the argument from design."[46]

Like the notion of purposeful evolution, the ecosystem served as an ultimate standard of morality, changing the very meaning of life. Just as evolution-as-progress seemingly enhanced the significance of humans, so ecosystems seemed to diminish it. As eugenics measured people by where they fit on the scale of being, the ecological vision judged them on whether they performed or usurped their proper role in the ecosystem.

This was the rationale of the Endangered Species Act. The task was not merely to rescue creatures that humans put at risk. It was to stop all extinctions. Fighting change would become the guiding vision. And like all teleological theories, the ecosystem idea would have implications far transcending science. The federal government would seize upon the idea as a rationale for extending its control, even as, unwittingly, true believers, guided by the metaphor of nature as a harmonious organism, went in search of places where it might be found. And these two quests would lead both sides into the "ancient forest."

10

THE BIRTH OF
BIOCENTRISM

LIKE MANY RECENT ARRIVALS to the Golden State, Bill Devall was on a spiritual journey but had not yet reached his destination. Having cast off old beliefs, he needed a new philosophy. And this day he found what he was searching for, an idea so mind-blowing it would change the world!

After graduating from the University of Kansas and enrolling in the Ph.D. program at the University of Oregon, Devall joined the faculty at Humboldt State at Arcata, California, in 1968, while completing his dissertation on the governance of the Sierra Club. But his sociologist colleagues didn't give a fig for the environment. So he designed a specialty for himself, calling it political ecology.[1]

When he arrived, Devall found the campus in turmoil over Redwoods National Park. The Sierra Club, students felt, had caved in to political pressure, accepting a park that was too small. "That experience taught me," Devall said, "that the conventional politics of give and take practiced by Sierra was self-defeating. The club didn't listen to the grassroots. The drama of David Brower's firing happened before my eyes. It seemed to symbolize the contrast between establishment environmentalism and the no-compromise approach."

So Devall sought an alternative ideology, an intellectual compass that would give direction to his dissatisfaction. Then, as he was walking through the college library one day in 1975, he recalled, "this article sort of fell into my lap." The article, from the obscure Norwegian journal *Inquiry*, was the translation of a 1973 address delivered by a Norwegian philosopher, Arne Naess, at the Third World Future Research Conference in Budapest a year earlier. The paper was titled "The Shallow and the Deep: Long-Range Ecology Movements."

There were, Naess said, two kinds of environmentalism. Shallow environmentalism was the parochial movement practiced by mainstream conservationist groups. Single issue–oriented, it pursued politics as usual, placed man at the center of the universe, and aimed at protecting "the health and affluence of people in developed countries."

Deep ecology, by contrast, proposed a basic realignment of the relations between people and nature. Combining ecology and philosophy into what Naess called "ecosophy" — the "philosophy of ecological harmony or equilibrium" — it applied ecology to all problems. Based on the insight that everything is interdependent, it sought to sustain balance in ecosystems, since these, and not their individual members, are the fundamental units of nature. This aim in turn demanded what Naess called "biospherical egalitarianism . . . the equal right [of all things] to live and blossom." Since living creatures depend on one another, all life is equally important. All *things* are created equal![2]

With deep ecology, ecosystem science had come home to roost. The concept of the organic community, which originated centuries ago as philosophic monism, and which was inserted into biology by Haeckel, Clements, Tansley, and the Odums, had become a philosophic doctrine once again. A new generation, borrowing the ecosystem metaphor from science, would put it to political uses no one anticipated.

This was a sledgehammer of an idea with which to change the world. For Devall, things suddenly fell into place. He would be the apostle of deep ecology! The next year he introduced the idea to America in a half-page article written for the tiny journal *Econews*, then followed it with a piece for the *Humboldt Journal of Social Relations* called "Streams of Environmentalism: Reform vs. Deep Ecology." Soon he teamed with the philosopher George Sessions of Sierra College, near Sacramento, churning out tracts to sell the idea. And it spread like lightning in August.[3]

By appealing to nature, Devall evinced a classical response in his search for political values. Just as Plato appealed to nature to justify benevolent despotism, Aristotle to champion Athenian democracy, Hobbes to argue for absolute monarchy, and Locke to defend liberalism, so Devall invoked nature to justify the principle of biocentric equality. Yet, however attractive, his idea was no less arbitrary than those advocated by earlier political philosophers. Nature was not necessarily "egalitarian." It could just as easily be characterized as a hierarchy, as Aldo Leopold described it in *Sand County Almanac*, as a "biotic pyramid." Though all things are mutually dependent, they are also predatory. Wolves eat elk, which consume grass. A hierarchical metaphor of nature seemed more likely to justify human domination.[4]

The notion of the individual as a subordinate member of an indivisible organic community of interdependent parts — the idea on which biospherical egalitarianism rested — was not so much an insight of empirical biology as one of German metaphysics. Georg Wilhelm Friedrich Hegel, teaching at the University of Berlin in the early nineteenth century, developed the doctrine to justify the restoration of the Prussian monarchy following the Napoleonic wars. Known as the "organic theory of the state," Hegel's philosophy asserted that the Prussians were connected to one another by tradition, language, and folklore. This was the national spirit of which the state was a manifestation.[5]

Hegel was both a monist and a holist, who, like Devall, applied his ideas to politics. Everything in the universe, Hegel believed, is composed of spiritual substance; only complex wholes, and not their parts, have independent reality. Likewise, people are merely elements in a larger system which is the state, and have no status apart from the state. The "highest duty" of the individual, Hegel wrote, "is to be a member of the state."[6]

As the philosopher Walter Stace explains, for Hegel "the state is a true individual. It is a person, an organism [in which] the life of the whole appears in all the parts. This means that the true life of the parts, i.e., the individuals, is found in and is identical with the life of the whole, the state." Hence, Hegel opposed liberalism and individualism. "Liberalism sets up, in opposition to [Prussian holism], the atomistic principle which insists upon the sway of individual wills." This "makes it impossible firmly to establish any political organization."[7]

To be sure, by early nineteenth-century standards Hegel was a highly principled, ethical thinker. His was intended as a moral holism, and the Prussian state he advocated was not totalitarian but benevolent. Nevertheless, his supposition that individuals are subordinate to higher values inspired both fascism (an amoral spiritual monism) and communism (a materialistic monism).[8]

"The Fascist conception," wrote Mussolini, "is for the individual insofar as he coincides with the State. . . . Fascism reaffirms the State as the true reality of the individual." To liberals, wrote Mussolini's minister of justice, Alfredo Rocco, in 1925, echoing Hegel,

society . . . is merely a sum total of individuals, a plurality which breaks up into its single components. . . . This doctrine which I call atomistic . . . reveals from under a concealing cloak a strongly materialistic nature. . . . The true antithesis [of liberalism] . . . is to be found in the doctrine of Fascism. . . . Each society . . . exists in the unity of both its biological and its social contents. . . . Instead of the liberal-democratic formula, "society for the individual," we have "individuals for society."[9]

Hegel, wrote Karl Marx's collaborator, Friedrich Engels, "was the most encyclopedic mind of his time." Indeed, Hegel's philosophy — complex, obscure, thorough, fascinating, and subtle — dominated European politics and scholarship for nearly a century. His monism was a fecund idea with prolific implications which opened up entirely new horizons for scholarship. Just one of his seminal insights — that things can be understood only within a larger context — not only prompted Marx to argue that individuals are subordinate to the social class to which they belong, but also gave birth to the science of sociology (i.e., studying people within the greater social setting).[10]

In 1866 Ernst Haeckel, embracing holism and monism, conceived the idea of studying living things within the context of their environment, which at first he believed was entirely material but later apparently came to see as infused with spirit. Individuals, Haeckel argued, following Hegel, do not have a separate existence; they are merely parts of larger wholes — the tribe, the nation, the environment.[11]

Haeckel was not merely a scientist. An ardent German nationalist, he was also a Darwinian and — like several Save the Redwoods League founders — a believer in eugenics. But, unlike the American conservationists, he promoted his racism as social policy, actually advocating preservation of the biological purity of the German people through euthanasia and careful breeding. As the historian Daniel Gasman has noted: "Disaster was on the horizon, he [Haeckel] preached, unless Germany acted radically and forcefully to bring itself into harmony with the laws of biology. . . . What was needed for Germany . . . was a far-reaching cultural and not a social revolution. . . . The Monists were, therefore, true practitioners of conservative religion."[12]

Nature was both a source of truth and a value worthy of worship. But the German people were cut off from nature. To reestablish this connection, said Haeckel, the state must mimic the organic structure of the environment. This reasoning led Haeckel to reject humanism and to found a political movement, the Monist League, to promote his ideology. If living things are interconnected parts of organic nature, the Monists reasoned, then differences between humans and other creatures are matters of degree, not kind. And since people derived their identity through their race — whose interests were represented by the state — then the state was the highest authority, and liberal concepts of freedom and justice were invalid. Liberalism was an enemy of the state, and of race.[13]

In short, ecology, like Darwinism, was adapted for political uses almost from the start. Its prominence by the 1920s prompts the Oxford historian Anna Bramwell to ask later if it should be called "a German disease." Haeckel's idea that humans should be close to nature and that his countrymen must revive "the German spirit" helped to fuel the "Volkish" movement — an effort to reestablish people's connection with nature by reviving early Celtic rural conditions. Nationalists and agrarians believed, according to Bramwell, that "Germans had been victims of forcible denaturalization from the days of the Roman Empire. The alien Christian Judaic civilization had blocked man off from the natural world, and all the anti-life manifestations of urban living stemmed from this false ethic."[14]

Hence, they believed that preserving society required the reestablishing of connections with nature by reviving the primitive agrarian culture, or *Volk*, and ridding Germany of everything — and everybody — that was unnatural. Society must promote biological fitness through "racial hygiene" and euthanasia.[15]

The desire to subordinate people to organic nature led directly to racism. "The 'scientific' element of racialism can be traced back to Haeckel," writes the philosopher Karl Popper. Haeckel, as Robert Jay Lifton observes, in part quoting the historian George L. Mosse, "a towering figure in German biology and an early Darwinian, was also a racist, a believer in a mystical *Volk*, and a strong advocate of eugenics who 'can be claimed to be a direct ancestor' of the Nazi 'euthanasia' project." Indeed, as Daniel Gasman calls "Germany's major prophet of political biology," someone who contributed significantly to the development of Nazi ideology: "The writings of Haeckel and the ideas of his followers . . . were proto-Nazi in character, and [as] one of the most powerful forces in nineteenth and twentieth-century German intellectual history, may be fully understood as a prelude to the doctrine of National Socialism."[16]

"We do not need to strain at gnats to show that there was a strain of ecological ideas among Nazis: the evidence is ample," writes Bramwell. As the historian Robert A. Pois observes, National Socialism was "a religion of nature," which called "for the establishment of a utopian community, the *Volksgemeinschaft*, rooted in a perceived natural order." Throughout Hitler's political career, writes Pois, "he would continually emphasize the importance of recognizing nature's power over man. He scoffed at the notion of humans ever having the ability to 'control' or 'rule over' nature. . . . Hitler sounded remarkably like contemporary environmentalists who, with ample reason, proclaim that a sharp-tempered Mother Nature . . . will eventually avenge herself upon those who, at least since the onset of industrialization, have tried her patience." He believed in "the sanctity of nature."[17]

Indeed, Nazism was based largely on biological theory. As Hitler's confidant Rudolph Hess insisted, the movement was nothing more than "applied biology" for restoring the "vitality of the German race." It sought "biological renewal" through building, said Heinrich Himmler's legal aide, Werner Best, an "organically indivisible national community." And those who opposed these goals merely revealed themselves to be "the symptom of an illness which threatens the healthy unity of the . . . national organism."[18]

Decrying man's alienation from nature, many Nazi thinkers — among whom can be counted the philosopher Martin Heidegger — opposed what they saw as unnatural and decadent about modern living. Heidegger complained that "technological domination spreads itself over the earth ever more quickly, ruthlessly, and completely. . . . The humanness of man and the thingness of things dissolve into the calculated market value of a market which . . . spans the earth." Likewise, the Nazis blamed capitalists for driving farmers off the land and into towns in an effort to obtain cheap labor, thus undermining rural culture and promoting factory farms that used poisonous synthetic chemicals. Reestablishing the connection with nature, they believed, required crushing unnatural, non-German values. Private property had to be abolished, since it promoted commercialism, consumerism, and urbanization. Forests and wildlife, symbolizing Germany's pre-Roman past, had to be preserved.[19]

Therefore, soon after seizing power in 1933, the Third Reich launched a ruralization program to create a new, more primitive Germany. Subdivisions and private property were declared illegal. Vivisection was banned, and Hitler's Germany became the first European country to establish nature preserves. In 1940 hedgerow and copse protection ordinances were passed "to protect the habitat of wildlife."[20]

"SS training," reports Bramwell, "included a respect for animal life of near Buddhist proportions." Meanwhile, the Nazi regime embraced organic agriculture. Hess promoted experimentation in "bio-dynamic farming," including tests that featured feeding babies organically grown food. Himmler, who, like Hitler, was a vegetarian, created several or-

DISCOVERY: NATURE IS AN ANCIENT FOREST

ganic farms, including one at Dachau which produced herbs for SS medicines. His staff, reports Bramwell, "sent him papers on B vitamin shortages as a cause of matriarchal societies," and other "studies were made on the degenerative effect of artificial fertilizer."[21]

To anyone who cares about the earth, the Nazi-ecology connection is profoundly disturbing. To be sure, contemporary environmentalism neither is nor could ever conceivably produce anything approaching the horrors perpetrated by the Third Reich. The mere fact that Nazis believed in ecology does not mean that ecology leads to Nazism. Presumably the Nazis also brushed their teeth, but that doesn't mean that everyone who practices oral hygiene is at risk of becoming a genocidal maniac.[22]

It is equally certain that the modern ecological perspective differs in countless ways from the beliefs of Haeckel or Hitler. Nevertheless, a troublesome puzzle remains. As Bramwell observes, it is important to know whether "the existence of ecological arguments so similar to today's in the Third Reich [is] . . . significant or just an embarrassing accident." This is a matter, she correctly insists, to "be taken seriously." Bramwell herself concludes that there is no necessary connection between ecology and National Socialism. She rightly notes that the ecological movement spans today's spectrum of ideologies, from leftist "Greens" in Germany to cultural conservatives in England. Similarly, Gasman observes, there is good ecology and bad ecology. The fact that Haeckel's ideas had unsavory consequences is not a reason for dismissing the science entirely.[23]

And surely they are both correct. Ecology cannot be blamed for the emergence of Nazism. This political movement was a product of many factors, not the least of which were the unique historical and cultural circumstances in which Germany found itself following the First World War. Moreover, ecology was by no means the only source of Nazi biological science. Haeckel also advocated eugenics, a racist doctrine with dangerous social implications. And National Socialism was fed by several other intellectual streams, such as the pseudoscientific pronouncements of the Nazi ideologist Alfred Rosenberg, who likened Jews to bacteria infecting the body politic.[24]

European ideas, moreover, undergo a curious kind of deconstruction when they cross the Atlantic. Americans are influenced by abstract political assumptions, but they rarely examine these closely or remain slavishly obedient to them. In the Old World, political ideas are clearly articulated and divide parties along rigid ideological lines. But when these same ideas arrive in the New World, they are quickly homogenized. Concepts that were neatly delineated in France or Germany become vague and inexact and lose their political import.[25]

Also, American environmentalism is a product of many unique historical factors, not just German ecology. The preservation movement has long exhibited distinctly indigenous roots, derived in part from the animism of Native Americans, the wilderness experience, and the pantheistic tradition of the Puritans. Neither has environmentalism ever been a distinctly right-wing movement. Rather, as Bramwell herself notes, over history ecology parties have spanned the political spectrum from socialism to liberalism to moderate Republicanism, as well as fascism.[26] Efforts to save the earth come from diverse individuals, motivated by every conceivable concern. For most people, worry over the environment springs from the heart, not from theory. It is a legitimate response to the soul-destroying ugliness and overcrowding of cities and suburbs and to America's inability to stop the spread of this blight into the countryside.

Nevertheless, despite these differences there were two specific ideas, derived in part from Haeckel and embraced by many American conservationists, whose political effects, when combined with traditional American values, could not be anticipated — namely, holism and monism. Throughout history such philosophies, when applied to politics, usually served to justify suppression of the individual by the state or society, even when, as with Hegel, that was not their original intent.[27]

It is a small step from saying, with Haeckel, that by virtue of being interconnected parts of organic nature humans do not differ fundamentally from other creatures to saying that people have no special rights. And it is an equally short jump from asserting, like Tansley, that ecosystems are the "fundamental units of existence" to holding that their requirements take precedence over human needs.[28]

And, indeed, Bill Devall would soon make this intellectual leap. In 1985 he and George Sessions invoked an eerily Hegelian holism to justify "biocentric equality." The "real work" of becoming a "whole person," they wrote, involves the "realization of 'self-in-self' where 'Self' stands for organic wholeness. This process of the full unfolding of the Self can also be summarized by the phrase, 'No one is saved until we are all saved,' where the phrase 'one' includes not only me, an individual human, but all humans, whales, grizzly bears, whole rain forest ecosystems, mountains and rivers, the tiniest microbes in the soil, and so on."[29]

So, naturally, Devall would conclude that biocentrism reveals the "inadequacies" of human rights. "Rather than use the term 'rights,' " he would write in 1987, "I prefer to speak of the 'inherent worth' of all beings. . . . A thing is right when it tends to protect the integrity, stability and diversity of the biotic community. It is wrong when [it] tends otherwise."[30]

The fact that Haeckel's science strongly influenced the Nazis, therefore, did not imply that all ecology was politically dangerous. It did, however, suggest that holistic ideas such as those embedded in systems ecology would have surprising and perhaps undesirable effects. And indeed, following the Second World War, as the ecologist Frank Golley notes, "within German biology there was much outright hostility to holistic, ecosystem-oriented work" for this reason. Rather, it was in America, where most biologists, who seldom study philosophy, did not know the risks, and where the pantheism of John Muir, Aldo Leopold, and Rachel Carson had already fertilized the soil in which monism and holism might take root, that the ecosystem idea quickly caught on.[31]

This was the beginning of an era of experimental political chemistry, of the mixing together of New and Old World ingredients which had never been combined before. No one knew, or could know, what would happen. The result would be neither left- nor right-wing but both, together with something entirely new. The idea of the ecosystem would energize people of myriad political persuasions, sending the movement off in countless and contradictory directions. But, despite their differences, these disparate movements would share allegiance to holism and monism.

By the 1960s writers such as Eiseley and Commoner were preaching the gospel of ecology to a generation of students already alienated from the "Judeo-Christian tradition." The day after Christmas 1966, the Berkeley historian Lynn White, speaking to the American Association for the Advancement of Science, provided another pseudoscholarly rationale for this rejection: Western civilization, argued White, was wreaking environmental havoc around the globe precisely because it was a Judeo-Christian culture. Our religious tradition taught us that we were apart from and superior to other things, that the world was created for our benefit.[32]

This was, of course, nonsense. Such a thesis could not explain, for example, why many Buddhists in Malaysia like to eat monkey brains while the animal is still alive, why Shinto Japan is the world's largest importer of tropical hardwood (using 200 million square meters of this material each year for chopsticks alone), why Chinese flood-control engineers are probably responsible for more soil erosion than any other people alive, or why Arab farmers have been desertifying the Middle East for the last three thousand years.[33]

Whether true or not, White's speech fired the imagination of many, including Devall. "The predominance of masculine imagery and the domination of Nature . . . in the west," he would write later, "has been well-documented." The domination of nature, he went on, is preached not only by the Bible, which exhorts us to "subdue" the earth, but also by humanism, which places mankind at the center of the universe. By contrast, he suggested, to regain a sense of ecologic sensitivity Americans must search for "the future primitive."[34]

This quest took many eastward, where they hoped to find wisdom in the ideas of Lao-tzu and Buddhism. Some went to Nepal to find themselves. Others decided that America must revive its pre-Columbian past and realize that Native American civilization, not Judaism or Christianity, is the repository of ecological virtue. These Americans, blaming Judeo-Christian culture for alienating man from nature, set out to save the world by dismantling technological civilization and returning culture to its primitive roots. The "back to the land" movement was reborn, and new philosophies such as "bioregionalism," dedicated to dismantling the state and reinstalling simpler societies, captured the fancy of activists.[35]

Meanwhile, similar ideas were being revived in a different form in Europe. Even as Devall was discovering deep ecology, the conservative German writer Herbert Gruhl, who had coauthored the Club of Rome's *Limits to Growth* in 1972, published *The Plundering of a Planet*, which became a bestseller in Germany. In 1978 Gruhl would form Grüne Aktion Zukunft (Green Action Future) as a national political party. Disillusioned with progress and technology, Gruhl, a former Christian Democrat, wanted Germany to return to an earlier, simpler era.[36]

Later his group formed a coalition with left-wing activists, who would soon be known as "fundies." They would create the world's first ecology party, known as "the greens" (Die Grünen). Taking "biospherical egalitarianism" as far as it could go, the Greens not only questioned the rights of industrial nations to take resources from the Third World but also challenged man's rights over nature. All *things*, they said, were created equal. Humans must stop trying to control nature and one another. All modern institutions — the church, business, political parties, the state — are hierarchies. So all the excesses and injustices of modern industrial society — resource depletion, economic exploitation, sexism, everything! — goes out once one adopts the ecological model.[37]

These currents were swirling in the air as Devall stumbled upon Naess. The Judeo-Christian tradition was out, and the ecosystem was in.

Prompted by these values, deep ecologists therefore unwittingly embraced ideas that synthesized an American religion of nature with German metaphysics: a holism that supposed individuals were only parts of a larger system and had no independent standing; antipathy to Judaic and Christian values of humanism, capitalism, materialism, private property, technology, consumerism, and urban living; reverence for nature; belief in the spiritual superiority of primitive culture; a desire to go "back to the land"; support for animal rights; faith in organic farming; and a program to create nature reserves. Heidegger was once again in vogue. Sessions would write in 1979, "Martin Heidegger is perhaps the one *major* philosopher . . . to provide a radical critique of the Western philosophic enterprise as paving the way for the technological mentality and society."[38]

No one noticed the checkered past of these ideas. Most activists, products of an educational system that had ceased to teach history, knew little about the heritage of political ecology. Cloaked in the attractive guise of environmentalism, and combined with the homegrown primitivism of Thoreau and Muir, it touched the taproot of a generation.

Deep ecology became the catechism of a new ethic which radical activists and environmental writers rushed to embrace. In 1981 the American philosopher Paul Taylor would call a similar constellation of concepts "the biocentric outlook on nature," and soon "biocentrism" would eclipse deep ecology as the rallying cry of the radical movement. It embodied, said Taylor, what "we have learned from the science of ecology: the interdependence of all living things in an organically unified order whose balance and stability are necessary conditions for the realization of the good of its constituent biotic communities."[39]

Thus, like Haeckel, the founders of deep ecology, Arne Naess and Bill Devall, transformed ecology into a political theory which carried a revolutionary insight: *politics rests on ecology.* They had revived a political biology whose central premise was that a government which violates the laws of ecology cannot stand. Preservation laws thus acquired an ethical dimension. More than biological strategies for saving the cogs, they came to be perceived as nothing less than a Bill of Rights for the animal kingdom.

So, in the few short decades since its revival in America, ecosystems ecology had taken three wrong turns. First, by employing concepts referring to unverifiable holistic entities such as ecosystems and their properties, it was no longer science but philosophy. Second, many practitioners were embracing unsubstantiated hypotheses concerning the balance of nature and the need for biodiversity. And now, third, a growing cadre of environmental philosophers was transforming the doctrine into political theory.

Followers of ecosystems ecology had crossed the line from fact to value. Not only were living things interdependent, they said, but this diversity was also intrinsically sacred. Unwittingly they had exhumed the ghosts of Hegel, Haeckel, and Heidegger. But no one asked where these ideas would lead.

11

THE OWL
SHRIEKED

ERIC FORSMAN WALKED QUICKLY up the path. Something, he feared, was amiss. Three days earlier he had fitted a radio transmitter on an owl for the first time — fastening it like a tiny backpack — to track the bird so he could measure its home range. Then he had returned to his university office in Corvallis. Now he was back, trying to locate the creature. But his radio receiver was silent. He got no signal at all. He couldn't understand. The battery was brand-new.[1]

Walking up a canyon trail near Blue River Reservoir, along the boundary of the H. J. Andrews Experimental Forest in Oregon's Cascade Mountains this summer day in 1976, Forsman was studying the elusive northern spotted owl. After three years' work he had completed a master's thesis at Oregon State University on the creature's distribution and abundance. Now he was collecting data for his doctoral dissertation on its habitat requirements by tracking birds at Andrews and in an O&C Forest just west of Lorane, Oregon.

But he couldn't believe his bad luck. The owl was the first he had radio-collared, and already it was lost. Abruptly his radio emitted a faint squeak, then lapsed into silence again. What was going on? Finally, as he reached the ridgetop overlooking Mill Creek, the owl's signal came in loud and clear. The bird was now a full three miles from where he had collared it. Spotted owls, he suddenly realized, had an extraordinarily large home range.

The implications of this discovery, Forsman knew, were profound. Spotted owl numbers, he had discovered in his master's work, were declining. And now this bird's flight revealed that the species's range was staggeringly large. The creature depended on thousands of acres of old-growth forest — just the kind loggers liked to cut. This finding had powerful political implications. Yet available knowledge on the bird remained skimpy. The owl was hard to find. By 1980 Forsman and his colleagues had managed to put radio collars on just fourteen individuals. The scientists needed to know much more.[2]

Forsman did not realize it yet, but he would soon be in the hot seat. Both environmentalists and loggers would want him to reach conclusions supporting their agenda, and would be ready to level heavy artillery at him if he did not. Yet, though he may have known more about the bird than anyone else alive, he nevertheless understood almost nothing at all. When the politics started up, he and his colleagues would have to decide: Were data on fourteen owls sufficient to justify turning the entire Pacific Northwest on its head?[3]

For Forsman, curiosity about these birds came naturally. Growing up in Eugene, where his father was a carpenter, Forsman was an avid hunter and fisherman. Like his mother he became an enthusiastic birder, and was particularly fascinated by raptors — hawks, falcons, and especially owls. The idea of flying creatures hunting at night intrigued him. While in high school he started studying the great horned owl, but it was the northern spotted, a bird he had never seen, that especially attracted him. A smaller, less aggressive western cousin of the barred owl, the spotted — just sixteen inches long, brown and dark-eyed, with white-speckled head and chest — was a mystery bird. Only twenty-four of them had ever been seen in Oregon.[4]

Forsman's interest persisted when he matriculated at Oregon State in 1966, majoring in fisheries and wildlife. Then, in the summer between his sophomore and junior years, an event occurred that would change his life. He had taken a job as a seasonal fire lookout for the National Forest Service. One evening, sitting on the porch of the Blue River guard station in Willamette National Forest, he heard a barking sound. At first he thought it was a dog. But the station sat in the middle of wilderness, far from other humans and their pets. Listening carefully, he realized the source of the sound: a spotted owl.[5]

Knowing that they were very territorial at this time of the year — early June, their nesting season — Forsman hooted back. The animal responded. Forsman hooted again. The reply came again, this time closer. The conversation continued. Suddenly, two owls appeared, sitting on the branch of a tree at the edge of his yard. They did not fly away as Forsman approached. They were remarkably tame.

Forsman and a friend and raptor specialist, Richard Reynolds, enthusiastically spent the remainder of their spare time that summer hooting for owls. They successfully called spotted owls several times. But they still knew almost nothing about the creatures. Forsman wanted to learn more.

After graduating in 1970, Forsman was drafted into the army and sent to Germany. Stationed in the Harz Mountains near the Czechoslovak border, he took walks in the woods, hooting for tawny owls, another relative of the spotted. While in Europe, he corresponded with his former professor Howard M. Wight at Oregon State. A pioneer in the study of nongame species, Wight had a particular interest in nesting birds. When Forsman suggested that he might do his dissertation on the northern spotted owl, Wight leaped at the idea.

Wight knew that almost nothing was known about this bird. Like other nongame species, it had received little attention from wildlife biologists. At the time, most studies focused on game animals that could be hunted or caught. Only creatures deserving death, it seemed, merited scientific attention. In 1926 a bird collector named Stokely Ligon wrote a short paper about the spotted owl in New Mexico, and in 1942 the ornithologist Joe Marshall wrote a journal article about the diet and habitat of the spotted owl. Yet for years the only standard reference was a 1938 book on the life histories of birds by a man named A. C. Bent.[6]

So in March 1972, three days after returning to Oregon from Europe, Forsman was back looking for owls in the forest. But almost immediately he began to fear that he might not find enough individuals to study. Not knowing the range of the species, he checked scattered locations throughout Oregon — the Klamath Mountains, the coast range, and the Cascades. At night he would walk the woods or drive along roads, stopping every quarter mile to call owls, by voice or with a tape recorder. To locate nests, he attracted roosting owls with live mice, then followed on foot as the birds flew home with their catch. Enlisting the help of state and federal biologists, he conducted extensive searches for owls throughout western Oregon.[7]

Now he had taken the next step: conducting radiotelemetry research at Andrews and the O&C forest. These places seemed ideal for study. Fully 65 percent of Andrews and 20 percent of the O&C lands were covered by old growth or mature trees. But the more he looked, the more concerned he became. Nearly half the owls he located lived in trees painted with blue or yellow marks, indicating that they were slated for cutting. Indeed, nesting in tree cavities on average more than eighty-five feet above the ground, spotted owls seemed to depend on large, unbroken stands of multilayered forest, where the overstory consisted of conifers 140 to 600 years old and the understory layers were dominated by younger shade-tolerant species such as western hemlock, western red cedar, Port Orford cedar, grand fir, white fir, Shasta red fir, western yew, vine maple, canyon live oak, California laurel, and tan oak.[8]

Their prey was a cafeteria of species characteristic of coniferous forests, including dusky-footed wood rats, deer mice, western red-backed voles, snowshoe hares, bushy-tailed wood rats, pocket gophers, twenty-three different kinds of birds, two families of reptiles, crayfish, terrestrial snails, twenty-nine genera of insects, and several kinds of spiders. But their principal prey in western Oregon was flying squirrels, which typically made up 20 to 30 percent of their diet. And these cute little rodents were most common in mature forests.[9]

It was clear to Forsman and his colleagues that old growth and mature forests constituted the owl's "preferred habitat." Of forty-seven nests they located, thirty were in cavities in old-growth conifers and seventeen were on platforms of sticks or other debris in mature conifers. Although the owl ranged from western Oregon to the eastern slope of the Cascades, more than 98 percent of the owls Forsman found lived amidst "old-growth conifers or mixtures of mature and old-growth conifer." None were found in forests younger than thirty-six years old.[10]

Living in these condemned neighborhoods, the birds seemed to be in decline. Mating on average every other spring, they usually raised only one or two owlets at a time. Yet the mortality rate of these young, as with the offspring of most predatory birds, was extremely high. They died in a variety of ways: some starved; others were eaten by predators or consumed by disease or exposure; still others fell or jumped from the nest too early. Even after successfully leaving the nest, of the twenty-nine owlets Forsman followed only nineteen survived until August. One was killed by a great horned owl. The others simply disappeared. Checking historical territories on annual intervals and finding some abandoned, Forsman calculated that the owl population was declining at the rate of 0.8 percent a year. "The principal cause of site abandonment," he and his colleagues concluded, "was timber harvest."[11]

To be sure, not all the evidence implicated logging. Some birds were living in areas where as much as 77 percent of the trees had been clear-cut. Nevertheless, finding the preponderance of data disturbing, Forsman started to express his concern to anyone who would listen. And many did. In the summer of 1973 the U.S. Fish and Wildlife Service had begun compiling a list of potentially endangered species for congressional consideration of the endangered species bill. Hearing of Forsman's work through Wight, the service included the northern spotted owl. The same year John McKean, director of the Oregon Game Commission, set up a state Endangered Species Task Force to inventory endangered species in Oregon. Wight was appointed to the task force and began to supply his colleagues with data collected by Forsman.

At Wight's urging, the task force agreed to recommend giving special attention to protection of old-growth forests, and the spotted owl in particular. In response, it recommended that state and federal agencies set aside three hundred acres of old-growth habitat around approximately one hundred spotted owl nests Forsman and others estimated to exist as an interim step until permanent spotted owl guidelines could be established. As McKean's committee had no enforcement authority, this amounted merely to a request for voluntary forest reserves. The Forest Service and Bureau of Land Management refused to comply. But with this suggestion for owl set-asides, McKean had fired the first volley in a new kind of war. Not merely a contest between economic and environmental concerns, it would be a battle of values and ideas, where victory would belong to the side that could capture the American mind.[12]

In 1973 the new project leader of the Forest Service's Forestry and Range Sciences Laboratory in LaGrande, Oregon, Jack Ward Thomas, came to the Corvallis office of the U.S. Fish and Wildlife Service's Cooperative Wildlife Research Unit at Oregon State University, seeking wildlife habitat studies suitable for government funding. Howard Wight, as unit leader, urged support for Forsman.[13]

Behind Thomas's good ol' country boy manner hid a sharp scientific mind. Grandson of a dairy farmer and son of a postal worker and contractor from Handley, Texas, Thomas liked to hunt, fish, and tell jokes. He would not lay eyes on a spotted owl until more than a decade later, when he would be approached to develop a scientifically credible strategy for the little troublemaker. Even then he tried to avoid encountering the bird, but was unsuccessful. But he knew that in the past most wildlife research had focused exclusively on game animals, and he realized that this was a mistake. So when Wight suggested that the service support Forsman's study of owls, Thomas jokingly replied, "Hell, Howard, what's the bag limit on those?"[14]

Then Thomas authorized the grant.

Thomas's visit to Corvallis symbolized the convergence of concerns over threatened species and ecosystems. Just as Forsman's owl study prompted him to worry more about the fate of forests, so did Thomas, by studying forest and rangeland as wildlife habitat, start down a trail that would lead eventually to the owl. Arriving at his new post in La-Grande in 1972, after having worked for twenty years in Texas, West

Virginia, and New England, Thomas immediately set out to devise a novel strategy for managed forests.

Beginning in 1969, insects had been massively invading the nearby Blue Mountains National Forest. As a result of decades of fire suppression, ponderosa pine stands had given way to later successional tree species such as grand fir and white fir, which were susceptible to defoliation by tussock moths and spruce budworm. In an attempt to end the outbreak, in 1976 the Forest Service, following what was standard procedure under these conditions, conducted aerial spraying with DDT.[15]

This action was, in effect, like flogging a dead horse. The insects, having eaten themselves out of house and home, were dying out anyway. But they left behind thousands of dead fir trees with considerable commercial value, which the service was eager to salvage. Thomas and his associates were asked to devise a harvest plan that considered impacts on vertebrates and protected myriad wildlife species.

The Texan was the right man to ask. He was aware of the national controversy generated by clear-cutting in Montana's Lolo National Forest in 1970. And he had been research scientist in the Monongahela National Forest in West Virginia when a clear-cutting controversy erupted that would change forest management forever. While working in West Virginia, Thomas watched as the Forest Service significantly increased its clear-cutting of eastern hardwoods. And he was struck by the public's reaction. Unlike Westerners, who had become accustomed to seeing forests turned into ugly patchworks, Appalachians were conservative people who loved their forests. Hunters in the region returned to the same area year after year. When they came back to find their favorite groves clear-cut, they got mad.[16]

When loggers created what some considered a particularly ugly scar just outside Richwood, West Virginia, outraged citizens asked Lawrence Beitz, owner of a small insurance firm and a member of the Richwood Federation, a local booster group, to investigate. Beitz, who thought he knew silviculture better than the Forest Service, was furious. By his reckoning, the clear-cut area had been mostly immature wild cherry. As far as he was concerned, even-age forest management didn't make sense where there were up to seventy-five different kinds of trees, many of them tolerant species needing shade. But foresters, wishing to encourage commercially valuable shade-intolerant trees, disagreed. So Beitz asked the local forest supervisor: Why not allow these trees to mature before harvesting? According to Beitz, the ranger, considering him just an ignorant hillbilly, told him to get lost.

Instead, Beitz went to Governor Arch Moore, who created a commission to investigate and put Beitz on it. When, by 1973, the state still had not stopped the Forest Service from clear-cutting, the Izaak Walton League, of which Beitz was also a member, went to federal court. Nonselective logging, the league's suit alleged, violated the intent of the Organic Act of 1897 establishing the Forest Service, which permitted cutting only designated mature trees. It argued that clear-cutting was illegal because it was indiscriminate, felling young as well as old trees.[17]

By the time the Izaak Walton League went to court, Thomas was already in LaGrande. But he had learned enough from his West Virginia experience to realize that public values were changing, and that clear-cutting, no matter how "correct" it seemed to the Forest Service, was unlikely to gain public acceptance. He sought to find a way to salvage moth-killed trees in the Blue Mountains while preserving the habitat of all the region's vertebrates. In later years this became known as "retaining biodiversity."[18]

So he began an effort that resulted in a book, *Wildlife Habitats in Managed Forests — the Blue Mountains of Oregon and Washington*, published in 1976. Rather than focusing on maximum production of timber or enhancing prominent game species such as mule deer and elk, this scheme catalogued all the fauna of the forest, then devised an approach for evaluating the effect of various management actions on species welfare.[19]

And what this study found was astounding. Altogether, it revealed that the Blue Mountain forests were home to 379 kinds of vertebrates — birds, mammals, and reptiles. Debris, which earlier foresters believed to be biologically useless, performed a vital role in the forest ecosystem. Snags provide habitat for insectivorous cavity-nesting birds — chickadees, woodpeckers, sapsuckers, nuthatches, and flickers — which "play a significant role in regulation of insect populations" that attack younger forests. The abandoned cavities provide habitat for many additional species of vertebrates such as flying squirrels and saw-whet owls. Dead and down woody matter — rotting logs — render a critical service to mineral cycling and nutrient immobilization. And they provide habitat for mice, coyotes, and many small mammals, such as gopher snakes, dusky shrews, yellow pine chipmunks, and long-tailed voles.

The year before Thomas completed this study, the federal court had found in favor of the Izaak Walton League and halted clear-cutting in national forests nationwide. The decision threatened to reduce national timber harvests by as much as half. The Forest Service and the timber industry went into a state of shock.[20]

Responding to the court decision, Congress in 1976 passed the National Forest Management Act. This law was intended both to protect the environment and to make clear-cutting legal. Relying partly on testimony from Thomas, it embraced a "holistic" or ecosystem approach to silviculture, requiring that the Forest Service "provide for diversity of plant and animal communities based on the suitability and capability of the specific land area," provide "protection of forest resources . . . range, timber, watershed, wildlife and fish," and allow clear-cutting only where "the potential environmental, biological, aesthetic, engineering, and economic impacts . . . have been assessed."[21]

This was just what Thomas had pioneered in the Blue Mountains. Following passage of the law, his study would be incorporated into the Wildlife Habitat Relationships Program of the Forest Service, and would be put to work in every service region. He was a man ahead of his time; but his time — the age of the ecosystem — had come. Yet, as with the Endangered Species Act, it would bring complications few anticipated.

It was a warm June day in 1974 when James Monteith came to Eugene to take the reins of the fledgling Oregon Wilderness Coalition. The group, eventually called the Oregon Natural Resources Council, had been established just two years earlier by student activists with the Sierra Club and Wilderness Society as a watchdog on the Forest Service. To comply with the 1964 Wilderness Act, the service in 1972 had completed a Roadless Area Review and Evaluation, or "RARE I" — inventorying areas eligible for wilderness designation. But the results of this study had been profoundly disappointing to environmentalists, who had hoped for far more wilderness than the service recommended. Eager to campaign for more wilderness preservation, and realizing that they had no activist network in Oregon, they created the coalition. But now there was much more on the agenda.[22]

As the coalition's second full-time staffer, Monteith was the right man at the right time. He embodied the conflicting ideals and intellectual ferment that swirled through the Oregon campuses in those days. His uncle had been the senior engineer in the Olympic National Forest; his father was a banker whose principal job was lending money to Weyerhaeuser and other timber companies. He grew up in Klamath Falls with friends who came from logging families, and who dreamed of driving logging trucks someday.

But Monteith marched to a different drummer. Driven by intellectual curiosity, he set his sights high. Deciding to be a doctor, he matriculated at Oxford University in England, then transferred to Massachusetts Institute of Technology as a premed student. Through his studies

Monteith was drawn to cell biology, then to marine biology. This intellectual curiosity next led the peripatetic student to Stanford, then, in quick succession, to the University of Oregon, the University of Alaska, and back to Stanford, where he finally earned a bachelor's degree.

Fascinated with fur-bearing animals, in 1973 he entered the Oregon State master's program, intending to study fisher and marten with Howard Wight. These were exciting times. Corvallis was buzzing with debates over trees and forest creatures. The university had started coniferous forest biome investigations to develop an inventory of life forms in virgin forests. Discoveries about nutrient cycling and hydrology were being made regularly. Meanwhile, disturbing rumors were circulating: that fishers were disappearing, that streams produced less water after surrounding forests were clear-cut, and that the spotted owl was in trouble.

But most exciting of all, Monteith thought, was the idea of the ecosystem. Rain forest studies were in their infancy, but scholars had already begun to suspect the global role played by these systems. They began to share their concerns with students and friends, fostering an easy camaraderie with environmentalists. They all sensed that they had embarked on a great adventure together. But by 1974, Wight was dying of cancer and could not take Monteith as a student. Disappointed, Monteith wandered to Mexico, then returned to Eugene to take the coalition job. Prompted by his fascination with ecosystems, Monteith decided that the coalition should focus on two things: free-flowing rivers and old-growth forests. Even environmentalists, Monteith felt, had missed the forests' importance, instead lobbying to establish alpine "rock and ice" wilderness. Back in Corvallis, the Oregon State Forestry School, he felt, was filled with hack professors teaching that old growth was biological desert. Powerful timber interests so dominated university teaching that the introductory course in forestry was known as "Weyerhaeuser I." This industry power cast a pall, making Monteith and his friends feel like members of an underground plotting to overthrow a king.

But even coups d'état need luck, and activists found it. The 1969 National Environmental Policy Act already gave them a strong weapon for challenging government projects that failed to consider all their biological consequences. And in 1976 they were suddenly handed another major weapon — the National Forest Management Act. This law decreed far more than holistic harvest policy. It also established a labyrinthine public planning process which ensured, as the historian David A. Clary observes, "the eternal generation of turgid documents to be reviewed and revised forever. Planning became an end in itself."[23]

The new law was an invitation for do-it-yourself activism, tilting the playing field toward environmentalists, who now had limitless opportunities to appeal and halt Forest Service harvest plans. No longer would lumbermen's buttoned-down lawyers dominate timber planning. Now any scruffy activist with a typewriter could stop a timber sale in its tracks.[24]

Indeed, the Oregon Wilderness Coalition would soon be far from alone. Throughout the Northwest, seeing the implications of the new laws, activists organized. In 1978 the National Wildlife Federation established an Environmental Law Clinic on the University of Oregon campus to pursue forest litigation. In 1982 this organization, with Yale Law School graduate Terry Thatcher as staff counsel and Oregon State alumnus Andy Stahl as staff forester, would move to Portland, setting as its priorities preserving salmon and forests. In 1987 the Sierra Club Legal Defense Fund would open offices in Seattle, where Stahl would join them. Together these groups would find a winning issue: the spotted owl.[25]

Meanwhile, by 1979 down in the redwood country town of Garberville, California, the "man who walks in the woods" was the man of the hour. Robert Sutherland adopted that title for himself because he believed that all names had once had a meaning that had been lost, and because he thought that everyone is entitled to choose his or her own, conveying that person's essence. So instead of Robert, which he'd had no role in choosing, he opted for the moniker "the man who walks in the woods" — or "woods" for short — because it best described him. And now, to stop a logging juggernaut, he was being asked to live up to his name.[26]

The fine old conservative Union Lumber Company — the same firm that had supported Emanuel Fritz's research and led the charge of sustainable forestry in the 1920s — had been sold to the multinational giant Georgia-Pacific. To Sutherland this new owner seemed to possess a time horizon that stretched no further than the next quarterly earnings report. Convinced that money should grow faster than trees, Georgia-Pacific was intent on getting its investment out of the forests as quickly as possible so it could be invested elsewhere.[27]

Following this philosophy, Sutherland believed, the corporation began chopping its way up a remote part of Mendocino County's North Coast — the so-called Lost Coast — through magnificent redwood groves adjacent to an area where the state planned to establish the Sinkyone Wilderness State Park, and through lands important to Native Americans. Eventually it would threaten a particularly exquisite stand known as Sally Bell Grove. A nearby resident, Richard Gienger, declared a one-man war on the company, cofounding a group called the Sinkyone Council. Sometimes sleeping in the forest to monitor loggers' progress, he met with politicians and corporate executives and organized hikes into the woods.[28]

Gienger's SOS reached Garberville, fifty miles away. Outraged, the community decided to help. But saving Sally Bell clearly required more than a one-man suicide squad. The Sinkyone, they realized, was just one of many issues erupting in the region. Dealing with multiple threats demanded a multipurpose, heavy-duty, straight-shooting gang that could write petitions and file lawsuits like the big boys. So Gienger and Gregory ("Obie") O'Brien, an activist from the nearby town of Whitethorn, asked Sutherland to restart a dormant environmental effort called the Environmental Protection Information Center, or EPIC.

An ex–Haight-Ashbury hippie, son of a Nobel prize-winning scientist and self-taught naturalist, Sutherland was the right person for the job. Now thirty-five, he had grown up in university communities in Saint Louis and Cleveland. After dropping out of Case Western Reserve University, he spent several years studying art in New York City, then joined the great westward migration of rootless youth to California. In San Francisco he drifted from job to job, working as a mailman, an apartment manager, a longshoreman, and even for a while owning his own flower shop.

This was a spiritual odyssey for Sutherland. He was intensely interested in religions, which he believed are repositories of cultural wisdom. Societies are as stable as their faiths are profound, he thought. Our degenerate age reflected the decayed state of its main religions — Christianity and Judaism — which primarily taught how to worship Mammon. Sutherland concluded that this spiritual crisis was largely due to our failure to take responsibility for our inner lives. We were no longer being taught how to deal with problems such as desire, pain, and loss. And this omission, Sutherland decided, was the source of our environmental crisis. Not finding sustenance in religion, Americans were trying to satisfy their emotional need by overconsuming material things, seeking to fill their emptiness with wealth and possessions.

So environmentalism, Sutherland thought, was a living spiritual alternative to these decaying old creeds. It taught that overconsumption would not quench our spiritual thirst. Instead, it permitted us to realize wholeness again through deeper awareness of our oneness with nature, for "nature is a metaphor for a healthy and natural inner life."[29]

By 1973 Sutherland's religious quest had drawn him to Garberville.

Willing to be "financially poor" in exchange for living a "spiritually rich" life, he camped in the forest. When a wildfire destroyed his few possessions, he moved onto a remote spit of land belonging to friends, where he built a small cabin, without telephone, water, or electricity. He spent his days reading biology and philosophy, and walking, walking, walking in the woods, driven by a passion to understand each and every creature there. Refusing to own a car, he hitched rides into Garberville when he needed supplies.

Sutherland had joined the back-to-the-land movement. The mirror opposite of the forty-niners who came to Sutter's Mill searching for wealth, a new generation of pilgrims was flocking into this tiny former logging community, seeking spiritual renewal.

Garberville was living proof of the resilience of nature. During the postwar building boom of the late fifties and early sixties, when a fortune could be made cutting trees, thousands of loggers had combed through the surrounding forests, felling everything in sight.

As quickly as it had come, the boom collapsed. The mills went bankrupt, leaving behind scarred and eroded hills. The town declined. Then, around 1968, the Berkeley and Haight-Ashbury diasporas began. Soon another boom erupted as thousands of settlers drove into town in Volkswagen microbuses to spend their meager savings on raw land. Hippies, freaked out by the Vietnam war, the military-industrial complex, and the King and Kennedy assassinations, sought soft landing spots to drop acid and drop out. Many migrated north, igniting the back-to-the-land movement. Opportunistic Garberville landowners began selling their cut-over land at fire sale prices.[30]

Seeking self-knowledge in nature, and willing to live as frugally as necessary to be left alone, the newcomers settled into the patchwork of clear-cuts interspersed between groves of remaining old growth, building ramshackle huts out of secondhand lumber. The old-time inhabitants had never seen anything like these people. Scruffily dressed and possessing an easy confidence, they were everything loggers were not: they preferred pot to alcohol, free sex to family life, frugality to wealth, New Age spirituality to mainstream religion, and hair to haircuts. But, most significant, they were far better educated than their neighbors. Most, like Sutherland, had some college education and came from upper-middle-class families. They were smart and resourceful.

It was only a matter of time before their talents would shine. Many began growing marijuana, thereby quickly transforming this activity into a major and lucrative industry. Then some turned their attention to activism. A local firm, the Barnum Timber Company, started spraying pesticide on its groves, which lay in a mosaic surrounding Garberville's hippie shacks. These people were outraged. They had come north to escape the poisons of technology. They kept organic gardens and believed in health foods. And pesticides were death on pot. They couldn't tolerate cut-and-run loggers spoiling the ecological purity of their lives![31]

Ruthanne Cecil was especially angry. After working as a secretary in San Francisco, she had moved to Garberville in 1973, when she was twenty-seven. Seeking a solitary place to write poetry, she bought some land for $175 an acre and built her own cabin for $600. Four months after she finished her cabin, Barnum started spraying. The toxic herbicide 2,4,5-T drifted for miles. Complaining about the smell, she organized a meeting with Sutherland and others at the old school building in Garberville on October 21, 1977. Agreeing to form EPIC, they filed suit against Barnum.[32]

The company was so astounded at meeting environmental resistance that it soon capitulated. But EPIC never followed up on its victory. Formed as an ad hoc group mainly to fight the spraying, it simply disbanded once the battle was over. So Sutherland continued to pursue environmental issues on his own. Surviving on savings and piecing together a living as an environmental consultant, he got by, and gradually became drawn into the Sinkyone dispute. When Gienger and O'Brien asked him to restart EPIC he agreed, but only if they did it right this time. They would formally incorporate as a tax-deductible organization, fund-raise, and put together a professional team for challenging timber harvest plans.[33]

The time was ripe for environmental conflict. Fifteen years of nearly continuous struggle over Redwood National Park had badly polarized the region. Ever since Congress first created this sanctuary in 1968, the Sierra Club had campaigned for its expansion. Deeming the park's watershed to be exposed to erosion caused by logging on its boundaries, the club demanded the high ground as a buffer. And although it eventually won — in 1978 Congress added 48,000 acres to the park — the fight once again left all parties dissatisfied. Only one fifth of the expanded park had any old growth, mostly in small, isolated groves. Over 90 percent of Redwood Creek was logged over. Rather than saving many big trees, Redwood was a memorial to their death. Over half had been clearcut, yet taxpayers would eventually pay $1.4 billion for the land. So while environmentalists got the park, loggers got the trees.[34]

And now, thanks to such environmental laws, problems were multiplying. The new rules mandated revolutionary changes in forestry. Yet neither the government nor mainstream conservation groups would enforce them. Playing the role of policeman, Sutherland decided, would be EPIC's job. He would begin by suing Georgia-Pacific over the Sinkyone. In logging the Lost Coast it had not considered the cumulative impacts, a possible violation of California's Environmental Quality Act. Only the Pacific Lumber Company, lying in Scotia just thirty miles down the road, was still a good corporate citizen, Sutherland thought. Too bad the other timber giants didn't follow Palco's example.[35]

Stanwood A. Murphy, Jr. — whom everyone called "Woody" — was angry. When his father, Stanwood Senior, died at the helm of the Pacific Lumber Company in 1972, Woody, then twenty-one, had joined the Palco Forestry Department, marking trees. Now, seven years later, he was a hook tender, earning less than a first-year log truck driver. Meanwhile, his family and friends owned 20 percent of the company![36]

After her husband's death, Stanwood's widow, Suzanne, although still a member of the board of directors, kept out of the company's daily affairs. Woody's younger brother, Warren, took a desk job and would eventually be made chief of timber operations. But Woody stayed in the woods, and therefore never got promoted.

Something had gone sour, Woody thought. Even as the state government was rewriting the rules of forestry, things weren't right at Palco. The year before his father died, Woody had quit college and begun running heavy equipment, then worked on a company woods construction crew. In 1974 he returned to college, got married, and earned a technical forestry certificate and associate arts degree before returning to work for the company in 1976.

But when he came back, he found Harvey ("Jup") Holt, Jr., who had been a mere timber faller two years earlier, promoted to siderod. As the foreman in charge of two or more logging crews, or "sides," a siderod is middle management within the woods hierarchy. It was the position Woody Murphy sought. The promotion looked like nepotism, since Jup's father, Harvey Senior, was woods superintendent and ran the whole operation.

Woody knew that by choosing to work in the woods rather than at company headquarters in San Francisco, he had put his chances for advancement at risk. The new managers were coat-and-tie people who never rolled up their sleeves. A team of blueblooded Stanford graduates and members of the Bohemian Club, they seldom ventured among the workers in Scotia. None had worked his way up through the ranks. They were out of touch.[37]

After Stanwood's death, Edward M. Carpenter, company president and Palco old-timer, became chairman of the board. He was succeeded by Robert Hoover, member of a prominent southern California lumber family. In 1975 Hoover had been followed by Gene Elam, a business school bean counter. Palco, Murphy feared, was becoming just another business. And he wasn't alone in believing that the leadership was out of touch. "They were a silver-spoon set, a crushed pineapple kind of team," recalled Lloyd Hecathorn, a former vice president for sales with rival Arcata Redwood.[38]

Meanwhile, a newcomer had arrived in Scotia. John Campbell grew up on an Australian farm before traveling to New York. While in America he met and married Edward Carpenter's daughter Cynthia. Eventually moving to Scotia, he joined the company as a sales trainee, and was made resident manager in 1977.

This was the wrong management at the wrong time, Murphy thought. Humboldt County was a mess. The expansion of Redwood National Park had been a disaster for the local economy and the U.S. taxpayer. Congress had approved the most expensive preservation purchase in history for a park few would visit. Now most of the loggers had left or were leaving.[39]

The Arcata Lumber Company had taken the money it had received from Uncle Sam and run, selling most of the remaining timber to the Simpson Lumber Company and transforming itself into a printing giant with plants virtually everywhere but Humboldt County. Simpson, too, had been forced to sell most of its old growth. Unemployment, hovering between 14 and 18 percent before park expansion, surged even higher. The towns were plagued by symptoms of bad times — an increase in crime, wife-beating, alcoholism, and divorce.[40]

Neither the fight over Redwood Park nor the brewing battle of the Sinkyone affected Pacific Lumber. It was the only company that still owned significant stands of old-growth redwood, and the only firm still practicing Emanuel Fritz's selective cutting. At current harvest rates Palco could cut old growth forever.[41]

Scotia remained an island surrounded by storms. But Murphy could see that Palco's time would come soon. In 1973 California had just passed its own version of the National Forest Management Act, called the California Forest Practices Act. This meant that timber couldn't just be cut wherever people wanted to anymore. Private landowners even had to ask state permission to harvest trees on their own lands! Yet, perversely, some old state laws had encouraged bad forestry, Murphy thought. Until 1977 Palco, like other companies, had to pay taxes on standing timber inventory. This was an incentive to cut. The fewer trees a company had, the less it paid in taxes.[42] It didn't take a genius, Woody mused, to see that by passing conflicting laws, government had inadvertently set a trap for industry. Pacific Lumber was headed for trouble. But did those hothouse plants at the company offices in San Francisco see it coming?

As usual, Tom Hirons was worrying about money — and the future of logging, which was almost the same thing.

In 1978 Thurston Twigg-Smith, owner of Shiny Rock Mining, which was the financial backer of Hirons's first logging effort, North Fork Logging, decided to withdraw his support. The rate of return, he told Hirons, simply wasn't great enough. So Hirons borrowed money from his banker in Mill City to start again. By mortgaging everything he owned, he raised the $225,000 necessary to buy his old equipment — yarder, log loader, D-6 cat, crummy, pickup, fire truck, and miscellaneous rigging and tools — back from Twigg-Smith. He decided to call his new venture Mad Creek Logging, which, under the circumstances, seemed appropriate.[43]

For 1978 was a risky time. By the mid-1970s logging had reached a new high. Private corporations, having run out of old growth on their own lands, were bidding more often on public timber. Everyone caught the speculative fever. People who didn't even own mills were purchasing standing timber like commodity brokers in Chicago buying platinum futures, hoping to sell their rights later for a profit. Prices soared, spurring a feeding frenzy among loggers.

But when inflation reached double digits after Jimmy Carter became president, interest rates soared, and these speculators got stuck with a lot of inventory — trees that they had bought but had not yet cut. This excess of supply threatened small family mills with financial ruin. To rescue them, the government agreed to buy the timber back. But then the Forest Service and Bureau of Land Management found themselves with extra inventory — both the old trees which had been sold and repurchased and new allotments they had planned to sell all along. They began selling not just the new stands but the backlog as well. Cutting reached new highs, which was bad for both business and the forests.

Meanwhile, Hirons couldn't understand Forest Service logging rules, which required burning slash and permitted cutting too close to streams. Slash, he knew, contained vital nutrients. Why not just let it rot? Hirons, who liked to fish, was especially concerned about the streams. He could see that trees were important to them. Their roots stabilized soil, reducing erosion. Their cover kept water temperatures cool, slowing evaporation and sustaining aquatic life. And deadfall acted like dams, limiting runoff.

He and the trees, Hirons felt, were in the same situation: both were being swept along by distant forces over which they had no control.

12

THE RELUCTANT
RESEARCHERS

By 1979 FORSMAN and his colleagues knew enough about the owl to be concerned but not enough to be certain that their worry was justified. The more they studied the bird, the more land it seemed to require. In comparison with the tawny owl, for example, which needs just 30 acres, the home range areas of the spotted owl were huge — between 2,840 and 10,440 acres. And since much of that was diminishing old growth, the prognosis was not encouraging. Yet their data remained skimpy: after four years they had managed to fit radio transmitters on only six pairs of birds.[1]

But politics would not wait for science. Events were occurring in rapid succession. In 1976 the McKean Task Force, citing regulations adopted to implement the Forest Management Practices Act, which called for maintaining well-distributed, viable populations of native species, recommended a long-term goal of maintaining "400 pairs of spotted owls on public lands in Oregon," and as an interim policy urged agencies to "protect spotted owl sightings and nest sites consistent with the specific habitat requirements as described by Forsman."[2]

In 1977 the Forest Service and the Bureau of Land Management accepted the McKean spotted owl management plan, agreeing to set aside 300 acres for each of four hundred pair. The same year the Forest Service, in an attempt to inventory the lands eligible for wilderness designation, began a comprehensive second Roadless Area Review and Evaluation, which became known as "RARE II." In 1978 the McKean Task Force was replaced by the Oregon-Washington Interagency Wildlife Committee, which recommended more efforts to search for the owl. And in 1979 Washington state established its own Spotted Owl Working Group.[3]

Meanwhile, the timber industry became increasingly nervous. The federal spotted owl set-asides would proscribe logging on 120,000 acres containing at least $10 billion worth of timber. RARE I had already put 17 percent of Northwest forests into wilderness, and RARE II would lock up even more. Yet the larger the amount of forest set aside, the more difficult it would be to practice sustainable logging on what remained. Long-term forestry, the industry argued, requires a large timber base.[4]

Yet, because of events far away, the stakes were rising. In 1967 the Tennessee Valley Authority began construction of a major public works project, called Tellico Dam, on the Little Tennessee River. Promising to inundate thousands of acres of fertile farmland, the dam had little economic justification. It was pure pork. Activists were furious but unable to stop it. Then, when the Endangered Species Act became law, they found a way.[5]

The ichthyologist James D. Williams was working in the Office of Endangered Species in Washington when he got a call from David Etnier, a former colleague at the University of Tennessee. Tramping along the banks of the Little Tennessee River, Etnier had found a kind of minnow he had never seen before. Curious, he began to search for the fish in other streams, but to no avail. Apparently the creature lived nowhere else. It ought to be listed as an endangered species, Etnier told Williams.

"Okay," Williams replied, "but there's a problem. The law may not allow us to list a species that doesn't have a name." Williams suggested that Etnier write a scientific article defining the new species right away. Then they could try to list it.

Within a few months Etnier had written a draft, which would eventually be accepted by the *Proceedings of the Biological Society of Washington.* But Williams did not wait for its publication. Instead he immediately proposed the listing, which was announced in the *Federal Register.* As the fish still did not have a name, the notice referred to it by its genus only, as *Percina sp.* This was in effect a promissory note, saying, "a minnow to be named later."[6]

Soon the world knew this fish's name: snail darter. Etnier and Williams had handed environmentalists a golden sword with which to slay the dragon. Reacting immediately, activists sued to stop construction of the dam, claiming that by threatening to destroy the minnow's critical habitat, Tellico would violate section 7 of the Endangered Species Act. In response, the TVA noted that the environmental impact statement had passed two federal court reviews. It claimed — rightly, as it turned out — that the darter was not endangered but also lived else-where.[7]

The case went to the Supreme Court, which in 1978 ruled against the dam, even though this project was under way six years before Congress passed the Endangered Species Act. The Court nonetheless ruled that it was "the plain intent of Congress to halt and reverse the trend toward species extinction, whatever the cost." Clearly, it claimed, "Congress viewed the value of endangered species as 'incalculable,'" hence surely worth more than a $100 million dam project.[8]

Thus did one form of extremism — construction of a dam that would harm both people and nature — provoke another. In judging the intent of Congress, the Court was, of course, mistaken. The ruling went far be-yond what Dingell and his committee colleagues had intended. They had not supposed that more than a few hundred creatures would be listed, and had specifically noted that any attempt to do too much for endangered species invited "dismantling civilization." But the Court, offended by the stupidity of the Tellico project, decreed endangered species to be of absolute value, thereby inadvertently endorsing biocen-trism as the law of the land.[9]

Nevertheless, in the short term advocates of development won. Sena-tor Howard Baker of Tennessee shepherded legislation through Con-gress exempting Tellico from the act, and the dam was eventually completed. But the political shock waves from the episode reverberated all the way to the Northwest. Suddenly the stakes over endangered species were infinitely higher. No longer did people suppose that the law was merely symbolic. Now they realized that, like some of the crea-tures it sought to save, it had very sharp teeth.[10]

The snail darter was not the only creature that demonstrated the power of this law. Other hitherto obscure life forms suddenly had major political significance. Already by 1975 the Smithsonian Institution had recommended investigating twenty thousand species for the endan-gered species list. In 1976 the National Wildlife Federation successfully sued to stop construction of a highway interchange in Mississippi be-cause it threatened sandhill crane habitat. In 1978 a rare wildflower called the Furbish lousewort temporarily halted a $650 million hydro-electric project in Maine.[11]

With the darter decision the Supreme Court fired a shot heard 'round the country. Suddenly it was clear that the Endangered Species Act ap-plied not just to a few politically popular whales, cranes, and cats but to virtually every creature on earth, including even the slimy snail darter, described by Laura Manning as "an uncuddly lower taxonomical species ungraciously blocking a major public work."[12] And conservationists and loggers now realized that the spotted owl was not just another bird. It was the king in a game of chess. Whoever captured it won.

Owl biologists were not the only scientists caught in converging political currents. Jerry Franklin, chief plant ecologist at the U.S. Forest Service Pacific Northwest Forest and Range Experiment Station at Oregon State University in Corvallis, would also be feeling the heat. Old-growth forests, he and his colleagues decided, far from being the "biological deserts" earlier scientists had described, actually contained living riches never before dreamed of.

Franklin's epiphany was the indirect consequence of Eugene Odum's successful effort to gain U.S. participation in the International Biological Programme. Born and raised in Camas, Washington, where his father was a pulp mill worker, Franklin attended Oregon State University and received his doctorate in botany at Washington State University. For most of the next thirty years, he did research at the Forest Service's laboratory at Corvallis and at H. J. Andrews Experimental Forest, which was run jointly by Oregon State University and the Forest Service.[13]

In 1970 Oregon State University received funding from the National Science Foundation to take part in the Northwest Coniferous Biome Project, a part of the International Biological Programme's effort to survey different ecosystems. But which one should the university study, and where? The most logical research site was the university's own research forest. Not far from Corvallis, it was convenient for faculty. But Franklin loved Andrews. It was farther away, high in the Cascades. He relished its remoteness, and sought to explore its damp forests whenever he could.

Andrews had been a pioneer in forest research ever since it was founded in 1948. It specialized in studies that looked beyond the time horizon of loggers and examined long-term changes. To Franklin it was the natural place to begin. Even though it was a two-hour drive from campus, it offered large areas of undisturbed habitat to study. The Forest Service, moreover, was already monitoring low-elevation watersheds there, and its forests had a lot of old growth, trees that no one — he thought — had examined closely before.

After lobbying successfully to conduct the biome research at Andrews, Franklin helped organize a team of faculty and Forest Service scientists which included Arthur McKee, biome research coordinator, and Fred Swanson, a postdoctoral geologist whose specialty was the geomorphology of mountain landscapes. Together they decided to begin by examining watersheds. And the most accessible streams in Andrews lay at lower elevations, in old-growth forest.[14]

These scholars therefore began to study old growth, not because they were prescient, but because Andrews was an enjoyable place to satisfy their intellectual curiosity, and it was convenient and interesting to do so. At first Franklin and his colleagues did not realize that old trees possessed special biological significance. So what they eventually concluded surprised everybody, especially themselves. Quite inadvertently they reached conclusions that would challenge ideas which had guided forestry for more than three hundred years.[15]

Old-growth forests, the team decided, were more complicated than anyone had previously realized. They were extremely diverse, with greater variations in tree size and more patchiness of the understory than in younger stands. Rather than being even-aged, these were communities in which the young and the old lived side by side. And far from being nearly devoid of life, they provided habitat for a variety of plant and animal species, such as mosses and lichens, small mammals, cavity-nesting birds, and a multiplicity of invertebrates.[16]

The old-growth Douglas fir forests west of the Cascades in particular, these scientists thought, were unique, exhibiting unusual paths of energy flow. In more typical ecosystems energy flows from green leaves or grass to herbivore to carnivore; but here in old growth, energy traveled from foliage to roots, fungi, bacteria, nectar, fruits, seeds, litter and coarse detritus, and a variety of fungivores and seed eaters, which are directly utilized by carnivores.[17]

Snags and fallen logs, they found, provided habitat for nesting birds and were reservoirs of carbon. A Douglas fir snag stays standing for up to 75 years, and a western red cedar snag for over 125. These dead trees were homes to predatory insects which preyed on insects that destroyed trees. They stored carbon that would otherwise escape to the atmosphere, the scientists thought. And though they had long known that early successional species, such as red alder, play an important role as nitrogen fixers, these researchers discovered that arboreal lichens, which live in old-growth Douglas fir forests, performed that role as well.[18]

The beneficial effects of old-growth forests on streams and rivers Franklin and his colleagues considered particularly profound. Fallen logs slow runoff, thus discouraging bank erosion. Forest litter provides energy to aquatic communities. The closed canopy of big trees shields streams from the sun, keeping water cool for trout and salmon.[19]

Rather than being mere fodder for loggers, therefore, old growth, they concluded, was a critical component of overall forest health. If timber-land were to retain its productivity — its ability to sustain life — over the long term, it needed careful management. Yet logging practices seriously damaged the old trees that were left behind, and dispersed-patch clear-cutting fragmented the forest. The stands that remained were often too small and isolated, the scientists thought. When virgin forests become patchworks of clear-cuts, they hypothesized, trees are vulnerable to invasions of plants that alter the ecology. The patches of remaining old-growth habitat can become too small to sustain some vertebrate populations.[20]

Logging roads aggravate forest dismemberment, they thought, becoming avenues for the invasion of diseases such as cedar root rot and black stain root disease, as well as exotic plants and destructive insects. Clear-cutting sometimes destroys critical organisms needed for regrowth. For example, the scientists found that the vigorous regeneration of plants after disturbance requires certain kinds of fungi, which feed on green plants. They found that when this vegetation is removed by logging, the fungus declines, and the ability of the system to regenerate is weakened. And, the Andrews team decided, that contrary to what loggers believed, even-aged management as currently practiced, does not mimic patterns of natural disturbance, such as fire, which commonly leaves more live trees and woody debris. With no deadfall or slash, they claimed, the cut-over areas do not provide good habitat for reptiles and amphibians or certain common birds, nor do they sustain some seeds and spores needed for complete ecosystem regrowth. Clear-cuts leave streams without shade and remove the logs that act as bulwarks against erosion.[21]

As these studies progressed, more biologists joined the chase. In 1973 Glen Juday, an Oregon State doctoral candidate, began studying old growth in the coast range. Others, such as Forsman, examined old-growth fauna. By 1980 the National Science Foundation was sponsoring the Long-Range Ecosystem Project at Andrews, exploring how forests change over centuries.[22]

Andrews Forest had become a hotbed of intellectual ferment. The atmosphere was charged with energy by the exultation of discovery. But despite the excitement, each scholar's work remained highly specialized, and thus the team published little that informed the world about the breadth of their discoveries. With only a small amount of data collected in a few places, they told themselves they didn't know enough to reach definite conclusions. Some, such as Franklin, formulated a hypothesis: that old-growth forests play a beneficial role in maintaining overall forest health. But it needed testing, and this would take time.

By delaying publication, Juday recalled, the team members remained isolated from one another. One researcher did not know what the others had discovered. Each worked in his own subspecialty, but no one saw the big picture. Then, in early 1977, a forest planner from the Suislaw National Forest approached Franklin. The National Forest Management Act, he said, mandated management of all types of forest, including old growth. But the scientific literature did not even provide a good definition of these mature stands. Could the Andrews team prepare a working description for him?

In response, Franklin invited members of the Andrews research community to a retreat at the Wind River Experimental Forest within the Gifford Pinchot National Forest in south-central Washington. They assembled around a table. "Okay," Franklin said, "Each of us is aware of the bits and pieces. Let's share ideas and put it all together."

Each took his turn, explaining what he was finding and what he thought important. The experience hit Juday with the force of a hammer blow. Not only did the researchers find their ideas converging, but, when put together, he believed, their collective insights signaled a major crisis. Each had been silently raising questions about Forest Service orthodoxy, which called for removing the last of old growth at the earliest possible time. But no one scientist had posed the collective scientific argument for persuasively opposing this policy. Now they could put together the ideas they needed to argue for preserving old growth.

They agreed that each attendee would write a section of a paper, which, when assembled, would lay out better strategies for forest management. Later in the spring of 1977, each researcher sent a draft of his contribution to Franklin, who put together the final document in a Tokyo hotel room while attending a forestry convention in Japan. Titled "Ecological Characteristics of Old-Growth Douglas-Fir Forests," the monograph challenged virtually all conventional forestry wisdom. Old growth, its authors argued, is a biological cornucopia — highly productive, retentive of nutrients, and possessing a structure that "is more heterogeneous than that of young forests."[23]

Old forests are "optimum habitat" for a variety of animals, including goshawks, northern spotted owls, Vaux swifts, pileated woodpeckers, Hammond's flycatchers, pine grosbeaks, Townsend's warblers, silver-haired bats, long-eared myotis, long-legged myotis, hoary bats, red tree voles, northern flying squirrels, California red-back voles, coast moles, and martens. They contain large amounts of decaying litter, which supplies energy to streams. They are home to nitrogen-fixing epiphytes that fertilize forest floors.

Both protecting and re-creating these biological riches, the authors urged, should be a priority of silviculture: "Foresters wishing to maintain or create ecosystems with old-growth characteristics can tie management schemes to maintenance or development of the four key structural components — live large, old-growth trees, large snags, and large logs on land and in streams." Protection required saving snags and creating buffer zones around streams. Re-creation of old growth demanded long-term vision, as "approximately 175 to 250 years are required to develop old-growth forests under natural conditions."[24]

After Franklin wrote a draft, he circulated it among the contributors. But they did not publish immediately. Juday suspected that some felt inhibited because the subject was so explosive. Like the men who had learned the secret of the atomic bomb, he believed, many of the participants at the Pinchot Forest conference realized that their ideas were so radical that they seemed too dangerous to put into words. Saving old growth required such fundamental change that the public might not accept it. Why, then, bother to sound the alarm?[25]

Others simply claimed that they felt no urgency, or they feared that they didn't know enough to draw conclusions. Rescuing old growth forests, said Franklin, was not a matter "of survival — of life and death." It did not affect "environmental quality and the quality of life." He knew that "substantial acreage of old growth" had already been reserved. "There is no positive evidence," he said, "that any species relies exclusively on old growth."[26]

By stimulating multidisciplinary cooperation, the ecosystem model seemed to open up fruitful avenues for research. Nevertheless, these scholars had good reasons for their caution. For most scientists still did not share their views. The Andrews research, critics noted, focused exclusively on small areas of Douglas fir forests. By contrast, studies of redwood forests which began in 1971 raised questions about the ecological indispensability of old growth and confirmed that clear-cutting, by mimicking the effects of fire, actually helped perpetuate this tree species.[27]

And many of the team's conclusions regarding Douglas fir were criticized as either unoriginal, false, or merely untested hypotheses. Foresters had long known that the removal of downed logs from streams harmed fisheries, for example, and silviculturalists had realized for years that fungi beneficial to trees lived in the soil. But the evidence suggested that these organisms persisted after logging and did not, as the Andrews team averred, disappear. Its claim that trees over 120 years old played a vital role in maintaining critical forest components was said to rest on theory, not evidence.[28]

But the most important criticism was that the Andrews team's views on old growth did not pass the test of science. They rested on hypothesis, not verified theory. And the perspective of their work was too narrow. A complete study of Northwestern forests would require the contributions of a variety of scholars representing a range of different fields, including silviculture, evolutionary biology, anthropology, archaeology, paleontology, ethnology, and even sociology and economics. But the Andrews group consisted entirely of ecologists who subscribed to the ecosystem idea. Inevitably, therefore, they had ignored the potential insights of these other fields.[29]

In particular, the other disciplines would have helped resolve the dispute over the roles that disturbances — both human and natural — played in Northwestern forests over time. Nearly all silviculturalists continued to believe that perturbations, including clear-cuts, were essential for Douglas fir, and that old groves lacked the virtues of younger stands. The Andrews team challenged that position, suggesting instead that the effects of clear-cutting often differed from those of natural disturbances such as fire, wind, and volcanic eruptions, and that old growth was in fact valuable. Settling this dispute required a look backward, into prehistory.[30]

The Andrews research was curiously static, focusing narrowly on the functions, such as nutrient cycling and energy flow, that maintained forest ecosystems. Tilting toward balance and away from change, these Oregon State scholars paid little attention to the history of disturbances in the region.

Yet abundant evidence suggested that natural and human disturbances had played key roles in creating modern forests. Rather than an unchanging forest primeval, studies of pollen and plant microfossils revealed the region to be a place of tumultuous chaos, continually convulsed not just by fire but also by drastic temperature shifts. When the Cordilleran ice sheet, which covered much of the area, began to recede 20,000 years ago, it left behind a sand-swept region dotted with proglacial lakes fed by melted glaciers. As the land dried out and the weather warmed, these places turned into open parklike tundra, covered by grasses, sedges, sagebrush, crowberry, and moss campion, and inhabited by animals such as lemmings, Arctic ground squirrels, caribou, and muskoxen, as well as native people, who hunted and set fires.[31]

Beginning 14,000 years before the present, lodgepole pine colonized the tundra, soon joined by Engelmann and Sitka spruce, western and mountain hemlock, grand fir, red alder, and Sitka alder. Then, during the early millennia of the interglacial period known as the Holocene, which began 10,000 years ago, the climate became drier, resulting in intense fires which promoted the growth of early successional plant species associated with the plains, such as prairie herbs, oaks, and bracken fern.[32]

Douglas fir made its appearance at this time, but remained rare. The climate was still too cold and dry, and young trees were overly sensitive to fire. Not until around 6,000 years ago, as the weather became wetter and fire frequency decreased, did Douglas fir, western hemlock, and western red cedar appear in abundance, creating closed-canopy forests whose characteristics continued to be redefined by fire. During the last 1,000 years, tree ring studies reveal large stand-replacing fires swept the region on average every 80 to 250 years, some leaving vast areas blackened and nearly devoid of trees.[33]

Not truly ancient, therefore, "old growth" is a relatively new arrival, and has continued to change. As the palaeogeographer Cathy Whitlock writes, these forests "developed relatively recently on an evolutionary time scale and probably do not represent a coevolved complex of species bound together by tightly linked and balanced interactions. . . . It is clear that vegetation has responded continuously to a varying array of climatic conditions. . . . No millennium has been exactly like any other during the last 20,000 years." Thus, "conservation efforts that emphasize the preservation of communities or vegetation types will probably be unsuccessful because future climate changes quite likely will dismantle the community or vegetation type of concern."[34]

This conclusion was later echoed by the palaeohistorian Margaret Bryan Davis, who observes: "An historical perspective leads one to question the importance of stability relative to mechanisms that allow communities to change. During the Quaternary Period the forests with which we are familiar seldom maintained a constant species composition for more than 2000 to 3000 years at a time. The evidence . . . suggests that forest communities in temperate regions are chance combinations of species, without an evolutionary history."[35]

Added to these climatic shifts were those caused by humans. By periodic burning, native peoples removed the forest canopy, creating open savannas. And archaeological, ethnological, and historical evidence suggests that the impact, beginning about 15,000 years ago, was extensive. Mounting data from tree ring studies reveal that, owing to wildfires that

periodically convulsed the region, including many that were set intentionally, the amount of forest cover — and indeed the extent of old
growth — fluctuated wildly.[36]

In short, the Douglas fir forests of the Pacific Northwest were not
"ecosystems" in which creatures coevolved over a period long enough
to establish functioning networks. Nor is such inconstancy new. Scholars have long recognized that associating a particular plant community
with a specific geographic area is the height of folly. "Anyone who has
tried to define a plant community and to solve the impenetrable maze
of cause and effect relations that exist in it at a point in time must have
wondered how he could ever hope to project it backward into history
without either losing it completely or merely compounding his un-
solved problems," wrote the plant ecologist Hugh M. Raup in 1942. It
therefore "seems extremely difficult to derive principles by which we
could reconstruct the area for past times."[37]

Given this evolutionary turbulence, it is clear that so-called natural
conditions never existed. Yet such conditions are precisely what the
Andrews foresters sought to define. Mature trees, they believed, were
essential components in a healthy forest ecosystem. So they had to decide: What is "old growth"?

This was not an easy question. As Jerry Franklin and his colleagues
reported, "An old-growth forest is more than a collection of some large,
old trees." Rather, it is a full panoply of plants, animals, and soil existing in specific relations and conditions at particular times, characterized by uneven age distribution, a rich understory, and late successional
vertebrate and invertebrate populations.[38]

Scholars offered many criteria for defining this complexity, such as
stipulating the number, variety, and age of trees, the presence of a multilayered canopy, the vegetative constituency in the understory, and the
number of snags and downed logs per acre. Franklin and his colleagues
concluded that "forests typically begin exhibiting old-growth characteristics at about 175 to 250 years."[39]

In 1986 the Forest Service's Old-Growth Definition Task Group offered a range of alternative definitions, among them, a specification that
"Old-Growth Douglas-Fir on Western Hemlock Sites" exhibit, at a minimum, "two or more" tree species in a range of ages, of which eight per
acre must be over 200 years old. Still later, the Wilderness Society
would distinguish between "super" old growth, with trees over 700
years old (stands that seldom, if ever, existed on National Forest lands);
"classic" stands, consisting of at least eight trees per acre over 300

years; and "early" old growth, containing at least eight trees over 200 years old per acre.[40]

In short, characterizations of old growth were subjective, reflecting the values and interests of those who sought to define it. And, given the complexity of these definitions, it was extremely difficult if not impossible to determine the relative proportion of prehistoric forests that at any given time fit these descriptions. By examining pollen samples, palaeobotanists could say whether particular kinds of plants existed at specific locations at certain times; and by studying tree rings and charcoal deposits, they were able to estimate fire intervals and tree sizes at study sites as far back as 1,000 years. But that would not tell them how extensive these groves were, nor how they had changed over the millennia. And these research tools still might not provide a complete picture of the complex, multilayered features of prehistoric forests.[41]

This temporal perspective therefore demanded that scientists take a closer look at past change. It raised critical questions about the role that disturbances, both natural and human, played in creating forest conditions. How did the "patchiness" created by intentional burning or by past volcanic eruptions differ from the "patchiness" following clearcutting? Which definition of "old growth" best describes prehistoric forests? How did the area covered by mature forests vary over millennia?

But rather than focusing on such questions, the Andrews team emphasized ecosystem continuity. They were, after all, following in the footsteps of Tansley, Hutchinson, and the Odums. The goal of the Coniferous Biome Project was, as Joel B. Hagen notes, "the production of large systems models, as tools for both understanding and managing ecosystems."[42] The Andrews group's emphasis on ecosystem relationships therefore marked a turning point in which many forest ecologists would endorse notions of permanence and direction. A telltale sign of this shift was the sudden teleological assumption, made by both the Andrews scientists and activists, that once upon a time "original conditions" existed in which most of the Northwest was blanketed with "old growth," and that these constituted the "natural" state that forests "ought" to exhibit.

"At the time of settlement," Forsman's colleague Charles Meslow surmised, "perhaps 60 to 70 percent of that forest was old growth." Now, he suggested, perhaps as little as 10 percent remained. Franklin concurred, suggesting that only "17 percent of the original area" of old growth survived. Environmentalists quickly followed suit. The "once vast ancient forest," the Sierra Club's William Arthur lamented, has been reduced to 10 percent of its original size. And in 1990 the Wilderness Society would announce, "Today, only 10 to 15 percent of the original endowment of old growth in the region is left." The media repeated these figures often. These claims presupposed a starting point for nature, before man, when everything was perfect, and these conditions had to be recaptured.[43]

But no "original" conditions ever existed. Evidence from tree ring studies reveals that, because of periodic wildfires, including those set intentionally, the kinds of forests in prehistory that fit minimal definitions of old growth varied widely. Subsequent research would paint a picture of the past that differed dramatically from what anyone had previously supposed.[44]

Science, Jack Ward Thomas observed, is a debate in process, not a body of answers. And done correctly, the Andrews scientists clearly believed, it cannot be hurried. Proceeding carefully throughout the 1970s, they pursued their studies but published little. Much research remained to be done, and a lack of consensus prevailed. Even Thomas (who was not working at Andrews) still couched his remarks hypothetically, saying, "If old growth does make up a unique ecological community . . ."[45]

But politics would not wait for science. Word about old growth and owls was already spreading through the activist community. The state universities had become hotbeds of political and scientific ferment over old growth. In their small-town atmosphere, stories about the plight of forests and birds circulated with the speed of flight. Coffeehouse debates raged, with unedited mixtures of hearsay and science. Rumors and reports about discoveries circulated regularly. Because of his early proselytizing, Forsman's fear for the spotted owl was out of the bag. Word of the Andrews studies spread.[46]

In Corvallis and Eugene many academics had close ties either to the environmental community or to the timber industry. Everybody knew everybody else. Activists attended the McKean committee's meetings. James Monteith and Howard Wight had been close friends. Andy Kerr, an Oregon State undergraduate and activist with the Oregon Natural Resource Council, remembers visiting Forsman with Monteith and seeing his first owl — one with an injured wing which Forsman was repairing — in the scientist's back yard.

Andy Stahl — an Oregon State undergraduate who would join the Oregon Loggers' Association before suddenly switching sides and going to work with the Environmental Law Center — was the son of a University of Oregon professor of molecular biology. But Glen Juday was chief honeybee, spreading the pollen of ecological wisdom among activists. In 1973 he began work on his doctoral dissertation in botany, "The Location, Composition, and Structure of old growth Forests in the Oregon Coast Range." Franklin sat on his dissertation committee. That same year Juday became an environmental lobbyist, helping to write the Oregon Natural Reserves Act, then served as chairman of the board that carried out that program. Simultaneously he joined the Mary's Peak (Corvallis) chapter of the Sierra Club, eventually serving as its chairman. He was friendly with Eric Forsman.[47]

Together with Monteith, Juday launched an old growth preservation campaign. To locate groves for his studies, Juday obtained satellite images of the coast range. The pictures were dismaying. The extent of the cut-over was staggering. Likewise, virtually every owl nest he and Forsman located lay in a timber sale area.

Juday resolved to warn the world. Blowing up 100-square-mile photos and gluing them together, he constructed a huge map of western Oregon. Covering an entire wall, it made a dramatic picture. Oregon appeared like a patchwork quilt, with no continuous stands of old growth. He showed his construction to anyone who would look. But, as Monteith had found, many environmentalists were not interested. Few wanted to challenge the loggers. Sierra officials were lobbying hard for rock and ice wilderness, and did not want to campaign for forests. Mainstream activists feared that the more forest was set aside, the less alpine terrain would be protected.

So Juday, Monteith, and a few others decided to go it alone, adopting what Juday called the "adopt-a-wilderness strategy." Picking an area in the Suislaw National Forest along Drift Creek, where old growth remained, Juday and Kerr, armed with chain saws, reopened an old trail, took everyone they could — including Congressman Les Aucoin — into the area, then showed them the map. Eventually, in 1984, this area would be designated the Drift Creek Wilderness, as a culmination of RARE II.

Slowly Juday mobilized conservationist interest. In 1978 he created a stir by reading a paper at Lewis and Clark College in Portland. During a conference on the National Forest Management Act, he not only extolled the ecological characteristics of mature forests but also severely criticized existing harvest policies. Since "the elimination of old growth on forest industry lands is now virtually complete," he said, public lands "hold the key to the future." Yet "until recently, national forest management generally tried to harvest old growth as early as possible and replace it with younger rapidly growing stands, thereby maximizing wood yields." This policy, he insisted, had to change.[48]

But, despite Juday's efforts, few other scholars were willing to go public with their concerns. Feeling the political heat, environmentalists suspected, these government-funded scientists were terrified of making mistakes. As the researchers' silence persisted, paranoia became pandemic among activists. Because Franklin, Forsman, and Meslow received support from the Forest Service, activists were convinced that their research was being suppressed. This suspicion grew the longer the Franklin monograph remained unpublished. Bootleg copies of the document circulated in the university communities, further convincing many that the scholars were being muzzled. Activists, many of whom had already read excerpts, badly wanted to see the paper published as proof that science was on their side. But they weren't willing to wait.

Despite the reticence of scientists, the entire Northwest conservation community began to rally around the issue of old growth. Within the space of five years — from 1975 to 1980 — its interest had shifted from setting aside rock and ice wilderness to saving mature forests. Dark, mysterious, ancient, and spiritually evocative, they seemed to embody nature's permanence.

In 1977 Sydney Herbert, a Eugene social worker, happened to read a monograph by a former Reed College student named Cameron La Follette, titled *Saving All the Pieces: Old Growth Forests in Oregon*. Published by the Oregon Public Interest Research Group, an Oregon State undergraduate activist organization, La Follette's work was in part a compendium of interviews with Thomas, Franklin, and other scholars at Andrews. It was the first opportunity for many outside Corvallis to learn about rising scientific consciousness of old growth. Moved by La Follette's essay, Herbert decided to fight for the trees. As conservation chair of the Lane County (Eugene) Audubon Society, she organized a joint conference in Portland with the Forest Service, Bureau of Land Management, and League of Women Voters. Here Franklin read his paper publicly for the first time.[49]

Soon old growth conferences followed in rapid succession. The Lane County Audubon Society resolved to fight for the owl. Mention of threatened links in forest "ecosystems" stirred activists' imaginations. The title of La Follette's monograph, invoking Aldo Leopold's machine metaphor of nature, "to keep every cog," signaled that biocentrism was an idea whose time had come. The very year of Herbert's conference, 1978, a poll of members of the mainstream conservation group Resources for the Future found that 83 percent disagreed with the statement that "plants and animals exist primarily for man's use."[50]

Whereas previously almost all wildlife research was directed toward commercially valuable game species, now, thanks to the Endangered Species Act, activists, scientists, and government officials had strong incentives to study nongame creatures as well. Looking for marbled murrelets and silverspot butterflies for the first time, they were shocked to discover that such hitherto ignored creatures were hard to find. Sometimes, as with the snail darter, this meant not that there were few of the creatures but only that techniques for finding them were in their infancy. But these searches nevertheless spurred concern. The more researchers looked, the more they found; and the more they found, the more they worried about what might be lost.

Around the country environmentalists were pressuring scientists to make quick determinations as to the rarity of ecosystems or the genetic uniqueness of creatures. Whenever scholars concluded that an ecosystem was rare, activists wanted to put it under protection. But all ecosystems are rare because each spot on earth is unique — "like a fingerprint," as the ecologist Allan Savory put it. Hence, the quest for protecting unusual ecosystems inadvertently espouses preserving everything.[51]

The earlier evolutionary perspective had assigned top priority to "higher-order" species. It put emphasis on progress, and therefore on more complex life forms such as redwoods, grizzlies, and humans. But the notion that nature is an intact machine implies that all parts have equal value. Everything plays an indispensable role in the ecosystem. Therefore, priorities shifted away from saving blue whales and spotted cats to worrying about ants and boring beetles. Scholars and activists became ecological miniaturists, as if suddenly they were afraid to put their feet down for fear of inadvertently stepping on a spider.[52]

So it was with old growth. Concern about abstract ecosystems encouraged a fascination with the intricacies of forest dynamics, which in turn drove conservationists to shift their priorities from mountains to trees, from trees to owls, and eventually from owls to invertebrates. Attention to the microcosm replaced concern for the macrocosm. Environmental focus narrowed to the size of a pencil point, channeling political energies until they could cut through opposition like a laser beam.

Activists mobilized for owls and trees. In 1978 the Lane County Audubon Society challenged a Forest Service timber sale on the grounds that it had failed to take into account the cumulative impact on the owl as a species, and thus violated the National Environmental Policy Act. This was the first attempt in history to use the owl as a reason for stopping logging. In 1980 the Environmental Law Clinic and Oregon Wildlife Federation challenged the Forest Service's first Spotted Owl Management Plans, which called for a 300-acre minimum for each pair.[53]

But these challenges boomeranged. The appeals were rejected, while the wood products industry, now aroused, began to fight back. Ever since Tellico, loggers had taken notice of Forsman's frolics through the woods. Now they put pressure on the National Wildlife Federation to drop its sponsorship of the law clinic, which in 1982 it did. Some in the timber industry suggested that Terry Thatcher's aide Andy Stahl had spied for the environmentalists when he was working for the Oregon Loggers' Association. Thatcher began to fear that the clinic might lose its adjunct status with the University of Oregon. Conservationists suddenly found themselves fighting on several fronts at once: filing administrative appeals to timber sales, going to court, fending off industry counterattacks. And they continued to lose.[54]

The problem, Stahl realized, was that they could not prove that they had science on their side. Politics had outstripped biology. Establishing that they occupied the ecological high ground became especially critical for conservationists following the snail darter fiasco. Fearful that another uncharismatic creature might materialize to scuttle its cherished pork projects, in 1978 Congress modified the Endangered Species Act, permitting the interior secretary to convene a cabinet-level Endangered Species Committee — dubbed the "God Squad" — empowered to override section 7 protection of endangered species habitat when such action was deemed necessary to save jobs. And if the darter could weaken the act, so could the owl.[55]

Before they pressed the bird's case further, therefore, these activists wanted proof that their biological claims were beyond dispute. To sway judges and federal agencies, they needed good, solid scientific journal articles. Appeals based on campus scuttlebutt wouldn't fly.

Environmentalists had the idea — the ecosystem. Now they needed research to validate this vision. But scientists still weren't publishing. What was holding them up?

13

THE NEW
FORESTRY

EARLY ONE MORNING IN JUNE 1980 a helicopter carrying Jerry
Franklin and several other biologists landed high on the slopes of Mount
St. Helens in Washington state. The machine's big blades churned a
black cloud of ash as the scientists scrambled out. The landscape, covered with volcanic dust, looked like the surface of the moon.[1]

Just two weeks earlier, on May 18, this long-dormant volcano had
erupted with a ferocity not witnessed in the lower forty-eight in historic
times. The mountain literally blew its top, igniting an avalanche that
swallowed lakes and covered portions of its slopes with debris more
than six hundred feet deep. A cubic mile of hot volcanic material shot
into the atmosphere, spreading a layer of ash over farms and forests up
to a thousand miles away.[2]

Pyroclastic flows — gasified volcanic material heated to over 500 degrees — turned lakes to steam and melted snow fields and glaciers,
sending mudflows raging down the mountain, filling in lakes and
streams and creating new ones in their place. Elsewhere on the mountain a layer of ash — air-fall tephra — covered everything up to a foot
deep.

Franklin and his colleagues, including Fred Swanson and Art McKee,
were sent by the Forest Service to assess the damage. The devastation
was so complete, they assumed that nothing could have survived. All
life would have been either sterilized by the searing heat or smothered
by debris and dust.

But that was not what they found. No sooner had Franklin disem-
barked from the helicopter than he spotted several fireweed sprouts.
And as the researchers trudged across the slope, they encountered one
living thing after another: thistle, pearly everlasting, brackenfern, vari-

ous herbs and legumes, fire fungi, animals such as deer mice, ants, and pocket gophers. Excited, Franklin worked his way down a small stream. Where the water had washed away the tephra, these plants grew in even greater profusion. And at the bottom of the brook he found salamanders, frogs, crawfish, and nymphs.[3]

As the researchers continued their work over the next two summers, they catalogued a profusion of living creatures. The mountain had been reborn. Altogether, 90 percent of the plant species that existed before the eruption had returned. And, even more surprising, this revival seemed to break the rules of seral succession. Conventional biological wisdom following Clements asserted that after a disturbance such as a volcanic eruption, succession must begin anew. First would come invading plants, fireweed and thistle, gradually followed by grasses, forbs, berries, herbs, and nitrogen-fixing deciduous trees such as red alder. Only much later, after more than twenty years, would these plant communities give way to pine and fir.[4]

But regeneration on Mount St. Helens followed this scenario in only a few spots. Even after this cataclysmic eruption, life was not totally destroyed. Rather than starting from scratch, regeneration took what Franklin described as a "multiplicity of . . . successional pathways." While some areas were dominated by early successional species, the biologists found that many other places merely mirrored the composition that had existed before the blast.[5]

Weedy herbs, such as bunchberry dogwood and deerfoot vanillaleaf, resprouted on the clear-cut sites, just as they had before the eruption. Deep-rooted perennials such as blackberry and brackenfern, and animals that live below ground such as ants and pocket gophers, survived intact. In other places shrubs, tree seedlings, and saplings of shade-tolerant conifers such as western and mountain hemlock and Pacific silver fir, buried in snowdrifts, survived, thereby accelerating succession by favoring growth of these late successional species. Many organisms also persisted in aquatic environments. Some, such as salamanders, frogs, and crawfish, lived on in the mud of stream bottoms. Trout remained in lakes that had been ice-covered.

Most significant were residuals left by old growth — seeds, scattered large trees, dead logs, snags, and rotting organic matter. These carbon sources were the structural component from which much rebirth emerged, providing seedbeds, habitat for insects, and energy for streams. Countless seeds and spores survived in rotting logs, snags, and humus. The researchers concluded: "The diversity of recovery patterns of Mount St. Helens . . . makes apparent the inadequacies of simple models in characterizing or explaining successional patterns. . . . The type of pre-eruption ecosystem and its physical condition . . . became the important determinants of ecosystem recovery."[6]

It was clear that the keys to this revival were the living things and organic matter that survived the disturbance. Franklin called these "biological legacies" — material that ensures the continuity of forest regrowth following a catastrophe. And though natural disturbances and clear-cuts differ widely in their effects and severity, the latter, he said, typically leave less behind. Logging produces even-aged stands that do not mimic nature well because it reduces and simplifies the biological legacies:

> The effects of clearcutting are not ecologically comparable to the effects of most natural disturbances, including wildfire. Levels of biological legacies are typically high following natural disturbances, leading to rapid redevelopment of compositionally, structurally, and functionally complex ecosystems. Traditional approaches to clearcutting purposely eliminate most of the structural and much of the compositional legacy in the interest of efficient wood production.[7]

Old growth, the researchers concluded, is critically important to the perpetuation of forest life. Instead of following a pattern of even-aged growth, succession involves a complex interaction between the old and the new. With the concept of biological legacies, Franklin and his colleagues found what they thought was the missing link in understanding forests. Before the Mount St. Helens eruption they were beginning to understand the role that late successional plants and animals play in nutrient cycling within mature forests. But they had no direct evidence of how these communities contribute to the functioning of forests over time.[8]

The St. Helens study, they thought, filled this blank. At last they had an answer to Leo Isaac. Far from being a worthless biological desert, old growth is a key to sustaining the forest's ability to recover from disturbance. By contrast, clear-cutting does not mimic natural calamities. Once the trees are removed from a grove and slash is burned, the biological legacies are greatly reduced, and that patch of ground may take centuries to recover, or even in extreme cases might never be the same.[9]

If valid, the implications of this epiphany were enormous. They seemed to imply that old growth is essential for sustaining forests through time. This conclusion suggested that harvesting timber could not mean simply clear-cutting big trees but requires more complex management strategies, calling for a shift in perspective. "What matters," says Franklin, "is not only how much you take but also how much you leave behind." Loggers must do whatever is necessary to preserve biological legacies — leaving snags, downed logs, and slash; protecting watercourses; and severely limiting clear-cutting.[10]

Franklin dubbed this hypothesis and its prescriptions the "New Forestry." It did not advocate locking up forests to ensure that they would reach, or remain at, climax. Its goal was not merely to preserve old growth but to sustain the uneven-age complexity of forests. This required a diversity of age classes, a mosaic of old, intermediate, and young trees. And keeping this kind of landscape demanded multifarious strategies that sometimes included clear-cutting but more often required various degrees of selection cutting. In any case, the chain saw remained a legitimate tool. "Environmentalists must stop relying on setting aside preserved lands as the only approach to the protection of ecological values," Franklin wrote.[11]

Despite its subtleties, the New Forestry represented another shift of silivicultural fashion, a tilt away from disturbance and toward stability. Ever since Clements, the tide of forestry opinion had alternated between theories suggesting that if left alone, biological systems experience uninterrupted development, and those claiming that disturbances are so frequent that the end state of harmony never arrives.[12]

As the ecologists F. Herbert Bormann and Gene E. Likens wrote in 1979:

> Ecology, like all other fields, is affected by the swinging pendulum of opinion. For decades Clementsian notions of succession and climax thoroughly dominated much ecological thinking and buttressed land-use policies that assigned disturbances a minor role in most naturally occurring ecosystems. Quite properly, these ideas have come under attack, and the concept of catastrophic disturbance, particularly fire, as an integral part of the structure and function of temperate forest ecosystems has gained enormous ground.[13]

But now Franklin and the New Foresters had revived the doctrine of continuity. This debate centered on the question of whether living communities are primarily products of internal or endogenous (also known as autogenic) factors such as nutrient cycling, recruitment, and competition, or of external, exogenous (or allogenic) forces such as fire, weather, volcanoes — and clear-cutting.[14]

Steady-state theorists believed that the endogenous forces promoting equilibrium shape ecosystems. Therefore, they supposed that only stable climax communities are truly healthy, and they viewed outside perturbations — especially those caused by humans — as threatening ecological collapse. By contrast, disturbance advocates presumed that disruptions are the greatest determinants of species composition and are necessary to ensure that flora and fauna continue to adapt to change. Hence, they welcomed exogenous events and the arrival of early successional communities.[15]

Until 1970 most ecologists, influenced by Hutchinson and the Odums, favored the steady state. But during the next decade, even as this idea became gospel among environmentalists, many scholars abandoned it.[16]

Prominent among those holding countervailing views were silviculturalists. In 1977 Chadwick D. Oliver, former Harvard Silviculture Research Fellow and professor of silviculture and forest ecology at the University of Washington, reported that for over three hundred years the Harvard Forest in Massachusetts had been shaped primarily by exogenous forces, including hurricanes, fires, and clear-cutting, and that the results of human disturbances did not differ significantly from those of natural ones. A former student of Yale University's David M. Smith, who in turn had been a research assistant under Leo Isaac, Oliver concluded that forests are shaped not by inexorable processes but by random events.[17] "There is accumulating evidence," he wrote, "that several different forest communities could potentially inhabit the same area for an indefinite period. This is contrary to the idea that a single species or group of species is predestined to dominate an area as 'climax' vegetation in a steady-state equilibrium."[18]

But whereas most silviculturalists usually favored disturbance, ecologists either waffled or came to this epiphany late. The difference reflected biases shaped by the methodologies of the two fields. Silviculturalists were empiricists who studied trees by testing different methods of seeding and cutting. They worked at forest "experiment stations." So they saw nothing wrong with human intervention in plant growth.[19]

By contrast, those ecologists who were not abstract theorizers and therefore already enchanted with equilibrium mathematics were field scholars whose research involved little manipulation of natural systems. Usually using passive techniques of observation and measurement, they preferred to study islands, national parks, and wilderness, where, they supposed, they could view nature "undisturbed." Thus, they actively looked for places where endogenous forces predominated.[20]

Even so, by the 1970s many ecologists had begun to doubt the equilibrium hypothesis. Among these converts was F. Herbert Bormann. A prominent and charismatic Yale professor, he was a firm believer in the steady-state theory until he participated in one of the few experimental efforts by ecologists. This long-term study of forest dynamics, conducted at Hubbard Brook in New Hampshire and involving more than sixty senior researchers, convinced Bormann that disturbance was the critical factor in ecosystem development.[21]

In a 1972 prize-winning essay written with coauthor P. L. Marks, Bormann observed that "successional species, specially adapted to exploit disturbed conditions, ought to be considered integral components of the larger ecosystem, despite the fact that they are typically absent from the terminal, climax community." Other scholars reached similar conclusions. In 1979 a University of Wisconsin botanist, Orie L. Loucks, concluded that forests experience "periodic perturbations" on an average interval of fifty to two hundred years. These "waves" of disturbance keep forests healthy, and "any modifications of the system that preclude periodic, random perturbation and recycling would be detrimental to the system in the long run."[22]

The same year Bormann and Likens, drawing further conclusions from Hubbard Farm, concurred in part that though steady states may have existed in forests in damp and stable climates, human activity such as clear-cutting "produces a pattern of recycling through time quite similar to that proposed for natural ecosystems subjected to severe exogenous disturbances at short intervals."[23]

To such scholars it seemed that Franklin was to some extent merely reinventing the wheel. The Mount St. Helens studies revealed what they already knew — that disturbances come in every shape and size: fire, winds, floods, erosion, siltation, landslides, avalanches, glaciers, volcanoes, ice storms, mammal browsing, insects, disease. And though each perturbation differs in severity and effect, none annihilates everything. Nor, they supposed, was Mount St. Helens an example of the most dramatic recovery. By 1986 data would show that the mountain was experiencing "dieback" as some of the vegetation Franklin had seen recovering suffered a relapse.[24]

To silviculturalists in particular, the New Forestry was a step backward. Its focus on biological legacies put too much emphasis on continuity and could lead to diminishing the forest's resilience to disturbance. Nor were legacies necessarily benign. Sometimes detritus left after a disturbance created even greater perturbations. Snags and deadfall from the 1933 Tillamook burn in western Oregon, for example, provided fuel for two subsequent fires which sterilized the soil and delayed regeneration. And although biological legacies might sometimes accelerate the return of forests to climax conditions after a disturbance, there was no special virtue to that, unless one already assumed that old growth was good. So Franklin's argument seemed circular: it held that since old growth is good, preserving old growth legacies is good.[25]

Thus, within the space of a decade conventional ecological wisdom had swung from steady-state to disturbance theory and was on its way back, even as forestry fashion swayed from clear-cutting to selection cutting to clear-cutting and was headed back to selection again.

But in one important respect the New Forestry was novel: its values represented a fundamental break with scientific tradition. Recognizing evolution to be chaotic and random, silviculturalists believed that there was no condition that plant communities "ought" to be in. The only measure of a forest's value was its potential benefit to society. But the New Foresters, by advocating that woods were healthy only when endogenous succession predominated, implicitly established a scale of values independent of human needs.[26]

The logic of the ecosystem had come full circle: the belief that nature was organized into systems had led to suppositions that nature is directional. This encouraged a bias toward stability and old growth, which in turn encouraged the belief that "ecosystem health" has intrinsic value. Following this logic, the New Forestry preached that timber harvests were justified only insofar as cutting contributed to forest fitness. Wood production was subordinated to the goal of maintaining internal ecosystem processes. As a report by British Columbia's Ministry of Forests put it, the New Forestry became "an attempt to define forest management with timber production as a by-product of its primary function: sustaining biological diversity and maintaining long-term ecosystem health."[27]

This was a social choice, not a scientific conclusion, a point recognized by Jack Ward Thomas, who, despite often allying himself with the Andrews team, did not even consider himself a New Forester. Scholars, according to Thomas, were merely facilitators. The nation, not scientists, must decide, he said (quoting former Bureau of Land Management director Marion Clawson), "for whom and for what" forests are to be managed. Thus, it was the role of science not to tell people what importance to place on trees but only to implement environmental goals after society had chosen them.[28]

But others assumed roles as more than facilitators. Franklin, in particular, became an advocate, preaching his gospel of forest fitness to the public. His articles began to read like Moral Rearmament manifestos, laced with emotive references to the "integrity of our forest and stream ecosystems," the "value" of legacies, and the danger that clear-cutting can "increase the potential for catastrophe." He went on a crusade. "Let us adopt a forest ethic," he wrote. "Let us approach forest ecosystems with the respect that their complexity and beauty deserve."[29]

Unconsciously, therefore, ecologists were rejecting three hundred years of the positivist tradition of scientific objectivity which had made modern science possible. With the advent of the New Forestry, the latent teleology of the ecosystem idea became manifest. "We can no longer see science as the source of value-free information," the historian Peter J. Bowler observed, describing this broad trend within environmental thinking. "The use of scientific ideas to uphold social values has been so obvious in this area that more perceptive scientists have given up pretending that they have a method for gathering purely objective knowledge."[30]

The separation of fact from value had come to an end, and no one knew where it would lead.

Every age has its celebrity scientist, embodying the values of the time. In the seventeenth and eighteenth centuries physicists such as Galileo and Isaac Newton were the star scholars, whose work supported the Enlightenment worldview that the universe is rational and truth absolute. In the first half of the twentieth century Sigmund Freud and Albert Einstein captured the popular imagination, turning their respective fields of psychotherapy and physics into major industries and projecting a portrait of humans as irrational and truth as relative.

But as this system of star scientists evolved, it increasingly reflected the workings of a curious feedback loop. Whereas classical theorists such as Galileo and Newton became prominent by affecting public opinion, modern wise men, such as Freud and Einstein, rose to popularity in response to changes in public taste. Freudian psychology was acclaimed in part because people were ready for a theory to justify sexual liberation. And the physicist's stature rose as world powers raced to build atomic bombs.

Likewise, by the early 1980s a new era had dawned — the Age of the Ecologist. It was the biologist who was now the celebrity scholar, and this too was largely a product of shifting public values. The ecosystem had captured the public imagination, leading to the passage of laws and the funding of bureaucracies dedicated to preserving stability. This created job opportunities for those who believed the doctrine, thus providing incentives for touting the steady-state theory and guaranteeing that skeptics would be ignored by grant makers and the media.[31]

As the social status of the ecologists waxed, that of silviculturalists waned. Their debate — stability versus disturbance — was the intellectual nexus of the contest between humanists and biocentrists, and it would have profound consequences for society. But few heard this dialogue because ecologists, the darlings of the pop culture, got all the jobs and monopolized the media. By 1993 Thomas would be named chief of the Forest Service and Franklin would become president of the Ecological Society of America. Scientists such as Paul Ehrlich and Edward O. Wilson were offered large speaking fees and put on the boards of foundations, and were quoted often in the *New York Times*, while Oliver and other doubters seldom gained a hearing outside the scholarly community.

Driven by politics, biocentrism became ascendant. Even as evidence accumulated against the stability hypothesis its influence mounted, as its believers assumed positions of power and prestige.

This values revolution was sweeping the Forest Service as Franklin trudged the slopes of Mount St. Helens. The National Forest Management Act demanded more interdisciplinary planning, which in turn required more ichthyologists, limnologists, botanists, taxonomists, conservation biologists, and other life scientists. The agency began hiring these professionals while simultaneously engaging fewer silviculturalists and foresters.[32]

In 1970 fewer than one hundred wildlife or fisheries biologists worked in the Forest Service. By 1981 there were 520, amounting to 6 percent of the professional workforce. Between 1978 and 1981, 25 percent of the natural resource managers hired in the intermountain and Pacific Northwest were wildlife or fisheries biologists, 16 percent range conservationists. Fully 45 percent of the natural resource personnel hired between 1978 and 1981 by the two western Forest Service regions were women.[33]

These newcomers brought with them radically different values. The typical forest ranger was trained in silviculture and had grown up in a logging or farming community. He was usually a white male who began to work for the agency between eighteen and twenty-four years of age. He believed that wood production was the most valuable use for forests. Many of the newcomers, by contrast, had grown up in cities and suburbs, entered the agency at an average age of thirty, and developed allegiances formed not within the government but in the academic world as well as in their families and larger social environment.[34]

Old-time rangers embraced what sociologists called the "dominant resource management paradigm." They believed that forests possess utilitarian value and should be managed rather than left alone. Knowing even before they entered college that they wanted to join the Forest Service, they exhibited what Thomas called "dog loyalty" — unquestioning obedience to the agency and an acceptance of authoritarian governmental decision-making by experts. By contrast, the new professionals subscribed to the "new resource paradigm." They believed that nature has intrinsic value, and they wanted the forests left alone. Few had experience with logging. Most thought that environmental protection was more important than wood production. Joining the agency at an older age, usually after graduate school, they exhibited "cat loyalty," insisting on more democratic, participatory decision-making and the right to dissent.[35]

According to a Louis Harris poll in 1979, Forest Service employees were already more "save/conserve or protection oriented" than the general public. Women in entry-level jobs were most environmentally oriented, followed by men at entry level, then new forest supervisors.[36]

Gradually the Forest Service began to exhibit a two-tier structure, with younger baby-boomer biocentrists at the bottom and older forest rangers at the top. The silviculture-educated foresters were bossing biologists who had spent more time in school but less in the woods. But as the older generation began to retire, the new cohort moved up, and the influence of ecological values grew.[37]

Owing to these demographic forces, the biocentrist vision became ascendant, not merely in the environmental community but in the Forest Service as well. As politics outstripped science, agency and environmentalist values forged beyond what the researchers knew. Franklin, Thomas, and their colleagues recommended managing forests, not neglecting them. But preservationists in and out of government wanted to stop harvests altogether. So, rather than endorsing the New Forestry, they were accepting only those parts of the theory they liked. They overlooked the researchers' management prescriptions but embraced their idea of biological legacies, claiming that it proved the importance of old growth.[38]

Hence, the New Foresters unwittingly gave environmentalists more ammunition with which to wage their campaign against logging. And as the 1980s progressed, this misuse of science would continue. A new breed of activist emerged who would make yesterday's radicals — Monteith, Stahl, and even Kerr — appear stodgy by comparison.

The New Forestry, as Mike Roselle, a leader of the radical activist group Earth First!, would cry, "is a kinder and gentler rape of the forests." Instead of embracing the doctrine, they would make political use of it in ways its practitioners had never imagined. Indeed, Roselle and his fellow biocentrists were already finding creative ways to escalate the conflict.[39]

III

RESPONSE: THE BIOCENTRIC REVOLUTION

1982–1990

And we are here as on a darkling plain
Swept with confused alarms of struggle and flight,
Where ignorant armies clash by night.

Matthew Arnold

Note this, you proud men of action. You are nothing but the unconscious hodmen of the men of
ideas.

Heinrich Heine

14

NIGHT ON
BALD MOUNTAIN

"LOOK MEAN," MIKE ROSELLE SAID. At 10:15 on the morning of April 27, 1983, he stood in front of the bulldozer, holding hands with Steve Marsden, Kevin Everhart, and Pedro Tama, wearing the tallest cowboy hat he could find and sporting Tony Llama boots with heels higher than a Radio City Rockette's. At six-foot-five in his socks, Roselle could stare down John Wayne.[1]

"Shut her down, we're not moving!" the four shouted, holding an Earth First! banner (naturally displaying the exclamation point, which they deemed mandatory).

The catskinner, Les Moore of the Plumley Construction Company dropped the blade, jumped off the 'dozer, and started for them, his fists balled into grimy knots. But at ground level these dudes in their Hopalong Cassidy costumes were a lot bigger than they seemed from atop the D-8.

As Roselle remembers it, apparently aware that the nearest support was half a mile away, Moore stopped. Cursing, he climbed back on the cat and began dislodging dirt on the high side of the road cut, above the protesters. But his tactic backfired. Boulders rolled down to the feet of the four, creating a protective wall before them. Moore gave up. Backing up the big machine, he dropped the blade and cut the engine, waiting for reinforcements to arrive. But the enemy troops arrived first.

Other Earth First!ers, dressed in Woolrich shirts and down jackets, materialized out of the woods. Linking arms, they joined the fearsome foursome. Then Dave Foreman strode up the hill dressed in fatigues, leading a gaggle of reporters carrying television cameras and sound equipment. A few minutes later the road crew straggled up hill. Soon more than fifty people stood around the 'dozer. Road workers and Earth First!ers were really having at each other now — arguing, spitting, and cursing — in front of furiously scribbling reporters and whirring video cameras.

Three hours later, as Josephine County deputies arrived and arrested Roselle and his friends, the cameras continued to roll. The story made the evening news. Stations around the country showed this same footage, over and over. Each time it played, the incident looked bigger. On the small screen the crowd seemed large, and viewers couldn't tell that this whole carefully planned incident had been orchestrated by four unshaven guys in cowboy hats.

Just as the Civil War began when a few South Carolina coast artillery-men fired on Fort Sumter, so these unkempt radicals, who had hiked twenty-five miles cross-country to stop construction of the Bald Mountain Road through Oregon's Siskiyou Wilderness, fired the first shots in what would turn out to be the greatest environmental battle of the century.

"The blockade of the Bald Mountain Road," Roselle announced immediately afterward, "had begun, after months of planning and preparations; so too, began the nonviolent struggle to save all wilderness."[2]

The Forest Service, Earth First!ers thought, was subverting preservation efforts by building roads into wilderness before it could be protected. It was giving away the store to loggers. Yet mainliners — vested bureau-cratic-political-environmental types with groups such as the Sierra Club and the National Wildlife Federation — were letting the feds get away with it.[3]

This made the Earth First!ers damned mad. And now that they had entered this range war, they planned to take no prisoners. They were not concerned about habitat, the buzzword among do-gooding yup-pie enviros. They just wanted to save wilderness. To them the late Pleistocene was the good old days. They wanted to make the world safe for hunter-gatherers, and Bald Mountain was where they chose to start.

"It's time for a warrior society to rise up out of the Earth and throw it-self in front of the juggernaut of destruction, to be antibodies against the human pox that's ravaging this precious beautiful planet," Foreman would write. But rather than crossbows or six-shooters, their weapon would be television. "Monkeywrenching can also be seen as a sophis-ticated political tactic that dramatizes ecological issues and places them before the public when they otherwise would be ignored in the media," declared Foreman. And that would prove more than a match for muscle-bound heavy equipment operators armed with wrenches and chains.[4]

Bald Mountain lay near the Kalmiopsis Wilderness in the Siskiyou National Forest in southern Oregon. It was not particularly attractive land. It had no lakes. Much of it looked like a desert. But parts contained beautiful old-growth Douglas fir forests. Ever since 1936, when the famed Forest Service preservationist Robert Marshall urged that a million acres of the Kalmiopsis be preserved, conservationists had fought to save this region, but with little success.

RARE I had set aside a mere 77,000 acres. The 1979 Oregon Wilderness Act expanded the Kalmiopsis only slightly, which was a major disappointment to environmentalists. And now the Forest Service seemed to be accelerating road building into the remaining undisturbed forests, apparently intent on rendering further preservation efforts moot. Once roads and clear-cuts disturbed the primeval scene, the land could no longer be called wilderness.[5]

Such, Earth First!ers were convinced, was the tactic behind the Bald Mountain Road. The Forest Service had first conceived the idea for the thoroughfare in 1978. Running along the northern boundary of the Kalmiopsis, it was to ride the high ridge from Flat Top to Bald Mountain between the Illinois River and Silver Creek, opening up 150,000 acres of big trees to cutting. This two-lane blacktop would destroy portions of the popular Illinois River trail and come within a foot of the Kalmiopsis boundary.[6]

The plan was a direct assault on biocentric sensibilities. Outraged, Andy Kerr of the Oregon Natural Resources Coalition went to court to stop the road. The Sierra Club funded the suit but, fearing a backlash against environmentalists, wouldn't use what Kerr thought was the best legal strategy: the argument that the Forest Service had failed to complete an environmental impact statement on the road, as required by the Environmental Policy Act. And when they lost in lower court, the club refused to support an appeal.[7]

This appeared to torpedo the coalition's legal initiative. But Roselle and Everhart, like the Lone Ranger and Tonto, arrived to save the day. When, in the winter of 1983, frozen pipes burst in their Goose, Wyoming, home, turning the floor into a skating rink, they piled into their "Lumbago" motor home and hit the road, looking for a good fight.

Roselle wanted an issue to galvanize the activist community — the old antiwar radicals who had gone soft growing pot — something to show the public that the Forest Service planned to eliminate all wilderness. When he and Everhart arrived in the Northwest, they toured the national forests, warning supervisors that they intended to stop the road building, legally or illegally.

In Grants Pass, Oregon, they found the activists in a serious state of depression over the lost lawsuit. So Roselle suggested a blockade. And when all except Marsden and Tama rejected the idea, the four decided to go it alone.

This was psychological warfare. When the catskinners arrived at Bald Mountain, they freaked out as the four men suddenly appeared, looking like giant Hobbits, and announcing that they planned a nonviolent protest to stop the construction. The road gang had heard of protests in Chicago before, but what the hell were potheads doing in the woods? How many of them were there?

After scaring the crew silly, the four turned around and walked twenty-five miles back the way they had come. This set the stage. Disappearing into the mountains like Cochise preparing an ambush, they gave the construction crew the creeps, unsettling their nerves as planned. And the next day, when the eco-commandos returned in cowboy costume, Earth First!'s guerrilla theater was born.

But the warriors did not stop there. Kerr, still fuming over the Sierra Club's dropping his lawsuit, asked Roselle if he would file the appeal. Earth First! would be listed as first plaintiff, he explained, followed by the coalition. Since the public already thought that Roselle's merry pranksters were off the wall, he reasoned, Earth First! had no reputation to lose by pursuing a high-risk legal strategy.[8]

Roselle accepted. Flooded by contributions following the Bald Mountain blockade, he and his friends holed up at Grants Pass and, without a lawyer, typed out their own legal brief to stop the road.

The issue was more than a highway, even more than saving wilderness. These activists were not simply protesting; they were acting out of an idea. "Our vision," Foreman said, "is that we really have to *have a vision*. We aren't willing to have our vision defined for us by the modern corporate state." Saving the Kalmiopsis was a way to fight for biocentrism, to stop the relentless advance of mankind! Bald Mountain would be to our civilization what Stalingrad was to Hitler, Tours was to the Saracens, Vienna to the Huns: the beginning of the big rollback.[9]

Earth First!ers were challenging civilization as well as its discontents, the whole enchilada. They were princes of disorder, a kind of ecological clockwork orange. Today the Kalmiopsis, tomorrow Manhattan! For if you can stare down a bulldozer, where might it end? By pulling up every nail hammered home during the last four hundred years!

The emergence of Earth First! signified something big and strange going down in America. By the early 1980s new biocentrist groups were multiplying like Elvis impersonators — Sea Shepherds, Robin Wood, Greenpeace, Friends of the Wolf, Friends of the Earth, Earth Island Institute, Rainforest Action Network, countless smaller organizations in eastern Europe and the Third World, and a wolfpack of animal rights groups, such as the Animal Liberation Front, Band of Mercy, Hunt Saboteurs, and People for the Ethical Treatment of Animals (PETA).

Combining a desire for a spiritual revival with media savvy and a knack for forming alliances through networking, these new activists were changing the rules of the game. And Roselle was one of the chief architects. Born in Louisville, Kentucky, one of nine children, Roselle was orphaned at the age of four. Brought up in a right-wing blue-collar culture, he started out in life supporting George Wallace because, as he explains, his parents did. But as a teenager he did a complete flip-flop, turned leftward, and never looked back. In high school he supported Eldridge Cleaver for president. He started hanging out with friends who listened to underground radio. And in the late sixties he dropped out of high school, enrolling in the Youth International Party (Yippies) to fight against the war in Vietnam.[10]

But the Yippies gradually split apart. Abbie Hoffman and Jerry Rubin, Roselle thought, spoiled by success, had neglected the nuts and bolts of party organization and strategy. Then these leaders committed the unpardonable sin — they supported George McGovern for president. Needing to separate himself from this co-optation, Roselle, along with an old-time leftist and marijuana missionary, Dana Beal, split the Yippies to found the Zippies. Along the way he discovered guerrilla theater.[11]

No one knows where or when guerrilla theater started. A kind of subversive drama, it may have originated with traveling road shows during the Middle Ages. Some Earth First!ers claim their use of it was inspired by the early Spanish "mudhead cantinas," in which peasants would put on plays to mock the nobility. The idea was to make fun of authority, undermining its mystique with satire. But the modern version married this idea with television. It first caught the nation's attention in Chicago, during the police riots at the Democratic National Convention in 1968. Roselle was thirteen at the time. The violence and the subsequent show trial of the Chicago Seven were rich material for television; and video, Roselle discovered, was an enormously effective medium for bringing home the emotion of an event. The more blood and guts on the screen, the better it played in Peoria.

But after Nixon ended the draft, the antiwar movement died. Roselle, burned out, was sick of leftist politics, with its naiveté, name-calling, backstabbing, ideologies, and endless debates. He was tired of being so alienated from mainstream society that average people "couldn't stand being in the same room with us." Roselle's final disaffection with leftist politics probably came when the Zippies took over McGovern's campaign office in Miami Beach. "Beal embarrassed everybody by getting up and saying, 'The question here is marijuana,'" says Roselle. But while many burned-out activists would "just say 'fuck' and take pot," Roselle wanted to find a new cause.

Deciding to be a "redneck environmentalist," he retreated first to the Everglades, then to the Smokies. When the war ended, he went west, working as a roughneck in the oil fields of Utah and the Dakotas. Then he moved to Colorado because he had been told that there was more wilderness there. But the central Rockies weren't as unspoiled as he had imagined. A lot of the landscape, he found, was marred by open pit mines and other developments. Seeking real wilderness, he headed north, to Jackson, Wyoming, where he went to work in the kitchen of the Cowboy Bar. Wanting to "go straight," he began to dabble in conventional environmental politics, cofounding the Wyoming Wilderness Association.

The bouncer at the Cowboy was Howie Wolke, a burly fellow with a habit of rolling up his sleeves to show off his biceps. Son of a traveling salesman, Wolke grew up in a suitcase. Born in Brooklyn, he studied forestry at the University of New Hampshire. In college he briefly joined the antiwar movement but never felt comfortable with confrontational politics. By the time he met Roselle, Wolke was the Wyoming representative of David Brower's new group, Friends of the Earth. He began to educate Roselle, asking his friend to write environmental articles, dragging him to meetings, and enlisting his help in recruiting blue-collar workers into the conservation movement.[12]

But these were frustrating times. The Forest Service, Roselle and Wolke thought, was screwing the wilderness, and mainstream environmentalists were letting them get away with it. RARE II was a major disappointment. In 1979, after inventorying 62 million acres, the agency recommended a mere 15 million for wilderness status. And most of this was "rock and ice," not the lush green lands needed by most wildlife.[13]

The following April, Wolke asked Roselle to join him for a hike in Mexico's Sonora Desert. In Tucson they hooked up with three of Wolke's friends who were equally disillusioned with conventional politics: farrier and general misfit Dave Foreman; mountain climber and Sierra Clubber Ron Kezar; and self-styled "outlaw buckaroo songwriter" and "environmental gunslinger," originally from the Adirondacks ("home of acid rain"), Bart Koehler.[14]

Foreman was another burned-out case. Recovering from a divorce, he quit a job as issues coordinator for the Wilderness Society. He was drinking heavily at the time, suffering from what Roselle termed "postdivorce stress," and he was on an odyssey from right to left, even as Roselle seemed headed in the opposite direction. Their political evolution intersected at Sonora.

A fourth-generation New Mexican, Foreman was a Neanderthal conservative. Son of an army officer, a former highly decorated Boy Scout and, later, Young American for Freedom, he had campaigned for Barry Goldwater for president in 1964. Eager to serve in Vietnam, he had volunteered for the marines after graduating from college. But he soon found that he didn't fit into the military either. Deemed a troublemaker by the marines, he was given an undesirable discharge. After a stint at horseshoeing school, he began working at a trading post on the Zuni reservation. While there, he joined a Santa Fe group that founded a second Black Mesa Defense Fund (to rival Marc Gaede's), and by 1978 found himself chief lobbyist for the Wilderness Society, sitting in an office in Washington, D.C., just four blocks from the White House.

But the Wilderness Society was too stodgy for Foreman — a "bunch of raging moderates," he recalled, playing footsie with the Carter administration. Frustrations began to pile up, such as "the staff trip near Lake Tahoe," he told one writer, when Wilderness Society executive director Bill Turnage "poured Perrier water from his French ceramic canteen and I had to eat a raw steak in front of him to get even."

Then there was the old growth issue. RARE II, completed in 1979, designated fifteen million acres as wilderness. Foreman was outraged and wanted to sue the Forest Service for more. But Turnage refused. Anxious to avoid a bitter and divisive battle and preferring the old style tactic of quiet lobbying, the director considered a court fight premature.[15]

This pussyfooting was the last straw. It was time, he thought, "for a new joker in the deck." He decided to quit. Wifeless and about to be jobless, Foreman jumped into the Volkswagen microbus with Kezar,

Koehler, Roselle, and Wolke, and the magnificent five headed south for Mexico, seeking spiritual enlightenment and Mexican beer.

But from the moment they met, Foreman and Roselle didn't like each other much. Roselle thought that Foreman was an unstable right-wing fanatic who seemed more afraid of the Russians than of developers. He wanted to build a bomb shelter in a mineshaft, for God's sake! And to Foreman, Roselle was just another hippie along for the ride.

The five spent a few days hiking in Mexico's Pinacate Desert, near Baja California, drinking beer, shooting the bull, and baying at the moon. At the end of the trip, on April 2, 1980, they gathered in a bar at San Luis Rio Colorado, at the Mexican-U.S. border. Lubricating their brains with Pacifica beer, they got an idea: to create a militant group that "would make the Sierra Club look moderate"— Earth First!, always to be spelled with an exclamation point. Its motto would be "No compromise in defense of Mother Earth."

Returning home, they hit the ground running. In Jackson, Roselle and Wolke drew up a list of wildernesses they wanted to save and a catalogue of people who might help. Roselle designed the logo — a green fist — to symbolize "the Earth, the cycle of life, and the coffee stain on an environmental impact statement." By summer Foreman had published the *Earth First Newsletter*, sending it out to names on his Rolodex, and proposing the most audacious set of preservation ideas ever put into print.

Declaring that "large sections of Earth should be declared off-limits to industrial human civilization, as preserves for the free-flow of natural processes," they proposed a "Wilderness Preserve System" that would push people off 716 million acres, including most of Nevada (50 million acres), half of Idaho, much of Nebraska and the Dakotas, most of the Sierras, the entire California North Coast, and 4.5 million acres of the Oregon Cascades. It would drain the reservoirs of the Snake, Colorado, and Missouri rivers and create a 3-million-acre condor sanctuary just north of fashionable Santa Barbara. Nor were Americans the only people to be run off the land. Much of the globe would be zoned, including large expanses of Australia, the Amazon, Tierra del Fuego and Patagonia, New Guinea, Borneo, Greenland, Baja; the Galapagos, Falklands, and South Georgia islands; the Sahara, the Congo, and Siberia; the Tien Shan, Gobi, and Sinkiang regions of Central Asia; and the oceans.[16]

That same summer the group organized a wilderness get-together called the Round River Rendezvous, and sent out invitations to "get drunk, get laid, and get beat up by Howie W." Then Foreman, Koehler, and Kezar jumped into the microbus, inaugurating what would become an annual whistle-stop tour around the country, giving speeches, singing songs, discussing issues, and plotting strategy.

"We were mad," Roselle recalls. "We didn't know what would work, but were willing to try anything." That meant what Foreman called "nonviolent direct intervention — with wit." That is, guerrilla theater and creative monkeywrenching — burning billboards, spiking trees, disrupting power lines, destroying bulldozer engines, and generally making life miserable for road builders, developers, power companies, loggers, and other "greedheads" who might dare to trespass in wilderness. Ed Abbey, who lived near Foreman in Tucson, became a kindly stepfather to the Earth First!ers, reveling in the fact that their lives imitated his art.[17]

By the end of the year their newsletter had more than 1,500 subscribers, and by 1983, with its name changed to the *Earth First! Journal*, it was on its way to becoming a cult classic. Filled with scatological humor, articles on deep ecology, and news from the boondocks written by irreverent, angry pseudonymous authors with names like "Miss Ann Thrope," "Randall Restless," "Arthur Dogmeat," and "The Friends of the Wild Dawgs from Hell," it became "must" reading for the Mercedes and BMW commuters of Silicon and Mill valleys who were seeking the vicarious thrills of primitive chic. The *Journal*'s "Ask Ned Ludd" column was a special hit. Sort of a "Dear Abby" for ecoteurs, it gave advice on every kind of sabotage from tree spiking to shooting cattle.

The Round River Rendezvous became the Earth First!ers' annual "tribal gathering." Setting up tents in dusty backcountry, they smoked pot, drank beer, had sex, and put on mud cantina minstrel skits, in which clay-caked performers in loincloths threw dirt and sprayed Cool Whip on one another, chanting obscene doggerel about shit-kicking greed bags and defecating multinational corporations.[18]

It was Woodstock every summer. The atmosphere was charged with sexual energy. Bare-chested men and women sat in empowerment circles holding hands and sharing thoughts about art for the earth, music for the earth, and the earth for the earth, as others squatted in the lotus position on the dusty ground seeking nirvana, and bearded men and floppy-breasted women sat in clusters under trees, strumming guitars or singing about the rape of the earth and the virginity of owls. Many trekked to nearby streams to skinny-dip or sit on rocks, occasionally retreating to tents to make love and plan actions.

The shows, the wit and humor, the contempt for authority, the sex and pot, the enjoyment of shocking middle-class prudes, the promise of action, the allure of a hunter-gatherer life, and the idealism were a potent mixture. Despite a mere $3,000 budget, even in its first year Earth First! attracted followers like flypaper catches gnats.[19]

The timing was perfect. Ronald Reagan had just been elected president on a platform of private enterprise which seemed to say, "Greed is good." His interior secretary, James Watt, seemed intent on developing every last square inch of the continent. Environmental fundraisers capitalized on this image, and by demonizing Watt scared millions into joining the movement.[20]

Employing professional direct-mail solicitors, who typically took fifty cents of every dollar raised, environmental groups grew exponentially — hiring lawyers, raising salaries, building fancy new office buildings, moving their headquarters to Washington, D.C. — and became more like the federal bureaucracies they were dedicated to fighting. "The worst thing Watt ever did," Foreman would reportedly lament, "was to drive another 100,000 into joining the Wilderness Society." As these groups grew bigger and stodgier, the more alienated activists flocked to Earth First! The movement became a lightning rod for the disaffected.[21]

After March 21, 1981, when Foreman, Wolke, and four others unrolled a 300-foot black plastic replica of a cement fracture over the face of the Glen Canyon Dam in Arizona, the whole country knew Earth First! The "cracking" of Glen Canyon was to environmentalists an unfurl heard 'round the world.[22]

Staunchly antiorganization, Earth First! had no paid staffers, no building, no prized five-oh-one-see-three status with the IRS. It was a spontaneous movement. Anyone who chose to call himself an Earth First!er could do so. This reflected not merely a commitment to anarchism but also an awareness that a group advocating or plotting illegal acts was guilty of conspiracy and could be put out of business by the FBI. But if isolated monkeywrenchers also happened to call themselves Earth First!ers, well, it was not the movement's responsibility.[23]

Rather than becoming a formal group, therefore, in the spring of 1982 the Earth First! Foundation was established as a distinct entity for fundraising. And among its board members was Bill Devall. While visiting Arcata on his road show in 1982 Roselle met Devall, who explained his philosophy of deep ecology. "I liked that," Roselle remembered, "liked calling myself 'deep' and others 'shallow.' " Devall joined the movement and immediately, in Roselle's words, began to have "a lot of effect" on the organization.[24]

Indeed, Earth First!, deep ecology, and the ecosystem idea were made for one another. What Wolke later called "The Earth First! whole ecosystem approach" had already been spelled out in the wilderness plan, which declared that "the central idea of Earth First! is that humans have no divine right to subdue the Earth, that we are merely one of several million forms of life on this planet. We reject even the notion of benevolent stewardship as that implies dominance. Instead we believe, as did Aldo Leopold, that we should be plain citizens of the land community."[25]

This deep ecological perspective also justified monkeywrenching. As Foreman explained: "'I am protecting the rain forest' develops to 'I am part of the rain forest protecting myself. I am the part of the rain forest recently emerged into thinking.' When we fully identify with a wild place, then, monkeywrenching becomes self-defense, which is a fundamental right."[26]

Ecotage, wrote Earth First!er Christopher Manes, "follows from the idea of the Ecological Self articulated by Arne Naess, Devall, and other Deep Ecologists. If our selves belong to a larger self that encompasses the whole biological community in which we dwell, then an attack on the trees, the wolves, the rivers, is an attack upon all of us. Defense of places becomes a form of self-defense, which in most ethical and legal systems would be ample grounds for spiking a tree or ruining a tire."[27]

Our real identity, then, is not our individual selves but the larger ecosystem of which we are a part. The long shadow of holism, the idea of individuals as mere cogs in a big, glorious machine, emerged as the central notion of the Earth First! protest. Soon the sense that ecosystems, not people, are the fundamental units of nature would be endorsed by academics as well. "Morality is derivative of the holistic character of the ecosystem," the philosopher Holmes Rolston III would write in 1986, summarizing this popular view. "The preservation of the ecosystem [is] in human self-interest, for the 'self' has been so extended as to be ecosystemically redefined."[28]

Just so, the spiritual pilgrimage of these activists had led them from Ralph Waldo Emerson's pantheism to Hutchinson's New Ecology, to Naess's Deep Ecology, to Hegel's metaphysics, to the Tucson Raiders' ecotage. Armed with their new idea, Earth First!ers took to their tools, busting machines and sabotaging logging with abandon — flattening tires, pulling survey stakes, felling power lines, cutting fences, spiking roads, billboarding, pulling up animal traps, setting off smoke and stink bombs, dumping garbage on the porches of loggers and other enemies of the earth, jamming locks, shooting out subdividers' windows with slingshots, vandalizing enemy cars, destroying computers, trashing condos, spray-painting messages on buildings, and generally finding imaginative ways to undermine, rip up, tear down, mess around with, hinder, block, harm, destroy, or render useless the material possessions of others.[29]

And the biggest innovation was tree spiking, which Earth First! introduced in the Siskiyou Mountains in Oregon in 1983. Within a few months the tactic had spread like kudzu through Georgia. Driving sixty-penny nails — or, even better, ceramic spikes, which cannot be found by metal detectors — into trees turned forests into time bombs. When a chain saw hits a spike, it bounces back violently, threatening to cut the operator severely. When a mill band saw hits a spiked log, it shatters, sending shrapnel through the body of anyone standing nearby.[30]

Thus, tree spiking was a devilishly effective means of discouraging logging. But the costs of monkeywrenching, including tree spiking, would become stupendous. By the late 1980s estimates of the damage would range from $20 to $25 million a year. The Association of Oregon Loggers calculated that each act of sabotage cost the equipment owner from $60,000 to $100,000.[31]

Even as Earth First!ers found their calling, tensions continued to simmer between Foreman and Roselle. Foreman was a macho wilderness freak who had declared war on the twentieth century. He believed in deep ecology, and, his critics thought, was mesmerized by the sound of his own voice. Considering himself a "tribal leader" of a neo-Neolithic renaissance, he strode around in marine fatigues like Che Guevara. He truly believed that civilization is a plague on the earth, and had no interest in the political games people played. He focused instead on rolling the clock back. Monkeywrenching, he believed, "symbolizes our fundamental strategy for dealing with the mad machine."[32]

By contrast, Roselle never shook his leftist roots. He was a reformer, not a destroyer. He didn't blame the human race but wanted to change the ways people live. More attracted to nonviolent tactics, he felt uncomfortable with Earth First!'s anarchist image and its association with mayhem. He saw social injustice as the principal cause of environmental decline. Unlike Foreman, who opposed all agriculture, he objected only to "mechanized farming." Hence, Roselle never completely trusted Foreman, whom he felt sometimes "went off the deep end" and "could explode any day."

"I always felt sooner or later," he said, "Dave and I would have to get settled on the whole left-versus-right thing. . . . When we have the revolution we want, we will end up shooting each other." But in the meantime, their alliance cemented by a mutual concern for wilderness, each put these uneasy thoughts aside.[33]

15

THE NETWORK

EARTH FIRST! HAD FOUND how to capture the public imagination. Following the cracking of Glen Canyon and the blockade of Bald Mountain, they were on their way to becoming multimedia folk heroes. But Earth First! was merely a fraction of a widening movement devoted to deep ecology and ecotage. Activist groups reproduced like amoebas, multiplying by dividing. Splinter cells split again as each explored new ways to press the edge of the envelope of protest. Meanwhile, they maintained ties to one another, creating a web of relationships not unlike their beloved ecosystems themselves, giving the movement a power and diversity of which few outsiders were aware.

One of these rebels was the early Greenpeacer Paul Watson, who, objecting to the group's prohibition against destroying property, left in 1977 to found the Sea Shepherds Conservation Society. Watson was an impatient man. Born in Toronto in 1950, growing up there and in New Brunswick, motherless since the age of twelve, he drifted away from home when he was sixteen, riding the rails to Vancouver, where he enlisted as a deck hand on a Norwegian freighter, the *Bris*. By the early 1970s, back in school studying communications, he became acquainted with the works of Marshall McLuhan and the idea that "the medium is the message," an insight he would apply to his new venture.[1]

His split with Greenpeace came during a seal hunt in Canada. "There was this man with a club about to hit a seal pup," he remembered. "The only way I could save the pup's life was to take away the man's club. Which I did. I threw it in the water."

For this Greenpeace threw Watson out. By casting the spear, he had broken Greenpeace's rule against violence. But, Watson objected, violence is only the intentional causing of physical harm to people and animals. Destroying property is not violence. Taking this principle with him, he and several friends founded Sea Shepherds. He saw himself as following the Isaac Asimov trilogy: Sea Shepherds would reform the reformers "exactly like the split that occurred in *Foundation II*."[2]

With a $120,000 gift from Fund for Animals president Cleveland Amory, Watson purchased a rusty trawler, which he dubbed the *Sea Shepherd*, and — because it lacked refrigeration — decided to run as a vegetarian vessel. With funding from the Royal Society for the Prevention of Cruelty to Animals (RSPCA), Watson then set off on his first campaign, to Newfoundland's Labrador Front seal pup hunt. Soon he would be calling Sea Shepherds "the navy of which Earth First! is the army."[3]

Steering a port course, Sea Shepherd began taking risks that Greenpeace avoided — photographing whaling operations in Siberia; blockading the port of St. John's, Newfoundland; sabotaging fishing in the Faroe Islands; reportedly hiring frogmen to blow up the pirate whaling ship *Sierra* in Lisbon harbor. And as the Sea Shepherd began to be noticed, Greenpeace followed suit. A kind of Gresham's law operated, whereby extremism drove out moderation. Greenpeace, anxious not to be outdone by the more radical Sea Shepherds, began to adopt more aggressive tactics as well.

So the environmental movement, its ranks swelling with the impatient and disaffected, sailed into uncharted waters. The line separating environmentalists from animal rights activists began to blur as both, believing that all living things have a "right to live and blossom," followed the star of biocentrism.

One of Watson's early recruits, Alex Pacheco, within three years would become a major force on his own as co-leader of the aggressive animal rights group People for the Ethical Treatment of Animals (PETA). Pale and thin, seemingly worn beyond his years, Pacheco looks like Michael J. Fox with frown lines — part waif, part yuppie. Born in Joliet, Illinois, of a Mexican father and an American mother, raised in Mexico and Ohio, Pacheco took a radical turn after a horrifying epiphany: while a junior at Ohio State University, he visited a slaughterhouse in Toronto.

"The stench and blood and suffering went beyond my imagination," he said. "I came home and picked up Peter Singer's book *Animal Liberation*, reading the chapter on farm animals. Right then I became a vegetarian."[4]

Returning to college, Pacheco attended a talk by Cleveland Amory, founding father of the U.S. animal rights movement. Moved by the talk, he asked Amory how he could get involved in the movement. The older man suggested that he join the Sea Shepherds.

Pacheco spent the summer with Watson during their famous campaign, which ended when their ship, *Sea Shepherd*, rammed the pirate whaler *Sierra* off Portugal. And after the Portuguese government threatened to confiscate Watson's ship to compensate *Sierra*'s owners, Pacheco was present when a nighttime explosion — set off, insiders say, by hired German frogmen who attached plastic explosives to its hull — sent *Sierra* to the bottom.[5]

Named "Sea Shepherd of the year" that summer, Pacheco left in September for England, where he spent six months with the Hunt Saboteurs, a group dedicated to direct action in protest of blood sports. More advanced in guerrilla tactics than American animal activists, the "Sabs" profoundly impressed Pacheco. "Some actually had scars on their faces where they had been whipped by huntsmen," he recalled. "I had never seen such bravery."

Returning to the United States in 1980, Pacheco enrolled in environmental studies at George Washington University and took a job with the Washington, D.C., Humane Society. There he met Ingrid Newkirk, who ran the society's dog pound. An Englishwoman raised in India, Newkirk, at twenty-nine eight years older than Pacheco, was already a successful activist. Applying knowledge of animal protection she had acquired from the RSPCA, Newkirk founded the Cruelty Department of the Humane Society's animal shelter.

The meeting of Pacheco and Newkirk produced a synergistic chemistry, combining the former's ideas with the latter's activism. They became lovers. "Alex taught me so much in such a short time," Newkirk said. Until she met Pacheco, Newkirk had not supposed that animals actually had rights. Rather, she thought that cruelty was wrong because it offended human values. "But Alex introduced me to Singer's book, and made me realize other living things have rights just as we do."[6]

Indeed, *Animal Liberation*, which first appeared in 1975, became the bible of the animal liberation movement. Articulating the biocentrist idea, Singer argued that all living things are equal. We are not morally entitled to kill, eat, breed, skin, capture, train, or experiment with animals.[7]

In Singer, Pacheco and Newkirk had found a whole new ideology, giving their activism a direction. In the summer of 1980 they founded PETA, and soon Pacheco went to work, under cover, at the Institutes for Behavioral Research in Silver Spring, Maryland, a laboratory studying the effects of nerve damage from spinal cord injuries and strokes, run by the psychologist Edward Taub. Its research consisted of experiments on monkeys. The animals were "differentiated," a procedure whereby nerves in the spinal column are severed, rendering some limbs useless.[8]

Believing laboratory conditions in Silver Spring to be intolerably filthy and inhumane, Pacheco secretly visited the lab at night and on weekends. An accomplice waited outside with a walkie-talkie while Pacheco took pictures and went through Taub's private files, photocopying documents and taking slides. Then Pacheco called the police. Based on Pacheco's findings, the National Institutes of Health found the lab "grossly unsanitary" and determined that it lacked proper veterinary care. Taub was convicted on six counts of cruelty to animals.[9]

Taub protested his innocence. Some of Pacheco's photos were "staged," he said. And he marveled at how Pacheco had used the media. "The search and seizure in my laboratory was planned well in advance to have maximum media coverage," he said. "It was a circus. The press was there before the search began. There was a virtual mob of media people."

Taub spent six years and his life savings fighting the verdict. "I thought I would never get a job in my profession again," he said. Eventually Taub was exonerated. Three peer reviews supported him, as did the Guggenheim Foundation, which, after careful examination of the Silver Spring case, gave him a fellowship. Still later, the Maryland Court of Appeals overturned his conviction. But as far as Taub is concerned, the damage was done. "This kind of mud," he said, "tends to stick."[10]

Meanwhile, long before Taub was vindicated, the Silver Spring bust had turned Pacheco and Newkirk into celebrities. Tens of thousands of unsolicited dollars arrived in the mail. Known as the "dynamic duo," the two were off and running. By then the animal rights movement was exploding. The cause became another battleground on which deep ecologists confronted a society bent on the domination of nature. Whereas in the past those involved in preventing cruelty to animals had supported their cause by appealing to human sympathy, the new breed of liberationists cited biospherical egalitarianism. For them there was no difference between the exploitation of animals and the subjugation of workers or women. Animal rights were as important as human liberty.[11]

Because of this reasoning militancy became a growth industry. Replacing what was known as "animal welfare"— a timid and stodgy cause pursued at weekly Humane Society meetings by little old ladies in Reeboks — the new animal rights based on biocentrism attracted younger, more violently inclined followers. Liberationist cells began to proliferate without end: Band of Mercy, Animal Liberation Movement, Animal Liberation League, True Friends, Humans against Rabbit Exploitation (HARE), Trans-Species Unlimited, Animal Rights Network, Feminists for Animal Rights, International Network for Religion and Animals, National Alliance for Animal Legislation, Farm Animal Reform Movement, and many, many others. Vying with one another in a form of do-it-yourself extremism, many escalated the action. Some, not content simply to boycott cosmetic manufacturers to protest the Draize test — the laboratory procedure of putting drops of a product into the eyes of animals to measure toxicity — began to vandalize the shops of furriers and invade laboratories to free experimental animals.[12]

By the time Mike Roselle donned his cowboy hat on Bald Mountain, green groups were springing up throughout Europe and North America. And though not formally allied, they had close ties to one another. Exemplifying the essence of networking, group members attended one another's meetings; the groups maintained overlapping board memberships and shared many members.[13]

In 1983 Die Grünen, having embraced biocentrism, stunned the world by capturing 5.6 percent of the vote and twenty-seven seats in the German federal elections. Soon this party's ideas were spreading across Europe like a brushfire. Die Grünen had a franchisable idea with which to replicate ecology parties around the globe like McDonald's restaurants. By the early eighties there were viable green parties in every country of western Europe, as well as Canada, Australia, Japan, and New Zealand. And they were taking root in the United States as well.[14]

In 1982 two part-time instructors at Berkeley, Charlene Spretnak and Fritjof Capra, visiting Germany on lecture tours, discovered Die Grünen. "We felt an immediate resonance with Green politics," they observed later. Returning to the States they wrote *Green Politics*, introducing most Americans to Die Grünen for the first time. The response was electric. A radically egalitarian platform dedicated to the fight against sexism, imperialism, and social injustice was just what many had been looking for.[15]

So, in the midst of the political doldrums of the Reagan years, when the country seemed numbed by Republican placebos, these people became electrified by a new mission. By August 1984, in part because of Spretnak's initiative, activists from New York and California met at Macalester College in Saint Paul, Minnesota, to found the American green movement. Calling themselves the Committees of Correspondence (after a group of the same name during our Revolutionary War), they hammered out a platform, adopting "ten key values": "ecological wisdom, grassroots democracy, personal and social responsibility, non-

violence, decentralization, community based economics, postpatriar-
chal values [i.e., feminism], respect for diversity, global responsibility,
and future focus."[16]

The same year Roselle's friend Dana Beal organized a series of punk
rock concerts, the "Rock Against Reagan" tour. Part of the Yippies'
"Freeze Reagan and Bush" campaign, it was planned to culminate with
a performance in Dallas during the Republican convention. It was
so popular that the Yippies suddenly found their ranks swelling with
all sorts of people who had never been Yippies before. Coming from
respectable middle-class backgrounds, these new recruits did not want
to be called Yippies. So that fall, Beal, following the suggestion of
Hans-Georg Behr, a visiting German Green, decided to change the
name of their movement from the Yippies to the North American
Greens.[17]

Soon green groups were spreading across the continent like leafy
spurge: Ecology Forum, Mississippi Watershed Alliance, North American Bioregional Congress, Institute for Social Ecology, Clamshell Alliance, League for Ecological Democracy, Chicagoland Green Network,
Venice (California) Greens, Upper Valley Greens, Central Vermont
Greens, Merrymeeting Greens, New Haven Green Party, Southern California Green Assembly, San Francisco Greens, Burlington (Vermont)
Greens, New York Green party, New England Committees of Correspondence, East Bay Green Alliance, Mid-Atlantic Greens, Hollywood
Greens, the East Bay Green Alliance, Santa Monica/Venice Greens, the
Los Angeles Green Alternative, the Southern California Green Assem-
bly, and the Pacific Northwest Greens from the Cascadia bioregion.[18]

In 1982 David Brower, now the graybeard of environmental action,
founded Earth Island Institute. Two years later he would help Earth
First!er Randy Hayes create Rainforest Action Network. Hayes was
later joined by Roselle. By 1977 Greenpeace had become an international organization which would eventually grow to be the world's
biggest environmental group, with offices from Washington to Ham-
burg to Moscow. Then in 1982 Greenpeacer Klaus Sheerer, a former
East German sea captain, objecting to the highly centralized decision-
making structure of Greenpeace, founded Robin Wood. Soon his little
army had invaded a nuclear power plant at Cattenom, France, planting a
flag on its cooling tower. Eventually it would have cells throughout
France, Germany, and eastern Europe.[19]

As these groups multiplied, they began to resemble the interconnected ecosystems they were determined to save. Watson, Amory,
Devall, Pacheco, Foreman, Roselle, Beal, Hayes, Brower, and Sheerer

became the political image of a biological metaphor, a network of relations as incestuous as the family tree of European royalty.

The Fund for Animals coordinated planning with PETA and the New England Anti-Vivisection League. PETA allegedly created an underground group, True Friends, and seems to have had ties to the Animal Liberation Front. Sea Shepherds owed its existence to Amory, and its leader, Watson, would found a Canadian group, Friends of the Wolf, and launch into tree spiking. The North American Greens served as a bridge between Germany's Greens and Earth First! through the Beal-Roselle connection. Watson and Foreman, introduced to each other by Marc Gaede, became friends, cementing ties between Earth First! and Sea Shepherds. Greenpeace had spawned both Sea Shepherds and Robin Wood. And so on and so on.[20]

Because these groups were small, their influence escaped public attention. But their strength derived from networking, not size, an informal cooperation fused by commitment to the same ideal.

On the surface the fecund idea of biocentrism seemed anything but a shared ideal. It looked to be multiplying ideologies like a virus. Splits were forming between Marxist materialism and spiritual environmentalism, anarchism and mainline politics, the agendas of nonviolence and those of terrorism, growth and no-growth, income redistribution and environmental regulation.[21]

There were green "cultural feminists," such as Spretnak, who believed that sexism was a consequence of "patriarchal perspectives" associated with the old hierarchical paradigm, which would go away once we adopted a true biospherical egalitarianism. There were "Luddites," such as Kirkpatrick Sale, who wanted to dismantle modern society. There were Aquarians and coevolutionists who wanted to take over the "tiller of creation." There were animal liberationists taking aim at "species chauvinism," and left-wing pragmatists who wanted to graft the Greens and the Democratic party together. There were green union leaders who saw "social justice" issues as paramount, and preservationists who believed saving grizzly bears and old-growth forests was most fundamental. There were splits between primitivists — who believed that the golden age was in the past — and futurists who believed that it lay in the future. And there were splits within these splits.[22]

Just as Hegel's holism gave birth to a plethora of mutually antagonistic ideologies, from Lenin's international communism to Hitler's national socialism, so now biocentrism spurred conflict between disciples of every ideologue from Mao to Muir. And the cacophony was so loud, the divisions so numerous, that no one noticed the disputants actually agreed on first principles. All supposed that everything was interconnected. All were suspicious of reason and traditional science. All agreed that man must be not lord and master of the universe but a biotic citizen of it. And all unconsciously embraced Ernst Haeckel's desire to reconnect society with nature.

Arne Naess's Hegelian ideas had become a full-fledged architectonic for cultural revolution. Western civilization, nearly all activists believed, had taken a wrong turn somewhere between the fall of Troy and the Renaissance, and for the first time had reached what Fritjof Capra, the former French student radical turned philosopher, called the "turning point." Foreman, Roselle, and Watson embraced deep ecology, and Devall served as their philosopher laureate.

Earth First!ers, said Foreman, are "the dog-soldiers of bioregionalism." He was a misanthrope and proud of it. "I see us as the warriors of the bioregional tribe. Our philosophy, our worldview, our religion, must be one of Deep Ecology. Biocentrism. . . . We recognize that we are part of the natural ecosystem in which we dwell. We are . . . turning away from hierarchy to tribalism." And bioregionalism, as the ecopoet Gary Snyder, one of the gurus of the movement, explained, "is a family-scale way of actualizing deep ecology."[23]

Deep ecology, wrote Devall's coauthor George Sessions, is "a religious and philosophical revolution of the first magnitude." It is, said the bioregionalist Kirkpatrick Sale, "a natural and organic response to what is arguably the most profound contemporary trend of all: the disintegration of the established forms and systems that have characterized the Western world." It is, wrote Capra, a "newly emerging social force," which they called "the rising culture."[24]

Dubbing deep ecology "the new paradigm," they aimed to replace the Judeo-Christian, positivist, materialist, consumerist, capitalist, hierarchical, nature-dominating values of the old order. And the principal focus of this rebellion was to refute what they called "Cartesian dualism."[25]

René Descartes, the seventeenth-century French mathematician and philosopher, had propounded the idea that reality consists of two "substances," ideas and things, and that humans, having both minds and bodies, are composites of these two kinds of reality. And although this was merely a restatement of the Judeo-Christian idea that people possess both bodies and souls, it served as the focus of the biocentric rebellion.[26]

By suggesting that the mind is distinct from the physical world, bio-centrists argued, Descartes laid the groundwork for the alienation of man from nature. This dualism explained everything they felt was wrong with civilization: it combined the Greek penchant for intellectu-alizing experience, the Jewish and Christian emphasis on dominating nature, and the proclivity of modern science for treating nonhuman creatures as mere objects.[27]

"One of the things we are suffering with in modern society right now," Foreman wrote in 1985, "is Cartesian dualism, the idea that you can separate the observer from that which is observed. This idea is the basis of modern science. . . . It's the basis of the fallacy that every-thing out there is mere mechanism, mere resource, mere *stuff* — things to be manipulated. . . . It's not Ronald Reagan or Walter Mondale that's the issue, it's the system they represent." By contrast, to "talk of Green politics, bio-regionalism, bio-centrism, [is to] stand up for values, for ideals, for dreams, for *reality*. To ask the deep questions, to get us back to the good old Neanderthal, Aborigine, Bushman, Lakota conscious-ness."[28]

But if biocentrists rejected dualism, what did they replace it with? One alternative, known as pluralism, holds that the world consists of many substances. But this philosophy isolates things from one another to an even greater extent. Whereas dualism creates an unbridgeable gulf between two substances, mind and body, pluralism alienates all things from one another.[29]

By repudiating pluralism and dualism, Foreman and his fellow bio-centrists had implicitly endorsed the only alternative — monism. The universe, they believed, is infused with and united by spirit. Unknow-ingly they were treading a well-beaten path blazed by Hegel and Haeckel. Nevertheless, their critique of dualism and endorsement of monism would catch on, and by 1991 even Senator Al Gore would de-nounce Descartes and embrace the idea of a unitary reality infused with spirit. "The Cartesian approach to the human story," Gore wrote, "al-lows us to believe we are separate from the earth, entitled to view it as nothing more than an inanimate collection of resources that we can ex-ploit however we like; and this fundamental misperception has led us to our current crisis."[30]

"The cleavage in the modern world between mind and body, man and nature, has created a new kind of addiction," Gore added. "I believe that our civilization is, in effect, addicted to the consumption of the earth it-self." Bemoaning the consequent "spiritual loss," Gore pushed for a new vision in which a sacred spirit, or God, rather than being separate from the world, is "manifest" in everything. Only when we realize that "the image of God can be seen in every corner of creation" will we be able to heal "the long schism between science and religion."[31]

By 1983, therefore, monism and holism had united to drive activists. But ideas do not show up on television, and only occasionally appear in magazines. Both the visual and the print media were instead obsessed with finding stories that offered color and action. So they missed the true significance and power of this new movement. Biocentrism was overlooked amidst the reports of profane escapades.

Radicals, moreover, encouraged this obsession with the visual. Not only did they recognize its power to change public values, but also they saw themselves as imitating art, from *Foundations* to *The Monkey-wrench Gang*, then *Ecotopia*, and finally *Foundations II*. They were living fantasies, larger than life! And so the legend of Earth First! grew. In December 1983 an article appeared in *Outside* magazine making Earth First!ers look, said Roselle, "like Victor Mature playing Samson." The next year an *Esquire* story again depicted them as bearded, macho outdoors lunatics. Soon editors all over the country were sending stringers to Round River Rendezvous and to covert "actions" to bring back stories of mayhem in the boondocks.[32]

Earth First!, Greenpeace, and other bioregional groups had discovered what worked. Spiking trees, ramming ships, scaling buildings, and dressing up as bears, owls, and other woodland creatures, they put on performances that cried out for television coverage. It was not long before the networks were beating a path to their door. Eventually everyone this side of Mars would see video images of brave Sea Shepherds and Greenpeacers steering their little Zodiacs between whale and harpoon.

But as they watched, few in the press or public were aware that this was just the tip of an iceberg, the visual manifestation of an idea that was neither entertaining nor colorful, but that would prove to be more powerful and longer lasting than the radical movement itself.

These biocentric ideas and mediagenic images came together that morning on Bald Mountain. By standing tall in front of the bulldozer, Roselle had set the precedent for the kind of protest that would be repeated again and again throughout the Northwest. He and his friends were bringing national media attention to the plight of old growth, which had been largely ignored by the mainstream press.

Also, they had seemingly accomplished the impossible — to make the Sierra Club look moderate. This encouraged mainline groups to join the conflict, and opened the pocketbooks of the trendy rich who sought vicarious means to fight for spotted owls and old growth. Soon the newly established Seattle office of the Sierra Club Legal Defense Fund would be escalating the issue to another level.[33]

Just before the 1983 Round River Rendezvous at Little Granite Creek Canyon near Goose, Wyoming, Roselle learned that he had won his lawsuit over the Bald Mountain Road. The courts agreed that the Forest Service must complete an environmental impact statement, assessing the ecological implications of the road, before proceeding with construction. Earth First! had won its first — and what would prove to be its only — lawsuit.[34]

Popping champagne corks, Roselle and his friends believed that the stage was set for even greater successes. As Stewart McBride, the *Outside* reporter, was attending the Rendezvous, they sensed that great publicity was on the way. But their victory would be short-lived. Within a year the Oregon Wilderness bill was signed, again excluding Bald Mountain from protection.[35] The war was escalating, and the Earth First!ers needed to find an even bigger issue than Bald Mountain, an issue that, loaded with symbolism, would distill the conflict over forests to its essence — a confrontation between the forces of good and evil.

And indeed, unknown to them, such a conflagration lay just ahead, in the sleepy town of Scotia. Pacific Lumber was a time bomb about to go off. And when it did, Earth First! would get not only its publicity but also more grief than Roselle could have imagined. The battle of Redwood Summer loomed, a conflict that would fracture Earth First! like a raw egg hit by a hammer, changing the mainstream movement in ways no one had anticipated.

16

WALL STREET
FORESTRY

WOODY MURPHY STOOD BY HIS PICKUP, watching a loader stack Douglas fir logs onto waiting trucks. Things were looking up. At last he had the job he wanted. Repeatedly passed over for promotion at Pacific Lumber, he finally quit in 1983 to form his own logging company. Meanwhile, his brother Warren, moving up in the Palco hierarchy, had just been made director of lumber operations.[1]

Woody's mobile phone rang. It was Warren.

"Get to a secure line as soon as possible," Warren said mysteriously. Woody, wondering what it was all about, drove to a pay phone in Dunsmuir, about eight miles from the logging site, and called his brother back.

"A guy named Charles E. Hurwitz wants to buy the company," Warren told him. Neither had ever heard of Hurwitz. But they soon learned. Often referred to as "the billionaire from Houston," Hurwitz had a reputation for purchasing undervalued companies then selling off their assets to liquidate his debt. At 5:30 that morning, September 30, 1985, Hurwitz had awakened company president Gene Elam with a telephone call to announce his intention to purchase Pacific Lumber — 100 percent of the stock in cash — for $36 a share, or $746 million. Then, to the startled and still groggy Elam, he drawled wryly, "I suppose you won't need a shower to wake you up."[2]

The brothers drove to see Bill Bertain, who had just moved his office to a new location in an old frame house on Eureka's J Street. From that moment on, Bertain remembers, "it was war." Together they began to plot a defense against what they felt was Hurwitz's "pitiful offer." Although Woody no longer worked for Palco, he, along with Warren, their mother, Suzanne Murphy Beaver, and other members of the extended family, still owned around 20 percent of the company.

Meanwhile, Elam looked for expert help. He contacted Palco's San Francisco law firm, Pillsbury, Madison, and Sutro, which in turn hired the New York merger specialists Wachtell Lipton and the Wall Street investment firm Salomon Brothers.[3]

Two days after Hurwitz's phone call Elam convened an informal meeting with top management and the Salomon representative, Roger Miller. The group sat around the table in stunned silence as the balding and bespectacled Elam, evincing deference to Miller, discussed whether their best strategy was defense (incurring more debt or seeking a "white knight"), offense (suing Hurwitz), or surrender. Miller urged caution, suggesting that they might lose if they decided to fight.[4]

In fact, Palco was a fatted calf for Hurwitz. Before the offer company stock was trading for $33 a share, while conservative estimates put its true value, based on the large tree inventory, at $70. Even this would turn out to be a gross underestimate. But the board members had almost no idea what the company's value was. They were not even aware how many trees Palco owned. The lords of Scotia were in over their heads and knew it. Blueblooded babes in the woods, they felt themselves no match for a Wall Street fighter like Hurwitz.[5]

In the Old West, before land went to patent, cattlemen often fought to protect their grazing lands. But more effective than force, many stockmen found, was fear. It was better to scare away trespassers than to shoot them. Ranchers would hire a gunman with a quick-draw reputation and spread stories of their new employee's homicidal prowess. By promoting this ornery image, a rancher could chase interlopers off the range without firing a shot.

So it was with Hurwitz. Though not so well known as his confederates Ivan Boesky and Michael Milken, he had nevertheless quietly gained a reputation as one of the baddest corporate raiders, a shark among sharks during this heyday of Reaganite free market feeding frenzy. Not someone to let the green grass grow under someone else's feet, Hurwitz, critics charged, did well by doing ill. In the fight for Pacific Lumber, his infamy would be a weapon, sowing fear and confusion into the ranks of the Palco board.[6]

Shortly after Elam received the fateful call, company managers began to play catch-up, studying the career of this enigmatic Texan. And what they learned only fed their unease. Forty-five years old, tall, and well-dressed, Hurwitz avoided publicity like an albino does the sun. So he went largely unnoticed during the period of leveraged buyout mania which consumed the financial world at that time. Raised in Kilgore,

Texas, two hundred miles northeast of Houston, Hurwitz came from an Orthodox Jewish family, grandson of a rabbi and son of a clothing retailer. Believing in the value of knowledge, he invariably outresearched his opponents. He knew the edge that comes with superior information, and had assembled teams of highly qualified experts who produced exceptionally thorough data.[7]

His reputation as a shark originated in 1969, after he sold a mutual fund he had established, the Hedge Fund of America, reportedly at a loss. Deciding that his forte was in buying stock, Hurwitz purchased a cash-rich private mutual fund, the Summit Group, which he then took public. In 1971 the Securities and Exchange Commission charged him with artificially inflating the price of securities in the public offering of Summit, which had since gone bankrupt. Without admitting guilt, he signed a consent decree, barring him from violating securities laws.[8]

After taking over Federated Development — a company with vast real estate holdings in the Southwest — in 1971, he soon had shareholders chewing their proxy ballots. To increase his control of Federated, he engineered a 1-for-40 reverse-share split that, according to the investment newsletter *13D Opportunities Report*, "wiped out over 200 shareholders," thus reducing their number so that Federated "would no longer be required to report its financial results to the S.E.C."[9]

In 1982 Hurwitz tried this ploy again, proposing a 1-for-600 reverse-stock split, to reduce the company's outstanding shares from 329,000 to 547. Enraged shareholders sued, and the plan was dropped. In 1977 the New York superintendent of insurance filed suit against Hurwitz for mismanagement and fraud for allegedly "upstreaming" (transferring) $834,000 from Summit to one of its parent companies, also owned by the Texan. He settled by paying what the New York Insurance Department called a "considerable sum of money."[10]

In 1978 the Property Trust of America sued Hurwitz for falsely claiming that he had acquired shares of the trust for "investment purposes." He dropped the purchase bid after a temporary restraining order was issued against him. The same year Hurwitz obtained control of McCulloch Oil, founded by the man who had invented the chain saw, which he dubbed MCO Holdings and stripped of everything but $10 million in cash. MCO became the holding company that controlled his empire.[11]

In 1982 Hurwitz acquired Simplicity Patterns, the cash-rich distributor of women's dress patterns. Two years later, in December 1984, he sold the clothing operation and changed the company's name to Maxxam Corporation. Maxxam, along with Federated, supplied the money he used to launch his takeover attacks.[12]

Along the way, Hurwitz gained fame for "greenmail." Four or more times — for sizable investments in Castle and Cook, a Hawaiian real estate company; Armsted Industries, a railroad and building products firm; UNC Resources, a high-tech aerospace firm; and Alamito, a Southwestern electric utility — he used either Simplicity (Maxxam) or Federated to buy into a firm, then allowed the company's board to buy him out at a premium.

In April 1983 Hurwitz bought his way into the savings and loan club when Federated acquired a controlling interest in the United Financial Group, a Texas-based holding company that owned United Savings Association of Texas — the state's fourth largest, with sixty-six branches throughout Texas. Soon after, the company, like other S&Ls, joined the real estate race, buying $23 million worth of apartments and condominiums around Houston and Brownsville by the end of the year.[13]

By using Maxxam and Federated to buy and strip companies, then employing the cash-rich empty shells to purchase other businesses, Hurwitz constructed, piece by piece, a nearly impenetrable maze of interlocking corporations. At the top stood Federated and MCO Holdings. The latter controlled the Maxxam Group and MCO Properties, while Maxxam Group in turn controlled Maxxam Properties (MPI) and the MXM Corporation. And Hurwitz ran the whole show. He was chairman of the board and chief executive officer of the Maxxam Group, Federated, and MCO Holdings, and director of Maxxam Properties and MCO Properties.[14]

So the more the Palco board heard about Hurwitz, the less they liked. He was a figure from their worst nightmares. They had learned their trade at Stanford and in the tranquil forest; he had honed his skills in the Wall Street jungle, after graduating with a degree in business from the University of Oklahoma in 1962. Treating laws like flexible fly rods, he snagged the big fish. And now he had Palco on the hook.

They did not know, however, how carefully Hurwitz had cast for this trophy.

Planning had begun in December 1984. United Savings was a money spigot, and the sale of Simplicity's pattern business to Triton Groups that month left Hurwitz awash in liquidity. Hurwitz had the organization and the cash. All he needed was another target.[15]

Wasting no time, immediately after the Simplicity sale Hurwitz assigned Robert Rosen, vice chairman of Maxxam, who worked in the New York office, to develop a short list of possible takeover candidates. Michael Milken's investment firm, Drexel Burnham Lambert, was asked to help. In May Maxxam raised $150 million through a Milken-backed junk bond offering to finance future acquisitions. By August MCO Holdings had raised another $35 million.[16]

After several failed acquisition attempts Rosen had enlisted the help of Bob Quirk, a Drexel securities analyst and expert on the forest products industry, to examine timber takeover targets. Quirk compiled a list of eight to ten companies, one of which was Pacific Lumber. Palco seemed ideal. "We saw a company," Hurwitz would say later, "with little debt, no concentration of ownership, and some timber assets that appeared to be essentially free from foreign competition."[17]

And the company was ripe for picking. Grossly undervalued, it had little debt. It possessed 197,000 acres of the most valuable redwood forests on earth. A single tree can be worth $30,000 on the stump and yield enough lumber to supply decks and siding for an entire housing subdivision. It owned several subsidiaries, such as Victor Welding, which were cash cows, producing $28 million in operating income in 1984. It had a worker pension plan worth $97 million — $60 million in excess of what was needed to cover liabilities. On June 24 Hurwitz secretly began buying Palco stock.[18]

Indeed, Hurwitz understood Palco's assets better than the company's own board. For these old-time timber people had almost no idea how many trees they owned. Taking a timber inventory is what foresters call "doing a cruise." But because California's forest tax was calculated on the basis of standing volumes, managers apparently believed it better not to know how much the company's trees had grown. Palco had not done a cruise since 1955–56. Instead, it had made estimates based on assumed growth rates. With this theorizing, management guessed its holdings at 5.2 billion board feet, an inventory Salomon Brothers would estimate in October 1985 to be worth between $1.07 and $1.2 billion, bringing the per share value of Palco, net of liabilities, to between $60.28 and $77.96. Even this, however, was a gross undervaluation. The company had been such a good conservationist that its trees had grown more than management realized.[19]

But Hurwitz and Milken knew. During the summer of 1985 they had quietly conducted cruises of their own. On July 30 Milken had hired the Arcata firm of Western Timber Services to do a cruise, which found between 4.25 and 5.35 billion board feet. Not trusting this report, on August 14 they engaged the respected Portland firm of Mason, Bruce, and Girard, which put the figure between 6.6 and 8.9 billion board feet, with the "'best estimate' as 8 billion."[20]

Bingo! Palco had as much as 60 percent more timber than its own directors thought. The entire inventory was worth at least $2 billion. This meant that Palco shares, which were selling at $33, might be worth as much as $90. The company was a steal. In early August Rosen started negotiations with the Irving Trust Company to see if the bank would put up the money to buy Pacific Lumber. It would later be charged that Hurwitz joined with Milken in the familiar Wall Street game of tit for tat, each agreeing to purchase the other's junk bonds. As the Federal Deposit Insurance Corporation would put it: "At the direction of the Milken group USAT [United Savings] purchased approximately $1.4 billion of Drexel underwritten junk bonds. In exchange, the Milken group financed a number of schemes for Charles Hurwitz, the primary owner of United Financial Group."[21]

By midsummer Hurwitz had the money. In addition to $150 million from the Drexel pool, he had secured a $300 million line of credit with Irving Trust and another $450 million from Milken's junk bonds. Proceeding with utmost secrecy, by early August Hurwitz had acquired $14.5 million worth of Palco shares. But there were two problems.[22]

The first was the Hart-Scott-Rodino Act, which required Maxxam to notify Pacific Lumber of its takeover plans when it purchased $15 million of the timber company's stock. This would have alerted the Palco board, giving it time to construct a defense. The second impediment was article 6 of Palco's own articles of incorporation, which required that a proposed hostile merger with anyone owning 5 percent or more of Palco stock must be approved by 80 percent of the holders of the outstanding shares. This provision would in effect allow the Murphy family to stall or perhaps even veto the transaction.[23]

To avoid triggering Hart-Scott-Rodino, Hurwitz needed to "park" stock — to find someone to buy and hold shares for him until the takeover attempt became public. But stock parking is illegal. Nevertheless, on August 8 Hurwitz told the Los Angeles stockbroker Boyd Jeffries that he would be interested in purchasing 500,000 shares of Palco stock, and Jeffries began buying large blocks from institutional funds around the country. By August 6 Maxxam had stopped buying Palco stock and did not resume purchases until September 27, the last trade date before the tender offer. That day Hurwitz bought 539,600 shares, worth $15 million, from Jeffries at $29.10, almost $4 below the $33 that Palco was trading at that day, thus gaining control of more than $28 million of Palco stock without triggering Hart-Scott-Rodino.

This looked like stock parking. As Congressman Thomas Bliley of Virginia subsequently put it to Hurwitz during hearings on the takeover: "I am a little confused. . . . You talked to him [Jeffries] on August

8, you said, 'Boyd, I am interested in Pacific Lumber, if you can acquire 500,000 shares for me, I will buy them.' . . . And then you tell me that you didn't have any explicit or implicit agreement with him to buy those shares and suddenly you buy 400 some odd thousand from him on the 27th at $29.10, which is approximately $4 less than the market at the time."[24]

But, as Hurwitz explained to Bliley, it wasn't stock parking if he and Jeffries did not have a prior agreement that the latter would buy stock for him at a prearranged price. And in spite of the four-dollar discount Jeffries gave Hurwitz, the Texan insisted that he had struck no such deal. Likewise, equally equivocal circumstances allowed Hurwitz to avoid the 80 percent rule of article 6. Immediately after Hurwitz's first tender offer at $36, Boesky began buying Palco stock. By October 21 he had purchased more than 5 percent of the company's stock — all of which he eventually sold to Maxxam.

What roles were Boesky and Milken playing? Were they merely opportunists driving up the price of Palco's stock, thus fattening Drexel's commission before selling their shares to Maxxam at a premium? Or were they, as Bill Bertain suspected, Hurwitz's agents, doing double duty by parking stock so the Houston billionaire could avoid the 5 percent rule while simultaneously acting as "black knights" to stampede the board in Hurwitz's direction?[25]

Whatever the intent, Boesky and Milken, like Jeffries, helped Hurwitz. In effect, if not technically, they had parked stock for him, allowing Maxxam to escape the provisions of both Hart-Scott-Rodino and article 6. The law was bent like a graphite fly rod, and all Hurwitz had to do was reel in the big sucker.[26]

Immediately after the $36 offer was announced, the price of Palco shares rose to above $38. On October 2 Maxxam boosted its offer to $38.50. Calling this bid "unconscionable," Elam described Hurwitz as "a notorious takeover artist . . . who knowingly engaged in a pattern of racketeering activity consisting of multiple acts of securities fraud."[27]

Meanwhile, Bertain recalls, the Palco board "snapped into inaction." While they simultaneously resolved both to defend and counterattack, their decisions led inexorably to surrender. As defense, at its first full meeting on October 9, the board unanimously rejected the Maxxam tender offer. To put the excess $60 million in retirement funds out of Hurwitz's reach, they amended the rules so that, in event of an unapproved change of control, the money would go immediately to existing employees and retirees. They resolved to seek alternative bidders, or "white knights." And to make the takeover more expensive for Hurwitz, they approved generous "golden parachute" provisions for their own officers.[28]

To retaliate, the same day Palco filed suit to block the Maxxam offer, citing numerous violations of federal securities laws and the Racketeer Influenced and Corrupt Organizations Act (RICO), and alleged that Hurwitz's background and experience "demonstrate a conspicuous absence of the integrity, competence and fitness necessary to control or manage a substantial business enterprise."[29]

Saying that "the purported financing for the MXM tender offer — consisting of virtually 100 percent borrowed funds — is illusory," the Palco suit alleged that Maxxam had made an illegal deal with Drexel, devising "a fraudulent and deceptive scheme to conceal their intention to acquire Pacific Lumber," whereby Maxxam "was to receive a majority interest in Pacific Lumber, while Drexel was to receive warrants for stock in Maxxam and huge fees totaling many millions of dollars."[30]

But this was whistling in the dark. "Everybody was walking around like peacocks," remembers one board member, "like they knew what they were doing when in fact nobody did." Indeed, ignorance and incompetence, Bertain thought, ruled the board throughout October. Not trusting company management, Bertain hired the San Francisco law firm of Khourie and Crew to help the Murphys.[31]

Why, Bertain wondered, had Palco not immediately taken the necessary steps to borrow $200 million or so and declared a special dividend in that amount, thereby providing a premium to the shareholders at least equivalent to that offered by Hurwitz, and thus rendering the company much less attractive to a takeover artist? This added debt would have forced Hurwitz to raise more cash, buying time. And why did the company not tell the whole world how much timber Palco had? Once the shareholders knew, they would lose interest in the Hurwitz deal, and environmentalists would rally to the company's side.

Instead, the company had hired Salomon Brothers as consultants — a firm Bertain would later discover was simultaneously working for Hurwitz, in November marketing $1 billion in mortgage-backed securities for his Texas Savings and Loan. To compound this error, on October 11 the board acceded to Salomon's request to amend the New York firm's compensation contract, agreeing to pay Salomon more if the takeover succeeded than if it failed.

To Bertain the arrangement seemed crazy: Palco agreed to pay Salomon $2.5 million if the company remained independent. But if the takeover was successful, the consultant would receive a percentage of the purchase price above $38.50 a share. This meant that if Hurwitz purchased Palco at, say, $38.51, Salomon would receive a fee of $4.3 million, and thus be rewarded $1.8 million for failure.[32]

Throughout October the board seemed to do nothing right. Some of its letters to possible white knights didn't go out until October 16. And although this search received a hundred responses, only three or four potential buyers actually sent emissaries to Scotia, and none made competing bids. Palco blamed the bad housing market.[33]

Meanwhile, Hurwitz stepped up the pressure, wielding first a stick, then a carrot. On October 18 he filed suit in Maine against the board, challenging the golden parachute and retirement fund amendments. Their perks threatened, the board members' resolve weakened. Elam agreed to meet with Hurwitz. After an abortive encounter on October 19, they assembled again two days later, when Hurwitz raised his bid to $39.50 a share, then to $40. At that Elam surrendered, shaking hands on the deal. The next day Elam presented the offer to board members, urging them to take it. After Miller likewise argued that it was a good deal, they agreed, but reluctantly. "We were scared," one board member said later.[34]

Fear and greed were good reasons for capitulation. The board faced an exquisite dilemma. If they made public Salomon's estimate that Palco stock was worth twice the tender offer, they would also have to admit that no cruise had been done in nearly thirty years, thus invoking the wrath — and lawsuits — of shareholders. Admitting they did not know how much timber Palco had would have been equivalent to pleading guilty to incompetence. Yet hiding the true value would mislead investors into believing that Hurwitz's bid was a generous one. The only way the board could escape accountability for the error was to capitulate before it was revealed, then seek protection from litigation. And that was what Hurwitz offered.

As part of the deal, Hurwitz promised to restore the golden parachute provisions and to sweeten the severance package of top management by $751,501. He pledged not to reduce executive salaries for three years, and to make an effort to put Elam on the executive committee of the board of directors of Maxxam. But, most important, he agreed to indemnify board members against subsequent stockholder suits.[35]

By October 24 the deal was done. The board sent a letter to shareholders, along with a news release stating — in an opinion joined by Salomon — that $40 was a fair price and recommending the merger, but without saying that Salomon had estimated Palco's net worth to be perhaps over $70 a share.[36]

Hurwitz had bought a company that owned at least $2 billion in trees for $823 million by amassing a total debt of $750 million, mostly in junk bonds requiring balloon payments beginning in 1990. Palco's debt, which was $46 million in 1985, would jump to $591 million in 1986, and nearly $750 million in 1987. Wall Street was ecstatic. "A brilliant investment coup," *13D Opportunities Report* called the merger. Hurwitz would tell Congress that the deal "was good for the company, good for its shareholders, good for employees, and good for the somewhat depressed North Coast California logging community." But few in Scotia believed these claims.[37]

Life in the Peace Zone, they felt, had come to an end. Experiencing the first change in Palco's ownership in their lifetimes, workers walked around in a daze, worrying about pensions, housing, and the college scholarship program. Their fix, they felt, revealed the truth of the axiom that no good deed goes unpunished. If Palco had squandered the fortune of the forests as the other companies did, Hurwitz would have had no interest in it.[38]

"It felt like someone had died," recalled one employee, Fred Elliott. People began counting their pennies, spending only on necessities even as Christmas approached. Two hundred workers and their friends put an ad in the *Eureka Times Standard* on November 17 with the headline "Heritage in the Balance." The notice read:

> In all earnestness, we do not feel that a company of real estate investors from the East Coast can manage resources such as ours with the consideration that has been shown all these years by the Murphy Family. We wish to protect the integrity of our company, which has served our community so well. The fight is not over. . . . It is our sincere belief that if the company's leadership were back in the hands of the Murphy Family, the company's business, our environment, and the communities in which we live will continue to prosper.[39]

On December 16 Hurwitz came to Scotia and talked to the workers, who had assembled in the company's magnificent Winema Theater, built entirely of redwood. His visit was intended to mollify fears, but it didn't. "There's a little story about the Golden Rule," Hurwitz told his audience, "He who has the gold, rules." Suddenly the magnitude of the change hit home. Gone was the Murphy paternalism. Gone was the collegiality between management and workers. What — and who — would be next?[40]

Bertain and the Murphys continued the fight, suing Hurwitz on their own. But on February 6 San Francisco Federal District Court judge William Schwarzer, an appointee of Hurwitz's sometime business partner former President Gerald Ford, found against them. Hurwitz's purchase of Palco was complete. The winds of change had reached Scotia, bringing gusts signaling the approach of a giant storm.[41]

Kelly Bettiga was tired. Before the takeover his work on the cleanup detail of Mill B had begun at 4:00 in the afternoon and ended at 1:00 A.M. On that schedule a man could get a decent night's sleep. But then Hurwitz moved the day shift to 5:30 in the afternoon. That meant he didn't get off until 2:30 in the morning, which made it hard to get enough rest, especially since he was taking college classes now. But there was nothing he could do about it.

Down at the repair department Peter Kayes, a blacksmith, sensed his days at Palco were numbered. He didn't mind when management announced it was increasing timber harvests by 20 percent, which, although requiring longer hours also meant more money. But first the company began hiring gyppos instead of taking on more full-time employees. Then it eliminated the pension fund, promising to replace it with a retirement insurance policy, which, it said, was just as good. So now Kayes, like most of his friends, were anxious. Loggers and cutters wondered if they might lose jobs to the gyppos, and everyone started to speculate about the future.[42]

They were feeling the sudden transformation that came to Scotia in the spring of 1986. Soon after the takeover Hurwitz stepped up production. Sixty-hour work weeks became common. Timber crews worked overtime in the forests. In June Elam left the company and was replaced by Hurwitz's associate William Leone. Warren Murphy was out after coming to work one day to find his desk emptied. Several other oldtimers switched sides. Robert Stephens, the chief forester, who had been wanting the company to clear-cut for years, was elated.[43]

The liquidation began. To pay debts, Hurwitz sold the welding division for $325 million and the San Francisco headquarters for $32 million. Then, as Hurwitz had promised, the employee pension fund went to help pay off the debt. Now Palco was searching for a cheap insurance policy to replace it.[44] In March Hurwitz's new board of directors hired a consultant, Wyatt and Company, to solicit bids for a pension insurance plan. Five companies responded. In addition, a member of the Maxxam board directed Palco to solicit a bid from Executive Life, run by Fred Carr, who had helped Hurwitz with the takeover by eventually buying $343 million of the Drexel junk bonds.[45]

Then in July Palco hired its own consultant, Conning and Company, to evaluate the companies from whom Palco had received bids. Conning assigned Executive Life an A rating, as compared with AAA and AA for the others — Metropolitan, Prudential, Equitable, and Aetna — suggesting that Carr's company was less safe than the rest. Nevertheless, over the objections of Palco officers, Maxxam insisted that Carr get the business.[46]

Meanwhile, Maxxam turned its attention to timber harvests. In June a Palco junk bond offering through Drexel announced that to "generate additional cash flow," the company expected "to increase the timber harvest to a level which may equal approximately two times Pacific Lumber's 1985 harvest." Its consultants Hammon, Jensen, Wallen, and Associates insisted that this would not deplete the forests. Since there was 30 percent more timber than had been realized, Palco could sustain this higher cut rate, they said, for twenty years. At that time, when "the majority of the forest will . . . be comprised of second growth trees," Palco could reduce harvest rates back to 1985 levels "and continue at that harvest level in perpetuity."[47]

In short, Maxxam would skim the excess timber which earlier management never knew it had, then return to a "sustained yield" policy. The only casualty would be old growth. So Hurwitz immediately accelerated harvests from 137 million board feet a year to 248 million board feet. Palco added three hundred employees, ordered longer work weeks, and bought a new sawmill. The cutting began.[48]

Many workers knew this couldn't last. Hurwitz was sending them on a voyage without enough fuel for the return trip. Even if the consultants were right, the big trees would be gone within a couple of decades, making Mill B, which specialized in the big logs, a dinosaur, and putting hundreds out of work. The people of Scotia were watching their lives wither away, one giant tree at a time. And who would save them?

17

OCCURRENCE AT
ALL SPECIES GROVE

IT WAS SEPTEMBER 30, 1987. Tarzan, otherwise known as Greg King, was wondering if he would ever get down from these trees alive. Here he was, having climbed more than thirty feet up a tree only once before (at his first tree-sit a few weeks earlier), swinging on a Tyrolean traverse that connected his tiny platform with Jane's, 150 feet from the ground above a giant banner proclaiming "Save the Old Growth — Earth First!!" as a gang of angry loggers threatened to cut him down.[1]

His companion, Jane, also called Mary Beth Nearing, stood on her three-by-six perch in a tree at the same height fifty feet away as television and newspaper reporters, standing behind the line of loggers, snapped photos, panned video cameras, and shouted questions at her. Banners reading "Pacific Lumber Stop the Plunder" and "Hurwitz Out of Humboldt" fluttered in the light afternoon breeze.[2]

At dusk three days earlier the two had sneaked into this old-growth redwood stand belonging to the Pacific Lumber Company. Working all night with the help of a well-organized team of Earth First!ers, they had hoisted two tree-sitting platforms and six hundred pounds of gear, including a CB radio to communicate with Earth First! lookouts, a cellular telephone to talk to the press, and enough food for two weeks.

At 5 A.M. King and Nearing ascended to their perches, determined to show the world that Hurwitz was destroying this exquisitely beautiful thousand-acre stand of ancient trees, which they called All Species Grove. But their first day up, no one came. The horrible prospect loomed that Palco and the press might not find them. Then, serendipitously and mysteriously, a helicopter landed in the clear-cut two hundred yards away, and an Associated Press reporter jumped out. As the chopper idled, the journalist, nervous about being discovered by Palco security, hurriedly interviewed the two by shouting questions from the base of their trees.

By nightfall, the journalist's story went over the wire, alerting both Palco management and other media. The next morning King and Nearing watched as a thirty-five-ton bulldozer cut a skid road toward them, followed by a dozen angry men in cork boots.[3]

"We're going to take your trees down," one said. King, terrified, picked up his cellular phone and called the sheriff, who asked, "What do you want me to do?"

But the loggers did not fell their trees. Under strict orders from management not to harm the sitters, they cut down the megaton goliaths that surrounded the couple instead. Enraged that by halting the harvest King and Nearing were shrinking their paychecks, the timber fallers wielded chain saws with enthusiasm, sending two-hundred-footers crashing and thwacking like thunder to the ground, and causing King and Nearing's trees to sway like schooner masts in a typhoon. After the cutters had created a clearing, they brought in blinding floodlights to illuminate the place at night, and stationed eight men to guard the two protesters.[4]

Then the newspaper reporters and television crews came, forming a thin line outside the loggers' defensive perimeter, where they took pictures and shouted questions as King conducted interviews on his cellular phone.

Thus, Palco played into Earth First!'s hands. The ugly scene created by its cutting looked dramatic on television. Stories of the tree-sit went out over the news wires. Interviews appeared in the *Santa Rosa Press-Democrat, Eureka Times-Standard, San Francisco Examiner, Los Angeles Times,* and television stations throughout the state. By the end of the week King and Nearing, whom the press had dubbed Tarzan and Jane, were cult folk heroes.

They had triumphed. But how were they going to escape?

It had been a helluva year. Just eighteen months earlier Greg King, a quiet, mild-mannered Bruce Wayne sort of guy, had been writing for *The Paper,* a Sonoma County journal. Now he was miraculously transformed into the scourge of Pacific Lumber — a nemesis who, in the eyes of loggers, was not so much Batman as the Joker.

King's family was one of the oldest in California. After settling by the Russian River in the 1860s, the first King made his fortune in timber. There was even a mountain chain named for the family — the King Range, now a conservation area. Greg himself grew up in Guerneville, just five miles from his family's original homestead, before attending the University of California at Santa Cruz.

After graduating from college in 1985, King joined *The Paper*, and soon found himself transformed from advocacy journalist to tree-sitting activist. Living in an apartment that overlooked a redwood grove belonging to the Louisiana Pacific Corporation, King one day saw cutters felling the trees. Angry and curious, he investigated. This led to a series of articles exposing Louisiana Pacific's "questionable compliance with state regulations," for which he won the Lincoln Steffens investigative journalism award, given by the Sonoma County Press Club.[5]

On a visit to Humboldt County in March 1986 to research these stories, King heard rumors about Palco's plans to double its harvests. Stopping by the EPIC offices in Garberville, he met Earth First! activist Darryl Cherney, who was on his own voyage of self-discovery. Soon Cherney would be contributing to King's education as an activist.

Compared with Waspy Westerner King, Cherney, a refugee from New York City, might have come from the other side of the moon. Growing up in Manhattan, where his father was a junior high school principal, Cherney was child actor, starring in thirty-five commercials before he was twelve. After receiving a bachelor's degree in English and a master's in urban education from Fordham University, he took a job as a record publicist before deciding that selling music was "corrupt." He next served a stint as a typing teacher at a business school in Times Square before quitting, again, for what he described as "moral reasons."[6]

Turning to a psychic, he experienced a mystical awakening and embraced vegetarianism and the occult. Traveling where "the spirit took him," he hitchhiked west, in 1985 settling in Garberville, where, heeding the call of the wild, he soon earned the nickname "Feral Darryl." He had found his calling: he would dismantle civilization cog by cog, turn cities into wilderness, and get humankind back in touch with its Pleistocene roots.

When they first met at the EPIC offices, Cherney invited King on a trip to Sally Bell Grove, but the reporter was unable to go. Instead, determining to find out more about Palco's activities, King obtained a copy of the Drexel securities prospectus announcing plans to double the rate of cut. Probing further, he found that Palco had filed forty-seven new timber harvest plans, covering ten thousand acres, with the California Department of Forestry, which must approve all cuts. Shocked, King wrote the department protesting its decision.[7]

Slowly, the battle was joined. In July 1986 the *San Francisco Chroni-*

cle published an open letter from Donald R. Nelson, business representative of the International Woodworkers Union local, to California's governor, senators, and other high officials, decrying the fact that "200,000 acres of prime Redwood timberland is being clearcut, divided, and sold off in chunks." Calling this "the greatest man made disaster ever to befall the Redwood Forests of Northern California," Nelson predicted that Scotia "will soon become a thing of the past, a subdivision will most likely replace it."

"Your help is needed, N O W ," he begged. "The people's right of eminent domain must be asserted to prevent the destruction of the economy of Humboldt County and Northern California."[8]

Despite his pleading, by fall the department had approved the company's plans calling for cuts of 10,289 acres. Fifteen of these, King would later learn, were clear-cuts covering 1,622 acres. In each of the two previous years Palco had applied for and received permission to harvest around 5,000 acres. But in actuality, he believed, the company had cut only 1,000 acres each year. Thus Hurwitz was free to carry out these approved but unrealized cuts as well, allowing him to take a total of 18,000 acres in a year.[9]

This was too much! King was steadily being drawn to shed his journalist's cloak of objectivity and don the mantle of an activist. Now he would pass the point of no return. In early November, realizing a long-time ambition, he accepted the editorship of the *North Coast News*. But immediately fate intervened to prevent his taking the desk job. Two days after accepting the post, King, still curious about the Palco story, persuaded Chuck Powell, a member of Garberville's Chamber of Commerce who ran a local janitorial service, to show him the Palco lands.[10]

Early on a November morning the two, along with an Earth First!er everyone knew only as "Mokai," drove up a rough dirt road into the mists of the high mountains of this coastal range to a place King dubbed Owl Creek Grove. Standing on a high point, King recalled, they saw "a legendary forest: steep, classic California coastal ridges, flowing for miles into the far distance, divided by year-round streams, and choked with huge redwood trees that sprouted before Christ's birth. This particular area was approximately 8,000 acres — never logged, rarely even walked upon."[11]

Later King would learn that this was not the unbroken, contiguous forest he had imagined. But at the time it appeared to be wilderness, and in it he also saw ugly signs of man's presence. Creeping down a steep slope marked by the deep scars of raw dirt dug by tractors, King and his friends spotted cutters, brandishing chain saws that buzzed like hornets, felling a tree two thousand years old. As they watched, Palco's director of forest operations, Robert Stephens, appeared. Accusing them of trespassing, he insisted that they leave, adding, "Don't come back, okay?" They hiked back to their car, where Palco security men waited to escort them off company lands.

Returning to Garberville, King phoned his publishers and resigned from *The Paper* then turned down the *North Coast News* job. He would move to Humboldt County, he told them, join Earth First!, and help stop the destruction of the forest.[12]

King wasted no time. Immediately after quitting *The Paper*, he wrote an article for the *Earth First! Journal* titled "Old Growth Redwood: The Final Solution." He had already helped Earth First! stage its first protest — on October 22 at Pacific Lumber headquarters in San Francisco — where he, along with David Brower, Dave Foreman, and Karen Pickett (Mike Roselle's wife) protested Maxxam's "evil plans" and "corporate greed." Other rallies followed, including one in Arcata in November and another in Scotia in December, where more than seventy Earth First!ers gathered to pray and sing and bash Hurwitz.[13]

In early January 1987 King moved permanently to Garberville and began writing to federal and state officials and conservation groups. He also contacted timber industry heads to ask for a meeting, threatening that if they didn't reach accommodation, "this will be a battle with years of litigation and civil disobedience."[14]

In response, Palco's executive vice president for timber operations, John Campbell, invited King to meet him at his Scotia office. But the two just talked past each other. Why, King asked, was Campbell willing to destroy the forest? The company man pointed out the window at the luxuriant stand of second-growth trees on the hillside. "Those trees," Campbell said, "were planted eighty years ago. Look at them now. We are not destroying forests, we are growing them. But if you accomplish your goal and stop logging, will you accompany me to the mill to say who should be laid off? Should I start with those fifty years old and work down, or those fifty and work up?"[15]

Campbell just couldn't understand, King thought. Second growth did not provide the conditions needed for the fertile understory critical to ecosystem health.

After the meeting the younger man returned to Garberville, realizing that there was no alternative to war. He would have to orchestrate a campaign to stop Palco. But this required strategy, planning, and, most important of all, good intelligence. He had to know what Palco was doing in the woods. So in late January King, Cherney, and Mokai took another exploratory hike, this time into the Shaw Creek Grove in the Owl Creek drainage, on Pacific Lumber lands. In this exquisite cathedral of tall trees, they found surveyors' ribbons, designating routes for roads, strung like Christmas tinsel on branches.

In February King, along with Nina Williams and Kurt Newman, undergraduates at Humboldt State, walked up the Lawrence Creek drainage, where they discovered a particularly beautiful flat stand which in April Earth First!ers would dub All Species Grove. And in March King tramped alone, thirty-five miles in two days, through the heart of Palco lands. On a ridge top he could see the entire drainage of the Little South Fork Elk River, including each of its many tributaries, and farther east the South Fork itself. Marching across this country, King came to one tiny feeder stream after another, rivulets that ran into the Little South Fork. He was, King felt, sitting at the top of the world, in the ur-forest where all the waters of the earth originated.

He decided to call this magnificent wilderness "Headwaters Forest." It was just too stupendous to let Hurwitz destroy it![16]

King's metamorphosis from reporter to activist continued, even as the venue of his education shifted northward. In March he was drawn to Oregon, where he gained his first combat experience. The locus was the Kalmiopsis, where in 1983 Roselle and friends had captured the imagination of this restless generation with his blockade of the Bald Mountain road. Despite Earth First!'s successful lawsuit to stop the road, in 1984 Senator Mark Hatfield had pushed through the Oregon Wilderness bill, which opened vast areas of Oregon's national forests to logging — including the Kalmiopsis. And once again Earth First! responded in force.[17]

Suddenly forests throughout Oregon became battlegrounds, as volunteers poured in from all directions to block roads, harass loggers, and picket Forest Service offices. The first hot spot was Breitenbush Springs, a rustic spa on the Middle Santiam River in the Willamette National Forest near Mill City. A countercultural resort surrounded by old-growth Douglas fir, frequented by hippies and pot farmers, Breitenbush possessed a chemistry made for conflict.[18]

It soon came. During the summer of 1985, loggers and Forest Service officials descended on the spot with chain saws and skyhooks. Local residents, supported by Earth First!ers, calling their forest "Millennium Grove" in honor of the longevity of the trees there, responded with anger. A rock climber and activist named Mike Jakubal, who called himself "Doug Fir," drove eight-inch pinions into the sides of a tree and scrambled up, hauling a plywood sheet and supplies of food and water after him. When loggers came the next day, he was perched on a platform eighty feet up, draped with an American flag and a banner proclaiming "Ecotopia Is Rising." Now this was novel! Loggers couldn't cut trees if people lived in them. Tree-sitting became a soaring success, snapping the imagination synapses of activists everywhere.[19]

By the spring of 1986 the Oregon Forest conflict had shifted to the Kalmiopsis again. Earth First!ers led by Jakubal, Mokai, and Nearing conducted action after action as contingents from the Golden Triangle and the Bay area, seeking to reinforce their Oregon brothers and sisters, filtered north in sixes and sevens to stage a protest, sing songs, spike trees, dress in animal costumes, smoke pot, lock themselves to bulldozers, bury themselves to the neck in the middle of logging roads, get arrested, and generally have a good time.[20]

In March three Berkeleyites were drinking beer in a pub after listening to Paul Watson tell a campus audience about ramming pirate whalers, chasing seal clubbers, and harassing dolphin killers, when they heard that Roselle was headed for the Kalmiopsis. Jumping in their car that night, they drove north, eventually landing in the Grants Pass jail and being featured in stories carried on three local television stations and in three newspapers, including the state's largest, the *Portland Oregonian*.[21]

In April the self-styled "Arcata Eight Affinity Group" traveled to the Kalmiopsis to celebrate John Muir's birthday. As some strummed guitars, others locked the gate to the Hobson Horn Timber Sale, to which another protester had chained himself with Kryptonite bike locks. At the invitation of Mokai, King also went to the Kalmiopsis, where he met Nearing and earned his spurs by spending a night in the Grants Pass jail. Then, hardened by conflict, he returned to Garberville. In April King and Mokai, working in the EPIC offices with a half dozen Humboldt State students, published a tabloid, *Old Growth in Crisis*, with photographs and stories, most of which were written by King.

Leading with the headline "CDF/Maxxam Devastate Last Virgin Redwoods — CDF: Big Timber's Rubber Stamp," a phrase that would have political implications later on, the tabloid offered hyperbolic stories titled "Watersheds Ravaged, Ask the Fish," "Forests Needed for All Species' Survival," "Where Have All the Critters Gone?," and "Maxxam: State Supported Terrorists."

Throughout it exuded romantic primitivism. "Almost 500 years ago,"

King wrote, "when Europeans came to this continent, they found an incredible expanse of forest stretching from coast to coast. It has been said that a squirrel starting on the east coast could traverse the country without touching food on the ground if it was so inclined." "Elegant and self-sustaining," King continued, "the old-growth forest is an ecological dance of organisms and processes." It is "a source of biological diversity, the cushion that provides resilience and stability to the biosphere."[22]

Once again Hutchinson's mantra — that biodiversity produces stability — was proving an incentive to activists, while the notion of a forest primeval revealed itself to be among the most enduring of American myths. Left alone, nature does not tend toward equilibrium but lurches wildly, propelled by rapid shifts in species composition, climate, and other conditions. Nearly all experts on prehistory agree that Native American hunting and burning radically altered the landscape before the first settlers arrived, and that forests, rather than shrinking, are perhaps more extensive in modern times than before Columbus landed. Far from being a land where a squirrel could jump from limb to limb across the continent, North America, according to the historian Stephen Pyne, was a place "where it was nearly possible to drive a stagecoach from the eastern seaboard to Saint Louis without benefit of a cleared road."[23]

The University of Wisconsin geographer William M. Denevan agrees:

> The Native American landscape of the early sixteenth century was a humanized landscape almost everywhere. Populations were large, forest composition had been modified, grasslands had been created, wildlife disrupted, and erosion was severe in places. Earthworks, roads, fields, and settlements were ubiquitous. With Indian depopulation in the wake of Old World disease, the environment recovered in many areas. A good argument can be made that the human presence was less visible in 1750 than it was in 1492.[24]

In short, as the ecological historian Charles Kay writes, "The modern concept of wilderness as areas without human influence is a myth." The continent, says Kay, "was not a 'wilderness' waiting to be discovered, instead it was home to tens of millions of aboriginal peoples before European-introduced diseases decimated their numbers." These peoples "structured entire plant and animal communities" by limiting wildlife populations with their hunting and "purposefully modifying the vegetation with fire." Game, relentlessly hunted, was usually scarce, and vegetation, rather than consisting mostly of mature forest, was constantly being renewed by frequent burning. Only animals such as bison, whose migrating herds periodically escaped pursuing hunters, persisted in relatively large numbers.[25]

The sights King saw from his ridge top, in particular, had been profoundly shaped by humans. Aboriginal peoples in California had long altered their environment through agriculture and, most especially, their use of fire. By coppicing (trimming), weeding, cultivating, and tillaging (digging for roots), Indians encouraged the growth of some plant species and discouraged others. Along the Sierra Nevada the Maidu, Miwok, and Mono tribes pruned redbud to stimulate production of long blood-red sprouts cherished for basketry. Pomo women in central California pruned sedge fields to produce white root, a rhizome also prized for basketry.[26]

And throughout the state Indians intentionally ignited forest fires. In California, writes the archaeologist Henry Lewis, burning was not a "forest management program" but a "hunting-gathering management program" intended to drive game and improve habitat. It was designed to reduce old-growth stands, which did not support many large mammals, and increase early successional plant communities, which provided better conditions for both edible berries and game. This burning transformed forests into savannas and early successional plant communities chock full of the nuts, game, berries, and shrubs the indigenous peoples used for food and tools. Only later, after settlers began suppressing fires, did these open places shrink and forests spread.[27]

By burning, many California tribes turned forests into fields. Along the North Coast they burned to promote oak, which provided acorns, mock orange for making arrows, and elderberries for musical instruments. In 1916 a Yurok Indian told an interviewer, "Our legends tell when [our ancestors] arrived in the Klamath River country that there were thousands of acres of prairie lands and with all the burning that they could do the country has been growing up in timber more and more." Trinity County (adjacent to Humboldt), now largely forested, was open prairie prior to the arrival of Europeans. Areas of the north fork of the Eel River, near Scotia, which are forests today were once open fields used by the first settlers as grazing pastures for cattle and sheep.[28]

But after more settlers came and began suppressing fires, the forests spread. In 1910 the University of California forest historian Willis Linn Jepson reported that "with an increasing control of annual fires, the forests and woods of this whole region are showing a decidedly aggressive character and are encroaching steadily on the barren lands. There is today more wooded area in Humboldt County than when the white man came over a half-century since."[29]

By 1985, after nearly a century of fire suppression, firs were shading out the oak, and ponderosa pine, once an abundant shade-intolerant species, was almost entirely gone. According to one study, during this period Douglas fir increased by 500 percent, while oak woodland decreased by around 80 percent. In Oregon and Washington the area of protected Douglas fir wilderness had grown from 3 million acres in 1970 to over 5 million in 1987. Remaining old growth was twice the amount that had been harvested since 1950, and over half of that lay in preserves that were off-limits to logging.[30]

And, surprisingly, studies suggested that redwoods covered most of their original range. A 1988 review of biogeographical literature by the Humboldt State University forester Lawrence Fox found that estimates of the "natural range" of redwoods (based on soil and weather conditions) ranged from 1.9 and 2.17 million acres. Using color infrared aerial photography and older NASA photos, Fox determined that the big trees still occupied around 1.95 million acres.[31]

So, how should these groves best be protected? If not by clear-cutting then by Fritz's selection cutting? Or by pure preservation? King did not say. And in fact there was no simple answer, although many studies showed that, often, clear-cutting was best. A rudimentary "New Forestry" program had been introduced to the redwood region in the early 1970s. And although this research was never as intense as its counterpart in Douglas fir forests to the north, biologists had learned enough to know that there are no simple answers.[32]

In 1971 the silviculturalist Anthony Smith urged "a New Forestry program," consisting of "timber harvesting and management methods that protect and conserve the soil, water, wildlife, vegetation ecosystem, recreational opportunities, scenery, and the timber itself." And in 1973 the forest ecologist Peter Twight expanded on what such ecological management must amount to: "In the redwoods this means the use of selection or group selection cutting rather than the now well-documented destructive practice of large-block clearcutting in old-growth redwood."[33]

In 1979 the city of Arcata began to experiment with Twight's New Forestry in its 1,200-acre second-growth redwood forest. Like the New Foresters of Oregon, the Arcata team — including experts in wildlife, silviculture, watershed, soils, fisheries, ecology, and economics —

found that spotted owls and other "old-growth sensitive species such as salamander" were concentrated in portions of the second-growth redwood forests that contained residual large trees, snags, and downed logs that remained after the original harvest of the old-growth timber in the late 1800s.[34]

But selection, they found, was not the panacea they had expected. In 1990 the forester Phillip Lowell wrote: "Both foresters and researchers began to question the concept of selective harvesting as experience and measurement began to show that in many areas selection did not deliver the expected responses. . . . There is increasing evidence that clearcutting as a silvicultural method and an ecological mechanism is an extension of nature's method of perpetuating redwood as a forest type."[35]

Other scientists reached similar conclusions. After "cutting trials" at Casper Creek in Jackson State Forest near Fort Bragg, the California Department of Forestry concluded that "selection logging to improve the growth response is too late when the stands are beyond eighty years. Mortality is heavy."[36]

In these experiments, begun in 1959, silviculturalists established different "test blocks." Some stands were clear-cut, others thinned by varying amounts, and still others left untouched. The state found that the more trees they cut, the greater the redwood regeneration. The undisturbed stands experienced almost no regrowth of any kind and the heaviest mortality; the areas of light selection encouraged resurgence of shade-tolerant grand fir and hemlock. But in the clear-cuts redwood sprang back in profusion, covering almost 93 percent of the area.[37]

Such discoveries prompted some silviculturalists to adopt more complex strategies resembling those at Andrews Experimental Forest. Rather than using one cutting system, the Arcata experimenters combined many techniques. In some places, next to mature stands they thinned older trees or made very small (six-acre) clear-cuts. In others they promoted green trees and mixes of hardwood and softwood. Along stream corridors they kept late successional stands intact. They left the rotten logs and a minimum of five snags per acre, scattered slash, and replanted.[38]

Private forest owners, including Simpson Timber, developed similar strategies. And, as a result of this mixed management, by 1985 redwood forests were growing as they never had before. New forests were adding volume at the phenomenal rate of 2.9 percent a year, and in some places growth was exceeding 6 percent. Since 1975 the number of softwood trees of all species in the region that were five inches in diameter or larger increased 55 percent. Growth was exceeding harvest by 658 million board feet a year.[39]

Later a University of California study would show that the outlook for continued sustainable forestry on private lands was excellent, concluding: "Prospects are good that the private timber harvest in California can be maintained at or around recent levels for the foreseeable future, provided forest practice regulations do not become significantly more restrictive."[40]

Thus, by the time King's tabloid appeared, historians and archaeologists knew that undisturbed redwood wilderness was a myth, and scientists had accumulated nearly fifty years' experience, beginning with Fritz's "wonder plot" experiments, suggesting that there was no single royal road to forest health. Sometimes even clear-cutting was best.

But King's errors went unchallenged. Emotion and plausibility, not truth, count in politics. Regardless of their ecological attributes, clear-cuts are ugly as sin, and few can watch a thousand-year-old giant redwood cut down without feeling a strong sense of loss. By treating these magnificent trees merely as capital assets to be liquidated as if they were so many car parts, Hurwitz offended the sensibility of the public.

So the tabloid said what many were ready to believe. By giving harvested stands appealing names such as All Species Grove and Headwaters Forest, it conveyed an aura of romance that heightened the feeling of an Eden in decline. By locating groves on a map, it gave the public its first glimpse of Palco's intentions. By inviting activists to protest, it served as a call to arms.

And the timing was perfect. People had already begun to pay attention. Prompted by Earth First!, in January the *San Francisco Chronicle* ran a story on the takeover. At the same time, KUED-TV of San Francisco aired a piece sympathetic to Earth First! which was later broadcast in part on PBS's *MacNeil-Lehrer News Hour*. In February *Business Week* ran a story titled "A Takeover Artist Who's Turning Redwoods into Quick Cash." In March the *Santa Rosa Press-Democrat* headlined "Take-Over Mania among the Redwoods."[41]

King's tabloid reaffirmed this view of the Palco buyout. In April the *Los Angeles Times* covered the story again, titling its piece "Old Redwoods, Traditions Felled in Race for Profits." Soon politicians also started to pay attention. In late April state senator Barry Keene introduced a bill in the California Assembly that would limit what Palco could cut.[42]

King was following the rules of environmental politics: by orchestrating a campaign that demonized the enemy and satisfied the media's craving for drama, he would enlist politicians to force Palco's surrender. But down in Scotia, Palco's managers, did not yet understand. They continued to suppose that the old rules of forestry and free market economics still applied. Surely people were reasonable! Headwaters was private property. Palco owned the trees and had a right to harvest them. And who were a scraggly band of college kids to lecture experts on silviculture?

In an open letter to Palco employees that appeared in Humboldt County newspapers in March, Robert Stephens charged that King "has no accurate knowledge of the true composition of the timber stands" and "is dedicated to bringing about a total halt to all cutting of old growth trees." By contrast, company harvests, he insisted, had been planned by professionals and reviewed by "the California Department of Forestry, Department of Fish and Game, Mines and Geology, Water Quality, Cal-Trans [Department of Transportation] and state parks."[43]

But Stephens was no match for King and Earth First! By April these activists had become whirlwinds, writing letters and articles, organizing actions. King wrote a story for the *Eureka Times-Standard* rebutting Stephens's open letter to workers. In May he published a press release charging that the state Fish and Game Department believed that Pacific Lumber's logging was "eliminating wildlife." In June he wrote another piece, "Unprotected Redwoods," in the *Siskiyou Journal.* Throughout this period he kept readers of *Earth First! Journal* informed on the progress of the campaign.[44]

In March 1987 King infiltrated the Maxxam stockholders' meeting in Santa Monica, at the elegant Miramar Sheraton, where he confronted Hurwitz directly, threatening, "We will not let this [logging] go unchecked." In Fortuna on May 7, King and other Earth First!ers protested Palco harvest plans at a meeting of the State Department of Forestry.[45]

From their outpost in Garberville, King and his followers contacted Earth First!ers in New York, Houston, Los Angeles, and San Francisco, inviting them to participate in a national day of direct action on May 18. They networked with local activists throughout the region, cultivated media contacts, and assigned volunteers to study state timber harvest files and aerial photos to keep tabs on Palco.[46]

Small actions — roadblocks, tree spiking, and peaceful protest — proliferated throughout the region. Giving in to the protests, the Department of Forestry asked Palco to withdraw or rewrite several forest plans. Encouraged by this sign of official weakness, activists pressed even harder. The conflict escalated and tempers rose. Then tragedy struck.[47]

18

THE AGE OF
EXTREMISM

ON MAY 8, 1987, GEORGE ALEXANDER was so concerned about the condition of his saw that he almost didn't go to work. A twenty-three-year-old millworker at the Louisiana Pacific plant in Cloverdale, in Sonoma County, Alexander, just married with a wife three months pregnant, operated the big band saw that makes the first rough-cut in giant logs as they come into the mill.

Even in the best of times Alexander's job — known as off-bearer — was a dangerous one. But that day Alexander felt especially uneasy. The saw was in bad shape. Not only was it undersized, but it was overdue for repairs. Designed for old-growth logs, it was fifty-two feet around and nine and a half inches wide, and "so powerful," he told Earth First!er Judi Bari later, "that when you turned it off you could make three more cuts through a twenty-foot log before the saw stopped." If a band saw hits a knot or a metal object such as a nail or a choker chain, saw teeth fly off, or the saw breaks. To protect himself Alexander wore a heavy facemask. But this day that wasn't enough.

As he made a center cut through a long, thin "pecker pole," the blade hit an eleven-inch nail, countersunk into the log so that Alexander, who always inspected logs before sawing them, did not see it. The saw exploded like a bomb, throwing Alexander nearly thirty feet. A twelve-foot section broke off its track, sending shrapnel through his mask, hitting him in the throat and face, breaking his jaw in five places, knocking out a dozen teeth, and nearly severing his jugular vein. He fell to the floor, the blade wrapped around him. As other workers used a blowtorch to remove the blade from his face, Alexander's friend Rick Phillips held his artery together until the ambulance arrived.[1]

Amazingly, the press did not hear of the story until a week later, just before Earth First!'s National Action Day of protest against Pacific Lumber. Then local newspapers played the story big. The *Eureka Times-Standard* carried the headline "Earth First!! Blamed for Worker's Injuries." The *Press-Democrat* proclaimed "Tree Spiking Terrorism." Millworkers and their families were outraged. The Mendocino County sheriff called the incident a "heinous and vicious criminal act."[2]

And Earth First!ers further enraged their critics by failing to be contrite. Greg King, who said he himself had never spiked a tree, was quoted by the *Los Angeles Times* as saying, "There would be no spiking were it not for . . . greed." Dave Foreman announced that he was "more concerned about old-growth forests" than about Alexander. And an anonymous group of Earth First!ers sent a letter to Pacific Lumber's offices in Scotia warning that similar "accidents" could happen there as well.[3]

Among activists, only a newcomer to Earth First! named Judi Bari, who would figure prominently later, seemed scandalized by the incident, lamenting that Earth First! displayed "moral arrogance" and "practically no sympathy for this innocent man who had just been through such a terrifying ordeal caused by a spiked tree. And after advocating the tactic for years, even putting out a manual on how to do it, when the shit came down they tried to disassociate."[4]

Indeed, rather than revealing self-doubt, most Earth First!ers confirmed their antihumanism. Despite heightened tensions, they went ahead with their direct action day on May 18 with simultaneous protests at Maxxam's New York City and Santa Monica headquarters, MCO's Houston offices, Pacific Lumber's Mill Valley offices, and the company's loading dock in Carlotta, in Humboldt County.

But these protests did not start as planned. The day before, Mokai and four companions had organized a tree-sit for All Species Grove. But before the three climbers — Kurt Newman, Oregonian Larry Evans, and Sonoma Earth First!er Darryl Sukovitzen — could haul up their platforms, company security men arrived, trapping the men halfway up the trees in their climbing harnesses. It became a waiting game.[5]

As Mokai hid in the bushes watching the scene through his binoculars, Sukovitzen stood in his spurs 150 feet off the ground with Palco security officials beneath him. Evans was 120 feet up in his stirrups and harness, tied to the ropes with climbing aids. Newman was only sixty feet above the ground. Then sheriffs arrived as other protests unfurled a thirty-foot "Save the Redwoods" banner on the road and another that read "Stop Maxxam," featuring a blood-spattered skull and crossbones.

Turning to his friends, Evans reportedly remarked, "It's only pain."

But finally the cold became too much, and he came down, surrendering to authorities. Sukovitzen followed later, and the next morning, when company officials sent one of their own climbers up to get Newman, he surrendered as well and was promptly arrested.[6]

The next action went better. In Santa Monica, where Earth First!ers were protesting what they called the "North Coast Clearcutting Machine," one, dressed as Mother Earth with vines winding over her dress, tried to carry a baby Sequoia Redwood into the Maxxam offices. In Mill Valley protesters cemented tree stumps to the front door of Palco's sales office.[7]

In Houston fifteen Earth First!ers stood in front of Maxxam headquarters carrying cardboard redwoods, three live cedars, a banner proclaiming "Hurwitz Is Destroying America," and a stuffed dummy labeled "Charles Hurwitz — Corporate Vampire." Demonstrating the art form of guerrilla theater to their sweating fellow Texans on this hot, muggy day, they conducted a mock trial on the sidewalk, in which a jury of trees, finding Hurwitz guilty, invoked "the Golden Rule" and chopped him down while chanting, "Charles Hurwitz, you can't hide. We charge you with arborcide!"[8]

In New York on Park and Madison avenues, Earth First!ers, along with their "sisters and brothers from Greenpeace, the Greens and Rainforest Action Network," dressed as owls and other "non-human species facing extinction due to the clearcutting of their habitat" and chanted "Wall Street Out of the Wilderness!"[9]

But the biggest event took place at the Palco log dock in Fortuna. It had been organized with the care of a Delta Force commando raid. There were "affinity groups" for media contacts, video crews, reconnaissance scouts, tree climbers, jail support and telephone crews, drivers to pick up forest action crews, lawyers, musicians, radio-phone operators for the rented two-way radios. There were teams of fundraisers, blockaders, fence jumpers, base camp maintainers, rally coordinators, and "woods action" guides to lead supply crews and journalists to the backcountry action. There were people stationed at phones to keep track of who was going to jail and where, and to help them get out.[10]

The event opened and ended with activists sitting in a circle on the road leading to the loading dock for prayer ceremonies led by Native Americans for, as one said, "spiritual assurance that what you are about to do or have done is for the benefit of all." But sandwiched between these peaceful interludes was pure mayhem.[11]

A large crowd swarmed around the gate to the log deck, blocking what Earth First!ers called "probably the world's major transport route for old growth Redwood." Suddenly three women, including Karen Pickett, leaped the barrier and sprinted for a stack of logs as sheriff's deputies stationed inside the gate raced to intercept them. The women, carrying a banner, and the cops, all running at top speed, collided at the logs. But while the officers struggled to subdue the three, other women, garlands in their hair, crossed the barrier as well, scrambled onto the pile of logs, and, pursued by another contingent of cops, began to dance from log to log.

In short, as Mokai would write later, "it was a successful action . . . thirteen local arrests, five more in Mill Valley. . . . We gained national news with a report on the 'Today Show.'" Pacific Lumber helped to seal their victory by filing a lawsuit against the protesters for $42,000 in damages, thus generating even more publicity for the happy warriors.[12]

They had become a hot news item. The combination of theatrical irreverence for authority and unctuous love of the land was too potent a mixture for the media to resist. The *Los Angeles Times* covered National Action Day in depth. Stories appeared in *Business Week*, *Newsweek*, *Forbes*, the *Philadelphia Inquirer*, and in countless television broadcasts, including the *CBS Evening News with Dan Rather*. Coaxed by Cherney, the national media began to beat a path to King's door. In the weeks that followed, King and his friends would be enlisted as guides by a host of luminaries, such as CBS's Ray Brady, to lead trespassing trips into Headwaters. And when these scribes returned to their offices in New York or Los Angeles, they would write their stories, flogging Hurwitz and sanctifying the hardy little band of ecoteurs.[13]

Thus the spin was set. The press had decreed that corporate greed was destroying virgin forests. Hurwitz, epitome of Wall Street avarice, was a demonic environmental destroyer. The story would be rewritten again and again as journalists searched their thesauruses for adjectives, adverbs, and nouns sufficient to convey the evil they had found in the north woods. "Razing the Giant Redwoods," *Newsweek* declared in July. "Raiding the Redwoods," reported *California Business*. The headlines blared through 1988 and 1989: "Wall Street Sleeze" (*Amicus Journal*), "Timber Wars" (*California Journal*), "Angry Harvest" (*Corporate Finance*), "A Raider's Ruckus in the Redwoods" (*Fortune*), "California's Chain Saw Massacre" (*Reader's Digest*), and "Milken, Junk Bonds, and Raping Redwoods," by *End of Nature* author Bill McKibbon in *Rolling Stone*.[14]

This publicity began to move law and politics, giving EPIC no time to rest. The previous December Robert Sutherland's group had finally achieved victory in its battle to rescue Sally Bell Grove. In a complicated settlement, the Trust for Public Lands agreed to purchase this 7,100-acre tract — including seven miles of coastline and most remaining old growth — for Sinkyone Wilderness State Park.[15]

But EPIC could not savor its victory. "Even as we were popping champagne corks over Sally Bell," Sutherland recalls, "we were worrying about Maxxam." And, indeed, in June the Garberville group petitioned to stop the harvests, repeating King's charge, made in his tabloid, that the Department of Forestry had merely "rubber-stamped" Palco's plans. In response, Pacific Lumber announced that it would halt logging on some acreage pending a hearing on the suit.[16]

As the activists found, their work had just begun. The movement was fighting on more fronts than any army since the Seven Years' War, when Frederick the Great of Prussia simultaneously clashed with Russia, Austria, France, Saxony, and Sweden. Skirmishes occurred throughout the summer and fall all over the country, beginning in May, when the Rainforest Action Network, led by former Earth First!er Randy Hayes, launched "Whopper Stopper Month" to protest Burger King's use of "rainforest beef."[17]

They continued in the Kalmiopsis, where tree-sitting was perfected to an art form; in Arizona, where the Nomadic Action Group battled to save the Grand Canyon from uranium mining; in Aspen, where activists protested new ski runs; in Washington, D.C., where a hundred waffle-stomping Greens stood in front of the offices of the World Bank in a rally to save the rain forests; in Muskwa Valley, British Columbia, where three women from Friends of the Wolf parachuted out of light planes to intercept government predator control agents; in Missoula, where a hundred primitivists from five states marched in the "Forever Wild Rally"; in Sacramento, San Franciso, and Santa Cruz, where animal rights activists protested mountain lion hunts; on Mount Graham in Arizona, where Earth First! sought to stop construction of an astronomical observatory on critical habitat for the endangered Mount Graham red squirrel; in the high desert of southeastern Utah, where dusty idealists struggled to save the "pygmy forest"; and in San Diego and Sacramento, where nature lovers dressed as owls, desert tortoises, bighorn sheep, banded geckos, chollas, tarantulas, and coyotes pleaded for passage of the California Desert Wilderness bill.[18]

They seemed to be everywhere! They surfaced in Hanford, Washington, when twelve agents clad as custodians climbed the fence of a nuclear facility with mops and buckets to "clean up" the nuclear reactor.

They wouldn't budge from the Wolf River in Wisconsin, where, teaming with Chippewa Indians, they forced Exxon to abandon plans for an underground zinc-copper mine. They were found crawling through the mesquite of Four Notch Forest in Texas when the Forest Service sought to use napalm and a fifty-two-ton tree crusher to destroy trees killed by the pine bark beetle.[19]

Simultaneously seeking publicity and anonymity, illegality and legitimacy, accountability and irresponsibility, they danced before the public under playful aliases: Mudslide Slim, Oldpantheist, Australopithecus, Bruce Budworm, Pirate Jenny, Wilderness Woman, Mary Sojourner, Lone Wolf Circles, Millipede, Spud Buster, Jean Ravine, Tecalote, Jack Pine, the Erinyes, the Rogue, the Bunchgrass Rebel, and Friends of the Wild Dawgs from Hell. And they entertained! People smiled when New Mexico Earth First!ers, declaring All Species Day in the Pecos Wilderness, performed a puppet drama called "The Elk Mountain Controversy" to publicize a proposed timber sale.

And they laughed when, in Contra Costa County, California, a group calling itself the Strawberry Liberation Front sought to pull up strawberry plants sprayed with a gene-altering substance that made them more resistant to frost. And they chortled when the like-minded Potato Liberation Front of Tulelake, California, apparently believing that vegetables should live organically or die, proudly claimed responsibility for uprooting thousands of potatoes at night to save them from the hubristic hands of genetic engineers.[20]

And they loved to read about the cracking of the dams at Hetch Hetchy in Yosemite, and Elwha River in Washington, even though that joke was not new.[21]

And the activists networked! Keeping in touch by computer and phone, they bounced around the country in search of action, wherever they found it. In Paoli, Indiana, the Woodpecker Rebellion Anti-Clearcutting Pow Wow, brought together strategists from twenty states to plan future actions. And rendezvous happened everywhere — in West Virginia, Four Corners, the eastern Sierra Nevada, and of course at the Grand Canyon, where participants in the Round River Rendezvous sat and sang:

> The earth is our mother,
> Sisters and brothers,
> She's a member of the family,
> It's up to you and me,
> So pick up a monkeywrench,

A little sledgehammer,
But if you're not careful,
You're gonna end up in the slammer.[22]

It seemed such good, innocent fun! No one got hurt, and the cause was so justified! Or so it seemed, especially to affluent urbanites. Through their tongue-in-cheek derring-do, the activists began to make ecotage respectable and helped to lower the standards of civility another notch. Inspired by the fiction of Abbey, Asimov, and Callenbach, they crisscrossed the boundary between truth and reality so many times that no one could tell the difference.

To television audiences accustomed to fictionalized nonfiction, they had become another miniseries: entertaining but hardly real, and sometimes a little too long. Earth First! bumper stickers began appearing on BMWs, Jaguars, and Mercedeses belonging to an affluent elite that got vicarious pleasure imagining long-haired ecofreaks torching a power pole. To these chic urbanites who followed Earth First!'s antics, the people of Mill City, Oregon, or Scotia, California, might as well have been living in another universe. Northwest mill towns simply didn't exist in the national imagination. The nation, having shed tears for whales and wolves, had none left for the down-and-out of Eureka. Like the Earth First!ers themselves, the public reserved their sympathy for other species.

Earth First! was clearly part of something big, a cross-cultural phenomenon sweeping the globe. Even as King organized early protests against Maxxam, ecotage elsewhere — and responses to it — had already reached entirely new levels of imagination and violence.

In July 1985 in Auckland, New Zealand, French frogmen blew up the Greenpeace ship *Rainbow Warrior*, killing a passenger. Meanwhile, the French secret service had so thoroughly infiltrated Greenpeace in France that most of its original members temporarily left the organization, joining Robin des Bois, the French affiliate of the German group Robin Wood.[23]

In June 1986 in Phuket, Thailand, demonstrators fearing poisonous waste from a tantalum plan rampaged, causing $25 million in damage.[24]

In August 1986 Robin Wood ecoteurs infiltrated the nuclear power plant at Niederaichbach in Bavaria, northeast of Munich. Climbing up a lightning rod to a platform on the circulation tower, they unfurled a sign reading "One Ruin Is Enough! Stop Ohu!" then waited for police to arrive.[25]

In October 1986 the Munich chapter of Robin Woods blocked the Alpenstrasse with an artificial landslide, to demonstrate the dangers of soil erosion, while that same month in Kapit, Borneo, local people and their Friends of the Earth leader were arrested for blocking a logging road in the Sarawak rain forest.[26]

In November 1986 two Sea Shepherds — Ron Coronado, an American, and David Howitt, an Englishman — dressed in black fisherman's sweaters and knit caps, broke into a whale processing plant near Reykjavík, Iceland, and spent the next eight hours destroying equipment, ultimately doing $1.8 million worth of damage. Using monkey wrenches and sledgehammers, they destroyed the refrigeration plant, allowing forty tons of whale meat to spoil. They poured cyanic acid into computers and file drawers. Then they calmly drove to Reykjavík harbor and, using jimmies and bolt cutters to open sea valves, scuttled two whaling ships.[27]

This was an age of commitment! Applying what they had learned in college, the ecoteurs made their highest goal not thought but action. Activists who had got their education not by studying Aristotle and Rousseau but by occupying Old Main, Mau-Mauing professors, leading teach-ins, or participating in the Paris student revolts had found their calling. They had finally and completely rejected the scholarly neutrality their professors once preached. Reason was a crutch and science a tool of authority.

And so, quite spontaneously around the world, a new epoch began.

During that summer of 1987 John Campbell stood looking out his office window one day at Mill B, trying to understand why harvesting Headwaters had become so controversial. By accelerating the cut, Palco was merely following the same policy the Forest Service was pursuing in the Douglas fir stands to the north: to spur regeneration and improve forest health by eliminating decadent old growth.[28]

The last battle over Redwood National Park, Campbell thought, should have settled the redwood preservation issue once and for all. That park was intended to save the "last" old growth. Its 78,000 acres, along with the 172,000 acres of coast redwood land in state and other public preserves — altogether containing 89,000 acres of magnificent old growth — ought to have been enough to satisfy even the most demanding environmentalists. Or so Congress thought when it spent nearly $2 billion on the park, which few now visited. Yet here were Earth First! and EPIC, once again crusading to save "the last redwoods." And the press supported them.

Why, Campbell wondered, didn't someone remind people that red-woods are a renewable resource that grows like crabgrass! A single acre of eighty-year-old trees adds enough wood in five years to build a good-sized house. But "preserving" forests was a recipe for their death. Mature trees do not grow; they shrink. Eventually they die of old age, disease, or fire. The only way to rejuvenate the woods is to harvest them.

And Pacific Lumber had been such a good citizen! Hurwitz was getting a bad rap. Palco had begun to increase harvests even before the Maxxam buyouts. And there was nothing sinister about takeovers. They were a sign of the times. Anyone who ran the company would do what Hurwitz was doing — responding to economic pressures and shareholder demands.

And since the takeover nothing but good things had happened. Palco had added three hundred employees and substantially increased its local tax payments. It was modernizing the mills at Scotia and Fortuna, purchasing a new facility at Carlotta, and installing new dry kilns and planing facilities. It planned to add over a thousand acres of timberland and spend $50 million to build an environmentally sensitive cogeneration plant, altogether a reinvestment of more than $100 million in Pacific Lumber after the acquisition.

Also, since the 1970s Palco had raised and released over half a million salmon and steelhead. It was building a new fish hatchery and hiring a full-time fisheries biologist. It already employed another biologist to give advice on habitat improvement and protection of a variety of species, including the northern spotted owl.[29]

Didn't people understand that Headwaters was private property? Why did the press not report these facts? Instead the media was providing knee-jerk propaganda for preservationists, who acted as though Headwaters belonged to them, and as though the Fifth Amendment provision of property rights had never been written.

Some of Campbell's workers were equally bemused. Many cutters in particular hated the Earth First!ers because of their tree-sitting and their threats of spiking. Under Hurwitz they were earning more money. The company still provided the same bonuses — housing and $8,000 in annual scholarship support for their children. And although Hurwitz had cashed out the pension plan, he had promised to honor his commitments there, too.

What, if anything, was wrong? To those whose universe was defined by the *Wall Street Journal*, nothing. Hurwitz had behaved like any other businessman; he was maximizing profits. To be sure, when the old growth was gone, investors would have to pay the piper. But this would not happen until 2007 at the earliest, which meant, in business terms, never. No shareholder would wait that long for a return on his investment. And if Maxxam thought no further than its next quarterly earnings statement, well, so did General Motors. Hurwitz should not be blamed for the myopia that afflicted the entire American corporate culture.

The takeover was considerably less immoral than John D. Rockefeller's secret 1870 scheme, known as the South Improvement Company, that drove many competitors out of business, and Hurwitz was not so different from Save the Redwoods League cofounders Duncan McDuffie, whose wealth came from subdivisions, and Stephen Mather, who made millions mining borax. Hurwitz never said, as William Henry Vanderbilt once did, "Let the public be damned."[30] If he had been living a century earlier, he'd have been a Horatio Alger hero. He'd be cast in bronze in Houston.

Nevertheless, nineteenth-century robber barons did not exclusively characterize the economics of their times. Their tactics were a sign that old Protestant values were in decline. The earlier era also had its share of businessmen, such as the Murphys, who, believing in noblesse oblige, practiced paternalism — as much for profit as to ensure that they might be counted among the Calvinist elect. This paternalism nevertheless reflected long-range concerns, arising from a belief that a happy, married worker was a better worker, and a worker with no desire to join a union. Stability ensured self-interest.

Reaganism was supposed to return the country to the values of that era. It was guided by the free market ideas of the eighteenth-century English economist Adam Smith, who argued that when people follow their own self-interest, an "invisible hand" ensures that everyone benefits. Yet the Reaganites carried Smith's theory one step further. Not only did the free market serve the public economic interest, they argued, but also it provided the best means of protecting the environment. Thus, economists were the experts of choice, hired to show that environmental goals were best achieved by incentive-based strategies. Think tanks dedicated to "free market environmentalism" sprang up around the country.

But now there was a fly in the libertarian ointment, and its name was Charles E. Hurwitz. As the very model of a free marketeer, he proved, said environmentalists, that no "invisible hand" operated to ensure environmental protection. And to the press and the public these arguments made sense. Free market theories may have won people's minds, but ecosystem protection captured their hearts.

Thus, the issue went beyond science into the rarefied air of national values. As the conflict escalated, the contestants forgot what the fight was about. Although biologists knew little about biodiversity in climax redwood groves, one thing was certain: the harvesting of another 45,000 acres would not be an environmental catastrophe.

Why, then, should these redwoods be saved? Bill Bertain, the Murphys, and many residents of these north woods communities believed that the trees should be used but also conserved for the benefit of the rural culture. Therefore, they endorsed the ideal of selective cutting and sustainable forestry promoted by Emanuel Fritz and described in the 1905 National Forest Service Organic Act as "community stability." This was the kind of management most forest ecologists supported as well. Thinning forests and prescribed burning, they believed, sustained biological diversity more effectively than locking land up as wilderness.

But these voices could not be heard above the rage of Wall Streeters and radicals alike, both of whose agendas would mean the death of rural culture and sound forestry. These two factions were mirror images of each other. One sought to maximize profits, the other to dismantle the American economic system. One held that only the free market could guarantee public benefit; the other believed the big trees should be saved, regardless of the human cost. One invoked property rights, the other confiscation. The north woods communities found themselves trapped in a no man's land between conservatives who would strip the forests for cash and radicals who would lock the people out. Either way the mills would close.

Thus, many Palco workers felt caught in the middle. They didn't like the environmentalists, who seemed to have an insatiable urge to lock up the land. Yet Hurwitz gave them reason to worry about the future. Although they were working six ten-hour days a week, they were convinced that this pace could not continue. Hurwitz wanted to take 200 million board feet out of the forest annually. At that rate in twenty years all the wood would be gone, and with it their jobs.[31]

The Palco takeover and its aftermath revealed an epidemic loss of balance. Since the 1960s mainstream America had touted moderation but practiced extremism, preached conservation and practiced profligacy, extolled reason while engaging in the politics of emotional manipulation. The country had become a land of activists. The generation that tore colleges apart in the 1960s had carried their love of engagement with them. Some went to Wall Street, others to the woods. So while investment bankers, corporate chieftains, and bond brokers pursued wealth by whatever means worked, activists pushed for preservation without restraint. Anarchy became a way of life, not just for the radical environmentalists but for the speculators of Wall Street as well.

By embracing Reaganism, entrepreneurs like Hurwitz inhabited the empty shell of Lockean liberalism. This philosophy had degenerated into a doctrine of freedom with the ethics squeezed out. And its death created a vacuum waiting to be filled. Activists, committed to commitment, offered an alternative, however confused. Finding libertarian selfishness wanting, they tapped the universal desire of people to believe in something larger than themselves. They offered a purposive theory of nature that gave meaning to life. Thus their biocentrism, by conferring a higher value on ecosystems than on individuals or private property, had broad appeal precisely because it seemed to justify rebellion.

Hurwitz and the environmentalists, therefore, were made for each other. Neither knew limits, and both were playing a game without rules. So as the battle over old growth evolved, a curious reversion occurred. The Darwinian struggle that had captured the imagination of early conservationists was revived. But whereas a century earlier the locus of this struggle was the marketplace, now it was the media. Contestants battled to capture the American mind, to prove that they held the moral high ground so as to get the coercive powers of the machinery of government to enforce their agenda. In this arena business was no match for its opponents. Entrepreneurs, to be sure, could accumulate obscene amounts of wealth. But they could never undo the damage their greed did, not so much to the environment (for this was minimal) as to the ideals on which sound social policies depend.

Indeed, during Reagan's second term, even as Wall Street's leveraged buyout mania reached fever pitch, as free market economists churned out papers on the virtues of self-interest, as the communist empire began to crumble — as, in short, on the surface things seemed to be aiming toward a return to Jeffersonian liberalism — in fact everything was headed in the opposite direction. The defense of democracy itself was left by default to economists, who usually justified liberty not on ethical grounds but on the grounds of its efficiency. Free enterprise, they noted, was the best way to maximize wealth.

Libertarian economists omitted the message of Locke's *Essays on the Law of Nature,* delivered in lectures at Oxford in the early 1660s, not only that natural law conferred property rights but also that "we can equate with our law . . . moral good or virtue." Instead, like Marxists, they appealed to materialism and, extolling self-interest, discounted altruism. Conservatives and liberals alike forgot what Locke had said about the state of nature: that it is a "state of liberty, yet it is not a state of license." Together these two opposing sides drove the final nails into the coffin of the classical idea that men, left alone, would exercise their reason for mutual benefit. And, as Locke knew, once people abandoned this belief, once they became Hobbesians who supposed that human relations were a "war of every man against every man," they would demand authoritarian government to protect people from one another.[32]

And this was happening. Quietly, without fanfare, the Palco battle set a profound political precedent. It evoked extremism on both sides. But the country was already so polarized over the environmental issue that many Americans noticed only the excesses committed by the side to which they were opposed. Environmentalists and the press railed against Hurwitz's accelerated cuts. Conservatives and libertarians complained about assaults, by activists and the state, on Palco's private property rights. Few noticed that both sides were correct, and that the real dangers lay beyond this anarchy, in the absolutism that would follow.

By August 1987 Mike Roselle's Nomadic Action Group, working alongside King, having temporarily concluded its campaign in the Kalmiopsis, returned to Garberville to launch new actions in Headwaters. On August 9 King and a friend, Rita Urn, hiked into the forest at midnight, camping on the Little South Fork Elk River. The next day they moved through dense old growth to the northeast panhandle of Headwaters. This last virgin tract in Elk Head Springs consisted of countless tiny pure streams separated by slopes of massive trees and thick undergrowth reaching overhead. Now, King noted, it was "under destruction," and this made it perfect for tree-sitting. The wall of old growth standing next to clear-cut lent itself nicely to the display of banners. And the contrast between clear-cut and virgin stands would impress reporters.[33]

Having done their reconnaissance, the duo went back to Garberville and waited for the logging to begin. On August 20 bulldozers began ripping a road through the stand. On August 27 the Nomadic Action Group arrived. Fifteen people carried five hundred pounds of climbing gear, food, and clothing eight miles to base camp. Leaving a watchman on the main haul road with a portable CB, they got to work at dusk. By 5:00 A.M. the climbing crew, led by Mokai, had installed platforms and girth hitches for hanging supplies 150 feet up in two trees, each eight feet in diameter.[34]

Using mechanical ascenders, King, who had never climbed a big tree before, pulled himself up the fixed ropes to the platforms as Mary Beth Nearing ascended the other tree. Then they hauled up enough food, clothing, and water for two weeks.

After two days of waiting without being seen, suddenly they were the center of attention. A cutter noticed a banner reading "Free the Redwoods" and ran over, calling to his friends. At the same time, other loggers found a gaggle of Earth First!ers padlocked to 'dozers, yarders, loaders, skidders, crummies, and other heavy equipment, worth millions, parked nearby. The grove soon filled with gawking lumberjacks, sheriff's deputies, and company security. An officer shouted to King that he was trespassing. King bellowed back that Maxxam had "abrogated its right to private property via its destruction of same!"[35]

The usual game began — Bugs Bunny versus Elmer Fudd, Wile E. Coyote versus Roadrunner. The impish prey would outsmart the plodding predator!

As loggers cut and hauled logs around the two tree-sitters, Palco security chief Carl Anderson sent a tree climber up to tear their banner down. When it was gone, King unfurled another that read "Two Thousand Years Old/Respect Your Elders."

Score one for Bugs Bunny!

Soon Anderson had stationed security troops to watch the pair and installed floodlights that saturated the area with blinding white light. He had the sitters trapped, he thought.

But rappeling down the dark side of the tree trunk, out of sight of the watchmen, King and Nearing instead ran off into the night unnoticed. Reaching the nearest road, they met their support team carrying supplies: smoke bombs, a sixpack of beer, and a portable stereo loaded with reggae and Doors tapes.

Score two for the Roadrunners!

Savoring their escape, the couple opened their beers and, King recalled, "shared the glory of our small group. We were free, happy Earth First!ers caught in a maddening world of environmental imprisonment."[36]

Still, the Elk Head Springs action had missed certain crucial elements: press and television. So a few weeks later King and Nearing were at it again, this time with the media in tow. Now known as Tarzan and Jane, they were back in their treetop retreats, driving Palco security nuts. As he swung on the traverse at All Species Grove, on his way to Nearing's tree to make lunch, King knew from the sound of frustrated voices below that he was winning.[37]

To make the story even better, this time they did not escape. By giving themselves up after a week in the trees, the protesters got more publicity. The *Eureka Times-Standard* ran a headline, "Treetop Protesters Climb Down," and Palco officials ritualistically swore to prosecute for trespassing. But, like Elmer Fudd and Wile E. Coyote, Palco had been outfoxed again. It did not know how to beat an enemy who wanted to get arrested.[38]

Soon there was more bad news for Hurwitz. In October the *Wall Street Journal* reported congressional subcommittee charges that Boyd Jeffries "appear[ed] to have parked stock for Houston investor Charles Hurwitz." Congress had also found, the *Journal* said, "'significant evidence' of insider trading in connection with the 1985 acquisition of Pacific Lumber Company by Maxxam Group, Inc., which Mr. Hurwitz controls," and that "a Maxxam official consciously sought to evade government oversight under the Hart-Scott-Rodino antitrust act."[39]

The same month a second group, calling itself "Concerned Earth Scientist Researchers," filed suit against Palco to stop the harvests, and on November 4 Judge Frank Peterson found in favor of EPIC, blocking harvest on three hundred acres. Proving the potency of a seed sown earlier, the judge charged that the Department of Forestry had "rubberstamped" this sale, thus borrowing a phrase from EPIC which the Garberville group had in turn taken from King's tabloid. Meanwhile, Senator Barry Keene's hearings to end Headwaters clear-cutting continued. And state assemblyman Byron Sher produced a legislative counsel's opinion asserting that the State Board of Forestry must require companies such as Palco to manage for sustained yield.[40]

It seemed Earth First!'s finest hour. Throughout the Northwest the political momentum for forest protection was building. Indeed, it had become an avalanche that would soon inundate everyone, including the environmentalists themselves.

19

THE PARADIGM SHIFT

THE VOICE ON THE PHONE said, "We've got another one."

This morning in January 1987, Andy Stahl, the peripatetic activist, had just settled into his new office of the Sierra Club Legal Defense Fund in Seattle. Having left the National Wildlife Foundation's Environmental Law Center earlier that year, he was perfectly placed to lead the fight to save old growth. But the message Stahl received suggested that events were overtaking him.

The caller was his contact within the U.S. Fish and Wildlife Service. "Somebody's petitioned to list the owl — again," the official said, adding, "a group from Cambridge, Massachusetts, called GreenWorld. And this time it's serious."

Things were getting out of hand, thought Stahl. The Northwest environmental community had been carefully crafting a campaign to put the issue of old growth on the national agenda. To rescue Oregon forests from logging, environmentalists reasoned, they needed a theme that would play in Peoria.[1]

This motif, of course, included the spotted owl, and petitioning to list the bird was part of their long-range strategy. But they weren't ready to launch a major media blitz yet, and a poorly worded petition could ruin everything. The Northwest wilderness bills had just been signed into law, enlarging the no-logging portion of national forests to 31 percent of their total land area, and the region remained badly polarized. The timber industry wasn't in the mood to give another inch.[2]

"We were not prepared to walk into the teeth of the dragon," Stahl recalled. The Endangered Species Act was up for renewal, and a provocative listing at this point could jeopardize the law. The last thing he needed was another snail darter fiasco! That controversy had set the conservation movement back years because, by calling attention to an ugly minnow, it had opened the act to public ridicule.

Avoiding another public relations disaster required careful preparation. An environmental campaign, like selling soap, depended on the right packaging. Yet the publicity build-up was still in its infancy. They had not even thought of the expression "ancient forests" yet. But the issue was developing a momentum of its own. Stories about the owl May were appearing in national magazines. In May 1986 *Ranger Rick*, the children's environmental journal published by the National Wildlife Federation, introduced "Tricksy," the spotted owl. In October the Audubon Society initiated its "Adopt-a-Forest" program in Northwestern public forests. Soon after, *National Park* magazine published an article on the owl as well.[3]

And now the GreenWorld petition was jumping the gun. Stahl felt like a wagon master about to be trampled by his own team of oxen. He needed to slow it down. But could he do it?

If events were moving too fast, Stahl was partly responsible. Convinced that the key to the conservationists' victory lay in science, he had helped generate owl research that would turn the tide in their favor. Now understanding itself would become a road-kill victim of the speeding owl bandwagon, rendering scholarship irrelevant.

As soon as the Andrews Forest team published its paper on old growth in 1981, the push and shove between activists and government inexorably inflated concern for the little bird. At first this awareness grew almost imperceptibly. In 1981 the Portland office of the Fish and Wildlife Service declared the owl "vulnerable" but not in need of listing. That same year, on the recommendation of Charles Meslow and Eric Forsman, the Oregon-Washington Spotted Owl Subcommittee — successor to Oregon's Spotted Owl Task Force — revised the 1977 Oregon Spotted Owl Management Plan and increased the recommended acreage for each nesting pair from three hundred to one thousand acres. In 1984 the U.S. Forest Service issued the final Pacific Northwest *Regional Guide*, upping owl protection from three hundred acres for each of 112 pairs to one thousand acres for 375 pairs.[4]

Environmentalists, however, believed even this insufficient to rescue the owl. In supporting the larger figure, Forsman, they suspected, was holding back. But, as his doctoral dissertation had not yet been published, they couldn't be sure. So in 1984 they filed a Freedom of Information Act request to obtain his data. And, indeed, the data seemed to confirm their worst suspicions. The average old-growth area required by nesting owl pairs was a whopping 2,264 acres. The smallest area used by any pair of birds Forsman had studied was 1,008 acres. Stahl accused Forsman of being "politically conservative, not scientifically conservative." Forsman and his colleagues "were asking for the owl what they thought they could get, not what the bird needed." The biologist's recommendation for thousand-acre owl habitat zones was inadequate even by his own evidence![5]

Consequently, convinced that the *Regional Guide* established insufficient habitat for spotted owls, in October 1984 the National Wildlife Federation, the Oregon Wildlife Federation, the Lane County Audubon Society, and the Oregon Natural Resources Council appealed the decision of the regional forester, arguing that the plan required a full environmental impact statement. And in March 1985 Deputy Assistant Secretary of the Interior Douglas MacCleery partially sided with the environmentalists, ordering the Forest Service to complete a supplemental environmental impact statement before the plan was implemented. He refused to comply with the activists' demand to halt timber sales until the statement was completed.[6]

So the environmentalists continued to press their case. At the heart of the issue was the question: How much old growth did the owl require? Environmentalists wanted to allot each of a thousand pairs 2,200 acres. They knew that the Forest Service didn't have the data to support its contention that saving one thousand acres of habitat for each of 375 owl pairs was sufficient. But proving the government's claims unfounded required that the critics have impeccable science on their side.

Lacking that scholarship, Stahl decided to generate some. He would find a reputable scientist to write a solid paper for a scholarly journal. Through his father's connections with the National Academy of Sciences, he obtained the name of a demographer, Russell Lande, who was summering in Maine. Locating the professor, Stahl flew to Portland, where Lande met him at the airport. The two drove to West Boothbay Harbor, where, over a lobster dinner, Stahl explained his problem: he needed a paper to prove that logging hurt owls.[7]

Lande knew little about birds. He had never seen a spotted owl. He was a numbers cruncher. But he had an idea how to help. In 1979 an entomologist named Richard Levins had developed a mathematical model showing how much pesticide was necessary to eliminate an insect population. Lande proposed using Levins's reasoning to calculate the extent to which forest fragmentation would wipe out the owl. But, as Stahl explained to Lande, not only would the paper have to exhibit impeccable scholarship, but also it had to be timely and written in terms a judge could understand. So the two collaborated. Stahl put Lande in touch with scholars who supplied the data and, Stahl says, later helped find peer reviewers willing to write supporting letters.[8]

The paper was ready by June 1985. And, indeed, its argument exhibited compelling simplicity. Levins's theory about insect extinctions, Lande argued, showed that a creature could become extinct if its habitat were spread in patches over a wide region. Employing the principle of "island biogeography" originated by Robert MacArthur in the 1950s, he wrote: "We conclude from this model that implementation of the Forest Service management plan is likely to cause . . . extinction. . . . Only a plan involving preservation of the great majority of the remaining old growth forest is likely to promote long-term persistence of the northern spotted owl population."[9]

Bingo! With this do-it-yourself science, environmentalists had the weapon they needed to win their war. When the manuscript was finished, Stahl called a press conference to announce its findings. Almost immediately the political tide turned in the environmentalists' favor. Lande's paper quickly helped Stahl and others convince the Forest Service to halt six timber sales. Soon it would be swaying the courts as well, thereby opening the door to a round of legal battles that promised to last longer than an owl's lifetime.[10]

The Lande paper would set the format for much science to follow. Nevertheless, on close inspection it was an exercise in scientific woolgathering, a collection of calculations based on scanty evidence and laced with false assumptions. To reach his conclusion, Lande assumed an owl population of 2,500, whereas by 1989 more than 6,000 would be counted by censuses that had explored less than 40 percent of the bird's optimal habitat. He accepted that old growth was an absolute requirement for the owl, which even Forsman did not believe. And he presumed to know how much remaining forest was old growth, though this was still a hotly contested subject. He conjectured that in pre-Columbian America, 60 to 70 percent of forest was old growth, a figure over twice as large as the one palaeobotanists generally accepted. He assumed that Forsman's data on survival were accurate, even as scholars were raising serious questions about their reliability. Using flawed equilibrium mathematical models, Lande falsely concluded that healthy bird populations should persist indefinitely in a state of mythical "stability."[11]

The Bureau of Land Management would later find that 64 of 131 pairs of spotted owls lived in regions with less than a thousand acres of old growth, and eleven pairs inhabited areas with no big trees at all. But Lande, who did not even see his first owl until 1989, assumed that none could reproduce in stands under two hundred years old! Most important, the demographer wrongly supposed that the bird's survival depended on the fate of a relatively small fraction of Northwestern forest. In calculating habitat available to the owl, he did not consider 25 million acres of private timberland, 5 million acres in four eastern slope national forests, and millions of acres of available habitat in California. He omitted prime habitat in wilderness areas, wild and scenic rivers, riparian zones, special interest areas, and Bureau of Land Management lands. The bird, he reasoned, depended entirely on management areas designated in the *Regional Guide*. Thus, he assumed that a mere 7.6 million acres was available to the owl, whereas in fact the bird had access to more than 53 million acres. Later he would admit that the land his model did not consider — wilderness, national parkland, and other set-asides — would alone be sufficient to ensure the bird's survival.[12]

With this paper environmentalists captured the political ground while simultaneously writing a new chapter in the continuing corruption of science. They would convince courts that the Forest Service had little scholarship on its side — which was true — and they made a plausible case for listing the owl as endangered. And in undertaking this project both Stahl and Lande clearly were motivated by the highest ideals. But, according to Stahl's account of the paper's gestation, Lande had reached his conclusion before obtaining any data, and, knowing little about the biology himself, had depended on an activist (Stahl) to locate the scientists who would supply him with the figures. Since the article attacked the *Regional Guide* by name, it had an overtly political purpose. Abandoning even the pretense of objectivity, it set the precedent for advocacy science which tacitly followed ancient teleological notions of the balance of nature.[13]

Scholarly caution was still justified. In fact, no one knew what was happening to the owl — neither scientists, public officials, nor environmentalists. No one knew how many birds there were, what prey they preferred, or how much old growth they needed, if any. And Forsman's data were pitifully inadequate to answer these questions. He had fitted a mere fourteen birds with radio transmitters and tracked the home ranges of just six pairs. His telemetry was extremely limited.[14]

Despite the inadequacy of his data, the Corvallis biologist nevertheless repeatedly insisted that old growth was the bird's "preferred habitat," citing as a possible reason for this "that the principal prey utilized

RESPONSE: THE BIOCENTRIC REVOLUTION

by the owls (flying squirrels) were most numerous in older stands." Hence, he urged "that a system of old-growth management areas be established."[15]

Forsman has since complained that he was misunderstood, that he never said the owls depend exclusively on mature forests. But although his early papers did indeed record finding birds in second growth, he minimized the significance of this, suggesting, as he did in 1977, that "second-growth forests provide, at best, marginal spotted owl habitat." In fact, it appears that Forsman quickly concluded that the owls prefer old growth, for that is where he spent the most time looking for them. His searches for the birds consumed a full twelve months annually in Andrews, predominantly an old-growth forest, and a mere three months in the O&C study area, where 70 percent of the land had been clear-cut within the previous forty years.[16]

Whatever the case, using Forsman's data, nearly all the spotted owl researchers assumed, like Lande, that the owl was an old-growth species. Yet they had only a hypothesis, not a proven theory. A creature might occupy a particular area for many reasons: because conditions for food and reproduction were optimal there; because competition from other species had driven it there; or because weather, pollution, successional changes, or human or other natural disturbances had displaced it from other, better environments. No one knew which of these reasons applied to spotted owls found in mature forests. Indeed, there was ample evidence, many scholars suspected, that old growth was not optimal for the owl at all, and that the creature's primary habitat might be mixed forest communities that had experienced selection logging.[17]

This hypothesis derives from a scholarly field known as "source-sink dynamics." Whereas all living things require a "source" habitat where births outnumber deaths, the biologist H. Ronald Pulliam, the founder of this field, wrote in 1985, "a large fraction [of a population] may regularly occur in 'sink' habitats, where within-habitat reproduction is insufficient to balance local mortality." In some circumstances "only a small fraction of the population may be breeding in a source habitat. . . . Clearly, if the reproductive surplus of the source is large and the reproductive deficit of the sink is small, a great majority of the population may occur in the sink habitat." For this reason, "an investigator could easily be misled about the habitat requirements of a species. . . . Population management decisions based on studies in sink habitats could lead to undesirable results."[18]

Thus, old growth could be the owl's sink habitat and second-growth or disturbed forests the source. The scientists simply did not know because no relevant studies had been done. Although many owls nested in mature stands, they may not have been able to survive without early successional habitat. In fact, abundant evidence suggested this to be true. Beginning in April 1985, a team of biologists from Humboldt State University and the California Department of Fish and Game began sampling spotted owls on national forest and private lands at Willow Creek near Eureka. Two thirds of their study area had been logged, and timber harvests continued. Nevertheless, not only did the researchers discover double the number of owls estimated by the Forest Service, but also they found that the birds were multiplying.[19]

Likewise, a Forest Service study in central Oregon in 1986 found owls throughout both new and old stands, but on average their home range contained only 20 to 50 percent old growth, distributed in a patchwork pattern. In 1988 Charles Meslow himself would find an exceptionally high density of owls in extremely fragmented forests of the southern Cascades. A year later another study revealed the densest congregation of owls yet — more than double the population Forsman had found at Andrews — in a managed private forest in northwestern California where no tree was over eighty years old.[20]

The more scholars looked, the more birds they found. By 1989 the actual counts had risen to over six thousand despite the fact that some 60 percent of available habitat remained to be censused. In California spotted owls were especially abundant. Unlike those at Andrews — whose principal prey was flying squirrels — Golden State owls preferred dusky-footed wood rats, which live in open-canopied younger plant communities.[21]

These discoveries cast doubt on the supposition that owls were an old-growth species. If California owls preyed principally on dusky-footed wood rats, it was inconceivable that genetically identical and contiguous Oregon owl populations depended exclusively on flying squirrels and other climax prey species. As the University of Arizona ecologist Michael L. Rosenzweig put it, "No predator such as the owl could be so prey-specific."[22]

Rather than a simplistic preference for squirrels and old trees, then, the owl's needs seemed complex and variable. Studies would find that birds living in wet areas with large amounts of old growth actually reproduced more poorly than owls in drier forests composed of only half old growth. By 1993 demographic studies in checkerboard O&C lands near Eugene, Oregon, would find owls increasing faster than in surrounding old growth.[23]

These data did not necessarily falsify the "old-growth species" hypothesis. They merely suggested the need to test it. Source-sink dynamics, according to Rosenzweig, shows "that it may be optimal — actually optimal — for a bird to choose a habitat in which it cannot reproduce itself successfully." Identifying the owl's source habitat required field experimentation, such as measuring nesting success in different habitats, tracking birds after old growth was logged, studying competitive interactions or dispersal behavior. Determining why birds occupied a particular place called for studying intraspecific competition, dispersal, and other behavioral patterns.[24]

But virtually no such work was being done. Instead, government biologists sought to explain away the inconvenient findings. The abundance of owls in early successional California stands was dismissed as irrelevant to the "plight" of their more northerly cousins. The plethora of industry-sponsored studies revealing owls to be abundant and increasing in young forests was dismissed as coming from a biased source. Birds found in young tree communities were deemed "floaters" or refugees from groves destroyed by clear-cutting. Potential distinctions between preferred and critical habitat were ignored.[25]

Most research, following Lande, focused not on behavioral studies but on demographic analyses of population trends. Highly theoretical, and not requiring scholars to spend much time in the woods, demography became the quick and dirty way to support predetermined policy conclusions. But, lacking data to support its assumptions, this methodology remained suspect.[26]

Demographics are notoriously uncertain. Successful long-range predictions — even of human population changes — are almost never achieved, even when forecasters have all the relevant information. And anticipating short-run population trends requires accurate censuses showing current numbers and fecundity of females in each age group, as well as death rates. But owl demographers did not have these figures. Like surveyors attempting to triangulate the height of a mountain without knowing their own altitude or distance from the summit, they had to guess, extrapolating from spot observations of field researchers to fabricate population and mortality figures and estimates of the number and fecundity of young females in the population.

Hence, spotted owl policy would be built on the thin air of uneducated guesswork. Rather than testing Forsman's hypothesis, state and federal governments and the courts constructed policy on it, then justified their decisions by appealing to the problematic conclusions of demography. And once the bird was listed, the Endangered Species Act would permanently prohibit most relevant behavioral studies, for the manipulation of forests this testing demanded — such as felling mature trees to determine the effects of logging on owl dispersal — would violate the law's prohibition against damaging "critical habitat."

As a result of this failure to test the "old-growth species" hypothesis, the owl had become another victim of the growing influence of the idea of the stable ecosystem. Wildlife biologists had come to assume that wherever creatures lived was best for them, and that if their numbers declined, this was proof that their "ecosystem" had been "disturbed." To rescue them required reestablishing the balance by insulating the system from interference.

This assumption inevitably favored climax communities, spelling catastrophe for many species the scientists sought to save. In England, for example, the biologist M. R. Young noted that creatures thriving on private land that had been kept in early successional condition by its owners suddenly disappeared once the land began to be managed as a "protected" sanctuary. "When bought for conservation purposes," Young writes, "management was changed . . . to a more non-interventionist system, with the result that rides [paths] shaded over and blackthorn and other shrubby species became scarce. In consequence, many butterflies, including the nationally rare black hairstreak, disappeared from the wood."[27]

Although the Endangered Species Act permitted active management, by 1987, owing in large measure to the influence of biocentrism, the "hands-off" form of preservation was unofficial U.S. policy, wreaking havoc on a host of plants and animals. In Mendocino County the lotus blue butterfly has recently become extinct, two scientists reported, apparently because of "a decline in early successional habitat supporting its principal host plant *Lotus formosissimus.*" In Oregon the silverspot butterfly, which depends on grasslands, was declared endangered as forests increasingly colonized its territory.[28] In New York, the Karner Blue butterfly seems headed for extinction for similar reasons. In Yellowstone, grizzly bears continue to decline, in part due to shrinking early successional habitat. In Texas, black-capped vireos have become endangered, as too much protection destroys its preferred vegetation of oaks, sumacs and shrubbery — conditions which, before European settlement, had been sustained by burning and soil erosion. And in wilderness areas, wildlife sanctuaries and national parks throughout the country, spreading climax forests are decimating the habitat of countless other creatures that depend on early successional conditions.[29]

. . .

Driving this infatuation with pure protection was a rising public concern for creatures deemed "symbols of wilderness." These were the "canaries in the mine," the "barometer species" so dependent on "undisturbed" ecosystems that they could not "tolerate" humans. Before activists elevated the spotted owl to this status, they exploited Yellowstone grizzlies for a similar purpose, citing the bear's plight to argue for expanded "protection" of the "Greater Yellowstone Ecosystem." And prior to the grizzly it was the California condor, another "symbol of wilderness" whose voyage to the brink of oblivion graphically revealed the dangers of environmental mythology.

For millennia the condor, a giant member of the vulture family with a wingspan of ten feet, soared over California skies from Santa Barbara to the Sierras. But during our century it has been in deep jeopardy. For more than forty years nearly every conceivable effort was made to save the species. The Forest Service established the Sespe Condor Sanctuary near Fillmore in 1946. Other havens, including wilderness areas, were created later. The National Audubon Society inaugurated a system of full-time condor wardens in 1965. The condor was classified as an endangered species in 1966, and again in 1973. Hunting and predator control were restricted in their range. In 1980 the Condor Research Center, an ambitious research project, opened in Ventura, run jointly by the U.S. Fish and Wildlife Service and the National Audubon Society.

Despite these efforts, condor numbers plummeted toward zero. In 1965 the wild population ranged from 80 to 120 birds. By the spring of 1986 only six — a cohort containing just one breeding pair — remained. Why did the bird continue to die out, despite all that was done to save it?

The principal culprit, according to Noel F. R. Snyder and his wife, Helen, biologists in charge of the condor recovery program from 1982 to 1986, was that conservationists were misled by romantic ideas about wilderness. As early as the 1940s biologists mistakenly concluded that the condor was "an incredibly shy and sensitive creature, almost completely intolerant of the presence of man." So dubbed, it became "a living symbol of wilderness . . . a sacred spirit." Consequently, "preserving an image of the condor as a paragon of wilderness [became] more important than saving the condor itself." Efforts were devoted almost entirely to protecting the scavenger from human interference. The need for ensuring condor habitat became a fashionable argument for creating more wilderness. Yet by seeking to "preserve" habitat, conservationists diminished the early successional conditions — open meadow and savannas — on which the bird depended.

As the Snyders argue, this wilderness mystique was both false and destructive. Far from being shy, the condor was "one of the most approachable large birds we have ever encountered," they say. Yet environmentalists' desire to protect the bird thwarted the only strategy — captive breeding — that could save it — claiming that "death with dignity" was preferable.

Most condors died from eating shards of lead from bullets in the carcasses of game animals. But since they ranged over great distances, and since their foraging habits were so well established, they were doomed. Experts realized that the species could be saved only by rearing a new generation with less self-destructive foraging habits. This required capturing and breeding birds to build up their numbers, then releasing their progeny in more secure surroundings. So, despite staunch opposition from the Audubon Society, the capture-breeding program was finally launched in 1982, accumulating eight pairs of birds by 1986.

By that year the wild population was terminally ill. Only one breeding pair remained. Experts were convinced that the condor faced certain extinction and should be captured for breeding. Even so, the Audubon Society fought like fury to prevent it. Mesmerized by the myth of the "symbol of wilderness," it went to court to halt capture of the birds. Fortunately the courts rejected Audubon's case, and the last condor was brought in from the cold on Easter Sunday, 1987. The breeding program at the Los Angeles and San Diego zoos then proceeded at full speed, with great success. Recently authorities have begun releasing birds into the wild again.[30]

Yet even as biologists were learning the folly of dubbing condors "symbols of wilderness," environmentalists in the Northwest, not coincidentally led by the Audubon Society, were repeating the same mistake with the spotted owl. By ordering a supplemental environmental impact statement for the *Regional Guide*, Douglas MacCleery had raised the political stakes, transforming the conflict into a bona fide national issue. The Sierra Club Legal Defense Fund joined the fray, and Stahl moved to the fund. Then, in the fall of 1985, the Audubon Society received a grant from an anonymous donor to evaluate the condition of and prospects for the bird.[31]

Putting together a six-person advisory panel of biologists, the society held hearings in Sacramento and Vancouver, Washington, in December. Relying heavily on demographic calculations by Lande and others, it justified protection not with scientific evidence but with what would become a popular argument in the age of biocentrism: an appeal to ignorance.

It was not possible to say, the Audubon Society observed, that the owl was an endangered species. The owl's decline could have natural causes, particularly competition with its close relative the barred owl. "Insufficient data exist," it noted, to say whether northern and California spotted owls were distinct subspecies. And although demographic data suggest that the owl may be headed for extinction, perhaps within twenty years, "we hardly think the situation is this dire."

If the rate of decline were as great as Forsman and others suggested, the panel remarked, then "we could project back just four generations" — roughly twenty years — "and expect to find over 38 million pairs of owls, an absurdity." Other predictions "may be close to representative or they may be wildly optimistic. There are no data to tell us." As for "simulation models," apparently a reference to Lande's study, these "require more accurate estimates of the parameters and their variability than are currently available." Nevertheless, while acknowledging that almost nothing is known about the spotted owl, the panel recommended preserving a whopping amount of habitat: providing each of 1,500 pairs with areas ranging from 4,500 acres of old growth in Washington state to 1,400 acres in California, with "linkages" between these places.[32]

The panel therefore used scientific caution to reach a politically radical conclusion. The owl, not people, it said, should have the benefit of the doubt. Its recommendations risked putting thousands of people out of work simply because the owl may — or may not — be at risk. Saving the ecosystem was deemed more important than preserving the health and well-being of logging communities.

The Audubon recommendations revealed that concern for the owl was reverberating throughout the environmental community. Among those also worried was a teenager named Eric Beckwith.[33]

The boy's father, Steve, had been a doctoral candidate in biophysics, working on his dissertation in cellular biology in the late 1960s, and his mother, Yahdi, had earned a degree in English and anthropology, when, burned out and caught up in back-to-the-land fever, they dropped out of academe and went as deep into the hills as they could go — to the end of the road, at the farthest extent of the power grid in the Sierra Nevada Mountains. There the family — also including Eric's younger brothers Willow and Kale — operated a native plant nursery.

Combing the woods in search of seeds, the Beckwiths concluded that the Forest Service was "vacuuming the landscape." So they got interested in forest planning, eventually establishing their own organization, the Sierra Biodiversity Institute. Along the way Eric, self-taught since the age of eleven, became intensely interested in biology and conservation. Fearing that mainstream environmental groups were not doing enough, he decided to help save old growth himself. When a Forest Service scientist told him that the best strategy was to "get the Endangered Species Act involved," he devised a plan. Obtaining a copy of the law from the Defenders of Wildlife, he found that any "interested person" could petition to list a creature.

So Eric sat down and wrote Secretary of the Interior Donald Hodel a letter asking that the northern spotted owl be listed as an endangered species. Signed by both Eric, then nineteen, and Willow, fifteen, it amounted to saying, as Steve summarized it, "Hey, guys, this is wrong."

The service is required by law to respond to every petition and investigate the status of the species in question, even if the request is the whim of teenagers. By writing, Eric and Willow had triggered the process. Bureaucratic wheels began to turn, sending alarms throughout the environmental establishment. The boys' action, these professionals fretted, was premature. Eventually they intended to petition to list the owl as part of a carefully planned campaign for forests. But this was too early.

Representatives of several groups phoned the Beckwiths, pleading with Eric to drop the petition. One was Stahl, who suggested that a premature listing might jeopardize the Endangered Species Act. Eric, however, refused to budge. Then Steve himself drafted a letter to the service withdrawing the petition, which Eric and Willow reluctantly signed.

But that was just the beginning. Although Stahl had put off the Beckwiths, he now faced another premature petition, this time from Green-World. Getting its phone number from the Fish and Wildlife Service, he called. "I think maybe [the group] was a guy and his girlfriend," Stahl told writer William Dietrich. "The calls I would get from him were always from a telephone booth, with traffic in the background." The group's director, Max Strahan, a long-time radical activist with a physics degree from the University of Massachusetts and a deep suspicion of mainstream groups, refused to withdraw his petition. The die was cast. Realizing that they had to go along or be left behind, by August 1987 the Sierra Club Legal Defense Fund, along with twenty-eight other groups, had filed a second petition to list the owl. Featuring Lande's paper, it presented, they supposed, an airtight case.[34]

The courts evidently thought so as well. When, in December 1987, the Forest Service rejected the petition, saying that a proposed listing of the northern spotted owl was "not warranted at this time," twenty-five environmental groups filed suit in Seattle challenging the decision. In November 1988 federal district court judge Thomas S. Zilly would side with the activists, calling the decision "arbitrary and capricious and contrary to law" and requiring the service to do a second status review. By April 1989 the service had reversed itself and declared that listing the owl as a threatened species did in fact warrant review.[35]

Events then moved quickly. In 1988 Washington state listed the owl as endangered and began work on a recovery plan. The same year the Oregon Wildlife Commission reaffirmed the owl as "threatened" and considered protecting it on private lands under the state's Forest Practices Act. Oregon's Interagency Spotted Owl Subcommittee proposed new guidelines, for the first time taking into consideration the owl's entire range. In August the Bureau of Land Management, the Forest Service, and the National Park Service agreed to cooperate on ensuring the viability of the owl population.[36]

Lawsuits proliferated like flies on carrion, as every effort to sell timber by the Bureau of Land Management or Forest Service was met with an equal and opposite court challenge by environmentalists. In 1986 the BLM, deciding that a supplemental environmental impact statement was not needed, announced two hundred more timber sales in owl habitat. In October environmental groups, led by the Portland Audubon Society, sued to stop the sales. Then in 1987 activists led by the Seattle Audubon Society filed suit to enjoin logging in nearly three hundred spotted owl sites, and the case began a long journey through the courts.[37]

In December 1988, after completing its supplemental environmental impact statement for the *Regional Guide,* the Forest Service announced its intention to establish a Spotted Owl Habitat Area network, setting aside between one thousand and three thousand acres for each nesting pair. The decision was attacked by both sides. Nine environmental organizations, charging that it did not address the needs of animals for continuous habitat as Lande had argued, filed suit in February 1989. In March district court judge William Dwyer granted the environmentalists' motion for an injunction, stopping 163 planned sales.[38]

Biocentrism thus worked its way from thinkers such as Bill Devall, to activists such as Stahl, to the scientist Lande, to the Audubon Society, the courts, and ultimately into legislation. This in turn provoked strong opposition from those who supported the old order. Both sides sought to enlist the powers of the state in their cause. And as government intruded into the debate, the stakes rose and chaos spread.

Fearing that those who refused to play would surely lose the game, other antagonists — environmentalists, biologists, lumber executives, mill owners, and bureaucrats at all levels — joined the fray. But by seeking to control their own fate, they inadvertently transformed the issue into an industry for courts, agencies, law firms, and lobbyists, who, though knowing nothing about ecology, would nonetheless consume money, time, jobs, and lives.

Like blind men building a mechanical elephant, each of the players picked up hammer and wrench and, working separately and often secretly, fashioned gears, soldered wires, and pounded sheet metal. One built a leg, another the tail, a third the trunk. Then suddenly this creation, like a dreadful android, sprang to life, catching its builders in its gears as it lurched, uncontrolled, toward unknown destinations, without purpose, limit, or remorse.

In his preface to the 1787 edition of his philosophical classic *The Critique of Pure Reason*, Immanuel Kant likens his own effort to the undertaking of Copernicus, the sixteenth-century Pole who revolutionized astronomy. For 1,400 years the prevailing geocentric theory of planetary motion, developed by the Egyptian Ptolemy in the second century A.D., held that the earth was the center of the universe, and that the sun, planets, and stars revolved around it. Copernicus argued that the sun was the center around which the earth and other planets orbited.

In one sense the Copernican theory changed nothing, and in another it altered everything. The sun still rose in the east and set in the west, and our experience of the heavens remained the same. But the passage of the sun across the sky meant that the earth must be spinning on its axis; and this realization transfigured for all time how people felt about their environment. Suddenly they realized that they were not the still center of the universe.

Copernicus therefore achieved a real revolution. And Kant would do the same. In exploring knowledge, the philosopher suggested, "we should then be proceeding precisely on the lines of Copernicus' primary hypothesis. Failing of satisfactory progress in explaining the movements of the heavenly bodies on the supposition that they all revolved round the spectator, he tried whether he might not have better success if he made the spectator to revolve and the stars to remain at rest."[39]

So Kant constructed a philosophy that was equally revolutionary. We can understand only what we construct, he argued in the *Critique*. Our environment appears to us not as it is "in itself" but as we make it. Our predetermined concepts — which he called "categories"— shape reality. Just as Copernicus showed that the sun appears to cross the sky only because we ourselves are moving, so Kant claimed that our view of nature is formed by what we put into the picture.[40]

The Copernican revolution was what the historian of science Thomas S. Kuhn in 1962 called a "paradigm change." By "paradigm," said Kuhn, "I mean to suggest that some accepted examples of actual scientific practices . . . provide models from which spring particular coherent traditions of scientific research. These are the traditions which the historian describes under such rubrics as 'Ptolemaic astronomy' (or 'Copernican'), 'Aristotelian dynamics' (or 'Newtonian') . . . and so on."[41]

A scientific revolution, Kuhn suggested, occurs when scientists replace one paradigm with another. Such shifts not only alter our perspectives of nature but also profoundly change politics and society:

> Political revolutions aim to change political institutions in ways that those institutions themselves prohibit. Their success therefore necessitates the partial relinquishment of one set of institutions in favor of another, and in the interim, society is not fully governed by institutions at all. Initially it is crisis alone that attenuates the role of political institutions as we have already seen it attenuate the role of paradigms. . . . At that point the society is divided into competing camps or parties, one seeking to defend the old institutional constellation, the others seeking to institute some new one. And, once that polarization has occurred, *political recourse fails.* . . . Parties to a revolutionary conflict must finally resort to the techniques of mass persuasion, often including force.

Similarly, Kuhn concludes, "like the choice between competing political institutions, that between competing paradigms proves to be a choice between incompatible modes of community life."[42]

With these words Kuhn provided the intellectual framework with which to understand the environmental revolution. So it was not surprising that "paradigm shift" became the activists' favorite buzzword. Devall called for a "radical critical analysis of the dominant social paradigm." His sometime coauthor George Sessions viewed environmental adversaries as "separated by competing paradigms." Fritjof Capra claimed that "the paradigm that is now shifting has dominated our culture for several hundred years." Marilyn Ferguson observed that "the paradigm of the Aquarian Conspiracy sees humankind embedded in nature."[43]

But these observers did not fully appreciate what this shift meant. To be sure, they correctly noted that it replaced individualism and positivism with holism and the intuitive appreciation of nature. But, unlike Copernican theory, biocentrism did not reveal objective attributes of nature; it only changed our perspective of it. Like Kant's categories, it provided concepts with which observers could construct a new *perception* of reality.

This paradigm shift, in short, lay entirely in the eye of the beholder. Sudden concern about the owl derived not from ecological calamity but from a new interpretation of how nature ought to behave. Once society embraced a teleology that demanded balance, then actions such as logging took on new meaning. What had previously been seen as ordinary and even beneficial was suddenly perceived as an ecological catastrophe.

Quite unconsciously biologists accepted this notion, thereby transforming their discipline from science to metaphysics, promoting a foreboding of doom, and provoking a political crisis which ensured, as Kuhn put it, that contending parties would "finally resort to the techniques of mass persuasion, often including force."[44]

20

WOBBLIES AND
YELLOW RIBBONS

JUDI BARI AND DARRYL CHERNEY, singing "You Can't Clear-Cut Your Way to Heaven," walked slowly down the Jack of Hearts Road. Behind them forty "eco-avengers" shuffled forward with Luna, an ancient woman draped in an Earth First! flag. On the heels of this ragged parade a fifteen-truck convoy followed, impatiently grinding in low, carrying Mendocino County sheriff's deputies, federal marshals, Bureau of Land Management officials, Louisiana Pacific security guards, and uniformed officers of the California Highway Patrol.[1]

Out of sight, someone — perhaps Jakubal, originator of tree-sitting — raced ahead, planting traps for the trucks. So, as the mechanized column inched forward, it encountered a succession of artful barricades — boulders strategically placed to demolish oil pans, mountains of slash and bumper-height logs laid across the narrow dirt road, and piles of sticks hiding what Cherney called a "boulder surprise" inside.

Bari was having the time of her life. Here in the "Cahto wilderness" near Latonville, California, in October 1988 she was enjoying her first backwoods action. Although she hadn't seen any big trees yet, the whole show — the singing and high jinks, the chaos, the sense of community and comradeship as the Earth First!ers and locals got together, cooked food, and sang — was great fun. She now knew that she had a home in Earth First! And though she didn't realize it yet, she would soon be molding it to reflect her own distinctive philosophy of protest.

It had been a long odyssey for Bari, filled with fits and starts, but always progressing toward a developed political philosophy. Growing up in a Baltimore suburb, one of three girls, she was born into radicalism. Her Italian-Catholic father, a diamond setter, and her Jewish mother — one of the first women to graduate from Johns Hopkins University with a doctorate in mathematics — were committed socialists who identified closely with the labor union movement.[2]

A National Merit semifinalist, Bari matriculated at the University of Maryland just as the campus burst into protest over the war in Vietnam. She spent her college career, she recalled, "going to riots." Finding herself more interested in politics than academics, she dropped out, eventually moving to a "hippie house" in Tacoma Park, Maryland, dubbed "Buffalo House," where she and her boyfriend experimented with drugs and spent evenings reading American history and communist literature to each other.

Gradually she meandered down an uneven path toward labor activism. While working at a supermarket in Hyattsville, Maryland, she concluded that the local unions didn't care about workers displaced by new automated checkout machines. Organizing a strike of the rank and file, she was promptly fired then driven from the union. During this fracas the union accused Bari of conspiring with Michael Sweeney, another rump activist who lived a continent away, in San Diego. Former editor of the Stanford University undergraduate newspaper, Sweeney had written a paper condemning the union. Although his polemic had been circulated throughout the leftist underground, Bari had neither read it nor heard of him. But now, eager to learn about the man with whom she was accused of plotting rebellion, she found a copy of his paper and wrote to him.

The two began corresponding but, living thousands of miles apart, did not meet. Meanwhile, Bari continued to read "everything I could get my hands on" concerning labor history. And one movement, in particular, impressed her: the Industrial Workers of the World, or IWW, also known as the Wobblies. Founded in 1905, embracing socialism and militant tactics, this group instigated major strikes of textile workers during the second decade of this century.

The Wobblies, Bari discovered, used two strategies: "boring from within" and "dual unionism." The first emphasized quiet organization and recruitment at the shop level; the second implied creation of an organization outside the existing union structure. This latter idea, in particular, appealed to Bari, who soon found a way to apply it.

Taking a job with the Postal Service bulk mail center near Washington, D.C., Bari discovered that conditions there reminded her of "a nineteenth-century sweatshop." Workers, mostly black, were represented by three unions, which, she felt, tolerated long hours in a dangerous and dirty environment. She decided to try dual unionism. After building a new organization, she launched another wildcat strike, which was dramatically successful. The Postal Service agreed to improve working conditions; the chief union representative on the shop floor resigned, and Bari became shop steward.

Meanwhile, Bari, who had broken up with her boyfriend, sent Sweeney, who had just divorced, a copy of the shop-floor newspaper she was publishing. Then she invited him to visit. "And the moment we met," she says, "we decided to have a baby together." They launched into a bicoastal relationship, taking turns visiting each other. Despite "kicking and screaming" over her reluctance to leave Maryland — her home and scene of her greatest political triumph — Bari eventually moved to Santa Rosa and the two were married. Drawn into domesticity, she became a full-time housewife, serving first as caretaker for Sweeney's children, Zachery and Colleen, while his ex-wife went to law school, then as mother to their two own — Lisa, born in 1981, and Jessica, who arrived in 1985.

The couple bought a dilapidated house, which Bari, teaching herself carpentry, worked on for five years, "redoing everything." Eventually the couple sold their home "for a big profit" and began renovating another. Meanwhile, "to prevent brain death," Bari helped publish an anti–nuclear power newspaper. While she was pregnant with Jessica, her activist flame rekindled, she joined Pledge of Resistance, a Quaker movement dedicated to defending the Nicaraguan Sandinistas. Attending training seminars in peaceful resistance, Bari was impressed with Gandhi's philosophy of nonviolence. Thus, her activist philosophy began to fill out: first dual unionism, then nonviolence. But it lacked a third element which would serve as her guiding star.

After buying a piece of unimproved land in Mendocino County, Bari and Sweeney set out to build a new house from the ground up. But this venture did not work out. Living in a ten-by-twenty-foot unheated garage with two young children while they worked on the house, the couple began to fight. He moved out into a trailer in the driveway.

Eventually divorcing Sweeny in 1987, Bari decided to remake herself. Having launched Lisa on a Suzuki violin course, Bari, who had played the instrument as a child, took it up again, writing songs as well. Working as a carpenter, she was soon studying yet another subject: the environment. While building a 2,500-square-foot weekend home for a Bay Area doctor, Bari noticed some particularly beautiful red-grained knotless siding and paneling. She asked Gary Ball, a bookkeeper for the Yurt Works, a company specializing in alternative prefab houses, what the wood was. "It's redwood," he said, and, pointing to a piece of paneling, added, "That tree must have been over a thousand years old."[3]

Then Ball — a recent émigré from Colorado who, along with his wife,

Betty, had founded the Mendocino Environmental Center — gave Bari a picture of a Palco clear-cut to show her what the land looked like once the trees were removed. Bari was outraged. She had been building a yuppie second home out of trees born before the Battle of Hastings. Feeling duped, she sent the doctor a housewarming present — a picture of a clear-cut, to remind him where his wood had come from.

This epiphany launched Bari on the road to environmental activism. Still angry, she wrote a song lamenting the death of redwoods, called "Paradise." Her friends loved it, and persuaded her to sing it at a songfest in Ukiah, where the featured performer would be Darryl Cherney, locally famous for his defense of Headwaters.

When the two met that evening, Bari immediately felt attracted to Cherney. "Darryl was electrifying onstage," she recalled. "He got my attention. He was funny, and had everybody dancing and singing." They soon became an item. Almost immediately, Cherney asked Bari to join Earth First! But she had mixed feelings. On the one hand, she felt that the movement was too macho, too violent, too sexist. But on the other, she was attracted to the idea of industrial sabotage. "Darryl persuaded me. He said, 'Yeah, Earth First! is male-oriented, macho, but it is completely decentralized, so you can form your own local chapter the way you want." Taking Cherney's advice, Bari joined the fledgling Mendocino chapter of Earth First!, recently started by Cherney and the Balls. And with this step she forged the third link of her activism — biocentrism.

"What I took from Earth First!," she says, "were three ideas: first, biocentrism; second, the spirit of no compromise; and third, the idea of direct action as the primary tactic. . . . The first and most important was biocentrism, the greatest advance in thinking in twenty years. Humans are part of nature — that's not opinion, but fact. Direct action means leverage at the point of production. . . . If you take a few people and try to lobby Congress, you would be looking into the void. But a handful blocking a logging road can have a big impact. I saw that as a very powerful philosophy."

So she became Cherney's lover and joined Earth First! despite its "antiworker and antiwomen" orientation. And after coming aboard, she was pleasantly surprised to find a number of very capable women already in the group. Several of the women in the movement, including Kelpie Willsin and Karen Pickett, were "some of the strongest" she had ever met.

Bari campaigned to reshape Earth First! She would turn the movement from a macho, romantic tribal cult into a blue-collar, community-based bastion against multinational capitalism. Angered by the activists' indifference to the tragedy of George Alexander, she recruited women and timber workers, and focused on issues — such as mill closures and the use of dioxins in the workplace — that directly addressed worker concerns. At the national Round River Rendezvous in the summer of 1988, held on Mount Leona in Washington state's Kettle River Range, Bari convened a feminist caucus to discuss the low status of women in Earth First! Later she led a mixed-company sensitivity session to talk about these concerns.[4]

Her unionism began to take root. Before the California regional rendezvous that fall, Bari announced that she would offer a workshop on the Wobblies, and was astounded when two real live Wobblies contacted her, offering to help with instruction. This movement, she thought, had disappeared sixty years earlier. Instead, she found, it had enjoyed a continuous, if marginal, existence right up to the present.[5]

The workshop was a smashing success, as Bari convinced her comrades that Earth First! and the Wobblies were made for each other. This old union, she explained, had preached "No Compromise" and "Direct Action Gets the Goods" since 1905. It was among the few groups in U.S. history to advocate sabotage openly. It had introduced tree spiking back in the 1917 Pacific Northwest timber strike, and its black cat sabotage symbol had just been found on a decommissioned bulldozer in Missoula, Montana. Partnership with the Wobblies, as she told fellow Earth First!ers, was "a coalition with definite possibilities."[6]

Armed with these ideals, Bari set out in search of proletarian brethren to befriend. And a golden opportunity presented itself in Scotia, as the fight over Headwaters began to take on social as well as environmental dimensions.

The previous February Congressman John Dingell's House subcommittee investigating the Palco takeover had asked the Federal Trade Commission to examine whether Maxxam had illegally engaged in stock parking to avoid triggering Hart-Scott-Rodino. The congressman was also raising questions about Maxxam's liquidation of $50 million from its employee retirement fund, and the apparent sweetheart purchase of an annuity contract from Executive Life, run by a big investor in Hurwitz's junk bonds, Fred Carr. The workers' interests, Dingell complained, had not been represented in the deal: "The employees are being asked to finance the takeover and get none of the benefits of ownership."[7]

In September 1989, employees would bring suit against both Maxxam and Executive Life to rescind the annuity purchase and (their attorney,

Jeffrey Lewis, would tell Congress that the deal "may have a potentially devastating effect on my clients, as well as tens of thousands of other workers, retired workers, and families across the country").

Meanwhile, in August 1988 several Palco employees, led by Peter Kayes, electrified fellow workers by unveiling the Employee Stock Ownership Plan (ESOP), a proposal to buy the company back from Hurwitz. At a September meeting at the Eureka Inn to discuss ESOP, more than four hundred people showed up.[8]

And as workers were organizing in October 1988, Bill Bertain, representing several Palco shareholders, filed *Thompson v. Maxxam*, a lawsuit against several premerger Palco executives, as well as against Boesky, Milken, Drexel, Maxxam, Hurwitz, and the investment banking firm Salomon Brothers, for forcing his clients to "sell their stock . . . at a price below its true worth because of the fraud and breach of duty of the defendants in connection with the takeover of Pacific Lumber by Maxxam Group and Drexel Burnham Lambert."[9]

This conflict was like honey to a bear for Bari. Hearing of the ESOP fight, she and Cherney drove to Eureka and called a meeting of Palco employees, urging them to join the Wobblies. But although they recruited one employee, Peter Kayes, the effort quickly fizzled. Playing hardball, Hurwitz warned his employees that he would never sell. Few came to Bari's meeting, and eventually Kayes left the company. Rather than realizing a worker revolution, ESOP had been reduced to another socialist fable.[10]

It was not working-class consciousness but biocentrism that drove the conflict. Pursuing their ideal, activists energized politicians and the courts, thereby elevating the dispute about trees into a titanic struggle between different ways of life.

In January 1988 at a national Restore the Earth conference held on the Berkeley campus, Earth First! proposed using public funds to buy Palco land, creating a Headwaters Forest Wilderness Complex. Almost immediately the state director of forestry, Jerry Partain, endorsed the idea, proposing to purchase the old growth with a bond issue. Then in February state assemblyman Byron Sher put forward a bill that would outlaw clear-cuts, but in May withdrew his bill after receiving assurances from Palco that the company would end all clear-cutting.[11]

That same month Cherney traveled to Wall Street, where he sat on the steps of the New York Stock Exchange singing, "All we are saying is give trees a chance" to a John Lennon tune. As the *Earth First! Journal* complained that "major conservation groups still sit on spineless duffs, watching the last unprotected primeval redwoods fall," Greg King and others, following what was by now a familiar tactic, reoccupied All Species Grove to slow logging until EPIC could get a friendly judge to issue a restraining order. By the end of the year EPIC had filed five lawsuits against Palco, three times succeeding in stopping Palco timber harvests, as Hurwitz and Campbell, like wounded bears, fought back.[12]

The environmentalists' most powerful weapons were the California Forest Practices Act, which gave the state authority to say how trees on private lands could be cut, and the state's Environmental Quality Act, requiring that wildlife populations be maintained at self-perpetuating levels. Although there was no evidence that any wildlife was in fact declining, these laws propelled public agencies onto a collision course with one another. The California Division of Forestry and Board of Forestry sided with the timber industry, while the Department of Fish and Game and Water Quality Control Board joined with environmentalists.[13]

And as Headwaters sucked state agencies and politicians into its collapsing orbit, Luddism reigned supreme within Earth First! In December 1987 a band calling itself "Mindless Thugs Against Genetic Engineering" poured 250 pounds of salt on a strawberry patch near Brentwood, California. As part of an experiment, the fruit had been sprayed with genetically altered bacteria intended to make it more resistant to frost. The group also sprayed the patch with a fire extinguisher full of ammonia and a slow-acting herbicide.[14]

Activists vied to outdo one another's extremism. "Stumps Suck! Wimps! Sissies! You Earth First!ers are all a bunch of moderate pukes. We're tired of your pussyfooting tactics and waffling tendencies," someone calling himself "The Avenger" announced in the Earth First! Journal in March. "We have no further patience for milketoast [sic] wilderness proposals which speak in acres, not continents. . . . No more nonviolent disobedience for us. . . . A new group is emerging. We are Stumps Suck! Our tactics include terrorism, coercion, and dumping sawdust on people's doorsteps. We don't mess around!"[15]

High on the list of Earth First! targets was the Forest Service. In April, Earth First! staged a "National Day of Outrage Against the Forest Service" in cities across the country, including Portland, San Francisco, Denver, and Duluth; Laconia, New Hampshire; Hamilton and Missoula, Montana; Salt Lake City; and, of course, Washington, D.C. Dubbing Forest Service employees "Freddies" (an acronym for "Forest Rape Eagerly Done and Done in Endless Succession"), protesters took up positions around Forest Service offices chanting, "No more roads! No more clear-cuts! No more cutting of old growth! No more grazing. No more herbicides and pesticides!"[16]

Others took aim at Smokey the Bear. In Denver, Earth First!ers staged a performance by "Smokey," who committed suicide by drinking (western) hemlock; elsewhere, according to Karen Pickett, confrontations with this hapless ursine "ranged from one in San Francisco that ended with Smokey and a friend escorted away in handcuffs by federal police, to a Montana encounter that evolved from coffee and doughnuts into a high-volume free-for-all between Earth First!ers, Freddies and loggers, to Sequoia's formal challenge to mud-wrestle with a Mendocino National Forest ranger."[17]

Forest rangers throughout the country began to quake behind their desks with apprehension. In Missouri agency employees, forewarned of the protest and fearing that office equipment might be sabotaged with super glue, hid their computers. In Florida officials searched protesters, confiscating at least one bag of sawdust, before allowing them to meet with the local Forest Service supervisor. To the delight of Earth First!ers, in Portland a ranger warned the Northwest Forestry Association, "We hear that Earth First! people are going to do some significant things to get our attention. . . . They have made our lives somewhat miserable."[18]

This, as events in Okanogan, Washington, revealed, was an understatement.

The Okanogan incident began quietly enough.

In early July 1988 a local logger parked his heavy equipment in the Okanogan National Forest near a grove slated for harvest. Fearing ecotage, he stationed two eighteen-year-old boys armed with shotguns in a trailer next to the equipment. He had reason to be nervous. Environmentalists had already characterized the stands he was slated to log as the "best lynx habitat in the south forty-eight." That spring someone had shot a hole in a helicopter that was lifting logs out of the forest. Another chopper had crashed, killing a passenger, and when authorities reached the scene, they found an Earth First! sticker on the cockpit bubble. The operator of a head rig at a nearby mill was injured when the saw hit some object, perhaps a tree spike. Then residents in this sleepy community noticed a suspicious increase in the number of campers pitching tents in the nearby national forest.[19]

So, naturally, the boys standing in the clearing that night jumped when they heard someone climb into the cab of a log loader. Getting out their guns and a high-powered spotlight, they flushed an Earth First!er hiding behind a rock. Terrified, guards and intruder ran in opposite directions. Coming down the hill, one watchman shone his light on the loader just as another Earth First!er jumped off. He fired his gun into the air, sending three or four more intruders crashing through the bush.

This incident should have alerted the Forest Service but didn't. The next day, Okanogan County sheriff Bill Tweed received a call from the local ranger, who told him, "We may have a little minor demonstration down here. We expect a maximum of eight, outside, and if it gets really wild, maybe twenty people."[20]

Instead more than 120 showed up, led by Cherney. Singing songs and carrying Earth First! banners and posters protesting the extinction of lynx, the activists rioted. Armed with super glue to pour into computers, they charged the ranger station as Forest Service personnel barricaded the doors. Unable to penetrate the defenses, the activists laid siege to the building, covering air conditioning vents with cow manure and refusing to allow the occupants to leave. Eventually, Sheriff Tweed and his deputies arrived, arrested twenty-four demonstrators, and relieved the federal garrison.

Throughout the spring and summer of 1988, events unfolded with the remorseless logic of anger. So long as the activists refused to compromise, the loggers would not compromise either. Feeling trapped and abandoned, the people of the logging communities suppressed their fear and loathing until it surfaced again at an event called the Silver Fire Roundup.

Ever since the Bald Mountain Road fight of 1982, Grants Pass in Josephine County, Oregon, near the Kalmiopsis, had been a favorite target for the marauding Nomadic Action Group. These locals had closely followed the trial of Kelpie Willsin and five others — known as the "Sapphire Six"— who had been convicted by a county judge for locking themselves to a yarder to protest the Sapphire timber sale, and who had also been sued by the company that owned the equipment, Huffman and Wright, for $57,818 in damages.[21]

Nevertheless, the locals were unprepared for what happened after lightning fires swept the Kalmiopsis on August 30, 1987, scorching 96,000 acres around Silver Creek near the Bald Mountain Road. As was customary, the Forest Service proposed a "salvage" harvest of 247 million board feet to remove burned timber. Most foresters believed that the alternative — leaving the dead trees — was wasteful, dangerous, and ecologically damaging. The first time a fire strikes, it usually burns only enough of the outer layer of the tree to kill it, leaving the rest unscathed. Over time the remaining wood becomes tinder dry, providing explosive fuel for subsequent conflagrations. Yet the lumber, if harvested quickly, can be very valuable.[22]

Few in Oregon old enough to remember had forgotten the famous Tillamook burn, and how salvage had saved a forest. This conflagration, the historian Stephen Pyne observes, consuming a great stand of virgin timber, "was a 300,000-acre fire that burned intermittently for eighteen years," a cyclic holocaust that first erupted in 1933 then broke out again in 1939, 1945, and 1951, with small burns occurring between the bigger ones. Tillamook's first iteration erupted like a thermonuclear device, devastating a vast region so completely that less than one live tree was left standing per square mile. "The devastation, covering some 311,000 acres," wrote a local historian, "was unbelievable."[23]

But rather than discouraging future fires, the first burn, by killing trees, merely dried the wood, which ignited subsequent flareups. Tillamook was a major economic disaster for the state. Foresters realized that something clearly had to be done, for left alone, charred areas were not regenerating but flaring continuously. Two months after the first burn the state forester announced: "The only hope lies in salvage, but the enormous amount of timber involved makes it impossible to log it all before decay and insects take a large toll. . . . It is a stupendous problem and necessitates concerted private and public action to remove all possible values." Thus began what Pyne describes as "the greatest salvage operation in American history." Beginning in 1933, it continued into the 1950s. The burn business boomed. Eventually more than two hundred logging companies would work on salvage simultaneously, and nearly all sound timber would be harvested. Fire roads were punched through the area, and avenues of snags were felled for firebreaks.[24]

But, as the salvage continued, it became clear that Tillamook would not regenerate without help. When the burning resumed, writes Pyne, it "obliterated refugia left by the original fire, devastated reproduction, and pushed back the green borders from which reseeding might occur. The Tillamook had been burned by man and logged by man; it would also have to be restocked by man."[25]

In 1948 Oregon voters approved a constitutional amendment to authorize bond issues to pay for reseeding, and the next year reforestation began. More than 73 million trees were planted and 97,679 acres seeded. Designated Tillamook State Forest in 1973, the area flourished. Fifty years after the first fire, it had become the pride of the state, a lush forest of Douglas fir, Port Orford cedar, and pines, many over two feet in diameter, once again supporting commercial logging.[26]

. . .

Tillamook stood as a shining example, illustrating how dangerous it is to let snags stand and how wise forestry can benefit both man and nature. Foresters therefore were dumbfounded when activists opposed the sale, suggesting that fire salvage "was like mugging a burn victim" and insisting that "not one burnt stick" should be taken by loggers. The issue of cutting dead trees escalated into yet another political fight. By February the *Earth First! Journal* was calling for "ecological jihad." Responding to these protests, the Forest Service sought compromise, reducing the allowable salvage to 157 million board feet. But environmentalists were unwilling to negotiate, and on July 8 the National Wildlife Federation, the National Audubon Society, the Wilderness Society, the Oregon Natural Resources Council, and other groups filed for a temporary restraining order against the Silver Creek harvest.[27]

Loggers were frantic. Every time they compromised, it seemed, the activists wanted more. First the environmentalists had objected to building roads, then to cutting old growth, now to taking dead trees. Where would it stop? Even a court delay would ensure that the trees would rot before they could be harvested. As these woodsmen fretted, another calamity occurred, underscoring their pain: the Medco plywood plant in Grants Pass shut down, putting 180 people out of work.[28]

The local communities had to fight back, to organize. But how? Looking for ideas, James Peterson, publisher of a small wood products magazine called *Evergreen*, drove from Grants Pass to Libby, Montana, in May to attend the Great Northwest Log Haul. Organized by a Montana logger, Bruce Vincent, himself a victim of Earth First! ecotage, the meeting was intended as a protest against Earth First! attacks. Sort of a woodsmen's teach-in, the log haul was a smashing success. Thousands of loggers came, and CBS's *60 Minutes* covered the event.[29]

While in Libby, Peterson and Vincent discussed their fix. Loggers and others who worked the land, they agreed, were scattered and isolated from one another. Unlike environmentalists, they could not network easily and were unable to fashion coordinated responses to attacks. So the two mapped a plan for a grassroots coalition that would link ranching, farming, mining, and logging people together.

Returning home, Peterson called a meeting of Oregon loggers to plan a response to the attacks that were destroying their way of life. Together with Grants Pass gyppo Bob Slagle, he conceived the idea for the Silver Fire Roundup, setting the date for August 27, 1988, at the Josephine County Fairgrounds. They asked all loggers to come wearing yellow ribbons, just like the strips people had tied outside their homes when American embassy personnel in Tehran were being held prisoner by

Iranian militants. Feeling themselves captives of hostile foreign forces, they saw the yellow ribbons as a symbol of their solidarity, too.

To announce the roundup, logger Greg Miller hiked Interstate 5 from Eugene to Grants Pass, tying yellow ribbons to posts along the way to guide out-of-state truckers to the fairgrounds. The response was overwhelming. The first logging truck rolled into the fairgrounds at 10:45 the morning of August 27; the last arrived at 7:45 that evening. Altogether 1,526 trucks from five states were parked at the fairgrounds, and approximately another three hundred were pulled up on the tarmac across the highway at the cement plant.[30]

"Left unsalvaged, the burned area will take five hundred years to recover," Congressman Bob Smith shouted from a stage atop a flatbed truck. ". . . If there's going to be a spotted owl set-aside, why not set aside for the freckle-faced logger as well?" Don't call the opposition "environmentalists," Bruce Vincent urged the crowd. "We are the environmentalists. They are the terrorists, obstructionists, and preservationists."[31]

Following the foundup, Peterson, Slagle, and others founded the Yellow Ribbon Coalition. They would borrow tactics from the environmentalists, become a grassroots group, and fight fire with fire! They had drawn a line in the sand. No activist, they decided, should be trusted. As the *Earth First! Journal* later observed, this was "the first year when *all* environmentalists in Oregon were labeled extremists."[32]

By the time Bari walked into Cahto, therefore, both the Douglas fir and the redwood regions had splintered into myriad shards of hatred, dismay, misery, and paranoia. Chasms lay between logging towns and Earth First!, between state agencies serving logging constituents and those representing environmentalists, between Palco and politicians in Sacramento.

Quickly the yellow ribbon became the symbol activists loved to hate. Loggers had chosen these ribbons as their symbol, environmentalists mistakenly suggested, because yellow bands were used to mark trees for cutting. Bari joined in the condemnation, referring to the "Nazi-like Yellow Ribbon Campaign, where workers, their families, and local businesses are asked to fly yellow ribbons to show solidarity with management against the environmentalist 'threat.'"[33]

Of course, she had things backwards. Loggers thought of themselves as entrepreneurs, not workers, and the yellow ribbon was a spontaneous expression of fear and comradeship among people under siege. The loggers viewed the Earth First!ers as fanatics bent on putting them out of business. The gulf between the two continued to grow. Forces were pushing people apart, not together. Bari's romantic socialist ideals of worker solidarity could not be heard above the cacophony of conflict. And just around the corner lay the second battle of Millennium Grove, otherwise known as the "Easter Sunday Massacre," which would push Earth First! and loggers to the brink of total war.

21

THE EASTER SUNDAY
MASSACRE

A COLD WIND BLEW as Tom Hirons, Larry Robertson, and six other cutters and loggers drove up the road in snowmobiles. Scanning the way ahead nervously, they felt like cowboys riding through Indian country, expecting an ambush. Everyone in Mill City had seen the Earth First! leaflets promising a big action at Breitenbush this Easter weekend, 1989.[1]

As the caravan rounded the corner, Hirons and Robertson saw the smiling face of a man — who they later learned was Earth First!er Leo Hund — buried to the neck in a pile of rocks in the middle of the road. Behind Hund the route was strewn with boulders and blocked by a chain stretched between trees. The loggers carefully drove around the Earth First!er, rolled the rocks away, removed the chains, and eventually reached the stand slated for cutting. But no sooner had they arrived than the woods came alive.

Men and women in parkas and wool shirts jumped from behind trees, followed by television camera and sound men. Around fifty activists, having arrived the night before on snowshoes and cross-country skis, were chained to Douglas firs with Kryptonite bike locks, sitting in tree platforms, or, like Hund, buried in the ground. Others ran, spitting and cursing, shouting "murderers!," as the cutters walked to their equipment cache to find their chain saws demolished.

The Second Battle of Breitenbush had begun. Fought just twenty miles northeast of the site of the 1986 conflict of Millennium Grove, near the North Santiam River in Willamette National Forest, it would become known as the Easter Sunday Massacre. It was the first time these woodsmen, who regularly risked their lives felling trees, felt fear. That morning, as the snow fell hard against their faces, they suddenly became aware of the full fury of the forces aligned against them and saw with cruel clarity that their way of life was coming to an end.[2]

For the loggers things had been going wrong for months. In January the Fish and Wildlife Service, acceding to circuit court judge William Dwyer's order, had reopened review of the petition to list the spotted owl as an endangered species. In March Dwyer, acquiescing to a petition filed by nine environmental groups led by the Seattle Audubon Society, issued an injunction halting 135 Forest Service timber sales. Then, in the ongoing lawsuit brought against the Bureau of Land Management by the Portland Audubon Society, district court judge Helen Frye suspended another two hundred timber sales on O&C lands.[3]

By these acts the courts reflected a shift in the prevailing cultural winds. The biocentric vision was spreading throughout America. Environmentalists knew that the public itself would serve as jury in any court of last resort. And now that the owl had become a national issue, they were using it as an effective fundraising tool to support broader publicity efforts. They became spin doctors, successfully convincing the nation that logging was ecologically evil and must be halted, and that because they assaulted nature, loggers did not deserve consideration.

In 1988 two conservation groups — the Wilderness Society and the National Wildlife Foundation — launched a media campaign that would prove particularly successful in tilting sympathy away from the loggers. With grants from the Andrew W. Mellon Foundation, the Pew Charitable Trust, and the W. Alton Jones Foundation, they published a series of books, *National Forests: Policies for the Future*, framing an argument that would serve to deny responsibility for the human suffering their protests caused.[4]

Preserving the remaining old growth, the Wilderness Society authors argued, would not hurt loggers because the industry was dying anyway. Forest depletion and mill mechanization were already producing long-term declines in employment, and whether or not old growth was spared, these would continue. "Between 1980 and 1985," the authors wrote, "the number of jobs in logging, lumber, and wood products manufacturing in western Washington and Oregon dropped from 82,000 to 71,500" despite the cutting of record volumes of trees.

With no change in historic cutting levels on the national forests, the baseline projection demonstrates that the annual timber harvest in the area will fall 16 percent by the year 2030. A total of 8,200 jobs will be lost to the reduced timber harvest alone. Old-growth protection is shown to exacerbate the situation, reducing the timber cut 22 percent by the year 2030 and eliminating 2,300 jobs in addition to projected job losses under the baseline scenario.

This analysis demonstrates, according to the authors,

the need to rethink conventional wisdom which holds that the amount of logging — particularly cutting the big old trees — is the key to a prosperous, growing economy in the Pacific Northwest. This view certainly did not prevent the loss of 13 percent of the timber industry's work force between 1980 and 1985, while logging on both the national forests and other lands reached record levels. Nor will it stem the loss of 26,450 more jobs to labor-saving technology over the next 45 years.[5]

This argument, suggesting that preservation would not hurt loggers very much — costing "only" an additional 2,300 jobs above those lost to technology — soon became a litany among the media and conservationists. But, like many statistics, these told a misleading story. Rather than supporting a mere 71,500 jobs in Oregon and Washington, as the authors claim, the wood products industry sustained 110,000 workers in Oregon alone, according to the University of Oregon economists Mark T. Spriggs and Gerald S. Albaum. And this does not include indirect employment for services such as trucking and paperboard manufacture. Nor is there a simple relation between productivity and employment, as the Oregon State University forest economist Brian Greber observes. Technological improvements "can result in less jobs, more jobs, different jobs or no change at all." Thus, although mechanization did take a slow toll on mill jobs from the 1960s on, it had almost no effect on cutters and loggers, whose tools had not improved much since the invention of the chain saw. Jobs in this category actually *increased* over a forty-year period — from 1.2 jobs per million board feet cut in 1947 to 1.5 per million in 1987.[6]

Also, instead of disappearing, other wood products jobs merely shifted in response to changes in market demand. As mill mechanization displaced workers, new positions appeared with firms specializing in finished lumber products, such as truss and I-beam construction. Indeed, by the most objective measure — the number of wood products jobs per million board feet of timber cut — employment had remained stable for a generation. In 1947 8.2 billion board feet were taken from Oregon and

Washington forests, and the number of jobs per million board feet harvested was 9.3. In 1987 the same amount of timber was harvested, while the number of jobs per million board feet had shrunk only slightly to 8.9.[7]

"Rather than causing job losses," writes Greber, "technological improvements allowed many timber mills to survive in a competitive international marketplace during the 1980s." And though "mill modernization did cause job losses in the early 1980s, from 1970–9, technological improvement in the Pacific Northwest actually created more jobs in the wood products industry, during a trend towards greater utilization of wood and new types of products."[8]

In fact, the biggest employment decline had occurred earlier, not as a result of mechanization but from the expansion of wilderness. RARE I and new national parks and recreation areas put 3.6 million acres, or 17 percent of Douglas fir public forests, off-limits to logging, and subsequent wilderness legislation withdrew another 7 percent, or 2 million acres, so that by 1989 over half of the region's old growth had been protected.[9]

In sum, preservation, not technology, had cost jobs. And the creation of still more sanctuaries would be a devastating blow. Even conservative federal estimates of job losses from owl protection were more than ten times the Wilderness Society figures. Several economists predicted that over 100,000 workers would be laid off, resulting in losses of $2.5 billion from the local economy and more than $270 million in taxes to local governments for fire and police protection, schools, roads, and social services.[10]

In western Washington, according to Robert G. Lee, professor of forest sociology at the University of Washington, saving remaining old growth would reduce Forest Service receipts by 25 percent and O&C income by two thirds, and it would diminish local government income up to 50 percent, for everything from hospitals and law enforcement to social services and libraries. In 1991 Lee wrote:

Indication of the magnitude of social costs associated with the economic dislocation can be gained from a recent study of social costs associated with timber industry job losses in Washington State. . . . Analysis predicted that total additional social costs in unemployment insurance, welfare, social security, training, wages lost, and taxes lost would total $165 million within the first year of the dislocation of 7,560 timber industry workers. This estimate did not include the increased costs of psychological counseling, law enforcement, education, or loss of asset value in homes, businesses,

THE EASTER SUNDAY MASSACRE

and equipment. It also did not consider the social costs of indirect job losses, or many of the other less easily measured costs.

The impact of such job loss on rural communities in timber-dependent regions of western Washington, Lee continued, "would be so severe that it can be most accurately described as a major disaster." By comparison, "the Washington State floods of last winter [1990–91] caused $41 million in property damage and took one life. There was an outpouring of sympathy and a national disaster was declared to provide support for rebuilding. . . . Yet there has been little effort by state or federal officials to develop strategies for the planned disaster inflicted on timber-dependent communities."[11]

This projected calamity was unique in only one way: rather than being caused by bad weather, an earthquake, or an economic downturn, it was the intentional consequence of political decisions. The nation, Lee suggested, ignores and invites the loggers' plight because it deems them to be guilty of an ecological crime. This makes them victims of what he, following sociologist Susan Opotow, calls "moral exclusion." Those deemed to live outside the "moral community" to "which moral values, rules, and considerations of fairness apply," writes Opotow, are seen as "nonentities, expendable, or undeserving; consequently harming them appears acceptable, appropriate." Likewise, says Lee, "moral exclusion of those who 'harm or abuse the environment' has been one of the most prominent expressions of the emerging cultural theme associated with environmental preservation." Activists, he observes, call loggers "buffalo hunters," "destroyers," "tree murderers," and "rapers of the land." The press "frets about owls and trees but reveal indifference to [the loggers'] plight."[12]

And indeed the nation had lost sympathy for loggers, as another popular argument revealed. The Forest Service, according to this view, was selling timber at a loss. These deficit timber sales, it was claimed, merely subsidized overharvesting and should therefore be stopped. Embraced by both environmentalists and Reaganites, this rationale pushed liberals and conservatives into the antilogging camp. "Free market" economists cited below-cost timber sales as proof that the Forest Service lacked incentives to conserve. And for environmentalists it showed that the agency remained a captive of the wood products industry. Both called for an end to "subsidies."[13]

This complaint, however, had less to do with logging than with environmentalism itself. The elaborate planning process mandated by the

National Forest Management Act had caused agency costs to double since 1964, even as harvests remained roughly stable. Owing to the rising expense of this paperwork, along with proliferating litigation, the service became virtually the only timber producer in the United States to lose money. Even state governments such as Montana's spent half as much on logging its lands as did the Flathead National Forest in that state.[14]

Moreover, rather than signaling a genuine concern about subsidies, the "below cost" issue reflected a shift in perspective. Few complained that federal outdoor recreation user fees covered just 3 percent of costs, that the public subsidy per wilderness visit per day was actually between $14 and $25, that national park entrance charges covered only 7 percent of operating costs, or that Forest Service subsidies of outdoor activities almost equaled those for grazing and logging combined.[15]

Instead, protests centered on the 25 percent of income from timber sales turned over to local governments in lieu of taxes. If these disbursements were subtracted, the agency did not lose money. Complaints about deficit timber sales rested on a semantic sleight of hand signaling that the nation no longer believed in Pinchot's goal of "community stability." What once was deemed the federal obligation to pay a fair share of local taxes was suddenly seen as a "subsidy." This shift in attitude toward loggers was part of a disturbing return to caste and class in America. As *The Atlantic Monthly* reported in 1994, the rich were getting richer and everyone else poorer at an accelerating rate. Since 1972 wages for the bottom 60 percent of male workers fell a staggering 20 percent, and the median male income dropped 12 percent. The number of young men between eighteen and twenty-four earning under $12,195 annually more than doubled during the 1980s. The percentage of young women earning under that amount rose from 29 to 48.[16]

As upward economic mobility slowed, social lines hardened and sympathy for the less fortunate diminished. Just so, affluent urban America lost touch with its more humble rural roots and sought to justify this detachment by claiming a higher allegiance to the "ecosystem." This idea was capturing the minds and hearts of many, including the men and women who worked for what had long been silviculture's champion — the Forest Service itself.

Ever since passage of the 1976 National Forest Management Act, this agency's values had shifted steadily toward biocentrism. But this emerging institutional consciousness went undetected. Then, in January 1989, a Willamette National Forest employee named Jeff DeBonis brought the evolution into the open. After returning from a University of Oregon "ancient forest" seminar, he sent a fighting memo to his colleagues.

Between 1979 and 1989, DeBonis wrote, the timber harvest on federal lands in Oregon had increased 18.5 percent. He continued:

> In that same period, employment in the wood products industry dropped 15 percent. The point here is that the claim by the timber industry that employment is tied to the harvest level in the National Forests is simply not true. The real impact on employment in the wood products industry is the automation and modernization of mills. . . . Even if the current, unsustainable level of harvest were to continue for the next forty-five years, the Pacific Northwest wood products industry would lose at least 35,000 jobs.

If all the ancient forest left on federal lands in the Pacific Northwest were saved, DeBonis added, it would translate into only 2,300 jobs lost. "We, as an agency," he concluded, "are perceived by the conservation community as being an advocate of the timber industry's agenda. Based on my ten years with the Forest Service, I believe this charge is true. I also believe, along with many others, that this agency needs to re-take the moral 'high-ground,' i.e., we need to be advocates for many of the policies, goals, and solutions proposed by the conservation community."[17]

DeBonis was correct that timber *harvests* had increased during the previous decade because the market had driven up prices. Forest Service timber *sales*, however, had remained flat during the period. Criticizing the service for the upsurge of cutting, therefore, seems partisan at best. Indeed, the figures he cites were identical to those published in the National Wildlife Federation–Wilderness Society study. And in March 1987 he founded his own advocacy group, the Association of Forest Service Employees for Environmental Ethics (AFSEEE), which by summer was off and running. Publishing a newsletter, *Inner Voice,* it became a national force. Its income would grow from $19,566.92 in 1989 to more than $680,000 in 1992. Well funded by the W. Alton Jones Foundation, the Rockefeller Family Fund, and other philanthropies, it represented the revolution in values overtaking the Forest Service. According to University of Idaho Resource Recreation and Tourism specialists Greg Brown and Charles C. Harris, AFSEEE members strongly support the "New Resource Management Paradigm," which stresses agreement with the ideas of "nature for its own sake," "environmental protection over commodity outputs," the "New Forestry," and "consultative and participatory decision making." Representing the younger, newer recruits, it was the future of the agency.[18]

The new metaphor for nature, therefore, inserted yet another player into the old-growth game, tilting the board ever more steeply in favor of the owl. But as national values changed, as the ecosystem idea captivated an ever larger public, and as environmentalists demonized forestry, the loggers of Mill City remained unaware of their isolation.

Until Breitenbush. That Easter Sunday, when activists, writers, and television crews jumped out of the woods, these people sensed with sudden clarity that the rest of the country was playing a joke on them. They were alone, and now they knew it.

Not that they hadn't expected trouble. In fact, they knew it was coming. Ever since the 1986 Battle of Millennium Grove, friction between Earth First!ers and loggers had continued. It reached a peak that fall when the Forest Service conducted its North Roaring Devil timber sale on the south fork of the Breitenbush River. The Oregon Natural Resources Council, insisting that this was spotted owl habitat, asked the courts for an injunction to stop the sale. So when, in January 1989, Portland judge James Burns rejected the environmentalists' request, and the Forest Service and the Bugaboo Timber company announced their intent to log Breitenbush "upon spring thaw," everyone knew that disorder was on the way.[19]

When spring came, Jim Morgan, the Mill City mill owner who had purchased the timber, asked Hirons to escort the cutters to the site. A few days before operations were to begin, Hirons, Robertson, and a crew rode to the Breitenbush unit by snowmobile, caching their chain saws and other equipment in places where they hoped activists wouldn't find them.

But when the loggers returned to the cutting site on Easter Sunday to find the activists waiting for them, they realized how wrong they were. Not only had Earth First! found their supplies, but so had CBS television, *Good Morning America*, the *Today Show*, and the whole damned world! Having lost in court, the protesters had arrived in force, intent on direct action. In addition to encountering rocks, logs, and strange people buried in the road and chained to the trees, Hirons's team found Jim Morgan's road grader destroyed. Someone had drained the oil from the transmission and transfer cases, then emptied a fire extinguisher into the housings and run the motor until the machinery seized.

Telling the others to "keep cool," Hirons phoned the Forest Service to send rangers and police to clear the area. Then he and his crew went home. The next day they returned with their wives, who came to lend moral support. Once again the Earth First!ers greeted them, this time with banners stretched across the logging road which read, "Save Our Old Growth."

As activists and journalists cavorted through the woods and the wives looked on with anxiety, the cutters went to work. Every time they felled a tree, Earth First!ers set off an electric foghorn, as if it were intended to signify the death moan of a dying tree. Its eerie groan, echoing through the canyon, made the workers, already nervous, jumpy as cats. "I think they were hoping to distract us," Larry Robertson recalled, "so that someone would get hurt and we would be forced to stop." There was a "tree witch," he remembered, who "put a curse on a lot of trees. On trunks she put painted sticks covered with feathers and shaped like a cross, then pretended to 'hex' the tree so that if anyone cut it, a terrible thing would happen to him."

And, indeed, as if by black magic, a tragedy occurred. A young hook tender, Steven Benham, had just attached a turn of logs. As the skycar lifted the load, the belly of the skyline swung, knocking the top off a snag. This debris crashed into another snag, which fell on Benham, killing him instantly.

Ordinarily loggers would have blamed this death on the "New Forestry" regulations requiring cutters to leave snags standing, a practice they knew was highly hazardous. But this time the accident seemed to reveal Earth First!'s powerful juju. Shaken, the loggers and their wives went home, following the ambulance.[20]

Their pain was palpable. But to the activists and reporters they were invisible. Andy Kerr of the Oregon Natural Resources Coalition saw the trees, not the dead Benson, as the sacrifice, commenting, "You win some, you martyr some." Catherine Caufield, covering the Breitenbush action for the *New Yorker*, did not mention the loggers at all. Instead she praised the Earth First!ers as dedicated grassroots activists, ignoring the fact that their protest was illegal and that they had damaged property belonging to people less affluent than they. "Ours was once a forested planet," she wrote, repeating the oft-cited myth. "Originally, the Pacific forest covered seventy thousand square miles of Canada and the United States. . . . In the United States, less than ten per cent survives."[21]

It was impossible for loggers to compete with such romantic nonsense. "The battle to preserve what remains of our ancient forests," Caufield continued, "is not driven by science or economics or an abstract respect for natural systems. . . . Across the Pacific region people have fought to save their patch of forest. . . . What has now come to be referred to as 'the ancient-forest movement' was not started by professional environmentalists in Washington, D.C., for some theoretical or bureaucratic reason. It was started and is being carried on by scores of local groups. . . . They are people with jobs and children, with ordinary lives."[22]

After Breitenbush such rhetoric cascaded forth from television and the press. In September an Audubon Society film, *Ancient Forests: Rage over Trees*, premiered on the Turner network, followed the next year by publication of the Wilderness Society book *Ancient Forests of the Pacific Northwest* by Elliott Norse; a *Life* magazine Earth Day 1990 issue focusing on "the miracle of trees," with a photo essay on ancient forests; a *Time* magazine cover story on spotted owls and ancient forests; and by the following September a *National Geographic* article on "the fate of the world's greatest rainforest."[23]

No mention was made of the "ordinary lives" of loggers, whose existence had become anything but commonplace. After Breitenbush, Mill City seethed with panic. The day of Benson's funeral an Earth First!er sent the young man's family a note saying his death was just retribution for his killing trees: a human's life for a tree's life.[24]

That made something inside these people snap. In one three-week period they had experienced the confrontation at Breitenbush; legislation had been introduced seeking to declare a nearby forest known as Opal Creek as wilderness; and Judge Dwyer had enjoined the 163 Forest Service timber sales. Then, in June, the U.S. Fish and Wildlife Service proposed listing the owl as a threatened species.[25]

Suddenly, as Robertson's sister Cherie Girod recalls, "People were out for total retribution and destruction. . . . Now there was 'a big ditch.' You were on one side or another, and you had to make clear where you belonged." A slim, attractive redhead in her forties, Cherie was the director of the Canyon Crisis Center in Mill City. Although her hobby was riding horses, she was spending most of her time holding a tiger by the tail.[26]

Like all logging communities, her town was tightly knit and conservative. Located in the Willamette Valley, Mill City, population 1,500, like hundreds of other towns in the state, was entirely dependent on logging. In 1988, according to government figures, the timber industry accounted for nearly a third of state personal income. The region served by the crisis center had a population of 40,000. Two thirds of these people earned their living directly from wood products, while the other third were merchants like Cherie's husband, Jim, who ran two small grocery stores.[27]

And now, Cherie realized, the town was coming apart. "I saw this woman pick up a head of lettuce in the grocery store and then just start crying. It was as though somebody just gave you the news you have a terminal illness and you don't know how much time you have and you have no control over what's happening. People talked about only one thing — the owl. It was like living with a time bomb, wondering how much time do I have in this job? Am I going to have a future? Am I going to have to say good-bye to it and find something else?"

All along Cherie had tried to help. With a degree in cultural anthropology and social psychology, she had joined the Canyon Crisis Center in early 1987. Founded to help battered and sexually abused women and children, the Center was associated with the Oregon Coalition against Sexual and Domestic Violence, and was not intended for men. But during 1987, as protests started and jobs disappeared, more and more men came in for aid.

"Every time a decision was handed down by the court, I didn't have to hear the radio to know," she said. "People would be walking around with their heads down, some crying. We would get men into our office who would not normally come. . . . Loggers, people of the earth, are stoic, very proud, and these men would come on the pretext of using the coffee machine. It would so happen that during the conversation they would talk of problems with the industry, then talk of friends who were having difficulties, then start to relate these to their own families and finally to themselves. But they insisted they weren't there for counseling. They couldn't admit that. They were just there to get a cup of coffee.

"But pretty soon they'd say, 'I don't suppose that there is anything you can do for me, anybody I can call, any telephone numbers, or any funds that are going to be set aside for dislocated workers,' or 'I never drank before but I find myself going to the tavern with my friend and it's sure upsetting my wife and I don't know what to do and it's really hard, she's having to take a job and here I'm laid off and the whole structure of the family's changing.'

"These things that so embittered these men and churned in their stomachs would start to come out. If they verbalized it to their fellow workers, they feared they would be called weak. And if they verbalized it at home, they would only make their wives and children more afraid."

These macho loggers had nowhere to go. She couldn't turn them away at the door. After all, even her father and brother were loggers. So, realizing that the county offered no support services for men, Cherie decided, "Okay, we're a full-service crisis center, we'll deal with anybody, no matter who it is." But the idea did not go over well with the Oregon Coalition against Sexual and Domestic Violence. "They thought of men as batterers, and that our job was to take care of the victims. . . . They saw no connection between economics and violence, and thought that if a man was going to batter you, he was going to do it no matter what's in his pocket."

So Cherie drove to Portland and appealed to the Department of Justice, which administered the state's Victims of Crime Act, a law designed to help battered women which also provided money for the center. Surely, she told officials, men could be victims as well. If so, then they were entitled to help. The officials were convinced. Back in Mill City, Cherie and her board of directors rewrote their mission statement, making the center a full-service group. And almost immediately they had more business than they could handle. By 1989 most forms of social dysfunction had doubled or tripled: domestic violence, suicides, child and teenage runaways, vandalism, aggression in school.

Children were the most frequent victims. "Teenagers are so self-centered that they believe any trouble at home is usually their fault. We'd pick up runaways who would tell us of mom and dad fighting over buying new clothes or shoes, complaining of the cost of paying for schoolbooks, or apologizing because whatever they set aside for college is being spent to keep the family going. So the kids reason if they leave, things will be better."

As the courts shut down or delayed timber sales, few millworkers were immediately affected because a lot of lumber was still in the pipeline. But cutters and loggers felt the impact right away. The number of employees at Hirons's company, Mad Creek Logging, would drop from twenty-five to nine by 1991. In 1989 many of these laid-off woodsmen, having exhausted their unemployment payments and lost their homes and cars, took their families into the national forest behind Mill City to live in tents. As these squatters began to arrive in the woods, rangers called Cherie, who organized relief convoys bringing blankets, soap, and other necessities. Volunteers from the Food Basket, run by the Canyonville Ministerial Association, an interfaith charity, brought food.[28]

Such were conditions in Mill City just before the Easter Sunday Massacre. And now, after Breitenbush, Girod and her husband were caught in the cross-fire. While he was away — biking cross-country to raise money for the Norm Becker Children's Hospital in Portland — Jim Morgan's sister called Cherie to tell her that someone was circulating a note saying that the Girods had sided with the Earth First!ers, and that many believed this because Girod was a hiker and a biker, and these were the sports of environmentalists.

Cherie, petrified that they might be cast out as pariahs, losing their business and even their lives in the process, immediately went on the local radio station to rebut the charges. Then she met with the employees of her husband's stores, telling them to put yellow ribbons and signs saying "We Proudly Support the Timber Industry" in the windows. She ordered forty-eight T-shirts for store workers to wear, sporting a logo with a log and an axe, which she designed herself. And she printed thousand of flyers supporting the industry to stuff in customers' grocery sacks. One evening she gave a speech at a loggers' rally in Slayton defending her husband, and the next day she wrote an article for the local paper stressing her support for the community.

Thus, the Girods' personal crisis quickly passed. But that, Cherie knew, had just been the beginning. "When the shutdown really comes, when the last timber runs through the pipeline, when most loggers lose their jobs, when the mill closes, when my husband loses his store and the newspapers go down, then this town is just a memory."

With Breitenbush the loggers' attitudes changed. Facing the abyss, they realized only they could save themselves. Before that spring, Hirons remembers, "we thought we should be reasonable. Throughout RARE I and II, we were willing to compromise. But that spring we realized environmentalists weren't interested in compromise. They wanted the whole pie."

As in Mill City, communities throughout the region were seized by anxiety. "We were blamed for everything by the media," Rita Kaley, a sales staffer with Hamel Lumber Company recalls. "Here in Hood River, many people didn't realize how many were involved in our industry. So we had a parade in early April, and over six hundred vehicles took part. That was happening all over."[29]

But eighteen-wheeler convoys wouldn't win this war. The loggers had to organize to face the threat. But how? Hirons, Morgan, Charles Janze, and John Kunzman, copying Bruce Vincent's Communities for a Great Northwest, set up a network called Communities for a Great Oregon. "And, God," says Hirons, "we got these groups just springing up left and right. Charlie Janze and I went over the whole state. Where there wasn't a group, we started one." Soon every town had its own. Canyonville started Save Our Sawmills (SOS), Mollala the Timber Action Committee, and so on throughout Oregon.

But loggers remained no match for environmentalists when it came to politics. There were too many organizations with too little networking between them. Attempts to bring folks together, such as the Yellow Ribbon Coalition and later the Oregon Project, failed because everyone wanted to lead and no one wished to follow. So although every town had a group, none had any idea what the others were doing. Loggers, it seemed, couldn't get their act together.

These frustrations climaxed during a stifling hot day in Eugene in late July 1989. The U.S. Fish and Wildlife Service was holding its first hearing on the listing of the spotted owl at the Lane County Fairgrounds. During a coffee break Charlie Janz from Eugene, Hirons and Jim Morgan from Mill City, Sue Morgan (no relation) from Canyonville, Rita Kaley from Hood River, Rick Sohn from Roseburg, and Evelyn Badger, wife of a Canyonville retail businessman, sat under a tree and discussed their fix.

"Our movement is floundering," Hirons told his friends. "Where's the control?" Each person there represented a group that didn't want to give up its autonomy. "So, finally," says Hirons, "everybody sort of stuffed their egos and said, 'Let's call it the Oregon Lands Coalition. We won't force any group to give up its independence. Instead, we'll create an umbrella group to coordinate us.'"[30]

The next week they met with around fifteen other community leaders in the offices of the Associated Oregon Loggers in Eugene. They passed a legal pad on which everyone wrote his or her phone and fax number and agreed to start sharing information. Choosing Valerie Johnson, daughter of a mill owner, as president, they opened an office in Eugene. Soon the coalition represented nearly sixty farm, ranch, and timber associations and more than eighty thousand members and seemed to have found the formula for success. But this was not the case. It still couldn't compete with environmentalists in the image department.[31]

The Oregon Lands Coalition would become the victim of a cruel paradox. Like its members, it enjoyed the worst of both worlds, being dismissed as a rich interest group even while it could not pay its staff. One of its principal opponents, the National Audubon Society, received megabuck support from multinational corporations to broadcast television specials about forest depletion, and in 1991 would reportedly spend more than twice the coalition's annual budget just on a new logo design and image survey. Yet the far less affluent coalition, which never received more than $10,000 from any source, was viewed by the public as representing big business.[32]

This was an irony of the 1980s: the mainstream environmental movement had grown into a giant self-perpetuating industry, yet the public continued to perceive it as small and altruistic. By 1990 the combined budget of the environmental "Group of Ten" — Natural Resources Defense Council, Wilderness Society, Sierra Club, National Audubon Society, Environmental Defense Fund, Environmental Policy Institute, National Wildlife Federation, National Parks and Conservation Association, Izaak Walton League of America, and Defenders of Wildlife — would exceed $250 million, and another group, Greenpeace USA (with an income of $50 million), was adding ten thousand new members a month.[33]

The National Wildlife Federation spent $60 million in 1988, and had just constructed a seven-story office building in downtown Washington, D.C. Its president, Jay Hair, reportedly rode to work in a chauffeur-driven limousine, and received a salary exceeding $200,000. Fred Krupp, director of the Environmental Defense Fund, received $125,000; Peter Berle, director of the National Audubon Society, earned $140,000. These Washington lobbyists also found lucrative ways to make money for their organizations. Direct-mail solicitations provided steady sources of income with little accountability. And by the 1980s a new reservoir of funds had materialized: lawsuits against the government.[34]

The Equal Access to Justice Act and many environmental laws contained "citizen suit" provisions requiring the courts to reimburse public interest groups for expenses incurred when they prevailed in court cases against the government. Other statutes stipulated that companies must pay punitive awards to conservation causes.[35]

The practice of awarding court costs began modestly in the early 1980s, when the Natural Resources Defense Council started recovering expenses after suing the Environmental Protection Agency for violating the Clean Water Act. But giveaways quickly grew. From 1983 to 1987 the council's income from court-awarded fees rose from $117,673 to $630,544, and before long other groups were padding down the yellow brick road as well. Suing to save the earth became a lucrative form of fundraising, raking in tens of millions of dollars annually.[36]

Owl advocates, in particular, tapped this source of income. The Seattle office of the Sierra Club Legal Defense Fund, often representing the Portland or Seattle offices of the Audubon Society, derived millions in income this way. And as their opportunities to make big money grew, these groups behaved more like the businesses they had become. The Sierra Club offered a credit card; the National Wildlife Federation sold millions of dollars' worth of merchandise, from coffee mugs to neckties. Thus, it should not have been surprising when, in March 1986, the federation — parent of the Portland Environmental Law Center, where Andy Stahl had once worked — sold the 357-acre Claude Moore Conservation Education Farm in Fairfax County, Virginia, to the development firm Miller and Smith for $8.5 million. It was among the last known nesting sites of the Henslow's sparrow, listed in Virginia as a rare species. Until Fairfax County saved the center by purchasing it from the developers, Miller and Smith had planned a subdivision, called Lanesmoore, containing 1,350 houses, condominiums, and apartments.[37]

As the incident was largely ignored by the press, the federation, like the other mainstream organizations, continued to enjoy a reputation as small and grassroots. By contrast, the Oregon Lands Coalition, truly tiny and representative, would soon be described by Greenpeace as among those groups that are "heavily financed by industry."

the tree symbol in the right margin

22

FORESTS
FOREVER

STANDING BY A PIÑON JUNIPER, a pretty shirtless woman with dark hair and tight jeans sipped beer as she said to the man she had just met, "I know ecologically it is best to have no children. But I went through a religious phase and had two kids. Now, would you believe it, my son's hero is Michael J. Fox, the guy in *Family Ties*"? Then she asked, "Do you have a tent where we could relax?"[1]

Near them, sitting on the dust in the hot sun, men and women sat in empowerment circles sharing their feelings. Nearby a bearded man wearing a loincloth squatted in the lotus position, eyes closed, reciting his mantra, oblivious to those around him. Clusters of people sat under trees, drinking beer. Others lay in their small backpacking tents, set up under trees, smoking pot, making love, or planning actions.

On the surface everything seemed as usual at Earth First!'s 1989 Round River Rendezvous. But the hilarity of this June gathering, held at Butterfly Springs in New Mexico's Jemez Mountains west of Los Alamos, masked changes and deep anxieties. Something was badly out of sync.

The predictable theatrics ensued — war dancing, naked Neanderthals, a man wearing women's underwear on his head, songs by Darryl Cherney and Judi Bari, and a performance by the "John Denver Re-Unification Army." The Mud Kachina performed, as men, sporting what looked like codpieces caked with mud, threw dirt at one another and shouted, "Spike a tree for Jesus!" Another performer urinated several times in front of the stage, saying, "Some things just can't be expressed in words."

But then Bari, attending her first Rendezvous, led the Redneck Women's Caucus in a staged "takeover" of the kachina; and while the significance of that would appear only later, it was another sign that fault lines were forming in the movement between machos and feminists, between "woo-woos" (wilderness romantics) and "rednecks" (eco-socialists like Bari), and between pacifists and the "tribal" leadership of Dave Foreman. But looming still larger was Foreman's arrest by the Federal Bureau of Investigation.[2]

One evening less than four weeks earlier, on Tuesday, May 30, 1989, according to FBI reports, Mark Davis, Marc Baker, and Katherine Millett walked up the dirt track that led from the Lake Alamo Road, near Phoenix, stopping when they reached the line transmitting electricity from the Harcuvar Substation, near Wenden, to the Central Arizona Project, a huge irrigation system for the Southwest. After assembling a propane and oxygen torch, they began to cut through a power pole. Their intent, said Jim Loyd, publisher of the La Paz County weekly newspaper, the *Gem*, was to "cut towers so that one would fall into another and create real fireworks in the desert."[3]

The three did not know that an FBI SWAT team of thirty officers, tipped off by an undercover agent within Earth First!, was squatting among the junipers around them. As the activists patiently guided the white flame of their torch through the base of the steel tower, the agents shot flares into the air, lighting up the night, and closed in. The Earth First!ers ran. One of the men, wearing boxes over his shoes to leave confusing footprints, hobbled clumsily into the desert and was quickly caught. So was the second man. But Millett disappeared. The soles of her shoes were taped, so her prints were easy to follow. But at the highway she vanished.

Reportedly borrowing a bloodhound named Buford T. Justice from the Tempe Police Department, and using two helicopters called *Black Hawk* and *Night Stalker*, federal agents searched unsuccessfully all night. At daylight they were joined by other bloodhounds and men on horseback from the state Department of Corrections. Later in the day Millett was arrested by Yavapai County officials at work in the Prescott office of Planned Parenthood.

Meanwhile, at 7:30 that morning, agents arrested Foreman at his home. Davis, Baker, and Millett were charged with destruction of an energy facility, destruction of property which affects interstate commerce, and destruction of government property and conspiracy. Foreman, who, according to the FBI, had told an undercover agent that he had given Davis $580 and would donate an additional $200 to buy equipment for later attacks on nuclear facilities, was indicted for conspiracy to destroy an energy facility. If convicted, each faced up to ten years in prison and $50,000 in fines.

This caper, the FBI claimed, was a trial run for the destruction of power lines feeding electricity to the Palo Verde nuclear power plant in Arizona, the Diablo Canyon nuclear plant in California, and the Energy Department's Rocky Flats plutonium fabrication plant in Colorado.[4]

The federal investigation began when the FBI planted an agent in the movement after someone had damaged power lines leading to Palo Verde in 1986. Since then, claimed the agency, Davis, Baker, and Millett had been extremely active. It charged that Davis and Millett sabotaged a ski lift north of Flagstaff in 1987, that Davis damaged another lift the following year, and that all three — calling themselves the "Ev Mecham Eco-Terrorist International Conspiracy," or EMETIC — had helped fell twenty-nine power poles leading to three Arizona uranium mines.[5]

Foreman's arrest struck the movement like a guillotine blow. After years of carefree derring-do and make believe, the activists were suddenly reminded that ecotage was a serious business with decidedly real consequences. Indeed, although they did not realize it yet, this confrontation between Earth First! and the FBI would not be the last. Within a year a far more tragic event would occur that would bring this escalating violence to an ugly climax.

As the Round River Rendezvous approached, tensions mounted. The Forest Service sent an Earth First! "specialist" to warn residents of the Jemez to beware of monkeywrenching. Soon the agency was blaming Earth First! for burning a barn, wrecking a grader, poisoning cows, threatening a loader operator, sabotaging wells, and monkeywrenching a windmill. A car belonging to the girlfriend of rendezvous organizer Rich Ryan was reportedly stolen and later found at the bottom of a ravine, and Ryan himself discovered the window of his own automobile smashed, a monkey wrench lying on its seat. Then the redneck faction got ticked off when woo-woos moved the date of the rendezvous up almost two weeks so they could attend the Rainbow Gathering, a national convocation of marijuana worshipers.[6]

By the time the convocation started, activists were paranoid — with reason. A phalanx of uniformed police stood at the parking lot by the trail head leading to their encampment. The surrounding woods crawled with constabulary from the Forest Service, the county sheriff's office, and the state police. And if the FBI had one known undercover agent in their group, Earth First!ers reasoned, surely there were more!

This pent-up fear and distrust built until it was ready to burst. Then, on the first night, Stumps Suckers burned the American flag and began handing out leaflets that read, "Factories don't burn down by themselves, they need help from you. Learn to burn." At that, as the *Earth First! Journal* writer known as "Loose Hip Circles" remarked, "the tension at Butterfly Springs almost went volcanic."[7]

With neither Roselle, Wolke, nor Foreman present during the first few days of the convocation, rumor gripped the participants. Everyone wondered: Would Foreman come? What would he do?

Foreman finally arrived Saturday evening, June 24, and gave a speech. It sounded like a swan song. Portraying himself as a martyr like Martin Luther King, he appeared both brave and afraid, implying that his own death was imminent but that he would fight to the end. Indirectly he addressed the Stumps Suckers, suggesting that if these radicals thought he was too moderate, they ought to leave. He seemed very much the tribal elder, leader of the folk, laying down the law, and like good followers his audience remained silent and respectful.

He was what he saw himself as, a warrior "of the bioregional tribe." But this macho Luddite cult was running out of steam. Even tree-sitting had become tiresome. By mid-May, Greg King admits, "I wanted to quit the movement." When Cherney asked him to do another tree-sit, King's reaction was:

> Great. Another tree-sit. Spend a few thousand dollars on a risky venture seemingly destined for early discovery by the dozens of spies I perceived to be lurking in every public head. Haul a quarter-ton of gear on not enough backs for too many miles and place neophytes at deadly heights to symbolically stop ubiquitous logging of the world's greatest forests. Spoon feed numb media news of continuous catastrophe only to have reporters cite sitters' height in the canopy, food consumed, and logger reaction as the most salient events of the day.[8]

So it wasn't surprising that after his arrest, Foreman and his audience were feeling the pressure. As Rich Ryan wrote, commenting on the rendezvous,

Pressure o yeah, pressure gonna drop on you . . .
Pressure drop, pressure o yeah, pressure gonna drop on you . . .
When you organized a rendezvous, pressure gonna drop on you . . .
No masking tape on your license plate, pressure gonna drop on you . . .
There's instigators, agitators, con-flagrators and infiltrators,
The FBI, the DOE, the DEA and some IOU's

We got eco-feminists, urban anarchists, eco-brutalists and w o o   w o o
Pressure drop, pressure o yeah, pressure gonna drop on you . . .[9]

The macho men had lost their nerve. The torch had been passed to
Bari and the Wilderness Women. As the men burned out, the women
were just getting started.

Although Bari was determined to chart a new, coalition-building, trade
unionist course, the conflict over old growth and owls would become
more polarized, not less so.

The deep divisions separating activists from loggers derived from the
nature of the conflict itself. The issue did not concern science. Conceivably, if it had, each side could have asked scholars to weigh the relative
costs and benefits of clear-cutting, preserving old growth, or fashioning
new logging practices. But while the activists touted "ecology" and loggers "wise use" of natural resources, neither side looked to scholarship
for resolution.

For one thing, academia itself was deeply politicized. Silviculturalists
and economists sided with loggers, ecologists and conservation biologists with environmentalists. And as the debate continued between forest ecologists such as Chadwick Oliver and proponents of the New
Forestry such as Jerry Franklin, the dialogue was ignored by the media.
The nation considered only extremes: industrial forestry or pure preservation of wilderness; defense of absolute property rights or the national-
ization of land.

Behind these polarities was a deeper division. Despite enormous popularity and influence, the environmental movement's agenda, based on
outdated biology, still lacked a clear sense of purpose. By embracing biocentrism, the environmentalists had confused science with philosophy,
facts with values, and truth with mythology. Meanwhile, the fundamental question — What is preservation? — remained unanswered.

As Douglas MacCleery, assistant director for forest inventory, planning, and ecology of the Forest Service, noted, no one had clearly defined what the issue was or why preservation was needed. Although
logging might reduce some components of old-growth forests necessary
to support all the creatures dependent on them — such as spotted owls,
flying squirrels, and murrelets — this harvesting was unlikely to harm
the successional processes which ensure that forests remain productive
and attractive. As MacCleery notes: "There are many areas of the world
in which old-growth has been gone for centuries. Some species loss
occurred that was associated with the loss of these old-growth components. But while such losses are certainly regrettable, the forest

ecosystem that exists remains productive and resilient. Forests in Scandinavia have been managed for human uses relatively intensively for six centuries or more. Yet a viable forest products industry continues to exist, as well as healthy populations of many wildlife species. So while the forest ecosystem has certainly changed, it is not on the brink of collapse."[10]

A reasonable response to such criticisms is that preservation is an aesthetic imperative. People seek to prevent changes in the landscape because they appreciate its look and feel. This is a good rationale. Beauty is important. But instead environmentalists cite grand theory, emphasizing "ecosystem health" and "preserving biodiversity." They summon the "sacredness" of nature, our innate "biophilia," and the requisites of a "new paradigm." The vagueness and appeal of these transcendental principles obscures their real, if unintended, effect: to justify coercion aimed at imposing a new set of values. If such a proposal were presented unambiguously, few Americans would agree to deprive people of liberty for offending the aesthetic sense of others; but they might agree to use force to realize a high ideal. They would never condone jailing people for cutting down a tree; but they could be persuaded to incarcerate citizens for destroying "critical habitat" of a "threatened" species, if this act harmed "biodiversity."

The fight over old growth and owls, therefore, really concerned questions of values that did not admit of compromise. This political cleavage did not, as Bari supposed, lie between socialism and capitalism. It did not pit workers against their employers. Rather, it separated biocentrism from humanism. It was a war of the upper-middle class against the working class; of the old-rich Mellons against the new-rich Hurwitzes; of affluent urbanites against the rural poor; of highly trained professionals against those who worked outdoors; of the government and media elite against hometown America; of college-trained exurbanite hippies such as Darryl Cherney and Robert Sutherland against poorly educated loggers, ranchers, and farmers.[11]

It was, in short, a class war. But, unlike the socialist scenario with which Judi Bari was familiar, this was a revolution from above, not below. By embracing both the old notion of worker solidarity and the new one of biocentrism, she — like conservative critics who believed environmentalism to be a communist conspiracy — confused one ideological struggle with another. Her attempt to rally the workers was bound to fail. Rather than promoting alliances, it would fracture the region further. By touting socialism and embodying biocentrism, Bari became Earth First!'s Princess of Disorder, inciting foes of both.

· · ·

Wherever Bari went, it seemed, strife followed. Indeed, some said she revealed a genius for angering people. In Maryland her post office co-workers reportedly dubbed her "Mafia Mama." And now, as Jonathan Littman observed, "with Cherney, Bari was having the time of her life. She was leading wild, unpredictable protest actions on the streets and in the woods. . . . But there were times when it seemed that the struggle was more important than the wilderness."[12]

Bari, however, was not just another crazy monkeywrencher with an authority hangup. She was more complex than that. Her idealism and confrontational style embodied all the complexities and contradictions of environmentalism.

The movement is a misplaced response to the dark side of our civilization. Ever since the Scotsman James Watt invented the steam engine in 1705, the industrial revolution has been inexorably transforming the globe into a place of anomie, escalating violence, and despair even as it has reduced death rates and raised economic living standards. Activists mistakenly suppose that these changes signal impending "ecological collapse." But technology's crime is not biological. It is aesthetic and ethical. We have created a world of luxury which is destructive because it spreads soul-destroying ugliness and undermines the cultural foundations that support our spiritual well-being.

"Fanaticism," George Santayana observed, "consists in redoubling your efforts when you have forgotten your aim." So environmentalists, mistakenly pursuing the wrong enemy, redoubled their efforts. Having fashioned ecological remedies for a cultural disease, they couldn't cure the patient — it merely got sicker. So they escalated their efforts again. In doing so they stepped onto a slippery slope that would inevitably culminate in violence. Pursuit of the mythical goal of "ecological health" led from the quiet negotiations of the Save the Redwoods League to the lobbying and litigation of the Sierra Club and eventually to the ecotage of Earth First! And as these tactics escalated, so did their consequences.

Thus, a movement that sought the stability of nature and the harmony of society was bound to result in tragedy. And Bari, who embodied this paradox, would almost be its martyr. More than most activists, she was aware that environmental problems were in reality cultural ones. Yet anarchy chooses its victims at random, without regard to fairness. Her very desire for social change would combine with her growing commitment to pacifism to ignite an explosion that nearly destroyed her and changed the radical movement forever.

· · ·

Returning from the Round River Rendezvous in July, Bari hit the ground running. On August 13, she led the California campaign of National Tree-Sit Week, dedicated to the theme "Save America's Forests." Over the following few days, as Earth First!ers conducted twelve sits in seven states, Bari and her compatriots launched three sits and twelve actions in Northern California alone. They took over Palco's sales office in Marin County, picketed a Forest Service office in San Francisco, hung a banner declaring "Clear-Cutting Is Eco-Terrorism" over the freeway in Sonoma County, blocked a Louisiana Pacific logging road and a Fort Bragg Georgia-Pacific mill, and staged the world's first "all-woman tree-sit."[13]

And as she rose to prominence, her enemies multiplied. In January 1989 Ukiah's police chief Fred Keplinger received a letter from an anonymous person identifying himself as "Argus," charging that "Earth First! recently began automatic weapons training" and that "Bari sells marijuana to finance Earth First! activities," and offering to work undercover for federal law enforcement officials.[14]

Then in August a logging truck rammed her car — also containing her two daughters, Cherney, a friend, Pam Davis, and her two children — from the rear as she drove through the town of Philo en route to the final demonstration of National Tree-Sit Week. The vehicle was sent flying through the air and crashed into a parked pickup truck. One child suffered facial lacerations, and Bari, with a concussion, back injury, and whiplash, was sent semiconscious to the hospital.[15]

Bari asked the Mendocino County district attorney to investigate the truck driver, Donald Blake, for "attempted murder." He had not used his brakes, she later charged, but hit her full speed. Authorities deemed Blake to be at fault but insisted on treating the crash as a traffic accident and refused to bring criminal charges. After the Blake incident Bari began to doubt herself. "I wasn't sure I could continue," she said. Like the bad-luck character in Al Capp's comic strip "Li'l Abner" who is followed through life by a pouring raincloud, Bari could not escape chaos. And that was a liability for the entire movement. "I wasn't sure it was right to lead people into situations where they could be killed," said Bari. She needed to rethink her mission. She needed to recharge her batteries. She needed to find a retreat. But where?[16]

As Bari pondered her next move, political and legal events raced at breakneck speed. In September John van de Kamp, the California attorney general, responding to calls for a mega-initiative to save the environment, introduced the California Environmental Protection Act of

1990 — proposition 128. Dubbed the "Big Green" by friends and the "Killer Watermelon" by enemies, it was a tossed salad that included imposition of a strict "zero-risk" standard for pesticides, a ban on offshore oil drilling, a tariff on oil shipped through California, creation of a $500 million oil spill cleanup fund, a host of regulations to combat "global warming," and establishment of an Office of Environmental Advocate, to be the state's chief preservation policeman with broad powers transcending those of other enforcement authorities.[17]

Backed by major environmental groups and many prominent politicians — including Jane Fonda's former husband, state assemblyman Tom Hayden — it took up thirty-nine single-spaced pages and included several forestry proposals, including a ban on clear-cutting, a one-year moratorium on logging mature redwoods, and floatation of a $300 million bond issue for the purchase of Headwaters Forest, by condemnation if necessary, if Pacific Lumber refused to sell.[18]

Soon after the Big Green was proposed, federal authorities escalated their involvement several notches. On October 4 six biologists, representing the Forest Service, the Bureau of Land Management, and the U.S. Fish and Wildlife Service, met in Portland under the leadership of Jack Ward Thomas to convene the Interagency Scientific Committee to Address the Conservation of the Northern Spotted Owl.[19]

The same month, on October 23, Congress, responding to industry's pleas for a reprieve, passed the Hatfield-Adams amendment, otherwise known as the "Northwest Compromise" of 1989, a rider to the 1990 fiscal year appropriations bill expanding spotted owl habitat areas and giving environmental groups a much larger role in the timber sale process in exchange for a temporary increase in logging.[20]

Instructing the bureau and the Forest Service to minimize fragmentation of "ecologically significant" stands of old growth in Oregon and Washington, it provided for citizen advisory boards to assist agencies in preparing and modifying sales. At the same time it encouraged plaintiffs in *Seattle Audubon Society* v. *Robertson* and other lawsuits to release 1.1 billion board feet from the timber sales which they had enjoined, and directed the Forest Service and Bureau of Land Management to offer 9.6 billion board feet of timber — the amount Congress supposed should have been offered during 1989 and 1990 but which had been held up by litigation.[21]

In the long run, the Hatfield-Adams amendment would make loggers the losers, since it represented the first time ever that old growth was recognized in the law. Nevertheless, the amendment split the environmental community down the middle. The Sierra Club Legal Defense

Fund opposed it, but the Sierra Club accepted it. The Wilderness Society supported it, but the Oregon Natural Resources Councils, the Audubon Society, and the National Wildlife Federation were opposed.[22]

Meanwhile, the contest between Pacific Lumber and EPIC continued like an endgame in chess. Every time the former filed a timber harvest plan, the latter would petition for an injunction. In 1987 the environmental group had stopped two clear-cuts in Headwaters totaling three hundred acres; and in 1988 it sued again to stop cuts on an additional two hundred acres.[23]

But Palco fought back. In October 1989 the company filed two more plans to log nearly six hundred acres. This put Department of Forestry director Len Theis on the spot. In addition to the spotted owl, his staff was beginning to worry about another creature soon to be put on the endangered species list — the marbled murrelet, a robin-sized shoreline seabird that reportedly prefers old growth. So his department postponed a decision on the Palco plans until January, pending wildlife studies.[24]

This merely increased environmentalists' anxieties. Fearful that Pacific Lumber would eventually win the right to log Headwaters, Robert Sutherland opted for another strategy. On October 18 EPIC joined a coalition of grassroots groups to file their own initiative with the attorney general. Written by Sutherland in cooperation with scores of other activists, it was titled The Forest and Wildlife Protection Initiative and Bond Act of 1990. But it was soon known as "Forests Forever."[25]

Bankrolled by the Illinois financier Harold Arbit, who would eventually contribute more than $940,000 out of total contributions of $1 million, Forests Forever was intended specifically to save Headwaters. The act would provide $710 million to purchase the forest, ban most clear-cuts, protect all old growth (not just redwoods), and prohibit harvesting trees faster than they could be replaced. It would also prohibit burning after logging, and would restructure the state Board of Forestry to limit industry positions. It not only stipulated that logging not harm any endangered species but also required the California Fish and Game Department to mitigate the impact of timber harvests on all wildlife.[26]

Industry was horrified. The Timber Association of California predicted that Forests Forever would shut down 85 percent of state logging activities, eliminate 176,500 jobs, and create a $22.7 billion loss to the state. Not to be outdone, therefore, in December a timber group, the Californians for Sensible Environmental Protection, marshaled a counterattack against Big Green and Forests Forever. Their bill, with the mischievous title Global Warming and Clear-Cutting Reduction,

Wildlife Protection, and Reforestation Act of 1990, was quickly dubbed "Big Stump" by environmentalists. The industry proposal would provide $300 million to aid private and public tree planting and reforestation, restrict clear-cutting in some areas, authorize but not appropriate funds for purchase of 1,600 acres of old growth, and allow lifetime timber harvesting plans.[27]

Together Big Green, Forests Forever, and Big Stump drew a line in the sand. The future of California's forests, it seemed, would be decided in the ballot box. The complex debate over trees that engaged Sir John Evelyn, Henry David Thoreau, Bernhard Fernow, Gifford Pinchot, Frederic Clements, Emanuel Fritz, Leo Isaac, Jerry Franklin, and Chadwick Oliver would be resolved by millions checking "yes" or "no" in polling booths. And for the very landscape most people wanted to preserve, all these resolutions posed great dangers.

Big Stump was an "agricultural" approach that would institutionalize plantation forestry and neglect the wildlife and plant diversity many deemed important. By contrast, Big Green and Forests Forever invited a plague of disasters for both man and nature.

Ruinous fires would be the most immediate and dramatic of these calamities. As scientists have known for some time, fire plays a vitally important ecological role. It is nature's way of renewing itself. But there is a darker side to such conflagrations as well. While small, cooler, "ground" fires regenerate critical vegetation, superhot "crown" fires can destroy both seeds and organic matter in the topsoil, producing soil erosion. And as forests age, crown fires become more likely. Trees die and dry out; flammable detritus accumulates in the duff; and the probability of big burns increases. Fuel buildup can be prodigious. According to Bruce M. Kilgore, the National Park Service's regional chief scientist, "In one year an acre of forest converts solar energy into vegetative matter equivalent to 300 gallons of gasoline."[28]

Preventing destructive fires, therefore, requires reducing fuel loads by logging or periodic burning. In presettlement times Native Americans played this role, igniting woods frequently to improve wildlife habitat, clear campsites, drive game, and make openings for trails. But when the Indians were evicted from their land, combustible material proliferated and calamitous fires became commonplace. By the turn of the century, wildfires were consuming between 20 and 50 million acres annually. In response, the federal government inaugurated a policy of fire suppression. In 1911 Congress passed the Weeks Act, authorizing federal matching funds for state fire control agencies. In 1924 the Clarke-Mc-

Nary Act spurred further federal-state cooperation. And in 1945 the Forest Service launched its "Smokey the Bear" public education campaign, convincing an entire generation that forest fires are evil.[29]

This program, though touted as highly successful, created the conditions for calamity. Fire can never be prevented, only postponed. The government should have launched instead a program of prescribed fire — intentionally lighting frequent small blazes to mimic aboriginal burning and prevent a buildup of combustibles. But whereas silviculturalists in the South had long practiced this system and continued to do so, Pacific Northwest foresters, dismissing prescribed burning as "Paiute forestry," rejected it.[30]

Owing to the policy of fire suppression, therefore, by the late 1980s Western forests, especially unmanaged wilderness, were tinderboxes. The Forest Service had reduced wildfires by 90 percent — to between 2 and 5 million acres burned annually — but seventy years of fire "prevention" had increased fuel loads dramatically. Meanwhile, as populations grew and wilderness areas multiplied, another danger materialized: what fire ecologists call the "city-wildlands interface." Towns and suburbs spread into aging protected forests, provoking, as Anthony R. O'Neill, vice president of the National Fire Protection Association of Quincy, Massachusetts, put it in 1988, "a national crisis." O'Neill explained: "The devastation in the United States has been growing at an incredible rate. As more people throughout the nation move from urban areas to more rural settings they are exposing their homes and their families to highly combustible environments. . . . The result of this migration has been tragically clear: wildfires which heretofore posed a threat to wildlands alone, are now taking lives and property."[31]

The correct response to this danger would have been both to continue judicious logging and to replace fire suppression with careful prescribed burning. Rather than waiting for lightning to start fires in the dry season — when they might be impossible to control — foresters should have intentionally ignited small fires in the winter, spring, and fall, when they could be controlled. Yet, though this option was ecologically right, it remained politically incorrect. Thanks to decades of fire suppression, forests "preserved" in wilderness were long overdue for combustion. Prescription burns in these forests could flare out of control. Indeed, this had happened in Sequoia National Park, where in 1977 a fire set by rangers on Redwood Mountain destroyed several giant trees and injured others. That flareup, says Bruce Kilgore, "scorched larger trees to the extent that insects are now removing the remaining overstory from the cover. The burn objectives, in retrospect, were not met, and the addition of the remaining trees to the dead fuel category will prevent establishment of regeneration for many years."[32]

Nor was Redwood Mountain an aberrant event. Accidental cremation of sequoias continued until it became a political issue. When, in 1985, a prescribed burn at a grove known as Broken Arrow, immediately adjacent to the Giant Forest Lodge and easily visible to Sequoia National Park visitors, went awry, environmentalists led by David Brower campaigned to end the burning.[33] Such misadventures were not inevitable. If not for politics and preservation law, averting burn kills would have been easy. This would merely have required bulldozing firebreaks through the woods and removing excess debris by truck, *before* a stand was ignited. But environmentalists objected to such intrusions into nature; the Wilderness Act, defining these sanctuaries as places "where the earth and its community of life are untrammeled by man," forbade them; and — after Sequoia — few park superintendents wanted to risk the controversy intentional burns would inevitably generate.[34]

Preservation, therefore, was a recipe for holocaust. And in 1988 it struck, dramatically, in Yellowstone. Between 1886 and 1972 officials in this national park had actively sought to suppress fires, so fuel loads had grown enormously. By 1972 Yellowstone was an explosion waiting to happen. "It is likely that crown fires would take place now if fires were introduced," wrote a University of Montana botanist, J. R. Habeck, that year, an event that would result in "total stand destruction." In 1980 George E. Gruell, a Forest Service scientist, reported on a study he had just completed in the Bridger-Teton National Forest along Yellowstone Park's southern boundary that "the likelihood of large, high-intensity fires is considerable in some areas because of great, contiguous fuel accumulations."[35]

Experts urged the Forest Service to begin prescribed burning. "Because of unnatural fuel accumulation . . . during the past half century," wrote Kilgore in 1982, "some planned prescribed burns may be essential in parks and wildernesses as a prelude to allowing lightning-caused fires to burn. . . . Simply allowing lightning-caused fires to burn is often not acceptable."[36]

Instead, in 1972 Yellowstone authorities introduced "natural fire management." Under this regime lightning-caused fires that did not endanger human life or buildings would be allowed to run their course.[37] This was, in effect, a decision to wait for disaster to strike. And sure enough, in 1988, following two years of drought in the northern Rockies, it came. Lightning and human-caused blazes, consuming more than a million acres in and around the park and requiring more than nine thousand firefighters to contain, burned for more than two months, threatening lives, historic buildings, and several Montana towns. Vegetation and wildlife were victims as well. Flames sterilized soil in the watersheds of the Lamar and Gibbon rivers, causing mudslides and massive soil erosion. And they killed so much whitebark pine — whose nuts are a principal food of the threatened grizzly bear — that later a conservation group, the Great Bear Foundation, would suggest to listing this tree as an endangered species![38]

By 1989 it was clear that the preservationist agenda would aggravate an already calamitous wildlands fire situation. Communities across the country were at risk. And though the damp Oregon and Washington forests (which typically experience infrequent but extremely "hot" conflagrations) would be relatively unthreatened at first, passage of either Big Green or Forests Forever was likely to decimate the California forests. As Douglas MacCleery observed: "The further south along the coast you go, the more intense the fire problem becomes. The forests of northern coastal California are absolutely unsustainable in a preservation mode. Fire *must* be reintroduced on a controlled basis in these forests in order for them to be sustainable."[39]

In short, preserving old growth, as Chadwick Oliver put it, not only favored late successional species at the expense of other forms of life but also increased "the risk of a very large disturbance destroying a forest." According to what Oliver called the misguided "steady-state" theory of ecosystem stability, preservationist policies would ultimately produce the "timber famine" which everyone sought to avert.[40]

Nor, many scientists believed, was fire the only risk. Restricting Northwest logging would drive up the price of lumber, thus accelerating cutting in other parts of the country where trees did not grow as fast, or in Third World rain forests, where environmental protection was weak or nonexistent.[41]

Reducing harvest levels, moreover, was unnecessary. The industrialized world was not running out of trees. As an exhaustive study of this question concluded in 1990: "At present, [the world's] forest and woodland . . . is still nearly three times the area of land in cultivation. Surprisingly too, the forests of the developed countries of the temperate world (including China) show a slow but steady net increase due to forest reversion, as marginal land is abandoned and agricultural production is concentrated in more favorable areas and as active replanting programs are instituted."[42]

The chain saw, many ecologists therefore believed, remained a useful tool for forest conservation. Rather than commodity management, as embodied in Stumps Suck, or the steady state regimes of Big Green and Forests Forever, they favored what Oliver dubbed the "constant change" program, whereby

> silvicultural operations are used to coordinate changing forest stand structures to maintain all habitats and reduce risks of uncontrollable natural disturbances, using techniques such as thinning, uneven-age management, even-age management, controlled fires, creating snags, and replanting open areas. Maintaining forest within this variation will involve removal of timber and other products and creating employment and other values as byproducts of these efforts.[43]

Unfortunately, political events would not permit such a rational approach. Instead, the countdown to confrontation continued.

Seeking renewal, in September Bari and Cherney attended a workshop run by two dedicated pacifists, Larry and Sheila Wilson, at the Highlander Research and Education Center in New Market, Tennessee. Combining the philosophy of pacifism with trade unionism, Highlander was the Harvard of nonviolent protest, having trained such luminaries as Rosa Parks, Martin Luther King, Stokely Carmichael, and Andrew Young. And it was just what Bari needed.[44]

Her trade unionism reinforced by Highlander, Bari returned to California to find laborers to organize. When some Georgia-Pacific workers claimed that they had been poisoned by a chemical known as dioxin, she ghosted a three-thousand-word condemnation of the company and helped workers file an OSHA complaint. When in November a Louisiana-Pacific worker named Fortunato Reyes was crushed to death by a tray of logs at the Ukiah Louisiana-Pacific planing mill, she helped to publicize the tragedy. Then, on December 12, she got her biggest opportunity yet: Louisiana-Pacific announced plans to build a $100 million manufacturing plant in Mexico. Loggers and environmentalists were outraged. To Bari it seemed that the industry, having cut most of the trees, was about to run. The announcement appeared to validate Bari's claims that environmentalists and not industry were on the side of workers.[45]

Louisiana-Pacific sprang into being in 1974 when the giant wood products company Georgia-Pacific Corporation, deemed a monopoly, was split by court order. One company became two: Georgia-Pacific, based in Atlanta, with $10.2 billion in assets, and the $2 billion Louisiana-Pacific, headquartered in Portland. Along with the $2.4 billion Pacific Lumber, these were the "Big Three" wood products companies in Northern California.[46]

Under the leadership of its president and chief executive officer, Harry Merlo, Louisiana-Pacific, lacking the big timber base of its parent, became known as an aggressive, and, according to its critics, even ruthless company. Unlike Georgia-Pacific, which remained unionized, Louisiana-Pacific, with mills in Cloverdale, Ukiah, Samoa, Big Lagoon, and Eureka, busted the union and became an open shop in 1986. The world's largest producer of common grades of redwood lumber, it emerged as a favorite on Wall Street in 1989, when its earnings jumped 42 percent in one year.[47]

Called "visionary" by one industry analyst, Merlo gave Louisiana-Pacific a reputation as the "leanest, meanest" concern in the business. His company was, said experts from the investment firm Paine Webber, "best positioned to benefit from current timber product trends." And his Mexican venture was one of the reasons why. In the late 1970s he had introduced a new product, waferwood — lumber made of wood chips glued together. Now the $1 billion Mexican plant would manufacture this product in quantity. "We're chewing everything up and putting it back together," Merlo reportedly explained when the new product was introduced. Waferwood was a wonderful marketing concept because it allowed the company to use every scrap of wood. "We need everything that's out there," said Merlo. "We don't log to a 10-inch top, or an 8-inch top, or a 6-inch top. We log to infinity. Because we need it all. It's ours. It's out there, and we need it all. Now."[48]

Such remarks made Merlo the man environmentalists loved to hate. Among the best and brightest free market whiz kids, he became, like Hurwitz, a perfect foil for Earth First!, easy to depict as a Hollywood bad guy who gets rich raping the forests and screwing the workers. It was therefore inevitable that Bari would lead the charge against Merlo. The two embodied the clash of values — one sanctifying profit and private property, the other despising both. And waferboard became the icon of this conflict. To Wall Street this innovation, which utilized every last scrap of wood, symbolized efficiency. To Earth First!ers it represented the ultimate intrusion of capitalism into nature, ensuring that every fragment of the forest carried a price tag.[49]

By the end of the year both sides were eyeing each other like Union and Confederate troops before the Battle of Gettysburg. Louisiana-Pacific's decision to build the Mexican plant divided the region like a cleaver. Palco's harvest plans galvanized opponents, and the state initiatives raised the stakes for both sides.

In January biologists from the Department of Forestry reported that Palco's proposed cuts at Headwaters threatened wildlife, including the marbled murrelet. Simultaneously, the Department of Fish and Game opposed the harvest. Palco even angered the Save the Redwoods League, which in December urged "that the company seriously consider refraining from logging this last large tract of old-growth Redwoods until sufficient public funds are available to purchase these Redwoods at fair market value."[50]

Cornered by this opposition, Palco and Louisiana-Pacific held a "timber summit" with prominent state assemblymen. The ensuing "nine-point agreement," brokered by U.S. representative Doug Bosco, state senator Barry Keene, and assemblyman Dan Houser, included a two-year moratorium on logging in Headwaters; a ban on clear-cutting; an end to log exporting; and establishment of a blue-ribbon panel of experts to audit Palco's rate of harvest, inventory, and general forest practices — all on condition that environmentalists would not hinder the company's operations elsewhere.[51]

With this agreement both sides sought to buy time. The real issue, everyone knew, would be decided in the ballot box in November, when state voters would choose between Big Green, Forests Forever, and Big Stump. To get on the ballot required 372,178 signatures, and the campaign to gather this support drew people into the vortex of conflict.[52]

Indeed, as the Forests Forever sign-up campaign gathered steam, Earth First!ers were seized by fear. The more likely it seemed that their initiative would succeed, the more extreme and desperate they believed the wood products companies would become. Realizing that, if Forests Forever were to pass, logging could come to an end after November, timber barons might try to cut all their trees beforehand.[53]

This concern turned to certainty when, in March, Earth First!ers claimed to have found that Palco was secretly bulldozing a new road into Headwaters. John Campbell, who had been appointed president of Palco in 1989, insisted that the company was merely clearing an old access trail for biologists to study wildlife, but the environmentalists refused to believe him. The Sierra Club Legal Defense Fund asked a district judge to find the company in contempt of court for breaking the ban on Headwaters logging. And whatever trust may have existed between industry and activists evaporated.[54]

Apparently, Earth First!ers thought, nothing short of a major campaign of protest would bring Hurwitz and Merlo to heel. They had to prevent the multinational corporations from logging off the land before Forests Forever became law.

All they needed was a plan.

23

FRED, THE WALKING
RAINBOW

AT THE TIME it seemed fortunate but later, perhaps, a cruel twist of fate. If Judi Bari's three-year-old daughter Jessica had not caught pneumonia, her mother would not have taken the girl to the Ukiah Hospital for treatment. If Bari had not gone to the hospital, she would not have talked to the man who called himself "Fred, the Walking Rainbow." And if she hadn't had a conversation with this unique person, Redwood Summer might never have happened.

Like most people, Bari tried to avoid Rainbow. This countercultural figure had been on a pilgrimage, bicycling around the Northwest on a strange custom-made bike, towing his few possessions in a small trailer, peddling, as it were, the message of peace. On arriving in a town, Bari was told, he would go straight to the local radio stations and newspapers, persuading them to announce his entrance. But as he traversed the region he found that the environment, not peace, was the most popular issue. So he switched causes. On arriving in Ukiah and learning that Bari was the leading environmental activist, he tried to meet her. He began bugging Bari by telephone, insisting on an interview.

And she kept turning him down. But when he phoned again — just after she had been up all night with Jessica at the hospital, then spent several hours as a panelist at a conference before returning to her vigil at the hospital — Bari was too fatigued to resist his entreaties. Dog-tired, she agreed to meet Rainbow at the hospital.

Bari was sitting beside her sleeping daughter's bed when Rainbow entered the hospital room, wearing long, flowing white robes. The man, Bari thought, talked as though he had invented environmentalism. His nonsequential patter was hard to understand. But for a brief moment his mind seemed to clear, as he uttered one lucid fragment: "We've got to bring people in like they did in Mississippi."

"At that moment," Bari recalled, "a light bulb went on over my head."

Of course, she realized, that was exactly what they needed to stop Hurwitz and Merlo from cutting their timber before Forests Forever became law: a summer of protest such as the one that brought thousands of civil rights protesters south in the 1960s.[1]

Like blacks during those awful days, the environment was a victim of discrimination. And, similar to Southern civil rights workers at that time, Earth First!ers had become targets for violently inclined local rednecks. Yet, just as the campaigners for racial justice eventually won by attracting supporters from outside the region, Earth First!ers could do likewise. Their campaign must be *nationalized*.

Bari talked with Mike Roselle, who liked the idea. "We had exhausted nearly everything to keep the issue alive," says Roselle. "We were being attacked, beaten, threatened. We figured we had the support of college students around the country and wanted to bring them in, to keep the issue focused on logging."[2]

What they needed, they decided, was a "Mississippi Summer in the California Redwoods." They also knew that, like the efforts of Martin Luther King, the campaign must be nonviolent. And that, they soon discovered, was going to be a problem.

Since visiting the Highlander Center, Bari had been attracted to the idea of nonviolent protest. But she remained, she said, "in denial" about Earth First! mischief. She was having too much fun to stop. As she talked with workers, however, she became increasingly uncomfortable about tree-spiking. Having established a rapport with Georgia-Pacific millworkers over the dioxin fight, she had high hopes for the Wobblies. Yet this stratagem was alienating the workers. If Earth First! was to win the hearts and minds of loggers, it would have to throw its nails away.

Until January 1990 Bari repressed these ideas. Then a millworker from Roseberg, Oregon, named Gene Lawhorn contacted her. Lawhorn, says Bari, was "smart and radical." He had helped organize against the Yellow Ribbon Coalition. So when she came to Eugene to speak at an environmental law conference, she persuaded the meeting's organizers to invite Lawhorn as well.

At the conference, in front of the audience, Lawhorn let Bari have it. While he admired her group, he said, he couldn't tolerate tree-spiking. It was sheer hypocrisy, he lectured, to insist, as Earth First! did, that this was not an act of extreme violence. Everyone in the hall waited for Bari to answer. Earlier she had told the conference about the plans for a Mississippi Summer, so when the microphone was handed to her this time, she added, "As the Earth First! organizer, I publicly renounce tree-spiking." She received a standing ovation.

Pete Roselle, who was in the audience, immediately called a meeting of Earth First!ers attending. Debate was heated. Eventually they agreed to seek to persuade their respective groups to renounce tree-spiking. If successful, they would issue simultaneous press releases announcing the decision.

Yet giving up tree-spiking seemed almost too radical. Many in the local chapters were fiercely resistant to the idea. Eventually one group — Northern Oregon Earth First! — refused to sign the press release. Others, including Bari's California contingent, insisted that any public renunciation be couched very carefully.[3]

But after Earth First!ers caught Palco apparently building the road into Headwaters, Bari did not wait for this dispute to be resolved. Instead, in early March at a gathering of ten California colleges in Sacramento organized by the Student Environmental Action Coalition, she asked for "Freedom Riders for the forest" to come to Mendocino, Humboldt, and Del Norte counties that summer to "defend the redwoods with nonviolent civil disobedience."[4]

Her call was published in the student newsletter and distributed to colleges across the country. Promising to provide housing, campsites, guides, and other support, she pledged to carry out "rolling waves of actions" to protest logging. The campaign "will be decentralized, and non-hierarchical, with actions based as much as possible on existing affinity groups and local support based as much as possible on existing coalitions."[5]

Then, in late March, Northern California Earth First! issued press releases signed by Bari, Cherney, King, Roselle, Pam Davis, and four others announcing Mississippi Summer and an end to tree-spiking. This was followed on April 11 with a series of press conferences along the North Coast to explain the decision. "With thousands coming to California" for Mississippi Summer, the press release announced, "renunciation of tree spiking will surely take the edge off potential violence."[6]

And, indeed, Bari told the *Santa Rosa Press-Democrat* reporter Mike Geniella, "we're trying to impress on everyone the need to understand the volatility of the situation here, and the importance of nonviolence. . . . We don't want people to direct anger toward the timber workers." Earth First!, Bari promised, would set up base camps through-

RESPONSE: THE BIOCENTRIC REVOLUTION

out the region to offer training in nonviolent tactics and would organize cadres of protesters to invade logging operations throughout the three-county region.

"This is not a retreat," the official statement read. "It is an advance toward joining Northern California woodworkers in the fight to save the planet." In fact, this move to pacifism was highly equivocal and not destined to allay loggers' fears. Because of fierce resistance within Earth First!, the press release was hedged with qualifications.[7] While declaring that "loggers and millworkers are our neighbors . . . not our adversaries," the statement nevertheless conceded that Earth First! would continue selling Foreman's monkeywrenching manual *Ecodefense* and "singing 'Spike a Tree for Jesus,'" albeit with "disclaimers." It warned that the "decision is not made for all Earth First!ers" and "is not irrevocable, should the forest situation worsen." Noting, "It is completely understandable that someone would still spike trees," it decreed, "we will not condemn tree-spiking."[8]

These caveats embarrassed Bari, who thought them hypocritical. Yet not even she would renounce monkeywrenching. Tree-spiking, she felt, was immoral, but ecotage, such as destroying bulldozers or chain saws, was "merely stupid" because it alienated workers. Yet, apparently indifferent to the fact that many gyppos mortgaged their homes to buy a yarder, her press release explicitly endorsed the tactic, noting that "equipment sabotage is a time-honored tradition among industrial workers."[9]

Thus, the campaign was fated to enrage nearly everyone. The *Earth First! Journal*, displaying surprising journalistic cowardice, commented, "The whole issue is very controversial . . . and we do not intend to cover the inevitable debate." Arcata Earth First! testily announced: "We . . . do not agree with non-feral Darryl Cherney's recent statement advocating no tree-spiking. . . . Companies do not have rights, only 'Mother Earth' has rights. We must save all trees."[10]

This hostility did not lessen even when, in mid-April, Bari and her comrades agreed to change the name of the campaign to Redwood Summer. Many detested the idea, no matter what it was called. In late April the Redwood Coast Watersheds Alliance, a coalition of seventeen antilogging watchdog groups, announced that it was "not working on or associated with" Redwood Summer. Leaders of the Forests Forever initiative also refused to support the campaign. And Gail Lucas, chairwoman of the Sierra Club's California Forest Practices Task Force, along with eleven other club leaders, condemned Mississippi Summer, fearing that it could lead to violence and would undermine support for the Forests Forever initiative: "We believe that what is needed is action at the polls by the people of the state of California, not recruits who, however well-intentioned and well-briefed in nonviolent protest, present a potential for violence."[11]

For loggers, the Redwood Summer announcement came at a terrible time. That spring a series of calamities increased their sense of being under siege. The first of these fell in early April when the Interagency Scientific (or Thomas) Committee made its conclusions public.[12]

This panel consisted of six federal scientists, including Eric Forsman and Charles Meslow. But whereas in the 1970s political pressure had encouraged researchers to minimize the spotted owl's habitat needs, now the same forces were giving a reason for maximizing it. The pendulum of popular opinion and federal action had tilted toward the bird. Forsman and Meslow were already on record as believing owls to be an old-growth-dependent species in decline. They were not likely to retract these claims.

Not surprisingly, therefore, the Thomas Committee concluded "that the owl is imperiled over significant portions of its range because of continuing losses of habitat from logging and natural disturbances" and recommended what its supporters quickly dubbed the "ecosystem" approach to conservation. Abandoning the strategy of setting up spotted owl habitat areas for one to three pairs each, it urged "protecting larger blocks of habitat — which we term Habitat Conservation Areas," ensuring "connectivity" between the areas to minimize fragmentation.[13]

Loggers were stunned. The Thomas report would rule at least a third of forests in the region — more than 8.4 million acres — off-limits to logging, including 1.4 million acres of private lands. This was, of course, in addition to the 5.6 million acres already in national parks and wilderness areas. The Northwest Forest Research Council reported that this would require setting aside $95 million worth of timber for each pair of owls.[14]

Even the government estimated that the plan would diminish federal timber sales by 40 percent and cause a direct loss of 27,705 jobs. O&C harvests in the Salem and Eugene districts would be reduced by 74 percent. The industry estimated that it would lessen Northwest timber harvests by 50 percent, destroy 50,000 jobs, and eliminate $1.2 billion in payrolls. The federal government would lose $1 billion in revenues and county governments $500 million annually, resulting, wrote the Association of O&C Counties, in what amounted to a gross understatement, "substantial reductions in public health services, law enforcement, and social services."[15]

RESPONSE: THE BIOCENTRIC REVOLUTION

Another problem, in addition to the hardships the plan would cause, was the fact that its conclusions rested on flawed science. It offered no evidence that old growth was essential for the owls or that their numbers were truly declining. On the contrary, data revealing an abundance of birds in young stands and clear-cuts continued to mount. But this evidence was explained away. Without studies to determine if logged stands were sources or sinks for spotted owls, the committee merely assumed birds in these areas to be "floaters . . . possibly the result of an influx of individuals displaced by timber harvest."[16]

Since it had little relevant research to rely on, the committee employed a strategy widely used in government wildlife studies. Known as "the Delphi approach," it sought to answer questions not by study but by taking opinion surveys among scientists. "Delphi" refers to the town in Phocis in ancient Greece which was the site of the Pythian Apollo, the greatest oracle of antiquity. For thousands of years pilgrims with a problem traveled to this town on the slopes of Mount Parnassus to ask the oracle to foretell the future. Likewise, the Delphi approach seeks to foresee the future by polling wise men and women — that is, scientists. Carefully chosen for their political reliability, these gurus (almost without exception scholars receiving funds from the government) are asked to answer specific questions about situations which they have not studied and about which they are given only sketchy information.

This method of prediction is no more reliable than reading sheep entrails. Nevertheless, it had become the primary method by which agencies such as the U.S. Fish and Wildlife Service and National Park Service did "science" because of its many political advantages. It allowed agencies to make decisions that looked authoritative. It did not require actual research, hypothesis formation, and testing, which is expensive and takes time. It protected bureaucrats from criticism, allowing them to say that their decisions were supported by a consensus of experts. And it was used with devastating effect by the Thomas Committee.

How closely spaced must habitat conservation areas be? "Because we know of no objective criteria for setting such a distance," the committee averred, "this decision was based on a Delphi Approach." Thus, it concluded, "consensus exists among biologists that, all else being equal, continuous suitable habitat supports more individuals of a species targeted for conservation than does fragmented [discontinuous] habitat."[17]

In addition to the Delphi approach, the Thomas Committee used another gambit popular with federal scientists: shifting the burden of proof to those who challenged their claims. Traditional science tests a hypothesis by seeking to falsify it under carefully controlled conditions. Only after repeated falsification attempts fail is a scholar justified in claiming his hypothesis to be confirmed. But the Thomas Committee simply declared that the lack of contradictory evidence was sufficient reason to justify endorsing its own hypotheses concerning the condition and needs of the owl. The very absence of data became "confirming evidence" for its conclusions!

The committee conceded, for example, that it had no confirmation that the owls actually depended on old growth. Instead, it claimed, such knowledge was impossible to obtain, but the dearth of data to the contrary justified asserting that it was true: "Unequivocal determination of whether habitat use or preference reflects the true 'needs' of a species could be settled only through experimentation, which we consider unfeasible." Indeed, the committee wrote, "the full range of a species' needs cannot be determined. . . . It is generally unknowable and unresearchable."[18]

Thus, the Interagency Scientific Committee recommended the economic devastation of a region based on assumptions it believed to be "unknowable and unresearchable." The industry was outraged, calling the Thomas report "the Facade of Science." But environmentalists were ecstatic. "It's ecosystems we're talking about — entire interrelated ecosystems in a natural forest," Bruce N. Apple, director of the National Wildlife Federation Pacific Northwest Resource Center in Portland, told the Associated Press. "It's not just spotted owls. It's all plant species, fish and wildlife. . . . That's what Jack Thomas is telling them. It's basically what the conservation community has been telling them for years. The spotted owl is nothing but a canary in a coal mine."[19]

Following the announcement of the panel's conclusions, loggers went on the warpath. On April 13 the Oregon Lands Coalition, already representing fifty-three separate grassroots woods and ranch groups, staged the biggest protest ever seen in Portland. More than thirteen thousand timber workers and their families, along with one thousand trucks, converged on Portland's Courthouse Square in protest.[20]

Meanwhile, in Mendocino County, millworkers were fuming over job losses. They were already angry at the Louisiana-Pacific Corporation — owner of 316,000 acres in the county — for deciding to build the mill in Mexico. Their fury grew white hot on March 29 when the company cut 195 jobs in Ukiah, Covelo, and Oroville, claiming that environmental protests had denied access to national forest timber. Compounding the calamity, on April 14 the grand old Redwood Empire sawmill in Philo closed its doors, putting another thirty-five people out of work because, said its president, of "uncertainties surrounding the proposed timber ballot initiative."[21]

Both sides believed that events were proving them right. Earth First!ers claimed the mill closures showed that timber companies had practiced "cut and run" logging. But loggers were equally certain that it demonstrated protesters were destroying their jobs. Declining living standards fueled their suffering and self-righteousness. These emotions, combined with the ambivalence many activists felt toward the pacifist declaration, put the two cultures on a collision course.

Appointing herself spokesman for millworkers, on April 3 Bari marched into a meeting of the county Board of Supervisors, charging the company with "corporate crimes," including "ecosystem liquidations," intended to "feed the gluttony of a millionaire" and proposing that the county acquire Louisiana-Pacific's holdings and "operate them for the public good." Then she and Cherney broke into song, "The Ballad of Harry Merlo," concluding with the line "L-Po, what have you done to Mendocino?"[22]

With friends like that, loggers thought, they didn't need enemies. Spring had summoned their worst nightmares. The Thomas report and the mill closures were bad enough. But the Forests Forever initiative drive, collecting signatures at a record rate and clearly destined for the November ballot, raised the prospect that electoral whim could end their way of life forever. Now Redwood Summer and Bari's move to acquire Louisiana-Pacific sent them into a fury. Tensions ratcheted upward.

In early April Pacific Lumber reported that spikes in a redwood log had destroyed a sixty-foot saw blade. That same month unknown arsonists burned an expensive giant automated logging machine called a feller-buncher, which belonged to a small company, Okerstrom Logging. This $700,000 device harvested logs up to only twenty-eight inches in diameter, and so was hardly a threat to old growth. Yet it had been a target of Earth First!ers for over a month, who charged that it put people out of work. Bari, writing in the *Earth First! Journal*, called the mysterious conflagration a "happy ending." But when asked if she had been involved, she told newsmen, "It wasn't me. I was home in bed with five witnesses."[23]

Contributing to the climate of violence was Cherney, who, Bari says, was becoming "increasingly unpredictable." As Jonathan Littman writes, he "was becoming a walking metaphor for the capricious side of Earth First!! Around Foreman, he would rant militantly about tree spiking. Around Bari, he would wax eloquent about worker empowerment." Gradually Bari began to leave Cherney out of her efforts. This seemed to grate on the man and confirmed Bari's suspicions that, deep down, Cherney, too, was a male chauvinist. Their relationship worked only so long as she played number two. So, as his envy waxed, their relationship waned.[24]

In March, CBS's *60 Minutes* asked Cherney what action he would take if he were terminally ill. He answered, "If I knew I had a fatal disease, I would definitely do something like strap dynamite on myself and take out Grand Canyon Dam. Or maybe the Maxxam Building in Los Angeles after it's closed up for the night." Such flaky unpredictability terrified north country communities, which did not know how to respond. So when another pamphlet — which Earth First!ers insisted was a fake — urged more monkeywrenching, it set off another round of anger and fear. Convinced that radicals planned to sabotage their equipment, loggers from Fort Bragg to Eureka slept with their equipment throughout Earth Day weekend, out in the pouring rain.[25]

Then came the "Earth Night" fiasco. Unable to control his impulse for mischief, Cherney drew a poster that featured a picture of what looked like aliens from outer space approaching a bulldozer. "Earth Night 1990," the poster read, "Go Out and Do Something for the EARTH at Night." So, apparently acting on Cherney's advice, unknown activists toppled a power pole, cutting electricity to 92,000 customers, that Sunday night near Santa Cruz. As soon as repairmen restored power a few hours later, a 100-foot steel tower, its support bolts cut with a chisel, crashed to the ground. After workers had patched it, a third incident occurred. Around nine in the morning a 2,000-foot span of line fell in Morgan Hill, shutting off electricity to another 50,000 customers for the entire day.[26]

A band calling itself the "Earth Night Action Group" sent a handwritten communiqué to the power company claiming responsibility. Everyone figured that Cherney was involved. The FBI investigated. Loggers circulated Cherney's poster with his name and address on it. Then Bari raised tempers further by refusing to condemn the action. "I think they were pretty heroic," the *Press-Democrat* reported her as saying. "Who's the terrorist? The person who takes down a couple of power lines, or a corporation that operated on an earthquake fault? . . . I'm sorry that some ice cream in people's refrigerators might have melted."[27]

Conflicts came thick and fast. In San Francisco the same Sunday, between three hundred and five hundred protesters broke windows at the Bank of America then threw golf balls, rocks, and eggs at police and overturned newsstands. On Tuesday police arrested thirteen more, including Cherney and King, on the Golden Gate Bridge. The ecoteurs had arrived before dawn, clad in mountain climbing gear and carrying cellular phones so that they could remain in contact with radio stations. Scrambling along the bridge's traverse lines, they tried to unfold a 130-foot netlike banner with lettering eight feet tall proclaiming: "Save This Planet. Defend Ancient Forests. Fossil Fuel Prohibited. Earth First!!"[28]

By May 1 everyone was on edge as an overflow crowd crammed into the meeting of the Mendocino County Board of Supervisors to discuss Bari's proposed summer campaign. "Call off this Mississippi madness," the head of a local logging firm pleaded. A fourth-generation logger, Jerry Philbrick, warned that there would be trouble "when the first guy comes on my property or damages my equipment." Another logger, Larry Loop from Fort Bragg, complained of "the duplicity of the ringleaders when they disavow terrorism to suit their purposes."[29]

Maribelle Anderson, co-owner of a small timber firm, complained, "I don't think these people's lives should be sacrificed for a media event." Others demanded that the supervisors denounce the campaign. The sheriff announced that the county faced huge expenses if thousands of college students joined the protest. Each incident, he said, could cost local taxpayers $30,000 to monitor and control.

When Bari complained of the "lynch mob" atmosphere, supervisor Marilyn Butcher lashed back, "Judi, you've brought this on yourself."

"Well L-P and G-P brought it on themselves," Bari retorted.

At that point sheriff Tom Shea stood up and, saying, "I don't have time for this," walked out of the room, followed by Butcher.[30]

Still, Bari could not call off the "Mississippi madness." The campaign could not be stopped.

Immediately following their early April press release, Bari's team, including Cherney, King, Davis, and the co-directors of the Ukiah Environment Center, Gary and Betty Ball, had thrown themselves into organizing Mississippi Summer — picking base camps, rounding up lawyers for jail support, writing and printing instructional pamphlets and videos, speaking at or sending mailings to colleges, and inserting announcements in a variety of publications.[31]

Cherney wrote in the *Earth First! Journal*, "Thousands of students, activists and retirees are being summoned to northern California to non-violently put their bodies on the line in defense of the most famous ecosystem in the world."[32]

By the May 1 supervisors' meeting recruits were already arriving in force. The *Santa Rosa Press-Democrat* reported, "'The Mississippi Summer in the California Redwoods' is getting off to an early start." Protesters were arriving from New York, Texas, Chicago, and other places where expressions such as "old growth" carried mystical implications. About seventy-five gathered early Thursday morning, May 3, outside Sanctuary, near the site of Bari's first action, the Cahto Wilderness, to stage yet another protest against the Eel River sawmill. In response, loggers circled their wagons. Louisiana-Pacific workers reportedly began stringing barbed wire around some facilities, and Georgia-Pacific, fearful of Earth First! actions in its forests and mills, ended its public mill tours and closed its forests to public use.[33]

An irresistible force was headed straight for an immovable object, and Bari stood at the point of collision. Bari's effort to chart a course between the moderates and the radicals had merely angered both. Tucson Earth First! claimed that "leftists" had taken over Redwood Summer. Some Humboldt County Earth First!ers denounced Bari as a traitor. Challenging her promise of nonviolence, they declared, "We intend to spike trees, monkeywrench, and even resort to violence if necessary." Meanwhile, loggers merely saw the renunciation of tree-spiking as hypocritical. They loathed Earth First!, led by Luddite eco-anarchists, but they feared this feminist union organizer with a clear political agenda.

So rather than helping the cause of peace, this effort paradoxically had the opposite effect. It made everyone mad. Like Mahatma Gandhi and Martin Luther King, Bari would find pacifism a powerful stimulant to the homicidally inclined.

A new and ominous dimension to the conflict was emerging. KDAC radio in Fort Bragg launched a campaign of criticism against Bari. Death threats, which had appeared singly, started arriving in bunches. First came harassing phone calls, then letters foretelling her death. The threats included:

- A photo of Bari framed in the cross-hairs of a rifle scope.
- A letter telling her, "GO BACK TO WHERE YOU CAME FROM . . . YOU WON'T GET A SECOND WARNING."
- A note from self-described "Tasmanian Teens" advising, "The next time you try to stop a logging truck remember that accidents happen! Have a nice summer!"
- A handwritten missive from "stompers" to Bari, King, and Cherney, giving "fair warning. . . . If law enforcement fails, our justice will be

swift and very real. We know who you are and where you live. If you want to be a martyr, we will be happy to oblige."

- And a poster with the words "Humboldt and Mendocino County's [*sic*] Welcome's Dirt First to a Mississippi Summer," displayed over the drawing of a hangman's noose.

By mid-May, Bari, Cherney, Davis, and King were receiving computer-generated threats in volume. "Dear Judi," read one. "It has come to our attention that you are an Earth First! lesbian whose favorite pastime is to eat box lunches in pajamas. . . . No longer can sleazy dikes like you operate with impunity through the guise of anonymity. We know who you are, where you live, and continue to home in on you . . . but you don't know who we are. How does it feel, eco-freak, to have the tables turned?" It was signed "Committee for the Death of Earth First! Brought to you by Fed Up Americans for Common Sense."[34]

These were too vulgar and ungrammatical to be fakes. But, despite repeated requests, the authorities refused to investigate. Earth First!ers, local officials assumed, not loggers, were the real threat to peace in Mendocino County. And on May 8 an event occurred to convince them that they had good reasons for thinking so.

That morning R. P. Sherbin, plant manager of the Louisiana-Pacific mill in Cloverdale, arrived at work to find the building vandalized and the wooden deck stained and covered with debris. A burst and capped gas can lay on the deck, and a small cardboard sign propped against a nearby tree read, "LP Screws Millworkers." The wreckage included small pieces of plywood, foam, duct tape, a pocket watch, and wires, some scorched. A section of two-inch galvanized pipe approximately nine inches long lay on the front lawn. Both ends had been capped, but one cap was missing. The sheriff, noting that these were the "remains of an exploded pipe bomb," concluded that "some type of destructive device had been exploded" — surely, it seemed, set by someone sympathetic to Earth First![35]

This incident received little attention in the press. But it did not go unnoticed by the Federal Bureau of Investigation, whose agents, along with officials from the Bureau of Alcohol, Tobacco, and Firearms, had coincidentally been conducting an antiterrorist bomb class for local law enforcement officers in Eureka at the time. Pupils at this school had been shown how to build devices exactly like the one found at Cloverdale. The countdown to Redwood Summer had just begun, yet the lives of Bari and FBI agents were already intersecting. As it always does, anarchy had invigorated the forces of authority, providing an excuse for repression.[36]

On the evening of Tuesday, May 22, Bari parked her car next to the Willits police station and entered the Frontier Restaurant next door. Around forty people were there, half of them loggers, the others activists. Frightened by the ferocity that had surfaced on May 2 in Ukiah, both sides had sought this meeting to lessen tension. And indeed, Bari thought, the climate was improving. They had even achieved a truce of sorts, each side agreeing not to use violence first.[37]

After the meeting Bari drove home to be with her old friends, the folk singers Utah Phillips, Joanna Robinson, and Dakota Sid, who were visiting. The next afternoon the four caravaned to Oakland — Bari driving her white Subaru, the others their recreational vehicle — stopping at 3237 California Street, headquarters of Seeds for Peace, a pacifist support group, which had promised to provide food and other support.

Cherney was there when they arrived, along with Shannon Marr of Seeds and another activist Bari did not know named David Kemnitzer. The singers left, but the four activists stayed until 11 P.M., planning Redwood Summer. This was to be their final strategy session. The campaign, they decided, would feature four large actions — one at Samoa, against Louisiana-Pacific; one at Fort Bragg, against Georgia-Pacific; one in Sequoia National Forest; and, in Fortuna, as a finale over the Labor Day weekend, a convocation against Pacific Lumber they would call "Redwoodstock."

The meeting went well, except that Bari and Cherney, who had just broken up, fought continually. By the time it ended, she didn't want to be near her former lover. So, rather than stay at Seeds with Cherney, she accepted Kemnitzer's invitation to spend the night with him and his wife.

After following Kemnitzer to his home, Bari parked her car on the street and unloaded everything — musical instruments, files, and clothes — taking three trips to do so. After breakfast the next day, Cherney and Marr arrived. The Earth First!ers were scheduled to give a concert that evening in Santa Cruz. For Cherney it would be the first of a ten-gig tour of California colleges; but Bari planned to return home after the first performance, to continue the planning of Redwood Summer.

In the meantime Bari and Cherney needed to rehearse with their banjo player, George Shook, who was staying at Seeds for Peace. Since Marr was familiar with Berkeley's streets, she volunteered to lead the way there. After rehearsing at Seeds, Bari, Cherney, and Shook planned to drive on to Santa Cruz.

Around 11:30 Bari packed her car. When she threw her duffle bag behind the driver's seat, she did not notice the little package wrapped in a blue towel. Instead, with Cherney beside her and Marr leading the way in a little Datsun B210, the three set off to meet Shook.

They never made it.

24

STEPPING ON
AN ANTHILL

JUDI BARI KNEW INSTANTLY a bomb had hit her. In fact, she was half expecting it.

Trying to keep up with Shannon Marr's Datsun, Bari drove fast down Oakland's Park Boulevard in her white Subaru station wagon on the way to Seeds for Peace. Darryl Cherney sat beside her. It was Wednesday, May 24, 1990, at about 11:50 A.M. As they approached the intersection with MacArthur Street, Bari touched her brakes.

The explosion was deafening. Drifting out of control, her car careened across the street, colliding with a signpost on the opposite curb. Smoke poured out the windows. Cherney was only slightly injured. But the explosion broke Bari's pelvis in ten places, pulverized her tailbone and two lower vertebrae, perforated her colon like a piece of Swiss cheese, and temporarily cut off feeling in both legs.

Fireman Thomas Veirs, using a reciprocating saw, sliced away the driver's side pillar and door, as well as a section of a pedestrian guard rail against which the car rested. Paramedics then reached through the opening to cut off Bari's clothes, but Veirs noted that the force of the blast had already torn away the woman's jeans. She complained of pain in her back and legs, so Veirs stood behind her and, after putting his foot through a hole in the car floor, sliced away her seat belt and reclined her seat back, trying to relieve her suffering until paramedics could lift her onto the stretcher.[1]

During his lunch hour Federal Bureau of Investigation Special Agent Timothy S. McKinley decided to shop for an apron which his child needed to wear in a school play. But as he drove through Oakland just past noon, he heard a radio report that "a car bomb with several injured had occurred at the intersection of MacArthur Boulevard and Park Street." Being nearby, he decided to investigate.

When McKinley arrived, the Oakland police were already there, along with Special Agent James Flannigan of the Bureau of Alcohol, Tobacco, and Firearms. Within a few minutes officers from the Alameda County Sheriff's Department bomb squad arrived, followed by an FBI antiterrorist expert, Special Agent Frank Doyle, Jr.

McKinley found Oakland homicide detective Sergeant Mike Sitterud examining "a heavily damaged Subaru station wagon, white in color." The vehicle sat partially on the sidewalk at the intersection, pressed against a guard rail. Its glass was gone, the roof bulged outward like a bubble, and "a large hole was blown through the floor of the vehicle approximately under and to the rear of the driver's seat."[2]

Sergeant Sitterud and his partner, Robert Chenault, had been at the Oakland police station, serving on standby homicide duty, when their boss, Mike Sims, asked them to respond to the explosion. Chenault drove to the hospital, arriving just as the ambulances arrived carrying Bari and Cherney. He found Bari, suffering from a shattered pelvis and multiple internal injuries, being rushed to the trauma room, then to surgery. Sitterud went immediately to the intersection, arriving at 12:20 as the firefighters were cleaning up. Chenault, driving from the hospital, joined him a few minutes later.[3]

The officers surveyed the scene. McKinley noticed that "several construction-type nails were embedded in those portions of the driver's seat which were relatively still intact." Walking back to MacArthur Boulevard to the point of ignition, he found "fragments of pipe caps, fragments of the threaded portion of a length of what appeared to be pipe with a diameter of 2.5 to 4 inches, numerous nails, duct tape, and near the point of ignition, a chunk of pipe split open and laid nearly flat by the force of the explosion."[4]

The driver, McKinley learned, had been "severely injured in the blast," and her passenger, "one Darryl Cherney," was also injured, but "to a lesser degree." Chenault told McKinley that both victims were members of Earth First! The FBI agent was familiar with this group, which he described in his report as "aggressively involved with efforts to control or restrict logging in the Ukiah, California, area." Calling his San Francisco office from a pay phone at a gas station across the street, he requested record checks on the victims, and alerted FBI Special Agent John Raikes, an expert on terrorism.[5]

Later, Sitterud would testify, Raikes "gave us a considerable briefing on [Bari and Cherney]. He told us that . . . these people, in fact, qualified as terrorists, and that there was an FBI investigation going on other incidents where these individuals were suspects."[6]

The Oakland detectives dutifully put this down in their books that day. "Injury victims," Sitterud wrote, "are apparent radical activists with recent arrest for illegal demonstration on Golden Gate Bridge. Earth First! leaders suspected of Santa Cruz power pole sabotage, linked to federal case of attempted destruction of nuclear power plant power lines in Arizona." Bari and Cherney, Chenault said, are "members of a violent terrorist group involved in the manufacture and placing of explosive devices." The two, he concluded, "were transporting an explosive device in their vehicle when the device exploded."[7]

From the very first moments, local investigators, prompted by the FBI, decided that Bari and Cherney had built the bomb themselves. Propelled by certainty, they sought evidence against the couple, interrogating Marr, Kemnitzer, and Cherney and searching Seeds for Peace and Kemnitzer's home. They inspected Cherney's van, finding "a plastic pipe nipple with metal end caps and 6–8 pieces of one half inch 12 inch long rebar sharpened at one end (These items are a road spiking kit to blow out lumber truck tires). There additionally were red wires and alligator clips."[8]

By three o'clock they had booked Bari on charges of possessing a booby trap and violating state explosive laws, and sent an officer to guard the suspect who, at the time, was unconscious in the operating room, under anesthesia.[9]

It was as though someone had stepped on an anthill, Kelpie Willsin remembers. By afternoon, right after the bombing, she and Karen Pickett, both Earth First!ers, had converted Pickett's house into a command center. People were scurrying all over the place, and everyone was angry. The FBI came and went. Police ransacked Seeds for Peace. Congressman Ronald Dellums called for an investigation. Reporters interviewed everything that moved. The Berkeley Environmental Center was in total chaos.

Meanwhile, the phones were driving Willsin crazy. Activists were calling from around the country. The entire public interest community rallied to the defense. Even the conservative old National Wildlife Federation called to offer support. Willsin asked for volunteers to man a fifty-person round-the-clock vigil at the hospital. And, of course, she asked each group that called to join in Redwood Summer, a crusade that before the bombing few had wanted to join.[10]

· · ·

Gary Ball was in his office at the Ukiah Yurt Works when his wife, Betty, called. Judi and Darryl, she told her husband, had been bombed. She heard it on the radio. Gary called the hospital, hoping to be told the report was a hoax. On learning it was true, he informed Mike Sweeney, Bari's ex-husband, so that he could come and take care of the children. Rushing to the Environment Center, Ball found "all hell had broken loose." People streamed through the door bringing get-well cards, volunteering to man the telephones.

Meanwhile, Betty Ball called Karen Pickett's house, reaching Kelpie Willsin, who phoned Pickett at the Berkeley Ecology Center. Pickett hurried to Highland Hospital, where she found Cherney in robe and slippers. Police had taken his clothes and shoes and told him not to leave. At 3:00 P.M. he was led away for questioning. The police and FBI wanted to talk with Pickett as well. When officers insisted that she accompany them to headquarters or face arrest, Pickett "began to feel something was weird." She called Willsin and got the name of a lawyer, Susan Jordan, before leaving with the authorities.[11]

Released at six that evening, Pickett returned to the hospital and stood outside Bari's door, using the hall phone to call the media. Meanwhile, at the police station Sitterud was questioning Cherney. At 2:00 A.M. the detective booked the activist and took him to jail. Soon Willsin arrived at the lockup with fifty Earth First!ers, establishing an all-night vigil outside the entrance.[12]

Before dawn the next morning Sitterud and Chenault flew in an FBI helicopter to Redwood Valley, near Ukiah, where they searched Bari's home. In the early afternoon they continued on to Garberville to comb through the flotsam of Cherney's one-room cabin. At Bari's they seized a treasure trove of apparent bomb-building materials, seemingly identical to those used in the Cloverdale and Berkeley bombs, including rolls of gray duct tape, black plastic tape, solder and soldering iron, light switch and light bulb socket, black electrician's tape, carpenter's glue, finishing nails, a pipe vise, black, red, and white wires, nine-volt Duracell battery, blue towels, and two pipe wrenches.[13]

None of these items had undergone laboratory analysis yet, and they also happened to be exactly the things likely to be found in the home of a professional carpenter such as Bari. Nevertheless, authorities now believed they had found the smoking gun. They could tighten the noose. So, even as Sitterud and Chenault conducted their north country helicopter sorties, Oakland Alameda County municipal judge Horace Wheatley was setting bail for Bari and Cherney at $100,000 for crimes related to possession and transportation of a bomb. Afterward, Bari, semiconscious and in guarded condition, was moved to the prison ward of the hospital.[14]

As investigators sought to prove the couple's guilt, Earth First!ers rushed to fill what they called the "Judi Gap." Redwood Summer must go on, they resolved. Karen Wood, member of the "Sapphire Six" and veteran of the Easter Sunday Massacre at Breitenbush, came from Oregon to help. Pickett's house became headquarters. The women divided the responsibilities: Wood would protect Bari, Pickett assumed liaison with other groups, and Willsin devoted herself to the campaign. The Balls and Pam Davis organized things in Ukiah. Roselle would raise money. Sweeney took care of the children.[15]

The strategy remained unchanged. There would be four large actions: at Samoa against Louisiana-Pacific, at Fort Bragg against Georgia-Pacific, in Sequoia National Forest, and, as a grand finale, "Redwoodstock" on Labor Day weekend, aimed at Pacific Lumber in Fortuna.[16]

Logistics and tactics were planned with the care of the D-Day invasion. A main office in San Francisco greeted and oriented out-of-state volunteers, sending them to nonviolence prep classes run with the aid of Greenpeace. A communications nerve center at Alder Point was prepared to make daily news reports. Information "nodes" were established at the Redwood Action Center in Sylvandale, under the command of Ed Denson; the Mendocino Environment Center in Ukiah, captained by the Balls; and the Northcoast Environment Center, run by Tim McKay. Recruiting offices were opened in Michigan, New Hampshire, Nevada, Vermont, Texas, and Wisconsin.[17]

Seeds for Peace readied itself to serve thousands, assembling large movable kitchens, portable toilets, and wastewater treatment facilities. Base camps were prepared near every major anticipated action. The network of camps and nodes was connected by a sophisticated communications system with telephones, fax machines, and computers lent by Greenpeace.

Multimedia efforts attracted and trained volunteers. The team issued a statement of seven goals for Redwood Summer which included resolves to "Save and Protect the Old Growth Ecosystem" and "Acknowledge that the Earth and all species have equal rights." It broadcast running news reports and calls for volunteers over the worldwide environmental computer network, Econet. The Mendocino Environment Center produced a video, "Redwood Summer," which was distributed throughout the country. Organizers assembled a 350-page informational packet, "Welcome to Redwood Summer," which offered a masterly blend of history, tactics, and propaganda sufficient to convince those who knew nothing about ecological issues that he or she was an expert.

Incoming recruits received a basic training that included indoctrination in the philosophy, history, and practice of civil disobedience, consensus decision-making, conflict resolution, and dealing with the law. They were given instructions on the booking process, contacting a lawyer, serving time, "jail solidarity," and defending against Mace, tear gas, and other police weapons.

The stage was set for confrontation. As prologue, small skirmishes began in early June, including a "cat-and-mouse" action at Tailed Frog Grove near Eureka, a log export protest at the Sacramento Export Docks, and the "Squirrel Brothers Tree-Sit" at Fortuna. These warmed up the audience. On June 8 Palco president John Campbell, speaking to a breakfast meeting of the Santa Rosa Sunrise Rotary Club, promised that his company would "raise an aggressive counterattack this summer and fall."[18]

On June 20 activists as far away as Milwaukee gathered to launch the campaign. And on June 21 Pickett and the pseudonymous "Woody Joe" opened the curtain on the first act, announcing in the *Earth First! Journal*, "Redwood Summer Goes On!" They proclaimed: "Now is the time to make a stand for the trees, for the frogs, for the owls, for the rivers. Now is the time to stand firm against the onslaught of greed and corruption, destroying the forests of the Pacific Northwest and attacking those who defend them." The drama had begun; and Earth First!, as the writer Alexander Cockburn observed, had an "appointment in Samoa."[19]

From that moment on events unfurled as in a classic tragedy, replete with plots, subplots, and tragic heroes. The season progressed by point and counterpoint. As confrontations between activists and loggers held center stage, the FBI continued its vendetta against Bari and Cherney, while the larger environmental community, like a Greek chorus, played the role of moral observer. A decade of monkeywrenching had finally led to tragedy, and ironically it was Bari, the would-be pacifist, who had suffered most.

But the actors were too engaged to remember the warning of another chorus, in Aeschylus' *Agamemnon:*

> Justice so moves that those only learn
> who suffer; and the future
> you shall know when it has come; before then,
> forget it.[20]

Like the Trojan warriors who, in the heat of battle, forgot their original purpose had been to return the kidnapped Helen, these combatants lost sight of the issues. Activists chanted slogans about trees and owls as they confronted jeering loggers in the mill towns, but the words had become mantras without meaning, sounds signifying anger without an object.

Neither did Earth First!'s critics understand what the fight was about. The loggers and their conservative allies believed that it concerned money and jobs, and that they were fighting the resurgence of communism, whereas in fact their enemy embodied the more revolutionary ideas of biocentrism.

The original *casus belli* — preservation of the environment — was forgotten. Redwood Summer became a generic ideological battle, inviting participants to fight for the cause of their choice. The investigators' pursuit of Bari revived a range of political agendas, attracting the aging radical left, from Peace and Freedom party stalwarts to graying Black Panthers, who had never stopped seething over the persecution of Angela Davis, Huey Newton, and the Chicago Seven. Becoming the newest martyr to the excesses of mainstream authority, Bari was dubbed the "Chico Mendes of the First World."[21]

Outside police headquarters fifty people, called by Seeds for Peace, maintained constant, silent watch. Periodically up to two hundred faithful assembled for noisier protests. Another round-the-clock congregation stood outside the hospital. Pickett organized a drive to raise bail money for Cherney. After he was released on bond, Cherney kept up a steady stream of public pronouncements.[22]

Countless groups rushed to the activists' side. Within hours of the bombing, Congressman Dellums's legal counsel, H. Lee Halterman, began pestering authorities with complaints and questions. Susan Jordan took charge of the legal defense. Letters of support poured in from Greenpeace, the Toxics Coordinating Project, the Pesticide Action Network, Friends of the Earth, the Environmental Project on Central America, World Rainforest Movement, International Indian Treaty Council, Rainforest Action Network, Earth Island Institute, the National Lawyers' Guild, the National Organization for Women, and many other organizations.[23]

News of the event galvanized the international green community with electrifying speed. On May 26 thirty-seven groups from thirteen countries, ranging from London's Gaia Foundation to Australia's Rainforest Action Group, declared, "We support grassroots community organizers like Judy [sic] Bari and Darryl Cherney in these work [sic] to stop the destruction of some of America's most important redwood forests."[24]

Representatives from these and other movements met to fashion a defense strategy. Greenpeace hired a private investigator to help Bari's and Cherney's attorneys. On June 1 Friends of the Earth called for a "full investigation of bombing incident . . . which injured two environmental organizers of the redwoods campaign." A May 30 *San Francisco Bay Guardian* editorial opined: "Perhaps Bari and Cherney are guilty. But the authorities should never have assumed so from the start. The investigation ought to consider all the likely suspects — including logging companies and government agents."[25]

Indeed, as the prosecution of Bari continued, questions lingered: Why were authorities so quick to accuse? Why had the FBI investigated no other suspects?

To catch their quarry, the investigators needed to connect the bomb to Bari. This meant finding the answer to a critical question: Where was it at the moment it exploded? Like Agent McKinley, the Alameda County bomb squad observed that, "the device was underneath and possibly just to the rear of the driver's seat." But after the FBI arrived, the Oakland detectives apparently changed their minds. That evening, Detective Sitterud reports, "S. A. Frank Doyle briefed meeting [of the investigation team] on . . . fack [sic] that the bomb had been on the floor behind the driver's seat."[26]

The Oakland police already knew Doyle, a twenty-year veteran of the international and domestic terrorism squad. Reportedly, he had been an instructor at the Eureka bomb school a month earlier, where a department officer had been a student. The bomb components, Doyle said, included a battery, mechanical watch, electrical wires, pieces of a pipe nipple about two inches by twelve filled with explosives and capped at both ends, and "numerous nails bound together by silver duct tape for shrapnel effect." Glued to a board and wrapped in a blue towel, it was about a foot square and three inches high, making a package that would fit neatly under the driver's seat.[27]

But Doyle insisted that the bomb had detonated behind Bari's seat, not under it. This not only contradicted the observations of the other officers but also defied the physical evidence, which clearly showed a hole directly under the seat. Yet the implications were crucial. If the bomb was behind the seat, Bari, who had placed her bags there that morning, must have known it was there.

Yet later examination would reveal a flaw in this hypothesis. The device had two triggering mechanisms. The first consisted of a watch with the minute hand removed and a screw inserted at the nine o'clock position on the face. When the hour hand touched the screw, it completed the connection. The second was a motion sensor designed to detonate at the slightest movement. It consisted of two wires, one carrying a positive and the other a negative electric current, which were looped over a small ball bearing that sat in a hole in the board. When a turn or a bump jarred the bearing out of the hole, it would roll and hit the wires, making contact between the positive and negative terminals, completing the circuit.[28]

Once the timer circuit closed, even slight jarring would ignite the bomb — but not before. The clock therefore served as a safety feature. By setting it ahead, its builder had protected himself, or herself, against premature detonation as it was placed in the car. This meant that when the device exploded, the hour hand was already touching the clock screw — virtual proof that Bari could not be guilty. If she had built the device herself, she would have set the clock ahead to preclude the possibility of premature explosion. No one would knowingly drive around with an armed motion-sensing bomb under — or even behind — their seat.

Then there was the most disquieting evidence of all: the "Lord's Avenger" letter. Sent to *Santa Rosa Post-Democrat* reporter Mike Geniella, it was postmarked May 25, the day after the explosion.[29]

"I built with these Hands the bomb that I placed in the car of Judi Bari," the letter began. "Doubt me not for I will tell you the design and materials such as only I will Know." And, indeed, the Avenger must have made the bomb. Three pages long, and expressing an ominous religiosity, the letter contained an exact description of it, including information not yet made public, along with an account of how it was placed in Bari's car and why.

"I come forward now emboldened by the Spirit of the Lord to spread the Message spoken by the bomb so that All will hear it and take it into there [sic] Hearts," the missive continued.

"This Woman Possessed of the Devil set herself on the Honest men of toil who do Gods work to bring Forth the bounty that He has given us to Take, All the forests that grow and all the wild creatures within them are a gift to Man that he shall use freely with God's Blessing to build the Kingdom of God on Earth. . . .

"'And God said,'" the Avenger continued, quoting the Book of Genesis, 'Let us make man in our image, after our likeness; and let them have dominion over the fish of the sea, and over the fowl of the air, and over the cattle, and over every creeping thing that creepeth upon the earth.'"

Then the writer explained how he had built and planted both the Cloverdale and Berkeley bombs: "The hand of the Watch Moved once again and the bomb was Armed and my Faith was Weak and I was Deaf to His Words as he instructed me. The Devil Hissed into my other ear that I should use Cunning and turn Judi Baris poison against her. . . . The Devil moved my hand to bomb in Cloverdale to bring Infamy down on Judi Bari."

After depicting the Cloverdale mechanism in detail — even describing the kind of wax placed on the pipe threads, the flashlight filament, and the epoxy glue — the Avenger offered a similarly precise description of the Berkeley bomb, explaining the explosive's three-to-one ratio of potassium chlorate to aluminum powder, the yellow sponge used to silence the ticking of the watch, and the blue towel that covered it.

Then, the writer concluded, "I put the bomb in her car whilst she was at the meeting with the loggers. The wicked shall know no refuge. . . . If you Heed not this Warning and go into the forests to do Satan's Bidding surely you will Suffer the Punishment of demon Judi Bari. . . . 'I will early destroy all the wicked of the land; that I may cut off all wicked doers from the city of the Lord' [Psalms 101:8]. I HAVE SPOKEN. I AM THE LORD'S AVENGER."

Laboratory analysis concluded that whoever wrote the letter planted both bombs. But the Avenger's missive did not fit into the neat case the authorities sought to build against the two activists. In fact, it raised more questions than it answered.

Its author claimed to be an enemy of Earth First! and to have placed the bomb in Bari's car while it was parked next to the Willets police station as she attended the May 22 "no first strike" meeting at the Frontier Restaurant. But that was forty hours before it exploded, and the timer could be set no more than twelve hours ahead. If the Avenger did place the bomb that night, it should have detonated when Bari first drove the car the next day.

Indeed, the Avenger anticipated and sought to resolve this puzzle, suggesting that divine intervention had delayed detonation so that Cherney could be blown up as well:

And the Bomb was Hidden and the hour hand Moved. But it did not Explode! The Lord had Made another Miracle. He had stopped the hand of the watch by His Divine Intervention. I was seized by Doubt and Confusion but my Faith told me that a Higher Purpose must be at Work. For two nights and two days the hand was stayed until the Demon was joined in her car by the VERY SAME man who had helped her Mock and Insult the Faithful outside the Abortion Clinic that day years ago. PRAISE GOD!

The Lord's Avenger letter therefore muddied the waters. It should have prompted police to look for suspects among loggers and anti-abortionists. Instead, the authorities discounted the missive's pro-logging and anti-abortion remarks as a ruse by environmentalists and as evidence that if Bari had committed one crime, she must have committed the other, too. They made no effort to trace the sources of earlier death threats. They never seriously considered any logger or pro-life activist a suspect. Instead, throughout June and July they pursued a media campaign aimed at convincing the public of Bari's guilt.[30]

Rather than dropping charges, prosecutors postponed the scheduled May 29 arraignment of Bari and Cherney until June 22. The police then transferred the half-conscious Bari from the prison ward into a private room and removed her guard. Fearing that whoever sought to murder once might try again, Pickett recruited bodyguards for her fallen comrade.[31]

Assistant district attorney Chris Carpenter explained that arraignment had been delayed because "I just want to have all the facts before we make a decision." But it was only a tactical retreat. Investigators continued to insist that Bari and Cherney were guilty. As late as July 5 police were still telling the press that the finishing nails linked Bari and Cherney to the bomb. Yet six days earlier, on June 29, the FBI had concluded that "a separate determination [of buyers of the nails] is not feasible" because, as their distributor, Pacific Steel and Supply of San Leandro, California, had told agents, the same batch had been distributed widely throughout Solano, Mendocino, and Humboldt counties.[32]

On July 11 the *San Francisco Chronicle* reported that Sitterud still believed that "the bomb was built at the Mendocino County home of one of the victims" — more than a month after FBI experts had concluded that the bomb was indeed under the seat and not behind it, and nearly three weeks after laboratory analysis had conclusively proved that none of the tape, solder, wires, or batteries taken from Bari's and Cherney's houses matched those used to make the bombs.[33]

But by then it was obvious to everyone but the authorities that Bari and Cherney were innocent, and these attempts to create a political climate favorable to the prosecution backfired. Rather than convincing the public of Bari's guilt, the campaign merely provoked outrage.

The press overwhelmingly sided with Earth First! Bari's arrest, wrote *Press Democrat* columnist Howard C. Hughes on June 21, has "*déjà vu* written all over it." The expression 'Mississippi Summer,' he continued, "is not a misnomer . . . because two committed environmental activists appear to have been targets of an assassination plot while being themselves discredited as the perpetrators of their own explosive fate." The real problems, he suggested, were "the high crimes and misdemeanors of the whole subcult of covert operators spawned in our midst behind the deceptive cloak of national security."[34]

As the day of arraignment approached, a slew of environmental leaders published a press release denouncing the "campaign to slander movement." A pro-Bari environmental consortium led by David Brower, calling itself the Alliance for Activists' Rights, held a rally on the steps of the Alameda County Courthouse calling "for a thorough and impartial investigation into who was truly responsible for the murder attempt against these activists as well as serious investigation of the numerous death threats they have received. Further, we demand that the authorities desist in their campaign to discredit the legitimacy of their struggle."[35]

Bowing to pressure, prosecutors again postponed arraignment, this time until July 18. The investigation was losing momentum even as, in Samoa, Redwood Summer opened to the deafening roar of bad rock music.

25

REDWOOD
SUMMER

HISTORICAL TURNING POINTS seldom have dramatic beginnings. Rather, they start quietly in the minds of ordinary people. New ideas incubate and gain popularity over a period of years, until some event sparks a transformation that gives them legitimacy. Then, suddenly, the world is turned upside down. Beliefs that before were sacrosanct are quickly discarded, and new ones, hitherto deemed too radical, assume the mantle of orthodoxy.

Thus, the first skirmishes between colonial minutemen and British soldiers at Concord Bridge in 1775 did not cause the American Revolution. The origins of that war can be found much earlier, when settlers first encountered notions of democracy articulated by philosophers such as John Locke. Similarly, the French Revolution had already begun before an angry mob stormed the Bastille on July 14, 1789. The revolt was inspired by ideas such as those contained in Montesquieu's 1748 book *Spirit of Laws*, and Jean Jacques Rousseau's 1762 treatise *The Social Contract*, which converted a generation to the ideas of liberty, equality, and fraternity.[1]

So it was with Redwood Summer. Strictly speaking, this campaign, although dramatic, accomplished little. Indeed, it would seem to have been a failure, leading directly to the destruction of radical environmentalism. Nevertheless, it represented a cultural crossroads, signaling that biocentrism, long perceived as the subversive religion of a radical fringe, now enjoyed legitimacy. For although this doctrine had been quietly winning converts among moderates, many of these new disciples kept their apostasy quiet. Biocentrism remained an official heresy, condemned by conventional wisdom — until the bombing of Judi Bari. Then conventional environmentalists who had hitherto been critical of Earth First! rushed to the radicals' defense, thereby helping to validate both the movement and its ideology. And Redwood Summer's pacifist theme would shatter Earth First!, sending forth a diaspora of activists who carried their ideas into the political mainstream.[2]

And so it began. Two days before the summer solstice, at base camp "Honeydew," perched on a curve of the Mattole River just off Highway 101 near Eureka, gender-balanced "affinity groups" of five to fifteen people — bearded activists, pencil-thin aging hippies, retired schoolteachers, stout grandmothers, and pubescent junior high schoolers — gathered for the grand opening of Redwood Summer.[3]

Everyone had an assigned role — as either facilitator, vibes-watcher, spokesperson, or support person. Seeds for Peace was cooking. Econet had broadcast the action widely. Media managers had alerted newspapers and radio and television stations within three hundred miles and handed out press releases and informational packets to journalists as they straggled into the clearing.[4]

The next morning this motley congregation walked under a cloudless sky to the beach at the end of the peninsula across Highway 101 from Louisiana-Pacific's Samoa mill, stopping at a wooden stage set up by Earth First! A thin blue line of helmeted policemen stood on the shoulder of the road watching as Cherney gave television interviews and others played Frisbee or sunned themselves on the sand. Speakers clumped to the rostrum to harangue the crowd. A rock band, Clan Dyken, began to play, and people danced on the dunes.

Then, as if on cue, everyone ran across the highway, breaching the ranks of police officers, and headed for the mill and export dock. As a logging truck arrived at the entrance gate, the crowd swarmed over it, backing up traffic. Getting into it now, the band turned their speakers around, aiming them at the crowd.

"Women, children, teenagers, freaks, has-beens, intellectuals, hippies, straights, senior citizens, everyone was dancing on the highway," observed a participant who called himself "Ricky in the Hills." The band continued to play as the riot squad arrived in vans and began pulling demonstrators off the truck, arresting and handcuffing them. The crowd chanted, "The whole world is watching! The whole world is watching!" and gave each captive an ovation as he or she was led away. By evening more than forty people had been arrested.

"Oh, wow!" exclaimed Ricky. "I've just returned from the best demonstration I have ever been on. . . . What a demonstration, what a victory, I'm floating, one of the best days of my life. . . . Mama mia, this is the real thing."[5]

And so it seemed to newcomers. But not to Earth First! veterans.

As the drama continued, the entire country became a stage. Two days after Samoa, the U.S. Fish and Wildlife Service announced its intention to list the northern spotted owl as a threatened species. The following Monday *Time* magazine carried a cover story about owls and forests, while in Eugene leaders of the Ancient Forest Alliance held a "mapping summit" to redraw wilderness boundaries. On Tuesday, June 26, as Bari's house was searched a second time, the Bush administration appointed a task force to consider alternatives to the Thomas report. And by July congressional subcommittees were deeply engaged in debates over a plethora of "ancient forest protection" bills. Later that summer, on August 20, the Senate would pass the Packwood amendment, restricting log exports. And by September Bush's owl task force would formally endorse the Thomas report.[6]

But owls were only the beginning. Soon environmental groups would petition to list the Pacific yew tree as threatened. The marbled murrelet, a robin-sized sea bird, and several strains of Columbia River sockeye salmon would be added to the endangered list, steps requiring protection of still more habitat. The entire Northwest, it seemed, was being set aside for a Disneyesque menagerie of obscure life forms. In California alone, ninety-five creatures had been classified as endangered or threatened. By the year 2000 the number would grow manyfold.[7]

Ignoring the admonitions of Paul R. Ehrlich and Richard W. Holm — as well as most evolutionary biologists — that the concept of subspecies has no genetic foundation, the endangered species list came to represent the triumph of splitters over joiners as government biologists, propelled by the Endangered Species Act's unintended mandate to halt evolution, dissected subspecies into increasingly smaller "distinct populations" held to be at risk.

Rather than testing to determine if candidate species possessed unique genes, the Fish and Wildlife Service increasingly classified creatures according to where they lived. Nearly every copse, field, and island was seen to possess irreplaceable specimens that required federal protection. Even a partial list of California's endangered and threatened species reads like an atlas of the state:

Truckee Barberry, San Clemente Island broom, San Clemente island bush-mallow, El Segundo blue butterfly, Palos Verde blue butterfly, San Bruno elfin butterfly, Bakersfield cactus, Mojave tul chub, California condor, Loch Lomond Coyote-thistle, Shasta (placid) crayfish, Santa Cruz cypress, Antioch Dunes evening-primrose, Eureka Valley evening-primrose, Eureka dune grass, Solano grass, San Clemente Island Indian paintbrush, San Clemente Island larkspur, Santa Barbara Island liveforever, Presidio (Raven's) Manzanita, San Diego Mesa-mint, Loma Alta mint, Armagosa niterwort, desert pupfish, Yuma clapper rail, Fresno kangaroo rat, Morro Bay kangaroo rat, Tipton kangaroo rat, Santa Cruz long-toed salamander, San Joaquin kit, San Clemente loggerhead shrike, San Francisco garter snake, Colorado River squawfish, Lost River sucker, Modoc sucker, San Mateo thornmint, Armagosa vole, Contra Costa wallflower, Santa Ana Rover wooly-star, San Joaquin wooly-threads, Delta green ground beetle, Valley elderberry longhorn beetle, San Benit evening-primrose, Ash Meadows gumplant, Coachella Valley fringe-toed lizard, Kern primrose sphinx moth, Sacramento River winter run Chinook salmon, Guadalupe fur seal, San Clemente sage sparrow, desert tortoise, Lahontan cutthroat trout, Little Kern golden trout, Paiute cutthroat trout.[8]

As the list lengthened, Redwood Summer lurched onward. While some activists sat in noisy "vigil" outside John Campbell's home in Redway, fourteen women dressed as mushrooms, insects, and stumps and calling themselves "Urban Earth Women" occupied Palco offices in Mill Valley. Seventy-five others protested at the California Department of Forestry headquarters in Santa Rosa. In early July, Grandparents for Old Growth began picketing Palco offices in Scotia as other activists lined the entrances of Louisiana-Pacific mills in Willits and Calpella. Fifty people barricaded the entrance to Jackson State Forest to protest a clear-cutting experiment. Another contingent occupied Louisiana-Pacific's Osprey Grove, where, Earth First! claimed, "nests of spotted owls and ospreys have been found."[9]

Each of these events provoked arrests — which was, of course, what Earth First! wanted. Activists kept score by counting incarcerations. So every parry by authorities merely encouraged a counterthrust. Loggers and local constabulary may have seen the campaign as deadly serious, but to volunteers like Ricky it was a game. A new generation, nostalgic for Vietnam war protests it had never known, carried the cudgel.[10]

Bari, like the unfortunate millworker George Alexander, it would seem, had learned better. What began as a fun game had become a high-stakes roll of the dice, claiming victims at random. When Bari was released from traction on July 3, doctors told her she might not walk again. On July 12 she was moved to a rehabilitation center near Santa

Rosa to begin physical therapy and learn to use a wheelchair. The pain never ceased. "Late at night," the *San Jose Mercury-News* reported, "after the parade of reporters and supporters has gone home, Judi Bari reaches for her pillow. Only then does she sob and wish that she would die. Only then does she admit to herself that her life has changed forever."[11]

She had become a latter-day Joan of Arc whose fiery fate served as the symbol of protest. On July 13 Dellums asked the House of Representatives Subcommittee on Civil and Constitutional Rights to "conduct an inquiry into the character of this investigation and the [FBI's] earlier involvement in monitoring/infiltrating this organization."[12]

On July 16 the Alliance for Activists' Rights held another press conference demanding "Congressional and State of California investigations into FBI and Oakland Police Department conduct in the Earth First!! bombing case." The same day, heads of Friends of the Earth, the Sierra Club, the National Wildlife Federation, the National Parks and Conservation Association, and the National Audubon Society wrote Senator Joseph Biden, chairman of the Senate Judiciary Committee, demanding "a full, independent investigation of the bombing incident as well as an investigation of the charge that the rights of the bombing victims have been violated."[13]

These efforts were only partly successful. On Tuesday, July 17, the Alameda County prosecutor dropped charges against the couple, but investigators remained dedicated to convicting them. On July 20 San Francisco FBI agents sent a teletype message to Director William Sessions, still insisting that "there may be evidence sufficient to charge the two subjects" and that "conviction is the ultimate aim."[14]

As the FBI quest continued, the curtain rose on the second act of Redwood Summer, at Fort Bragg. As usual, the event had been well prepared. On July 10 a base camp had been established near the Georgia-Pacific mill on private land, at Branscomb. More than 150 press passes had been issued. The night before the biggest crowd of activists yet — more than 1,500 — had poured into the encampment, ready to march.

But this time the timber community was ready as well. A pro-logging organization, Community Solidarity Coalition, was prepared for Earth First!'s arrival. On Friday night loggers had felled trees across the intersection of Highway 128 and Branscomb Road, temporarily halting incoming traffic. Cops had come from every town within 120 miles. And when Saturday arrived, Earth First!ers found 1,500 angry citizens there to greet them.[15]

The loggers stole Earth First!'s parade. Before the activists assembled,

Solidarity supporters marched down Harold Street. Five women wearing big floppy hats rode a "Timbermobile," made from a hollowed-out redwood trunk, through what the *North Coast News* described as "a sea of yellow ribbons, T-shirts and balloons." A small boy drove a miniature tractor towing a tiny trailer with small logs. Adults and children carried signs that read, "Families First," "Salaries, Not Welfare," "Hippies Are Parasites," and "Eat Spotted Owls for Dinner!"[16]

"Timber workers and their families," observed one writer, Greg Goldin, "lined the streets as a half-mile-long train of air-horn blasting Kenworths, Peterbilts and Freightliners . . . rumbled down Harold Street, shuddering the moist air, past Paul Bunyan Park (notably devoid of a single tree), toward a cookout featuring red meat, soda pop (no beer allowed), the national anthem and a colorguard flag presentation at Green Memorial Field."[17]

At the park the crowd applauded when a speaker told them, "We are at risk. We are endangered. We have a family-habitat crisis." It chanted along with two former high school cheerleaders who recited in singsong, "We led cheers twenty years ago on this field . . . families first! Save our jobs. . . . Two, four, six, eight, who do we appreciate? Millworkers!"[18]

At the other end of town, a singing and dancing Redwood Summer army climbed over log barricades and assembled in an empty lot belonging to Georgia-Pacific. After listening to speeches by Cherney, Cockburn, and others, it headed down Main Street toward Georgia-Pacific headquarters and directly toward the waiting loggers. It was "scary and awesome," Kelpie Willsin remembers. Carrying signs that read, "Respect the Aged, Hands Off Old Growth," and "Georgia-Pacific Don't Steal Our Children's Future," the ragtag troops shuffled down the street as angry men and women, many wearing Solidarity T-shirts and carrying "Support Our Timber Industry" signs, stood behind the thin line of helmeted police, taunting them.

"Go home!"

"Fuck you, hippie. Get out of our town. Get off of welfare. You deserve a bullet in the head. Darryl, where's Judi?"

The two cultures collided at the corner of Main and Redwood streets. At the intersection the march halted as the enemies stood eyeball to eyeball. As tension became almost unbearable, the marchers began to sing "America the Beautiful." The crowd fell silent. Then, one by one, they joined in as well.[19]

Another successful demonstration, it seemed. But veteran Earth First! watchers knew that something was amiss. The problem wasn't loggers.

Opposition at Fort Bragg may have been stronger than at any earlier event, but there was nothing new about it. Rather, the problem was that environmental extremism had begun to imitate itself. The movement had traveled full circle — from the reality of the Tucson Raiders to Edward Abbey's fiction, back to real-live monkeywrenching, and now to imitating its past.

When Goldin asked Mokai and another Earth First! leader to explain their long-term strategy for saving redwoods, his question was "scorned as 'sequential thinking.'"

"Think like an artist," Goldin was told. Then the two activists began to chant, "Jah love and protect I and I. Jah and the Earth together, nothing can stop them." Goldin, hoping to find evidence of deeper thinking, was disillusioned. "When the affinity groups finally did map out their twilight marauding," he wrote, "they emerged with actions reflecting the same gutlessness and foolhardy glee that dominated the other self-indulgent activities of base camp: tree-hugging, skinnydipping, 'grief circles' and the party-line assertion that male testosterone was ultimately responsible for environmental rape."

"Could this be all there was left of Redwood Summer?" Goldin asked. "What had become of Judi Bari's wondrous vision of thousands, perhaps tens of thousands, of protesters converging on timberland to block the decimation of the forest? Had it come down to scampering into the woods in midnight sorties to place timbers across logging roads, escaping arrest under cover of darkness? Had it come down to impersonating twinkle-toed spirits and wood nymphs?"[20]

Just before the battle of Fort Bragg, a group of long-haired men and women wearing T-shirts and cutoffs sat holding hands in a clearing in the woods of the Gravelly Mountains, overlooking Montana's magnificent Madison River Valley. Below, flags flew from trees. One banner read, "We Have a Dream: Equal Rights for All Animals." Another read, "Recycle or Die!" A slightly pop-eyed man in their midst was burning incense. The circle chanted, "Earth is my flesh / water is my blood / air is my breath / fire is my feeling."[21]

This "woo-woo workshop" at the 1990 Round River Rendezvous was dedicated to exploring the spirituality of nature. Everyone was "sharing" his or her most intimate feelings: a former Baptist preacher's wife recounted how she suddenly became convinced that God did not exist, and another announced, "I am the incarnation of the tree, fighting for itself. That is the highest form of spirituality."

Later, women sat in one circle and talked about empowerment. Men gathered a hundred feet away and discussed how to nurture their feminine feelings. As the men held hands in an effort to sensitize themselves, two of their dogs began to snarl and snap viciously at each other. The session was interrupted until the dogfight was ended. Then everyone stood up, linked arm in arm, and howled like wolves.

Compared with previous rendezvous, this meeting, ten years after the founding of Earth First!, was listless. Only around three hundred people showed up during the week, and most were onlookers. Foreman and Roselle were conspicuous by their absence. Howie Wolke stayed just one day.

A large proportion of attendees were middle-class lawyers and college professors who walked around like couch potatoes looking for a sofa. Everyone remained sober, kept their clothes on, and held hands a lot. To be sure, the workshops spanned a wide range of subjects, from "nonviolence" to "political assassination" to "self-vasectomy." Some ritualistically promised direct actions against logging and mining. But there was also talk about ending illegal acts altogether and "working together" with loggers to protect the wilderness.

Paradoxically, what in California was supposed to be Earth First!'s finest hour seemed to signify imminent burnout. What was the source of this malaise? Much could be attributed to the movement's success. Publicity had attracted an upscale cohort more interested in feminism and philosophy than in tree-sitting. And the message of biocentrism — that all creatures are equally important — recruited animal rights advocates less interested in wilderness than in achieving a Bambi-like intimacy with wildlife.

The very thirst for novelty that a decade earlier had prompted the media to glorify Earth First! now caused them to lose interest. Electronic journalists in particular had no patience with repetition. And now, thanks to its early popularity, monkeywrenching had escalated, attracting the attention of law enforcement. Foreman was scheduled to go on trial in October, and fear of FBI infiltrators was spreading paranoia.[22]

But as powerful as these negative influences may have been, they did not reflect the real source of Earth First!'s problems. The cause was ideological — a nasty internecine fight between the Californians and the Arizonans over the nature of biocentric protest.

Differences that had long simmered between Roselle and Foreman had come to a boil. Foreman sought to roll the clock back to the Pleistocene, not set it forward to some Orwellian socialist utopia. He wished to dismantle civilization, not reform it. To his mind the major threats were technology and overpopulation, not capitalism. Roselle, and now Bari, couldn't abide Foreman's macho tribal leader stuff. If Earth First! remained a bunch of wilderness freaks, they insisted, it would never become a mass movement. Capitalism, not the human race, threatened nature. The system must be reformed, not destroyed.[23]

Redwood Summer precipitated the break. Since early spring Foreman had been objecting to the campaign. He supported tree-spiking and didn't want to turn Earth First! into a labor union. Yet the campaign embodied Roselle's and Bari's most cherished ideals of worker solidarity and grassroots democracy.

The split came in mid-July. The organization's "California crazies," Foreman told the press, were "more interested in the wildness within than the wildness out in the forests." Earth First! has been "taken over by leftist politicos more interested in the class struggle than the rhetoric of ecology." Then, in a letter to Earth First!ers, Foreman and his wife, Nancy Morton, announced their "retirement":

> Sensing an influx into our gene pool by those more adapted to a social and economic justice worldview than an ecological one . . . we cannot escape the fact that we are uneasy with much in the current EF! movement. We therefore have come to the irrevocable decision to leave. . . . This letter announces that decision. . . . We see happening . . . an effort to transform an ecological group into a Leftist group. We also see a transformation to a more overtly counterculture/anti-establishment style, and the abandonment of biocentrism in favor of humanism. I want a no-fault divorce.[24]

Wolke and Bill Devall followed Foreman to the door. Saying that the "new guard" was "aligned with the left," Wolke complained, "I'm tired of being sidetracked by eco-feminism, sanctuary, anarchy, woo-woo, coalition building, bleeding heart humanists against misanthropy, sexist animal lovers for gay rights, and all of the other egotistical fodder for human chauvinistic cause-lovers. . . . I'm tired of hearing myself. You're probably tired of hearing me, too."[25]

The movement, Devall said, had lost its identity: "When EF!ers began taking themselves too seriously and began being taken too seriously by the mainstream media, the movement lost a vital element — playfulness. It seems that during the serious 1990s, drugs, sex, rock n' roll, and tree spiking are the four great sins. . . . Maybe I'm not leaving the Earth First! movement. Maybe the movement is leaving me."[26]

Roselle and Bari were unmoved. Foreman, said Roselle, is "red-baiting. . . . We don't need Foreman in Earth First!! if he's going to be an unrepentant right-wing thug." Rejecting the accusation that she was a "humanist," Bari replied, "Dave Foreman would like to keep the movement small and pure. But profound social changes don't happen without mass movements."[27]

Indeed, Bari was right, but for the wrong reasons. Despite her romantic ideas about workers, she was not a traditional socialist. The conflict as she saw it was not between biocentrism and humanism but between two interpretations of holism, one conservative, the other radical. Just as Hegel had been the philosophical ancestor of both Marx and Mussolini, so now the old Prussian had inspired two kinds of unwitting environmental imitators.

The Arizonan's biocentrism prompted him to reject everything that did not contribute to the stability of ecosystems. This implied a rejection not only of humanism but of most humans as well. Concerned that economic development and overpopulation were upsetting the balance of nature, he embraced those things — even, apparently, AIDS — which reduced the numbers of people. By implication, only those who, like himself, represented "the part of the rain forest recently emerged into thinking" deserved to exist.

This elitism and misanthropy inexorably implied primitivism and tribalism, a yearning to return to a time when only a few hunter-gatherers, led by chiefs such as himself, roamed the earth. It was also the unstated philosophy of most mainstream upper-class conservationists. White, predominantly male and Republican, with names such as Rockefeller, Mellon, and Grosvenor, the superrich had given millions to the movement. They sat on the governing boards of conservation groups, where their relatives or friends often acted as staffers. They served on prestigious environmental policy panels, and their protégés regularly assumed leadership of federal land management agencies.

Through their foundations, such as the Rockefeller Brothers Fund, Alton Jones Foundation, and Pew Charitable Trust, they wielded enormous influence over both environmental interest groups and federal preservation agencies. They underwrote the costs of preservation studies which environmental groups periodically undertook as "non-lobbying" efforts to influence government.[28]

But they shared few interests with average Americans. Members of a class that was losing its privileges, these scions of Oyster Bay and Grosse Point families did not benefit from the 1964 Civil Rights Act, women's liberation, or equal employment opportunities. Instead, the world they knew was falling apart: game was disappearing where their parents had once safaried in Kenya; salmon were dwindling at the family's beat on the Miramichi River in New Brunswick. And they perceived these losses not merely as an end to their Camelot but as representing the inexorable death knell of history.

By contrast, the Californians' biocentrism led to an egalitarian absolutism. If all things are interconnected, then all creatures are equal, including all people — at least all those who don't mistreat the earth. Instead of looking backward, they looked forward to Ecotopia. Rather than governance by tribal elders, they espoused a politics that demanded consensus in grassroots "affinity groups" but resorted to force — through either monkeywrenching or government coercion — against those who did not share the proper "affinities."

As carping between these factions continued, Redwood Summer began to fall between the cracks, even as authorities stepped up efforts to catch the activists. "Tensions had been mounting all summer long," Goldin wrote. "A vigilante group, 'Mothers' Watch' drew up a blacklist of businesses to be boycotted for advertising in a pro-environmentalist newspaper. A petition drive has been started in Miranda to ban from the schoolhouse *The Lorax*, Dr. Seuss' allegory of the disappearing forest."[29]

The third major action took place as planned in Sequoia National Forest July 27–30. But many attending thought that it was a failure. Only three hundred people took the scheduled early morning march down a logging road to occupy a small logging site. The scene lacked focus and — worst of all! — wasn't fun.

"Abysmal" is the way one participant described the Sequoia action in the *Earth First! Journal:* "Last night was an example of what EF! has grown into. First a lousy acoustical duo, then a really fine electrical San Francisco country-rock group with a loud generator that seemed to unplug itself three times to the increasing approval of listeners." The protesters had "created a nasty amount of erosion by rolling logs and boulders downhill to create roadblocks that a D-6 Dozer can clear in a half minute. . . . Efers deflated six tractor tires. . . . This is not monkeywrenching. It's stupid vandalism. . . . It's crisis time at Earth First!!"[30]

As Devall observed, fun had been the real appeal of Earth First! But now this sport was being squelched by humorless feminism and the heavy hand of the law! No longer infused with a hallucinogenic sense of freedom, the atmosphere at Earth First! actions had grown heavy with puritanism and foreboding of impending doom.

Just as the Sequoia action ended, two hundred federal troops, supported by the Departments of Justice and Agriculture, swooped into the region, combing for drugs. Called Operation Green Sweep, the raid reportedly netted one thousand marijuana plants. It also sent a signal to local pot farmers that Humboldt County was no longer a safe haven. One of Garberville's major industries had been dealt a severe blow.[31]

Meanwhile, the FBI, still convinced that an environmentalist had built the bomb that injured Judi Bari, continued to bypass attempts to investigate loggers and spread an ever-widening net over Earth First! The agency collected the names of activists who had written to regional newspapers. It asked police to submit names of "prominent environmental activists" and to produce "any and all examples of typewriting or handwriting originating from the environmental movement." It invited managers of local timber companies to submit "any documentation" on the "environmentalist/redwood timber issue." Its agents interviewed loggers asking them to submit lists of those they feared most. And on August 21 one agent noted that "individuals suspected of being a core group capable of engaging in violent activity include . . . Bill Devall, Greg King . . . and Darryl Cherney. . . . Cherney hangs out with Mike Rozelle" [sic]. The agency began collecting all available material about Earth First![32]

Because of FBI harassment of them and the agency's refusal to investigate loggers, the Earth First!ers sensed that they were the casualties of an official conspiracy. Redwood Summer made everyone feel like a victim. Leaderless and lacking a clear sense of purpose, it ran out of control, striking real terror into the hearts of northern communities.

On August 17 John Campbell was giving a talk at the Redwood Region Conservation Council Educational Symposium to the faculty of Humboldt State University in Korbel when demonstrators assembled outside. Shouting and banging on walls, they successfully disrupted the meeting. As Campbell left and headed for his car, protesters grabbed at him to make a "citizen's arrest" for alleged forestry rules violations. Shaking free, Campbell jumped into his car. But as it moved, demonstrators surrounded the vehicle, forcing it to stop.

"One protester bashed the hood," said Jan G. Petranek, a college staffer and former journalist accompanying Campbell. Another protester, Richard Serina of San Jose, "jumped on the hood and crashed his fists against the windshield six or eight times. From all sides, demonstrators closed upon the car. Police officers pulled people off the car. One officer yelled to Campbell, 'Get out of there.' Campbell started to drive and found openings between the protesters."

Terrified, the two men drove off, Serina still clinging to the hood. "Seventy-five yards down the road," continued Petranek, "we pulled off to the side and asked Serina to get off the hood. Looking at us, eyeball to eyeball, through the windshield, he refused. By then, the protesters had caught up to the car, so we started driving again."

A short way down the road, the two men stopped again, begging Serina to get off. "Then he looked at us and said, 'My friends are coming.' We looked back and three of his fellow protesters were rounding the corner on foot. Again we started to drive off. Serina looked at us and said, 'Bad press.'" This tragicomic chase continued, stopping and starting until the state police arrived and removed Serina. Petranek was shaken. But for Campbell the incident was not over. Earth First!ers, accusing the Palco president of making Serina a "hood ornament," redoubled their harassment.

Setting up sleeping bags by his house, they banged drums throughout the night, maintained blockades during the day, and once dumped a road-killed deer into his swimming pool. Under siege, neither Campbell nor his wife could leave home without a sheriff's escort. At night Campbell, and especially his wife, lay terrified, listening to the chants and banging and wondering if the Earth First!ers would break in.[33]

And so Redwood Summer proceeded. Throughout August actions were continuous, with rallies at the Eureka courthouse, Osprey Grove, Wall Street, Mill Valley, Carlotta, Sacramento, Headwaters, Founders' Grove, and Maxxam's Los Angeles headquarters. On August 14 Bari made her first public appearance since the bombing, at a demonstration in front of San Francisco's FBI headquarters, where two hundred people demanded, "Defend Mother Earth and Sister Judi."

During "Take Back the Redwoods Week" (August 20–26), Willits activists staged a bicycle protest, while in Scotia an Earth First! "hostile takeover" of Maxxam was met by angry loggers and millworkers wearing yellow ribbons. On August 27 twenty women, declaring "class liberation," invaded a course taught by Carleton Yee, a member of the State Board of Forestry, demanding that Humboldt State teach the "Gaia" principle. In Richardson Bay, Marin County Greens and the West Marin Action Group teamed up with Redwood Summer sailors to form a "Peace Navy Flotilla," protesting the liquidation of ancient forests.[34]

The pace quickened as the traveling troupe of eco-thespians prepared for the final act, "Redwoodstock: The Ultimate Log Jam."

We live in an age of movie sequels, television reruns, and Elvis impersonations. And Redwood Summer, patterned after Mississippi Summer, proved that imitation had become the sincerest form of conflict as well.

RESPONSE: THE BIOCENTRIC REVOLUTION

In 1968 Columbia University students occupied five campus buildings to contest the university's connections with the military-industrial complex, thus firing the first shots in a generational war that encompassed more than civil rights, Vietnam, and the environment.[35]

The fuller dimensions of this cultural rebellion were made manifest the following year at a four-day rock concert in Woodstock, New York. As the *New York Times* commented: "The dreams of marijuana and rock music that drew 300,000 fans and hippies to the Catskills had little more sanity than the impulses that drive the lemmings to their death in the sea. They ended in a nightmare of mud and stagnation that paralyzed Sullivan County for a whole weekend. What kind of culture is it that can produce so colossal a mess?"[36]

Perhaps this criticism was too harsh. Nevertheless, the question remains: What sort of society produces a Woodstock? Twenty-one years later, here in the Northwest, came the answer: a society that is undergoing a philosophical revolution.

"Why does no one find it remarkable," the novelist Walker Percy once asked, referring to a great civilization which disappeared around three thousand years ago, "that in most world cities today there [is] not one single Hittite, even though the Hittites had a great flourishing civilization?" He persisted, "Where are the Hittites? Show me one Hittite in New York City."[37]

Likewise, we may ask, why are Bosnia and Somalia collapsing? Why do civilizations die? Environmentalists claimed to have the answer. The earth, they said, is fragile. Societies die when they decimate the environment on which they depend. And once ravaged, the earth does not recover. Men are "brute destroyers," George Perkins Marsh wrote, who "destroy the balance which nature had established." Thus, "nature avenges herself upon the intruder," reducing the human condition to one of "deprivation, barbarism, and perhaps even extinction."[38]

Subsequent writers expanded on this myth. In his 1948 book *The Plundered Planet*, Fairfield Osborn wrote that because "man is destroying the sources of his life," civilization is "facing its final crisis." And in his 1989 bestseller Bill McKibbon lamented that "the end of nature" means "we have a crisis."[39]

But these writers had things backward. Civilizations, not nature, are fragile flowers, and when they disappear, they are gone forever. By contrast, the earth eventually recovers from abuse. Reminders of this are all around us: the Yucatan jungle reclaimed the temples of the great Maya civilization that disappeared suddenly eight hundred years ago. In Europe, Celtic and Roman ruins lie scattered in verdant fields where farmers fear financial ruin because they produce too much. The Inca and Aztec societies were destroyed, but the genes of these ancient people are still alive in the Central and South American Indians of today. Since Columbus, Native American numbers have plummeted, but perhaps more of the continent is covered by forest today than ever before.[40]

Most societies do not die because they destroy their environment. Rather, the environment suffers when societies die. The disappearance of ancient Sumer precipitated desertification of the Fertile Crescent; the Roman conquest of Carthage spread the sands of the Sahara. And today it is chaotic countries such as Somalia and Rwanda that have experienced the worst forms of ecological depredation. Water purification plants don't work when engineers are murdered. Farmers cannot plant fields if marauding gunmen steal their seeds.[41]

To survive, cultures must not only remain free from foreign conquest, but also sustain an internal chemistry of trust and cooperation that derives from a broad sense of shared history and values. These attributes form the deep structure of society. Without them the economic, educational, legal, and social institutions cease to work, and no amount of governmental tinkering can revive them. Yet in America by 1990 this social glue was dissolving in the solvents of economic and environmental extremism. Wall Street raiders, pursuing private agendas, ripped at the fabric of mutual trust, while activists conducted a direct assault on the nation's sense of shared values.

This was the import of Redwood Summer. Many activists who, two decades earlier, had rejected history and philosophy, occupied "Old Main," and sanctified "relevance" now looked back at this shredding of the past with nostalgia. Seeking to reenact the Columbia takeover and Woodstock bacchanalia, they divided the nation further.

By Labor Day in Scotia it was déjà vu all over again. A tense, terrified, and hostile logging community once again awaited invasion by unpredictable and sybaritic hippies. "Call off 'Redwoodstock,'" pleaded a local paper. "Redwood Summer proponents have made their point time and time again. . . . The whole state and nation now know how they feel about redwoods and trees in general."[42]

But the enemy, compelled to relive its past, could not stop. Once again it established a base camp — this time on a sandbar on the Eel River at Fernbridge, near Fortuna. Once again, it offered all-day concerts and a multitude of workshops. And once again it set out to confront the enemy.[43]

On Labor Day morning six hundred protesters, chanting "This land is your land" and "We shall overcome," marched across the old bridge at Fernbridge. On the other side, waiting for them, a hundred young loggers stood by parked pickups, drinking beer and wine coolers. Walking through this gauntlet, the contingent, pelted with eggs and water balloons, continued down Highway 101 to Palco's Fortuna mill, where it was met by another phalanx of loggers and their wives shouting, "Go home! Go home!" "Jobs first!" and "Hemp-hemp hooray."[44]

And, like every sequel, this one was tamer than its predecessors. The combatants had run out of energy. After it was over, everyone went home, and along the North Coast one could almost hear an audible sigh of relief.

As the curtain came down on Redwoodstock, Bari remained at home near Willits. Every move she made, every second of the day, pain reminded her of her loss. Obsessively seeking justice, she devoted herself to the task of achieving public exoneration and finding the real culprit. Was it someone, she wondered, who worked for the sheriff or the FBI?[45]

Both the people and their environment had become casualties. North Coast communities, burdened with debts and hard feelings, remained in a daze. Policing Redwoodstock alone had cost Humboldt County taxpayers $400,000. With Foreman's departure Earth First! self-destructed, and a nasty fight brewed between Roselle and the Tucsoners over control of the *Journal*. Greg King, also the target of death threats, was in hiding. Others were merely burnt out. "I went home and painted my refrigerator," Karen Wood says.[46]

What, then, had been accomplished?

"By late August," Goldin observed, "Redwood Summer had given up even trying." It was "more like a cry in the wilderness than the sonic boom that had been promised. . . . Greg King, the Earth First!!er who'd almost single-handedly brought the Headwaters Forest to national attention, had dropped out of sight altogether. Cherney, his ego a bit overstretched by the media attention following the bombing, only made appearances when the crowds swelled to his expectation."[47]

"In timber territory," observed the *San Francisco Examiner*, "it's been a summer of discontent. Logging families have been angered — and threatened — by the often obnoxious presence of 'unwelcome invaders' who trespassed on private logging jobs, linked arms around mammoth trees, blockaded roads, unfurled banners in the groves and attempted citizens' arrests on corporate executives." In turn, the paper continued, "environmentalists have been shot at in Willow Creek, beaten and stripped in Garberville, chased by a mob in Rio Dell, insulted on the streets of Fortuna. . . . More than 150 were arrested, many spent time in jail and many will return for court appearances."[48]

By fall the effort to save owls and old growth seemed stalled. Pacific Lumber was expected to win its court battle to harvest Headwaters. Although Foreman's trial had been postponed, his prospects for acquittal didn't look good. And in November California voters decisively rejected both Big Green and Forests Forever — revealing, in the words of University of Southern California political scientist Sheldon Kamieniecki, skepticism "about the government's ability to deliver." Conservatives rejoiced. Environmentalism, they thought, had peaked.[49]

But as usual these critics underestimated the power of an idea. Biocentrism — a political philosophy that had been gaining strength through three Democratic and four Republican presidential administrations — was immune to ephemeral fluctuations of partisan politics. Indeed, as it turned out, the very failure of Redwood Summer to fulfill its tactical agenda would ensure environmentalists of ultimate — if Pyrrhic — victory.

IV

CONSEQUENCES:
THE SEASON OF
OUR UNCERTAINTY

1991–

By wire and wireless, in a score of bad translations,
They give their simple message to the world of man:
"Man can have Unity if Man will give up Freedom.
The State is real, the Individual is wicked;
Violence shall synchronize your movements like a tune,
And Terror like a frost shall halt the flood of thinking."

W. H. Auden

That to which we are obligated is an effort to understand,
and that entails taking an exacting look at things. For
every recurrence of the inhuman will be disguised. It will
seek out unexpected locations and choose disguises to
make itself seem honorable. The decisive factor, then, is
that we recognize soon enough what is really beginning to
happen.

Christian von Krockow

26

DIASPORA

ADVOCACY WAS ASCENDANT at Ann Arbor. Men in rumpled shirts and women in dusty tweed jackets sat in the large University of Michigan auditorium in November 1992, listening to media mogul Ted Turner, oozing good intentions, announce in an aw-shucks voice that they could "change the world. . . . We must educate people. . . . That's why we've got a media."[1]

Although this was just its second annual meeting, this trade group, the Society of Environmental Journalists, already boasted eight hundred members. And already it faced a crisis. In the halls, on panels, and at dinner the scribes wanted to know what level of advocacy was acceptable. Almost imperceptibly this profession had ballooned, and many of its conscripts came from activist organizations.

So Turner was preaching to the choir. Lacking any pretense of objectivity, this was a meeting of biocentric true believers. The next apostle, Lester Brown, president of Worldwatch Institute, urged the assembled to help him remake society; and the third, Jeremy Rifkin, critic of genetic engineering and eating beef, announced that we were observing "an entire period of history moving into its twilight years," and urged journalists to hasten the environmental revolution. During the question and answer session, the same reporters who routinely threw hardballs at congressmen and presidents cheered with unreserved enthusiasm.[2]

This preoccupation with advocacy revealed a deeper dilemma. Biocentrism is a teleological view of nature, and those who think this way cannot, even in principle, distinguish fact from value. To understand a thing, according to this perspective, is to know how it ought to behave in nature. The attitudes of a generation that had rejected scholarly objectivity as irrelevant now infused journalism, whose tradition was one of political neutrality. Commitment to a cause collided with a heritage of detachment, and journalists did not know what to do.

Concern for forests and owls, wrote Andy Stahl and his Sierra Club Legal Defense Fund colleague Victor M. Sher in 1990, indicated that an "increased public awareness of natural ecosystems, particularly for their own inherent merit beyond their value to humans, was spreading. Biocentrism, the ideology that the earth and not humans is the center of all that is important, was coming of age."[3]

Indeed, the values emerging in Michigan revealed that the radicals had won by losing. As the 1990s began, their movement was disintegrating, not because it had failed but because it had succeeded. The need for protest disappeared once the national leadership had accepted their agenda. Leaving the movement, Earth First!ers and other biocentrists joined the establishment, bringing their philosophy with them. Abandoning jeans for gray flannel suits, they became missionaries with a zeal that would not accept rejection. Their diaspora fed the mainstream movement, transforming political ecology from heresy to orthodoxy and infusing the culture of upper-middle-class white urban professionals, including teachers, professors, and the press.

Ancient ideas of nature, revived by Haeckel, nurtured by Clements and Tansley, transformed into a mathematical discipline by Hutchinson and the Odums, popularized by Carson and Commoner, and promoted as a political ideology by Devall and Foreman, had become a dominant cultural theme of American politics.

After the split, Roselle went to Greenpeace and took control of the *Earth First! Journal*, moving it to Missoula, Montana. Others, later joined by Foreman, founded an alternative newsletter, *Wild Earth*, in Vermont. Devall enlisted with the IRA-HITI grant-making foundation (later called the Foundation for Deep Ecology) in San Francisco. Bart Koehler became director of the Southeast Alaska Conservation Council. Howie Wolke went over to the Alliance for a Wild Rockies, another preservationist organization. Randy Hayes was already at the helm of the Rainforest Action Network, and Denis Hayes, executive director of the first Earth Day, was ensconced as the president of a megaphilanthropy, Seattle's Bullitt Foundation.[4]

By 1990 the activist generation, having reached middle age, now populated the media, universities, and federal agencies. Individuals moved regularly among these professions, retaining their allegiance not to the employer for whom they worked at the moment but to the ideals that drove them. Radicals metamorphosed into journalists, then lobbyists, then federal bureaucrats, then foundation executives, and sometimes back again, even as mainstream environmentalists moved between government and activist groups which, in turn, maintained links with America's largest business corporations. Greenpeace publicist Peter Dykstra joined the Cable News Network. National Audubon Society staffer Amos Eno would become executive director of the National Fish and Wildlife Foundation, a nominally private group receiving public funds, which assists Fish and Wildlife Service conservation efforts. Destry Jarvis, formerly vice president of the National Parks and Conservation Association, a Park Service watchdog group, would join the Park Service. A former Friends of the Earth and World Resources Institute activist, Rafe Pomerance, went to the State Department.

President George Bush appointed Conservation Foundation president William K. Reilly administrator of the Environmental Protection Agency. The masthead of the foundation included the heads of America's major corporations (Campbell Soup, Exxon, Atlantic Richfield, Philip Morris); foundations (Mellon, Dodge, Smithsonian); and media empires (*National Geographic*, Times Mirror Company, RCA); as well as the names of prominent bureaucrats (William D. Ruckelshaus, former administrator of the Environmental Protection Agency) and politicians (former Arizona governor Bruce Babbitt).[5]

Along with journalists, these forces formed a phalanx that, often unintentionally, saturated public consciousness with the message of biocentrism.

It was Dave Foreman who once again symbolized the evolution of the movement. In August 1991, more than two years after his arrest, he and four co-defendants plea-bargained with prosecutors, each pleading guilty to one count. While his confederates were given jail sentences and stiff fines, Foreman, confessing to conspiracy to commit property damage, received a deferred five-year probationary term which, after time, could be reduced to misdemeanor property destruction.[6]

Benefiting from his notoriety, Foreman wrote *Confessions of an Eco-Warrior* and went on the lecture circuit. The arrest turned out to be a "bonanza," according to the *Washington Post*. "His college lecture business is booming; his new book has won him slots on Larry King's radio broadcast and the 'Today' show." And soon he found a vehicle to launch his biocentrism into the mainstream.[7]

In November 1991 Foreman and other activists met with Reed F. Noss, editor of the journal *Conservation Biology*, to found the Wildlands Project. "Designed to protect biodiversity in North America," wrote Charles C. Mann and Mark L. Plummer in the journal *Science,* "the project calls for a network of wilderness reserves, human buffer zones, and wildlife corridors stretching across huge tracts of land — hundreds of millions of acres, as much as half the continent."[8]

Altogether, Mann and Plummer observed, "the Wildlands approach calls for 23.4 percent of the land to be returned to wilderness, and another 26.2 percent to be severely restricted in terms of human use. Most roads would be closed; some would be ripped out of the landscape." It would mean "nothing less than a transformation of America from a place where 47 percent of the land is wilderness to an archipelago of human-inhabited islands surrounded by natural areas."[9]

Touted as reducing "ecosystem decay" caused by "fragmentation" of habitat, the Wildlands Project was a Luddite agenda wrapped in the guise of science. Project director David Johns, political scientist at Portland State University, proclaimed, "Here on the basis of sound, peer-reviewed science is what we think is necessary to keep ecological processes going or prevent a mass extinction event." But as Mann and Plummer note, "The Wildlands project has never been peer reviewed."[10]

In addition to entailing perhaps the forced relocation of tens of millions of people, the project risked ecological calamity as well. The "fragmentation" it sought to avoid was nothing more than the mosaic of vegetation needed to sustain biological diversity. It ignored the role the Native Americans had played in shaping their environment. Thus, it would "restore" nothing but instead produce conditions unique in natural history. Wildfires would be more numerous and intense, and some species of animals, once held in check by early hunters, would reach unprecedented numbers, posing unique dangers to humans, wreaking havoc on plants, and denuding the landscape.

Indeed, the preservation time bomb was already ticking. Owing to fire prevention and selective harvesting, *Abies* (true fir, as opposed to Douglas fir) and Douglas fir had colonized much of the inland West, growing where more shade-intolerant and fire-resistant larches and ponderosa pines once were found, while for similar reasons red maple had spread to places in Missouri and Arkansas where they had never existed before.[11]

By the early 1990s America was experiencing an unprecedented overabundance of certain wildlife. Protected deer, moose, and elk multiplied, destroying endangered plants and other vegetation on which the soil and many other creatures depended. In most states deer were perhaps five times more numerous than when Columbus landed. In parts of the West, including Colorado, elk, reintroduced after having been eradicated by hunters in the nineteenth century, thrived beyond expectation. Forty moose introduced into Colorado in 1979 had multiplied to more than six hundred by 1992. In Montana white-tailed deer, once confined to the northwest corner, were found throughout the state. In Wisconsin, deer densities had risen from four per square mile to forty since pre-settlement times.[12]

In the West several kinds of ungulates were destroying willow and aspen that sustained a host of creatures from beavers to grizzly bears. Deer, browsing through fields and forests like rototillers, pushed endangered plants to the brink of extinction. In Virginia they decimated flocks of migratory birds such as vireos, warblers, and ovenbirds. On Wisconsin's Madeline Island — which, says University of Wisconsin researcher Don Waller, was "crawling" with deer — "there is no woody plant regeneration at all. It looks like a clear-cut."[13]

Throughout Wisconsin deer had altered the landscape dramatically. On Nature Conservancy lands, according to Conservancy spokesperson Nancy Braker, they had destroyed the reproduction of orchids by nipping off flowers and seeds and had devastated the Canada yew — once a common understory shrub which contains taxol, a chemical used in cancer treatment. Likewise, deer had ravaged Wisconsin's white cedar and hemlock forests, destroying orchids and other plants such as the ram's head lady's slipper, listed as an endangered species.

Around Chicago deer were making parks "look like feed lots," according to Illinois Nature Conservancy director Steven Packard. They were eliminating many rare wildflowers, such as the white-flowered trillium, and had eaten all the endangered white-fringed orchids at the only park where this plant was still abundant. They consumed the last oval milkweed surviving in Illinois. And when the Conservancy put protective wire mesh over small white lady's slipper and yellow lady's slipper orchids, "deer actually ripped cages out of the ground," said Packard.

"The problem has gone past a few plants," said Waller. "We're talking about fundamental change in the north woods plant community." Indeed, only Native American lands still contained much original vegetation. As many Indians followed the rule "If it's brown, it's down," reservation deer densities remained under ten per square mile.

Because of an abundance of prey, predators multiplied as well. In the Rockies, mountain lions had become, according to experts, more numerous than before Columbus landed. Not coincidentally, the big cats began preying on pets and children. In Evaro, Montana, in 1989, a lion killed a six-year-old boy playing in his back yard; in 1991 one killed a high school boy in Colorado; and in 1994 another would kill a woman in California. Montana officials reported that since 1989 close encounters with cougars had multiplied fourfold. In Boulder County, Colorado, lion incidents increased more than 900 percent over the previous decade. Nationally lion assaults were ten times more frequent from 1970 to 1990 than between 1909 and 1932.[14]

These irruptions revealed the fundamental flaw in the ecosystem model — the notion that, left alone, nature would reach "equilibrium." Nevertheless, belief in the balance of nature remained strong in government and environmental circles. For the very biological failure of the ecosystem idea ensured its political success. Since no one could define the boundaries of a "self-sustaining ecosystem," its size was infinitely elastic. Whenever biota of a sanctuary failed to stabilize, this could be taken as proof that the true "ecosystem" must be larger, and hence the preserve must be expanded. And since equilibrium would never be reached, the rationale justified infinite growth of sanctuaries.[15]

Land management agencies and environmental groups used this argument repeatedly to justify enlarging wilderness. In 1980 the National Park Service claimed that Yellowstone National Park's 2 million acres was an "intact ecosystem" for its major mammalian species. When its grizzly bear population continued to decline, by 1986 the service, along with the Greater Yellowstone Coalition, defined the "greater Yellowstone ecosystem" as 6 million acres.[16]

Less than a year later the Congressional Research Office claimed that this "ecosystem" encompassed 12 million acres. By 1991 the Greater Yellowstone Coordinating Committee, a Park Service–Forest Service body, defined it as covering 18 million acres. And by 1992 some members of the coalition, realizing that grizzly populations were still dwindling, embraced the Wildland Project's idea that Yellowstone had to be linked to a chain of "ecosystems" throughout the Rockies.[17]

Thus, by providing a rationale for depopulating the earth one step at a time, the Wildlands Project carried ecosystem reasoning to its logical extreme. And Foreman's phoenixlike rise revealed how popular the idea had become. It was supported, according to Mann and Plummer, by luminaries such as Edward O. Wilson, Paul Ehrlich, and Michael Soule, the University of California at Santa Barbara conservation biologist who had helped Andy Stahl fashion arguments in favor of the spotted owl. And when, in 1987, a New Jersey couple, Frank and Deborah Potter, suggested creating a 139,000 square mile "Buffalo Commons" spreading over ten states in the Great Plains, their proposal was publicized by the

New Yorker, giving impetus to another activist program, "Cattle-Free by '93," aimed at evicting domestic livestock from Western rangelands.[18]

Promoted by government, activists, and scientists, biocentrism had become the philosophy of America's ruling classes — the media, government, universities, church hierarchy, and teaching professions. In 1989 Bill McKibben's book predicting "the end of nature" became a best-seller; National Park Service researcher David Graber would write in the *Los Angeles Times* that "human happiness, and certainly human fecundity, are not as important as a wild and healthy planet. . . . We have become a plague upon ourselves and upon the earth."[19]

The magazine and outdoor recreation industries, realizing that wilderness areas were the playgrounds of their customers, crusaded to "save the environment." Times Mirror Magazines, calling itself "America's leading publisher of leisure-oriented magazines," created the Washington-based Conservation Council, whose "goal is to get our 32 million readers personally involved in the conservation of natural resources . . . to harness the enormous power of our . . . readers at the ballot box and to focus attention on the environmental problems facing the country."[20]

Television, comic books, and children's literature spread a new green political correctness with Captain Planet and the Planeteers, Teenage Mutant Ninja Turtles, the Toxic Avenger. Full-length feature films such as *Ferngully, the Last Rainforest* sought to raise the biocentric consciousness of young people. In 1990 Congress passed the National Environmental Education Act establishing the Environmental Protection Agency's Office of Environmental Education, and indoctrination in biocentrism became national policy.

Classrooms turned into centers of activism. "Children are told to write letters to Congress, draft petitions, and boycott products," the magazine *Consumers' Research* noted. A "Save the Earth Action Pack" distributed to schools in 1992 by the Turner Broadcasting System even went so far as to tell children "to increase the amount of time and money" they gave to environmental lobbying organizations. The Rainforest Action Network put out an eight-page "school kit" as part of its program to add "a Fourth 'R'" — the Rainforest.[21]

To be sure, America's young badly needed a real understanding of nature. But this required the study of quantitative sciences that were not part of these curricula. Mathematical ability — absolutely essential for understanding the strengths and weaknesses of ecological thought —

was a disaster area. Virtually every survey ranked American students at or near the bottom among industrialized countries in this subject. But rather than addressing this deficiency, the green curriculum was attempting to spread the icing before the cake was baked. It pretended to teach ecology to students who did not yet have the tools to understand it.[22]

Indeed, even as politics and popular culture headed one way, the science of ecology was going the other. By 1990 evolutionary ecologists were winning their decades-long debate with systems ecologists. The former had long rejected the concept of a stable ecosystem, arguing that empirical science must stick to concrete individuals, not abstract wholes, and that if ecosystems were indeed to remain "in balance," then evolution — which requires disruptions — would be impossible. And, increasingly, mounting evidence — and even new theory — revealed these critics to be correct.

Among the new data was material supplied in a landmark 1985 collection of essays edited by the botanists S. T. A. Pickett and P. S. White, titled *The Ecology of Natural Disturbance and Patch Dynamics.* "The majority of both theoretical and empirical work," the book's editors observed, "has been dominated by an equilibrium perspective." As a corrective they presented pieces by various authors who, citing myriad empirical studies, painted a dramatically different picture of nature. As the environmental historian Donald Worster summarized their findings: "The climax notion is dead, the ecosystem has receded in usefulness, and in their place we have the idea of the lowly 'patch.' Nature should be regarded as a landscape of patches, big and little . . . changing continually through time and space, responding to an unceasing barrage of perturbations."[23]

In other words, the very "fragmentation" that environmentalists — and scientists such as Russell Lande — lamented was now revealed to be an absolute requirement for sustaining life! Simultaneously, the theme of instability was receiving support from the new science of "chaos theory," a line of inquiry, as Worster put it, which revealed nature to be "*fundamentally* erratic, discontinuous and unpredictable."[24]

The tide of science, it seemed, had shifted. As the *New York Times* reported in 1990:

The concept of natural equilibrium long ruled ecological research and governed the management of such natural resources as forests and fisheries. It led to the doctrine, popular among conservationists, that nature knows best and that human intervention in it is bad by definition.

Now an accumulation of evidence has gradually led many ecologists to abandon the concept or declare it irrelevant, and others to alter it drastically. They say that nature is actually in a continuing state of disturbance and fluctuation. Change and turmoil, more than constancy and balance, is the rule. As a consequence, say many leaders in the field, textbooks will have to be rewritten and strategies of conservation and resource management will have to be rethought.[25]

"There will always be people who will cling to old ideas," the *Times* quoted Dr. Simon A. Levin, Cornell University ecologist and president of the Ecological Society of America, as saying. "But certainly the center of the mass of thinking" among ecologists, he observed, has shifted away from equilibrium and "toward the fluctuating nature of natural systems." Likewise, as the *Times* quoted Pickett, "the balance-of-nature concept makes nice poetry, but it's not great science."[26]

But though it might seem that by 1990 chaos had replaced stability as conventional wisdom, this was not quite the case. In fact, the new developments amounted to a crisis for many ecologists, who, often unfamiliar with nonequilibrium mathematics, were slow to realize the implications of instability on their science and were reluctant to relinquish their beloved ecosystem. Cybernetic models of feedback loops seemed to them such beautiful conceptual tools that they hated to admit they didn't fit the facts. This meant they were back where they started, before the advent of Hutchinson's and Odum's New Ecology: with lots of data and no comprehensive analytical models for explaining them!

Thus, rather than serving as a reality check on pop ecology, science remained to a large extent part of the problem. By 1990 the federal government controlled nearly all environmental research, and its various agencies retained an interest in the outcome of ecological debates. Most wildlife biologists worked for the U.S. Fish and Wildlife Service and other preservation agencies. Since state and federal governments owned a third of the country's land area and all its wildlife, few ecologists could do research without permission from appropriate authorities. And as study became more expensive, scholars relied increasingly on public sources of financial aid.

The growing popularity of biocentrism exacerbated this politicization, making partisanship seem respectable. Motivated by teleological beliefs in the stability of ecosystems, researchers regularly crossed the line between science and partisanship. Prominent ecologists lost sight of their own limitations and began speaking on subjects such as psychology and sociology, about which they knew little. Ecosystem assumptions remained built into nearly all policy-oriented environmental research. Forced to choose between their models and the data, many scientists opted for the former, relying more heavily on computer modeling and less on real-world testing. And when their field studies failed to find projected equilibria, they took this as a sign that ecological catastrophe was imminent.[27]

Driven by this reasoning, many cyberneticists became the dismal scientists of the new age, trumpeting doom. Exercising mathematical imaginations, they conjured theories that scared the socks off society. Teaching that humanity was destroying the earth, they spread fear of global warming, ozone depletion, acid rain, dioxin, asbestos, and indeed anything that was new, was made by humans, or signified change. Symptomatic of this hysteria was the spreading fear of an "extinction crisis."[28]

First inspired by Norman Myers's 1979 book, *The Sinking Ark*, which estimated the rate of species loss at forty thousand a year, this fear quickly assumed a life of its own. In the 1980 *Global 2000 Report to the President*, Thomas Lovejoy predicted, "Of the 3–10 million species now present on the earth, at least 500,000–600,000 will be extinguished during the next two decades." This growing chorus was joined by Harvard's Edward O. Wilson, who, claiming that "we are in the midst of one of the great extinction spasms of geologic history," estimated worldwide species loss at 27,000 a year. Environmental groups capitalized on this concern. In a 1992 advertisement the World Wildlife Fund warned, "Without firing a shot, we may kill one-fifth of all species of life on this planet in the next twenty years."[29]

By the 1990s the "extinction crisis" had become conventional wisdom, preached on television and in schools across the country. Unfortunately, however, there was no evidence that it existed. Most claims rested on speculative assumptions about the number of living species, the rate of forest depletion, and the ratio of this decline to species loss, but these relationships were poorly understood. Even extinction crisis advocates admitted that their claims remained not only unverified but unverifiable![30]

Myers would confess, "Regrettably we have no way of knowing the actual current rate of extinction in tropical forests, nor can we even make an accurate guess." Wilson conceded that "the great majority of extinctions are never observed." UCLA conservation biologist Jared Diamond wrote: "North American and European birds — the world's best-monitored species . . . have actually suffered few recent extinctions. But most of the world's species live in the tropics, where there is no systematic annual monitoring." And this, he suggested, produces a "gross underestimation" of worldwide extirpations.[31]

In short, mass extinctions were supposedly occurring only where no one could witness them. Yet an exhaustive study — commissioned by the highly respected International Union for the Conservation of Nature — reported that "these and other data indicated the number of recorded extinctions for both plants and animals is very small. . . . Despite extensive inquiries we have been unable to obtain conclusive evidence to support the suggestion that massive extinctions have taken place in recent times as Myers and others have suggested." Indeed, the IUCN could only verify that "the current rate of extinction is about one [species] per year."[32]

Under scrutiny, proof of the extinction crisis evaporated. But fear of it remained because, as Wilson admitted, the issue concerned not facts but feelings. Humans have, he suggests, a psychological need to arrest change: "At the heart of the environmentalist world view is the conviction that human physical and spiritual health depend on sustaining the planet in a relatively unaltered state."[33]

Motivated by this desire, the nation ignored facts as public anxiety pushed the politics of endangered species. Critical habitat and new creatures were listed as endangered at an exponentially increasing rate. In February 1991 the Fish and Wildlife Service, citing impacts of even-aged forestry on habitat, determined that the Mexican spotted owl warranted listing. In April the service, along with the National Marine Fisheries Service, proposed listing Snake River sockeye and Columbia Chinook salmon as endangered. In May it proposed designating 11.6 million acres as critical habitat for northern spotted owls, including 3 million acres of private land — an action that, if realized, economists believed would claim 98,000 jobs. In the fall it listed three tiny Sonoma County wildflowers — the Sebastopol meadowfoam, Burke's goldfields, and Sonoma sunshine.[34]

In August 1992 five wildflowers — Cushenbury buckwheat, Parish's daisy, Cushenbury oxytheca, San Bernardino Mountains bladderpod, and Cushenbury milk-vetch — were added to the endangered species list, threatening operation of a major limestone quarry run by Mitsubishi, Pleuss-Staufer, Pfizer, and Riverside Cement. In September the Fish and Wildlife Service was forced by court order to list marbled murrelets as threatened before it could complete studies to determine if those living in Oregon, Washington, and California were genetically distinct from the 250,000 birds inhabiting southeastern Alaska.[35]

The same month the service accepted a petition to list the Southwestern willow flycatcher. In November it nominated the Delhi Sands flower-loving fly as an endangered species, thereby holding up a $250 million extension of the Ontario Airport runway near San Bernardino. And in January 1993 it announced a plan to protect the California spotted owl which would cost, according to a report in the *Los Angeles Times*, between five thousand and fifteen thousand jobs.[36]

By 1993 more than 1,350 domestic species were listed, and the waiting queue of creatures proposed for listing had passed 3,500 species. Overwhelmed by its mandate to save all "distinct populations" of every species, the service abandoned the pretense of science in an effort to keep up. Rather than seeking to save what was truly at risk, it focused on "charismatic megafauna."[37]

"On average," write Mann and Plummer,

the service spent more on subspecies than on full species, more on species with a low recovery potential than those with a high recovery potential, and despite congressional instructions to the contrary, fourteen times as much on "charismatic megafauna" as on other types of species. Perhaps most troubling, average federal and state disbursements are actually lower for endangered species than for threatened species. Two of the three most expensive species — the northern spotted owl ($9.7 million, the highest single expenditure) and the grizzly bear ($5.9 million) — are threatened, not endangered.[38]

Nevertheless, activists and the courts accelerated this slapdash process. In the spring of 1992 the Fund for Animals, along with other environmental groups, sued the government, demanding that it accelerate listing of species. And in an out-of-court settlement reached in December, the service promised to add four hundred species by 1996, effectively doubling the number on the list, and to expedite processing of another nine hundred species for which no scientific information existed.[39]

Since there was no way such wholesale listing could be guided by careful study, the service decided to process this volume not on a species-by-species basis but by area. Henceforward the government would pursue a "multispecies ecosystem approach," listing unique ecosystems rather than distinct populations.[40]

The same factors — hysteria over the "extinction crisis" and pressure to put more species on the list — drove owl science as well. Although the spotted owl had been designated as threatened on the supposition that fewer than three thousand survived, field studies continued to find more birds. By 1993 six thousand to nine thousand would be estimated to live in northern California alone, and perhaps an equal number in Oregon and Washington. Yet federal demographic studies continued to claim that the species remained in deep decline.[41]

The most influential of these reports was an analysis contained in the Fish and Wildlife Service's 1991 draft owl recovery plan and later distributed in revised form to the scholarly community. Coauthored by the service biologist David R. Anderson, lead author of the 1990 status review that led to the listing of the owl, along with his colleague Kenneth P. Burnham, the study suggested that the owl's decline was actually more precipitous than had hitherto been estimated. It would play a pivotal role in convincing Judge William Dwyer's court that even the Thomas recommendations were insufficient to save the species.[42]

Yet its predictions raised hoots of protest from many biologists. Like most owl researchers, Anderson and Burnham looked for owls only in old-growth habitat. They assumed, without solid evidence, that "any unknown emigration out of a study area is permanent." They did not rule out that decline could result from competition with barred owls or changes in the weather. They had little information on different age classes.[43]

Using simplistic mathematics to extrapolate from scanty data, they demonstrated why demographic studies so often contradict the empirical evidence. As Michael L. Rosenzweig observed in August 1992, commenting on the status of California spotted owls, such studies "have gotten nowhere. Moreover, from a theoretical point of view, there was every reason to expect that result." This kind of study, Rosenzweig noted, lacks "a practical strategy for discovering how owls rank their habitats," ignores competition between species, "does not use behavioral studies," and "does not distinguish successfully among habitats that are used, habitats that are preferred, and habitats on which the species must (or can) depend." Even worse, "none of the studies have measured dispersal. . . . The literature is full of long-term bird censuses that indicate fluctuating populations in response to unknown changes in background conditions. From storks to dickey birds, populations may go into decades-long decline, only to be followed by decades-long resurgence."[44]

Only one class of Northwest creatures was undeniably at risk: salmon and steelhead trout. Yet almost nothing was known about the extent and cause of their demise.

These anadromous fish, studies revealed, occupied mere fractions of their historic range. Coho salmon had disappeared from 46 percent of their original waters, summer steelhead from 35 percent, winter steelhead from 25 percent, chum salmon from 37 percent, sockeye from 49 percent, spring Chinook from 45 percent, and fall Chinook from 17.5 percent. But these data did not reveal the rate of these declines or when they began. They could not tell us whether, or to what extent, logging was the culprit.[45]

The dynamics of anadromous fish are hideously difficult to understand. Living at sea and traveling hundreds of miles to spawn, they are exposed to every kind of environmental variable, from ocean upwellings to urban pollution and agricultural runoff. Logging affected only one subset of these conditions. An independent biologist, Daniel Botkin, who led a team of scientists conducting an exhaustive 1994 study on salmon for the state of Oregon, observed: "Present scientific knowledge does not allow definitive answers based on a cause and effect approach. Given the complexity of the life cycle, and the many factors that could influence salmon, it is unlikely that a single list could be produced that would apply to all cases for all times. It is much more likely that one factor might play an important role in one watershed and another factor in some other watershed."[46]

Among the factors affecting salmon noted in Botkin's report were horizontal and vertical ocean currents, sea salinity, surface temperature changes and wind speeds, precipitation affecting snow depths and stream flows, irrigation, agricultural nutrients and pesticides, poaching, commercial and sport fishing, urban pollution, seal and sea lion predation, and channelization of streams by road builders.

To be sure, the Botkin study agreed that logging touched salmon in many ways. Clear-cutting removed shade which produced algae important to fish. It reduced stream litter and nutrient flow. But, equally, these scientists found some disturbances beneficial. Fish needed nutrients supplied by deciduous early successional trees, such as alder. And they spawned on gravel supplied by upper reaches of streams where banks had been eroded by logging, storms, or fire.[47]

In short, salmon and trout required the right mixture of continuity and disturbance. What had been the role of forestry in upsetting the rates of change? The data did not give a simple answer. Steelhead and coho declines correlated best with timber harvests, chum the least. The best available information on population trends — covering Oregon's Rogue and Umpqua rivers since 1972 — suggested that salmon abundance was more the result of dams and irrigation than variations in forest cover. But that did not rule out the possibility that logging practices changed "background" conditions, with long-term detrimental effects. It was simply not possible to say with certainty.

"We do not know." These were the most difficult words for a country consumed by environmental concern to utter. The niceties of science were left behind as the ripple effect of Earth First!'s diaspora spread across the continent. The ecosystem became the model for culture, and ecological survival was deemed to depend on promoting "diversity" by social engineering or by force.

Despondency became the measure of moral seriousness. If people believed that nature was threatened, they could not feel good about their society or the environment. If global survival depended on "balanced" ecosystems that did not exist, then catastrophe was imminent. If mythical "healthy" ecosystems maintained "all their parts," but no actual ecosystem was found to do so, then humans must be killing nature. And since individuals, left alone, would pursue "selfish" goals such as wealth and liberty, then a strong central government was needed to protect ecosystems from the onslaughts of humanity. Social and environmental ills were deemed consequences of irrationality and unlimited desire. Only the coercive powers of the state could protect us from ourselves.

We are reaching "the point beyond which an ecological collapse is inevitable," then-Senator Al Gore intoned in 1992, because "we have tilted so far toward individual rights." We need, Donald Worster would write, "a revised Constitution" because "a stable . . . society in equilibrium with the processes of nature cannot allow much freedom or self-assertiveness to the individual."[48]

So it was inevitable that government would invent a new class of crimes based on the allegation of harm done not to individuals or society but to ecosystems. And this extension of the concept of criminality would stigmatize many never before thought of as felons.

- Ocie Mills, fifty-four, and his son Carey, thirty-one, of Navarre, Florida, would be among the first. On May 15, 1989, they entered a federal penitentiary to serve twenty-one months for dumping nineteen loads of sand on a one-third-acre lot. An outspoken critic of wetlands law, Ocie had been targeted by the U.S. Army Corps of Engineers, according to an 1987 internal memorandum, because of "his documented furnishing of advice to others with intent to subvert the Corps Regulatory Program." On going to jail, Ocie Mills declared, "My family has been destroyed."[49]
- Fifty-nine-year-old John Pozsgai of Morrisville, Pennsylvania, was sentenced to three years for cleaning a vacant lot near his truck repair shop. His offense was putting dirt on the lot (which had been used as a dump for twenty years) after removing thousands of old tires and rusting car parts. According to the *Washington Post*, "The ordeal has bankrupted his family."[50]
- The Monday after Thanksgiving 1992, Vietnam veteran and environmental consultant Bill Ellen began serving a six-month sentence for "disturbing wetlands" while directing a private conservation project called Tudor Farms. With the enthusiastic support of Maryland officials, Ellen had been creating ponds and vegetation not just for migratory waterfowl but for many other species as well. His plans called for improving habitat of upland game birds and Delmarva deer, designing pools for otter and muskrat, and aiding recovery of the Delmarva Peninsula fox squirrel, an endangered species. But officials claimed that the ponds he had created harmed the environment because, among other things, ducks and geese defecated in them. Even the judge was dumbfounded, asking an expert government witness, "Are you saying that there is pollution from ducks, from having waterfowl on a pond — that pollutes the water?"[51]

And so it went. As environmental laws widened the concept of criminality, a technician would face prosecution for leaking the contents of refrigerators into the air; an immigrant farmer would have his tractor and disk confiscated and face punishment for inadvertently plowing a field supposedly inhabited by Tipton kangaroo rats; suburban residents would be threatened with fines and prison terms for disturbing endangered rat territory if they disked firebreaks around their homes.[52]

From the perspective of history this pattern was chillingly familiar, and some scholars raised cries of alarm. Before the International Earth Summit, held in Rio de Janeiro in June 1992, forty-six prominent American scientists, including twenty-seven Nobel Prize winners, joined with 218 scholars from other countries in an appeal to heads of state. They were worried, "at the dawn of the twenty-first century," by

> the emergence of an irrational ideology which is opposed to scientific and industrial progress and impedes economic and social development.
>
> We contend that a Natural State, sometimes idealized by movements with a tendency to look toward the past, does not exist and has probably never existed since man's first appearance in the biosphere. . . .
>
> We fully subscribe to the objectives of a scientific ecology for a universe whose resources must be taken stock of, monitored and preserved. But we herewith demand that this stock-taking, monitoring and preservation be founded on scientific criteria and not on irrational preconceptions. . . .
>
> We . . . forewarn the authorities in charge of our planet's destiny against decisions which are supported by pseudo-scientific arguments or false and non-relevant data. . . . The greatest evils which stalk our Earth are ignorance and oppression, and not Science, Technology and Industry, whose instruments, when adequately managed, are indispensable tools of a future shaped by Humanity, by itself and for itself, overcoming major problems like overpopulation, starvation and worldwide diseases.[53]

The scientists' appeal, however, fell on deaf ears, as events in the Northwest continued to propel, and be propelled by, the swift currents of biocentrism.

27

HOME, SWEET HOME

IN HIS NOVEL *Bleak House*, published in 1853, Charles Dickens tells the story of "Jarndyce and Jarndyce," a legal battle over a last will and testament that drags on for decades, until the entire value of the contested estate is consumed by court costs. Based on an actual case that continued even as Dickens wrote, it was a bitter satire of the English legal system. But the truth was worse: the real-life litigation that Dickens ridiculed began in 1798 and was not settled until the twentieth century.[1]

So it was in the Northwest, where politics and litigation over owls and forests took on Dickensian dimensions. The adversaries seemed intent on pursuing the conflict until it had exhausted the resources over which they were contending. The contest sucked ever larger armies into its expanding vortex, eventually consuming an entire nation. Yet as the stakes rose, the adversaries' goals became more obscure. One side fought for "preservation" and the other for "wise use," but neither knew what these phrases meant. They were blind soldiers stalking each other at night, in the fog, without a compass.

"Didn't Forests Forever lose last November?," the *Santa Rosa Press-Democrat* asked in 1991. It was hard to tell. Palco continued to honor the voluntary 1990 moratorium on Headwaters and would for at least another four years. Yet no sooner was the initiative defeated than Governor Pete Wilson put pressure on the state Board of Forestry to reject Pacific Lumber's harvest plan for the forest. Then mainstream environmental groups and timber companies began to negotiate reform of timber harvest practices, and the governor stressed the need for sustained yield. Before the spring was out, Louisiana-Pacific had announced it would end clear-cutting. All of these had been objectives of Forests Forever.[2]

Despite the initiative's defeat, the impetus of preservation could not be stopped. As events unfolded in the 1990s, direct action was no longer needed. A new stratagem had emerged: environmentalists delayed logging through lawsuits while their political allies sought a final solution in legislation. Everyone from Wilson on down played the game. And the contest over Owl Creek, a small unit of old growth near Headwaters where Greg King had first ignited conflict in 1986, thus became the alpha and omega of this Jarndycian contention.

Palco first submitted its plan to log this 237-acre site in April 1990, but was forced to withdraw it until additional wildlife studies could be done. After the company resubmitted its request in October 1990, the California Department of Forestry rejected the plan, citing inadequate protection for the owl. In March the state Board of Forestry overruled the department and approved the plan. The Sierra Club and EPIC immediately filed suit. The case went to the Court of Appeals, which sent the case back to the Humboldt County Superior Court. This body then asked the Board of Forestry to reconsider its approval, and in March 1992 the board reapproved the plan, provided Palco would conduct marbled murrelet surveys prior to, during, and after harvest.[3]

In June, after the initial surveys were completed, finding birds but no nests, Palco began logging. Immediately EPIC protested, and California Department of Forestry director Richard Wilson asked Palco to voluntarily halt logging until the matter was settled. Company president John Campbell complied. Although EPIC's Robert Sutherland called the logging "a deliberate and premeditated act to destroy murrelet nesting habitat," a five-member team of the Department of Forestry could find no evidence that murrelet nests had been destroyed during the operation. Nevertheless, logging was stopped once again, and Palco had to devise another plan to ensure that there would be no accidental "takes" of murrelets.[4]

When, in September 1992, Palco again sought to log the site, EPIC reopened its suit. And in November, after the First District Court of Appeals in San Francisco dismissed the case, EPIC immediately appealed.[5]

The legal obstacles apparently removed, Palco, needing logs to keep its mills going, began logging over the Thanksgiving weekend. Earth First!ers quickly occupied the site, slowing logging. Meanwhile, as the Fish and Wildlife Service had declared the murrelet a threatened species in September, EPIC sued again, claiming that Palco's action constituted a "take" of murrelets under section 9 of the act. Four days later the court granted EPIC's request for a temporary halt to logging.[6]

In December the U.S. Fish and Wildlife Service joined the battle, charging that Palco might indeed have violated the Endangered Species Act when it logged on Thanksgiving. The company insisted that the state had given it permission, but the Department of Forestry, while admitting it had "agreed" to the harvest plan, insisted that it hadn't actually given "permission." The same month Justice Zerne P. Haning of the state appeals court ordered Palco to stop logging "until further order of this court." The company appealed, requesting permission to remove the downed logs before they rotted. Activists protested, and another round was joined.[7]

In February 1993 the service field supervisor admitted that Palco might not have broken the law after all, and that murrelet "nesting has not been confirmed in the Owl Creek watershed." Furthermore, he said, no "Service 'approval' is required for logging on private lands under the Act." Nevertheless, the service continued its investigation, which it warned "could take a long time."[8]

Having successfully denied Palco use of Headwaters, activists and politicians sought to acquire it. In February 1991 a Wilson aide announced that the governor was committed to "protection of an ecologically significant portion" of the forest. Later the same month a coalition of thirty-three North Coast environmental groups formed the California Forest and Watershed Council, promising to launch another initiative campaign to save Headwaters. Simultaneously, a state Senate committee recommended $300 million in appropriations to acquire the forest. In March, state Senate majority leader Barry Keene proposed that California purchase Headwaters, and in April Wilson unveiled a fourteen-point program to preserve forests, suggesting a $628 million bond issue to acquire North Coast forests, including three thousand acres of Headwaters.[9]

Preservationists would not be denied. When it was clear that California could not afford to purchase the forest, they launched a campaign for federal acquisition. In the summer of 1992, over Palco's objections, Bay Area congressman Pete Stark introduced a bill in Congress to purchase 44,000 acres.[10]

A similar drama enveloped Douglas fir forests. While on Capitol Hill environmental lobbyists pushed for passage of the Ancient Forest Protection Act, creating a National Ancient Forest Reserve System, in Oregon and Washington a litigious pattern was repeating itself: as soon as the Forest Service, the Bureau of Land Management, or a private timber company announced a harvest plan, activists sued to stop it. And once the case got to court, it took on a life of its own. No sooner would an industry or agency think it had satisfied the courts than the goal posts would be moved — habitat requirements would be increased or a new species listed. Each time a new wrinkle was added, the court would issue an injunction to stop logging. And after each round more land was given up to the owl.[11]

Over twenty major lawsuits dragged on. Between May 1990 and October 1991 alone, the Seattle office of the Sierra Club Legal Defense Fund, often helped by the University of Oregon Environmental Law Clinic, was involved in at least thirty separate legal actions or decisions involving six major cases.[12]

In 1987 activists launched *Portland Audubon Society* v. *Hodel*, suing the Bureau of Land Management for failing to consider the impact that two hundred proposed timber sales would have on the owl. The case was dismissed in 1989, then reopened a year later. When bureau director Cy Jamison reduced the proposed timber harvests, environmentalists filed suit (*Lane County Audubon Society* v. *Jamison*), claiming that the Jamison plan violated section 7 of the Endangered Species Act, which required the Bureau to ask the U.S. Fish and Wildlife Service whether the proposed harvest threatened critical owl habitat or jeopardized the continued existence of the owl.[13]

In August 1990 preservationists amended an ongoing suit, *Northern Spotted Owl* v. *Hodel*, asking Seattle District Court judge Thomas Zilly to require the Fish and Wildlife Service to designate critical habitat for the owl. Complying with a court order, the service did so in July 1991, declaring in a biological opinion that fifty-two bureau timber sales would jeopardize the owl. When the agency asked that forty-four sales be exempted from this designation, in October 1991 Interior Secretary Manuel Lujan convened a cabinet-level Endangered Species Committee, known as the "God Squad," to consider this appeal. And after the God Squad excluded thirteen sales and required adoption of a draft recovery plan, activists challenged this decision in court, claiming that President Bush had improperly communicated with members of the committee.[14]

Just as *Portland Audubon Society* v. *Hodel* challenged the Bureau of Land Management, so *Seattle Audubon Society* v. *Robertson* took on the Forest Service. Filed in February 1989, it charged that the service had violated the National Environmental Policy Act (NEPA) in failing to address Russell Lande's thesis that logging harmed the owl. When, in October 1990, the service announced that it would harvest in a manner "not inconsistent" with the Thomas report, activists expanded the suit, demanding that the service develop its own specific plan and environmental impact statement.

In March 1991 Seattle District Court judge William Dwyer found in favor of the plantiffs, issuing an injunction temporarily barring timber sales in owl habitat on seventeen national forests in Washington, Oregon, and Northern California until the agency wrote another environmental impact statement for the owl. But when the service completed the plan in May 1992, the environmentalists went back to court again, insisting that the statement didn't go far enough.[15]

Once more Dwyer sided with the plaintiffs, ruling that the service plan did not address concerns expressed in the Anderson-Burnham demographic study indicating that the owls were declining by 6 percent a year, and did not consider how harvesting affected nonendangered, old-growth-dependent species. He ordered the service to complete a new supplemental environmental impact statement by August 1993.[16]

And so it went — with *National Audubon Society* v. *U.S. Forest Service*, challenging four timber sales in the Rogue River National Forest; *Sierra Club* v. *BLM*, seeking to end the right of way for private landowners to reach their properties in checkerboard areas; *Forest Conservation Council* v. *Roseboro Lumber Company*, seeking a court ruling that timber harvests on private lands constituted a "take" of spotted owls and was therefore a violation of the Endangered Species Act; *Sierra Club Legal Defense Fund* v. *National Marine Fisheries Service* over salmon; *Oregon Natural Resource Coalition* v. *Lowe*, claiming that 24,000 acres of old growth was not sufficient for late-successional species in Winema National Forest; *Oregon Rivers Council* v. *Robertson*, requiring forests to submit plans to the U.S. Fish and Wildlife Service over impacts on salmon; *Marbled Murrelet* v. *Lujan*, a request by the Seattle office of the Sierra Club Legal Defense Fund for the courts to make a summary judgment that the National Forest Management Act required the Forest Service to protect not only endangered species but all viable populations of all native vertebrate species; and on and on and on.[17]

The machinery of conflict fueled itself. For the Seattle office of the Sierra Club Legal Defense Fund in particular, owl litigation became lucrative, thanks to legal provisions allowing "public interest" plaintiffs to receive compensation from taxpayers for court costs.

Proving that biocentrism pays, on June 30, 1992, the Seattle office of the Sierra Club Legal Defense Fund was awarded $56,718 for disputing the adequacy of the government's designation of critical habitat for the species (*Northern Spotted Owl* v. *Lujan*). In September 1993 it would receive $220,000 for contesting God Squad recommendations. On January 14, 1994, it would be compensated $766,420.38 for successfully pursuing *Seattle Audubon Society* v. *Robertson*; received in August another $92,752.99 for *Lane County Audubon Society* v. *Jamison*; and later was awarded $1,005,000 for work done on *Portland Audubon Society* v. *Babbitt*.[18]

Litigation took its toll. "Most of the logging decline," the *Mendocino Press-Democrat* reported in January 1993, "so far has been traceable to court-ordered logging restrictions designed to protect the endangered northern spotted owl." In California national forest harvests had dropped by 40 percent since the 1980s and were expected to drop much further when the impact of California owl restrictions began to be felt. In Oregon and Washington, by the spring of 1993 national forest sales were just 10 percent what they had been in the last preinjunction year, 1990, and Bureau of Land Management sales had virtually stopped altogether.[19]

As harvests dropped, jobs disappeared. Despite the availability of some salvage timber and cuttings from private lands, 161 mills in Oregon, Washington, Idaho, and California closed between 1990 and 1993, equaling 29 percent of all operating mills, displacing 14,675 employees not including loggers and other non-millworkers. Altogether, since 1980 the region had witnessed the closure of 342 mills, with 32,208 mill jobs lost.[20]

Desperate, loggers fought back, meeting each activist thrust with an equal and opposite parry. The industry challenged adoption of the Thomas report; it sued to force the U.S. Fish and Wildlife Service to complete an environmental impact statement before designating critical owl habitat. It filed several suits challenging salmon protection. And it took on the issue of property rights. In *Sweet Home Chapter of Communities for a Great Oregon* v. *Lujan*, filed in 1991, it questioned whether the Endangered Species Act empowered the government to regulate harvests on private lands.[21]

But industry was not a main contender in this conflict. Rather, ordinary people were. While logging companies pursued legal responses and lobbying efforts, a new, multifarious, and chaotic grassroots campaign was sweeping across the continent, striking fear into the hearts of environmentalists.

Borrowing a phrase from Gifford Pinchot, who called conservation the "wise use of resources," this campaign would dub itself the "Wise Use Movement." But actually it represented several constituencies: "sagebrush rebels," who sought to privatize public lands; Western loggers and ranchers denied traditional access to public resources; and middle-class rural folk threatened by assaults on property rights. Had it not been for biocentric extremism, these groups might never have come together. But a shared sense of victimization provoked their merger, and almost by accident they realized their potent political strength.

The movement brought together farmers fighting National Park Service acquisition of their lands; ranchers fearing grazing and irrigation restrictions; older couples prevented by wetlands regulations from building retirement homes; small communities whose economic base was threatened by wilderness designation; families who found that the National Park Service had declared their property "national natural landmarks," thus subjecting them to myriad new federal regulations without their knowledge or consent; suburbanites whose back yards were designated critical habitat for endangered species; urban professionals who had purchased a lot for a summer cottage only to find that preservation regulations prevented them from building on it; and tens of thousands of other freeholders whose life savings had been put at risk by rules they had not known of and did not understand.[22]

Prompted by quiet desperation, mom-and-pop groups sprouted like wild asparagus in burgs such as Libby, Montana; Pocatello, Idaho; Tonopah, Nevada; Manitowoc, Wisconsin; Pohoa, Hawaii; East Liverpool, Ohio; Bleecker, New York; Hoonah, Alaska; Coronado, California; Gorham, New Hampshire; Frohna, Missouri; Escalante, Utah; Kane, Pennsylvania; Gillette, Wyoming; Alpine, Texas; Saint Croix, Indiana; Silver Bay, Minnesota; Marrero, Louisiana; Hayfork, California; Cozahome, Arkansas; Mentone, Alabama; and Taos, New Mexico.

Imitating their adversaries, they networked by phone, fax, and E-mail. But they did not come together until September 1990, when Tom Hirons, representing the Oregon Lands Coalition, led a lobbying pilgrimage to Washington, D.C., called the "Fly-In for Freedom." For three days the two hundred loggers and millworkers, wearing yellow ribbons and carrying signs reading "People Count Too," roamed Congress, explaining their plight to lawmakers. And, when they met property rights advocates, they realized for the first time they were not alone.[23]

Fly-ins became annual events. The following September nearly four hundred people came to Washington from twenty-six states, representing over one hundred organizations. Two months later, prompted by Dave Howard, a corporation executive turned woodworker from

Bleecker, New York, they met in Saint Louis to found a coalition of their groups, which they called the Alliance for America.

Alarmed by this upstart phenomenon, environmentalists sought ways to counter it. With foundation funding the Wilderness Society hired media strategy and political communications consultants MacWilliams Cosgrove Snider to review the Wise Use movement and suggest strategies for containing it. But what they found was not comforting to them.

A recent Roper poll, the Wilderness report said, suggested that Americans overwhelmingly favored "wise use" over pure preservation. By a margin of three to one they believed that conservation was compatible with economic use of natural resources, as opposed to believing that only strict preservation could save nature. Another survey had found that only a minority of respondents favored protecting the environment when doing so hurt the economy. Roper also observed that "there is some truth to the idea that environmental protection is something mainly affluent people can afford."

In short, potential support for Wise Use was huge. Only 22 percent of the populace, consisting of those with "a higher socioeconomic status than other Americans," Roper found, were hard-core environmentalists, whereas 28 percent, "the most socially and economically disadvantaged," considered themselves firm antienvironmentalists. The rest of the country — about half the population — stood between these extremes. Though sympathetic to environmental concerns, they did not necessarily favor pure preservation or measures that would hurt the economy or limit personal freedom.

Thus, the Wilderness Report concluded, "the battle lines are exquisitely captured by Roper's 1990 and 1992 polls. We have our base. The national Wise Use Movement is consolidating theirs. The fight is over the middle 50 percent of the population. "For environmentalists hoping to win the support of this uncommitted segment, the manual suggested tactics that would have warmed the heart of Senator Joseph McCarthy. It conceded that, rather than a front for industry, "Wise Use is a local movement driven primarily by local concerns, not national issues." Nevertheless it recommended tactics to paint Wise Use as a "far right," fanatically religious "pawn of powerful special interests."

Show how opponents "are ripping off America," it advised. "Expose the connections between Wise Use leaders and other extremists . . . expose the Wise Use/Japanese connection . . . prepare articles, monographs and books that expose Wise Use activities and leaders. . . .

Expose the Dan Quayle effect in government — a dozen years of administration's for-sale-to-the-highest-bidder gutting of environmental regulations on behalf of special interests."[24]

Environmentalists quickly embraced these suggestions. In 1993 the *Greenpeace Guide to Anti-Environmental Organizations* warned readers to beware of groups that used "deceptive jargon like *Wise Use, integrated resource management, sustainable development and multiple use.*" These groups, Greenpeace warned, are "heavily financed by industry." Wilderness Society president George Frampton — and late Assistant Interior Secretary — repeatedly sought to marginalize the movement, calling loggers "a mob," charging that they and other resource users had a "license to rob the federal treasury," and calling his adversaries "earth busters" and their movement "worst use."[25]

Meanwhile, foundations that supported environmentalism were spending millions to neutralize Wise Use. As their establishmentarianism left them with few troops in the field, philanthropic officials, according to tape recordings of a 1992 meeting of the Environmental Grantmakers Association, decided to create their own "grassroots" movement, using money in place of people. Pooling resources, they set up the Ancient Forests Campaign with a $500,000 annual budget under the umbrella of the Wilderness Society — dedicated, said one foundation staffer, to doing "non-lobbying education with Congresspeople." But they quickly found this "grassroots group," headquartered in Washington and with a budget nearly five times that of the Oregon Lands Coalition, insufficient.[26]

Needing bigger guns, several philanthropies, including the Pew Charitable Trust and the Bullitt and Alton Jones Foundations, joined forces, according to the tape recordings, "to set up a much more sophisticated media strategic coordination operation in Washington." In fact, they sponsored two efforts. The first, according to a Pew staffer, was run by Fenton Communications, a "full process public relations firm in Washington, D.C., that has done a fair amount of activist political work over the years for mainly progressive and left wing types of organizations, foreign governments, etc." The other was a national campaign conducted by Robert A. Chlopak, former head of the Democratic Senate Campaign Committee.

Fenton, according to the tapes, had sent Jeff DeBonis, Andy Kerr, and other activists to "major media centers . . . where they would spend two or three days with back-to-back meetings briefing editorial boards, news directors, feature writers, thereby producing a torrent of media." Meanwhile, Chlopak helped to arrange for the production of a film for national television by Paul Newman.

"Some day very soon," Newman told viewers, repeating the oft-told myth, "when most of the trees in America's national forests are gone, it will be too late to tell you that this is public land. Our land. And every day over six hundred acres of America's national forests are destroyed."

But despite their sophisticated media efforts, environmentalists remained concerned. "This is a class issue," one of the conferees conceded. "There is no question about it. . . . We have to face that fact. It's true. They're not wrong that we are rich and, you know, they are up against us. We are the enemy as long as we behave in that fashion."

"We have to have a strategy that is also addressing these concerns," said another. "That's the dilemma here. . . . It's not simply that they don't get it, it's that they do get it. They're losing their jobs."

"What we're finding is that Wise Use is really a local movement driven by primarily local concerns and not national issues," observed a third, who continued:

The more we dig into it . . . we have come to the conclusion that this is pretty much generally a grassroots movement, which is a problem, because it means there's no silver bullets, it means this is . . . something that is going to have to be confronted in states and communities across the country. . . . The movement is actually growing quickly at the grassroots as it finds its base. . . . In New England it's about the Adirondack Mountains, it's about private property rights movements, it's about the Northeastern forests. In the Southeast it's about coastal zone management and coastal development. It's about shrimpers in Louisiana not liking turtle exclusion devices. In the Midwest it's about farmland. In coastal Louisiana and Texas it's about . . . minerals development; it's about . . . you know, coal mining in those states.

"What they're saying out there," this foundation staffer summarized, is,

We are the real environmentalists. We are the stewards of the land. We're the farmers who have tilled the land and we know how to manage this land because we've done it here for generations. We're the miners and the ones who depend for our livelihood on this land. These guys live in glass towers in New York City. They're not environmentalists, they're elitists. They're part of the problem, and they're aligned with big government and they're out of touch. So we are the real environmentalists." . . . And when Joe Sixpack hears that message he goes, "You're right, dammit, people oughta be able to work." . . . And the minute the Wise Use people capture that high ground, we almost have not got a winning message left . . . in our quiver.

So what should they do? After admitting that Wise Use was a mom-and-pop movement, this speaker recommended smear tactics: "We need to expose the links between Wise Use and other extremists: the Unification Church, the John Birch Society, Lyndon LaRouche."

So the collision over forests continued. Environmentalists and Wise Users contended for the moral high ground, even though neither knew where it lay. One side preached of preservation and diversity and warned of ecological catastrophe but could not explain what these meant. The other stood for stewardship but had no plan for achieving it.

It was a collision of visions. Wise Users made their living from the land. They believed in nurturing nature for human benefit. They saw the earth as a garden that, given tender loving care, would bloom indefinitely. Environmentalists were college-educated urban professionals, many of whom had fled the city to seek solace in rural areas. They viewed the earth not as a garden but as home to creatures of equal value, in which humans occupy but one small space.

Hence, they disagreed about nearly everything. To Wise Users, nature was a pyramid with people on top. It was imperfect until "improved" by human labor. It had only extrinsic value but was infinitely fecund. To biocentrists it was a web in which humanity was enmeshed. It was perfect and had intrinsic value, but its riches were limited. One side idealized private enterprise, the other federal protection; one revered domestic livestock, the other native wildlife. One believed that forests could survive only if they were logged. The other insisted that people be kept away.

Although many on either side were well intentioned, each side distrusted the other. Biocentrists saw Wise Users as greedy destroyers of nature. Wise Users viewed biocentrists as socialists living in $250,000 wooden houses who yearned to return to caves.

Yet while both claimed to champion the environment, neither really did. The stewards put pocketbooks first, while the biocentrists gave primacy to aesthetics. Both frequently ignored science. The stewards oversimplified the challenges to active management, while the biocentrists failed to see the inadequacies of "hands-off" preservation policies.

Indeed, although each claimed to fight for the environment, even the best science could not define this goal. Rather than being one thing, preservation was many. And what, precisely, our national aims should be depended on what the country wished to save. Even if America had a clear idea of what it wanted, the science of life remained too primitive, too incomplete, to provide the answers that politics demanded of it.

Thus, environmentalists and Wise Users confronted each other's weaknesses while remaining blind to their own. The goals of preservation and stewardship were too fuzzy to serve as compasses. This offered the advantage to those who, rather than pretending to save the world, simply sought profit. And therefore it was not surprising that the biggest winner of the forest wars would be people like Charles Hurwitz.

Bill Bertain sat in his cluttered office in a two-story building on Eureka's J Street, waging his one-man war with Maxxam. His health deteriorating, more than half a million dollars in debt, and sometimes unable to meet house payments, he continued to pursue *Thompson* v. *Maxxam* at his own expense. And surely, he believed, Hurwitz must someday pay the piper. Perhaps the federal lawsuit would prevail. Perhaps the Labor Department or Federal Deposit Insurance Corporation would catch up with the Texan. Or perhaps Maxxam would be unable to make the $510 million in junk bond balloon payments due in 1993.[27]

But once again Hurwitz revealed a feline ability to land on his feet. Of all the contestants in this conflict, Hurwitz, who had helped to start it all, was the one most likely to come out smelling like a rose.

To be sure, Maxxam was under siege. Facing at least ten lawsuits brought by environmentalists, by the spring of 1993 it also had to contend with Bertain's $2 billion claim, the Department of Labor suit on termination of the pension plan, and FDIC charges stemming from the collapse of the United Savings Association of Texas savings and loan collapse.

But, as always, Hurwitz found a way to squeeze out of these tight spots. In February 1993 he solved his debt crisis. Borrowing $70 million more than he needed to pay off the $510 million in junk bonds, he had enough left over to cover fees and prepayment penalties and still give a $25 dividend to shareholders. In effect, Hurwitz had paid himself with borrowed money, thereby increasing his debt but obtaining it at the low interest rate of 7.95 percent. And even while the Sierra Club and Audubon Society were asking federal regulators to look closely at the deal, saying that it might be financed with trees, the bonds sold out "very, very rapidly," said a Palco spokesman, Dave Galitz.[28]

And where amidst these conflicting values over preservation, wise use, and money, Bertain wondered, did he fit in? Ordinary people such as himself aimed at something less lofty than saving civilization but more ambitious than just making money. Yet in the clash between advocates of grand ecological theory and prophets of the profit motive, something had happened to the American character. The middle had disappeared, leaving no ethical signposts for others to follow. Maybe the great environmental crisis and even Wall Street's excesses would vanish if Americans returned to basics such as the Golden Rule — the Bible's version, not Hurwitz's. Or was that too simple, and too difficult?[29]

28

THE FOREST SUMMIT

"SAVE THE TREES! Save the forests! Save the fish! Save the woods!" Denis Hayes stood on the podium like a priest before his congregation, chanting the four-line catechism as the crowd of fifty thousand repeated his words in unison. Billed a "rock concert for trees," this April Fools' Day 1993 meeting in Portland's Waterfront Park was one of many organized by environmentalists for President Bill Clinton's forest conference, to be held the next day.[1]

A woman dressed as a tree paraded through the crowd, followed by a gaggle of cameramen. Others carried signs reading, "Clear-Cutting Kills Salmon" and "It's the Habitat, Stupid!"[2]

The next day, as environmentalists' "Project Lighthawk" took journalists by helicopter to view clear-cuts, twelve thousand timber workers stood with their wives and children in the pouring rain at the same park. Invited by the Oregon Lands Coalition, they came by van and bus from tiny towns throughout the region to attend this "Forest Family Summit." As they huddled under umbrellas listening to speakers ask the new administration for balance, they could see the twin glass spires of the Oregon Convention Center across the river, where President Clinton, Vice President Al Gore, and four cabinet members were deciding their future.[3]

The mother of all environmental meetings, the Forest Conference raised the stakes for both sides. In calling it, the president had signaled that the Northwest conflict was no longer merely a regional issue. By promising to protect "both jobs and the environment" with a solution that would serve as the model for future preservation decisions, he ensured that the outcome would have nationwide implications. And by advancing an "ecosystem" approach for rescuing forests and threatened species, he revealed that biocentrism had come home to roost. Transcending partisan politics, it had infused the popular culture and become the law of the land. Now it was returning to its birthplace, the Pacific Northwest. And Bill Clinton would be the instrument of its homecoming.[4]

The president was another reed blowing in the ideological wind. After initially promising to fashion a fair solution to the forest fight, he quickly became a captive of the idea that emphasized deference to nature over justice to people. Immediately after the election, his administration — the first team of 1960s activists ever to lead the country — made "ecosystems management" official policy for most federal agencies and sought to impose an "ecosystems solution" on the forest crisis.[5]

The change came suddenly. Presidential candidate Clinton had stepped into the vortex of the storm in August 1992, promising that the "politics of blame will end," and offering "to work out a legislative solution." His would be, he said, a "constructive, hands-on role in seeking resolution of the crisis which is hurting so many of our timber families and dividing too many of our citizens in Oregon, Washington, and California."[6]

And, indeed, a "legislative fix" would have been sensible. No lasting peace could be achieved without revising laws — such as the Environmental Policy Act, the National Forest Management Act, and the Endangered Species Act — that encouraged litigation and polarization. But after the election, Clinton's perspective shifted. He populated his administration with apostles of the new order. Bruce Babbitt, president of the League of Conservation Voters, was made interior secretary; Wilderness Society president George Frampton became assistant secretary of the interior for fish, wildlife, and parks. Vice President Al Gore's protégée Carol Browner assumed the administratorship of the Environmental Protection Agency. At Frampton's urging another member of the orthodoxy, Mollie Beattie, took the helm of the U.S. Fish and Wildlife Service, declaring, "My job will be to keep the system in balance."[7]

This team realized the dangers of a legislative fix. Going to Congress would open Pandora's box. Existing laws, written during the golden age of environmental legislation, were the best friends activists ever had. Yet now Congress was tilting toward the Wise Use movement and might revise or gut these laws, given a chance. Besides, the Endangered Species Act was due for renewal in 1993, and opening the owl issue might invite scuttling it.[8]

By February, therefore, Clinton had withdrawn his promise of a legislative fix. Rather than seeking to change the laws, he would comply with them. This meant satisfying the courts, especially Judge Dwyer, who had decreed that the administration must produce a revised supplemental environmental impact statement on Northwest forest management by August 1993 — the same judge who had almost singlehandedly halted most logging on public lands in the Northwest. An administrative fix also meant complying with the Fund for Animals lawsuit, which required greatly accelerated listings of endangered species. And it had to satisfy activists who would sue if the plan were not to their liking.[9]

Only an omnibus strategy, the administration decided, could satisfy these conditions. Identifying 24 million acres of Northwest forests as one ecosystem might not be good science, but it would justify imposition of broad regulations with one stroke.

Chaired by Clinton and Gore, the conference was a star-studded media event. But the real agenda was conceived beforehand, when the administration asked Jack Ward Thomas to head a committee called the Forest Ecosystem Management Assessment Team (FEMAT) to produce an "ecosystems solution" within sixty days. Packed with architects of the New Forestry, including Jerry Franklin, Charles Meslow, and Eric Forsman, this body shut out all skeptics. Despite his expertise, Chadwick Oliver was not included. Robert Lee was initially part of the FEMAT team, but then resigned when he saw how science was being mishandled.[10]

Indeed, court evidence later revealed that the White House intentionally packed FEMAT with true believers to ensure a biocentrist outcome. As the government's attorney, Robert S. Whitman, would say later in court, the administration wanted to ensure that the team reached ecosystems conclusions. In balanced discussions, Whitman explained, Clinton "would not be able to control the policy parameters of the advisory committee." Instead, he "would have to hear from everyone. He would have to hear from people who disagree with an ecosystem approach to forest management." And that was the last thing the government wanted.[11]

Closeting themselves in a Portland office building, Thomas and his scientists went to work in secrecy. The team waited until the forty-third day of its sixty-day preparation period before inviting Oliver to visit. When Oliver finally met with Thomas, he asked: Who will judge the scientific soundness of the FEMAT report? By what criteria will it be evaluated? How will risk and certainty be measured?[12]

He got no clear answers. Concerned that others like himself had been excluded from the process, Oliver then wrote to Thomas and officials of the administration, with copies sent to Clinton and Gore, expressing concern about "bias" in the process. Earlier, on April 19, Oliver had written Clinton directly, urging that, rather than focus on old growth, the president should "encourage a fluctuating balance of all structures across the landscape" through fire, thinning, and pruning.[13]

As he later told *Evergreen* magazine:

> There is a sameness in our forests now where once there was a great deal of diversity. What we must do now is restore diversity, and the fastest way to do this involves the use of silvicultural techniques that mimic the kinds of natural disturbances and regrowth that gave us biological diversity in the first place. . . . The alternatives prepared for the President's consideration were too narrowly drawn, and reflect a steady-state view of nature, rather than a belief that nature is in a constant state of fluctuation.[14]

It is an unfortunate fact about ideological conflicts — whether religious or philosophical — that they are, even in theory, irreconcilable. Since adversaries start from contradictory assumptions, the force of reductionist logic inexorably leads them to draw polar-opposite conclusions. So it was in this dispute about nature. Like the Crusades, which pitted Christians against Muslims, it concerned ultimate beginnings that lay beyond the ability of science to understand. And as with the cold war between communism and capitalism, it was driven by starkly contrasting visions of utopia.

As an effort at reconciliation, therefore, FEMAT was bound to fail. And indeed its plan, dubbed "Option 9" and released on June 18, pleased neither side. "Report outrages environmentalists," declared the *Portland Oregonian* that month. "Outraged loggers reject plan," said the *Seattle Post Intelligencer*.[15]

While admitting that owl numbers probably exceeded eight thousand, FEMAT nevertheless pushed for maximum protection of old growth. Of 24 million acres of regional national forest land, less than 5 million would be made available for regulated timber harvesting. But not all the rest would be parks and wilderness. The plan also called for a variety of management zones, including late successional reserves, riparian reserves, experimental and adaptive management zones, "matrixes," and "administratively withdrawn areas." And, unlike wilderness, some of these areas would permit limited salvage and thinning of young trees.[16]

Yet even this limited intrusion into their sacred forests provoked activists. "Red alert!," cried the Sierra Club, which then launched "a lobby blitz to swamp the hill with grassroots pressure." The club promised, "If the Administration goes for [the FEMAT plan], we're going to blast it, bigtime!" In a June 15 memorandum, Western Ancient Forest Campaign director Jim Owens charged that "this plan is intended to maximize logging under the mantra of science, minimize ecosystem management and give federal agencies the latitude to break laws."[17]

And loggers were equally upset. The administration's own figures, they noted, revealed that Option 9 would reduce timber harvests by 75 percent, cost local economies $4.6 billion, and put another 67,000 to 85,000 people out of work. By protecting an area nearly six times the size of Connecticut, the Clinton plan mandated review and probable rejection of existing timber sales. Only after court approval, after lawsuits were resolved and federal harvest plans revised to comply with new regulations, would timber be available. This ensured that the wood "pipeline" would remain dry until most loggers had lost their equipment and gone on welfare.[18]

Predictably, therefore, both sides fought the report. Eventually environmental groups would launch five separate legal challenges to the Clinton plan; and in August the timber industry, represented by the Northwest Forest Resource Council, filed suit against the administration, claiming that by acting in secrecy and excluding dissident scholars such as Oliver, it had violated a "sunshine law" known as the Federal Advisory Committee Act (FACA), which required such meetings to be open and balanced.[19]

But, despite bipartisan disapproval of its specific proposals, philosophically Option 9 represented a triumph for biocentrism. Its aim, to restore the "presettlement conditions [of] late-successional and old-growth forest ecosystems" was nothing but a scientific fraud. Ecosystems were organizations of plants, animals, and soils which undergo changes over time, and whose final or "late successional" stage, barring disturbances, is old growth. By calling old growth an "ecosystem," FEMAT implied that mature trees belong to a biologically distinct category that *never changes* — which was an absurdity, like saying that people become a different species as they age. A classic example of teleological thinking, it defined an ecosystem in terms of its (desired) final, or end, state.

But though many scientists noted this linguistic legerdemain, few spoke out. Politics had swallowed up ecology. Either working for the Forest Service or dependent on federal approval to conduct research on public lands, most knew that open criticism could cost them their jobs and study opportunities. So instead they wondered quietly: What was the purpose of keeping forests in a permanent state of senescence?

To be sure, they noted, the plan contained constructive strategies, yet even these were modest and incomplete. Adaptive management areas offered opportunities for research and cooperation between scientists, activists, and local citizens. But they comprised only small acreages seemingly designed to test only one theory: the New Forestry. And the plan's restrictive rules for protecting wildlife prohibited much of the research — such as behavioral studies of owls — required for understanding.[20]

Likewise, proper care of riparian zones, they noted, was important for trout and salmon; but here, too, Option 9 missed the mark. The plan merely regulated forest cover, which constituted only one of many factors affecting fish abundance. And while it called for some salvage along streams, it did not permit all silvicultural techniques necessary for anadromous fish to survive. Successional species such as alder and cottonwoods were vital components of streamside habitat, providing nutrients, shade, and bank stabilization. But Option 9 permitted thinning only of *younger* trees, thus actually accelerating the disappearance of some of the plants anadromous fish need most.[21]

As the community of biologists quietly raised such criticisms, Oliver, already a pariah, pressed his own. "What has been proposed," he stated in an interview in *Evergreen* magazine, "may in fact place the region's forest ecosystems at greater risk than they face now." Rather than the "large reserves" demanded by the "steady state" concept of nature, Oliver had all along urged a "landscape approach" that presupposed "constant change" to "mimic, avoid, and mitigate the effects of large natural disturbances." Authorities, he urged, must manage all landscape types, not just "late succession and old growth," because this bias jeopardized endangered species that depend on early successional habitat. They should improve critical habitat, not just preserve what's left, and they should look for "other causes of species declines" in addition to changes in forest cover.[22]

Unmoved by these suggestions, the administration pushed ahead. In July it submitted the thousand-page supplemental environmental impact statement, incorporating Option 9, to Judge Dwyer. In October, Clinton fired National Forest Service supervisor F. Dale Robertson and appointed Thomas, despite complaints from seventy forest supervisors that this step politicized the position.[23]

Indeed, unknown to the public, the administration, under the rubric of "reinventing government," had adopted biocentrism as the guiding philosophy of all federal land management. Rather than giving public welfare the highest priority, the White House decided, federal agencies should put their principal focus on the loftier goal of ecosystem protection. This happened with astonishing speed following President Clinton's signing of the International Convention on Biological Diversity in June. Intended to protect the "variety and frequency of various types of ecosystems, diversity, and genes," this treaty required signatory governments to manage their biological resources to "promote the protection of ecosystems, natural habitats and the maintenance of viable populations of species in natural surroundings."[24]

The treaty set off a tidal wave of planning designed to analyze and control every square inch of American real estate. As a first step the administration established the President's Council on Sustainable Development. Composed of five cabinet members along with leaders of the National Wildlife Federation, the Sierra Club, the Natural Resources Defense Council, the Environmental Defense Fund, and the Nature Conservancy, it was to "develop policy recommendations for a national strategy for sustainable development that can be implemented by the public and private sectors."[25]

This strategy in turn triggered a plan to create a new agency that would map and computerize biodiversity data throughout the country. Conceived by the late Edward T. LaRoe, a scientist with the U.S. Fish and Wildlife Service, this new body would compile a national biological inventory to catalogue all life forms and identify sensitive areas. Its principal tools, LaRoe thought, should be a computer program known as the Geographic Information System (GIS), which included both a National Wetlands Inventory and a program for identifying "holes" in biodiversity called "GAP analysis." LaRoe reportedly went to the vice president with his idea, and Gore, a well-known "technology wonk," jumped at it.[26]

Once again, ecosystem computers would feed the machine of control. As Congressman Gerry Studds put it, the survey would have an "awesome mission — catalog everything that walks, crawls, swims, or flies around this country." It would, Secretary Babbitt's science adviser Tom Lovejoy reportedly concurred, "map the whole nation for all biology and determine development for the whole country and regulate it all because that is our obligation as set forth in the Endangered Species Act."[27]

And, most troubling, the administration proposed that the survey's data and planning would be exempt from the Freedom of Information

Act. Naturally this quest for secrecy worried many on Capitol Hill. Suppose, asked Congressman Richard Pombo, a survey researcher "improperly identified a particular plant or animal on someone's property, which turns out to be an endangered species. The landowner receives this information, and is not permitted to request that experts review it. The property owner may then be prohibited from adding a room to his home, installing a swimming pool, garage, or a shed, raising crops, grazing livestock, or improving his property in any way."[28]

Concerned about such potential abuse, in October the House denied the secrecy exemption and added restrictions to survey authorization, including amendments requiring the government to ask a landowner's permission before inventorying a property. But the administration would not be denied. Wishing to have no such limits, Babbitt withdrew the bill. Abandoning the attempt to achieve congressional authorization, he decided to create the new agency by executive order instead.[29]

But the survey was just a small part of a bigger plan. Under the rubric of both the treaty and "reinventing government," the administration asked federal agencies to conduct "national performance reviews" that included, in part, revising mission statements to give "ecosystems protection" the highest priority. An Interagency Ecosystem Management Coordination Group was established, including the Bureau of Land Management, Forest Service, Soil Conservation Service, National Park Service, Environmental Protection Agency, Fish and Wildlife Service, Geological Survey, Bureau of Indian Affairs, National Biological Survey, Department of Energy, Department of Defense, Bureau of Mines, Bureau of Reclamation, and Mineral Management Service.[30]

Each member agency of this group, assisted by environmental organizations such as the Nature Conservancy, would assess public and private lands to be placed in ecoregions, supplying information to the Biological Survey, which in turn would feed the data into a National Spatial Data Infrastructure, using a plan known as the National Hierarchical Framework of Ecological Units, utilizing the GIS and GAP analysis computer programs. Once this information was analyzed, special Ecoregional Technical Assistance Teams would travel the country to help agencies implement strategies for managing these regions.[31]

By fall this infrastructure was taking shape. In August the Environmental Protection Agency had completed the "ecosystem protection" portions of its national performance review, thereby quietly altering its mandate. Known as the "Edgewater Consensus," it would, according to a planning document, constitute "a fundamental reorientation of the Agency." Under the new rules its primary goal would no longer be to protect public health. Rather, it would seek to save nature instead. "Agency regulations," the National Performance Review declared, "have not been developed with full regard to ecosystem protection. . . . Historically EPA has primarily focused on the protection of human health with less consideration of the impacts on ecosystem issues. . . . EPA must make ecosystem protection a primary goal of the Agency." This would be accomplished by protecting "ecosystem stability" from "man-made stressors" that upset it, "such as over-grazing, unbridled commercial and residential development, over-population, pollution and a host of others."[32]

Gore had indeed reinvented government, but in ways few expected: government had shifted its goal from protecting people to that of safeguarding ecosystems from them.

"In Northern California five thousand people have already lost their jobs because of the controversy over the spotted owl," NBC Nightly News's Roger O'Neill told viewers on September 17, 1993, adding, "Some biologists agree now that the politics of environmentalism got in the way of careful science." The dirty little secret was getting out. Reporting from Eureka, O'Neill found the Northwest crawling with owls. "In fact," he reported, "thousands of so-called new owls have been found, almost entirely on private timber company land which has been logged before. The owls appear to be happy and content in Northern California for one simple reason: the dusky-footed wood rat. They love 'em. And as forest grows back [after being logged], the wood rat is everywhere."

As biocentric true believers pressed on, more people found that their claims did not fit the facts. Even computer modelers were having an increasingly hard time explaining away the evidence. More scientists, in particular, were raising questions about the dire predictions offered in the Anderson-Burnham study, which had prompted Judge Dwyer to halt logging in the first place. To pour water on this fire, the U.S. Fish and Wildlife Service held an emergency workshop of owl demographers in Fort Collins, Colorado, in December 1993.[33]

Attendees felt a great urgency to remain pessimistic. One participant, U.S. Fish and Wildlife Biologist Barry Mulder, said, "I can't emphasize enough about the expectations which the Administration, the Departments, and their local representatives have about the outcome of the workshop. Otherwise there would not have been so much pressure to bring a group together so quickly to do this analysis." Not surprisingly, therefore, conferees concluded that owls were continuing to decline at an increasing rate.[34]

But some industry and independent scientists left the meeting angry and confused. How, they wondered, could the workshop conclude that owls were declining when, for example, the government's own data revealed bird populations in the Bureau of Land Management's Salem district to be increasing in stands containing the smallest amount of old growth in any study area? Why did they find that owls in Andrews, which contains 60 to 70 percent old growth, were declining faster than those on Bureau lands containing only 20 to 30 percent old growth?[35]

And how could they say that the drop was steeper than Anderson and Burnham had originally thought when these authors had revised estimates of the decline *downward*, from 7.5 percent in 1992 to 4.5 percent in 1994? While insisting that the problem was worse than previously thought, government scientists had simultaneously hedged their bets, framing claims in language that would allow them to deny them later if evidence of owl abundance became incontrovertible. They were quietly crawling back off the limb, even as they pretended they weren't.

Industry scientists attending the meeting were outraged. Robert Taylor, former member of the faculty at Utah State University, who had recently joined the California Forestry Association, was mystified. "When the International Biosphere Program (IBP) closed down in the mid-1970s," he commented, "I had anticipated that I had seen the last global linear population model and that the ecological world had learned that linear models in populations dynamics are not merely misleading, they are active jokes."[36]

Larry Irwin, an ecologist with the National Council for Air and Stream Improvement, complained, "Well-known scientists are apparently becoming policy advocates on behalf of the Environmental Community." Current demography, Irwin commented, is not "relevant to anything. And, most certainly, current demography should not be used to judge whether the proposed forest policy from the FEMAT process is adequate or inadequate." Such modeling contains "well known flawed mathematical structure for predicting future populations." Additional studies "indicate that factors in addition to the amount of late successional and older forests influence owl population dynamics." These have found that "in steep areas with large amounts of old growth, owls reproduced at a much lower rate than in drier forests with 50 percent less mature old growth." In other words, lack of moisture, more than the age of the forest, might be the greatest determinant of owl numbers.[37]

Undeterred by such criticisms, the Fish and Wildlife Service escalated its efforts, applying "ecosystems management" to private property as well. On December 9, in a precedent-setting step, the agency filed suit against a private landowner in Washington state, claiming that logging within 1.5 miles of a spotted owl nest constituted a "take" that would "directly harm" the creature. And later the same month it found still another way to extend federal intrusion into the lives of ordinary people, as two Oregonians, Bill Arsenault and Dan Newton, discovered.[38]

In 1976, Arsenault, a sixty-six-year-old former electronics engineer from Southern California, retired and moved to Douglas County, Oregon. Settling onto a small ranch with 240 acres of timberland which he had purchased in 1971, he began to cultivate trees with the expectation that they would provide a retirement income, allowing him to harvest timber selectively, on a sustained-yield basis, into perpetuity. Arsenault's neighbor, Dan Newton, shared a similar dream. A trained forester, Newton had carefully restored forest that had been entirely cut over in the 1930s. By good stewardship over the previous decade he successfully restored the parcel to healthy woodland.[39]

But in December both men found themselves targets of the new policy. Authorized under section 4(d) of the Endangered Species Act to issue "protective regulations" for the bird, the service proposed drawing circles ranging from 1.5 miles to 2.7 miles in radius around each nest and designating these zones — from 4,760 to 14,200 acres in size — "special emphasis areas," where 40 percent of the habitat must be kept inviolate. Anyone cutting a tree in a prohibited zone would be charged with "harming" this species and would be liable to criminal penalties including a $100,000 fine and a year in jail.[40]

Arsenault's farm lay entirely within a proposed "emphasis area." As neighboring lands had already been logged, his groves contained the best habitat, and thus would be included in the zone to be ruled off-limits to logging. Meanwhile, parcels belonging to his neighbors which had already been harvested would go unregulated. He was faced with the choice of cutting all his trees before his neighbors could cut theirs or never being allowed to harvest them.

Newton's groves stood within one thousand feet of one nest and within 1.5 miles of another. Only he and another private farm had good habitat in the proposed emphasis area. If his neighbor logged his property first, leaving Newton's forest the only remaining habitat, then the regulations would prohibit him from logging at all.

In effect, section 4(d) meant that the best land stewards would suffer the most. As a social and ecological vehicle, the biocentrism bandwagon seemed without a driver. And by the end of 1993 it was clear that no one — neither the president, the Congress, the American people, nor even scientists — knew where that bandwagon was headed.

29

THE INFERNO

LARRY ROBERTSON SAT AT HOME, wondering when he would work again. After several years of finding only occasional jobs felling small trees, he now had to contemplate an entirely new career. But who would hire him, he wondered? If he had noticed the dead alder, things might have been different. Instead, when the mature myrtlewood he had been cutting fell, it dislodged the smaller tree. Rain-soaked and heavy, this snag smashed his shoulder, dislocating the socket and stretching nerves. His arm had become a dangling, useless appendage that was mending only slowly.[1]

Meanwhile, his sister Cherie Girod felt decidedly overworked, as the Canyon Crisis Center sought to stem the flood of runaway children, gang fights, teen pregnancies, suicides, troubled latchkey kids, and families that, having lost their homes, were camping in tents in neighbors' yards and surrounding forests.[2]

It was a time for reckoning. Exacting retribution on people and forests, Mother Nature punished without regard to guilt or innocence. Tom Hirons's employees had dwindled from twenty-seven to two. Thomas was running the Forest Service, and Jerry Franklin was president of the Ecological Society of America. In January 1994 an appeals court found in favor of Judi Bari, rejecting the FBI's claim of sovereign immunity and allowing her suit of false arrest to go forward. As the discovery phase of her case began, she sat in her tiny hippie shack surrounded by stacks of manuscripts, seeking justice.[3]

In March the Washington, D.C., Circuit Court found in favor of loggers in the *Sweet Home* case, decreeing that cutting trees did not constitute "taking" under the Endangered Species Act. To prove that a take had occurred, said the court, the authorities must, in effect, produce the body. That same month Federal District Court judge Thomas Penfield Jackson sided with the wood products industry in the FACA suit. The administration, the court said, had violated the law by failing to hold open meetings, and by not ensuring that Jack Ward Thomas's team at the Forest Service was not unduly influenced by environmental interests.[4]

Hurwitz continued to survive. In May he reached a record settlement with Bertain in *Thompson v. Maxxam*, agreeing that Maxxam — along with Drexel and the Boesky and Milken funds — would pay six thousand Palco shareholders around $140 million. And as EPIC's suit to stop logging on Owl Creek proceeded, the Texan reportedly met privately with Vice President Al Gore, seeking a deal on Headwaters. By August Palco had accepted Congress's buyout bills. This opened the way for federal purchase of 44,000 acres — worth, according to Salomon Brothers in 1993, $2 billion for the old growth alone, in 1978 dollars.[5]

Thus, Hurwitz got Bertain's shareholder lawsuit off his back and positioned himself to be handsomely rewarded with taxpayer money for accelerating the rate of redwood cut. Even his tarnished reputation showed signs of revival, as *Time* magazine asked, "Hero or villain?" Hurwitz, according to *Time*, "didn't fire anybody; he hired more workers and added a fourth mill. He continued a Pacific Lumber practice of giving a college scholarship to every employee's child who finished high school. Top hourly pay runs about $15–16 an hour in an area of high unemployment (higher than other companies)."[6]

Indeed, for those with ethical or ecological sensibilities, 1994 was not a good year. The administration, eager to impose ecosystem management, appealed both the *Sweet Home* and FACA decisions, then proceeded as if recent rulings had never happened. And it ignored mounting signs that its preservation policies were promoting social and environmental calamity.[7]

The Endangered Species Act had become a runaway train that no one could control. Almost totally ineffective and lacking a clear purpose, it was nonetheless costing taxpayers and the economy billions. And although it had expired in 1992, environmentalists, fearful that a hostile Congress might gut the law, had successfully lobbied to stall legislative consideration of its renewal. In the meantime, the old law remained in full force and effect.[8]

Through politically driven taxonomic gerrymandering which arbitrarily multiplied the number of subspecies and "distinct populations" at risk, the register of threatened and endangered domestic creatures had reached 895 by 1992 (the most recent year for which there are data), and the number of life forms on the international list had climbed to 532. Meanwhile, another 3,941 candidate species were being considered for listing.[9]

And once on the list, they seemed likely to remain there forever. While the U.S. Fish and Wildlife Service claimed that the act had slowed the disappearance of approximately 40 percent of plants and animals at risk, there was little evidence to credit the law for such rebounds. Indeed, only four species and one population had ever been declared recovered: three Palau Island doves, the Southeastern population of brown pelicans, and the American alligator. And of these only the alligator owed its improved status to the act. The others had been reviving before the act was passed, and were later removed from the list when their inclusion had been found to rest on a mistake. Similarly, although eleven kinds of animals had been "downlisted" from endangered to threatened, only one of these — the Aleutian Canada goose — owed its rebound to the act. Several were demoted to threatened status when they were found to be more common than had been thought. One of these was the snail darter.[10]

But though the law had failed to save creatures, it was a boon to bureaucratic budgets. In 1992 federal and state agencies spent $393,195,860 on endangered and threatened species, disbursing $297,072,623 for the "top ten" alone. Since it cost $39,000 to list a creature and another $68,000 to delist one, achieving recovery of 90 percent of the 895 listed species, according to one estimate, would eventually cost taxpayers up to $13.56 billion. And, as a result of the forest crisis, Pacific Northwest species topped this list of expenditures. By 1992 the Fish and Wildlife Service and National Forest Service together had spent more on the northern spotted owl than on any other species, ever: $9,853,570. Combined costs to all federal agencies for recovery efforts on behalf of the owl and Chinook and sockeye salmon that year was $152,415,671.[11]

These were merely direct expenses, for no one had calculated indirect costs stemming from increased federal staffers' time, lands acquisition for sanctuaries, public assistance to the jobless, reduced or terminated business activities, lost jobs, devalued property, forgone tax revenues, and of course legal fees. Nor had anyone calculated the human and economic impacts stemming from the termination or reduction of thousands of private enterprises affected by the act. But this cost was considerable. The service's creation of a preserve for the gnatcatcher in San Diego County, according to one estimate, would cost local residents $3.46 billion annually and eliminate 28,600 potential jobs.[12]

· · ·

Not surprisingly therefore, in the Northwest anxiety ruled. Thanks to logging shutdowns, counties, destitute of funds, were closing schools and hospitals. Poverty spread and families disintegrated. In Grays Harbor County, Washington, the number of food bank users had increased from three thousand to eighteen thousand since 1989, and nearly 90 percent of students in some schools were eligible for the federal food program. A culture of poverty emerged, as aid that attended to the needy — such as "breadbasket" programs and housing assistance — attracted urban poor to the logging communities, where they in turn introduced violence and street gangs.[13]

Since 1989, 168 mills had closed, and approximately twenty-two thousand jobs had been lost in Oregon and Washington because of federal timber reductions. In 1994 one mill was closing in the Pacific Northwest every other week. For the first time the United States was importing more than half the newsprint it consumed. Saving the owl had effectively shut down an area larger than Massachusetts, Vermont, New Hampshire, and Connecticut combined, costing the economy tens of billions of dollars and casting tens of thousands out of work.[14]

Timber harvests on regional federal lands dropped from 5.4 billion board feet in 1989 to less than 800 million in 1994. And almost nothing was coming into the pipeline. By December 1993 three years had passed without a meaningful federal timber sale. Contract volumes sank to 17 percent of 1989 levels, and were destined to hit virtually zero by 1995.[15]

As harvests dropped to a trickle, timber prices shot through the roof. By January 1994 they were rising to their maximum daily limit in trading at the Chicago Mercantile Exchange. The average cost of a new 2,000-square-foot home had risen $4,000. Stud prices were up a record 75 percent over the preceding four months. And although the Wilderness Society had produced a "study" denying that the owl-caused 20 percent drop in the nation's supply of softwood had had any effect on prices, virtually no independent economist supported this contention. A 1993 study by the University of California forest economist William McKillop found that Option 9 would cost America's consumers $4.6 billion in higher wood products prices, and another calculation concluded that the drop in timber production since 1992 had already cost the economy $20 billion.

These rising prices accelerated harvests elsewhere, unfortunately in places where trees did not grow as well. Already, shortly after the 1993 Forest Conference, Chadwick Oliver had written President Clinton, warning that "large-scale stopping of timber harvesting in the Pacific Northwest is increasing wood prices and causing substitution by harvesting more acres of less productive forests elsewhere and by increasing use of far more polluting steel, aluminum, concrete, and brick. This harvesting elsewhere is exporting the environmental problems and creating an 'environmental imperialism' . . . not protection of the environment." Furthermore, a preservation approach would only aggravate these problems.[16]

Now Oliver's prediction was coming true. As federal timber became less accessible, many companies redirected their attention to private stands or away from the Northwest to places receiving minimal moisture and less environmental protection. This trend, experts warned, would have global consequences. Just replacing the wood obtained from 100,000 acres of Northwest forests, one study found, required felling 1.53 million acres of Russian forest.[17]

America was robbing an indigent Peter to pay the rich Paul. Capitalizing on rising timber prices, and fearing that coming regulations would soon prevent their harvesting any timber at all, private landowners began stripping their lands. From 1992 to 1993 private harvests in Oregon alone jumped by a whopping 500 million board feet. And as prices continued to rise, loggers in the Midwest and northern Rockies started harvesting inferior grades of softwood in places that should have been left alone. The number of jobs on state and private lands in Idaho climbed 24 percent in just one year, from 1992 to 1993.[18]

Even the Sierra Club's Northwest regional director Bill Arthur and Wilderness Society president Jon Roush reportedly caught the timber fever. The former felled twenty loads of conifers at his summer residence north of Newport, Washington, next to a wildlife refuge in Colville National Forest, and the latter harvested 400,000 board feet on his Montana ranch. In Montana, which received less than a tenth the precipitation of Oregon's coast range, newspaper headlines told a disturbing story of carpetbagging loggers searching for cottonwoods along streams: "Desperate Timber Mills Looking at River Bottoms. Oregon Sawmill Looking for Montana Cottonwoods."[19]

The exodus was greatest to the Southeast, where most forests lay in private hands. As Northwest lumber and plywood capacity among the seven largest manufacturers decreased by 33.5 percent between 1978 and 1990, it grew by 121 percent in the Southeast. Already by 1987 this warmer region, less hampered by federal regulations, was producing more than 45 percent of the nation's timber growth and 55 percent of its harvests, despite possessing a mere 22 percent of its softwood growing stock.[20]

To be sure, the reduction of Northwest timber harvests did not spell doom for the entire regional economy. Logging job losses were tiny when compared with the overall employment picture in Oregon and Washington. And high-tech firms arriving in the region would probably create more positions than the wood products industry would lose. Rather, it was a way of life that was being lost. Possessing no more than an eighth grade education, the average logger would not find employment with the newly arriving companies. Rural towns would die.

Also, ironically, the environment would suffer. The great effort to save old growth would eventually destroy the very landscapes it was intended to preserve. For it demonstrated an important principle: that seeking to halt change merely accelerates it. Nothing more clearly revealed this truth than the rising threat of wildfire. In Oregon and Washington, studies confirmed, owing in part to preservation and fire exclusion, up to 20 million acres were overripe for burning. By seeking to save wilderness and endangered species, the nation risked destroying both.

In the spring of 1994 the congressionally established National Commission on Wildfire Disasters warned that the risks of conflagration had "reached critical levels over large areas of the western states." In 1988, it noted,

> 72,570 fires burned over five million acres of wildland, representing a 137 percent increase over the previous five year average. . . . In 1990, the Pinto fire in southern California burned 648 structures and cost $248 million dollars in damages. On October 20, 1991, the 1,600 acre East Bay Fire in Oakland, California, killed 25 people, injured 150 others, destroyed 3,354 single family homes, 456 apartments, and caused an estimated 1.5 billion dollars damage. Six days prior, in a community near Spokane, Washington, . . . 62 mile per hour winds fanned 92 separate fires that burned 114 homes and 35,000 acres.

Paradoxically, the commission averred, the country's preservation policies had triggered this holocaust. "In many forest situations, trees protected from fire's effects for many decades have grown to a size and density where the competition between them for moisture and nutrients has caused serious stress, resulting in epidemic outbreaks of opportunistic diseases and insects." As these trees died, they dried out, producing "a fire environment so disaster-prone in many areas that it will periodically and tragically overwhelm our best efforts at fire prevention and suppression." Consequently,

Public concerns for endangered species . . . may not always achieve the desired goal. Officials in southern California, following the 1993 firestorm, attributed the lack of prescribed burning that could have reduced or eliminated much of the destruction to public opposition, some of which was based on concern for the habitat of the Stephens kangaroo rat and the gnatcatcher.

A similar paradox is emerging in the Blue Mountains of eastern Oregon, where interim regulations imposed by the National Marine Fisheries Service, attempting to protect the habitat of endangered Pacific salmon species, now prohibit timber removal within 300 feet of primary fish-bearing streams. These forests, badly impacted by species shift, insects, and drought stress, are full of dead and dying trees — a wildfire disaster awaiting almost-certain fulfillment. When streamside forests burn under these conditions, stream habitats for endangered fish will be impacted far more seriously, and for far longer time spans, than would be experienced with careful forest treatment and fuel reduction.

Instead of wilderness protection, the commission urged, forests need active management, including "fuel reduction by mechanical removal through careful salvage logging, thinning, and other means," followed by "prescribed fire." But unfortunately, it observed, "public opposition to logging and other silvicultural actions in federal forests results in greatly increased costs and time delays which hamper timely action. Areas needing treatment in wilderness areas or parks, where logging and other silvicultural methods are not an option, present an additional challenge." The commission therefore recommended that the government "change land management techniques to focus on establishing and maintaining sustainable ecosystem conditions commensurate with commodity production, and demonstrating the benefits of such techniques to a skeptical public and Congress."[21]

In its race to make ecosystem management national policy, however, the Clinton administration ignored these warnings. In 1992 the National Forest Service had already announced its intention to implement ecosystem management. By 1993, 271 million acres — nearly four times the combined area of New York, Maine, Massachusetts, New Hampshire, Vermont, and Rhode Island — had been reserved as wilderness or national parks or restricted for other conservation purposes. Yet the federal government continued to spend over $300 million annually to purchase new refuges and wilderness areas. In March the U.S. Fish and Wildlife Service announced "an ecosystem approach to fish and wildlife conservation" that would include mapping America into fifty-two separate "ecosystem units." Shortly after, the Bureau of Land Management embraced ecosystems management, declaring that "all ecosystem management activities should consider human beings as a *biological resource.*" And in October the administration would persuade Congress to pass the 6.6 million acre Desert Wilderness bill, creating in California the biggest preserve south of Alaska.[22]

Meanwhile, the administration fine-tuned plans for implementing the biodiversity treaty, as the Senate began its consideration of the agreement. Once approved, it would remove preservation policy from the control of elected officials altogether, delegating this power to United Nations bureaucrats, State Department officials, and advisory committees representing environmental groups (which the UN euphemistically called NGOs, or "non-governmental organizations").[23]

To give a glimpse of what this meant, in September one such NGO committee produced a planning document titled "Global Biodiversity Assessment Section," which recommended implementation of Dave Foreman's Wildlands Project, that would call for the removal of human habitation from up to half the country's land area. Preventing habitat "fragmentation," the assessment stated, "means that representative areas of all major ecosystems in a region need to be reserved, that blocks should be as large as possible, that buffer zones should be established around core areas, and that corridors should connect these areas. The basic design is central to the recently-proposed Wildlands Project."[24]

On April 14, 1994, the administration submitted its "Record of Decision" to Judge Dwyer, incorporating FEMAT recommendations aimed at protecting a "functional and interconnected old-growth forest ecosystem." And in December the judge, rejecting challenges from both sides, approved the plan, paving the way for implementation.[25]

The record spread its net over virtually every creature that crawls, photosynthesizes, or swims. In addition to owls, salmon, murrelets, and eighty-seven other vertebrates, it promised to save more than one thousand other life forms including lichens, fungi, mosses, liverworts, saprobes, bryophytes, amphibians, mollusks, vascular plants, and arthropods. It would provide roosting sites for bats, restrict slash burning to protect arthropods, regulate moss collection to conserve bryophtes, and take steps to minimize soil disturbance.

To manage this ambitious system, the record proposed layers of bureaucracy — a labyrinth of validation steering committees, a Regional Interagency Executive Committee, Regional Ecosystem Office, Research and Monitoring Committee, and Province Teams. As with Option 9, it divided the 24 million acres of Northwest forests into congressionally reserved areas (7.3 million acres), matrixes (3.9 million), late successional reserves (7.3 million), adaptive management areas (1.5 million), administratively withdrawn areas (1.48 million), and riparian reserves (2.6 million). Only matrixes would be open to traditional "silvicultural activities," and even some of these, the record observed, contain nonforested areas "technically unsuited for timber production."

Although adaptive management areas would allow silvicultural experimentation, much of the rest would remain untouchable. The purpose of the largest category, late successional reserves, was nothing less than to keep forests in a permanent state of senescence. Rather than allowing selective cutting of *old* trees — so that stands would become more complex and uneven-aged over time — the record recommended the reverse: cutting only *young* ones under eighty years old (subject to permission of the Regional Ecosystem Office). This would advance the average age of forests until fire wiped them out. But even the prospects of thinning these young trees was uncertain. The record placed so many bureaucratic obstacles to active management that foresters were not often likely to receive the money and permission to thin, prune, or ignite prescribed fires.[26]

Option 9 revealed that as the long fight over forests and owls entered the final stages, its original purposes had been forgotten. In place of the initial aim of saving forests, the authors of the record of decision would "restore presettlement conditions" that never existed. And they seemed to have forgotten about owls altogether. Restoring "presettlement conditions," they claimed, meant promoting old growth until these forests covered 65 percent of the region.[27] But new evidence suggested that seldom, if ever, in any moment of prehistory, had late successional forests been so extensive. In fact, current old-growth conditions may already exceed the historic average.

In 1990 a fire history analysis by a Forest Service plant ecologist, Jan Henderson, suggested that by the year 2000 old growth would cover 40 percent of the Mount Baker-Snoqualmie and Olympic national forests, thereby actually surpassing averages for these areas between A.D. 1300 and 1800. Henderson also concluded that the amount of old growth had *increased* during the last century. Another recent study by the Bureau of Land Management found that in 1850 trees over two hundred years old constituted only 40 percent of the landscape in the Oregon coast range.[28]

But it was an Oregon State University graduate student, Bob Zybach, who most successfully exploded the old-growth myth. In what seems the most thorough investigation of the historical record so far, Zybach reviewed Bureau of Land Management maps from 1850, 1890, 1920, and 1940 and read notes of early explorers, diaries of settlers, ship logs, Geological Survey studies, interviews with Indians, and notations of early scientists, and examined data on pollen fossils and charcoal deposits.

Through this investigation he drew a very different portrait of the pre-Columbian Northwest. Rather than a "sea of old growth," the landscape, he suggested, was characterized by what early settlers called "green islands." The fragmentation which the government and the Wildlands Project sought to destroy had been the dominant regime for millennia!

"Forests were more open than they are now," he later told *Evergreen* magazine. "There were islands of even-aged conifers, bounded by prairies, savannas, groves of oak, meadows, ponds, thickets and berry patches." And, far from exhibiting the "complex structure" touted as necessary by the New Foresters — such as multilayered canopies, woody debris, and snags — these early stands, owing to frequent Indian burning, "were virtually free of underbrush and course woody debris that has been commonplace in forests for most of this century." Thus, Zybach concluded, "There's not a chance in the world the forest [Jerry Franklin] describes has existed here in the past 10,000 years. . . . The maps indicated that in the early 1800s, when white settlement began in the region, significant portions of what is now spotted owl habitat contained only small amounts of trees 200 years old or older, perhaps no more than five or ten percent." On average, Zybach concluded, old growth covered from 5 to 38 percent of the region over the last several thousand years, and today's "blanket" is "10 to 20 percent larger than it was 150 years ago, with most of the increase due to the growth of forest in areas once occupied by old burns, prairies, savannas and meadows."[29]

What the record's authors had ignored, Zybach observed, was that "virtually all of the forests we see today in the Pacific Northwest are the product of human intervention." Echoing a point made by virtually every ethnographer who has ever studied Native American cultural practices, he noted that the Indians' broadcast burning cleared underbrush and created patchworks of forests interspersed by prairie. These early peoples did not eat spotted owls; they pursued deer and elk. Therefore, they viewed old growth as biological desert. To produce the early

CONSEQUENCES: THE SEASON OF OUR UNCERTAINTY

successional conditions that favored game animals, they had to burn, which they did, constantly. "If the government's scientists were to construct an accurate portrayal of Indian land management practices," Zybach concluded, "their sea of old growth myth would vanish in a puff of smoke."[30]

As it had with the evidence about old growth, the record of decision disregarded owl science as well. As estimates of the bird's population grew to around 10,000, this gigantic management effort could hardly be justified as a way to save the creature. Whereas Endangered Species Act recovery plans set specific goals, indicating scientifically measurable criteria when a creature had recovered sufficiently to need no further federal protection, the record listed no such limitations. Rather, it proposed an open-ended enterprise which only a gigantic government could conceive but no one could accomplish. Demanding a budget of billions, preoccupying scores of state and federal agencies, geared for unlimited expansion, intended to regulate everything that moved, it was designed to last not until the time when owls, murrelets, and other creatures recovered but *forever*. Its approach "involved complex projections regarding the likely fate of species over the next fifty to one hundred years or more."[31]

Such hubris was inevitable. All along biocentrists had invoked the fate of the owl not because they were worried about the little bird itself, but because it was a tool for achieving broader antihumanist and primitivist goals. But as they approached total victory, this crutch was no longer necessary. With ecosystem protection they did not need to cite declining owl numbers to justify forest preservation. That required painstaking field research and yielded uncertain results. Now, by declaring the government responsible for all life, they could avoid science — and accountability — altogether.

And, indeed, Option 9 was just the beginning. Before the ink on that plan was dry, the administration had extended the concept eastward. In July 1993 it directed the Forest Service "to develop a scientifically sound and ecosystem-based strategy for management of eastside forests" — public lands east of the Cascade Mountains in Oregon and Washington. A year later it proposed a third, for the upper Columbia River drainage in Idaho, Montana, Utah, Wyoming, Nevada, and eastern Washington, called the Upper Columbia River Basin. Like Option 9, both the eastside and upper Columbia schemes would impose "ecosystem management strategies" controlling or limiting activities on public lands in order to sustain "ecosystem health." According to the government definition, "ecosystem health" means "ecosystem resiliency," and "resiliency" is equivalent to "biological integrity."

The ecosystem idea, in short, was too useful politically to be rejected simply because it was meaningless. As if to prove this point, in August Interior Secretary Babbitt denied the California Forestry Association's petition to delist the owl in that state, thereby confirming that no level of abundance would ever be sufficient to reverse the terrible trend of events.[32]

So instead of raising hopes that the end of the forest crisis was in sight, the government inspired fears that the fight might last forever. Oregonians, one survey found, remained "pessimistic about the prospects for resolving environmental and quality of life issues" and "unenthusiastic about at least some of the current prescriptions."[33]

People seemed trapped on a treadmill, condemned to repeat the same mistakes again and again. In "Redwoods: The Last Stand," intoned *Time* magazine in June, "a young activist fights a corporate raider to save an ancient California forest from being cut down." *Time* was not referring to Greg King. The story concerned a new activist incarnation — Doug Thron, age twenty-four, nature photographer, who, *Time* said, dropped out of Humboldt State University to become a permanent activist, trespassing thirty times on Palco lands in his effort to fight Hurwitz and save Headwaters.[34] Thron was ten years old when Foreman and his friends hiked out of the Sonora Desert to found Earth First! in 1980. Possessing an unquenchable thirst for environmental heroes, America had created a protest machine that no one knew how to turn off. Rushing blindly ahead, the nation seldom looked backward — and never learned from the past.

What could it have learned? On the slopes of Mount St. Helens, whose devastation inspired the New Forestry, time told a cautionary tale. Rather than ensuring glorious rebirth, by 1994 the "biological legacies" Jerry Franklin had identified had produced only a stunted and patchy forest. But next door, on 68,000 acres of Weyerhaeuser Company lands which had been equally devastated, a full forest had reappeared, containing trees up to forty feet tall. All known kinds of wildlife had returned. This spectacular growth had happened because, unlike the National Forest Service, Weyerhaeuser did not leave the land alone. Instead, it salvaged the old timber and planted over 18 million new trees.[35]

Far from harming forests, this old way of silviculture had husbanded them. Since 1952 net volume of timber per acre had increased 33 percent nationally. In 1991 net forest growth exceeded harvest by 33 percent. In the Northwest by 1991 net annual growth was 83 percent greater than in 1952. "Had there been no intervention on behalf of the spotted owl, twenty or twenty-five years from today, this region could have sustained a harvest level twice what it was in the 1940's," observed University of Minnesota forest scientist and then-incoming president of the forest products society Jim Bowyer in 1993.[36]

Farther south at Redwood National Park, near where this story began, all that remains is regret. As *Smithsonian* magazine reported in 1993:

> Twenty-five years after the establishment of the nation's first billion-dollar national park, 15 years after an expansion more than doubled its size, the trees are coming back, but the painful wounds left by a bitter battle over the park formation remain raw in the lives of the people. . . . Establishing the park with 78,000 acres of prime timberland triggered a downward economic spiral that stole good-paying jobs, savaged the timber industry and sentenced the area to chronic hard times and heartbreak: "We are fast becoming the Appalachia of the West," one ex-logger maintains.

Nor, notes *Smithsonian*, has the void been filled by tourism, as environmentalists promised:

> Redwood National Park is almost invisible to visitors. . . . Far from the projected million and a half tree lovers a year, tourist visits last year were estimated at 388,000. . . . "What they get are park-and-pee visitors," as one put it. . . . John Grobey, professor of economics at Humboldt State, shakes his head as he says that his most dire prediction, that the park would destroy the country's economic base, came true. "The taxpayers spent a lot of money, but not much came of it. Certainly not much benefitted the people here. They feel betrayed."[37]

The warnings were sounded, but few listened. And the light at the end of the tunnel was fire. By June it came, driven by hot, dry winds rolling up mountains like freight trains, pushing walls of heat that turned small stones red. As the disciples of biocentrism raced to consolidate their agenda, these flames, fueled by old growth that had become too old, sick, and dry, raced through the West, destroying homes and habitat, threatening towns, killing firefighters, sterilizing soil, and laying waste the very trees, plants, and animals preservationists sought to save.

By the time the embers cooled in October, more than 3.5 million acres had burned, nearly doubling the previous year's fire toll. Tens of thousands of acres of owl habitat went up in smoke, and the nation awaited another season.[38]

30

IN A
DARK WOOD

THE IMAGE REMAINED crystalline in the man's memory: The four-year-old boy sat on a boulder at the lakeshore with his nanny as his grandfather glided toward them in a canoe, holding up a large, silvery trout. It was the summer of 1939. And, like many recollections, it was tinged with sadness. His grandfather died a few years later, about the same time, he was told, that the species of trout the old man caught went extinct.

Then the man's mind flickered with an image of the boy at ten, sitting on giant breakwater boulders underneath a dilapidated dock on the Maine coast, watching fish swim at his feet, so clear and vivid he wanted to touch them. The deck above blocked the sun's glare, providing a picture-window view of subsurface sea life amidst barnacled pilings and waving bunches of seaweed. In the half-light he sat transfixed by a fluxing diorama of crawling and swimming lobsters, crabs, starfish, hermit crabs, mussels, snails, sole, cod, mackerel, blowfish, dogfish sharks, stingrays, cunner, and pollack.

While his father was fighting in Europe, the boy spent summer days in Maine like Huck Finn on the Mississippi, patrolling coastal waters in a small dinghy. If he was ashore and wanted to escape the grownup world (which was often), he climbed under loose planking on the dock and sat in silence, enjoying his hidden aquarium.

Now the man had returned to find the wharf gone, and so, too, most of the fish. Scuba divers told him that, except for a prodigious number of lobsters, the bay bottom seemed dead.

What had happened, he wondered? No one could say. The lake where his grandfather used to cast flies, Pleasant Pond, lay in the heart of the Maine woods and had been among the deepest and clearest in New England. His family had vacationed there for generations, angling for "Pleasant Pond trout" — a wild species, locals said, unique to the lake. But by the time the boy was a young man, this fish had disappeared, and baffling algae blooms had destroyed the lake's translucency. He could find only brook trout, a variety that was smaller and less brilliant than the one he remembered. The Pleasant Pond species, he was told, was gone for good.

This news reinforced his already bleak vision of decay. But then he met a state biologist who told him Pleasant Pond trout never existed! The fish his grandfather had caught were hatchery-reared brook trout, regularly planted by the Maine Department of Inland Fisheries since his great-grandfather was a boy. "Pleasant Pond trout" were the stuff of local lore, nothing more. The man's memory, the scientist suggested, rested on illusion.[1]

He found marine experts equally unsatisfying when he asked why so many coastal fish had vanished. Some suspected overfishing and pollution, but since no research had been done to confirm this, the puzzle remained. Focusing on commercially important species such as lobster and scallop, biologists had ignored economically insignificant creatures such as the cunner, which they hadn't even realized was missing.[2]

Sometimes, the man mused, the only record lies in memory. While apparent declines go unrecorded by science, they are reflected in the slow impoverishment of our lives. Perhaps in a few decades, he speculated, no one would recall the cunner — a small, ugly fish offering excitement only to little boys. On his deathbed Natty Bumppo, the hero of James Fenimore Cooper's leatherstocking tales laments, "How much has the beauty of the wilderness been deformed in two short lives!" Now he found himself thinking the same thing.[3]

Yet what did his loss signify, he wondered? How much represented his own nostalgia? In assessing decline, he speculated, can we distinguish reality from illusion? How much change is twilight and how much the dawn of another day? What carries the dirty fingerprint of man and what merely signals the ebb and flow of evolution? To be sure, many environmental problems are real in that they represent changes which threaten human health or deplete the aesthetic and spiritual richness of our lives. But do some reflect only a longing for a past that cannot be recovered or, worse, that never was? If he had been wrong about Pleasant Pond trout, might he be confusing decline with his own mortality? And what should be done? Should we restore the past? Can we?

. . .

Who has not felt the same pain and puzzlement? The sense of loss, more than anything else, is what powered the political forces of preservation. But though an honest emotion, it was sometimes hard to assess, and the salvation it sought never materialized. The environmental movement, which many desperately hoped would succeed, did not keep its promises. Embarking on a long voyage without a clear destination, it was hijacked by ideas and values that often destroyed the very things it sought to save. And, tragically, this failure was avoidable. Environmentalism is potentially worthy and even necessary. It need not be destructive. Now is the time to start over, and do it right.

"Midway in our life's journey," wrote Dante in *The Divine Comedy*,

> I went astray
> from the straight road and woke to find myself
> alone in a dark wood. How shall I say
> what wood that was! I never saw so drear,
> so rank, so arduous a wilderness![4]

So, too, in its quest for ecological deliverance, America wandered, and woke to find itself surrounded by arduous wilderness. In their 1935 book *Primitivism and Related Ideas in Antiquity*, Arthur O. Lovejoy and George Boas wrote:

> One of the strangest, most potent and most persistent factors in Western thought [is] the use of the term "nature" to express the standard of human values, the identification of the good with that which is "natural" or "according to nature." The primitive condition of mankind, or the life of "savage" peoples, has usually been extolled because it has been supposed to constitute "the state of nature." . . . Little, indeed, in the history of Western ideas about what is good or bad in conduct, in social and political institutions, and in art, is intelligible without a constant realization of the fact that the sacred word "nature" is probably the most equivocal in the vocabulary of the European peoples; that the range of connotation of the single term covers conceptions not only distinct but often absolutely antithetic to one another in their implications; and that the writers who have used it have usually been little aware of its equivocality and have at all times tended to slip unconsciously from one of its senses to another.[5]

Likewise, America was misled by the elusive implications of nature. This ambiguous and value-laden concept and its cognates influence policies to perhaps a greater degree than at any other time in history.

Confused assumptions about it pervade conservation laws, yet few seek to define it.

Rather than pursuing unambiguous goals, the environmental crusade was propelled by unexamined assumptions whose ambiguities went unnoticed. The country's legitimate desire to stem the tide of urban and suburban blight became confused with the goal of re-creating "presettlement conditions" which never existed. From America's long-term infatuation with primitive wilderness the movement derived the notions that preservation meant "restoring" these prehistoric "conditions" by leaving nature alone. From preservationists such as Thoreau and Muir it inherited a Calvinistic certainty in the righteousness of its cause which justified moral exclusion of those deemed to be damned.

Borrowing from European ideas, it transformed ecology from a promising science into a highly political one. From thinkers such as Hegel and Naess it derived a monistic metaphysics justifying activism and absolutism, and a belief that nature was the source of political truth. The vision of all things as interconnected led to the idea that all things were equally valuable. Positing ecosystem health as the supreme value diminished the standing of individuals.

Out of this odd coupling of mystical American ideals with systematic European philosophies rose a doctrine that was neither fascist nor entirely home-grown but something new — biocentrism, which held that the best way to preserve nature was to leave it alone, and that the supreme good to which society should dedicate itself is not human happiness but the health of nature. The ecosystem became the model for culture, and global survival was deemed to depend on promoting "diversity" by social engineering or by force.

The goal of natural preservation went almost entirely unexamined. And when policymakers occasionally did seek to define it, the results were intellectually embarrassing, as in 1990 when the National Parks and Conservation Association, at the invitation of the National Park Service, convened a blue-ribbon panel to reexamine national park objectives. The purpose of these preserves, the committee concluded, was to maintain "the biotic assemblages that existed, or would have evolved, without the 'discovery' of America by Columbus and subsequent European settlement."

This was an accurate portrayal of the presuppositions of federal policy. Indeed, it was not unlike FEMAT's objective of restoring "presettlement conditions." But by articulating it, the panel exposed its flaws. Resurrecting early landscapes entailed the impossible task of undoing five hundred years of history. And if by some miracle this could have been done, we would never have known it, for we cannot identify what "would have happened" had Columbus not discovered America any more than we can know what "would have happened" had Napoleon won the battle of Waterloo. It was an impossible and immeasurable standard.

This was the flaw underlying the preservationist movement: it rested on an unjustified conviction of certainty. It attributed objective validity to views that in reality merely reflected subjective tastes. It forgot that environmental beauty, like art, lay in the eyes of the beholder; that ecology is a tool, not an end in itself; and that nature is merely one among many values, not the supreme source of all that is good. By focusing on the mythical goal of "ecosystem stability," it did not recognize that the "health of nature" is a myth. It fought for wilderness because its supporters liked to hike, but rationalized this fight as a struggle to preserve "ecosystem health." It sought to save birds because these feathery creatures are pretty but justified this goal in the name of spurious "biodiversity."

Embracing teleology, it confused philosophy with science and fact with value. Filling a vacuum created by the death of the Lockean consensus, it embraced new values based on systems ecology, which from the beginning was less a preservation science than a program for social control. Supposing that protecting ecosystems was the highest imperative for government, it increasingly viewed the exercise of individual liberty as a threat.

Misled by the ecosystem model, it failed to develop a clear strategy for sustaining the very landscapes most people hoped to maintain. It would save "biodiversity" and "forest health" but did not know what these terms meant. It idealized Native Americans and sought to restore pre-Columbian conditions, but ignored how these peoples changed the landscape. Seeking to "save" everything, it promoted policies that favored climax communities rather than early successional ones. Attempting to halt change, it risked cataclysmic destruction. Eager to resurrect the past, it created regimes that were unique in natural history. And touting itself as guardian of the public interest, it lobbied for laws that destroyed cultures and put liberty at risk.

In short, it misdiagnosed the cause of America's ills. For most people preservation is an aesthetic and spiritual imperative which is satisfied by environments containing a variety of life forms. This does not mean only wilderness. It includes landscapes that people create as well. Anyone who has visited a Tuscan village or an English garden knows that humans can create scenes that are pleasing to the eye. But the movement was unable to conceive a way to stop social blight other than by creating wilderness. It therefore encouraged the spread of both until, today, in many areas, they are virtually contiguous to each other — where McDonald's restaurants stand cheek by jowl with "pristine wilderness."[6]

In this way all of us are forced to choose between pavement or wilderness when what we really want is livable communities. Ancient forests and wildlife sanctuaries have become playgrounds for urbanites sufficiently affluent to escape the city on weekends, but they do nothing to halt the cultural decay that propels this exodus. Instead, as we watch conflicts over forests and wildlife replay themselves again and again, we soil our nests and move on. We migrate from Boston or Philadelphia to Denver or Seattle in search of better communities, only to find the same disintegration at work there, too.

. . .

Today the crisis of spiritual and political values triggered by the triumph of positivist science continues. The nation remains fragmented. Many conservatives embrace free market philosophies dedicated exclusively to personal liberty. But shorn of the ethical foundations that liberalism once derived from natural law, this doctrine contributes little to maintaining standards of public or private conduct.

Repelled by this secularity and agnosticism, others seek spiritual foundations for their political beliefs. While a few experiment with less conventional alternatives, such as Eastern or New Age religions, many have returned to fundamentalist Christianity, transforming this movement from an evangelical to a political one. Or they flock to environmentalism, which, as another manifestation of the Puritan ethic, also represents a reaction to the excessive materialism of modern life.

Like many spiritual movements that achieve worldly power, therefore, environmentalism has lost its way. Bloated by wealth, mainstream environmental groups have become bureaucracies not unlike the public agencies they pledged to police. Occupying high-rent offices in the nation's capital far from the "ecosystems" they promised to defend, and heavily staffed with well-paid lawyers, these organizations are driven by ever greater pressures to increase income flow. They spread scare stories to stimulate public generosity and embrace litigation as a way of life.[7]

Federal agencies, recognizing the ineffability of ecosystem boundaries as an opportunity for expansion, jump on the bandwagon, enacting "remedies" that give them power over science. Unclear about fact-value distinctions, researchers cross the line between science and advocacy. Ecology, which as a pure interdisciplinary undertaking was essential for understanding the complexity of living systems, has been transformed into a semioccult Delphic priesthood, whose oracles are given the power to decide what is best for nature, and therefore who in society should sacrifice and who should benefit.

Somewhere along the line, too, the movement became a war launched by the haves against the have-nots. It is a situation analogous to what the late Christopher Lasch has called "the revolt of the elites" whereby "upper-middle-class liberals have mounted a crusade to sanitize American society." Indeed, Lasch could have been thinking of environmentalists when he added that "when confronted with resistance . . . members of today's elite betray the venomous hatred that lies not far beneath the smiling face of upper-middle-class benevolence."[8]

These currents have come together in the fight over forests and endangered species. Activists, loggers, and Wall Street raiders are walking metaphors of the age. The Pacific Northwest struggle became a proxy war between the philosophical forces of environmentalism, wise use, and the free market, exposing the flaws of each and ensuring that both man and nature would lose. Thus, it became the biggest, most protracted, and most costly environmental conflict in history, building with apocalyptic inevitability for more than thirty years. Its final eruption signals that environmentalism has come of age, yet simultaneously has been strangely transformed from a conservation crusade into a political one.

The movement is wrong on most key points. Contrary to what it insists, America is not running out of trees; old growth still covers most of its historic range; owls are probably not disappearing and may not even need old growth. Yet activists deny these truths because they do not fit the biases of biocentrism.

More than a mere conservation theory, biocentrism has emerged as a full-blown, soup-to-nuts political philosophy. No longer representing a single issue, it has, like classical nature-based ideologies, become a complete theory of government, offering an answer to the most fundamental questions of political obligation. But by abandoning all belief in the rationality and moral self-sufficiency of mankind — so necessary for maintaining democracy — it endorses a darker view of humanity.

In his 1958 address "Two Concepts of Liberty," the Oxford historian Sir Isaiah Berlin said that the central question of politics is: "Why should I (or anyone) obey anyone else?" Throughout history philosophers have offered two competing answers, which he defined as negative and positive freedom.

Negative freedom, Berlin suggested, is when "a man can do what he wants." According to this concept, endorsed by liberal theorists such as Locke and Mill, the state is entitled to use only the minimum coercion necessary to discourage behavior that limits the liberty of others.

By contrast, positive freedom, propounded by a variety of holistic thinkers from Eastern mystics to Plato, Rousseau, and Marx, "derives from the wish on the part of the individual to be his own master." In this sense we are free when we do what our "better" self wants. Unlike negative freedom, this idea can justify force — "to coerce men in the name of some goal (let us say, justice or public health) which they would, if they were more enlightened, themselves pursue, but do not, because they are blind or ignorant or corrupt." And throughout history this notion has led to tyranny:

> One belief, more than any other, is responsible for the slaughter of individuals on the altars of the great historical ideals — justice or progress or happiness of future generations, or the sacred mission or emancipation of a nation or race or class, or even liberty itself, which demands the sacrifice of individuals for the freedom of society. This is the belief that somewhere, in the past, or in the future, in divine revelation, or in the mind of an individual thinker, in the pronouncements of history or science, or in the simple heart of an uncorrupted good man, there is a final solution.[9]

Environmentalism, too, promises a final solution. Embracing positive freedom, it rests on the assumption that the primeval stability of nature is the supreme good. Thus, it suggests, we must let authorities define for us the "presettlement conditions" which we ought to desire.

But nature cannot be a transcendent good. Values do not exist like trees and stars. Rather, they are tags which sentient beings, whether godly or human, confer upon things to designate their importance to the evaluator. If consciousness did not exist, nothing would have value.[10]

Once we recognize that the balance of nature is not the supreme good, the house that biocentrism built collapses. We need no longer accept that environmental protection is a categorical imperative taking precedence over all other social duties. Then preservation fights are seen for what they are: conflicts between competing class, regional, vocational, recreational, and aesthetic interests. Since nature does not "prefer stability," this mythical state cannot constitute "ecological health." And once we reject the supremacy of stability, we no longer need rely on experts to tell us how to achieve it, nor need we suppose that "letting nature take its course" best protects those features we prize. If humanity is the standard of value, then policies must be measured by the extent to which they enhance human life. People choose the landscape they want, not the "ecosystem health" they are told to desire.

Likewise, the goals of preservationism evaporate. Its purpose cannot be to prevent "unnatural change" while permitting "natural" alterations because the two are indistinguishable. Yet neither can it be said to sustain evolutionary processes. Evolution does not need our help. And it becomes equally obvious that preservation cannot mean restoring and maintaining "presettlement conditions." Even if we could turn the clock back, how could we ever decide what moment of history to "restore" and why? Should America be returned to what it was in 1850, or 1492, or as it was fifteen thousand years ago, when woolly mammoths roamed freely, and before humans set foot on the continent?

What, then, is natural preservation, and how is it to be achieved? And how can we begin to resolve the crisis over values that began in the 1960s, when the Lockean consensus dissolved? Surprisingly, the answer may lie in the past.

One cannot think about aboriginal peoples without encountering paradoxes. For millennia societies worshiped primitive indigenous cultures but ignored or despised contemporary ones. And today, even as many extoll pre-Columbian Indians as ecological heroes, they decry the excesses of their modern descendants. While crediting early peoples with having kept the continent "pristine," environmentalists castigate and sometimes litigate against modern tribes for killing too many salmon, hunting marine mammals, overharvesting forests, and permitting mining on their lands. Indeed, Native Americans today seem no better at conservation than anyone else. This is puzzling. If their ancestors were such good land stewards, why did they not pass this ethic down to their descendants?

One reason is that presettlement Indians were not the good conservationists they are reputed to be. Rather than living off the land without depleting it, they altered the landscape profoundly, sometimes beneficially and sometimes not. Although their burning was almost uniformly beneficial, there is abundant evidence that they overhunted many game species to the point of local extinction. The diverse landscape the early settlers saw was not the product of a conscious and wise preservation philosophy but almost certainly the happy consequence of three conditions: no one tribe controlled the entire continent; tribal economies varied widely; and many peoples were nomadic.

Within its territory, many a tribe overused resources. But collectively these early peoples conserved because their diffusion (and often their mobility) ensured that all the land would not be subject to the same treatment. Some hunted buffalo, others deer. Some fished, others killed seals. Some collected berries, others raised corn. The great diversity of wildlife that amazed early explorers was also the result of the fact that the hundreds of tribes on this continent were often at war with one another. Several early accounts suggest that wildlife was scarce within tribal territories but abundant in the no man's land separating warring peoples.[11]

These regimes contrast starkly with contemporary land management. The United States government controls a third of the real estate in America, and has been moving ever closer to a single national preservation strategy. Whereas in 1968 the National Park Service was the only agency to practice "ecosystems management," today it is official doctrine for all federal land management. Laws such as the Endangered Species Act, the Wilderness Act, and the National Forest Management Act apply each year to ever vaster areas of the continent. And this monolithic approach has proved a recipe for disaster. Rather than producing diversity, it is resulting in a numbing uniformity.[12]

Therefore, a national preservation policy is clearly a contradiction in terms. Our much-increased capacity for destruction makes it even more imperative that, like the Indians, we embrace a diversity of landscape strategies. Any mistake made by uniform policies is multiplied many-fold across the entire continent. And present-day America, like that of the Indians, is composed of differing peoples with varying views about beauty and well-being. This means that preservation is not one thing but many. This is the real meaning of biodiversity: conditions that reflect the variegated interests of a heterogeneous society.

A truly ecological perspective recognizes that humans and their activities are part of nature, and that enhancing all aspects of their lives — including their surroundings — begins with cooperation between individuals, based on mutual trust. This means that rather than following one strategy, we should mimic the early Indians and encourage a multiplicity of regimes. Rather than halting or reversing disturbances, we should embrace change. Rather than excluding man from the garden, we should welcome his cultivation of it. Rather than feeling compelled by metaphysical imperatives to save pseudoscientific "ecosystems," we should seek to sustain a variety of landscapes simply because they please us. And rather than impose draconian environmental laws that divide society, we should encourage cooperation which builds trust and seeks to heal the social wounds that thirty years of philosophical conflict have caused.

This demystification and democratization of preservation would ensure the diversity of life that many environmentalists desire, and would redefine the role of ecologist from guru to guide. Instead of helping to shape policy objectives, as they often do today, these scientists would merely evaluate and implement mandates. They would address means, not define the ends.

Lying south of Mount Lassen in Northern California, surrounded by the Plumas National Forest, lies the village of Quincy. In the town's library a small miracle recently occurred which suggests that a new kind of environmentalism may be aborning.

Heavily dependent on federal timber, Quincy was deeply polarized by the split between activists and loggers. Environmentalist opposition to timber sales had pauperized the community. The Plumas National Forest budget declined by 40 percent in just a few years. Schools were losing counselors and sports programs; unemployment was growing. Desperate, county supervisor Bill Coates invited Tom Nelson, head of the local logging company, and Michael Jackson, a prominent town environmentalist, to meet with him in the library. He asked the men: Was there anything they could agree on?[13]

It turned out there was. Both conceded that fire was a problem. Quincy was surrounded by crowded and overly mature trees overdue for burning. The men sketched a plan for dealing with the threat, to thin and prune forests where possible. And after they had reached an initial accord, others joined them: environmentalists, college professors, loggers. Calling themselves the Quincy Library Group, they began by thinning a small watershed where no owls lived, then expanded their planning to cover two national forests, Plumas and Lassen, and the Sierraville district of Tahoe National Forest, an area of about 1.6 million acres.

Throughout they followed this rule: to discuss only matters they could agree on. The environmentalists were against logging in roadless areas, so they deferred debate about these places. Wilderness was put off-limits. That still left about two thirds of the forest open for selective cutting, enough to sustain the economy indefinitely, and far more than the 20 percent which FEMAT permitted in northern spotted owl country.

They kept things simple, focusing like a laser on helping local communities and thinning overaged forests. Rather than adopt problematic goals — such as those proposed by the New Forestry, which required making two hundred-year projections — they kept to a more modest landscape scale, improving stand conditions to minimize fire, and agreeing to proceed for five years then assess the results.

Fortunately, the California spotted owl had not been listed under the Endangered Species Act, and Quincy lay outside the region of the northern spotted owl, covered by the restrictive FEMAT plan. Otherwise the stringent rules governing this bird's northern spotted cousin would have prohibited their plan altogether. Nevertheless, although they agreed unanimously not to disturb owl nests, they faced obstacles. National environmental organizations remained suspicious of the plan because it entailed their loss of control. Some of these groups charged that local activists were caving in to industry. Federal regulations also presented severe hurdles. Some Forest Service personnel resented a civilian group's suggesting how to run "their" forests. Specialists such as hydrologists and timber and fire experts were reluctant to work together. Many managers preferred to build trails rather than promote silviculture.[14]

And research was a big disappointment. Originally they had hoped their project would be a laboratory for understanding forests and wildlife. They planned to invite ecologists such as Stephen Rosenzweig and Robert Taylor to study how burning stands and cutting trees affected owl populations. But government red tape and opposition from environmentalists — who did not want wildlife habitat to be disturbed by the scientists — killed the plan, at least temporarily.[15]

Their idea remained a fragile flower, vulnerable to the killing winds from Washington, D.C. The Forest Service was completing an environmental impact statement on the forest management plan for the region, whose conclusions might determine its fate. They hoped that their effort would be approved and that mainstream environmentalists would not sue. And they knew that if the California spotted owl were declared an endangered species, they might not be permitted to go forward.[16]

But whatever the outcome, one thing was certain: their insights would not die. "Like the carnival 'bump 'em cars,'" said one member of the Quincy team, "we hit a lot of walls, but keep going." And, indeed, locally based initiatives, each unique in its own way, are springing up in many places.

At Willapa Bay in Washington state, an environmental group called Ecotrust has been working with local citizens to promote sustainable industries. On the Coyote Valley Reservation in Northern California, the Intertribal Sinkyone Wilderness Council is coordinating an effort of ten tribes to establish an intertribal park dedicated to reviving plant diversity and finding new markets for traditional native uses of this resource. And in Grants Pass, Oregon, a coalition of loggers and conservationists has formed the Applegate Partnership, aimed at restoring both forest health and the local economy, and which, to its credit, FEMAT's forest plan will allow to continue.[17]

The possibilities are endless. For, unlike governments, civilizations, and even genes, ideas are immortal.

NOTES AND SOURCES

INDEX

NOTES
AND SOURCES

CHAPTER I. THE SEARCH FOR NATURE

1. Rachel Carson, *Silent Spring* (Boston: Houghton Mifflin, 1962), pp. 169–170.
2. See Stephen Fox, *John Muir and His Legacy: The American Conservation Movement* (Boston: Little, Brown, 1981), p. 292.
3. Ibid.; Michael J. Bean, *The Evolution of National Wildlife Law*, rev. ed. (New York: Praeger, 1983); and Samuel P. Hays, *Beauty, Health, and Permanence: Environmental Politics in the United States, 1955–1985* (Cambridge: Cambridge University Press, 1987).
4. A full list of environmental successes would be too lengthy to give here. As a general summary, see President's Council on Environmental Quality, *Environmental Quality: 22nd Annual Report* (Washington, D.C.: Government Printing Office, 1991). For improvements in public health and agriculture, see Dennis T. Avery, *Saving the Planet with Pesticides and Plastic: The Environmental Triumph of High-Yield Farming.* On automobile emissions, see Robert W. Crandall et al., *Regulating the Automobile* (Washington, D.C.: The Brookings Institutions, 1986). The figures on conservation restrictions on federal lands include only acreage managed by the National Forest Service, National Park Service, Fish and Wildlife Service, and Bureau of Land Management. On national parks and wilderness, see: General Accounting Office, *Federal Lands: Information on Land Owned and on Acreage with Conservation Restrictions* (Washington, D.C.: U.S. Government Printing Office, January, 1995); National Parks and Conservation Association, *New Parks, New Promise* (Washington, D.C., 1988), I-1; Ronald F. Lee, *Family Tree of the National Park System* (Philadelphia: Eastern National Park and Monument Association, 1972); U.S. Department of Agriculture, Forest Service, *Land Areas of the National Forest System as of September 1993* no. FS-383 (Washington, D.C.: Government Printing Office, 1994); Task Force on Outdoor Recreation Resources and Opportunities to the Domestic Policy Council, *Outdoor Recreation in a Nation of Communities* (Washington, D.C.: U.S. Government Printing Office, March 1988), pp. 1–13. The National Wildlife Refuge System also grew. By 1988 it totaled more than 88 million acres. See *Outdoor Recreation*, pp. 1–16.
5. Assessing a variety of polling data, in 1993 the Clearinghouse on Environmental Advocacy and Research reported, "The core group of bedrock support-

ers of the environment is still small." *Report on the Wise Use Movement*, rev. March 1993. In 1990 a national Roper poll found that "pro-environmental Americans are a minority today — only 22 percent of the public." In 1992 only 29 percent of respondents considered themselves "active" environmentalists. A 1991 Roper poll found that when asked whether saving species justified putting loggers out of work, "Americans voted in favor of the loggers, by a margin of 45 percent to 35 percent." Quoted from *Report on the Wise Use Movement*. In a 1992 Roper study respondents favored multiple use of natural resources over preservation, 70 to 26 percent. And although there have always been critics of environmentalism, what is new is that erstwhile supporters of the movement are becoming constructive critics of it. For a discussion of the backlash, see *Environment Reporter* 5, no. 4 (August 1993) and 5, no. 5 (September 1993). And for other examples of serious criticism of hitherto sacrosanct environmental policies, see Gregg Easterbrook, *A Moment on the Earth* (New York: Viking, 1995); Charles C. Mann and Mark L. Plummer, "The Butterfly Problem," *Atlantic* (January 1992); Charles C. Mann and Mark L. Plummer, *Noah's Choice: The Future of Endangered Species* (New York: Alfred A. Knopf, 1995); Charles T. Rubin, *The Green Crusade* (New York: Free Press, 1994).

6. "Aging Greenpeace Seeking New Directions," *Los Angeles Times*, September 6, 1994. After the 1992 general elections a Cable News Network exit poll found that the environment ranked last among voter priorities. On environmentalists' concern about the Wise Use Movement, see Carl Deal, *The Greenpeace Guide to Anti-Environmental Organizations* (Berkeley: Odonian Press, 1993), and David Helvarg, *The War Against the Greens* (San Francisco: Sierra Club Books, 1994). On the state of the parks, see Alston Chase, *Playing God in Yellowstone* (New York: Atlantic Monthly Press, 1980); Karl Hess, Jr., *Rocky Times in Rocky Mountain National Park* (Niwot, Colo.: University of Colorado Press, 1993); Charles E. Kay, "Too Many Elk in Yellowstone?," *Western Wildlands* 13, no. 3 (1987): 39–41, 44; William D. Newmark, "A Land-Bridge Island Perspective on Mammalian Extinctions in Western North American Parks," *Nature*, January 29,1987; National Research Council, *Science and the National Parks* (Washington, D.C.: National Academy Press, 1992); and 75th Anniversary Steering Committee, *National Parks for the 21st Century: The Vail Agenda* (Washington, D.C.: The National Parks Foundation, 1992). On the effects of environmental pessimism, see transcript of ABC News report, "Are We Scaring Ourselves to Death," aired April 21, 1994; and "John Stossel's Brand of Libertarian Journalism," *Environment Writer* 6, no. 10 (January 1995).

7. See Arthur O. Lovejoy and George Boas, *Primitivism and Related Ideas in Antiquity* (Baltimore: Johns Hopkins University Press, 1935); John Passmore, *Man's Responsibility for Nature* (New York: Charles Scribner's Sons, 1974).

8. The literature on this subject is voluminous. See, e.g., Heinrich A. Rommen, *The Natural Law* (London: B. Herder, 1955); Otto Gierke, *Political Theories of the Middle Age*, ed. F. W. Maitland (Cambridge: Cambridge University Press, 1900); John Plamenatz, *Man and Society* (London: Longmans, 1963).

9. Lovejoy and Boas, *Primitivism*.

10. See F. M. Cornford, ed., *The Republic of Plato* (Oxford: Oxford University Press, 1945); Ernest Barker, ed., *The Politics of Aristotle* (Oxford: Oxford University Press, 1950); Thomas Hobbes, *Leviathan*, ed. Michael Oakeshott (Oxford: Basil Blackwell, 1960); John Locke, *Two Treatises of Government*

(New York: Hafner, 1947); John Locke, *Essays on the Law of Nature*, ed. W. von Leyden (Oxford: Oxford University Press, 1954); Jean Jacques Rousseau, *The Social Contract* (London: J. M. Dent and Sons, 1958); Carl Cohen, ed., *Communism, Fascism, and Democracy* (New York: Random House, 1968).

11. J. W. Gough, *The Social Contract* (Oxford: Oxford University Press, 1963); José Ortega y Gasset, *Man and Crisis* (New York: Longmans Green, 1927).

12. Concern about preserving "shared values" in the "Judeo-Christian tradition" was very strong among educational reformers after the Second World War. See Harvard Committee, *General Education in a Free Society* (Cambridge, Mass.: Harvard University Press, 1945); and Gail Kennedy, *Education at Amherst* (New York: Harper and Row, 1955). For explanations of this "taproot" sense of culture, see Alston Chase, *Group Memory: A Guide to College and Student Survival in the 1980s* (Boston: Atlantic Monthly Press, 1980); and John Bonner, *The Evolution of Culture in Animals* (Princeton: Princeton University Press, 1980).

13. Charles Reich, *The Greening of America* (New York: Bantam, 1970); Daniel Bell, *Reforming of General Education: The Columbia College Experience in Its National Setting* (New York: Columbia University Press, 1966).

14. See Fox, *John Muir and His Legacy*.

15. As examples of the new environmental perspective, see Donella H. Meadows et al., *The Limits to Growth* (New York: Signet, 1972); James Rathlesberger, ed., *Nixon and the Environment* (New York: Village Voice Books, 1972); Barry Commoner, *The Closing Circle* (New York: Bantam, 1971).

16. Louis Hartz, *The Liberal Tradition in America* (New York: Harvest Books, 1955), p. 140; see also chap. 1.

17. John Locke, *Second Treatise*, chap. 2; cf. Locke, *Essays on the Law of Nature*.

18. Alston Chase, "The Rise and Fall of General Education," *Academic Questions* 6, no. 2 (spring 1993). See also Gerald Grant, "The Overoptioned Curriculum," in *Working Papers: Toward the Restoration of the Liberal Arts Curriculum* (New York: Rockefeller Foundation, 1979); E. A. Burtt, *The Metaphysical Foundations of Modern Science* (New York: Doubleday, 1954); I. Bernard Cohen, *Revolution in Science* (Cambridge, Mass.: Harvard University Press, 1985); Carl Hempel, *Aspects of Scientific Explanation* (New York: Free Press, 1965). The term *positivism* was introduced by the French philosopher Auguste Comte (1798–1857) in his book *Course of Positive Philosophy* (1830–1832).

19. Chase, "General Education." See also Christopher Jencks and David Riesman, *The Academic Revolution* (New York: Doubleday, 1969).

20. Chase, "General Education."

21. Ibid.; Reich, *Greening*, pp. 233ff.

22. James George Frazer, *The Golden Bough*, ed. Theodore H. Gaster (New York: Criterion Books, 1959), p. 74; Roderick Nash, *Wilderness and the American Mind* (New Haven: Yale University Press, 1967), p. 2.

23. J. E. Cirlot, *A Dictionary of Symbols* (New York: Philosophical Library, 1962), p. 107.

24. Michael Williams, *Americans and Their Forests* (Cambridge: Cambridge University Press, 1989), p. 10; Clarence J. Glacken, *Traces on the Rhodian Shore* (Berkeley: University of California Press, 1967), p. 294.

25. Williams, *Americans and Their Forests*; see also Nash, *Wilderness*.

26. Do people or ideas move history? The answer, of course, is both. For a discussion, see Isaiah Berlin, *The Hedgehog and the Fox* (New York: Mentor Books, 1957).

27. Barry Commoner offered the first popular articulation of this philosophy in 1971; see Commoner, *Closing Circle*.
28. Ibid.
29. The term *biocentrism* is an old one, even appearing in the *Oxford English Dictionary*. But its present meaning seems to have been introduced in Paul W. Taylor, "The Ethics of Respect for Nature," *Environmental Ethics* 3 (1981). The philosophy known as "deep ecology" shares this central idea of biocentrism (i.e., the notion sometimes called biospherical egalitarianism). See Bill Devall and George Sessions, *Deep Ecology* (Salt Lake City: Gibbs M. Smith, 1985).
30. For a description of these forests, see Williams, *Americans and Their Forests*. On some of the other fights over endangered species, see Mann and Plummer, *Noah's Choice*.
31. Steven Lewis Yaffee suggests, rightly, that "controversy of this magnitude and tenacity was inevitable somewhere on federal public lands, but most likely on national forests in the Pacific Northwest." See Steven Lewis Yaffee, *The Wisdom of the Owl* (Washington, D.C.: Island Press, 1994); see also William Dietrich, *The Final Forest* (New York: Simon and Schuster, 1992).
32. The California National Forests which serve as habitat for the northern spotted owl are Shasta-Trinity, Mendocino, Klamath, Six Rivers, and Modoc. U.S. Forest Service, *Land Areas of the National Forest System*. Forest Ecosystem Management Assessment Team, *Forest Ecosystem Management* (Washington, D.C.: Government Printing Office, 1993).
33. Susan Zakin, *Coyotes and Town Dogs* (New York: Viking, 1993), chap. 14.
34. Yaffee, *Wisdom of the Owl*; "Endangered Species Blueprint," *NWI Resource* 5, no. 1 (Fall 1994); William McKillop, "An Economic Analysis of the FEMAT Report," mimeo., October 26, 1993; American Forest and Paper Association, "The 1995 Outlook for the Lumber and Wood Products Industry," December 1994.
35. For a picture of the variety of players in this drama, see Dietrich, *The Final Forest*.
36. Laura L. Manning, *The Dispute Processing Model of Public Policy Evolution: The Case of Endangered Species Policy Changes from 1973 to 1983* (Ann Arbor: University Microfilms International, 1986); Steven Lewis Yaffee, *Prohibitive Policy: Implementing the Endangered Species Act* (Cambridge, Mass.: MIT Press, 1982); Chase, *Playing God*. For an example of one fight over endangered species, see Mark Jerome Walters, *A Shadow and a Song: The Fight to Save Endangered Species* (Post Mills, Vt.: Chelsea Green, 1992).

CHAPTER 2. CORK BOOT FEVER

1. Tom Hirons's story is based on interviews conducted between October 1991 and December 1994.
2. Dow Beckham, *Swift Flows the River* (Coos Bay, Ore.: Arago Books, 1990).
3. Larry Robertson's story is based on interviews conducted between January 1992 and December 1994.
4. In 1971 forty-one loggers lost their lives, which represented 3.8 fatalities for every thousand loggers. But, thanks to improving technology, mortality rates, adjusted for the logger population, have steadily declined. In 1994 ten loggers lost their lives, representing 1.1 death per every thousand. Informa-

tion compiled from state data by the Association of Oregon Loggers, February 1995.

5. Beckham, *Swift Flows the River*; Michael Williams, *Americans and Their Forests* (Cambridge: Cambridge University Press, 1989), chap. 4.
6. Beckham, *Swift Flows*.
7. Ibid.; Williams, *Americans and Their Forests*, chap. 7.
8. Williams, *Americans and Their Forests*, chaps. 8 and 9; Beckham, *Swift Flows*.
9. Williams, *Americans and Their Forests*; Beckham, *Swift Flows*.
10. Beckham, *Swift Flows*.
11. Interview with Ray E. Doerner, executive director, Association of O&C Counties, 1993; Elmo Richardson, *BLM's Billion-Dollar Checkerboard* (Santa Cruz, Calif.: Forest History Society, 1980), chap. 1; George Kraus, ed., "History of the Oregon Division of the Southern Pacific," from Erle Heath and Lindsay Campbell, eds., "From Trail to Rail," a series published in the Southern Pacific *Bulletin* between 1926 and 1931.
12. Richardson, *Checkerboard*; Williams, *Americans and Their Forests*, chap. 9.
13. This background information is drawn from the prologue to Richardson, *Checkerboard*; and Kraus, "History."
14. Charles McKinley, *The Management of Land and Related Water Resources in Oregon: A Case Study in Administrative Federalism* (Washington, D.C.: Resources for the Future, 1965), p. 192.
15. Richardson, *Checkerboard*, chap. 1; Kraus, "History"; Harold K. Steen, *The U.S. Forest Service: A History* (Seattle: University of Washington Press, 1976), chap. 10.
16. Richardson, *Checkerboard*, chap. 4; Kraus, "History."
17. Richardson, *Checkerboard*, chaps. 5–8; Kraus, "History"; McKinley, *The Management of Land and Related Water Resources in Oregon*; Bureau of Governmental Research and Service, *The O&C Lands* (Eugene: University of Oregon School of Community Service and Public Affairs, 1981); Robert G. Lee et al., *Social Impacts of Alternative Timber Harvest Reductions on Federal Lands in O&C Counties* (Seattle: University of Washington College of Forest Resources and Northwest Policy Center, 1991); Northwest Forest Resource Council, *BLM Lands: Sixty Years of Forestry Excellence* (Portland: Northwest Forestry Association, 1993).
18. John B. DeWitt, *California Redwood Parks and Preserves* (San Francisco: Save the Redwood League, 1985), pp. 7–8; L. K. Napton and Carlo De Ferrari, "Regional Historical Background, mimeo., n.d.; David Warren Ryder, *Memories of the Mendocino Coast* (San Francisco: privately printed, 1948), a history commissioned by the Union Lumber Company.
19. Ryder, *Memories*, pp. 5ff.
20. "Palco Past: A Social History of Scotia and the Pacific Lumber Company," mimeo., 1972, a history commissioned by the Pacific Lumber Company; Hugh Wilkerson and John van der Zee, *Life in the Peace Zone* (New York: Collier Books, 1971); "The Murphy Family and T.P.L. Co.," *Humboldt Historian* 25, no. 4 (July–August 1977); Frank J. Taylor, "Paradise with a Waiting List," *Saturday Evening Post*, February 24, 1951; S. B. Show, *Timber Growing and Logging Practice in the Coast Redwood Region of California* (Washington, D.C.: U.S. Department of Agriculture, 1932); Henry J. Vaux, *Timber in Humboldt County* (Eureka, Calif.: Department of Forestry, Humboldt County, 1955).
21. Ryder, *Memories*.
22. Wilkerson and van der Zee, *Life in the Peace Zone*; Taylor, "Paradise."

23. Douglas W. MacCleery, *American Forests: A History of Resiliency and Recovery* (Durham, N.C.: Forest History Society, 1992); Douglas S. Powell et al., *Forest Resources of the United States, 1992,* General Technical Report RM-234 (Fort Collins, Colo.: Rocky Mountain Forest and Range Experiment Station, U.S. Department of Agriculture, Forest Service, 1993); Douglas S. Powell et al., *Forest Statistics of the United States, 1992* (Washington, D.C.: FIERR Staff Report, Forest Service, 1993); George A. Craig, *California's Commercial Timber Situation after Fifty Years of State Regulation* (Oakland: privately printed, 1992).

24. Susan R. Schrepfer, *The Fight to Save the Redwoods: A History of Environmental Reform* (Madison: University of Wisconsin Press, 1983), pp. 5–6, 38–40; Donald Culross Peattie, *A Natural History of Western Trees* (Boston: Houghton Mifflin, 1950), pp. 15ff.; John W. Barrett, *Regional Silviculture of the United States,* 2d ed. (New York: John Wiley & Sons, 1980); Chadwick D. Oliver and Bruce C. Larson, *Forest Stand Dynamics* (New York: McGraw-Hill, 1990).

25. Barrett, *Regional Silviculture;* Peattie, *A Natural History;* John C. Merriam, "The Highest Uses of the Redwoods," messages to the Council of the Save-the-Redwoods League, 1922–1941 (San Francisco: Save the Redwoods League, 1944; Emanuel Fritz, "Twenty Years' Growth on a Redwood Sample Plot," *Journal of Forestry* 43, no. 1 (January 1945); Elwood R. Maunder and Amelia R. Fry, *Emanuel Fritz: Teacher, Editor, and Forestry Consultant* (Santa Cruz, Calif.: Oral History Office, Forest History Society, 1972).

26. Peattie, *A Natural History;* Fritz, "Twenty Years' Growth"; Barrett, *Regional Silviculture.*

27. Larry D. Harris, *The Fragmented Forest* (Chicago: University of Chicago Press, 1984); Peter D. A. Teensma, John T. Rienstra, and Mark A. Yeiter, "Preliminary Reconstruction and Analysis of Change in Forest Stand Age Classes of the Oregon Coast Range from 1850 to 1940," Technical Note 9217, U.S. Department of the Interior, Bureau of Land Management, October 1991; Peter H. Morrison, *Old Growth in the Pacific Northwest: A Status Report* (Washington, D.C.: Wilderness Society, 1988); Elliott A. Norse, *Ancient Forests of the Pacific Northwest* (Washington, D.C.: Island Press, 1990); Jerry F. Franklin et al., *Ecological Characteristics of Old-Growth Douglas-Fir Forests,* General Technical Report PNW-118 (Portland: Pacific Northwest Forest and Range Experiment Station, U.S. Department of Agriculture, Forest Service, February 1981).

28. Harris, *Fragmented Forest;* Franklin et al., *Characteristics of Old-Growth.*

29. DeWitt, *Parks and Preserves,* p. 7; Lawrence Fox III, "A Classification, Map, and Volume Estimate for the Coast Redwood Forest in California," prepared for the Department of Forestry, College of Natural Resources, Humboldt State University, April 1988.

30. Peattie, *A Natural History,* p. 15.

31. DeWitt, *Parks and Preserves;* Schrepfer, *Fight to Save the Redwoods.*

32. Robert G. Lee, "Social and Cultural Implications of Implementing 'A Conservation Strategy for the Northern Spotted Owl,'" College of Forest Resources, University of Washington, June 21, 1990, pp. 12 and 13; Robert G. Lee et al., *Social Impacts;* Robert G. Lee, *Broken Trust, Broken Land* (Wilsonville, Ore.: BookPartners, 1994). For a portrait of this culture, see David Seideman, *Showdown at Opal Creek: The Battle for America's Last Wilderness* (New York: Carroll and Graf, 1993).

1. Elwood R. Maunder and Amelia R. Fry, *Emanuel Fritz: Teacher, Editor, and Forestry Consultant* (Santa Cruz, Calif.: Forest History Society, 1972), p. 264; also interviews with Maunder and Fry. Fritz's life and thought have been reconstructed with the help of interviews, conducted in 1992 and 1993, with his daughter, Barbara Fritz, and his former colleagues, the silviculturalist Henry Trobitz and the forester Robert Grundman.

2. Maunder and Fry, *Emanuel Fritz.*

3. Michael Williams, *Americans and Their Forests* (Cambridge: Cambridge University Press, 1989); Clarence J. Glacken, *Traces on the Rhodian Shore* (Berkeley: University of California Press, 1967), pp. 484ff.

4. Glacken, *Traces*, p. 485.

5. Ibid., p. 486.

6. Howard K. Steen, *The U.S. Forest Service: A History* (Seattle: University of Washington Press, 1976); Carl Alwin Schenck, *The Birth of Forestry in America*, ed. Ovid Butler (Santa Cruz, Calif.: Forest History Society, 1974), chap. 1; David M. Smith and Stephen H. Spurr, "Silviculture," in *Encyclopedia of American Forest and Conservation History*, ed. Richard C. Davis (New York: Macmillan, 1983; David A. Clary, *Timber and the Forest Service* (Lawrence: University of Kansas Press, 1986).

7. George Perkins Marsh, *Man and Nature*, 3d ed. (Cambridge, Mass.: Harvard University Press, 1974), pp. 29–30.

8. Frederick Jackson Turner, *The Frontier in American History* (New York: Henry Holt, 1920), pp. 12–13; Clary, *Timber*, pp. 12–13.

9. Peter J. Bowler, *The Norton History of the Environmental Sciences* (New York: W. W. Norton, 1992), pp. 323ff.

10. Alston Chase, *Playing God in Yellowstone* (New York: Atlantic Monthly Press, 1986), chaps. 2–4.

11. Schenck, *Birth of Forestry;* Clary, *Timber.*

12. Steen, *Forest Service*, pp. 8, 24, 27.

13. Ibid., pp. 9–20.

14. Ibid.; Schenck, *Birth of Forestry.*

15. Steen, *Forest Service;* Clary, *Timber*, chap. 1.

16. Steen, *Forest Service;* Schenck, *Birth of Forestry.*

17. Steen, *Forest Service*, p. 325; Clary, *Timber*, chap. 2; Randal O'Toole, *Reforming the Forest Service* (Washington, D.C.: Island Press, 1988).

18. O'Toole, *Reforming*, p. 90; Steen, *Forest Service*, p. 325.

19. Clary, *Timber*, pp. 50ff.

20. Clary, *Timber;* Maunder and Fry, *Emanuel Fritz;* Gifford Pinchot, *The Uses of the National Forests* (Washington, D.C.: National Forest Service, 1907); Gifford Pinchot, *Breaking New Ground* (Washington, D.C.: Island Press, 1987).

21. Clary, *Timber;* Maunder and Fry, *Emanuel Fritz.*

22. Maunder and Fry, *Emanuel Fritz*, p. 100.

23. B. E. Fernow, "Division of Forestry," in *Department of Agriculture Yearbook* (Washington, D.C.: Department of Agriculture, 1897), p. 149.

24. Franklin Moon and Nelson Courtlandt Brown, *Elements of Forestry* (New York: John Wiley and Sons, 1924); Henry Solon Graves, *The Principles of Handling Woodlands* (New York: John Wiley and Sons, 1911); David M. Smith, *The Practice of Silviculture*, 8th ed. (New York: John Wiley and Sons, 1986); Chadwick D. Oliver and Bruce C. Larson, *Forest Stand Dynamics* (New York: McGraw-Hill, 1990).

25. Moon and Brown, *Elements*; Graves, *Principles*; Smith, *Silviculture*; Oliver and Larson, *Dynamics*.

26. Maunder and Fry, *Emanuel Fritz*; Moon and Brown, *Elements*.

27. Leo A. Isaac, *Place of Partial Cutting in Old-Growth Stands of the Douglas-Fir Region* (Portland: USDA Forest Service, March 1956).

28. Clary, *Timber*, pp. 46ff.

29. Ibid., pp. 48–49; E. T. Allen, "Red Fir," mimeo., 1903 p. 88; W. D. Hagenstein, "Douglas-Fir Forestry from Allen to Mendel," in *Douglas-Fir: Stand Management for the Future*, ed. Chadwick Dearing Oliver, Donald P. Hanley, and Jay A. Johnson (Seattle: Institute of Forest Resources, University of Washington, 1986).

30. Jerry Franklin, personal communication; Chadwick D. Oliver, personal communication; J. V. Hofmann, *The Natural Regeneration of Douglas-Fir in the Pacific Northwest*, USDA Bulletin no. 1200, 1924.

31. Clary, *Timber*, p. 49.

32. Daniel B. Botkin, *Discordant Harmonies* (Oxford: Oxford University Press, 1990), pp. 51–52.

33. Ibid., p. 52; H. D. Thoreau, "The Succession of Forest Trees; An Address Read to the Middlesex Agricultural Society in Concord, September 1860," in *8th Annual Report of the Massachusetts Board of Agriculture* (1860); Donald Worster, *Nature's Economy* (Cambridge: Cambridge University Press, 1977), p. 72.

34. Frederic E. Clements, *Plant Succession: An Analysis of the Development of Vegetation* (Washington, D.C.: Carnegie Institution, 1916); Bowler, *History*, pp. 374–376; 519–526; Joel B. Hagen, *An Entangled Bank* (New Brunswick, N.J.: Rutgers University Press, 1992); Frank Benjamin Golley, *A History of the Ecosystem Concept in Ecology* (New Haven: Yale University Press, 1993).

35. Clements, *Plant Succession*.

36. Bowler, *History*, p. 376.

37. Oliver, *Stand Dynamics*, pp. 200ff.; John W. Barrett, *Regional Silviculture of the United States*, 2d ed. (New York: John Wiley and Sons, 1980), pp. 463ff.; Jerry F. Franklin et al., "Modifying Douglas-Fir Management Regimes for Nontimber Objectives," in Oliver, Hanley, and Johnson, *Douglas-Fir*.

38. Smith, *Silviculture*; Oliver, *Stand Dynamics*.

39. Williams, *Americans and Their Forests*, pp. 323–324; see also Larry D. Harris, *The Fragmented Forest* (Chicago: University of Chicago Press, 1984).

40. Clary, *Timber*, pp. 156ff; Steen, *A History*, chaps. 10–11; Hagenstein, "Douglas-Fir Forestry"; Chadwick D. Oliver and Jerry F. Franklin, personal communication.

41. Isaac, *Place of Partial Cutting*, p. 46.

42. Oliver and Larson, *Stand Dynamics*.

43. Hagenstein, "Douglas-Fir Forestry"; Clary, *Timber*, pp. 183ff.

44. Maunder and Fry, *Emanuel Fritz*; Emanuel Fritz, *California Coast Redwood* (San Francisco: Foundation for American Resource Management, 1957); Dale Thornburgh, interview.

45. David Warren Ryder, *Memories of the Mendocino Coast* (San Francisco: privately printed, 1948); *Palco Past: A Social History of Scotia and the Pacific Lumber Company*, mimeo., 1972, a history commissioned by the Pacific Lumber Company; "The Murphy Family and T.P.L. Co.," *Humboldt Historian* 25, no. 4 (July–August 1977); S. B. Show, *Timber Growing and Logging Practice in the Coast Redwood Region of California* (Washington, D.C.:

U.S. Department of Agriculture, 1932); Henry J. Vaux, *Timber in Humboldt County* (Eureka, Calif.: Department of Forestry, Humboldt County, 1955).
46. Maunder and Fry, *Emanuel Fritz.*
47. Ibid.
48. Ibid.; Emanuel Fritz, "Twenty Years' Growth on a Redwood Sample Plot," *Journal of Forestry* 43, no. 1 (January 1945).
49. Fritz, "Twenty Years' Growth."
50. Maunder and Fry, *Emanuel Fritz*, p. 110. Not everyone agrees, even today, that selection is best. See Peter Cafferata, "Clearcutting versus Selection in Coastal Redwood Forests," *Newsletter*, Jackson Demonstration State Forest, May 1990; and James L. Lindquist, "Hare Creek Sprout Stocking Study on Jackson Demonstration State Forest," *California Forestry* (September 1989).
51. Maunder and Fry, *Emanuel Fritz*, p. 110; Myron E. Krueger, "Forestry and Technology in Northern California, 1925–1965," ed. Amelia R. Fry, University of California, Bancroft Library, Regional Oral History Office, 1968.
52. Maunder and Fry, *Emanuel Fritz*, p. 145; *Palco Past*, chap. 6, p. 3.
53. Susan R. Schrepfer, *The Fight to Save the Redwoods: A History of Environmental Reform* (Madison: University of Wisconsin Press, 1983), pp. 109 ff.
54. Ibid.; *Palco Past*; Hugh Wilkerson and John van der Zee, *Life in the Peace Zone* (New York: Collier Books, 1971).
55. Maunder and Fry, *Emanuel Fritz*, p. 264.

CHAPTER 4. THE ECO RAIDERS

1. This information comes from interviews with Marc Gaede, 1991–1995, whose responsibility in these exploits is only now being publicly revealed. At the time he was still the anonymous "Arizona Phantom" depicted by Susan Zakin in *Coyotes and Town Dogs* (New York: Viking, 1993); see pp. 41ff.
2. The September 1971 campaign to protest nuclear testing on Amchitka Island in Alaska by the Don't Make a Wave Committee (later known as Greenpeace) has often been called the first confrontational environmental protest. But the actions of Gaede and the American Indian Movement preceded this by almost a year. In fact, the idea for the Arizona action itself grew out of AIM's November 1969 occupation of Alcatraz Island. For the Greenpeace story, see Paul Watson, *Sea Shepherd* (New York: W. W. Norton, 1982); Michael Brown and John May, *The Greenpeace Story* (London: Dorling Kindersley, 1989); Robert Hunter and Rex Weyler, *The Voyages of Greenpeace* (Vancouver: Scrimshaw Press, 1978); Robert Hunter, *Warriors of the Rainbow* (New York: Holt, Rinehart and Winston, 1979).
3. Dave Foreman and Bill Haywood, eds., *Ecodefense: A Field Guide to Monkeywrenching* (Tucson: Ned Ludd Books, 1987); Dave Foreman, *Confessions of an Eco-Warrior* (New York: Harmony Books, 1991); Christopher Manes, *Green Rage* (Boston: Little, Brown, 1990).
4. Edward Abbey, *The Monkeywrench Gang* (Salt Lake City: Dream Garden Press, 1985).
5. *Encyclopaedia Britannica*, 11th ed., s.v. "Luddites."
6. Tom Miller, "Eco-Saboteurs: Lurkers on the Corporate Threshold," *Rolling Stone*, August 29, 1974.
7. Tom Miller, "What Is the Sound of One Billboard Falling?," *Berkeley Barb*, November 8–14, 1974.

8. Miller, "Eco-Saboteurs."
9. Stephen Fox, *John Muir and His Legacy* (Boston: Little, Brown, 1981), pp. 60–61.
10. Ibid., chap. 5.
11. Ibid., p. 107.
12. Ibid., p. 363.
13. Perry Miller, *The New England Mind: The Seventeenth Century* (Cambridge, Mass.: Harvard University Press, 1954), p. 207, chap. 8; Perry Miller, *Errand into the Wilderness* (New York: Harper and Row, 1964), chap. 8. See also Perry Miller, *Jonathan Edwards* (New York: Dell, 1949); Perry Miller, ed., *The American Transcendentalists* (Baltimore: Johns Hopkins University Press, 1957).
14. Quotations in Miller, *The New England Mind*, pp. 207, 209.
15. Miller, *Errand*, p. 195.
16. Ibid., pp. 202–203.
17. Ibid.; H. D. Thoreau, "Walking," in H. D. Thoreau, *The Natural History Essays*, p. 112. Emerson and Bushnell quotes from Miller, *Errand into the Wilderness*, pp. 189 and 202.
18. Fox, *John Muir*, pp. 4–7 and chap. 11.
19. Ibid., p. 144; Frederick Turner, *Rediscovering America* (New York: Viking, 1985). See also Alston Chase, *Playing God in Yellowstone* (New York: Atlantic Monthly Press, 1986), pp. 307–308.
20. Fox, *John Muir*, chap. 11; Chase, *Playing God*, chap. 16.
21. Sigurd F. Olson, "The Emergent God," in *Reflections from the North Country* (New York: Alfred A. Knopf, 1982), p. 164; Susan L. Flader, *Thinking Like a Mountain* (Lincoln: University of Nebraska Press, 1974), p. 18; Fox, *John Muir*, p. 231; Robinson Jeffers, *The Selected Poetry of Robinson Jeffers* (New York: Random House, 1927), p. 458.
22. Robert G. Lee, *Broken Trust, Broken Land* (Wilsonville, Ore.: BookPartners, 1994); Robert H. Nelson, *Reaching for Heaven on Earth: The Theological Meaning of Economics* (New York: Rowman and Littlefield, 1991).
23. Susan R. Schrepfer, *The Fight to Save the Redwoods: A History of Environmental Reform* (Madison: University of Wisconsin Press, 1983), chap. 1.
24. Ibid., pp. 11–13.
25. Ibid., chaps. 2–4.
26. Ibid., pp. 42–43.
27. Charles Darwin, *The Origin of Species by Means of Natural Selection; or, The Preservation of Favoured Races in the Struggle for Life* (New York: Modern Library, 1936); Madison Grant, *The Passing of the Great Race* (New York: Charles Scribner's Sons, 1916).
28. Schrepfer, *Fight to Save the Redwoods*, p. 50; John C. Merriam, "Are the Days of Creation Ended?," *Scribner's Magazine* 81, no. 6 (June 1927). John C. Merriam, "The Highest Uses of the Redwoods," in *Messages to the Council of the Save-the-Redwoods League, 1922–1941* (San Francisco: Save the Redwoods League, 1944).
29. Schrepfer, *Fight to Save the Redwoods*, chaps. 3 and 4.
30. Walt Whitman, "Song of the Redwood Tree," in *Leaves of Grass* (New York: New American Library, 1980), p. 180.
31. Schrepfer, *Fight to Save the Redwoods*, chap. 2; *Palco Past: A Social History of Scotia and the Pacific Lumber Company*, mimeo., 1972; "The Murphy Family and T.P.L. Co.," *Humboldt Historian* 25, no. 4 (July–August 1977).
32. John B. DeWitt, *California Redwood Parks and Preserves* (San Francisco: Save the Redwood League, 1985), p. 15.

33. Schrepfer, *Fight to Save the Redwoods*, chap. 8.
34. Ibid., chap. 9.
35. Carsten Lien, *Olympic Battleground* (San Francisco: Sierra Club Books, 1991). See also Irving Brant, *Adventures in Conservation with Franklin D. Roosevelt* (Flagstaff: Northland Publishing, 1988); Michael Frome, *Regreening the National Parks* (Tucson: University of Arizona Press, 1992).
36. Lien, *Olympic Battleground*.
37. Schrepfer, *Fight to Save the Redwoods*, chap. 8.
38. Ibid., chaps. 7–8, p. 116.
39. Ibid., pp. 117–120.
40. Lloyd Hecathorn, interviews, 1992–1994; Schrepfer, *Fight to Save the Redwoods*, p. 120.
41. Schrepfer, *Fight to Save the Redwoods*, p. 131.
42. Ibid., p. 150.
43. Ibid., chap. 10.
44. Ibid., pp. 158, 163–165; Paul R. Ehrlich, *The Population Bomb* (San Francisco: Sierra Club Books, 1968).
45. Schrepfer, *Fight to Save the Redwoods*, p. 160.
46. Ibid., pp. 184–185.

CHAPTER 5. REBELS WITH A CAUSE

1. *Audubon Magazine* (May 1970); Stephen Fox, *John Muir and His Legacy* (Boston: Little, Brown, 1981), pp. 325–326.
2. The Kent State killings took place on May 4, 1970.
3. José Ortega y Gasset, *Man and Crisis* (New York: Longmans Green, 1927).
4. Alston Chase, "The Rise and Fall of General Education," *Academic Questions* 6, no. 2 (Spring 1993); Alston Chase, "America Found and Lost: The Rise and Fall of Generation Education," a research project for the Exxon Education Foundation; Alston Chase, "Skipping through College: Reflections on the Decline of Liberal Education," *Atlantic* (September 1978); Gerald Grant, "The Overoptioned Curriculum," in *Working Papers: Toward the Restoration of the Liberal Arts Curriculum* (New York: Rockefeller Foundation, 1979).
5. In 1953 the first books that students enrolled in Harvard's Social Sciences 1 were asked to read were Ruth Benedict's *Patterns of Culture* and Margaret Mead's *Coming of Age in Samoa*. The lesson they were supposed to learn was that all value judgments are relative. On emotivism, see Charles L. Stevenson, *Ethics and Language* (New Haven: Yale University Press, 1944).
6. Charles Reich, *The Greening of America* (New York: Bantam, 1970); Arthur Levine, *When Dreams and Heroes Died* (San Francisco: Jossey-Bass, 1980); Howard R. Bowen, *Investment in Learning* (San Francisco: Jossey-Bass, 1978); David Riesman, *On Higher Education* (San Francisco: Jossey-Bass, 1980); Benson R. Snyder, *The Hidden Curriculum* (Cambridge, Mass.: MIT Press, 1971); Frederick Rudolph, *Curriculum* (San Francisco: Jossey-Bass, 1977); Lansing Lamont, *Campus Shock* (New York: E. P. Dutton, 1979).
7. Ecclesiastes 1:18. See also Francis Bacon, "The Advancement of Learning," bk. 1, in *The Works of Lord Bacon* (London: William Ball, 1837).
8. Edith Hamilton, *The Greek Way to Western Civilization* (New York: W. W. Norton, 1930), esp. pp. 133ff.; Aristotle, *Politics*, bk. 5; *Bulfinch's Mythology* (New York: Avenel Books, 1978); W. W. Tarn, *Hellenistic Civilization* (New York: World Publishing Company, 1961).

9. Hamilton, *The Greek Way*; H. D. F. Kitto, *Greek Tragedy* (New York: Doubleday, 1954).

10. *The Republic of Plato*, F. M. Cornford, ed. (Oxford: Oxford University Press, 1945), p. 215.

11. *Metaphysics*, bk. 12, and *Physics*, bks. 7 and 8, in *The Basic Works of Aristotle*, ed. Richard McKeon (New York: Random House, 1941). See also John Herman Randall, Jr., *Aristotle* (New York: Columbia University Press, 1962), pp. 133ff.

12. See particularly Aristotle's discussion of substance in *Metaphysics*, bks. 7 and 8.

13. *Aristotle: The Nicomachean Ethics*, ed. H. Rackham (Cambridge, Mass.: Harvard University Press, 1926), p. 33.

14. *Aquinas: Selected Political Writings*, ed. A. P. d'Entreves (Oxford: Basil Blackwell, 1959), pp. 127ff. For more on early natural law, see A. P. d'Entreves, ed., *Natural Law* (London: Hutchinson University Library, 1951); Otto Gierke, *Natural Law and the Theory of Society: 1500 to 1800*, trans. Ernest Barker (Boston: Beacon Press, 1960); Heinrich A. Rommen, *The Natural Law* (London: B. Herder, 1955). For positivist critiques of it, see Hans Kelsen, *General Theory of Law and the State* (New York: Russell and Russell, 1961); Hans Kelsen, *What Is Justice? Justice, Law, and Politics in the Mirror of Science* (Berkeley: University of California Press, 1960).

15. John Locke, *Two Treatises of Government* (New York: Hafner, 1947); Jean Jacques Rousseau, *The Social Contract* (London: J. M. Dent and Sons, 1958); John Locke, *Essays on the Law of Nature*, ed. W. von Leyden (Oxford: Oxford University Press, 1954).

16. E. A. Burtt, *The Metaphysical Foundations of Modern Science* (New York: Doubleday, 1954); I. Bernard Cohen, *Revolution in Science* (Cambridge, Mass.: Harvard University Press, 1985), esp. pp. 126ff.; John D. Barrow and Frank J. Tipler, *The Anthropic Cosmological Principle* (Oxford: Oxford University Press, 1986), chap. 2.

17. Burtt, *Metaphysical Foundations*; *An Essay Concerning Human Understanding by John Locke*, ed. A. S. Pringle-Pattison (Oxford: Oxford University Press, 1924); *The Leibniz-Clarke Correspondence, with Extracts from Newton's Principia and Opticks*, ed. H. G. Alexander (Manchester: Manchester University Press, 1956).

18. This was Bacon's fear. See Bacon, "Advancement of Learning," in *Works*.

19. Laurence Sterne, *Tristram Shandy* (New York: Modern Library, 1955), pt. 2, chap. 3.

20. Christopher Marlowe, *Doctor Faustus*, in C. F. Tucker Brooke and Nathaniel Burton Paradise, *English Drama, 1580–1642* (Boston: D. C. Heath, 1933); George Madison Priest, *Johann Wolfgang von Goethe: Faust* (New York: Alfred A. Knopf, 1959).

21. Alasdair MacIntyre, *After Virtue* (Notre Dame, Ind.: University of Notre Dame Press, 1981), esp. chap. 4; *Immanuel Kant's Critique of Pure Reason*, ed. and trans. Norman Kemp Smith (London: Macmillan, 1956), p. 29; Oswald Spengler, *The Decline of the West*, volume 1, trans. Charles Francis Atkinson (New York: Alfred A. Knopf, 1926); see esp. chap. 11, "Faustian and Apollinian Nature-Knowledge."

22. Mary Shelley, *Frankenstein, or, the Modern Prometheus* (New York: New American Library, 1965), pp. 199–200.

23. Frederick R. Karl, *A Reader's Guide to Joseph Conrad* (New York: Farrar, Straus and Giroux, 1960), p. 138; *The Portable Conrad*, ed. Morton Dauwen Zabel (New York: Viking, 1947), p. 540.

24. Ibid., p. 560.
25. Quoted from Laurence J. Peter, *Peter's Quotations* (New York: William Morrow, 1977), p. 280.
26. See Karl Marx and Friedrich Engels, "Manifesto of the Communist Party," reprinted in *Communism, Fascism, and Democracy*, ed. Carl Cohen (New York: Random House, 1968).
27. Benito Mussolini, "The Doctrine of Fascism," in *The Social and Political Doctrines of Contemporary Europe*, ed. Michael Oakeshott (Cambridge: Cambridge University Press, 1939).
28. Crane Brinton, "The Mid-Twentieth Century: The Anti-Intellectual Attack," in *Ideas and Men: The Story of Western Thought* (New York: Prentice-Hall, 1950), chap. 14.
29. Today it is difficult to imagine how powerful the ideas of Marx and Hitler seemed in the 1930s. See, for example, Hugh Seton-Watson, *From Lenin to Malenkov: The History of World Communism* (New York: Frederick A. Praeger, 1955); George L. Mosse, *Toward the Final Solution: A History of European Racism* (New York: Harper and Row, 1978); George L. Mosse, *The Crisis of German Ideology* (New York: Schocken Books, 1981).
30. During the twentieth century the belief that "value judgments" could not be rationally defended spread gradually, beginning with Nietzsche and G. E. Moore, then to the logical positivists, and finally, after World War II, to academia at large. The landmark books were G. E. Moore, *Principia Ethica* (Cambridge: Cambridge University Press, 1903); and A. J. Ayer, *Language, Truth, and Logic* (London: Gollancz, 1936).
31. All quotations from this source are from Carl Hempel, "The Logic of Functional Analysis," in *Aspects of Scientific Explanation* (1959; rpt. New York: Free Press, 1965), pp. 297–330.
32. Derek Bok, "The President's Report," reprinted in *Harvard Magazine*, (May–June 1978).
33. Chase, "The Rise and Fall of General Education."
34. Quoted in Susan Schrepfer, *The Fight to Save the Redwoods* (Madison: University of Wisconsin Press, 1980), pp. 126–127.
35. Loren Eiseley, *The Night Country* (New York: Charles Scribner's Sons, 1947), p. xi.
36. Charles Reich, *The Greening of America* (New York: Bantam, 1970), chap. 9.
37. Ibid., p. 278.
38. See, for example, Stewart McBride, "The Real Monkey Wrench Gang," *Outside Magazine* (December–January 1983).
39. Paul Watson, founder of the radical group Sea Shepherds, told the author, "We are the McLuhan generation." See Alston Chase, "The Age of Unreason," *Outside Magazine* (December 1990); Dave Foreman, *Confessions of an Eco-Warrior* (New York: Harmony Books, 1991); Christopher Manes, *Green Rage* (Boston: Little, Brown, 1990).
40. Paul Watson, *Sea Shepherd* (New York: W. W. Norton, 1982); Michael Brown and John May, *The Greenpeace Story* (London: Dorling Kindersley, 1989); Robert Hunter and Rex Weyler, *The Voyages of Greenpeace* (Vancouver: Scrimshaw Press, 1978); Robert Hunter, *Warriors of the Rainbow* (New York: Holt, Rinehart and Winston, 1979); David Day, *The Whale War* (London: Routledge and Kegan Paul, 1987); Rex Weyler, *Song of the Whale* (New York: Anchor Press, 1986).
41. Greenpeace, "The Greenpeace Philosophy," brochure.
42. Watson, *Sea Shepherd*.

43. This discussion is based on interviews with various residents of Ukiah, Willits, Garberville, Eureka, and Arcata, California, between 1992 and 1995.
44. Ernest Callenbach, *Ecotopia* (New York: Bantam, 1975).
45. Quoted in Linnie Marsh Wolfe, *Son of the Wildness: The Life of John Muir* (New York: Alfred A. Knopf, 1951), p. 77. Although Muir saw the universe as governed by teleological laws, he did not envision humans as the center of it; see, e.g., Fox, *John Muir*, p. 52.

CHAPTER 6. LIFE IN THE PEACE ZONE

1. This section is based on several interviews with Bill Bertain, 1992–1995.
2. Interviews with Bertain and Woody Murphy, 1993–94.
3. *Palco Past: A Social History of Scotia and the Pacific Lumber Company*, mimeo., 1972; Hugh Wilkerson and John van der Zee, *Life in the Peace Zone* (New York: Collier Books, 1971); "The Murphy Family and T.P.L. Co.," *Humboldt Historian* 25, no. 4 (July–August 1977); Frank J. Taylor, "Paradise with a Waiting List," *Saturday Evening Post*, February 24, 1951.
4. *Palco Past*; "The Murphy Family and T.P.L. Co."
5. Wilkerson and van der Zee, *Peace Zone*.
6. Ibid.
7. Ibid., p. 53.
8. Bertain, interviews.
9. *Palco Past*; Wilkerson and van der Zee, *Peace Zone*; "The Murphy Family"; "Pacific Lumber Company: History," mimeo., n.d.; Taylor, "Paradise."
10. "The Murphy Family"; Taylor, "Paradise."
11. "The Murphy Family"; Taylor, "Paradise."
12. *Palco Past*; "Pacific Lumber Company: History"; Wilkerson and van der Zee, *Peace Zone*.
13. *Palco Past*, pp. 4 and 10.
14. Ibid., chaps. 5 and 9.
15. Ibid., chap. 9. See also Susan R. Schrepfer, *Fight to Save the Redwoods* (Madison: University of Wisconsin Press, 1980), chaps. 1–5; John B. DeWitt, *California Redwood Parks and Preserves* (San Francisco: Save the Redwood League, 1985), p. 15.
16. Cubic volume of the company's redwood holdings would rise from approximately 5.2 billion board feet in 1956 to around 9 billion in 1985. See chapter 16.
17. Douglas W. MacCleery, *American Forests: A History of Resiliency and Recovery* (Durham, N.C.: Forest History Society, 1992); Douglas S. Powell et al., *Forest Resources of the United States, 1992*, General Technical Report RM-234 (Fort Collins, Colo.: Rocky Mountain Forest and Range Experiment Station, U.S. Department of Agriculture, Forest Service, 1993); Douglas S. Powell et al., *Forest Statistics of the United States, 1992* (Washington, D.C.: FIERR Staff Report, Forest Service, 1993); George A. Craig, *California's Commercial Timber Situation after Fifty Years of State Regulation* (Oakland: privately printed, 1992); Bruce Krumland and William McKillop, *Prospects for Supply of Private Timber in California* (Berkeley: University of California Agricultural Experiment Station, 1990); Douglas W. MacCleery, "What on Earth Have We Done to Our Forests? A Brief Overview on the Condition and Trends of U.S. Forests," in *National Forests, 1891–1991*, U.S. Department of Agriculture, Forest Service, April 6, 1993.
18. American Forest Council, California Redwood Association, Redwood Re-

gion Conservation Council and Timber Association of California, "The State of the Redwoods Today," 1990; California Forestry Association, "California Forests," 1991; William McKillop, "Timber Growth and Harvest Projections on California Private Lands," a talk presented to the Association of Consulting Foresters Conference, Auburn, Calif., April 23, 1992; W. D. Pine, "Humboldt's Timber: A Present and Future Problem," a report of the Humboldt County Board of Supervisors, 1952.

19. Because of the variety of definitions of "old growth," estimates of the area this age class covers vary widely. In 1990 the Forest Service estimated that nearly 20 percent of the national forest land base in the Pacific Northwest was old growth (see Forest Service Report PNW-447). Many experts think that this is in the range of the average amount of Douglas fir old growth existing over the last one thousand years. On Douglas fir conditions, see Powell et al., *Forest Statistics*; Peter H. Morrison et al., "Ancient Forests on the Mt. Baker–Snoqualmie National Forest," Wilderness Society, 1990; Peter D. A. Teensma, John R. Rienstra, and Mark A. Yeiter, "Preliminary Reconstruction and Analysis of Change in Forest Stand Age Classes of the Oregon Coast Range from 1850 to 1940," U.S. Department of Interior, Bureau of Land Management Technical Note T/N OR-9, October 1991; Russell G. Congalton, Kass Green, and John Teply, "Mapping Old Growth Forests on National Forest and Park Lands in the Pacific Northwest from Remotely Sensed Data," *Photogrammetric Engineering & Remote Sensing* 59, no. 4 (April 1993); Thomas A. Spies and Jerry F. Franklin, "Old Growth and Forest Dynamics in the Douglas-Fir Region of Western Oregon and Washington," *Natural Areas Journal* 8, no. 3 (1988); Jan A. Henderson, "Trends in Amount of Old-Growth Forest for the Last 1,000 Years in Western Oregon and Washington," a peer-reviewed analysis prepared for National Forest Service chief F. Dale Robertson, November 19, 1990; R. Neil Sampson et al., "Assessing Forest Ecosystem Health in the Inland West," Forest Policy Center, 1994; Charles L. Bolsinger and Karen Waddell, "Area of Old Growth Forests in California, Oregon, and Washington," Forest Service Pacific Northwest Research Station, Portland, March 10, 1993; William M. Denevan, "The Pristine Myth: The Landscape of the Americas in 1492," *Annals of the Association of American Geographers* 82, no. 3 (1992); Bob Zybach, "Native Forests of the Douglas-Fir Region: A Brief History of the Forests of Western Washington and Oregon from Prehistoric Times to the Present," mimeo., March 29, 1994; "Voices in the Forest: An Interview with Bob Zybach," *Evergreen Magazine* (March–April 1994); Douglas W. MacCleery, "Trend Highlights: Forest Resources of the U.S. Prepared for the 1993 RPA Assessment Updates," U.S. Forest Service report FS-6200-28b(3/92); Cathy Whitlock, "Vegetational and Climatic History of the Pacific Northwest during the Last 20,000 Years: Implications for Understanding Present-Day Biodiversity," *Northwest Environmental Journal* 8, no. 1 (1992); Peter H. Morrison, *Old Growth in the Pacific Northwest: A Status Report* (Washington, D.C.: The Wilderness Society, 1988). On redwood forests, see DeWitt, *California Redwood Parks*; Lawrence Fox III, "A Classification, Map, and Volume Estimate for the Coast Redwood Forest in California," Department of Forestry, College of Natural Resources, Humboldt State University, October 1989.

20. MacCleery, *American Forests*; Daniel D. Oswald, Frank Hegyi, and Al Becker, "The Current Status of Coast Douglas-Fir Timber Resources in Oregon, Washington, and British Columbia," in Chadwick Dearing Oliver, Donald P. Hanley, and Jay A. Johnson, eds., *Douglas Fir: Stand Management*

for the Future (Seattle: University of Washington College of Forest Resources, 1986); Thomas A. Spies, "Plant Species Diversity and Occurrence
in Young, Mature, and Old-Growth Douglas-Fir Stands in Western Oregon
and Washington," in Leonard F. Ruggiero et al., Technical Coordinators,
Wildlife and Vegetation of Unmanaged Douglas-Fir Forests, U.S. Department of Agriculture, Forest Service, General Technical Report PNW-GTR-
285, May 1991. Indeed, with the exception of tropical rain forests, forests
around the world have been on a rebound since the 1950s. See Michael
Williams, "Forests," in *The Earth as Transformed by Human Action:
Global and Regional Changes in the Biosphere over the Past 300 Years,* ed.
B. L. Turner II et al., eds. (New York: Cambridge University Press, 1990).

21. *Appalachia* (September 1991); MacCleery, *American Forests.*
22. An excellent account of harvest strategies is provided by Randal O'Toole,
Reforming the Forest Service (Washington, D.C.: Island Press, 1988), chap.
9. See also David A. Clary, *Timber and the Forest Service* (Lawrence: University of Kansas Press, 1986).
23. Leo A. Isaac, *Place of Partial Cutting in Old-Growth Stands of the Douglas-
Fir Region* (Portland: USDA Forest Service, March 1956); Chadwick Dearing
Oliver, Donald P. Hanley, and Jay A. Johnson, eds., *Douglas-Fir: Stand Management for the Future* (Seattle: Institute of Forest Resources, University of
Washington, 1986).
24. For a full account of harvest strategies, see David M. Smith, *The Practice of
Silviculture* (New York: John Wiley and Sons, 1986). See also Franklin Moon
and Nelson Courtlandt Brown, *Elements of Forestry* (New York: John Wiley
and Sons, 1924); Henry Solon Graves, *The Principles of Handling Woodlands* (New York: John Wiley and Sons, 1911).
25. Clary, *Timber.* For an account of the harvest strategies of the private companies, see W. D. Hagenstein, "Douglas-Fir Forestry from Allen to Mendel," in
Oliver, Hanley, and Johnson, *Douglas-Fir.*
26. As we shall see, this is precisely the harvest strategy which the Pacific Lumber Company would adopt in 1986.
27. Clary, *Timber,* pp. 18off.; "Hearing Record for the Proposed Shelton Cooperative Sustained Yield Unit," on file at the Olympic Forest supervisor's office, Olympia, Wash., September 18, 1946, quoted in O'Toole, *Reforming,* p.
20. U.S. Department of Agriculture, Forest Service, *Douglas-Fir Supply
Study* (Portland: Forest Service, 1969).
28. O'Toole, *Reforming,* pp. 14off.
29. MacCleery, *American Forests;* Powell et al., *Forest Resources of the United
States, 1992;* Jonathan H. Adler, "Popular Front: The Rebirth of America's
Forests," *Policy Review* (Spring 1993).
30. Northwest Forest Resource Council, *BLM Lands: Sixty Years of Forestry Excellence* (Portland: Northwest Forestry Association, 1993); Charles McKin-
ley, "The Management of Land and Related Water Resources in Oregon: A
Case Study in Administrative Federalism (Washington, D.C.: Resources for
the Future, 1965); Bureau of Governmental Research and Service, *The O&C
Lands* (Eugene: University of Oregon School of Community Service and
Public Affairs, 1981); Craig, *California's Commercial Timber Situation;*
MacCleery, *American Forests;* Oswald, Hegyi, and Becker, "The Current
Status of Coast Douglas-Fir Timber Resources in Oregon, Washington, and
British Columbia"; American Forest Council, California Redwood Associa-
tion, Redwood Region Conservation Council and Timber Association of
California, "The State of the Redwoods Today," 1990; Fox, "Classification,
Map, and Volume Estimate."

440

NOTES AND SOURCES

31. MacCleery, *American Forests*; American Forest Council, *State of the Red-woods*.
32. Herbert Kaufman, *The Forest Ranger* (Washington, D.C.: Resources for the Future, 1960).
33. Clary, *Timber*, pp. 180–188.
34. Schrepfer, *Fight to Save the Redwoods*, chap. 10.

CHAPTER 7. BUILDING AN ARK

1. Library of Congress, *A Legislative History of the Endangered Species Act of 1973, as Amended in 1976, 1977, 1978, and 1980*, February 1982. Scenes and background were reconstructed based on interviews with Earl Baysinger, Lee Talbot, Lewis Regenstein, Ray Erickson, and others.
2. Laura L. Manning, *The Dispute Processing Model of Public Policy Evolution: The Case of Endangered Species Policy Changes from 1973 to 1983* (Ann Arbor: University Microfilms International, 1986); Steven Lewis Yaffee, *Prohibitive Policy: Implementing the Endangered Species Act* (Cambridge, Mass.: MIT Press, 1982).
3. Baysinger, interviews; Manning, *Dispute Processing*.
4. Library of Congress, *A Legislative History*.
5. Ibid.
6. This remark was made to the author by a member of the 10th U.S. Circuit Court of Appeals. See also Daniel J. Rohlf, *The Endangered Species Act: A Guide to Its Protections and Implementation* (Palo Alto: Stanford Environmental Law Society, 1989); Yaffee, *Prohibitive Policy*.
7. Baysinger and Ray Erickson, interviews, 1991–1994. For another account of the fight to save a species and how this effort intersected with passage of the Endangered Species Act, see Mark Jerome Walters, *A Shadow and a Song: The Fight to Save Endangered Species* (Post Mills, Vt.: Chelsea Green, 1992).
8. Faith McNulty, *The Whooping Crane* (New York: E. P. Dutton, 1966).
9. Ibid.
10. Erickson, interview. An account of the evolution of the organization of the U.S. Fish and Wildlife Service can be found in Earl Baysinger, "Evolution of the U.S. Fish and Wildlife Service's Authorities and Responsibilities," mimeo., March 25, 1993.
11. Baysinger, Erickson, interviews. McNulty, *Whooping Crane*.
12. Rachel Carson, *Silent Spring* (Boston: Houghton Mifflin, 1962). Surprisingly, today, after nearly thirty years, the evidence overwhelmingly suggests that DDT is not dangerous to wildlife. See Gregg Easterbrook, *A Moment on the Earth* (New York: Viking, 1995), pp. 79–85; Dennis T. Avery, *Saving the Planet with Pesticides and Plastic: The Environmental Triumph of High-Yield Farming* (Indianapolis: Hudson Institute, 1995); McNulty, *Whooping Crane*.
13. It was a Mundt aid, Rod Kreger, who, according to Erickson, brought the whooper's plight to the senator's attention. See also Whooping Crane Recovery Team, *Whooping Crane Recovery Plan, 1986* (Albuquerque: U.S. Department of Interior, Fish and Wildlife Service, 1986). See also Yaffee, *Prohibitive Policy*, p. 190, n. 12, and pp. 27–28, 192.
14. Committee on Rare and Endangered Wildlife Species, Bureau of Sport Fisheries and Wildlife, *Rare and Endangered Fish and Wildlife of the United States* (Washington, D.C.: Government Printing Office, 1964).

15. P.L. 89-669, 89th Cong., H.R. 9224, October 15, 1966. Michael J. Bean, *The Evolution of National Wildlife Law*, rev. ed. (New York: Praeger, 1983); Yaffee, *Prohibitive Policy*, pp. 39–41; Baysinger, interview.

16. Baysinger, interview; Bean, *Evolution*, p. 22, n. 59.

17. See Bean, *Evolution*.

18. Alston Chase, *Playing God in Yellowstone* (New York: Atlantic Monthly Press, 1986), esp. chap. 10; H. Duane Hampton, *How the U.S. Cavalry Saved Our National Parks* (Bloomington: Indiana University Press, 1972).

19. Chase, *Playing God*, chap. 10.

20. Bean, *Evolution*, pp. 272–277; Yaffee, *Prohibitive Policy*, p. 192, n. 27.

21. Bean, *Evolution*; Yaffee, *Prohibitive Policy*.

22. Committee on Rare and Endangered Wildlife Species, *Rare and Endangered Fish and Wildlife of the United States*; Lewis G. Regenstein, "A History of the Endangered Species Act of 1973, and an Analysis of Its History; Strengths and Weaknesses; Administration; Probable Future Effectiveness," mimeo., December 1974.

23. Regenstein, "A History of the Endangered Species Act," Lewis Regenstein, *The Politics of Extinction: The Shocking Story of the World's Endangered Wildlife* (New York: Macmillan, 1975).

24. Paul R. Ehrlich, *The Population Bomb* (New York: Ballantine Books, 1968), pp. 75–76 and 124.

25. Carson, *Silent Spring*, p. 110; Bill McKibben, *The End of Nature* (New York: Random House, 1989); Fairfield Osborn, *Our Plundered Planet* (New York: Pyramid Books, 1948). On the inaccuracy of these predictions, see Gregg Easterbrook, *A Moment on the Earth* (New York: Viking, 1995).

26. Regenstein, "A History of the Endangered Species Act"; Yaffee, *Prohibitive Policy*, p. 47; Manning, *Dispute Processing*; David Zwick, "Water Pollution," in *Nixon and the Environment: The Politics of Devastation*, ed. James Rathlesberger (New York: Village Voice Books, 1972); Stephen Fox, *John Muir and His Legacy: The American Conservation Movement* (Boston: Little, Brown, 1981), chap. 9; Susan R. Schrepfer, *Fight to Save the Redwoods* (Madison: University of Wisconsin Press, 1980), chap. 9. This rising environmental concern was directly connected to peace issues. Schrepfer, for example, notes: "Behind the activism of the 1960s was the shadow of violence: the bomb, assassination, and war. . . . In the 1978 Resources for the Future Survey, 27 percent of the club's members testified to having participated in antiwar activities" (pp. 165–166). An excellent summary of public opinion concerning the environment during the mid-1960s is provided in Cecil Trop and Leslie L. Roose, Jr., "Public Opinion and the Environment," in Leslie L. Roose, Jr., *The Politics of Ecosuicide* (New York: Holt, Rinehart and Winston, 1971).

27. P.L. 91-135, 91st Cong., H.R. 11363, December 5, 1969; Regenstein, "A History of the Endangered Species Act"; Yaffee, *Prohibitive Policy*; Bean, *Evolution*, pp. 321–324.

28. Baysinger, interview; Regenstein, "A History of the Endangered Species Act."

29. Regenstein, "A History of the Endangered Species Act."

30. Ibid.; Paul and Anne Ehrlich, *Extinction* (New York: Ballantine, 1981).

31. Farley Mowat, *A Whale for the Killing* (Boston: Atlantic Monthly Press, 1972).

32. Donella H. Meadows et al., *The Limits to Growth* (New York: Signet, 1972). Countless other books stressing doom and protest appeared during this period. See, for example, Wesley Marx, *The Frail Ocean* (New York:

Ballantine, 1967); Garrett deBell, ed., *The Environmental Handbook: Prepared for the First National Environmental Teach-In, April 22, 1970* (New York: Ballantine, 1970); Roose, *The Politics of Ecosuicide*. Also, several books which had appeared much earlier were reissued, becoming bestsellers. See, for example, Aldo Leopold, *A Sand County Almanac* (New York: Ballantine, 1966), which first appeared in 1949, and Fairfield Osborn, *Our Plundered Planet* (New York: Pyramid Books, 1968), which was first published in 1948. Osborn was a founding member of the Save the Redwoods League.

33. Yaffee, *Prohibitive Policy*, p. 48; Bean, *Evolution*; Samuel P. Hays, *Beauty, Health, and Permanence: Environmental Politics in the United States, 1955–1985* (Cambridge: Cambridge University Press, 1987).

34. Baysinger, interview; Fund for Animals, press release, "Department of Interior Violates Endangered Species Act and Jeopardizes Future Survival of Tigers, Cheetahs, Leopards, and Other Spotted Cats," n.d. (late 1971); Lewis Regenstein, "Can Spotted Cats Survive Despite the Fur Industry?" *Washington Post*, August 9, 1971. This article had great influence on Congress. See Congressman Dingell's comments in Subcommittee on Fisheries and Wildlife Conservation, "Hawks, Owls, and Eagles," September 20 and 24, 1971, p. 113.

35. This account is drawn from interviews with Baysinger, Regenstein, and Lee Talbot.

36. Bean, *Evolution*; Yaffee, *Prohibitive Policy*; Manning, *Dispute Processing*.

37. Yaffee, *Prohibitive Policy*; Library of Congress, *A Legislative History of the Endangered Species Act of 1973*.

38. Library of Congress, *A Legislative History of the Endangered Species Act of 1973*.

39. Ibid.

40. Ibid.; Manning, *Dispute Resolution*; Yaffee, *Prohibitive Policy*.

41. Library of Congress, *A Legislative History of the Endangered Species Act of 1973*; Manning, *Dispute Resolution*; Yaffee, *Prohibitive Policy*.

42. Manning, *Dispute Resolution*; Yaffee, *Prohibitive Policy*.

CHAPTER 8. A LAW FOR ALL SEASONS

1. Library of Congress, *A Legislative History of the Endangered Species Act of 1973, as Amended in 1976, 1977, 1978, and 1980*, February 1982, p. 374.

2. Ibid., p. 145.

3. Ibid., pp. 356–357.

4. See esp. Barry Commoner, *The Closing Circle* (New York: Bantam, 1971), chap. 2.

5. Quoted in Frank N. Egerton, "Changing Concepts of the Balance of Nature," *Quarterly Review of Biology* 48 (June 1973).

6. Ibid.; Peter J. Bowler, *The Norton History of Environmental Science* (New York: W. W. Norton, 1992), pp. 14, 144, 170–173.

7. Samuel Willard, *A Compleat Body of Divinity* (1726), quoted in Perry Miller, *The New England Mind* (Cambridge, Mass.: Harvard University Press, 1954), pp. 225–226.

8. Charles Lyell, *Principles of Geology*, 3 vols. (London: John Murray, 1830–1833); Bowler, *Norton History*; Egerton, "Changing Concepts"; Joel B. Hagen, *An Entangled Bank* (New Brunswick, N.J.: Rutgers University Press, 1992).

9. Hagen, *Entangled Bank*, p. 1; Bowler, *Norton History*, pp. 366–367. See also W. A. Berggren and John A. van Couvering, eds., *Catastrophes and Earth History: The New Uniformitarianism* (Princeton: Princeton University Press, 1984). For American thinking on the question of balance at this time, see Frank N. Egerton, "Ecological Studies and Observations before 1900," in *Issues and Ideas in America*, ed. Benjamin J. Taylor and Thurman J. White (Norman: University of Oklahoma Press, 1976).

10. Bowler, *Norton History*, p. 333; Ernst Haeckel, *Generelle Morphologie der Organismen: Algemeine Grundzuge der organischen Formen-Wissenschaft, mechanisch begrundet durch die von Charles Darwin reformierte Descendenz-Theorie* (Berlin: Reimber, 1866); Susan L. Flader, *Thinking Life a Mountain* (Lincoln: University of Nebraska Press, 1974), p. 5. See also Donald Worster, *Nature's Economy: A History of Ecological Ideas* (Cambridge: Cambridge University Press, 1977), pp. 191ff.

11. Arthur O. Lovejoy, *The Revolt against Dualism* (La Salle, Ill.: Open Court, 1960); Bowler, *Norton History*, pp. 310ff.; Herbert Spencer, *The Data of Ethics* (New York: D. Appleton, 1880).

12. Ernst Mayr, *The Growth of Biological Thought* (Cambridge, Mass.: Harvard University Press, 1982), p. 121; see also Bowler, *Norton History*.

13. Frederic E. Clements, *Plant Succession: An Analysis of the Development of Vegetation* (Washington, D.C.: Carnegie Institution, 1916); Bowler, *Norton History*, pp. 374–376; 519–526; Frank Benjamin Golley, *A History of the Ecosystem Concept in Ecology: More Than the Sum of the Parts* (New Haven: Yale University Press, 1993).

14. Arthur G. Tansley, "The Use and Abuse of Vegetational Concepts and Terms," *Ecology* 16, no. 3 (1935).

15. Golley, *Ecosystem Concept in Ecology*.

16. Robert P. McIntosh, "Ecology since 1900," in Taylor and White, *Issues and Ideas*.

17. Commoner, *The Closing Circle*, chap. 2; J. E. Lovelock, *Gaia: A New Look at Life on Earth* (Oxford: Oxford University Press, 1987).

18. Steve Heims, "Encounter of Behavioral Sciences with New Machine-Organism Analogies in the 1940s," *Journal of the History of the Behavioral Sciences* 11 (1976); Donna J. Harawa, "The High Cost of Information in Sociobology of Communication Systems," *Philosophical Forum* 13 (1981–82); Peter J. Taylor, "Technocratic Optimism, H. T. Odum, and the Partial Transformation of Ecological Metaphor after World War II," *Journal of the History of Biology* 21 (1988).

19. G. Evelyn Hutchinson, "Homage to Santa Rosalia, or, Why Are There So Many Kinds of Animals?," presidential address to the American Society of Naturalists, Washington, D.C., December 30, 1958. See also Walter David Hellman, "Norbert Wiener and the Growth of Negative Feedback in Scientific Explanation, with a Proposed Research Program of 'Cybernetic Analysis'" (Ph.D. diss., Oregon State University, 1982); G. Evelyn Hutchinson, *The Kindly Fruits of the Earth: Recollections of an Embryo Ecologist* (New Haven: Yale University Press, 1979); G. Evelyn Hutchinson, "Circular Causal Systems in Ecology," *Annals of the New York Academy of Sciences* 50 (1948).

20. In other words, these research efforts all assumed the existence of — and at the outset searched for — ecosystems. And when they did not find things "in balance," they did not take this as disconfirming their hypothesis that balance does not exist in nature. Instead, they took it as evidence that the "ecosystems" had been "disturbed." As examples of these types of searches, see Lovelock, *Gaia*; and Raymond L. Lindeman, "The Trophic-Dynamic Aspect of Ecology," *Ecology* 23, no. 4 (1942).

21. Robert H. MacArthur, "Fluctuations of Animal Populations and a Measure of Community Stability," *Ecology* 36 (1955); Robert H. MacArthur, "Patterns of Species Diversity," *Biological Review* 40 (1965). See also Robert H. MacArthur and Edward O. Wilson, *Theory of Island Biogeography* (Princeton: Princeton University Press, 1967); Robert H. MacArthur, *Geographical Ecology: Patterns in Distribution of Species* (New York: Harper and Row, 1972). See also Robert M. May, *Stability and Complexity in Model Ecosystems* (Princeton: Princeton University Press, 1974).

22. Golley, *History of the Ecosystem Concept*, pp. 57–59.

23. Eugene Odum, "The Strategy of Ecosystem Development," *Science* 164 (1969). See also Lindeman, "The Trophic-Dynamic Aspect of Ecology;" Eugene Odum, *Fundamentals of Ecology* (Philadelphia: W. B. Saunders, 1953); Eugene Odum, "Historical Review of the Concepts of Energy Flow in Ecosystems," *American Zoologist* 8 (1968).

24. Golley, *History of the Ecosystem Concept*; Odum quoted from Hagen, *Entangled Bank*, p. 102.

25. Vincent Schultz and Alfred W. Kleinert, Jr., eds., *Radioecology: Proceedings of the First National Symposium on Radioecology, Held at Colorado State University, Fort Collins, Colorado, September 10–15, 1961* (New York: Reinhold, 1963); F. Ward Whicker and Vincent Schultz, *Radioecology: Nuclear Energy and the Environment*, 2 vols. (Boca Raton, Fla.: CRE Press, 1982); John N. Wolfe, Richard T. Wareham, and Herbert T. Scofield, "Micro-Climate and Macro-Climate of Neotoma, a Small Valley in Central Ohio," *Ohio Biological Survey Bulletin 41* 8, no. 1 (1949).

26. Golley, *History of the Ecosystem Concept*.

27. Alston Chase, "The Development of Environmental Science," a paper commissioned by Sigma Xi, the Scientific Research Society, 1991.

28. Lovelock, *Gaia*.

29. Hagen, *Entangled Bank*, chap. 9.

30. McIntosh, "Ecology since 1900"; Daniel B. Botkin and Matthew J. Sobel, "Stability in Time-Varying Ecosystems," *American Naturalist* 109, no. 970 (November–December 1975); Daniel B. Botkin, *Discordant Harmonies* (Oxford: Oxford University Press, 1990); K. E. F. Watt, "Use of Mathematics in Population Ecology," *Annual Review of Entomology* 7 (1962).

31. Bowler, *Norton History*, p. 536.

32. Ibid., p. 538.

33. Bowler, *Norton History*, pp. 529ff.; Hagen, *Entangled Bank*, pp. 147–151, 162–163. Indeed, the number of community ecologists who remained skeptical of the ecosystem idea was not only large but growing. See Robert H. Whittaker, *Communities and Ecosystems* (New York: Macmillan, 1975); Robert P. McIntosh, "Ecology since 1900"; Charles E. King and Peter S. Dawson, eds., *Population Biology: Retrospect and Prospect* (New York: Columbia University Press, 1983); Donald R. Strong, Jr., et al., *Ecological Communities: Conceptual Issues and the Evidence* (Princeton: Princeton University Press, 1984); P. S. White and S. T. A. Pickett, *The Ecology of Natural Disturbance and Patch Dynamics: An Introduction* (Orlando, Fla.: Academic Press, 1985); Donald Worster, *The Wealth of Nature* (Oxford: Oxford University Press, 1993), chap. 13; Robert P. McIntosh, "Succession and Ecological Theory," in *Forest Succession: Concepts and Applications*, ed. Darrell C. West, Herman H. Shugart, Daniel B. Botkin (Heidelberg: Springer-Verlag, 1992); Daniel B. Botkin, *Discordant Harmonies* (Oxford: Oxford University Press, 1990); George W. Salt, ed., *Ecology and Evolutionary Biology* (Chicago: University of Chicago Press, 1984).

34. Hagen, *Entangled Bank*, p. 163; Bowler, *Norton History*, p. 539.

35. Commoner, *Closing Circle*, p. 187.
36. Ibid., pp. 187–188.
37. Ibid., pp. 29–30.
38. Ibid., pp. 29, 33–35.
39. Ibid., p 37.

CHAPTER 9. A NEW METAPHOR FOR NATURE

1. See *The Dialogues of Plato*, ed. B. Jowett, 2 vols. (New York: Random House, 1937). This is a precise paraphrase of a conversation the author had with Lee M. Talbot, co-author of the Endangered Species Act.
2. Several architects and early proponents of the Endangered Species Act whom I interviewed gave these kinds of answers. When I asked Earl Baysinger what was the purpose of the act, he replied, "In my thirty-five years in Washington, no one has ever asked that question."
3. For an example of how persistent are the ambiguities and implied values of the ecosystem concept, see "Upper Columbia River Basin Purpose and Need Summary Working Draft," a 1995 administration ecosystem planning document, which alternately defines its goals as "forest ecosystem health" and "resiliency," which in turn it defines as "biological integrity."
4. Aldo Leopold, *A Sand County Almanac* (Oxford: Oxford University Press, 1949). The expression remained very popular among environmentalists. See Cameron La Follette, "Saving All the Pieces: Old Growth Forest in Oregon," Oregon Student Public Interest Research Group, March 1979; Rocky Barker, *Saving All the Parts* (Washington, D.C.: Island Press, 1993).
5. Robert P. McIntosh, "Ecology since 1900," in *Issues and Ideas in America*, ed. Benjamin J. Taylor and Thurman J. White (Norman: University of Oklahoma Press, 1976).
6. Daniel B. Botkin, *Discordant Harmonies* (Oxford: Oxford University Press, 1990), p. 33.
7. E. C. Pielou, *After the Ice Age: The Return of Life to Glaciated North America* (Chicago: University of Chicago Press, 1991); Charles A. Reed, "Extinction of Mammalian Megafauna in the Old World Late Quaternary," *BioScience* 20, no. 5 (1970); Charles A. Reed, "They Never Found the Ark," *Ecology* 50, no. 2 (Spring 1969); B. Kurten and E. Anderson, *Pleistocene Mammals of North America* (New York: Columbia University Press, 1980); S. D. Webb, "Ten Million Years of Mammal Extinctions in North America," in *Quaternary Extinctions*, ed. P. S. Martin and R. G. Klein (Tucson: University of Arizona Press, 1984); P. S. Martin, "Prehistoric Overkill: The Global Model," in Martin and Klein, *Quaternary Extinctions*; P. S. Martin, "The Discovery of America," *Science* 179 (March 1973); P. S. Martin and H. E. Wright, Jr., *Pleistocene Extinctions: The Search for a Cause* (New Haven: Yale University Press, 1967); Richard A. Kerr, "How Ice Age Climate Got the Shakes," *Science*, May 14, 1993; E. J. Butler and F. Hoyle, "On the Effects of a Sudden Change in the Albedo of the Earth," *Astrophysics and Space Sciences* 60 (1979); P. S. White and S. T. A. Pickett, *The Ecology of Natural Disturbance and Patch Dynamics: An Introduction* (Orlando, Fla.: Academic Press, 1985); Donald Worster, *The Wealth of Nature* (Oxford: Oxford University Press, 1993), chap. 13.
8. Pielou, *After the Ice Age*, pp. 186–189.
9. Ibid.; P. S. Martin, "The Pattern and Meaning of Holarctic Mammoth Ex-

tinction," in *Paleoecology of Beringia*, ed. D. M. Hopkins et al. (New York: Academic Press, 1982); E. Lucy Braun, *Deciduous Forests of Eastern North America* (New York: Free Press, 1950); Hugh M. Raup, "Trends in the Development of Geographic Botany," *Annals of the Association of American Geographers* 32, no. 4 (December 1942); Chadwick Dearing Oliver, "Forest Development in North America Following Major Disturbances," *Forest Ecology and Management* 3 (1980–81); Cathy Whitlock, "Vegetational and Climatic History of the Pacific Northwest during the Last Twenty Thousand Years: Implications for Understanding Present-Day Biodiversity," *Northwest Environmental Journal* 8, no. 1 (1992); Margaret Bryan Davis, "Quaternary History and the Stability of Forest Communities," in *Forest Succession: Concepts and Application*, ed. Darrell C. West, Herman H. Shugart, and Daniel B. Botkin (Heidelberg: Springer-Verlag, 1992).

10. Botkin, *Discordant Harmonies*, pp. 58–59.

11. Ibid., p. 45.

12. Ibid., pp. 15–20.

13. As an example of this "static" thinking in science and how it leads directly to land planning of the kind mandated by the Endangered Species Act, see Rexford Daubenmire, "The Roots of a Concept" and "The Scientific Basis for a Classification System in Land-Use Allocation," papers presented at the symposium "Land Classifications Based on Vegetation: Applications for Resource Management," Moscow, Idaho, November 17–19, 1987.

14. Library of Congress, *A Legislative History of the Endangered Species Act of 1973, as Amended in 1976, 1977, 1978, and 1980*, February 1982, p. 144.

15. McIntosh, "Ecology since 1900." See also Robert P. McIntosh, "Succession and Ecological Theory," in West, Shugart, and Botkin, *Forest Succession*.

16. Earl Baysinger, interview; Anne E. Magurran, *Ecological Diversity and Its Measurement* (Princeton: Princeton University Press, 1988), p. 1. For an examination of some of the confusions concern for biodiversity engenders, see A. Ross Kiester, "Natural Kinds, Natural History, and Ecology," *Synthese* 43 (1980).

17. Magurran, *Ecological Diversity*; Brian H. Walker, "Biodiversity and Ecological Redundancy," *Conservation Biology* 6, no. 1 (March 1992).

18. Ibid.; P. B. Medawar and J. S. Medawar, *Aristotle to Zoos: A Philosophical Dictionary of Biology* (Cambridge, Mass.: Harvard University Press, 1983).

19. The "bottleneck" idea is based on studies of the mitochondrial gene and is highly controversial. But the notion that humans are genetically very similar is not. See Ashley Montague, ed., *The Concept of Race* (Glencoe, Ill.: Free Press, 1964).

20. Paul R. Ehrlich and Richard W. Holm, "A Biological View of Race," in Montague, *The Concept of Race*, pp. 153, 155, and 177–178.

21. Richard Hartshorne, "The Nature of Geography: A Critical Survey of Current Thought in Light of the Past," *Annals of the Association of American Geographers* 29 (1939); Hugh M. Raup, "Trends in the Development of Geographic Botany"; J. Nicholas Entrikin and Stanley D. Brun, *Reflections on Richard Hartshorne's "The Nature of Geography"* (Washington, D.C.: Association of American Geographers, 1989).

22. H. G. Andrewartha and L. C. Birch, *The Distribution and Abundance of Animals* (Chicago: University of Chicago Press, 1954), p. 251; Faith McNulty, *The Whooping Crane* (New York: E. P. Dutton, 1966); David M. Raup, "Biological Extinction in Earth History," *Science*, March 28, 1986.

23. L. David Mech, *The Wolf* (New York: Natural History Press, 1970); Durward L. Allen, *Wolves of Minong* (Boston: Houghton Mifflin, 1979).

24. Pielou, *After the Ice Age*, chap. 7.
25. All claims suggesting that massive extinctions are imminent or under way are based on calculations (using ecosystem habitat models), not on empirical evidence — a point conceded even by those making these claims, such as Jared Diamond, Edward O. Wilson, and David Ehrenfeld. See Jared Diamond, "World of the Living Dead," *Natural History* (September 1991); Edward O. Wilson, ed., *Biodiversity* (Washington, D.C.: National Academy Press, 1988); T. C. Whitmore and J. A. Sayer, eds., *Tropical Deforestation and Species Extinction* (New York: Chapman and Hall, 1992); Julian L. Simon and Aaron Wildavsky, "Assessing the Empirical Basis of the 'Biodiversity Crisis,'" Competitive Enterprise Institute Environmental Studies Program, May 1993.
26. Steven Lewis Yaffee, *Prohibitive Policy: Implementing the Endangered Species Act* (Cambridge, Mass.: MIT Press, 1982), p. 18; Library of Congress, *Legislative History*, p. 141; Pielou, *After the Ice Age*, pp. 252ff.; Diamond, "Living Dead."
27. See definition of "critical habitat" in Endangered Species Act of 1973, sec. 3, 5(A), (i) and (ii).
28. Alston Chase, *Playing God in Yellowstone* (New York: Atlantic Monthly Press, 1986); Edwin Dobb, "Cultivating Nature," *The Sciences* (January–February 1992); and Daniel Botkin, *Discordant Harmonies*.
29. Aldo Leopold, speech at dedication ceremony for the University of Wisconsin arboretum, 1934.
30. Stephen Fox, *John Muir and His Legacy: The American Conservation Movement* (Boston: Little, Brown, 1981), pp. 358ff.
31. A. S. Leopold et al., "Wildlife Management in the National Parks," Report of the Advisory Board on Wildlife Management to Secretary of the Interior Udall, March 4, 1963.
32. Department of the Interior, National Park Service, *Administrative Policies for Natural Areas of the National Park System* (Washington, D.C.: Government Printing Office, 1968).
33. Chase, *Playing God*, chaps. 5–6; Charles E. Kay, "Too Many Elk in Yellowstone?," *Western Wildlands* 13, no. 3 (1987).
34. Jared Diamond, "Must We Shoot Deer to Save Nature?," *Natural History* (August 1992).
35. Lynn White, Jr., "The Historical Roots of Our Ecologic Crisis," *Science*, March 10, 1967, pp. 1203–1207.
36. This tradeoff is especially acute when it seems to pit human health against "biodiversity." For example, in 1991 several communities, on the advice of the EPA, stopped chlorinating drinking water. Shortly afterward a cholera epidemic spread to twenty-one countries, infecting a million people and causing over 8,500 deaths. See Carlyle Guerra de Macedo, Director, Pan American Health Organization, to William K. Reilly, Administrator, U.S. Environmental Protection Agency, May 1, 1991.
37. Botkin, *Discordant Harmonies*, pp. 68ff.; Charles C. Mann and Mark L. Plummer, "The Butterfly Problem," *Atlantic* (January 1992); Yaffee, *Prohibitive Policy*.
38. Library of Congress, *Legislative History*, p. 144.
39. Baysinger, interview.
40. Theodore Roszak, *Where the Wasteland Ends: Politics and Transformation in Postindustrial Society* (New York: Doubleday, 1972), p. 367.
41. Loren Eiseley, *The Unexpected Universe* (New York: Harcourt Brace Jovanovich, 1964), pp. 152–153.

42. Paul Sears, "The Steady State: Physical Law and Moral Choice," in *The Subversive Science*, ed. Paul Shepard and Daniel McKinley (Boston: Houghton Mifflin, 1969); Ian L. McHarg, "Values, Process, and Form," in *The Ecological Conscience: Values for Survival*, ed. Robert Disch (Englewood Cliffs, N.J.: Prentice-Hall, 1970); Thomas B. Colwell, Jr., "The Balance of Nature: A Ground for Human Values," *Main Currents in Modern Thought* 26, no. 2 (November–December 1969).

43. Donella H. Meadows et al., *The Limits to Growth* (New York: Signet, 1972), pp. 163ff.; Sigurd F. Olson, *Reflections from the North Country* (New York: Alfred A. Knopf, 1976), p. 136.

44. For a portrait of this despair, see Alvin Toffler, "Coda: Yearnings for a New Dark Age," in *Powershift* (New York: Bantam, 1990). For the Newtonian perspective, see H. G. Alexander, ed., *The Leibniz-Clarke Correspondence, with Extracts from Newton's Principia and Opticks* (Manchester: Manchester University Press, 1956). For an overview of earlier conceptions of nature, see John D. Barrow and Frank J. Tipler, *The Anthropic Cosmological Principle* (Oxford: Oxford University Press, 1986), chap. 2, "Design Arguments."

45. Charles Darwin, *The Origin of Species by Means of Natural Selection: or, The Preservation of Favoured Races in the Struggle for Life* (New York: Modern Library, 1936); see also Matt Cartmill, *A View to a Death in the Morning* (Cambridge, Mass.: Harvard University Press, 1993).

46. Quoted in Barrow and Tipler, *The Anthropic Cosmological Principle*, p. 31.

CHAPTER IO. THE BIRTH OF BIOCENTRISM

1. This account is based on interviews with Bill Devall in 1986, 1987, and 1994.

2. Arne Naess, "The Shallow and the Deep: Long-Range Ecology Movements: A Summary," *Inquiry* 16 (1973). See also Bill Devall and George Sessions, *Deep Ecology* (Salt Lake City: Peregrine Smith, 1985); Arne Naess, *Ecology, Community, and Lifestyle: Outline of an Ecosophy*, trans. David Rothenberg (Cambridge: Cambridge University Press, 1989).

3. According to Devall, George Sessions was walking down the same path at the same time. See Bill Devall, "Reformist Environmentalism," *Humboldt Journal of Social Relations* 6, no. 2 (1979); George Sessions, "Anthropocentrism and the Environmental Crisis," *Humboldt Journal of Social Relations* 2, no. 1 (1974); Bill Devall, "The Deep Ecology Movement," *Natural Resources Journal* 20 (Spring 1980); George Sessions, "A Short Informal Summary of My Philosophical Development as Pertains to the Deep Ecology Movement," mimeo., January 21, 1986. See also Michael Tobias, ed., *Deep Ecology* (San Diego: Avant Books, 1984).

4. See Devall and Sessions, "Biocentric Equality," in *Deep Ecology*, p. 67; Aldo Leopold, *Sand County Almanac* (Oxford: Oxford University Press, 1949), p. 214.

5. Hegel's theory of the state is developed in G. W. F. Hegel, *Hegel's Philosophy of Right*, trans. T. M. Knox (Oxford: Oxford University Press, 1942). See also "Organicism," pt. 2, sec. 2, in Carl Cohen, ed., *Communism, Socialism, and Democracy* (New York: Random House, 1962), pp. 264ff.; G. W. F. Hegel, *The Philosophy of History*, trans. J. Sibree (New York: Dover, 1956); K. R. Popper, *The Open Society and Its Enemies*, vol. 2, *The High Tide of Prophecy: Hegel and Marx* (London: Routledge and Kegan Paul, 1945); Wal-

ter Stace, *The Philosophy of Hegel* (New York: Dover, 1955); Bernard Bosan-
quet, *The Philosophical Theory of the State* (London: Macmillan, 1958).

6. *Hegel's Philosophy of Right*, sec. 258.

7. Stace, *Hegel*, p. 425; Hegel, *Philosophy of History*, p. 452.

8. See G. R. G. Mure, *The Philosophy of Hegel* (London: Oxford University
Press, 1965); J. N. Findlay, *Hegel: A Reexamination* (New York: Collier
Books, 1958).

9. Benito Mussolini, "The Doctrine of Fascism," in *The Social and Political
Doctrines of Contemporary Europe*, ed. Michael Oakeshott (Cambridge:
Cambridge University Press, 1939); Alfredo Rocco, "The Political Doctrine
of Fascism," in *Communism, Fascism, and Democracy*, ed. Carl Cohen
(New York: Random House, 1962), pp. 336, 343.

10. Friedrich Engels, *Ludwig Feuerbach and the End of Classical German Philosophy*, reprinted from Karl Marx and Friedrich Engels, *Basic Writings on
Politics and Philosophy*, ed. L. S. Feuer (New York: Anchor Books, 1959), p.
86. See also Karl Marx, *Critique of Hegel's "Philosophy of Right,"* trans. An-
nette Jolin and Joseph O'Malley, ed. Joseph O'Malley (Cambridge: Cambridge University Press, 1970).

11. Ernst Haeckel, *Generelle Morphologie der Organismen: Algemeine Grundzuge der organischen Formen-Wissenschaft, mechanisch begrundet durch
die von Charles Darwin reformierte Descendenz-Theorie* (Berlin: Reimber,
1866); Donald Worster, *Nature's Economy: A History of Ecological Ideas*
(Cambridge: Cambridge University Press, 1977), pp. 191ff.

12. Daniel Gasman, *The Scientific Origins of National Socialism* (New York:
American Elsevier, 1971), p. 23.

13. Ibid., pp. 20–23.

14. Anna Bramwell, *Ecology in the Twentieth Century* (New Haven: Yale University Press, 1989), pp. 175, 178. See also George L. Mosse, *The Crisis of
German Ideology: Intellectual Origins of the Third Reich* (New York:
Schocken Books, 1981); George L. Mosse, *Toward the Final Solution: A History of European Racism* (New York: Harper and Row, 1978).

15. On the eugenics of the Monist League, see Gasman, *Scientific Origins*, pp.
90–98. See also Popper, *The Open Society*, vol. 2. In 1900, Popper writes, the
Monist League conducted an essay competition whose subject was: "What
can we learn from the principles of Darwinism in respect of the internal and
political development of the state?" First prize was awarded to "a voluminous racialist work by W. Schallmeyer, who thus became the grandfather of
racial biology." Schallmayer's essay was titled "Heredity and Selection in
the Life of the Nations." "Hegel + Haeckel," Popper therefore concluded, "is
the formula of modern racialism" (p. 61).

16. Popper, *The Open Society*, 2:61; Bramwell, *Ecology*, p. 150; Robert J. Lifton,
The Nazi Doctors: Medical Killing and the Psychology of Genocide (New
York: Basic Books, 1986), p. 125; Gasman, *Scientific Origins*, pp. xiv, 150.
The German historian H. Schnadelbach wrote, "The general biologism in
the theory of culture . . . culminated in National Socialism." See H. Schnadelbach, *Philosophy in Germany: 1831–1984* (Cambridge: Cambridge University Press, 1984), p. 149.

17. Bramwell, *Ecology*, p. 195; Robert A. Pois, *National Socialism and the Religion of Nature* (New York: St. Martin's, 1986), pp. 30, 38.

18. Hess and Best quoted in Lifton, *The Nazi Doctors*, pp. 31, 129, 153, and
437–438; Bramwell, *Ecology*, pp. 196ff.

19. Martin Heidegger, "What Are Poets For?," in *Poetry, Language, Thought*
(New York: Harper and Row, 1971), pp. 114–15. On Heidegger's environ-

mentalism, see Gunther Neske and Emil Kettering, *Martin Heidegger and National Socialism*, trans. Karsten Harries and Joachim Neugroschelm (New York: Paragon House, 1990); Victor Farias, *Heidegger and Nazism* (Philadelphia: Temple University Press, 1987). On the ecological influences of the Nazis' "Back to the Land" movement, see Bramwell, *Ecology*, pp. 195ff.

20. Bramwell, *Ecology*; Mosse, *Crisis of German Ideology*. Among Nazi concerns was an obsession with "native," or *heimish*, plants and animals. In this respect German nature policy during the Third Reich was very similar to U.S. policy today, which dictates expenditures of billions of dollars to save indigenous plants and animals, while agencies such as the National Park Service spend tens of millions attempting to eradicate "exotic" species. For the Nazi fascination with native flora and fauna, see Gert Groening and Joachim Wolschke-Bulmahn, "Some Notes on the Mania for Native Plants in Germany," *Landscape Journal* 11, no. 2 (Fall 1992); Gert Groening and Joachim Wolschke-Bulmahn, "1 September 1939: Der Uberfall auf Polen als Ausgangspunkt 'totaler' Landespflege," *RaumPlanung* 46–47 (1989); Joachim Wolschke-Bulmahn, "Ethics and Morality: Questions in the History of Garden and Landscape Design," *Journal of Garden History* 14, no. 3 (July–September 1994); Joachim Wolschke-Bulmahn, *Biodynamischer Gartenbau, Landschaftsarchitekture und Nationalsozialismus*, address to the German Studies Association Conference, Minneapolis, October 1–4, 1992; Joachim Wolschke-Bulmahn, "Die Asthetisierung der Landschaft — Zum Einfluss der burgerlichen Jugendbewegung auf die Landespflege," *Natur und Landschaft* 66, no. 10 (1991); Joachim Wolschke-Bulmahn, "'The Peculiar Garden' — the Advent and the Destruction of Modernism in German Garden Design," *Proceedings of the Garden Conservancy Symposium*, March 12, 1993.

21. Bramwell, *Ecology*, pp. 195ff.

22. Indeed, in truth, history never repeats itself.

23. Bramwell, *Ecology*, p. 11; Gasman, interview.

24. Pois, *National Socialism*, p. 41. Hitler was influenced by Alfred Rosenberg, whose work *Der Mythus des 20. Jahrhunderts* contained an attack on Judeo-Christian dualism. "Belief in the Judaeo-Christian dualism," wrote Rosenberg, "could only lead to a situation in which the 'natural-grown Being of nature' would be crippled."

25. European political parties, for example, are far more sharply divided by ideology than American ones.

26. Bramwell, *Ecology*, pp. 11, 237ff.

27. See, esp. Popper, *The Open Society*.

28. Arthur G. Tansley, "The Use and Abuse of Vegetational Concepts and Terms," *Ecology* 16, no. 3 (1935).

29. Devall and Sessions, *Deep Ecology*, p. 67.

30. Bill Devall, "Deep Ecology and Its Critics," *Earth First! Journal* 8, no. 2 (December 22, 1987).

31. Frank Golley, *A History of the Ecosystem Concept in Ecology* (New Haven: Yale University Press, 1993), p. 175.

32. Lynn White, Jr., "The Historical Roots of Our Ecologic Crisis," *Science*, March 10, 1967.

33. See, e.g., Donald Worster, *Rivers of Empire* (New York: Pantheon, 1985).

34. Bill Devall, "New Age and Deep Ecology: Contrasting Paradigms," mimeo., 1981; Bill Devall, "Muir Redux: From Conservation to Ecology," 1982. Devall notes that "more and more intellectuals were questioning the premises

of humanism"; see Bill Devall, "John Muir and His Legacy," *Humboldt Journal of Social Relations* 9, no. 1 (Fall–Winter 1981–82).

35. See Alston Chase, *Playing God in Yellowstone* (New York: Atlantic Monthly Press, 1986), chap. 19; for an account of bioregionalism, see Kirkpatrick Sale, *Dwellers in the Land* (San Francisco: Sierra Club Books, 1985).

36. This account is based on interviews with several members of Die Grünen, including Carl Amery, Joachim Vielhauer, Joshka Fischer, Walter Ebermann, and Hans-Georg Behr. See also Alston Chase, "The Great, Green Deep-Ecology Revolution," *Rolling Stone Magazine*, April 23, 1987; Alston Chase, "It's Not Easy Being Green," *American Way*, April 15, 1990; Charlene Spretnak and Fritjof Capra, *Green Politics* (Santa Fe: Bear and Company, 1984); Sara Parkin, *Green Parties: An International Guide* (London: Heretic Books, 1989); Rudolf Bahro, *From Red to Green* (London: Verso Books, 1984).

37. Interviews with Charlene Spretnak, Fritjof Capra, and others. See Spretnak and Capra, *Green Politics*, chap. 2; Jonathon Porritt, *Seeing Green: The Politics of Ecology Explained* (Oxford: Basil Blackwell, 1984).

38. George Sessions, *Ecophilosophy* 2 (May 1979).

39. Paul W. Taylor, "The Ethics of Respect for Nature," *Environmental Ethics* 3, no. 3 (Fall 1981). See also Paul W. Taylor, "In Defense of Biocentrism," *Environmental Ethics* 5 (Fall 1983); Paul W. Taylor, *Respect for Nature: A Theory of Environmental Ethics* (Princeton: Princeton University Press, 1986). Today the term *ecocentrism* is replacing *biocentrism* among true believers.

CHAPTER 11. THE OWL SHRIEKED

1. Eric Forsman, interviews, 1992–1994.

2. Memorandum from E. Charles Meslow to Andy Stahl et al., "Old Growth Forest Retention for Spotted Owls — How Much Do They Need?," November 5, 1984; Eric Forsman and E. Charles Meslow, "The Spotted Owl," in *Audubon Wildlife Report, 1986*, ed. Roger L. DiSilvestro (New York: National Audubon Society, 1986); Steven Lewis Yaffee, *The Wisdom of the Spotted Owl* (Washington, D.C.: Island Press, 1994), pp. 36ff.; Eric D. Forsman, E. Charles Meslow, and Howard M. Wight, "Distribution and Biology of the Spotted Owl in Oregon," *Wildlife Monographs* (April 1984).

3. Forsman's master's thesis, completed in 1976, focused on behavior, not numbers and demographics. Not until he began work on his doctoral dissertation later that year did he begin to understand the range requirements and demographic factors that determined the needs and status of the bird. See Eric D. Forsman, "A Preliminary Investigation of the Spotted Owl in Oregon" (M.S. thesis, Oregon State University, Corvallis, 1976); Eric D. Forsman, "Habitat Utilization by Spotted Owls in the West-Central Cascades of Oregon" (Ph.D. diss., Oregon State University, Corvallis, 1980).

4. Forsman, interviews. See also William Dietrich, *The Final Forest* (New York: Simon and Schuster, 1992), pp. 47ff.; Yaffee, *Wisdom of the Owl*, pp. 14–34.

5. Dietrich, *The Final Forest*.

6. J. S. Legon, "Habits of the Spotted Owl (*Syrnium occidentale*)," *The Auk* 43 (1926); J. T. Marshall, Jr., "Food and Habitat of the Spotted Owl," *Condor* 44 (1942); A. C. Bent, "Life Histories of North American Birds of Prey," pt. 2, *U.S. National Museum Bulletin* 170 (1938).

7. Forsman and E. Charles Meslow, interviews; Yaffee, *Wisdom of the Spotted Owl*; Dietrich, *Final Forest*.

8. Forsman, Meslow, and Wight, "Distribution and Biology of the Spotted Owl."

9. Ibid.

10. Ibid.

11. Ibid; Forsman, "Habitat Utilization by Spotted Owl."

12. Forsman and Meslow, interviews; Yaffee, *Wisdom of the Spotted Owl*, pp. 20–21. The momentous implications of this beginning were not immediately apparent. As Yaffee notes, it seemed that the task force was "off to a reasonable start," even though "approaches established by the Task Force early on affected the course of the controversy in ways the scientists on the Task Force did not intend" (*Wisdom of the Owl*, p. 22).

13. Forsman and Jack Ward Thomas, interviews, 1992–1994.

14. Jack Ward Thomas, interviews. See also Dietrich, *Final Forest*, p. 53.

15. Thomas, interviews; U.S. Department of Agriculture, Forest Service, *Wildlife Habitats in Managed Forests, the Blue Mountains of Oregon and Washington*, Agriculture Handbook no. 553, September 1979, pp. 10ff.

16. Thomas, interviews; also interviews, July 1993, with Lawrence Beitz, former forest supervisor John Gill, and Jim Pack of the West Virginia Department of Natural Resources.

17. Thomas, Beitz, Gill, and Pack, interviews. See also Michael J. Bean, *The Evolution of National Wildlife Law*, rev. ed. (New York: Praeger, 1983), pp. 145n. and 198; David A. Clary, *Timber and the Forest Service* (Lawrence: University of Kansas Press, 1986), pp. 190–192.

18. Thomas, interviews.

19. Forest Service, *Wildlife Habitats in Managed Forests*.

20. See Bean, *Evolution of National Wildlife Law*, p. 198; Clary, *Timber and the Forest Service*, pp. 190–192.

21. Bean, *Evolution of National Wildlife Law*, p. 149.

22. James Monteith, interviews, 1993–1994.

23. Bean, *Evolution of National Wildlife Law*, pp. 149–150; Clary, *Timber and the Forest Service*, p. 193.

24. See Samuel P. Hays, *Beauty, Health, and Permanence: Environmental Politics in the United States, 1955–1985* (Cambridge: Cambridge University Press, 1987), p. 126.

25. Monteith, Terry Thatcher, Andy Kerr, Andy Stahl, and Max Axline, interviews, 1992–1994. See also Yaffee, *Wisdom of the Spotted Owl*, pp. 48, 74, 108.

26. Robert Sutherland, interviews, 1993–94.

27. Sutherland and Ruthanne Cecil, interviews.

28. Ibid.

29. Sutherland, interviews.

30. Sutherland and Cecil, interviews; interviews, 1992–1994, with Humboldt County residents including Cecelia Lanman, Chuck Powell, Kelly Bettiga, John Campbell, Bill Bertain, Lloyd Hecathorn, Tim McKay, Greg King, Peter Kayes, and Bill Devall. See also Paul DeMark, "EPIC, 10 Years Later: Still Fighting to Preserve the Environment," *Redwood Record*, February 18, 1987.

31. Cecil, interview; DeMark, "EPIC, 10 Years Later."

32. Sutherland, interview; DeMark, "EPIC, 10 Years Later"; "Environmental Education Center Being Formed Here," *Redwood Record*, March 30, 1978; EPIC, "Organizational History and Goals," n.d. For an overview of the

Sinkyone battle, see David Cross, "Sally Bell Redwoods Protected! Sinkyone Coast Purchased for Park," *Earth First! Journal* 7, no. 3 (February 2, 1987).

33. Sutherland, interview; "Environmental Education Center Being Formed Here"; EPIC, "Organizational History and Goals."

34. Susan R. Schrepfer, *The Fight to Save the Redwoods: A History of Environmental Reform* (Madison: University of Wisconsin Press, 1983), chap. 10; Bill Devall, interview; Edwin Kiester, Jr., "A New Park Saves the Tall Trees, but at High Cost to the Community," *Smithsonian* (November 1993).

35. See The man who walks in the woods, "Summary of EPIC Forestry Lawsuits," June 1992.

36. Interviews with Woody Murphy, 1992–1994.

37. Murphy, Powell, Kayes, and Hecathorn, interviews.

38. Hecathorn, interview.

39. Murphy, Bertain, and Hecathorn, interviews. See also "A New Park."

40. Murphy, Bertain, Hecathorn, and John Campbell, interviews; "A New Park"; Schrepfer, *Fight to Save the Redwoods*.

41. Council on Economic Priorities, Corporate Environmental Data Clearinghouse, *Maxxam: A Report on the Company's Environmental Policies and Practices* (New York: Council on Economic Priorities, 1991); Hammon, Jensen, Wallen, and Associates, "Analysis of the Effects of Increased Harvests on Pacific Lumber's Forest and North Coast Economy," report prepared for the Pacific Lumber Company, August 13, 1986.

42. Murphy, Campbell, and Bertain, interviews.

43. Tom Hirons, interviews, 1992–1995. See also David Seideman, *Showdown at Opal Creek: The Battle for America's Last Wilderness* (New York: Carroll and Graf, 1993), pp. 75ff.

CHAPTER 12. THE RELUCTANT RESEARCHERS

1 Memorandum, E. Charles Meslow to Andy Stahl et al., "Old Growth Forest Retention for Spotted Owls — How Much Do They Need?" November 5, 1984.

2. Quoted from Interagency Scientific Committee to Address the Conservation of the Northern Spotted Owl, *A Conservation Strategy for the Northern Spotted Owl* (Portland: Departments of Agriculture and Interior, May 1990), p. 53.

3. Ibid., pp. 52ff. See also Steven Lewis Jaffee, *The Wisdom of the Spotted Owl* (Washington, D.C.: Island Press, 1994), p. 53.

4. William Dietrich, *The Final Forest* (New York: Simon and Schuster, 1992), p. 77; Northwest Forestry Association, "Chronology of Compromise: Land Set-Asides in the Pacific Northwest," mimeo., n.d.; Northwest Forestry Association, "Shrinking Giant," n.d..

5. Laura L. Manning, *The Dispute Processing Model of Public Policy Evolution: The Case of Endangered Species Policy Changes from 1973 to 1983* (Ann Arbor: University Microfilms International, 1986), pp. 251ff.; Steven Lewis Yaffee, *Prohibitive Policy: Implementing the Endangered Species Act* (Cambridge, Mass.: MIT Press, 1982).

6. James D. Williams, interview, July 1993.

7. Charles C. Mann and Mark L. Plummer, "The Butterfly Problem," *Atlantic* (January 1992); Charles C. Mann and Mark L. Plummer, *Noah's Choice: The Future of Endangered Species* (New York: Alfred A. Knopf, 1995), app.

8. Michael J. Bean, *The Evolution of National Wildlife Law*, rev. ed. (New York: Praeger, 1983), p. 363; see also Mann and Plummer, "The Butterfly Problem."

9. Library of Congress, *A Legislative History of the Endangered Species Act of 1973, as Amended in 1976, 1977, 1978, and 1980*, February 1982, p. 144.

10. Plummer and Mann, "The Butterfly Problem"; Yaffee, *Prohibitive Policy.*

11. Manning, *Dispute Processing Model*; Yaffee, *Prohibitive Policy*; Charles C. Mann and Mark L. Plummer, *Noah's Choice: The Future of Endangered Species* (New York: Alfred A. Knopf, 1995), p. 165.

12. Manning, *Dispute Processing Model.*

13. Discussion of the research at H. J. Andrews Experimental Forest is based on interviews, conducted between 1992 and 1994, with Jerry Franklin, Arthur McKee, Glen Juday, Charles Meslow, Eric Forsman, and Thomas A. Spies. See also James Peterson, "A Kinder, Gentler Forestry," *Evergreen* (July 1990).

14. John J. Magnuson, "Long-Term Ecological Research and the Invisible Present," *BioScience* 40, no. 7 (July–August 1990); "H. J. Andrews Experimental Forest," mimeo., n.d.; Arthur McKee et al., "Research Publications of the H. J. Andrews Experimental Forest, Cascade Range, Oregon, 1948 to 1986," General Technical Report PNW-201, U.S. Department of Agriculture, Forest Service, Pacific Northwest Research Station, April 1987.

15. Their conclusions, however, would represent a shift in values more than new scientific discoveries. See chapter 13.

16. Jerry F. Franklin et al., "Ecological Characteristics of Old-Growth Douglas-Fir Forests," U.S. Department of Agriculture, Forest Service, General Technical Report PNW-118, Pacific Northwest Forest and Range Experiment Station, February 1981; Thomas A. Spies and Jerry F. Franklin, "The Structure of Natural Young, Mature, and Old-Growth Douglas-Fir Forests in Oregon and Washington," *Wildlife and Vegetation of Unmanaged Douglas-Fir Forests*, ed. Leonard F. Ruggiero et al., General Technical Report PNW-GTR-285, U.S. Department of Agriculture, Forest Service, Pacific Northwest Research Station, May 1991.

17. Franklin et al., "Ecological Characteristics of Old Growth"; Thomas A. Spies and Jerry F. Franklin, "Coarse Woody Debris in Douglas-Fir Forests of Western Oregon and Washington," *Ecology* 69, no. 6 (1988).

18. M. E. Harmon et al., "Ecology of Coarse Woody Debris in Temperate Ecosystems," *Advances in Ecological Research* 15 (1986).

19. Mark E. Harmon, William K. Ferrell, and Jerry F. Franklin, "Effects on Carbon Storage of Conversion of Old-Growth Forests to Young Forests," *Science* 247 (February 1990). See also James K. Agee and Mark H. Huff, "Fuel Succession in a Western Hemlock/Douglas-Fir Forest," *Canadian Journal for Resources* 17 (1987); Stanley V. Gregory et al., "An Ecosystem Perspective of Riparian Zones," *BioScience* 41, no. 8 (September 1991).

20. A. J. Hansen et al., "Conserving Biodiversity in Managed Forests," *BioScience* 41, no. 6 (June 1991); Jerry F. Franklin, "Scientific Basis for New Perspectives in Forests and Streams," in *New Perspectives in Watershed Management*, ed. Robert J. Naiman (New York: Springer-Verlag, 1991).

21. Gordon E. Grant and Fred Swanson, "Cumulative Effects of Forest Practices," *Forest Perspectives* 1, no. 4 (1991); F. J. Swanson, J. F. Franklin, and USDA Forest Service, "New Forestry Principles from Ecosystem Analysis of Pacific Northwest Forests," mimeo., November 21, 1991; Thomas A. Spies et al., "Trends in Ecosystem Management at the Stand Level," *Transactions, Fifty-sixth North American Wildlife and Natural Resources Conference*, 1991.

22. "H. J. Andrews Experimental Forest."
23. Franklin et al., "Ecological Characteristics of Old Growth."
24. Ibid.
25. There was some disagreement between Juday and McKee on this point. Juday stresses the conferees' awareness of the awesome implications of their work; McKee thinks this is exaggerated.
26. Interview with Franklin in Cameron La Follette, "Saving All the Pieces: Old Growth Forest in Oregon," Oregon Student Public Interest Research Group, March 1979, p. 44.
27. James Lindquist and Ron Mastrogiuseppe, "Dynamics of Second-Growth Forest Establishment in Redwood National Park," U.S. Department of Interior, National Park Service, mimeo., May 17, 1988; James L. Lindquist, "Hare Creek Sprout Stocking Study on Jackson Demonstration State Forest," *California Forestry Notes* (September 1989); Dale A. Thornburgh, "Historic Development of the Concepts of 'New Forestry,' 'Ecological Forestry,' or Forest Ecosystem Management in the Redwood Forests of California," memorandum, July 1993; Phillip Lowell, "A Review of Redwood Harvesting — Another Look," California Department of Forestry, 1990; Chadwick Dearing Oliver, "A Landscape Approach: Achieving and Maintaining Biodiversity and Economic Productivity," *Journal of Forestry* 90, no. 9 (September 1992); William Atkinson, "Another View of New Forestry," address to the Oregon Society of American Foresters, Annual Meeting, Eugene, Oregon, May 4, 1990; "Scientists Disagree on Balanced Cut," *Seattle Times*, April 21, 1993.
28. Chadwick D. Oliver, interviews, 1992–1994; Chadwick D. Oliver and Bruce C. Larson, *Forest Stand Dynamics* (New York: McGraw-Hill, 1990); Peterson, "A Kinder, Gentler Forestry"; Atkinson, "Another View of New Forestry."
29. Oliver, interviews; James Peterson, "An Alternative to the President's Proposal," *Evergreen* (September–October 1993); Bob Zybach, "Native Forests of the Douglas-Fir Region: A Brief History of the Forests of Western Washington and Oregon from Prehistoric Times to the Present," mimeo., March 29, 1994; "Voices in the Forest: An Interview with Bob Zybach," *Evergreen* (March–April 1994); Douglas MacCleery, "Some Thoughts on Sustainable Forest Management," mimeo., November 21, 1994.
30. The tendency to ignore the past is, of course, a consequence of the ecosystem perspective. So long as one supposes that nature tends toward a steady state, then the past is not deemed relevant. See Orie L. Loucks, "Evolution of Diversity, Efficiency, and Community Stability," *American Zoologist* 10 (1979); F. Herbert Bormann and Gene E. Likens, "Catastrophic Disturbance and the Steady State in Northern Hardwood Forests," *American Scientist* 67 (November–December 1979); P. L. Marks and F. H. Bormann, "Revegetation Following Forest Cutting: Mechanism for Return to Steady-State Nutrient Cycling," *Science*, May 26, 1972.
31. E. C. Pielou, *After the Ice Age: The Return of Life to Glaciated North America* (Chicago: University of Chicago Press, 1991).
32. Linda B. Brubaker, "Climate Change and the Origin of Old-Growth Douglas-Fir Forests in the Puget Sound Lowland," in Ruggiero et al., *Wildlife and Vegetation of Unmanaged Douglas-Fir Forests*; Cathy Whitlock, "Vegetational and Climatic History of the Pacific Northwest during the Last Twenty Thousand Years: Implications for Understanding Present-Day Biodiversity," *Northwest Environmental Journal* 8, no. 1 (1992); Margaret Bryan Davis, "Quaternary History and the Stability of Forest Communi-

ties," in *Forest Succession: Concepts and Application*, ed. Darrell C. West, Herman H. Shugart, and Daniel B. Botkin (Heidelberg: Springer-Verlag, 1992); E. Lucy Braun, *Deciduous Forests of Eastern North America* (New York: Free Press, 1950).

33. Brubaker, "Climate Change"; Peter D. A. Teensma, John R. Rienstra, and Mark A. Yeiter, "Preliminary Reconstruction and Analysis of Change in Forest Stand Age Classes of the Oregon Coast Range from 1850 to 1940," U.S. Department of the Interior, Bureau of Land Management Technical Note T/N OR-9, October 1991; James K. Agee, "Fire History of Douglas-Fir Forests in the Pacific Northwest," in Ruggiero et al., *Wildlife and Vegetation of Unmanaged Douglas-Fir Forests*; Peter H. Morrison and Frederick J. Swanson, *Fire History and Pattern in a Cascade Range Landscape*, General Technical Report PNW-GTR-254, U.S. Department of the Interior, Forest Service, Pacific Northwest Research Station, May 1990; John D. Walstad, Steven R. Radosevich, and David V. Sandbert, *Natural and Prescribed Fire in Pacific Northwest Forests* (Corvallis, Ore.: Oregon State University Press, 1990); Stephen J. Pyne, *Fire in America: A Cultural History of Wildland and Rural Fire* (Princeton: Princeton University Press, 1982).

34. Whitlock, "Vegetational and Climatic History."

35. Davis, "Quaternary History."

36. Pyne, *Fire in America*, pp. 71ff.; George R. Fahnestock and James K. Agee, "Biomass Consumption and Smoke Production by Prehistoric and Modern Forest Fires in Western Washington," *Journal of Forestry* (October 1983); Zybach, "A Brief History of the Forests of Western Washington"; William M. Denevan, "The Pristine Myth: The Landscape of the Americas in 1492," *Annals of the Association of American Geographers* 82, no. 3 (1992); Douglas MacCleery, "Understanding the Role That Humans Have Played in Shaping America's Forest and Grassland Landscapes," U.S. Department of Agriculture, Forest Service, mimeo., June 7, 1994; James K. Agee, "The Historical Role of Fire in Pacific Northwest Forests," in Walstad et al., *Natural and Prescribed Fire*; Omer C. Steward, "Fire as the First Great Force Employed by Man," in *Man's Role in Changing the Face of the Earth* (Chicago: University of Chicago Press, 1955); Stephen W. Barrett, "Indians and Fires," *Western Rangelands* (Spring 1980); Dean A. Shinn, "Historical Perspectives on Range Burning in the Inland Pacific Northwest," *Journal of Range Management* 33, no. 6 (November 1980); Charles E. Kay, "Aboriginal Overkill: The Role of Native Americans in Structuring Western Ecosystems," *Human Nature*, in press.

37. Hugh M. Raup, "Trends in the Development of Geographic Botany," *Annals of the Association of American Geographers* 32, no. 4 (December 1942).

38. Old-Growth Definition Task Group, "Interim Definitions for Old-Growth Douglas-Fir and Mixed-Conifer Forests in the Pacific Northwest and California," Research Note PNW-447, U.S. Department of Agriculture, Forest Service, 1986; Thomas A. Spies and Jerry F. Franklin, "Old Growth and Forest Dynamics in the Douglas-Fir Region of Western Oregon and Washington," *Natural Areas Journal* 8, no. 3 (1988); Malcolm L. Hunter, Jr., "What Constitutes an Old-Growth Stand?" *Journal of Forestry* (August 1989); Franklin et al., "Ecological Characteristics."

39. Franklin et al., "Ecological Characteristics."

40. Old-Growth Definition Task Group, "Interim Definitions"; Bruce G. Marcot et al., "Old-Growth Inventories: Statues, Definitions, and Visions for the Future," in Ruggiero et al., *Wildlife and Vegetation of Unmanaged*

Douglas-Fir Forests; Jerry F. Franklin and Thomas A. Spies, "Ecological Definitions of Old-Growth Douglas-Fir Forests," in Ruggiero et al., *Wildlife and Vegetation of Unmanaged Douglas-Fir Forests;* P. H. Morrison, *Old Growth in the Pacific Northwest: A Status Report* (Washington, D.C.: The Wilderness Society, 1988). See also Peter H. Morrison, *Ancient Forests of the Olympic National Forest* (Washington, D.C.: The Wilderness Society, 1990).

41. G. James West, "Holocene Fossil Pollen Records of Douglas Fir in Northwestern California, Reconstruction of Past Climate," presented at Sixth Annual Pacific Climate (PACLIM) Workshop, Asilomar, California, March 5–8, 1989; Brubaker, "Climate Change": Teensma et al., "Preliminary Reconstruction."

42. Joel B. Hagen, *An Entangled Bank* (New Brunswick, N.J.: Rutgers University Press, 1992), p. 175.

43. Meslow and Arthur quotes from Forest Ecosystem Management Assessment Team, *Forest Ecosystem Management: An Ecological, Economic, and Social Assessment* (Washington, D.C.: Government Printing Office, 1993); Jerry F. Franklin and C. T. Dryness, *Natural Vegetation of Oregon and Washington* (Corvallis, Ore.: Oregon State University Press, 1987); Spies and Franklin, "Old Growth and Forest Dynamics"; P. H. Morrison, *Old Growth in the Pacific Northwest: A Status Report* (Washington, D.C.: The Wilderness Society, 1988); Peter H. Morrison et al., "Ancient Forests on the Mt. Baker–Snoqualmie National Forest," Wilderness Society, 1990; Elliott A. Norse, *Ancient Forests of the Pacific Northwest* (Washington, D.C.: Island Press, 1990).

44. Zybach, "Native Forests of the Douglas Fir Region"; Teensma et al., "Preliminary Reconstruction and Analysis of Change"; P. J. Teensma and M. Yeiter, "Prehistoric Old Growth Timber in Northwest Oregon," Bureau of Land Management, 1991.

45. Quoted from interview in La Follette, *Saving All the Pieces,* p. 42.

46. Monteith, Juday, and Kerr interviews.

47. Forsman and Juday, interviews.

48. Glenn Patrick Juday, "Old Growth Forests: A Necessary Element of Multiple Use and Sustained Yield National Forest Management," *Environmental Law* 8 (1978).

49. Sydney Herbert, interviews, July 1993; Franklin, interview.

50. Resources for the Future, survey, 1978. See Susan R. Schrepfer, *The Fight to Save the Redwoods: A History of Environmental Reform* (Madison: University of Wisconsin Press, 1983), p. 236.

51. Allan Savory, interviews, 1988.

52. And emphasis shifted inexorably in a teleological fashion to "final" or climax forests rather than early successional ones.

53. Victor M. Sher and Andy Stahl, "Spotted Owls, Ancient Forests, Courts, and Congress: An Overview of Citizens' Efforts to Protect Old-Growth Forests and the Species That Live in Them," *Northwest Environmental Journal* 6 (1990).

54. Andy Stahl and Terry Thatcher, interviews.

55. Library of Congress, *A Legislative History of the Endangered Species Act of 1973, as Amended in 1976, 1977, 1978, and 1980,* February 1982, pp. 643ff.

458 | NOTES AND SOURCES

CHAPTER 13. THE NEW FORESTRY

1. Interviews with Jerry F. Franklin and Arthur McKee, 1992–1994.
2. Jerry F. Franklin et al., "Ecosystem Responses to the Eruption of Mount St. Helens," *National Geographic Research* (Spring 1985).
3. Ibid.; Jerry F. Franklin, "Scientific Basis for New Perspectives in Forests and Stream," in *Watershed Management: Balancing Sustainability and Environmental Change,* ed. Robert J. Naiman (New York: Springer-Verlag, 1991).
4. Franklin et al., "Ecosystem Responses"; Frederic E. Clements, *Plant Succession: An Analysis of the Development of Vegetation* (Washington, D.C.: Carnegie Institution, 1916). See also Frederic E. Clements and Victor E. Shelford, *Bio-Ecology* (New York: John Wiley and Sons, 1939).
5. Franklin et al., "Ecosystem Responses."
6. Ibid.
7. Franklin, "Scientific Basis for New Perspectives."
8. Franklin and McKee, interviews.
9. Franklin, "Scientific Basis for New Perspectives."
10. Ibid.; Franklin, interview, May 20, 1992. See also Franklin, "Scientific Basis for New Perspectives"; James Peterson, "A Kinder, Gentler Forestry," *Evergreen* (July 1990); Jerry F. Franklin, "An Ecologist's Perspective on Northwestern Forests in 2010," *Forest Watch* (August 1989); Jerry F. Franklin, "Thoughts on Applications of Silvicultural Systems under New Forestry," *Forest Watch* (January–February 1990). See also Jerry F. Franklin et al., "The Forest Communities of Mount Rainier National Park," Scientific Monograph Series no. 19, U.S. Department of the Interior, National Park Service, 1988; E. J. Swanson and J. F. Franklin, "New Forestry Principles from Ecosystem Analysis of Pacific Northwest Forests," *Ecological Applications* 2, no. 3 (1992); "Forest and Forestry," in *McGraw-Hill Yearbook of Science and Technology, 1992* (New York: McGraw-Hill, 1992).
11. Jerry Franklin, "Toward a New Forestry," *American Forests* (November–December 1989). See also Franklin, "An Ecologist's Perspective"; Franklin, "Scientific Basis for New Perspectives."
12. On the broader issue of stability versus disturbance, see Peter J. Bowler, *The Norton History of the Environmental Science* (New York: W. W. Norton, 1992), esp. pp. 543ff.; Daniel B. Botkin, *Discordant Harmonies* (Oxford: Oxford University Press, 1990); Frank N. Egerton, "Changing Concepts of the Balance of Nature," *Quarterly Review of Biology* 48 (June 1973); Robert P. McIntosh, "Ecology since 1900," in *Issues and Ideas in America,* ed. Benjamin J. Taylor and Thurman J. White (Norman: University of Oklahoma Press, 1976); Eugene P. Odum, "The Strategy of Ecosystem Development," *Science,* April 18, 1969; Robert P. McIntosh, "Succession and Ecological Theory," in *Forest Succession: Concepts and Application,* ed. Darrell C. West, Herman H. Shugart, and Daniel B. Botkin (Heidelberg: Springer-Verlag, 1992); Daniel B. Botkin and Matthew J. Sobel, "Stability in Time-Varying Ecosystems," *American Naturalist* 109, no. 970 (November–December 1975).
13. F. Herbert Bormann and Gene E. Likens, "Catastrophic Disturbance and the Steady State in Northern Hardwood Forests," *American Scientist* 67 (November–December 1979).
14. Ibid.; Chadwick Dearing Oliver, "Forest Development in North America Following Major Disturbances," *Ecology and Management* 3 (1980–81); C. D. Oliver and E. P. Stephens, "Reconstruction of a Mixed Species Forest

in Central New England," *Ecology* 58 (1977); F. J. Swanson, S. M. Wondzell, and G. E. Grant, "Landforms, Disturbance, and Ecotones," in *Landscape Boundaries: Consequences for Biotic Diversity and Ecological Flows*, ed. A. J. Hansen and F. diCastri (New York: Springer-Verlag, 1992).

15. See Orie L. Loucks, "Evolution of Diversity, Efficiency, and Community Stability," *American Zoologist* 10 (1970); A. S. Watt, "Pattern and Process in the Plant Community," *Ecology* 35 (1947); J. Roger Bray, "Gap Phase Replacement in a Maple-Basswood Forest," *Ecology* 37 (1956). Bormann seems to have changed his mind on this issue. See F. H. Bormann, "A Holistic Approach to Nutrient Cycling Problems in Plant Communities," in *Essays in Plant Geography and Ecology*, ed. K. N. H. Greenidge (Halifax: Nova Scotia Museum, 1969); David M. Smith, "Comments on the Research Program of Four Silvicultural Projects," Pacific Northwest Forest and Range Experiment Station, U.S. Department of Agriculture, Forest Service, August 16, 1966.

16. The high point of the popularity of the notion of stability came around 1970; then it began to wane. But paradoxically the New Foresters, somewhat unintentionally, put renewed emphasis on stability just as its influence began to wane.

17. Oliver and Stephens, "Reconstruction of a Mixed Species Forest." See also Chadwick Dearing Oliver, "Forest Development in North America Following Major Disturbances," *Forest Ecology and Management* 3 (1980–81); Chadwick Dearing Oliver, "Even-Aged Development of Mixed-Species Stands," *Journal of Forestry* (April 1980); Chadwick Dearing Oliver, "Silviculture," *Journal of Forestry* (April 1986). For a comparison of Franklin's and Oliver's views, see the articles by the two that appear in *Journal of Forestry* 91, no. 12 (December 1993).

18. Oliver and Stephens, "Reconstruction of a Mixed Species Forest." See also M. G. R. Cannell, D. C. Malcolm, and P. A. Robertson, *The Ecology of Mixed-Species Stands of Trees* (London: Basil Blackwell, 1992); R. H. Whittaker, "Dominance and Diversity in Land Plant Communities," *Science* 147 (1965).

19. That is, silviculture had remained an empirical discipline.

20. Supposing that by studying "wilderness" they would gain knowledge into "natural" conditions merely begged the question. Such a research agenda presupposed that "undisturbed" forests were "natural" ones.

21. Bormann and Likens, "Catastrophic Disturbance." For more on Hubbard Brook Farm, see Joel B. Hagen, *An Entangled Bank* (New Brunswick, N.J.: Rutgers University Press, 1992); Frank Benjamin Golley, *A History of the Ecosystem Concept in Ecology* (New Haven: Yale University Press, 1993), pp. 126 and passim.

22. Loucks, "Evolution of Diversity"; P. L. Marks and F. H. Bormann, "Revegetation Following Forest Cutting: Mechanisms for Return to Steady-State Nutrient Cycling," *Science* 176 (March 1972).

23. Bormann and Likens, "Catastrophic Disturbance." See also F. H. Bormann et al., "The Hubbard Brook Ecosystem Study: Composition and Dynamics of the Tree Stratum," *Ecological Monographs* 40, no. 4 (Autumn 1970).

24. Franklin concedes that his notion of "biological legacies" is not new. On the Mount St. Helens dieback, see Gerardo Segura, "Dynamics of Old-Growth Forests of *Abies amabilis* Impacted by Tephra from the 1980 Eruption of Mount St. Helens, Washington" (Ph.D. diss., University of Washington, 1991). By contrast, private lands that were equally devastated by the eruption but, unlike the public forests, were intensively reseeded fared much

460

NOTES AND SOURCES

better. See James A. Rochell, "Natural Resource Recovery Following the 1980 Mount St. Helens Eruption: Lessons in Ecological Resilience," in *Proceedings of the Fifty-fifth North American Wildlife and Natural Resources Conference*, Denver, March 16–21, 1990.

25. Leo A. Isaac and George S. Meagher, "Natural Reproduction on the Tillamook Burn, Four Years after the Fire," Pacific Northwest Forest Experiment Station, Portland, Oregon, January 10, 1938; Ellis Lucia, *Tillamook Burn Country* (Caldwell, Idaho: Caxton Printers, 1983); Chadwick D. Oliver and Bruce C. Larson, *Forest Stand Dynamics* (New York: McGraw-Hill, 1990), pp. 90ff.

26. That is, once the teleological perspective was adopted, there was no way, even for scholars, to distinguish between facts and values.

27. Doug Hopwood and Lasqueti Island, *Principles and Practices of New Forestry* (Victoria, British Columbia: Ministry of Forests, February 1991), p. 1.

28. Marion Clawson, *For Whom and for What?* (Baltimore: Johns Hopkins University Press, 1975); Jack Ward Thomas, "Forest Management Approaches on the Public's Lands: Turmoil and Transition," mimeo., n.d.

29. Franklin, "Toward a New Forestry." See also Peterson, "A Kinder, Gentler Forestry."

30. Bowler, *Norton History*, p. 547. Bowler also notes how wrongheaded this is: "No one can prove that a value-system is right by appealing to the facts of Nature, because the facts are always filtered through the value-systems of the underlying theories" (p. 548).

31. See Jerry A. Sesco, "Strategy for the 90's for USDA Forest Service Research," U.S. Department of Agriculture, Forest Service, 1992; James J. Kennedy and Thomas M. Quigley, "How Entry-Level Employees, Forest Supervisors, Regional Foresters, and Chiefs View Forest Service Values and the Reward System," survey for the Sunbird Conference, Second Meeting of Forest Supervisors and Chiefs, Tucson, Arizona, November 13–16, 1989; James J. Kennedy, "Symbolic Infrastructure of Natural Resource Management: An Example of the U.S. Forest Service," *Society and Natural Resources* 1 (1988); James J. Kennedy, "Understanding Professional Career Evolution — an Example of Aldo Leopold," *Wildlife Society Bulletin* 12 (1984); James J. Kennedy, "Conceiving Forest Management as Providing for Current and Future Social Value," *Forest Ecology and Management* 13 (1985).

32. Niels Elers Koch and James J. Kennedy, "Multiple-Use Forestry for Social Values," *Ambio* 20, no. 7 (November 1991); Greg Brown and Charles C. Harris, "The Implications of Work Force Diversification in the U.S. Forest Service," Department of Resource Recreation and Tourism, University of Idaho, mimeo., April 15, 1992; Greg Brown and Charles C. Harris, "The U.S. Forest Service: Changing of the Guard," *Natural Resources Journal* 32, no. 3 (1992); Greg Brown and Charles C. Harris, "The U.S. Forest Service: Toward the New Resource Management Paradigm?," *Society and Natural Resources* 5 (1992).

33. James J. Kennedy and Jack Ward Thomas, "Exit, Voice, and Loyalty of Wildlife Biologists in Public Natural Resource/Environmental Agencies," in *American Fish and Wildlife Policy: The Human Dimension*, ed. William R. Mangun (Greenville, N.C.: East Carolina University Press, 1992), p. 225.

34. Herbert Kaufman, *The Forest Ranger: A Study in Administrative Behavior* (Washington, D.C.: Resources for the Future, 1960); B. W. Twight, "The Forest Service Mission: A Case of Family Fidelity," *Women in Forestry* 7 (1985).

35. Brown and Harris, "Toward the New Resource Management Paradigm?"; Kennedy and Thomas, "Exit, Voice, and Loyalty."

36. L. Harris and Associates, *A Survey of the Public's Attitudes toward Soil, Water, and Related Resource Conservation Policy*, PB82-219975, National Technical Information Service, Springfield, Virginia, 1980. See also Kennedy and Quigley, "Entry-Level Employees"; *The Forest Service: An Agency in Transition: An Analysis of Changes in Personnel and Changing Employee Attitudes*, Public Timber Council, Forest Products Association, 1991.
37. Brown and Harris, "Toward the New Resource Management Paradigm?"; Brown and Harris, "Changing of the Guard"; Kennedy and Thomas, "Exit, Voice, and Loyalty."
38. Brown and Harris, "Toward the New Resource Management Paradigm?"
39. Interview with Mike Roselle, January 23, 1992.

CHAPTER 14. NIGHT ON BALD MOUNTAIN

1. This account is drawn from Mike Roselle, interviews, 1992; "Wilderness War in Oregon," *Earth First! Journal* 3, no. 5 (June 21, 1983); Christopher Manes, *Green Rage* (Boston: Little, Brown, 1990); Susan Zakin, *Coyotes and Town Dogs* (New York: Viking, 1993), pp. 236ff.
2. Mike Roselle, "Blockade Personal Accounts," *Earth First! Journal* 3, no. 5 (June 21, 1983).
3. Roselle, interviews; Howie Wolke, interview, June 17, 1992.
4. Foreman quotes from Manes, *Green Rage*, p. 84; and Dave Foreman, *Confessions of an Eco-Warrior* (New York: Harmony Books, 1991), p. 144.
5. Manes, *Green Rage*, pp. 84ff.
6. Ibid.; Zakin, *Town Dogs*, pp. 232ff.
7. This account is drawn from Manes, *Green Rage*; Zakin, *Town Dogs*; Roselle, interviews.
8. "Sue the Bastards!," *Earth First! Journal* 3, no. 5 (June 21, 1983).
9. "Earth First! Says 'No Compromise,' " *New Options*, February 24, 1986. See also Dave Foreman, address to the East Bay Green Alliance, Berkeley, October 23, 1985; Foreman, interviews, 1986–87.
10. Roselle, interviews, 1986–1992.
11. Roselle, interviews; Dana Beal, interviews, 1986–87. See Alston Chase, "The Great, Green Deep-Ecology Revolution," *Rolling Stone*, April 23, 1987; Alston Chase, "It's Not Easy Being Green," *American Way*, April 15, 1990.
12. Roselle and Wolke, interviews.
13. Ibid.; Manes, *Green Rage*, pp. 61ff.; Zakin, *Town Dogs*, esp. pp. 84ff.
14. This account is drawn from Foreman, Roselle, and Wolke, interviews; Manes, *Green Rage*; Zakin, *Town Dogs*; Stewart McBride, "The Real Monkey Wrench Gang," *Outside* (December–January 1983); Joe Kane, "Mother Nature's Army," *Esquire* (February 1987).
15. Andy Kerr, interview, June 26, 1992; Roselle and Foreman, interviews; Zakin, *Town Dogs*.
16. *Earth First! Journal* 3, no. 6 (July 21, 1983).
17. Roselle, interview. Foreman quote from McBride, "The Real Monkey Wrench Gang."
18. This account is drawn from Zakin, *Town Dogs*, pp. 141ff., and the author's experience of several Rendezvous.
19. Roselle, interviews.
20. On growth of the movement during this period, see Alston Chase, *Playing God in Yellowstone* (New York: Atlantic Monthly Press, 1986), pp. 330–331.
21. See Alston Chase, "Goose Music and Dr. Muir," *Outside* (November 1987); idem; "A Small Circle of Friends," *Outside* (May 1988).

22. Manes, *Green Rage*, pp. 3ff.; "Crack 'Em Up!," *Earth First! Journal* 2, no. 4 (March 20, 1992).
23. Dave Foreman and Bill Haywood, eds., *Ecodefense: A Field Guide to Monkeywrenching*, 2d ed. (Tucson: Ned Ludd Books, 1987).
24. "Foundation for EF!," *Earth First! Journal* 2, no. 4 (March 20, 1992).
25. Howie Wolke, "The Grizzly Den," *Earth First! Journal* 3, no. 4 (May 1, 1983); *Earth First! Journal* 3, no. 5 (June 21, 1983). See also Manes, *Green Rage*, pp. 70, 74.
26. Foreman, *Confessions of an Eco-Warrior*, p. 140.
27. Manes, *Green Rage*, pp. 176–177.
28. Holmes Rolston III, *Philosophy Gone Wild* (Buffalo: Prometheus Books, 1986), p. 24.
29. In short, the ecosystem idea emerged as a new form of collectivism, which, as Anna Bramwell notes, was neither left nor right. See Anna Bramwell, *Ecology in the Twentieth Century* (New Haven: Yale University Press, 1989).
30. Manes, *Green Rage*, p. 12.
31. Ibid., p. 9.
32. Ibid., p. 175.
33. Roselle, interview, August 5, 1989.

CHAPTER 15. THE NETWORK

1. Interviews with Paul Watson, 1987–1994; Paul Watson, *Sea Shepherd* (New York: W. W. Norton, 1982).
2. Watson, interviews, May and October, 1989; John May, interview, 1989. See also Michael Brown and John May, *The Greenpeace Story* (London: Dorling Kindersley, 1989); Robert Hunter, *Warriors of the Rainbow* (New York: Holt, Rinehart and Winston, 1979); David Day, *The Environmental Wars* (New York: St. Martin's, 1989); David Day, *The Whale War* (Toronto: Douglas and MacIntyre, 1987); Greenpeace, *The Greenpeace Book* (Vancouver: Orca Sound Publications, 1978); David McTaggert, *Outrage!* (Vancouver: J. J. Douglas, 1973); Richard Shears and Isobelle Gidley, *The Rainbow Warrior Affair* (London: Unwin Paperbacks, 1986).
3. Watson, interview; Watson, *Sea Shepherd*. See also Brown and May, *The Greenpeace Story*; Hunter and Weyler, *The Voyages of Greenpeace*; Hunter, *Warriors of the Rainbow*. The author spent a week aboard *Sea Shepherd* when it was docked in Seattle harbor during the summer of 1987. Later, Watson would help form another organization, Friends of the Wolf. See Robert Hunter and Paul Watson, *Cry Wolf!* (Vancouver: Shepherds of the Earth, 1985).
4. Alex Pacheco, interviews, May 1989. See Peter Singer, *Animal Liberation: A New Ethics for Our Treatment of Animals* (New York: Avon Press, 1975).
5. Much of the material on the ramming of the *Sierra* was supplied by sources who wish to remain anonymous. Other parts of the account are based on interviews with Paul Watson and Alex Pacheco. See also Watson, *Sea Shepherd*.
6. Pacheco and Ingrid Newkirk, interviews, May 1989.
7. Singer, *Animal Liberation*. Other popular texts among animal liberationists include Peter Singer, ed., *In Defense of Animals* (New York: Harper and Row, 1986); Tom Regan, *The Struggle for Animals Rights* (Clark's Summit, Pa.: International Society for Animal Rights, 1987); Tom Regan, *The Case for Animal Rights* (Berkeley: University of California Press, 1983). Animal

liberationists like to quote Jeremy Bentham's remark, "The question is not, Can they reason? nor Can they talk? but, *Can they suffer?*" But as every professional philosopher knows, Bentham was never able to provide a satisfactory justification for *human* rights. See Jeremy Bentham, *The Principles of Morals and Legislation*, chap. 17, sec. 1 (New York: Hafner, 1948).

8. Pacheco and Newkirk, interviews.

9. Ibid.; interview with Edward Taub, May 31, 1989. Also, interviews with Henry Heimlich, May 30, 1989; Robert White, May 25, 1989; Jane Goodall, June 1, 1989; and others. See also Alex Pacheco with Anna Francione, "The Silver Spring Monkeys," People for the Ethical Treatment of Animals, 1987; Edward Taub, "The Incident at the Primate Laboratory of Dr. Edward Taub," mimeo., n.d.

10. Taub, interview. Court of Appeals of Maryland, *Edward Taub* v. *State of Maryland,* September 1982; Decision of the Departmental Grant Appeals Board, Department of Health and Human Services, "Subject: Institute for Behavioral Resources — Dr. Edward Taub," Decision no. 538. See also Taub to Guggenheim Foundation, October 29, 1982.

11. Marjorie Spiegel, *The Dreaded Comparison* (Viborg, Denmark: VSP, 1988).

12. Patricia Gallagher, "Firms Face a Spreading Animal Rights Fight," *Cincinnati Enquirer,* October 23, 1988; William Booth, "A Preemptive Strike for Animal Research," *Science,* April 28, 1989; Foundation for Biomedical Research, "Animal Rights Movement Activities Summary," United States, mimeo., n.d.; Katherine Bishop, "Growing Militancy for Animals Rights Is Seen," *New York Times,* January 19, 1988; "Animal-Rights Raiders Ravage Arizona Labs, Spark Senate Warning," *Denver Post,* April 8, 1989; Gene Varn, "Group Frees US Animals, Burns Labs," *Arizona Republic,* April 4, 1989.

13. This networking was also accomplished by a variety of green publications, which appeared in profusion during the early 1980s, such as *Green Letter, Newsletter of the Cascadia Green Alliance, New Options, PETA News, The Trumpeter, Green Action,* and many others.

14. Charlene Spretnak and Fritjof Capra, *Green Politics* (Santa Fe: Bear and Company, 1984); Sara Parkin, *Green Parties: An International Guide* (London: Heretic Books, 1989).

15. Interviews with Spretnak, Capra, Kirkpatrick Sale, Dana Beal, Lorna Saltzman, John Gerding-Oresic, and other Greens, spring and summer 1986. See also Spretnak and Capra, *Green Politics.*

16. Spretnak, Sale, Saltzman interviews; Spretnak and Capra, *Green Politics.*

17. Beal, interviews, spring and summer 1986.

18. See Committees of Correspondence, "Building the Green Movement — a National Conference for a New Politics," Hampshire College, Amherst, Mass., July 2–7, 1987; UCLA Graduate School of Architecture and Urban Planning, "International Green Movements, and the Prospects for New Environmental/Industrial Politics in the U.S.," UCLA, April 17–19, 1986.

19. Randy Hayes and Klaus Sheerer, interviews. Also, interviews with French journalist Jean-Pierre Edin and several members of the French Robin Woods (Robin des Bois). See Alston Chase, "The Age of Unreason," *Outside* (December 1990); Alston Chase, "It's Not Easy Being Green," *American Way,* April 15, 1990; Wolpertinger, "Robin Wood," *Earth First! Journal* 7, no. 3 (February 2, 1987); Alston Chase, "Welcome to World War III," *Lear's* (December 1989). For news on Robin Wood, see "Aktionen" section of *Robin Wood* magazine.

20. Interviews with Pacheco, Newkirk, Amory, Watson, Foreman, Roselle, Beal, Gaede, Sheerer, and others.

21. Alston Chase, "The Great, Green Deep-Ecology Revolution," *Rolling Stone*, April 23, 1987.
22. Interviews with Spretnak, Beal, Sale, Gary Snyder, Willis Harmon, and others.
23. Foreman, interview, October 21, 1986; "Earth First! Says 'No Compromise,' " *New Options*, February 24, 1986; Dave Foreman, "Reinhabitation, Biocentrism, and Self-Defense," *Earth First! Journal* 7, no. 7 (August 1, 1987); Snyder, interview, April 23, 1986.
24. George Sessions, "Aldo Leopold and the Deep Ecology Movement," *Environmental Review* (June 1987); Sale, interview, December 13, 1986; Willis W. Harmon, "Colour the Future Green?," *Futures* 17, no. 4 (August 1985); Fritjof Capra, "Book Summary: The Turning Point," *Elmwood Newsletter* 1, no. 2 (1986); Sale, interview, December 13, 1986; Fritjof Capra, *The Turning Point* (New York: Bantam, 1983); Kirkpatrick Sale, *Dwellers in the Land* (San Francisco: Sierra Club Books, 1985).
25. Capra, *The Turning Point*; Sale, *Dwellers in the Land*; Bill Devall and George Sessions, *Deep Ecology* (Salt Lake City: Peregrine Smith Books, 1985); George Sessions, "Shallow and Deep Ecology: A Review of the Philosophical Literature," prepared for Earth Day X, The Humanities and Ecological Consciousness: A Scholarly Colloquium, University of Denver, April 21–24, 1980.
26. René Descartes, "Discourse on Method" and "Meditations on First Philosophy," in *The Philosophical Works of Descartes*, ed. G. R. T. Ross, 2 vols. (New York: Dover, 1931), vol. 1; Arthur O. Lovejoy, *The Revolt against Dualism* (La Salle, Ill.: Open Court, 1960).
27. See, e.g., Capra, *The Turning Point*; Devall and Sessions, *Deep Ecology*.
28. Dave Foreman, Address to the East Bay Green Alliance, Berkeley, October 23, 1985; Foreman, interviews, 1986–87.
29. One of the greatest pluralist philosophers of all time was Leibniz. See *Leibniz: The Monadology and Other Philosophical Writings*, ed. and trans. Robert Latta (Oxford: Oxford University Press, 1951); Bertrand Russell, *A Critical Exposition of the Philosophy of Leibniz* (London: George Allen and Unwin, 1958).
30. Al Gore, *Earth in the Balance* (Boston: Houghton Mifflin, 1992), p. 218.
31. Ibid., pp. 220, 253, 265.
32. Roselle, interview, July 7, 1992; Stewart McBride, "The Real Monkey Wrench Gang," *Outside* (December–January 1983); Joe Kane, "Mother Nature's Army," *Esquire* (February 1987).
33. Steven Lewis Yaffee, *The Wisdom of the Owl* (Washington, D.C.: Island Press, 1994); William Dietrich, *The Final Forest* (New York: Simon and Schuster, 1992).
34. Roselle, interview, July 7, 1992; Christopher Manes, *Green Rage* (Boston: Little, Brown, 1990); Susan Zakin, *Coyotes and Town Dogs* (New York: Viking, 1993).
35. McBride, "Real Monkey Wrench Gang"; Zakin, *Town Dogs*, pp. 259, 262–263.

CHAPTER 16. WALL STREET FORESTRY

1. Woody Murphy, interviews, 1992–1994.
2. Murphy and Bill Bertain, interviews, 1992–1994; David M. Abramson, "The Takeover," *Image*, July 13, 1986. Some material in this chapter is based on interviews with John Campbell, Robert Stephens, Peter Kays, Kelly Bettiga,

Doug Coleman, Chuck Powell, and Thomas B. Malarky, Jr., before his untimely death.

3. Subcommittee on Oversight and Investigations of the Committee on Energy and Commerce, House of Representatives, "Corporate Takeovers, October 5, 1987 — Pacific Lumber: A Case Study," February 8, 1988, no. 100-116, p. 10. See also *Pacific Lumber Company* v. *Charles E. Hurwitz et al.*, U.S. District Court, Northern District of California.
4. Abramson, "The Takeover"; Subcommittee, "Corporate Takeovers."
5. Murphy and Lloyd Hecathorn, interviews; Subcommittee, "Corporate Takeovers"; Abramson, "The Takeover"; Robert K. Anderberg, "Wall Street Sleaze," *Amicus Journal* (Spring 1988); John Goff, "Angry Harvest," *Corporate Finance* (April 1989); Ellen Schultz, "A Raider's Ruckus in the Redwoods," *Fortune*, April 24, 1989; Jack Epstein, "Raiding the Redwoods," *California Business* (September 1987); Mark Walters, "California's Chain Saw Massacre," *Reader's Digest* (November 1989); Bill McKibbon, "Milken, Junk Bonds, and Raping Redwoods," *Rolling Stone*, August 10, 1989.
6. Abramson, "The Takeover."
7. Michael Shnayerson, "Redwood Raider," *Houston Metropolitan* (January 1992). See also "Maxxam Makes a Brilliant Investment Coup with Acquisition of Pacific Lumber," *13D Opportunities Report*, 1984.
8. Subcommittee, "Corporate Takeovers"; Shnayerson, "Redwood Raider"; Schultz, "Raider's Ruckus in the Redwoods"; *Wall Street Journal*, May 5, 1978.
9. "Brilliant Investment."
10. Ibid.; *New York Times*, July 13 and August 10, 1980; *Forbes*, February 14, 1983; Shnayerson, "Redwood Raider"; Schultz, "Raider's Ruckus in the Redwoods"; Pamela Sherrid, "A Split Too Far?" *Forbes*, January 6, 1983.
11. See *Pacific Lumber Company* v. *Charles E. Hurwitz*, United District Court, Northern District of California, October 10, 1985; Epstein, "Raiding the Redwoods"; Subcommittee, "Corporate Takeovers."
12. Epstein, "Raiding the Redwoods"; Shnayerson, "Redwood Raider"; Schultz, "Raider's Ruckus in the Redwoods."
13. "Brilliant Investment," *13D Opportunities Report*.
14. Subcommittee, "Corporate Takeovers," p. 231. See also "A Takeover Artist Who's Turning Redwoods into Quick Cash," *Business Week*, February 2, 1987; Michael Parris, "Western Environmentalists' Enemy No. 1," *Los Angeles Times*, August 19, 1990; Robert Draper, "Charles Hurwitz," *Texas Monthly* (September 1994).
15. Subcommittee, "Corporate Takeovers"; Epstein, "Raiding the Redwoods"; Shnayerson, "Redwood Raider."
16. Subcommittee, "Corporate Takeovers." See also *Pacific Lumber Company* v. *Hurwitz*; *Stanwood A. Murphy, Jr.*, v. *Charles E. Hurwitz*, December 1, 1985; *Stanwood A. Murphy, Jr.*, v. *Pacific Lumber Company*, October 30, 1985; *Terry Russ* v. *Michael R. Milken et al.*, March 28, 1990 (*In re Boesky*).
17. Subcommittee, "Corporate Takeovers," p. 24.
18. Ibid.; Pacific Lumber Company, *1984 Annual Report*; "Statement of Jeffrey Lewis before the U.S. House of Representatives Select Committee on Aging, Subcommittee on Retirement Income and Employment," April 30, 1991; "Brilliant Investment"; *Labor Department* v. *Maxxam*, June 12, 1991. See also Shnayerson, "Redwood Raider."
19. Subcommittee, "Corporate Takeovers"; Pacific Lumber proxy statement, January 22, 1986.
20. Subcommittee, "Corporate Takeovers"; Maxxam tender offer, October 2, 1985. As it turned out, all these cruise estimates were too conservative.

21. Subcommittee, "Corporate Takeovers"; *Federal Deposit Insurance Corporation v. Milken*, December 30, 1988.
22. Subcommittee, "Corporate Takeovers."
23. Ibid.; *Pacific Lumber Company v. Hurwitz; In re Boesky; Murphy v. Hurwitz.*
24. Subcommittee, "Corporate Takeovers."
25. Bertain, interview.
26. At the conclusion of the hearings on the takeover, chairman John Dingell observed, "Even if no arrangement existed between Hurwitz and Jeffries regarding 'parking' of stock, there is significant evidence of a separate failure to file under the Hart-Scott-Rodino Act." Subcommittee, "Corporate Takeovers," p. 229.
27. Schultz, "Raider's Ruckus."
28. Bertain, interview; Abramson, "The Takeover."
29. *Pacific Lumber Company v. Hurwitz.*
30. Ibid.
31. Bertain, interview.
32. Securities and Exchange Commission, "USAT Mortgage Securities," registration no. 33-1692, received November 21, 1985; *In re Boesky*; Bertain, interview. Subcommittee, "Corporate Takeovers."
33. Abramson, "The Takeover"; Goff, "Angry Harvest"; Subcommittee, "Corporate Takeovers."
34. Subcommittee, "Corporate Takeovers"; *MXM Corporation v. Pacific Lumber Company*, October 18, 1985; Epstein, "Raiding the Redwoods"; Goff, "Angry Harvest"; Walters, "Chain Saw Massacre"; Schultz, "Raider's Ruckus."
35. Agreement and Plan of Merger by and among Maxxam Group, Inc., et al., and the Pacific Lumber Company, October 22, 1985. See also *In re Boesky*; Salomon Brothers, Inc., to Board of Directors, the Pacific Lumber Company, October 22, 1985.
36. *In re Boesky.*
37. In what was surely an understatement, Palco's 1986 10-K annual report observed, "The Company is highly leveraged." See Pacific Lumber Company, Form 10-K for the fiscal year ended December 31, 1986. See also Subcommittee, "Corporate Takeovers"; Pacific Lumber Company, prospectus, June 26, 1986; "Brilliant Investment"; Epstein, "Raiding the Redwoods"; McKibbon, "Milken, Junk Bonds."
38. Interviews with Doug Coleman, Kayes, Bettiga, and other Palco millworkers.
39. Abramson, "The Takeover"; Walters, "Chain Saw Massacre"; "Heritage in the Balance," *Eureka Times-Standard*, November 17, 1985.
40. Bettiga and Kayes, interviews; Bertain testimony, Subcommittee, "Corporate Takeovers"; Schultz, "Raider's Ruckus."
41. *Murphy v. Hurwitz.*
42. Bettiga, Kayes, and Coleman, interviews.
43. Warren Murphy, Robert Stephens, John Campbell, Malarky, and Bertain, interviews; Schultz, "Raider's Ruckus"; Goff, "Angry Harvest"; Abramson, "The Takeover"; Subcommittee, "Corporate Takeovers."
44. Goff, "Angry Harvest." The welding operation was sold in August 1987. See Bertain testimony, Subcommittee, "Corporate Takeovers"; Pacific Lumber Company, Form 10-K for fiscal year ended December 31, 1987. On the change of insurer, see Pacific Lumber Company, prospectus, June 26, 1986.
45. *Labor Department v. Maxxam*, June 12, 1991; V. C. Garner to Palco President, W. C. Leone, Palco interoffice correspondence, September 25, 1986;

NOTES AND SOURCES

William C. Leone to Vince Garner, "Subject: Annuity Purchase," interoffice memorandum, September 26, 1986; Wade Lambert, "United Financial Found Liable by FDIC," *Wall Street Journal*, May 22, 1992; United Financial Group, Inc., Form 10-K for fiscal year ended December 31, 1991; Fred Strasser, "Insurer's Collapse Entangles," *National Law Journal*, December 9, 1991.

46. Garner to Leone; Leone to Garner; "U.S. Sues Maxxam, MagneTeck for Buying First Executive Annuities for Pensions," *Wall Street Journal*, June 13, 1991; David Forster, "U.S. Sues PL, Maxxam over Pension Fund Snafu," *Eureka Times-Standard*, June 13, 1991; "Statement of Jeffrey Lewis"; Wade Lambert, "Thrift Regulators Allege Broad Abuse," *Wall Street Journal*, September 14, 1991.

47. Pacific Lumber Company, prospectus, June 26, 1986. For more on the stepped-up production, see Council on Economic Priorities, "Maxxam: A Report on the Company's Environmental Policies and Practices," May 1992; Friends of the Van Duzen, "A Summation of the Pacific Lumber Company's 1988 Timber Harvest Plans," mimeo., n.d.; Hammon, Jensen, Wallen, and Associates, "Analysis of the Effects of Increased Harvests on Pacific Lumber's Forest and the North Coast Economy," August 13, 1986.

48. Hammon, Jensen et al., "Analysis of Effects"; Campbell and Stephens, interviews; Council on Economic Priorities, "Maxxam: Report"; Pacific Lumber Company, prospectus, June 26, 1986; Goff, "Angry Harvest"; Schultz, "Raider's Ruckus"; Epstein, "Raiding the Redwoods."

CHAPTER 17. OCCURRENCE AT ALL SPECIES GROVE

1. Interviews with Greg King, 1993–94.
2. Mike Geniella, "'Tarzan,' 'Jane' Perch in Trees," *Santa Rosa Press Democrat*, October 1, 1987; "Environmentalists Taking a Leaf from Tarzan's Tree," *Los Angeles Times*, October 1, 1987; Mokai, "Tarzan and Jane Swing through Redwoods Again," *Earth First! Journal* 8, no. 1 (November 1, 1987).
3. King and Woody Murphy, interviews. King claims he was told that it was Woody Murphy piloting the chopper. Murphy emphatically denies that he was the one who landed with the helicopter that day.
4. King, Peter Kayes, and John Campbell, interviews.
5. King, interviews; "Lincoln Steffens' King," *The Paper*, July 3, 1986.
6. Susan Zakin, *Coyotes and Town Dogs* (New York: Viking, 1993), pp. 344–345; Jonathan Littman, "Peace, Love . . . and TNT," *AP World* (December 1990).
7. King, interviews. For the reply, see California Forest Practice Officer Tom Osipowich, to Greg King, November 1986.
8. Donald R. Nelson, "Open Letter to Doug Bosco, Barry Keene, Dan Hauser, Alan Cranston, Pete Wilson, and George Deukmejian," *San Francisco Chronicle*, July 30, 1986.
9. Ibid.; King, interview; Osipowich to King, November 24, 1986. Rather than citing this 1,622 figure, King publicly suggested that "PL has changed its silvicultural methods from selection cutting to clearcutting. Harvest plans include what are actually *called* clearcuts." Pacific Lumber strenuously denies it intended to clear-cut this much area. Campbell, interviews. See Greg King, "Old Growth Redwood: The Final Solution," *Earth First! Journal* 7, no. 2 (December 21, 1986).
10. King and Chuck Powell, interviews.

11. King, "Final Solution."
12. Ibid.; King, interviews.
13. King, "Final Solution"; Editor's Note, *Earth First! Journal* 7, no. 2 (December 21, 1986); Dale Champion, "Plan for Cutting Redwoods Stirs Protest," *San Francisco Chronicle*, October 23, 1986; Lee Fremstad, "Earth Lovers Wield Monkey Wrench to Save Environment," *Sacramento Bee*, October 23, 1986.
14. George Snyder, "Redwood Logging War in Humboldt County," *San Francisco Chronicle*, January 5, 1987.
15. King and Campbell, interviews.
16. King, interviews. See also Greg King, "Battle for the Last Redwoods," *Earth First! Journal* 7, no. 5 (May 1, 1987).
17. Zakin, *Town Dogs*, pp. 261–262; Christopher Manes, *Green Rage* (Boston: Little, Brown, 1990), pp. 84ff.
18. King, Tom Hirons, and Larry Robertson, interviews; Ron Huber, "Battle for Millennium Grove," *Earth First! Journal* 5, no. 7 (August 1, 1985).
19. Manes, *Green Rage*, pp. 100–101; Huber, "Battle for Millennium Grove."
20. Mike O'Rizay, "Freddies Murder Millennium Grove," *Earth First! Journal*, June 21, 1986; Rhoda Dendron, "Memories of a Tree Climber," *Earth First! Journal*, May 1, 1986.
21. David Barron, "CD Begins Anew in Kalmiopsis," *Earth First! Journal* 7, no. 5 (May 1, 1987).
22. Earth First! Siskyou, "18 Arrested in Three Actions in North Kalmiopsis," *Earth First! Journal* 7, no. 6 (June 21, 1987); North Coast California Earth First!, *Old Growth in Crisis!* 1, no. 1 (Earth Day, 1987).
23. Stephen J. Pyne, *Fire in America: A Cultural History of Wildland and Rural Fire* (Princeton: Princeton University Press, 1982), p. 48.
24. William M. Denevan, "The Pristine Myth: The Landscape of the Americas in 1492," *Annals of the Association of American Geographers* 82, no. 3 (1992). See also George E. Gruell, "Fire on the Early Western Landscape: An Annotated Record of Wildland Fires, 1776–1900," *Northwest Science* 59, no. 2 (1985); Stephen W. Barrett and Stephen F. Arno, "Indian Fires as an Ecological Influence in the Northern Rockies," *Journal of Forestry* 80, no. 10 (October 1982); C. Kristina Roper Wickstrom, *Issues Concerning Native American Use of Fire: A Literature Review*, Department of Interior, Yosemite Research Center, Publications in Anthropology no. 6, December 1987; Stephen W. Barrett, "Indians and Fire," *Western Wildlands* (Spring 1980); Dean A. Shinn, "Historical Perspectives on Range Burning in the Inland Pacific Northwest," *Journal of Range Management* 33, no. 6 (November 1980).
25. Charles E. Kay, "Aboriginal Overkill: The Role of Native Americans in Structuring Western Ecosystems," *Human Nature*, in press.
26. M. Kat Anderson, "California Indian Horticulture," *Fremontia* (1990); M. Kat Anderson, "Wild Plant Management: Cross-Cultural Examples of the Small Farmers of Jaumave, Mexico, and the Southern Miwok of the Yosemite Region," *Arid Lands Newsletter* 31 (Fall–Winter 1991); M. Kat Anderson, "California Indian Horticulture: Management and Use of Redbud by the Southern Sierra Miwok," *Journal of Ethnobiology* 11, no. 1 (Summer 1991); Shelly Davis-King, "Prehistoric Human and Natural Causes of Environmental Change, with Comments on the History of the Clavey River Watershed," mimeo., n.d.; M. Kat Anderson and Gary Paul Nabhan, "Gardeners in Eden," *Wilderness* (Fall 1991).
27. Henry T. Lewis, "Why Indians Burned: Specific versus General Reasons," in *Proceeding — Symposium and Workshop on Wilderness Fire*, Missoula,

NOTES AND SOURCES

Montana, November 15–18, U.S. Department of Agriculture, Forest Service, General Technical Report INT-182, April, 1985, p. 79; H. T. Lewis, "Patterns of Indian Burning in California: Ecology and Ethnohistory," *Anthropological Papers No. 1* (Ramona, Calif.: Ballena Press, 1973). See also Bruce M. Kilgore, "What Is 'Natural' in Wilderness Fire Management?," in *Symposium on Wilderness Fire*; George E. Gruell, "Indian Fires in the Interior West: A Widespread Influence, in *Symposium on Wilderness Fire*.

28. M. Kat Anderson, "From Burns to Baskets," *California Indians and the Environment* (Spring 1992); Thomas S. Keter, "Indian Burning: Managing the Environment before 1865 along the North Fork," paper presented to Society for California Archaeology, April 16, 1987, Fresno, California.

29. Keter, "Indian Burning."

30. Ibid.

31. Lawrence Fox III, "A Classification, Map, and Volume Estimate for the Coast Redwood Forest in California," prepared for the Department of Forestry, College of Natural Resources, Humboldt State University, April 1988.

32. Dale A. Thornburgh, "Historic Development of the Concepts of 'New Forestry,' 'Ecological Forestry,' or Forest Ecosystem Management in the Redwood Forests of California," memorandum, July 1993.

33. Anthony Smith, "A New Forestry Program," testimony submitted to the Subcommittee on Public Lands of the Committee on Interior and Insular Affairs of the U.S. Senate, April 4 and 5, 1971; Peter Twight, "Ecological Forestry for the Coast Redwoods," National Parks and Conservation Association, 1973.

34. Thornburgh, "Historic Development."

35. Phillip Lowell, "A Review of Redwood Harvesting: Another Look — 1990," California Department of Forestry, Sacramento, 1990.

36. James L. Lindquist, interview, 1993. Peter Cafferata, "Clearcutting versus Selection in Coastal Redwood Forests," *Newsletter*, Jackson Demonstration State Forest, May 1990; James L. Lindquist, "Hare Creek Sprout Stocking Study on Jackson Demonstration State Forest," *California Forestry* (September 1989).

37. Lindquist, interview; Lindquist, "Hare Creek Study."

38. Thornburgh, "Historic Development."

39. American Forest Council, California Redwood Association, Redwood Region Conservation Council and Timber Association of California, *The State of the Redwoods Today*, 1990. See also California Forestry Association, "California Forests," 1991; William McKillop, "Timber Growth and Harvest Projections on California Private Lands," a talk presented to the Association of Consulting Foresters Conference, Auburn, California, April 23, 1992.

40. Bruce Krumland and William McKillop, *Prospects for Supply of Private Timber in California*, bulletin no. 1931 (Berkeley: University of California Agricultural Experiment Station, 1990); Douglas W. MacCleery, "What on Earth Have We Done to Our Forests? A Brief Overview on the Condition and Trends of U.S. Forests," in *National Forests, 1891–1991*, U.S. Department of Agriculture, Forest Service, April 6, 1993.

41. George Snyder, "Redwood Logging War in Humboldt County," *San Francisco Chronicle*, January 5, 1987; "A Takeover Artist Who's Turning Redwoods into Quick Cash," *Business Week*, February 2, 1987; "Take-Over Mania among the Redwoods," *Santa Rosa Press-Democrat*, March 29, 1987.

42. Marie Gravelle, "Keene Bill Would Limit PL Timber Harvesting," *Eureka Times-Standard*, April 21, 1987. See also George Snyder, "Environmental-

ists Challenge Sonoma County Logging Plan," *San Francisco Chronicle*, April 18, 1986; Ilana DeBare, "Old Redwoods, Traditions Felled in Race for Profits," *Los Angeles Times*, April 20, 1987.

43. Pacific Lumber Company, "To Our Many Friends and Neighbors. . . . We Thought You Would Be Interested in the Following Letter — ," paid advertisement, *Eureka Times-Standard* and *Humboldt Beacon*, March 18, 1987.

44. Greg King, "Pacific Lumber Co. Letter Went Too Far," *Eureka Times-Standard*, April 16, 1987; Greg King, "Fish & Game Says Pacific Lumber/CDF Eliminating Wildlife," Humboldt News Service, May 11, 1987; Greg King, "Environment: Unprotected Redwoods," *Siskiyou Journal*, no. 30 (June–July 1987).

45. Mokai, "EF! Protests Maxxam Redwood Logging from California to New York City," *Earth First! Journal* 7, no. 6 (June 21, 1987); King, "Battle for the Last Redwoods"; Peter Braiver, "EF! LA Update," *Earth First! Journal* 7, no. 5 (May 1, 1987); John Soukup, "Arrests Follow Pacific Lumber Protests," *Humboldt Beacon*, May 20, 1987; Enoch Ibarra, "PL Foes in Fortuna for Harvest Protest," *Humboldt Beacon*, May 9, 1987.

46. Mokai, "EF! Protests Maxxam Redwood Logging."

47. Peter Page, "Old-Growth Logging Stopped by Partain," *Humboldt Journal*, May 8, 1987.

CHAPTER 18. THE AGE OF EXTREMISM

1. George Alexander, interview December 13, 1994. Alexander told this writer that the incident "ruined" his life, yet he received, he says, very little compensation. Today he still works for Louisiana Pacific. See also Judi Bari, "The Secret History of Tree-Spiking," pts. 1 and 2, mimeo., n.d.; Larry B. Stammer, " 'Eco-Terrorists' Focus of Mill Accident Probe," *Los Angeles Times*, May 15, 1987; "Tree Spike Blamed in Injury," *Oregonian*, May 16, 1987; Eric Brazil, "Tree Spiking in Mendocino Splinters All Sides," *San Francisco Examiner*, June 21, 1987; Mid-Atlantic Research Associates, "U.S. Ecoterrorists," *Early Warning*, July 18–July 24, 1987. In July the Pacific Lumber Company received an anonymous letter, warning that what happened to Alexander could happen to any of the company's loggers, as "trees may have been spiked with a ceramic material not detectable by a metal detector." Letter postmarked July 15, 1987.

2. Bari, "Secret History."

3. Stammer, "Eco-Terrorists."

4. Bari, "Secret History."

5. Mokai, "EF! Protests Maxxam Redwood Logging from California to New York City," *Earth First! Journal* 7, no. 6 (June 21, 1987). See also Socratrees, "Tactical Thoughts on the MAXXAM Protests," *Earth First! Journal* 7, no. 6 (June 21, 1987).

6. Greg King, interview; Mokai, "EF! Protests Maxxam Logging."

7. Mokai, "EF! Protests Maxxam Logging"; Peter Bralver, "Los Angeles," *Earth First! Journal* 7, no. 6 (June 21, 1987).

8. Jean Crawford, "Texas," *Earth First! Journal* 7, no. 6 (June 21, 1987).

9. Matt Meyers, "New York City," *Earth First! Journal* 7, no. 6 (June 21, 1987).

10. Mokai, "EF! Protests Maxxam Logging."

11. Socratrees, "Tactical Thoughts."

12. Mokai, "EF! Protests Maxxam Logging"; John Soukup, "PL Files Lawsuit against Protesters," *Humboldt Beacon*, July 25, 1987.

13. King, interview.
14. Pamela Abramson, "Razing the Giant Redwoods," *Newsweek*, July 6, 1987; Tom Abate, "Timber Wars," *California Journal* (August 1988); Robert K. Anderberg, "Wall Street Sleaze," *Amicus Journal* (Spring 1988); John Goff, "Angry Harvest," *Corporate Finance* (April 1989); Ellen Schultz, "A Raider's Ruckus in the Redwoods," *Fortune*, April 24, 1989; Jack Epstein, "Raiding the Redwoods," *California Business* (September 1987); Mark Walters, "California's Chain Saw Massacre," *Reader's Digest* (November 1989); Bill McKibbon, "Milken, Junk Bonds, and Raping Redwoods," *Rolling Stone*, August 10, 1989; Chris Bowman, "The Redwood Wars," *Sacramento Bee Magazine*, February 12, 1989.
15. David Cross, "Sally Bell Redwoods Protected! Sinkyone Coast Purchased for Park," *Earth First! Journal* 7, no. 3 (February 2, 1987); The Man Who Walks in the Woods, "Summary of EPIC Lawsuits," mimeo., n.d.; Greg King, "Liquidating the Last Redwood Wilderness," *Earth First! Journal* 7, no. 7 (August 1, 1987).
16. Robert Sutherland, interviews; The Man Who Walks in the Woods, "Summary"; Frank S. Petersen, Judge of the Superior Court, ruling, *EPIC v. Maxxam Corporation*, Superior Court of the State of California for the County of Humboldt, Case no. 79879, November 4, 1987; Mike Geniella, "Judge Bars Pacific Lumber Clear-Cutting," *Santa Rosa Press-Democrat*, November 10, 1987.
17. Randy Hayes, interview; Karen Pickett, "Stop Rainforest Destruction! May Is Whopper Stopper Month," *Earth First! Journal* 7, no. 5 (May 1, 1987); Karen Pickett, "Whopper Stopper Month Strikes Again — and Continues," *Earth First! Journal* 7, no. 6 (June 21, 1987); Karen Pickett, "Hamburger Connection Broken, Major Victory," *Earth First! Journal* 7, no. 7 (August 1, 1987).
18. Paul Watson, interview; Jericho Clearwater, "Kalmiopsis Shutdown!," *Earth First! Journal* 7, no. 7 (August 1, 1987); Randall Hayes, "Citizens Conference Demonstrates against the World Bank, Submits Demands," *Earth First! Journal* 7, no. 2 (December 21, 1986); Mary Sojourner, "Grand Canyon Uranium Heats Up," *Earth First! Journal* 7, no. 5 (May 1, 1987); John Patterson and Jean Ravine, "EF! Shuts Down Grand Canyon Uranium Mine," *Earth First! Journal* 7, no. 7 (August 1, 1987); Karen Pickett, "Bay Area EF! Update," *Earth First! Journal* 17, no. 5 (May 1, 1987); Peter Bralver, "EF! LA Update," *Earth First! Journal* 17, no. 5 (May 1, 1987); Enojado P. Desierto, "Mt. Graham Defends Herself," *Earth First! Journal* 17, no. 5 (May 1, 1987); Tom Skeele, "The Three Little Wolves and the Big Bad Pigs — Wolf Defenders Stop Aerial Hunt!," *Earth First! Journal* 8, no. 4 (March 20, 1988); Rock Chalktalk, "Montana Marches for Wilderness," *Earth First! Journal* 7, no. 4 (March 20, 1987); Randall Restless, "BLM vs. the Pygmy Forest," *Earth First! Journal* 8, no. 2 (December 22, 1987); Del Mar Man, "San Diego EF! Entertained in Wilson's Office," *Earth First! Journal* 7, no. 6 (June 21, 1987).
19. Barbara Dugelby, "The Battle of Four Notch," *Earth First! Journal* 7, no. 2 (December 21, 1986); Al Gedicks, "Indian-Environmentalist Alliance Stops Exxon Mine," *Earth First! Journal* 7, no. 3 (February 2, 1983); "Hanford Occupation," *Earth First! Journal* 7, no. 8 (September 23, 1987).
20. Homo Fragaria, "The Strawberry Liberation Front," *Earth First! Journal* 7, no. 6 (June 21, 1987); Spud Buster, "The Potato Liberation Front," *Earth First! Journal* 7, no. 6 (June 21, 1987).
21. Rabinowitz, "Down with the Elwha Damns!" *Earth First! Journal* 7, no. 7 (August 1, 1987).
22. Bob Kaspar, Tom Skeele, and Sally Miller, "Grand Canyon Round River Ren-

dezvous," *Earth First! Journal* 7, no. 7 (August 1, 1987); "Burn That Dozer!" *Earth First! Journal* 7, no. 7 (August 1, 1987); Bushjuan, "Woodpeckers' Rebellion," *Earth First! Journal* 8, no. 1 (November 1, 1987); "Woodpeckers' Rebellion Pow Wow," *Earth First! Journal* 7, no. 7 (August 1, 1987).

23. Richard Shears and Isobelle Gidley, *The Rainbow Warrior Affair* (London: Unwin Paperbacks, 1986); Sunday Times, *Rainbow Warrior* (London: Arrow Books, 1986).
24. Alston Chase, "Welcome to World War III," *Lear's* (December 1989).
25. Wolpertinger, "Robin Wood," *Earth First! Journal* 7, no. 3 (February 2, 1987).
26. Ibid.; Chase, "Welcome to World War III."
27. Paul Watson, David Howitt, and Ron Coronado, interviews; Paul Watson, "Raid on Reykjavik," *Earth First! Journal* 7, no. 2 (December 21, 1986).
28. John Campbell, interviews.
29. See Steven J. Kerns, "Wildlife Observations on the Lands of the Pacific Lumber Company, 1990 Spotted Owl Summary Report," Wildlife Resources Managers, prepared for the Pacific Lumber Company, January 1991.
30. William Henry Vanderbilt quoted in *New York Times*, August 25, 1918.
31. Interviews with Palco workers Peter Kayes, Kelly Bettiga, Gene Kennedy, and Doug Coleman.
32. John Locke, *Essays on the Law of Nature*, ed. W. von Leyden (Oxford: Oxford University Press, 1954); John Locke, *Two Treatises of Government* (New York: Hafner, 1947); Thomas Hobbes, *Leviathan*, ed. Michael Oakeshott (Oxford: Basil Blackwell, 1960).
33. King, interview; Greg King, "Redwood Tree Climbers," *Earth First! Journal* 7, no 8 (September 23, 1987).
34. King, interview; Greg King, "Redwood Tree Climbers."
35. King, "Redwood Tree Climbers."
36. Ibid.
37. King, interview; Mokai, "Tarzan and Jane Swing through Redwoods Again," *Earth First! Journal* 8, no. 1 (November 1, 1987).
38. Marie Gravelle, "Treetop Protesters Climb Down," *Eureka Times-Standard*, September 4, 1987.
39. Thomas E. Ricks and Daniel Hertberg, "Ex-Jeffries Aide May Have Parked Stock for Hurwitz, Congressional Report Says," *Wall Street Journal*, October 5, 1987. See also James B. Stewart, "Deals in Boesky Probe Show Increasing Links with Drexel Burnham," *Wall Street Journal*, December 5, 1986.
40. Frank S. Petersen, Judge of the Superior Court, ruling, *EPIC v. Maxxam Corporation*, Superior Court of the State of California for the County of Humboldt, Case no. 79879, November 4, 1987; Mike Geniella, "Judge Bars Pacific Lumber Clear-Cutting," *Santa Rosa Press-Democrat*, November 10, 1987; The man who walks in the woods, "Judge Blasts MAXXAM!," *Earth First! Journal* 8, no. 2 (December 22, 1987); Marie Gravelle, "Second Group Files PL Lawsuit," *Eureka Times-Standard*, October 10, 1987.

CHAPTER 19. THE PARADIGM SHIFT

1. Andy Stahl, interviews, 1992–1994; William Dietrich, *The Final Forest* (New York: Simon and Schuster, 1992), chap. 13.
2. The Oregon and Washington wilderness bills were passed in 1984. See Steven Lewis Yaffee, *The Wisdom of the Owl* (Washington, D.C.: Island Press, 1994); Dietrich, *The Final Forest*.
3. Liza Tuttle, "End of the Old-Growth Canopy," *National Parks* (May–June

1987). For the debate over what to call the forest, see Dietrich, *The Final Forest*; Susan Zakin, *Coyotes and Town Dogs* (New York: Viking, 1993).

4. Jerry F. Franklin et al., *Ecological Characteristics of Old-Growth Douglas-Fir Forests*, General Technical Report PNW-118 (Portland: Pacific Northwest Forest and Range Experiment Station, U.S. Department of Agriculture, Forest Service, February 1981); Interagency Scientific Committee to Address the Conservation of the Northern Spotted Owl, *A Conservation Strategy for the Northern Spotted Owl* (Portland: Departments of Agriculture and Interior, May 1990); Victor M. Sher and Andy Stahl, "Spotted Owls, Ancient Forests, Courts, and Congress: An Overview of Citizens' Efforts to Protect Old-Growth Forests and the Species That Live in Them," *Northwest Environmental Journal* 6 (1990); Yaffee, *Wisdom of the Owl*.

5. Stahl, interviews. See also memorandum from E. Charles Meslow to Andy Stahl et al., "Old Growth Forest Retention for Spotted Owls — How Much Do They Need?" November 5, 1984.

6. Stahl and Douglas MacCleery, interviews; Sher and Stahl, "Spotted Owls, Ancient Forests"; Yaffee, *Wisdom of the Owl*.

7. Stahl, interviews; Dietrich, *Final Forest*.

8. Stahl, interview; R. Levins, "Some Demographic and Genetic Consequences of Environmental Heterogeneity for Biological Control," *Bulletin of the Entomological Society of America* 15 (1969).

9. Russell Lande, "Report on the Demography and Survival of the Northern Spotted Owl," final corrected draft, June 1985; R. Lande, "Demographic Models of the Northern Spotted Owl (*Strix Occidentalis caurina*)," *Oecologia* (Berlin) 75 (1988).

10. Stahl, interviews; Yaffee, *Wisdom of the Owl*, pp. 98ff.; Sher and Stahl, "Spotted Owls, Ancient Forests."

11. Lande, "Demographic Models"; Interagency Committee, *A Conservation Strategy*. The number of owls seen on all surveyed public and private lands by 1989 was 6,059. See Northwest Forest Resource Council, "Comments Submitted to the U.S. Fish and Wildlife Service Regarding the Status Review Supplement, Revised Finding and Proposed Rule Determining the Northern Spotted Owl as a Threatened Species," December 20, 1989. Lande also disregarded the entire California northern spotted owl population. Robert Taylor and Larry Irwin, interviews; R. J. Gutierrez et al., "Dispersal Ecology of Juvenile Northern Spotted Owls in Northwestern California," Final Report on Cooperative Agreement, U.S. Department of Agriculture, Forest Service, PNW-82-226; M. S. Boyce and L. L. Irwin, "Influence of Habitat Fragmentation on Spotted Owl Site Occupancy and Reproductive Success in Western Oregon," proposal to the U.S. Bureau of Land Management, 1989. Even the National Audubon Society's blue ribbon panel observed, "Yearly adult survival is not well known." See National Audubon Society, "Report of the Advisory Panel on the Spotted Owl," Audubon Conservation Report no. 7, 1986.

12. Lande, "Demographic Models"; Lande, testimony, *Portland Audubon Society* v. *Lujan*. See also Northwest Forest Resource Council, "The Northern Spotted Owl — NFRC Summary of Issue," Portland, Oregon, February 1989; B. Cary, Janice A. Reid, and Scott P. Horton, "Spotted Owl Home Range and Habitat Use in Southern Oregon Coast Ranges," *Journal of Wildlife Management* 54 (1990).

13. Stahl, interview. In his court testimony Lande admitted that he was recruited by environmentalists.

14. Memorandum from Meslow to Stahl et al.

15. Eric D. Forsman, E. Charles Meslow, and Howard M. Wight, "Distribution and Biology of the Spotted Owl in Oregon," *Wildlife Monographs* (April 1984).

16. Eric Forsman, interviews; Eric D. Forsman and E. Charles Meslow, "Spotted Owl Abundance in Young Versus Old-Growth Forests, Oregon," *Wildlife Society Bulletin* 5, no. 2 (Summer 1977).

17. Interviews with Michael L. Rosenzweig, Robert Taylor, and others.

18. H. Ronald Pulliam, "Sources, Sinks, and Population Regulation," *American Naturalist* 132 (1988).

19. Alan B. Franklin et al., "Density of Northern Spotted Owls in Northwest California," *Journal of Wildlife Management* 54 (1990).

20. Cary et al., "Spotted Owl Home Range"; E. Charles Meslow, "Spotted Owl Monitoring; Medford Segment, Miller Mountain Study Area," Supplement no. PNW-86-390 to Master Memorandum of Understanding no. PNW 80-87, Oregon Cooperative Wildlife Research Unit, 1988; Larry L. Irwin et al., "Characteristics of Spotted Owl Nest Sites in the Wenatchee National Forest," 1989. The evidence of owl abundance in new forests is voluminous. See also E. Charles Meslow, "The Ecology of Spotted Owls in the Central Cascades, Western Oregon," Supplement no. PNW 87-406 to Master Memorandum of Understanding no. PNW-80-87, 1988; W. A. Neitro, "Fifth Affidavit of William A. Neitro," *Portland Audubon Society v. Lujan,* U.S. District Court of Oregon, 1989.

21. Rosenzweig, interviews; Interagency Committee, "A Conservation Strategy," pp. 201 ff.; C. Ogan and H. F. Sakal, "Spotted Owl Food Habits," U.S. Department of Agriculture, Forest Service, Redwood Science Laboratory, Arcata, California, 1990; K. Wallen, "Social Organization in the Dusky-Footed Woodrat," *Animal Behavior* 30 (1982); J. P. Ward and R. J. Gutierrez, "Spotted Owl Reproduction and Abundance in Northwest California," 1989; Larry Irwin and Steve Self, "Status of Northern Spotted Owls on Managed Forestlands in Northern California," a study conducted for the Timber Association of California, mimeo., December 13, 1989.

22. Rosenzweig, interviews; L. Goldwasser, M. Groom, and P. Kareiva, "The Effects of Model Structure and Annual Variability on Population Viability Analyses of the Northern Spotted Owl," Department of Zoology, NJ-15, University of Washington, n.d.

23. Taylor, interview. See also Gregg Easterbrook, "The Birds," *New Republic,* March 28, 1994.

24. Rosenzweig, interviews. See also Michael L. Rosenzweig, "The California Spotted Owl Report: An Evaluation," August 28, 1992.

25. See, e.g., Franklin et al., "Density of Northern Spotted Owls."

26. See, e.g., Barry R. Noon and Charles M. Biles, "Mathematical Demography of Spotted Owls in the Pacific Northwest," *Journal of Wildlife Management* 54 (1990).

27. M. R. Young, "Conserving Insect Communities in Mixed Woodlands," in *The Ecology of Mixed-Species Stands of Trees,* ed. M. G. R. Cannell, D. C. Malcolm, and P. A. Robertson (London: Basil Blackwell, 1992).

28. Charles C. Mann and Mark L. Plummer, "The Butterfly Problem," *Atlantic* (January 1992); Charles C. Mann and Mark L. Plummer, *Noah's Choice: The Future of Endangered Species* (New York: Alfred A. Knopf, 1995); Michael E. Fry and Nelson R. Money, "Biodiversity Conservation in the Management of Utility Rights-of-Way," *Proceedings, Fifteenth Annual Forest Vegetation Management Conference,* Redding, California, January 25–27, 1994.

29. Alston Chase, *Playing God in Yellowstone* (New York: Atlantic Monthly

Press, 1980); Mann and Plummer, *Noah's Choice*, chapters 5 and 7.

30. The foregoing discussion is based on Noel F. R. Snyder and Helen A. Snyder, "Biology and Conservation of the California Condor," *Current Ornithology* 6 (1989).

31. Stahl, interview; Yaffee, "Wisdom of the Owl"; National Audubon Society, "Report of the Advisory Panel on the Spotted Owl," Audubon Conservation Report no. 7, 1986.

32. Audubon Society, "Advisory Panel."

33. Interviews with Steven, Willow, and Eric Beckwith, 1992–1994.

34. Stahl, interviews; Yaffee, *Wisdom of the Owl*; Dietrich, *Final Forest* p. 83.

35. Yaffee, *Wisdom of the Owl*; Dietrich, *Final Forest*; Interagency Committee, "Conservation Strategy," pp. 54–55; Sher and Stahl, "Spotted Owls, Ancient Forests."

36. Interagency Committee, "Conservation Strategy"; Yaffee, *Wisdom of the Owl*.

37. Stahl, James Monteith, and Terry Thatcher, interviews. Interagency Committee, "Conservation Strategy"; Yaffee, *Wisdom of the Owl*; Sher and Stahl, "Spotted Owls, Ancient Forests."

38. Interagency Committee, "Conservation Strategy"; Sher and Stahl, "Spotted Owls, Ancient Forests."

39. *Immanuel Kant's Critique of Pure Reason*, ed. and trans. Norman Kemp Smith (London: Macmillan, 1956), p. 22.

40. Ibid., esp. "Transcendental Analytic."

41. Thomas S. Kuhn, *The Structure of Scientific Revolutions* (Chicago: University of Chicago Press, 1962), p. 10.

42. Ibid., pp. 93, 94.

43. Bill Devall, "New Age and Deep Ecology: Contrasting Paradigms," 1981; George Sessions, "Shallow and Deep Ecology: A Review of the Philosophical Literature," prepared for Earth Day X, The Humanities and Ecological Consciousness: A Scholarly Colloquium, University of Denver, April 21–24, 1980; Fritjof Capra, *The Turning Point* (New York: Simon and Schuster, 1982), p. 30; Marilyn Ferguson, *The Aquarian Conspiracy* (Los Angeles: J. P. Tarcher, 1980), p. 29.

44. Kuhn, *Structure of Scientific Revolutions*, p. 93.

CHAPTER 20. WOBBLIES AND YELLOW RIBBONS

1. Much of this account is drawn from Judi Bari, interviews, 1991–1994; see also Darryl Cherney, "Triple Victory in Three Day Revolution," *Earth First! Journal* 9, no. 2 (December 21, 1988).

2. See Jonathan Littman, "Peace, Love . . . and TNT," *AP World* (December 1990).

3. Gary and Betty Ball, interviews, 1992.

4. John Patterson, "EF! Howls at 1988 Rendezvous," *Earth First! Journal* 8, no. 7 (August 1, 1988).

5. Judi Bari, "California Rendezvous," *Earth First! Journal* 9, no. 1 (November 1, 1988).

6. Interviews with Bari, Karen Pickett, Karen Wood, and Kelpie Willsin, 1991–1994.

7. "FTC Asked to Investigate Pacific Lumber Takeover," *Ukiah Daily Journal*, February 11, 1988. See also Subcommittee on Oversight and Investigations

of the Committee on Energy and Commerce, House of Representatives, "Corporate Takeovers," October 5, 1987, "Pacific Lumber: A Case Study," February 8, 1988, serial no. 100-116. See also *Federal Deposit Insurance Corporation et al. v. Michael R. Milken et al.*, December 30, 1988.

8. *Clarence Kayes et al. v. Pacific Lumber Company et al.*, April 1990; "Statement of Jeffrey Lewis before the U.S. House of Representatives Select Committee on Aging, Subcommittee on Retirement Income and Employment," April 30, 1991; *Thompson v. Maxxam Group*, filed in Los Angeles Federal Court on October 21, 1988. This suit was later incorporated into other ongoing litigation known as *In re Boesky*. See also Gail Diana Cox, "Tall Timber Tension," *National Law Journal*, February 1, 1988.

9. "ESOP Update," *Takeback* (a newsletter of the Pacific Lumber Rescue Fund), 1, no. 1 (February 1989).

10. Bari and Peter Kayes, interviews.

11. Northcoast California Earth First!, "Earth First! Proposed Redwood Wilderness," *Earth First! Journal* 8, no. 4 (March 20, 1988); Byron Sher, "Sher Calls for Harvest Moratorium to Protect Critical Old-Growth Redwoods," press release, February 2, 1988.

12. Dennis Duggan, "A Street Filled with Angry Trees," *New York Newsday*, January 14, 1988; "In the Trees, again," *Eureka Times-Standard*, May 21, 1988; "EPIC Files New Lawsuit to Block Cutting of Old Growth," *North Coast News*, April 7, 1988; Mark Stein, "Small Environmental Group Has a Big Impact on Logging," *Los Angeles Times*, January 27, 1990; The man who walks in the woods, "Summary of EPIC Forestry Lawsuits," n.d.

13. The man who walks in the woods, "The California Forest Practices Act: It Is Tough Enough," *Forest Watch* (July 1986); EPIC to California Department of Forestry, April 5, 1988; Greg King, "Unprotected Redwoods," *Siskiyou Journal*, no. 30 (June–July 1987); Greg King, "Fish & Game Says Pacific Lumber/CDF Eliminating Wildlife," Humboldt News Service, May 11, 1987; Jerry Partain, "A Tale of Two Agencies," *The Lumberjack*, December 4, 1991.

14. Associated Press, "Vandalism Postpones Frostban Test, Earth First! Admits Role," *Eureka Press-Democrat*, December 3, 1987.

15. The Avenger, "Stumps Suck!," *Earth First! Journal* 8, no. 4 (March 20, 1988).

16. Karen Pickett, "Day of Outrage Shakes Forest Service Nationwide!," *Earth First! Journal* 8, no. 6 (June 21, 1988).

17. Ibid.

18. Ibid.

19. Mitch Friedman, "26 Arrested in Washington Demo," *Earth First! Journal* 8, no. 7 (August 1, 1988); Jim Weed, "Sheriff Jim Weed of Okanogan County, Washington," a speech delivered to Washington Contract Loggers Association, September 15, 1988, and reprinted in *Loggers' World* (November 1988).

20. Weed, "Sheriff Weed."

21. Interviews with Jim Peterson, Bob Slagle, Kelpie Willsin, and Karen Wood, 1993–94; Aaron Ellis, "Silver Fire Roundup," *Loggers' World* 13, no. 10 (October 1988); Karen Wood, "Sapphire Six Sued," *Earth First! Journal* 8, no. 4 (March 20, 1988); Karen Wood, "Sapphire Six Suit Approaches Decision," *Earth First! Journal* 9, no. 1 (November 1, 1988); Kelpie Willsin, "Another Kalmiopsis Kangaroo Court, *Earth First! Journal* 9, no. 2 (December 21, 1988).

22. Ellis, "Silver Fire Roundup"; Bobcat, "Mugging a Burn Victim: Salvage Logging in the North Kalmiopsis, *Earth First! Journal* 8, no. 4 (March 20, 1988); The Captain, "Kalmiopsis Fire: The Reality and the Politics," *Earth First! Journal* 8, no. 3 (February 2, 1988).

23. Elis Lucia, *Tillamook Burn Country* (Caldwell, Idaho: Caxton Printers, 1983), p. xxi.
24. Ibid.; Leo A. Isaac and George S. Meagher, "Natural Reproduction on the Tillamook Burn, Four Years after the Fire," Pacific Northwest Forest Experiment Station, Portland, Oregon, January 10, 1938; Stephen J. Pyne, *Fire in America: A Cultural History of Wildland and Rural Fire* (Princeton: Princeton University Press, 1982), pp. 331–334.
25. Pyne, *Fire in America*, p. 332.
26. Ibid.; Lucia, *Tillamook Burn.*
27. Bobcat, "Mugging a Burn Victim"; The Captain, "Kalmiopsis Fire"; Bobcat, "No-Compromise Politics Work," *Earth First! Journal* 8, no. 8 (September 22, 1988); "The Burn Returns," *Forest Log* (January–February 1992); U.S. Department of Agriculture, Forest Service, *Final Supplement to the Environmental Impact Statement for an Amendment to the Pacific Northwest Regional Guide, Spotted Owl Guidelines,* 1987.
28. Bob Slagle and James Peterson, interviews; Ellis, "Silver Fire Roundup."
29. Bruce Vincent, "A Logger's Story," *Evergreen,* June 1988.
30. Ellis, "Silver Fire Roundup."
31. Ibid.
32. Bobcat, "No-Compromise Politics"; Jim Peterson, "Where Do We Go from Here?," *Loggers' World* 13, no. 10 (October 1988).
33. Judi Bari, "Timber Wars," in *Timber Wars and Other Writings* (privately published, 1992).

CHAPTER 21. THE EASTER SUNDAY MASSACRE

1. Tom Hirons and Larry Robertson, interviews, 1992–1994.
2. Paul Roland, "Millennium Grove II: Breitenbush Blockade Draws National Attention to Ancient Forests," *Earth First! Journal* 9, no. 5 (May 1, 1989); Catherine Caufield, "The Ancient Forest," *New Yorker,* May 14, 1990.
3. Victor M. Sher and Andy Stahl, "Spotted Owls, Ancient Forests, Courts, and Congress: An Overview of Citizens' Efforts to Protect Old-Growth Forests and the Species That Live in Them," *Northwest Environmental Journal* 6 (1990).
4. *National Forests: Policies for the Future* (Washington, D.C.: Wilderness Society, 1988–89); see esp. vol. 2, *Protecting Biological Diversity,* by David S. Wilcove; vol. 4, *Pacific Northwest Lumber and Wood Products: An Industry in Transition,* by Jeffrey T. Olson (published in cooperation with the National Wildlife Federation); and vol. 5, *The Uncounted Costs of Logging,* by Richard E. Rice.
5. Olson, *Pacific Northwest Lumber,* pp. vi, viii, and 29.
6. Mark T. Spriggs and Gerald S. Albaum, "Examination of Economic Multipliers for the Oregon Wood Products Industry," Forest Industries Management Center, College of Business Administration, University of Oregon, September 1990; Brian J. Greber, "Technological Change in the Timber Industries in the Pacific Northwest: Historic Background and Future Implications," Oregon State University, November 22, 1991.
7. Paul F. Ehinger, "Comparison: Wood products conversion efficiency, 1947 and 1987, and Employment per MMBF of Timber Harvested and Processed Domestically," April 6, 1994.
8. Greber, "Technological Change."
9. By 1990 53 percent of total national forest land in Oregon and Washington

had been set aside for uses that excluded any timber harvesting. And, in contrast to the net loss of 2,300 jobs which the Wilderness Society claimed, in 1990 a joint Forest Service–Bureau of Land Management study predicted a reduction of 25,000 timber-related jobs alone. William MacCleery, interviews; "Oregon's Forests, 1994 Fact Book," *Evergreen Magazine* (1994); Northwest Forestry Association, "Chronology of Compromise: Land Set-Asides in the Pacific Northwest," mimeo., n.d.; Northwest Forestry Association, "Shrinking Giant," n.d.

10. In 1990 the timber industry predicted that the regional economy would lose 107,000 workers and $2.5 billion. See Northwest Forest Resource Council, "Briefing Packet: Northwest Forest Resource Council Spotted Owl Presentation," 1990; Institute of Forest Resources, University of Washington, "Three-State Impact of Spotted Owl Conservation and Other Timber Harvest Reductions: A Cooperative Evaluation of the Economic and Social Impacts," contribution no. 69, September 1990; Claire A. Montgomery, Gardner M. Brown, Jr., and Darius M. Adams, "The Marginal Cost of Species Preservation: The Northern Spotted Owl," 1991.

11. Robert G. Lee et al., "Social Impacts of Alternative Timber Harvest Reductions on Federal Lands in O and C Counties," College of Forest Resources, University of Washington, June 1991, pp. 15–16. See also Robert G. Lee, Matthew S. Carroll, and Kristin K. Warren, "The Social Impact of Timber Harvest Reductions in Washington State," in *Revitalizing the Timber-Dependent Regions of Washington*, ed. William Beyers et al. (Seattle: University of Washington, Northwest Policy Center, February 1991).

12. Robert G. Lee, "Moral Exclusion and Rural Poverty: Myth Management and Wood Products Workers," February 24, 1992; Susan Opotow, "Moral Exclusion and Injustice: An Introduction," *Journal of Social Issues* 46, no. 1 (1990). See also Robert G. Lee, "Social and Cultural Implications of Implementing 'a Conservation Strategy for the Northern Spotted Owl,'" College of Forest Resources, University of Washington, June 21, 1990; Robert G. Lee, "Institutional Stability: A Requisite for Sustainable Forestry," 1990 Starker Lectures, College of Forestry, Oregon State University; Robert G. Lee, *Broken Trust, Broken Land* (Wilsonville, Ore.: BookPartners, 1994).

13. See, for example, Randal O'Toole, *Reforming the Forest Service* (Washington, D.C.: Island Press, 1988).

14. Donald R. Leal, "Making Money on Timber Sales: A Federal and State Comparison," in *Multiple Conflicts over Multiple Uses*, ed. Terry L. Anderson (Bozeman, Mont.: Political Economic Research Center, 1994).

15. Theodore Sudia, interviews; William R. Burch, Jr., "Finding the Way Back: Park and Wildland Management as a Professional Public Service," George Hartzog Lecture, Clemson University, September 26, 1988; Richard W. Guilden, "An Economic Model of the Costs of Wilderness Management Incurred by the United States Forest Service" (Ph.D. diss., Yale University, 1979); "Tarnished Jewels: The Case for Reforming the Park Service," *Different Drummer* 2, no. 1 (Winter 1995). This "below cost" crusade reached its peak on February 17, 1993, when the Clinton administration proposed closing 62 of the nation's 156 national forests to logging because they were deemed to "lose money." In fact, this step, which failed, would have cost taxpayers nearly $1.5 billion while saving only $274 million. See Keith Schneider, "U.S. Would End Cutting of Trees in Many Forests," *New York Times*, April 30, 1993.

16. See "Lies, Damned Lies, and Statistics: How the Forest Service Timber Program Cost Taxpayers $499 million in 1992," *CHEC* (Portland), April 8, 1993;

Alston Chase, "Real Issues of Below-Cost Timber Sales Being Ignored," Creators Syndicate, May 10, 1993; *The Atlantic Monthly*, April, 1994.

17. Jeff DeBonis, "Background to AFSEEE's Development," Eugene, Oregon, n.d.; Ehinger and MacCleery, interviews. National Forest timber sales levels rose sharply after World War II, from around 5 billion board feet to between 9 and 12 billion by the late 1960s, where they remained until 1988. During this time, however, forest growth rates continued to rise, so that nationally forests continued to grow in volume. In the Pacific Northwest the timber harvest in 1987 was almost identical to the 1947 figure: 8,212 million board feet in 1947 and 8,215 in 1987.

18. AFSEEE (Association of Forest Service Employees for Environmental Ethics), Annual Report, Department of Justice, State of Oregon, Registration no. 50-15747, received September 14, 1993; *AFSEEE Activist* 1, no. 4 (November 1991); *Inner Voice* 3, no. 1 (Winter 1991); Greg Brown and Charles C. Harris, "The U.S. Forest Service: Toward the New Resource Management Paradigm?," *Society and Natural Resources*, September 14, 1991.

19. Hirons, Robertson, and Cherie Girod, interviews; Roland, "Millennium Grove II."

20. Hirons, Robertson, Girod, Kelpie Willsin, and Karen Wood, interviews.

21. Roland, "Millennium Grove II"; Caufield, "The Ancient Forest." According to an empirical study conducted by Utah State University researchers in 1995, users of wilderness in that state are "predominantly male, relatively young, well educated, white, and employed as professionals or executives." Their incomes "were also higher than those in the general population." Likewise, a 1982–83 national survey found that the average wilderness visitor earns more than $50,000 a year, and that 83 percent of African Americans have never visited a national park. According to the Northwest Forestry Association (personal communication), incomes of loggers and millworkers — before these timber wars — was about the median annual household income of $35,000. Today it is much less. See Donald L. Snyder et al., *Wilderness Designation in Utah: Issues and Potential Economic Impacts* (Logan: Utah State University, 1995), p. 76; Burch, "Finding the Way Back"; and Merle J. Van Horne et al., *1982–83 Nationwide Recreation Survey* (Washington, D.C.: National Park Service, 1984).

22. Caufield, "The Ancient Forest."

23. National Audubon Society, "Ancient Forest Chronology," mimeo., n.d.; Elliott A. Norse, *Ancient Forests of the Pacific Northwest* (Washington, D.C.: Island Press, 1990).

24. Hirons and Girod, interviews.

25. Interagency Scientific Committee to Address the Conservation of the Northern Spotted Owl, *A Conservation Strategy for the Northern Spotted Owl* (Portland: Departments of Agriculture and the Interior, May 1990); David Seideman, *Showdown at Opal Creek: The Battle for America's Last Wilderness* (New York: Carroll and Graf, 1993); Steven Lewis Jaffee, *The Wisdom of the Spotted Owl* (Washington, D.C.: Island Press, 1994); Sher and Stahl, "Spotted Owls, Ancient Forests."

26. Girod, interview.

27. Ibid.; Lee et al., "Social Impacts."

28. Girod, Hirons, Mark Silvernagel, and Bob and Jeanne Gaines, interviews.

29. Hirons and Rita Kaley, interviews.

30. Hirons, Kaley, James Peterson, Valerie Johnson, Mike McKay, and Evelyn Badger, interviews.

31. By 1993 the Oregon Lands Coalition would represent sixty-six groups and 83,000 families; interview with OLC executive director Jackie Lang.
32. In 1991 the Audubon Society reportedly spent $225,000 on the logo and survey. The same year the coalition's gross income was $107,857. Environmentalists' frequent complaints that the coalition is the "tool of industry" is a myth. By comparison, in 1992 AFSEEE's income was $367,129, and in 1988 the National Audubon Society's budget was $38,499,654. See Anne Raver, "Old Environmental Group Seeks Tough New Image," *New York Times*, June 9, 1991.
33. Bill Gifford and the Editors, "Inside the Environmental Groups," *Outside* (September 1990). See also John Lancaster, "The Environmentalist as Insider," *Washington Post Magazine*, August 4, 1991; Leslie Spencer with Jan Bollwerk and Richard C. Morais, "The Not So Peaceful World of Greenpeace," *Forbes*, November 11, 1991.
34. Alston Chase, "Goose Music and Doctor Muir," *Outside* (November 1987); Gifford et al., "Inside the Environmental Groups"; John Lancaster, "The Environmentalist as Insider."
35. Michael S. Greve, "Environmentalism and Bounty Hunting," *The Public Interest*, no. 97 (Fall 1989).
36. Ibid.
37. Chase, "Goose Music and Doctor Muir"; "A Small Circle of Friends," *Outside* (May 1988). In 1993 the Sierra Club Legal Defense Fund received $1,493,800 in court-awarded attorneys' fees and costs. See Sierra Club Legal Defense Fund, annual report, fiscal year 1992–93.

CHAPTER 22. FORESTS FOREVER

1. This account of the Round River Rendezvous is a personal report.
2. Associated Press, "Four Environmentalists Arrested on Nuclear Sabotage Charges," *Livingston Enterprise*, June 1, 1989; "Earth First! Activists Arrested," *Billings Gazette*, May 26, 1989.
3. Paul Feldman and Richard E. Meyer, "4 Held in Plot to Cut Lines Near Nuclear Plants," *Los Angeles Times*, June 1, 1989; Federal Bureau of Investigation, media release, May 31, 1989; Russ Hemphill, "FBI Says 4 Planned to Attack Palo Verde," *Phoenix Gazette*, May 31, 1989; Russ Hemphill and Dennis Wagner, "FBI Probe of Sabotage Led to Radicals' Arrest," *Phoenix Gazette*, June 1, 1989; Randy Collier, "Environmental 'Radicals' Arrested," *Arizona Republic*, June 1, 1989; Mark Shaffer, "Serious 'Monkeywrenchers,'" *Arizona Republic*, June 1, 1989, June 2, 1989; Jim Robbins, "Saboteurs for a Better Environment," *New York Times*, July 9, 1989; Gene Varn, "Environmentalist Held to Silence Him, His Supporters Say," *Arizona Republic*, June 2, 1989.
4. FBI media release; Feldman and Meyer, "4 Held in Plot."
5. Hemphill and Wagner, "FBI Probe"; "Update on 'Arizona Four' Arrests," *Earth First! Journal* 9, no. 6 (June 21, 1989); "Arizona Arrestees Released from Jail!" *Earth First! Journal* 9, no. 7 (August 1, 1989).
6. Rich Ryan, "RR Reflects on the RRR," *Earth First! Journal* 9, no. 7 (August 1, 1993); Dana Beal, Howie Wolke, and Dave Guterson, interviews.
7. Loose Hip Circles, "Riotous Rendezvous Remembered," *Earth First! Journal* 9, no. 7 (August 1, 1993).
8. Greg King, "Anti-MAXXAM Warriors Climb Back into the Trees," *Earth First! Journal* 9, no. 6 (June 21, 1989).

9. Ryan, "RR Reflects on the RRR."
10. Douglas MacCleery to author, July 6, 1994.
11. For one of the first developments of this theme, see William Tucker, *Progress and Privilege: America in the Age of Environmentalism* (Garden City, N.Y.: Anchor Press/Doubleday, 1982).
12. Jonathan Littman, "Peace, Love . . . and TNT," *AP World* (December 1990).
13. Judi Bari, interviews; Loose Hip Circles, "EF! Takes to the Trees," *Earth First! Journal* 9, no. 8 (September 22, 1989); Judi Bari, "Californians Start a New Fad: Tree-Sitting Becomes a Pastime," *Earth First! Journal* 9, no. 8 (September 22, 1989).
14. "Argus" to Ukiah Chief of Police Fred Keplinger, postmarked January 6, 1989.
15. Mike Geniella, "Logging Protesters Claim Pattern of Violence," *Santa Rosa Press-Democrat*, March 28, 1990; Bruce Anderson, "This Man Tried to Kill Us," *Anderson Valley Advertiser*, March 12, 1990; Alliance for Activists' Rights, "The Bombing of Judi Bari and Darryl Cherney: A Chronology of Events," mimeo., November 15, 1990. During the same month there was another violent incident in which Bari was involved, known as the Lancaster or Whitethorn action, when at least one shot was fired by a logger. See Mendocino County Sheriff's Department, press release, "The Incident in Whitethorn," August 16, 1989.
16. Bari, interviews; Bari to Susan Massini, Mendocino County Court House, March 14, 1990.
17. Teresa Simons, "Epic Struggle over Redwoods," *California Journal* (March 1990); California Coordinating Council, "The Good, the Bad, and the Ugly," leaflet, July 12, 1990; "'Big Green' Colors State Politics," *Los Angeles Times*, March 25, 1990; Brian Lantz, "'Big Green' Referendum in California Protects Pests, Endangers People," *New Federalist*, May 20, 1990. Steven Hayward, "The Big Green Monster," *Reason Magazine* (June 1990); Warren Brookes, "Revenge of the Killer Watermelon," speech given before the Pacific Research Institute for Public Policy, July 26, 1990.
18. Simons, "Epic Struggle"; Hayward, "Big Green Monster."
19. Interagency Scientific Committee to Address the Conservation of the Northern Spotted Owl, *A Conservation Strategy for the Northern Spotted Owl* (Portland: Departments of Agriculture and the Interior, May 1990).
20. National Audubon Society, "Ancient Forest Chronology," mimeo., n.d.
21. Most environmentalists view the Adams-Hatfield amendment, which they often call the "rider from hell," as a defeat, but in fact it was a victory for them. As Steven Lewis Yaffee writes: "Timber got the promise of a short-term federal timber supply at fairly high cut levels, but received it at a price of unprecedented environmental group input into the timber sale process and the explicit recognition of old growth in federal law, a change that was sure to come back to haunt them." Steven Lewis Yaffee, *The Wisdom of the Owl* (Washington, D.C.: Island Press, 1994), p. 122.; see also William Dietrich, *The Final Forest* (New York: Simon and Schuster, 1992), pp. 121–122.
22. Yaffee, *Wisdom of the Owl*, pp. 120–121; Dale Turner, "Sierra Club Undermined Efforts against Hatfield Rider," *Earth First! Journal* 10, no. 3 (February 2, 1990); Mitch Friedman, "The 1989 Timber Compromise: Will Environmentalists Never Learn?," *Earth First! Journal* 10, no. 3 (February 2, 1990).
23. *EPIC* v. *Maxxam I*, originally filed April 10, 1987; *EPIC* v. *Maxxam II*, filed October 15, 1987; The man who walks in the woods, "Summary of EPIC Forestry Lawsuits, current to June 17, 1992," n.d.; Bill Israel, "EPIC Timber

Battle Heats Up, Heads to Supreme Court," *Northcoast News* (February 1989).

24. Mike Geniella, "Headwaters Trees in Eye of a Storm," *Santa Rosa Press-Democrat*, January 14, 1990; Mark A. Stein, "Plan to Log Redwoods Hits a Buzz Saw of Opposition," *Los Angeles Times*, January 27, 1990; Greg King, "Headwaters Forest Alert!," *Country Activist* 6, no. 10 (November 1989); Jane Kay, "North Coast Split Over Logging of Old Growth," *San Francisco Examiner*, January 21, 1990; Earth First!, "Save Headwaters Forest," *Mendocino County Environmentalist*, January 1, 1990.

25. Mendocino-Lake Group, Redwood Chapter, Sierra Club, "Forests Forever," *The Spotted Owl* 2, no. 1 (November 1989).

26. Northcoast Environmental Center, "1990: Year of the Forest Initiatives," March 19, 1993; Mike Geniella, "'Forests Forever' Apparently Headed for November Ballot," *Santa Rosa Press-Democrat*, May 8, 1990; Jennifer Jennings, "Forests Forever," Planning and Conservation League, April 2, 1990; Bleys W. Rose, "Timber Issue Turns to Cost," *Santa Rosa Press-Democrat*, October 14, 1990; Donald R. Nelson, "Forests Forever for Whom?," *Santa Rosa Press-Democrat*, July 19, 1990; Steve Hard, "Redwoods Measure Gets State Nod," *Santa Rosa Press-Democrat*, January 1, 1990.

27. Steve Hart, "Timber Industry Vows 'True' Reform," *Santa Rosa Press-Democrat*, January 20, 1990; Tim Tesconi, "Farmers' Initiative Counters 'Big Green,'" *Santa Rosa Press-Democrat*, April 27, 1990; "'Phony' Timber Measures Biased," *Santa Rosa Press-Democrat*, May 4, 1990.

28. Stephen J. Pyne, *Fire in America: A Cultural History of Wildland and Rural Fire* (Princeton: Princeton University Press, 1982). Bruce M. Kilgore, "What Is 'Natural' in Wilderness Fire Management?," in *Proceedings: Symposium and Workshop on Wilderness Fire*, Missoula, Montana, November 15–18, U.S. Department of Agriculture, Forest Service, General Technical Report INT-182, April 1985; see esp. section titled "'Unnatural Buildup' Issues."

29. Pyne, *Fire in America*; Douglas W. MacCleery, *American Forests: A History of Resiliency and Recovery* (Durham, N.C.: Forest History Society, 1992); Omer C. Stewart, "Barriers to Understanding the Influence of Use of Fire by Aborigines on Vegetation," Proceedings of the Tall Timbers Fire Ecology Conference, vol. 2.

30. W. B. Greeley, "'Paiute Forestry,' or the Fallacy of Light Burning," *Timberman* (March 1920).

31. Anthony R. O'Neill, "A National Crisis," in William C. Fischer and Stephen F. Arno, *Protecting People and Homes from Wildfire in the Interior West*, U.S. Department of Agriculture, Forest Service, Intermountain Research Station, Ogden, Utah, General Technical Report 251, September 1988; see also MacCleery, *American Forests*.

32. Bruce M. Kilgore, Eric Barnes, David Brower, and David J. Parsons, interviews, 1988–89.

33. Although the ecological virtues and vices of the prescribed burns of sequoia continue to be debated, there is no doubt that they proved to be political problems. See McClatchy News Service, "State's Sequoias to Be Target of Planned Fires Once Again," *San Diego Tribune*, March 13, 1987; Kilgore and Parsons, interviews; Lin Cotton and Joe R. McBride, "Visual Impacts of Prescribed Burning on Mixed Conifer and Giant Sequoia Forests," presented at the Symposium on Wildlife Fire 2000, April 27–30, 1987, South Lake Tahoe, California; Eric Barnes, "An Introduction to the Fire and Landscape Issues in Sequoia and Kings Canyon National Parks, California," mimeo., December 1987; Norman L. Christensen et al., "Review of Fire Management Program

for Sequoia–Mixed Conifer Forests of Yosemite, Sequoia, and Kings Canyon National Parks," final report, February 22, 1987.

34. National Commission on Wildfire Disasters, report, 1994; Everett L. Towl, "Fire Management Policy and Programs for National Forest Wilderness," in *Proceedings: Symposium on Wilderness Fire.*

35. Department of the Interior, National Park Service, "Wildland Fire Management Plan for Yellowstone National Park," 1987; George E. Gruell, "Fire's Influence on Wildlife Habitat on the Bridger-Teton National Forest, Wyoming," vol. 2, USDA Forest Service Research Paper INT-252, Intermountain Forest and Range Experiment Station, 1980; Alston Chase, "Neither Fire Suppression Nor Natural Burn Is a Sound Scientific Option," *New York Times*, September 18, 1988; Alston Chase, "How Yellowstone Got Burned," *Outside* (December 1988).

36. Bruce M. Kilgore, "Fire Management Programs in National Parks and Wilderness," in *Proceedings of the Intermountain Fire Council and Rocky Mountain Fire Council*, October 20–22, 1983.

37. Department of the Interior, National Park Service, "Natural Fire Management Plan for Yellowstone National Park," 1972; Chase, "Neither Fire Suppression Nor Natural Burn"; Chase, "How Yellowstone Got Burned."

38. Interagency Congressional Oversight Task Force, "Greater Yellowstone Area Fire Situation, 1988, Phase 1" report, September 28, 1988; Greater Yellowstone Postfire Resource Assessment Committee, Burned Area Survey Team, Henry F. Shovic, Team Leader, "Preliminary Burned Areas Survey of Yellowstone National Park and Adjoining National Forests," draft, December 13, 1988; Department of the Interior, National Park Service, "The Yellowstone Fires: A Primer on the 1988 Fire Season," Yellowstone National Park, October 1, 1988; Greater Yellowstone Postfire Ecological Assessment Workshop, "Ecological Consequences of the 1988 Fires in the Greater Yellowstone Area," final report, 1988; Thomas M. Bonnickson, "Fire Gods and Federal Policy," *American Forests* (July–August 1989).

39. MacCleery to author, July 6, 1994; National Commission on Wildfire Disasters, report, 1994.

40. Chadwick Dearing Oliver, "Enhancing Biodiversity and Economic Productivity through a Systems Approach to Silviculture," mimeo., 1993; see also Chadwick D. Oliver, "A Plan to Help Timber Communities," *Seattle Times*, August 28, 1990.

41. John M. Perez-Garcia, "Global Forestry Impacts of Reducing Softwood Supplies from North America," CINTRAFOR working paper no. 43, Center for International Trade in Forest Products, University of Washington, May 14, 1993; Roger A. Sedjo, "The Global Environmental Effects of Local Logging Cutbacks," *Resources* (Fall 1994).

42. Michael Williams, "Forests," in *The Earth as Transformed by Human Action: Global and Regional Changes in the Biosphere over the Past Three Hundred Years*, ed. B. L. Turner III et al. (New York: Cambridge University Press, 1990).

43. Oliver, "Enhancing Biodiversity."

44. Bari and Larry Nelson, interviews.

45. Judi Bari, *Timber Wars and Other Writings* (privately printed, 1992); "IWA Rank-and-File Union Millworkers' Reply," *Mendocino Commentary*, no. 360, December 14, 1989; Keith Michaud, "Worker Killed at Ukiah's L-P Mill," *Ukiah Daily Journal*, September 15, 1989; Brooks Mencher, "Azevedo Controversy Escalates," *Fort Bragg Advocate News*, October 20, 1988; Mike Geniella, "L-P Rebukes North Coast Critics," *Santa Rosa Press-*

Democrat, January 10, 1990; Mike Gienella, "Humboldt Unions Take L-P Fight to Billboards," *Santa Rosa Press-Democrat*, December 12, 1989; Steve Hart, "Riggs: Halt Redwood Exports," *Santa Rosa Press-Democrat*, December 16, 1989.

46. Mike Geniella, "Timber Industry's 'Big Three,'" *Santa Rosa Press-Democrat*, May 7, 1990; Mike Geniella, "Scathing Memos Warned L-P Boss of Overcutting," *Santa Rosa Press-Democrat*, January 5, 1992; Steve Hart, "Assembly Bill Would Block L-P from 70,000 Acres of State Timber," *Santa Rosa Press-Democrat*, January 17, 1990.

47. Editorial, *Eureka Advocate-News*, January 16, 1992.

48. Geniella, "Timber Industry's 'Big Three'"; Mike Geniella, "Merlo: No-Limit Logging," *Santa Rosa Press-Democrat*, December 10, 1989.

49. Claudia Smith, "Debate Continues on Timber's Role in Local Economy," *Willits News*, January 24, 1990.

50. Save the Redwoods League, "Headwaters Forest Threatened by Logging," press release, December 5, 1989; Steve Hart, "Bosco Pledges L-P Sanctions If Area Jobs Cut," *Santa Rosa Press-Democrat*, December 27, 1989; Mike Geniella, "Environmentalists Blast Bosco," *Santa Rosa Press-Democrat*, December 28, 1989.

51. John Campbell, interviews; "Timber Pact Opens Door to New Talks," *Santa Rosa Press-Democrat*, February 10, 1990; Mike Geniella, "Activists Protest Timber Agreement," *Santa Rosa Press-Democrat*, February 13, 1990; Mike Geniella, "'Human Chain' Stops Timber Truck," *Santa Rosa Press-Democrat*, February 14, 1990; Mike Geniella, "Big Timber's Foes Not Calmed by Agreement," *Santa Rosa Press-Democrat*, February 10, 1990.

52. Geniella, "'Forest Forever' Apparently Headed for November Ballot"; Tesconi, "Farmers' Initiative Counters 'Big Green.'"

53. Kelpie Willsin and Karen Pickett, interviews; Steve Hart, "Big Timber Girds for Ballot Battle," *Santa Rosa Press-Democrat*, December 9, 1994.

54. "Logging Firm Accused of Building Illegal Road," *San Francisco Chronicle*, March 14, 1990; Mike Geniella, "Pacific Lumber Must Answer Road Challenge by Monday," *Santa Rosa Press-Democrat*, March 15, 1990.

CHAPTER 23. FRED, THE WALKING RAINBOW

1. Judi Bari, interviews; Jonathan Littman, "Peace, Love . . . and TNT," *AP World* (December 1990).

2. Mike Roselle, interview, January 23, 1992.

3. Bari and Roselle, interviews.

4. Mike Geniella, "Summer of Disobedience in the Woods," *Santa Rosa Press-Democrat*, March 13, 1990; Mike Geniella, "Redwood Wars Ready to Escalate," *Santa Rosa Press-Democrat*, March 25, 1990. See flyer, "Mississippi Summer in the California Redwoods — Organizing Meeting, Sunday, March 18, 1990, Mendocino Environmental Center, Ukiah," and similar flyers for April 8 in Garberville and May 13 in Laytonville.

5. Geniella, "Summer of Disobedience."

6. Northern California Earth First!, press release, *Earth First! Journal* 10, no. 5 (May 1, 1990); Southern Willamette Earth First!, statement, April 1990.

7. Mike Geniella, "Timber Activists Ax Tree-Spiking," *Santa Rosa Press-Democrat*, April 9, 1990; Darryl Cherney, Judi Bari, and North Coast California Earth First!, "Tree-Spiking Renunciation & Mississippi Summer in the California Redwoods," memorandum, March 28, 1990; Northern California

Earth First!, press release, "Northern California Earth First! Renounces Tree-Spiking," April 10, 1990; North Coast California Earth First!, "A Call for an End to Tree-Spiking," press conference statement, April 11, 1990.

8. Northern California Earth First!, press release.

9. Ibid.; Bari, interviews.

10. "Tree-Spiking Renounced behind Redwood Curtain," *Earth First! Journal* 10, no. 5 (May 1, 1990); Arcata Earth First!, news release, April 13, 1990; Mike Geniella, "Fight over 'Mississippi' Support," *Santa Rosa Press-Democrat*, April 17, 1990.

11. Bari, interviews; Mike Geniella, "Redwood Radicals Losing Support," *Santa Rosa Press-Democrat*, April 26, 1990. Sierra Club of California, "Sierra Club Reacts to Mississippi Summer," press release, April 16, 1990; Mike Geniella, "Sierra Club Cuts Radicals' Plans for Logging Protest," *Santa Rosa Press-Democrat*, April 15, 1990; Judy Nichols, "'Mississippi Summer' Stirs Sierra Club Split," *North Coast News* 4, no. 38 (April 19–May 2, 1990).

12. Interagency Scientific Committee to Address the Conservation of the Northern Spotted Owl, *A Conservation Strategy for the Northern Spotted Owl* (Portland: Departments of Agriculture and the Interior, May 1990).

13. Interagency Committee, *A Conservation Strategy*, p. 3.

14. Associated Press, "'Stark' Choice between Owls, People, Forest Group Says," *Santa Rosa Press-Democrat*, April 6, 1990.

15. Robert G. Lee et al., "Social Impacts of Alternative Timber Harvest Reductions on Federal Lands in O and C Counties," College of Forest Resources, University of Washington, June 1991; Preston et al., "A Facade of Science: An Analysis of the Jack Ward Thomas Report," report for the Association of O&C Counties and the Northwest Forest Resource Council, August 1991; North West Timber Association, "Summary and Critique of the Spotted Owl Conservation Strategy Proposed by the Interagency Spotted Owl Scientific Committee," June 1990.

16. Interagency Committee, *A Conservation Strategy*, p. 236.

17. Ibid., pp. 25, 303.

18. Ibid., p. 144.

19. Preston et al., "A Facade of Science"; Associated Press, "New Philosophy for Spotted Owl," *Livingston Enterprise*, April 5, 1990.

20. Oregon Lands Coalition, "Mayday! Mr. President," *The Seedling* 1, no. 6 (May 1990).

21. Mike Geniella, "Landmark Philo Mill Shuts; 35 Out of Work," *Santa Rosa Press-Democrat*, April 14, 1990; Keith Michaud, "Valley L-P Mill Closures Shock Lawmakers, Locals," *Fort Bragg Advocate-News*, April 5, 1990; Mike Geniella, "L-P Cutting 195 Mill Jobs," *Santa Rosa Press-Democrat*, March 29, 1990.

22. Bari, interviews; Keith Michaud, "Board Asked to Take over L-P," *Ukiah Daily Journal*, April 3, 1990.

23. "Spikes Found in Scotia Redwood Log," *Willits News*, April 27, 1990; Judi Bari and Darryl Cherney, "Ukiah Burning," *Earth First! Journal* 10, no. 5 (May 1, 1991).

24. Littman, "Peace, Love . . . and TNT."

25. Ibid.; Alliance for Activists' Rights, "The Bombing of Judi Bari and Darryl Cherney: A Chronology of Events," mimeo., November 15, 1990.

26. Littman, "Peace, Love"; South Humboldt Earth First!, Darryl Cherney, and Greg King, poster, "Earth Night 1990"; Mike Geniella, "Planned Summer Protests Draw Fire," *Santa Rosa Press-Democrat*, May 2, 1990.

27. Alliance, "The Bombing"; *Press-Democrat* News Services, "Earth Day Protests Turn Violent, *Santa Rosa Press-Democrat*, April 24, 1990.

28. Mike Geniella and Clark Mason, "Earth First! Climbs the Golden Gate," *Santa Rosa Press-Democrat*, April 25, 1990.
29. Kevin Murphy, "Loggers Call on Supervisors to Oppose Mississippi Summer," *Northcoast News*, May 3, 1990; Geniella, "Planned Summer Protests Draw Fire."
30. Murphy, "Loggers Call on Supervisors"; Geniella, "Planned Summer Protests Draw Fire."
31. Geniella, "Planned Summer Protests Draw Fire."
32. Darryl Cherney, "Freedom Riders Needed to Save the Forest," *Earth First! Journal*, May 1, 1990.
33. Clark Mason, "Summer Protests Get Early Start," *Santa Rosa Press-Democrat*, May 4, 1990; Tobias Young, "G-P Axes Mill Tours, Closes Off Land," *Santa Rosa Press-Democrat*, May 4, 1990.
34. Arcata Earth First! news release, April 13, 1990; Alliance, "The Bombing"; copies of death threat notes were supplied to the author by Bari.
35. "FBI Searching for Link to L-P Pipe Bomb," *Santa Rosa Press-Democrat*, May 26, 1990; Larry B. Stammer, *Los Angeles Times*, May 15, 1987.
36. Federal Bureau of Investigation, "Explosives — Materials Analysis — Chemistry — Document Fingerprint," report on Cloverdale incident, June 1, 1990.
37. This account is drawn from Bari, interviews; brochure, "Seeds for Peace . . . a History," n.d.; Mendocino Environmental Center, "Welcome to Redwood Summer," Redwood Summer informational packet, September 1990; Alliance, "The Bombing."

CHAPTER 24. STEPPING ON AN ANTHILL

1. Judi Bari, interviews; Alliance for Activists' Rights, "The Bombing of Judi Bari and Darryl Cherney: A Chronology of Events," mimeo., November 15, 1990; "Judi & Darryl Still Fighting Despite Bomb Damage," *Earth First! Journal* 10, no. 6 (June 21, 1990); Dennis J. Opatrny, "Judi Bari's Injuries Point to Hidden Bomb, Friends Say," *San Francisco Examiner*, July 6, 1990; FBI interrogation of paramedics Thomas Veirs, Patrice Skipp, and Brian Buckman, May 29–30, 1990.
2. Statement of Special Agent Timothy S. McKinley, FBI files, no. 016199, transcribed May 25, 1990.
3. M. Sitterud, investigation report, Oakland Police Department, RD no. 90-57171, May 24, 1990. See also affidavit of Sergeant Robert Chenault, Oakland Police Department, May 25, 1990.
4. McKinley, statement.
5. Ibid.
6. M. Sitterud, deposition in the case of *Judi Bari et al.* v. *Richard Held et al.*, November 15, 1993.
7. Sitterud, investigation report.
8. Ibid.
9. Arrest warrant, incident no. 1092, 3 P.M., May 24, 1990.
10. Kelpie Willsin and Karen Pickett, interviews.
11. Gary Ball, Betty Ball, and Karen Pickett, interviews.
12. Sitterud, investigation report.
13. Ibid.
14. The police had requested $250,000 bail be set for both Bari and Cherney. See Barry Witt, "Pair in Bombed Car Arrested," *San Jose Mercury News*, May 26, 1990.

15. Karen Wood, interview.

16. Mendocino Environmental Center, Redwood Summer information packet, September 1990.

17. This account is drawn from Pickett, Willsin, Wood, Tim McKay, Gary and Betty Ball, interviews; Mendocino Environmental Center, information packet; Earth First!, "Redwood Summer Handbook."

18. Earth First!, "Redwood Summer — a Chronology," mimeo., n.d.; Bleys W. Rose, "Timber Exec Fires Back at Protesters," *Santa Rosa Press-Democrat*, June 9, 1990.

19. Earth First!, "Redwood Summer — a Chronology"; Karen Pickett and Woody Joe, "Redwood Summer Goes On!," *Earth First! Journal*, vol. 10, no. 6, June 21, 1990; Alexander Cockburn, "Beat That Devil," *The Nation*, July 2, 1990.

20. Aeschylus, *Agamemnon*, in *Greek Plays in Modern Translation*, ed. Dudley Fitts (New York: Dial Press, 1952), p. 14.

21. Cockburn, "Beat That Devil."

22. Alliance, "The Bombing"; Pickett, interview; "Earth First! Arraignment," press conference, June 22, 1990.

23. Michael Collier, "Dellums Joins Call for Bomb Probe," *Oakland Tribune*, July 17, 1990; Jane Kay, "Lawmakers Asking Probe in Earth First Bombing Case," *San Francisco Examiner*, July 17, 1990; Jim Doyle, "Coalition Wants U.S. Probe of Earth First Blast," *San Francisco Chronicle*, July 17, 1990; Alliance, "The Bombing"; "Environmental Leaders Denounce Campaign to Slander Movement," press release, June 22, 1994; Environmental Project on Central America, press release, May 29, 1990; Greenpeace Action, "Statement of David Chatfield, Chairman," June 21, 1990; PAN North American Regional Center, press release, June 22, 1990; Toxics Coordinating Project, press release, June 21, 1990; International Indian Treaty Council, press release, May 25, 1990; Rainforest Action Network, press release, May 25, 1990; Earth Island Institute, press release, June 21, 1990; Peter Bahout, Executive Director, Greenpeace USA, et al., letter to public officials, July 16, 1990.

24. World Rainforest Movement, press release, May 26, 1990.

25. Pickett, interview; Friends of the Earth, press release, June 1, 1990; Editorial, "Earth First!, Terrorism and the FBI," *San Francisco Bay Guardian*, May 30, 1990.

26. For Alameda Bomb Squad report, see Alameda Technical Services incident form N.90-7181, May 24, 1990. As soon as the FBI entered the investigation, the Oakland police began to change their story, suggesting that the bomb went off behind, not under, the driver's seat. Chenault's affidavit reports, "Your affiant was advised by these F.B.I. Agents that the bomb device was on the floor board behind the driver's seat when it detonated." Sitterud at first hedged, saying, "It appeared that the device was underneath and possibly just to the rear of the driver's seat." Then, he reported being briefed that evening by Doyle: "S.A. Frank Doyle briefed meeting on known components of the bomb including fact that the bomb had been on the floor behind the driver's seat. Sitterud, investigation report.

27. Chenault, affidavit. Chenault also first placed the bomb behind, not beneath, the driver's seat.

28. FBI document no. 005204; Sergeant Michael Sitterud, affidavit for search warrant, register no. 9691, July 6, 1990.

29. "Lord's Avenger" to Michael Geniella, *Santa Rosa Press-Democrat*, postmarked May 25, 1990.

30. Sharon McCormick, "Evidence List Released in Earth First! Bombing," *San Francisco Chronicle*, May 27, 1990; Dean Congbalay, "Police Say Car Bomb Was in the Back Seat," *San Francisco Chronicle*, May 28, 1990; Mary Furillo, "Police Sent Out Bari's Picture," *San Francisco Chronicle*, June 13, 1990.
31. Pickett, interview; Sharon McCormick, "Earth First! Prosecutor Asks Delay," *San Francisco Chronicle*, May 30, 1990; Harry Harris, "Earth First! Pair Gets Own Private Eye," *Oakland Tribune*, May 29, 1990.
32. Paul Grabowicz, "Police Claim Nails Link Car Bomb to Activists," *Oakland Tribune*, July 6, 1990; Ronald E. O'Conner, president, Pacific Steel and Supply, to Stewart Daley, Federal Bureau of Investigation, June 26, 1990; Stewart Daley, transcription, dictated June 29, 1995.
33. FBI explosives-materials analysis," file no. 174-10707, June 14, 1990, concludes that material obtained from Bari's house and from the Oakland bomb "did not . . . originate from these [same] sources." See also Michael Taylor, "Court Records Released in Bombing; Officer Says Earth First Explosive Was Built in Victim's Home," *San Francisco Chronicle*, July 11, 1990; Michael Taylor, "Bomb Materials Linked to Victims," *San Francisco Chronicle*, July 6, 1990. FBI photos in the author's possession clearly show that the bomb had been placed under the driver's seat.
34. Howard C. Hughes, "Earth First! and Covert Ops," *Santa Rosa Press-Democrat*, June 21, 1990.
35. "Environmental Leaders Denounce Campaign to Slander Movement," press release, June 22, 1990; Alliance, "The Bombing"; "Earth First! Arraignment."

CHAPTER 25. REDWOOD SUMMER

1. For an explanation of Locke's influence on Montesquieu and the latter's influence on Rousseau, see John Plamenatz, *Man and Society* (London: Longmans, 1963). For an account of the influence of Montesquieu and Rousseau on the French Revolution, see Simon Schama, *Citizens: A Chronicle of the French Revolution* (New York: Alfred A. Knopf, 1989).
2. As a sign of this sudden respectability conferred on Earth First! after the bombing, see letter to Senator Joseph Biden from presidents and executive directors of Friends of the Earth, Sierra Club, National Wildlife Federation, National Parks and Conservation Association, and National Audubon Society, July 16, 1990.
3. Ricky in the Hills, "A Samoa Report," Mendocino Environmental Center, Redwood Summer informational packet, September 1990; Alexander Cockburn, "Appointment in Samoa I," *Anderson Valley Advertiser*, June 27, 1990; Alexander Cockburn, "Appointment in Samoa II," *Anderson Valley Advertiser*, July 4, 1990.
4. Cockburn, "Appointment II."
5. Ricky, "A Samoa Report."
6. National Audubon Society Ancient Forest Campaign, "Ancient Forest Chronology," mimeo., n.d.; "Bomb Victims' Homes Searched," *San Jose Mercury-News*, May 26, 1990; Steven Lewis Yaffee, *The Wisdom of the Spotted Owl* (Washington, D.C.: Island Press, 1994).
7. David Foster, "Law That Gives a Hoot Leaving Trail of Conflict," *Santa Rosa Press-Democrat*, September 2, 1990; Department of the Interior, U.S. Fish and Wildlife Service, *Endangered and Threatened Species Recovery*

Program, report to Congress, December 1990; "Endangered Species Blueprint," *NWI Resource* 5, no. 1 (Fall 1994).

8. Foster, "Law That Gives a Hoot."
9. John Campbell, interviews; Karen Pickett, "Redwood Summer Chronology," *Earth First! Journal* 11, no. 1 (November 1, 1990).
10. "44 Arrested at L-P Mill," *Earth First! Journal* 10, no. 7 (August 1, 1990); "Redwood Summer Activists Harassed by Police," *Earth First! Journal* 10, no. 7 (August 1, 1990); "Redwood Summer Activists Assaulted by Loggers," *Earth First! Journal* 10, no. 7 (August 1, 1990).
11. Linda Goldston, "Judi Bari Begins New Struggle," *San Jose Mercury-News*, August 6, 1990.
12. Representative Ronald V. Dellums to Representative Don Edwards, Subcommittee on Civil and Constitutional Rights, July 13, 1990.
13. Alliance for Activists' Rights, "Media Advisory," press conference, July 16, 1990; letter to Senator Joseph Biden from presidents and executive directors of Friends of the Earth, Sierra Club, National Wildlife Federation, National Parks and Conservation Association, and National Audubon Society, July 16, 1990.
14. Judy Nichols, "Redwood Summer Arrives," *North Coast News*, August 2, 1990; Katherine Bishop, "2 Won't Be Charged in Bombing Case," *New York Times*, July 18, 1990; Harold Maass, "Earth First! Activists Hurt in Blast Won't Be Charged," *Los Angeles Times*, July 18, 1990; Barry Witt, "D.A. Drops Charges in Activists' Bomb Case," *San Jose Mercury-News*, July 18, 1990; FBI memorandum from FBI San Francisco to Director FBI/priority, "Subject: Judith Beatrice Bari and Darryl Reed Cherney, bombing, July 20, 1990."
15. Interviews with Fort Bragg residents John Shemolino and Heather Drum and Earth First!ers Karen Pickett and Kelpie Willsin; "Two Thousand Rally at Fort Bragg," *Earth First! Journal* 10, no. 7 (August 1, 1990); Greg Goldin, "Lost in the Woods," *L.A. Weekly*, September 7–13, 1990; poster, "A Rally in Protest of Georgia-Pacific's Liquidation Logging," Fort Bragg, Saturday July 21, 1990.
16. Will Behr, "Timber Rallies Cool and Peaceful," *Fort Bragg Advocate-News*, July 26, 1990; Will Behr, "Coalition Turns Green Field Yellow for a Day," *Fort Bragg Advocate-News*, July 26, 1990; Marylou Hadditt, "Dialogue in Fort Bragg," *Santa Rosa Press-Democrat*, July 30, 1990; William Beradd, "We Didn't Hold No Parade," *Anderson Valley Advertiser*, July 25, 1990; AVA News Service, "Bosco Addresses Larouche Rally," *Anderson Valley Advertiser*, July 25, 1990; Judy Nichols and Gayle Caldwell, "Redwood Summer Arrives," *North Coast News*, August 2, 1990.
17. Goldin, "Lost in the Woods."
18. Ibid.
19. Ibid.; Willsin, interview.
20. Goldin, "Lost in the Woods."
21. This is an eyewitness account by the author. See also "RRR Rocks and Rolls in Montana," *Earth First! Journal* 10, no. 7 (August 1, 1990).
22. "Arizona 5 Trial Soon," *Earth First! Journal* 10, no. 8 (September 22, 1990).
23. Mike Roselle and Judi Bari, interviews; Judi Bari, "Breaking Up Is Hard to Do," in *Timber Wars and Other Writings* (privately printed, 1992); Judi Bari, "Expand Earth First!," *Earth First! Journal* 10, no. 8 (September 22, 1990); Judi Bari, "The Earth First! Divorce," in Redwood Summer informational packet.
24. Bleys W. Rose, "Earth First! Founder Makes It Official — He Quits," *Santa Rosa Press-Democrat*, August 21, 1990; Dave Foreman and Nancy Morton,

"Good Luck, Darlin'. It's Been Great," *Earth First! Journal* 10, no. 8 (September 22, 1990); Douglas Kreutz, "Earth First! Movement Has Lost 'Eloquent Voice,'" *Arizona Daily Star*, August 15, 1990; "Founder Leaving Earth First!," *Arizona Citizen*, August 14, 1990.

25. Howie Wolke, "Focus on Wilderness," *Earth First! Journal* 10, no. 8 (September 22, 1990).

26. Bill Devall, "Maybe the Movement Is Leaving Me," *Earth First! Journal* 10, no. 8 (September 22, 1990).

27. Bari, "Expand Earth First!"; Associated Press, "Founder Critical of Leftist Direction of Earth First!," *Santa Rosa Press-Democrat*, August 17, 1990; Mike Geniella, "Leadership Dispute Splits Earth First!," *Santa Rosa Press-Democrat*, August 12, 1990; Alexander Cockburn, "An Interview with Mike Roselle, Talkin' Earth First!," *Anderson Valley Advertiser*, August 4, 1990.

28. Foreman, *Confessions of an Eco-Warrior*, p. 140; Miss Ann Thropy, "Population and AIDS," *Earth First! Journal* 7, no. 5 (May 1, 1987). In 1994 there were 2,200 environmental grant-making foundations in America, which had made 36,000 grants since 1988. The top 600 of these had combined assets of $70 billion, and collectively gave more than $425 million in environmental grants each year. See Environmental Data Research Institute, *Environmental Grantmaking Foundations, 1995 Directory* (Rochester, N.Y.: Environmental Data Research Institute, 1995).

29. Goldin, "Lost in the Woods"; Pickett, "Chronology"; "Mother's Watch Blacklists Scores of County Businesses," *Willits News*, August 15, 1990.

30. J. P. Bernhard, "Sequoia Sayonara," *Earth First! Journal* 10, no. 8 (September 22, 1990).

31. Bari, interviews; Earth First!, Mendocino Environmental Center, Redwood Summer informational packet.

32. Mike Geniella, "FBI Investigates Radical," *Santa Rosa Press-Democrat*, August 16, 1990; Paul Grabowicz, "Earth First Probe Hits North Coast," *Oakland Tribune*, August 20, 1990; FBI investigation report no. 174A-SF-90788; Special Agent Richard W. Held to Michael Parkman, *Santa Rosa Press-Democrat*, August 6, 1990.

33. John Campbell, interviews; Pickett, "Chronology"; "Redwood Summer Anything But Nonviolent," *Humboldt Beacon*, August 30, 1990; Richard Mann, "Man Who Pounded on PL President's Car in Korbel Incident Gets Fine, 4 Months in Jail," *Arcata Union*, November 7, 1990.

34. Pickett, "Chronology."

35. On April 23–24, 1968, Columbia students seized five buildings in protest of the university's connections with the Institute of Defense Analysis, sponsored by the Pentagon. Similar disruptions occurred at Duke, Oregon State, and several other universities that same spring. Interestingly, students did not realize that ecosystems studies were also supported by the defense establishment — in particular the Office of Naval Research — for the purpose of refining the United States' ability to wage thermonuclear war. See David Wallechinsky and Irving Wallace, *The People's Almanac* (New York: Doubleday, 1975).

36. Wallechinsky and Wallace, *People's Almanac*, p. 255.

37. Walker Percy, *The Message in the Bottle* (New York: Farrar, Straus, and Giroux, 1954), p. 6.

38. George Perkins Marsh, *Man and Nature* (Cambridge, Mass.: Harvard University Press, 1974), pp. 37, 42–43.

39. Fairfield Osborn, *Our Plundered Planet* (1948; rpt. New York: Pyramid Books, 1968), book jacket; Bill McKibben, *The End of Nature* (New York: Random House, 1989), p. 78.

40. William M. Denevan, "The Pristine Myth: The Landscape of the Americas in 1492," *Annals of the Association of American Geographers* 82, no. 3 (1992).
41. Donald Worster, *Rivers of Empire* (New York: Pantheon Books, 1985).
42. Editorial, "Call Off 'Redwoodstock,'" *Redwood Record*, August 29, 1990.
43. Bill Israel, "Tense Logging Protest Caps Redwood Summer," *San Francisco Chronicle*, September 4, 1990; Associated Press, "Redwood Summer Ends with Peaceful Protest," *Sacramento Bee*, September 4, 1990; Rhonda Parker, "'Summer' Ends in a Standoff," *Eureka Times-Standard*, September 4, 1990.
44. Richard Mann, "Cooler Heads Prevail in Fortuna March," *Arcata Union*, September 11, 1990; Peter Bralver, "LA EF! Enjoys a Redwood Summer!," *Earth First! Journal* 10, no. 8 (September 22, 1990); Marie Gravelle, "One Arrest in Fortuna March," *Santa Rosa Press-Democrat*, September 4, 1990.
45. Bari, interviews.
46. Greg King and Karen Wood, interviews; Jerry Sena, "County's 'Hard Line' May Have Driven Redwood Summer Spending Higher," *Humboldt Beacon*, September 13, 1990; Richard Mann, "Redwood Summer Costs Still on the Increase," *Humboldt Beacon*, November 22, 1990; Douglas Kreutz, "Ending Role as Activists' Voice," *Arizona Daily Star*, October 20, 1990.
47. Goldin, "Lost in the Woods."
48. Jane Kay, "Bitter End to North Coast Summer of Discontent," *San Francisco Examiner*, September 2, 1990.
49. Marie Felde, "Logging Off: Redwood Summer's Protests End," *Oakland Tribune*, September 16, 1990; Rodney R. Jones, "New Solidarity for North Coast," *Santa Rosa Press-Democrat*, September 28, 1990. See also Karen Pickett, "Redwood Summer Retrospective," *Earth First! Journal* 11, no. 1 (November 1, 1990).

CHAPTER 26. DIASPORA

1. Eyewitness account of author, who attended and taped the Society of Environmental Journalists meeting, November 6–8, 1992.
2. The increase in environmental advocacy is in part a consequence of the fact that most journalists are poorly trained in science and therefore tend to oversimplify issues. See American Opinion Research, "The Press and the Environment: How Journalists Evaluate Environmental Reporting," 1993.
3. Victor M. Sher and Andy Stahl, "Spotted Owls, Ancient Forests, Courts, and Congress: An Overview of Citizens' Efforts to Protect Old-Growth Forests and the Species That Live in Them," *Northwest Environmental Journal* 6 (1990).
4. Interviews with Mike Roselle, Bill Devall, and Howie Wolke.
5. See, for example, Conservation Foundation, annual report, 1987.
6. David Quammen, "Reckoning," *Outside* (November 1990); Karen Pickett, "Four of AZ 5 Get Maximum Jail Time," *Earth First! Journal* 12, no. 1 (November 1, 1991); Tom Beal, "'Eco-Warrior' Explains His Radical Ways," *Arizona Daily Star*, June 30, 1991.
7. Dave Foreman, *Confessions of an Eco-Warrior* (New York: Harmony Books, 1991); John Lancaster, "The Green Guerrilla," *Washington Post*, March 20, 1991.
8. Dave Quammen, "Natural Acts," *Outside* (December 1993); Charles C. Mann and Mark L. Plummer, "The High Cost of Biodiversity," *Science*, June 25, 1993.
9. Mann and Plummer, "High Cost of Biodiversity."

10. Ibid.
11. Chadwick Oliver and Douglas MacCleery, interviews; National Commission on Wildfire Disasters, report, 1994.
12. Interviews with Kathi Green of Colorado Department of Wildlife; University of Wisconsin botanist Don Waller; Illinois Nature Conservancy director Steven Packard; Leopold Memorial Forest director Brent Haglund; Montana Department of Fish, Wildlife, and Parks lion expert Shawn Reilly; mountain lion researcher Maurice Hornocker; and others. See Alston Chase, "Wilderness in the Balance: As Endangered Species Rebound, Our Parks Pay the Price," *Condé Nast's Traveler* (June 1993); Alston Chase, "Too Many Bears," *New York Times*, September 2, 1993; Alston Chase, "Wild Thing," *Countryside Magazine* (December 1991); Alston Chase, "Horns of Dilemma," *Countryside Magazine* (Winter 1990).
13. This discussion is based on interviews with Don Waller, Nancy Braker, and Steven Packard.
14. Reilly and Green, interviews; Paul Beier, "Cougar Attacks on Humans in the United States and Canada," draft, Department of Forestry and Resource Management, University of California, Berkeley, mimeo., n.d.; Clair E. Braun, ed., *Mountain Lion–Human Interaction*, symposium and workshop, Denver, April 24–26, 1991; Carol Wilcox, "Searchers Find Body of CCHS Senior, 18, Mauled by Mountain Lion," *Clear Creek Courant*, January 16, 1991; Associated Press, "Cougar Attacks Five-Year-Old Girl," *Livingston Enterprise*, June 16, 1992; Associated Press, "Big-Cat Attacks Trouble Officials," *Billings Gazette*, July 25, 1990; Mike Aderhold, "Mountain Lion Situation," *Fish, Wildlife, and Parks News*, July 19, 1990.
15. Allan K. Fitzsimmons, "Ecosystems: Where Do They End?," *NWI Resource* (Summer 1993).
16. Alston Chase, *Playing God in Yellowstone* (New York: Atlantic Monthly Press, 1986); Alston Chase, "Unhappy Birthday," *Outside* (December 1991). By 1991 the Greater Yellowstone Coalition would define a "core" Greater Yellowstone Ecosystem as 13.9 million acres. See Dennis Glick, Mary Carr, and Bert Harting, eds., "An Environmental Profile of the Greater Yellowstone Ecosystem," Greater Yellowstone Coalition, 1991.
17. Congressional Research Service, "Greater Yellowstone Ecosystem," December 1986; Greater Yellowstone Coordinating Committee, "Vision for the Future: A Framework for Coordination in the Greater Yellowstone Area," draft, August 1990.
18. Anne Matthews, *Where the Buffalo Roam* (New York: Grove, Weidenfeld, 1992).
19. Bill McKibben, *The End of Nature* (New York: Random House, 1989); David M. Graver, "Mother Nature as a Hothouse Flower," *Los Angeles Times*, October 22, 1989.
20. Times Mirror Magazines, "Natural Resource Conservation: Where Environmentalism Is Headed in the 1990s," June 1992.
21. Thomas Harvey Holt, "Are Schools Turning Our Kids into Eco-Activists?," *Reason Magazine* (October 1991); Rainforest Action Network, "School Year Begins with a Fourth 'R' — the Rainforest," press release, August 17, 1993; Jonathan H. Adler, "A Child's Garden of Misinformation," *Consumers' Research* 76, no. 9 (September 1993).
22. Mary Jordan, "Students Test Blow Average: In World, U.S. Fares Poorly in Math, Science," *Washington Post*, February 6, 1992; Associated Press, "Small Improvement Seen in U.S. Students' Math Ability," *Washington Post*, April 9, 1993; Mary Jordan, "90 Million Lack Simple Literacy," *Wash-

ington Post, September 9, 1993; Associated Press, "'A Nation at Risk' Still May Hold True," *Bozeman Daily Chronicle,* April 25, 1993.

23. P. S. White and S. T. A. Pickett, eds., *The Ecology of Natural Disturbance and Patch Dynamics: An Introduction* (Orlando, Fla.: Academic Press, 1985); Donald Worster, *The Wealth of Nature* (Oxford: Oxford University Press, 1993), p. 165.

24. Worster, *Wealth of Nature,* p. 167; James Gleick, *Chaos* (New York: Penguin Books, 1987).

25. William K. Stevens, "New Eye on Nature: The Real Constant Is Eternal Turmoil," *New York Times,* July 31, 1990.

26. Ibid.

27. Paradoxically, their very failure to find equilibria has led many scientists to see this as confirming evidence of the stability hypothesis. They reason that the absence of equilibria merely proves that all ecosystems have been "disturbed" by humans!

28. See Daniel J. Rohlf, *The Endangered Species Act* (Palo Alto: Stanford Environmental Law Society, 1989), chap. 1, "An Introduction to the Extinction Crisis."

29. Edward O. Wilson, *The Diversity of Life* (New York: W.W. Norton, 1992), p. 280. None of these authors cite any direct evidence of these extinctions, however. See Norman Myers, *The Sinking Ark* (New York: Pergamon Books, 1979); President's Council on Environmental Quality, *Global 2000 Report to the President;* Edward O. Wilson, ed., *Biodiversity* (Washington, D.C.: National Academy Press, 1988). World Wildlife Fund quote from its 1992 fundraising letter signed by WWF Chairman Russell E. Train.

30. See Julian L. Simon and Aaron Wildavsky, "Assessing the Empirical Basis of the 'Biodiversity Crisis,'" Competitive Enterprise Institute Environmental Studies Program, May 1993.

31. Norman Myers, "A Major Extinction Spasm: Predictable and Inevitable?," in *Conservation for the Twenty-First Century,* ed. David Western and Mary C. Pearl (New York: Oxford University Press, 1989), p. 102; Edward O. Wilson, "Is Humanity Suicidal?," *New York Times Magazine,* May 30, 1993; Jared Diamond, "World of the Living Dead," *Natural History* (September 1991).

32. V. H. Heywood and S. N. Stuart, "Species Extinctions in Tropical Forests," in *Tropical Deforestation and Species Extinction,* ed. T. C. Whitmore and J. A. Sayer (New York: Chapman and Hall, 1992), pp. 93, 96. See also Charles C. Mann and Mark L. Plummer, *Noah's Choice: The Future of Endangered Species* (New York: Alfred A. Knopf, 1995).

33. Wilson, "Is Humanity Suicidal?"

34. National Audubon Society Ancient Forest Campaign, "Ancient Forest Chronology"; Carol Benfell, "Tiny Wildflowers to Stall Builders," *Santa Rosa Press-Democrat,* November 26, 1991; Associated Press, "Idaho's Sockeye Salmon Added to Endangered List," *Santa Rosa Press-Democrat,* November 15, 1991; Chronicle Wire Services, "Mexican Spotted Owl Protection," *San Francisco Chronicle,* February 1, 1992; Barry Meier, "Spotted Owl Dispute Jolts Another Timber Region," *New York Times,* February 1, 1992.

35. Linda Burgess, "Five Small Flowers Generate Major Conflict in Big Bear Area," *The Grizzly* 5, no. 47 (August 20, 1992). Federal Court Judge Barbara Rothstein gave the U.S. Fish and Wildlife Service until September 18, 1992, to decide whether to list these species. See Northwest Forest Resource Council, Legal Update no. 103A, September 16, 1992.

36. Department of the Interior, U.S. Fish and Wildlife Service, "U.S. Fish and Wildlife Service Accepts Petition to List Southwestern Willow Flycatcher," press release, September 4, 1992; Janet Zimmerman, "Fly's Status Sends County Officials Buzzing," *San Bernardino Sun*, November 20, 1992. By 1995, 962 species had been classified as threatened or endangered, and the candidate list totaled 4,114. Information supplied by the U.S. Fish and Wildlife Service, 1995. Mike Geniella, "U.S. Protection for California Owl," *Santa Rosa Press-Democrat*, January 15, 1993; California Forestry Association, "Forest Service Spotted Owl Guidelines Hinder State Economic Recovery Efforts," press release, January 14, 1993.

37. Department of the Interior, U.S. Fish and Wildlife Service, *Endangered and Threatened Species Recovery Program*, Report to Congress, December 1990. See also General Accounting Office, *Endangered Species: Management Improvement Could Enhance Recovery Program*, GAO/RCED-89-5, December 1988; U.S. Department of the Interior, *The Endangered Species Program, U.S. Fish and Wildlife Service*, audit report no. 90-98, September 1990.

38. Charles C. Mann and Mark L. Plummer, "The Butterfly Problem," *Atlantic* (January 1992).

39. Fund for Animals, "Lawsuit Challenges President's Rules Moratorium for Halting the Listing of Endangered and Threatened Species," press release, April 2, 1992.

40. Bruce Kenworth, "Settlement Ends Lawsuit over Endangered Species," *Oregonian*, December 16, 1992.

41. Federal Ecosystem Management Assessment Team (FEMAT), *Forest Ecosystem Management: An Ecological, Economic, and Social Assessment* (July 1993). By 1990 estimates for the northern spotted owl population had already reached ten thousand. See David Foster, "Phantoms in the Forest," Associated Press, August 28, 1990.

42. David R. Anderson and Kenneth P. Burnham, "Demographic Analysis of Northern Spotted Owl Populations," U.S. Department of the Interior, Fish and Wildlife Service, "Recovery Plan for the Northern Spotted Owl," draft, April 1992. See also Kenneth P. Burnham and David R. Anderson, "Estimation of Vital Rates of the Northern Spotted Owl," mimeo., January 12, 1993.

43. Anderson and Burnham, "Estimation of Vital Rates."

44. Michael L. Rosenzweig, "The California Spotted Owl Report: An Evaluation," August 28, 1992.

45. Daniel Botkin, interview; Daniel Botkin et al., *Status and Future of Salmon of Western Oregon and Northern California* (Santa Barbara, Calif.: Center for the Study of the Environment, 1994).

46. Botkin, interviews.

47. Botkin et al., *Status and Future of Salmon*.

48. Al Gore, *Earth in the Balance* (Boston: Houghton Mifflin, 1992), p. 278; Worster, *Wealth of Nature*, p. 111.

49. Melanie Hiett, "Mills Hope Court Victory Near," *Pensacola News Journal*, May 24, 1991. Appellants' opening brief before U.S. District Court, Northern District of Florida, *Ocie Mills and Carey C. Mills v. United States of America*, 1988; memorandum from Charles T. Myers III, Colonel, Corps of Engineers to Office of Counsel, "Subject: *United States v. Ocie Mills and Lewis W. Jenkins*," February 12, 1987. One judge in the Mills case called the Clean Water Act "a regulatory hydra . . . worthy of *Alice in Wonderland*" (see decision of Judge Roger Vinson, PCR 88-03100 and PCA 93-30428). And while environmentalists suggest that cases such as the Mills' are rare, unfortunately they are not. The Fairness to Landowners Committee claims to have documented more than one thousand such cases.

50. H. Jane Lehman, "A Changing Tide on Wetlands Decisions," *Washington Post*, January 18, 1992; Margaret Ann Reigle, "Eco-Con Creates Convicts?," *News from the FLOC* (August 1992).

51. Interviews with Bill Ellen and his wife, Bonnie Ellen; statement of facts, Ellen trial. Many people asked the Bush administration to pardon Ellen, but it refused. See Editorial, "EPA's Most Wanted," *Wall Street Journal*, November 18, 1992; "The Ellen Pardon," *Wall Street Journal*, January 15, 1993; memorandum, Bonnie Ellen to James Baker, "Pardon for Bill Ellen," October 27, 1992; "Bill Reilly's Family Values," *Washington Times*, September 28, 1992.

52. General Accounting Office, report on the Riverside, California, fires of October 1993; Ike C. Sugg, "Rats, Lies, and the GAO," Competitive Enterprise Institute report, August 1994.

53. Bruce N. Ames et al., "Beware of False Gods in Rio," June 1992.

CHAPTER 27. HOME, SWEET HOME

1. Charles Dickens, *Bleak House* (London: J. M. Dent and Sons, 1954). The novel originally appeared in serialized form during 1852–53. The case on which it was based was that of William Jennings, who died in 1798, leaving an estate worth millions.

2. Editorial, "A Losing Initiative Prevailing in Forests," *Santa Rosa Press-Democrat*, March 8, 1991; Office of the Governor of California, "Wilson Proposes Resourceful California — Major Environmental Plan 'To Invest in Our Children's Natural Inheritance,'" press release, April 22, 1991.

3. Manny Frishberg, "Pacific Lumber Calls Off Harvest in Marbled Murrelet Habitat," *Northern Mendocino Life and Times* (July 1992). California declared the marbled murrelet endangered in December 1991. See Karen Jeffries, "New 'Endangered' Bird," *Eureka Times-Standard*, December 8, 1991.

4. Frishberg, "Pacific Lumber Calls Off Harvest"; John Campbell, interviews.

5. The man who walks in the woods, "What's Happening in Owl Creek?," mimeo.; November 6, 1992.

6. Mike Geniella, "Pacific Lumber Wins Round in Owl Creek Fight," *Santa Rosa Press-Democrat*, November 24, 1992; Wayne S. White, field supervisor, U.S. Fish and Wildlife Service, to attorney Mark P. Harris, November 29, 1992; Mike Geniella, "Owl Creek Logging Challenged," *Santa Rosa Press-Democrat*, November 29, 1992; Karen Jeffries, "Garberville Environmentalist Group to Appeal Dismissal of PL Lawsuit," *Eureka Times-Standard*, November 28, 1992; Ron Sonenshine, "Protesters Arrested at Redwood Forest," *San Francisco Chronicle*, December 1, 1992.

7. Karen Jeffries, "PL Begins Harvesting Old Growth," *Eureka Times-Standard*, November 30, 1992; Mike Geniella, "Removal of Downed Logs Sought," *Santa Rosa Press-Democrat*, March 11, 1993; Karen Jeffries, "Federal Agency Joins Timber Talks," *Eureka Times-Standard*, November 25, 1992; Mike Geniella, "U.S. Wildlife Agency Raps Pacific Lumber," *Santa Rosa Press-Democrat*, December 1, 1992; Maitland Zane, "Judge Halts Timber Harvesting," *San Francisco Chronicle*, December 2, 1992; Karen Jeffries, "Federal Probe to Determine If PL Logging Violated Rules," *Eureka Times-Standard*, December 4, 1992; Mike Geniella, "Chasing Paper Trail in Cutting by Pacific Lumber," *Santa Rosa Press-Democrat*, December 8, 1992; Karen Jeffries, "PL Chief Defends Logging Decision," *Eureka Times-Standard*, December 9, 1992; Jessie A. Faulkner, "Courts Grant Permanent

Stay on PALCO's Owl Creek Logging," *Southern Humboldt Life and Times*, March 9, 1993.

8. U.S. Fish and Wildlife supervisor Wayne S. White to Don Forman, editor of the Sierra Club *Yodeler*, February 4, 1993; Karen Jeffries, "Probe of PL Will Take Time," *Eureka Times-Standard*, February 13, 1993.

9. Bill Israel, "Headwaters Forest Deal Near," *North Coast Journal* (February 1991); Richard C. Paddock, "Wilson's Formula to Save Redwoods," *Los Angeles Times*, April 22, 1991; Mike Geniella, "Activists to Create Own Timber Plan," *Santa Rosa Press-Democrat*, March 1, 1991; Associated Press, "Wilson Aide to Visit Headwaters," *Eureka Times-Standard*, March 28, 1991; Steve Hart, "Assembly OKs Bills to Slow Logging," *Santa Rosa Press-Democrat*, June 6, 1991.

10. Kevin Kean, "PL Slams Bill on Forced Sale," *Santa Rosa Press-Democrat*, September 11, 1992; William Kahri, "Logjam at Headwaters," *Sacramento Bee*, August 27, 1992; Mary Frishberg, "Time Runs Out for Possible Headwaters Forest Buy-Out," *Humboldt/Northern Mendocino Life and Times*, October 13, 1992.

11. "Statement of Rep. Jim Jontz on the Introduction of the Ancient Forest Protection Act of 1991," press release, January 31, 1991; Editorial, "Jim Jontz National Park," *Washington Times*, February 27, 1991; "De La Garza Introduces Old-Growth Forest Bill for Markup," news release, April 9, 1992.

12. This is the author's own count, intended to be conservative. See Victor M. Sher and Andy Stahl, "Spotted Owls, Ancient Forests, Courts, and Congress: An Overview of Citizens' Efforts to Protect Old-Growth Forests and the Species That Live in Them," *Northwest Environmental Journal* 6 (1990); National Audubon Society Ancient Forest Campaign, "Ancient Forest Chronology," n.d.; Northwest Forest Resource Council (NFRC), legal updates, 1990–91; Sierra Club Legal Defense Fund, "Chronology: Northwest Old-Growth Litigation and Related Developments," n.d.; Melanie J. Rowland, "Spotted Owl Litigation Primer," Washington Environmental Council, November 5, 1991.

13. Sher and Stahl, "Spotted Owls, Ancient Forests"; NFRC, legal updates; Steven Lewis Yaffee, *The Wisdom of the Spotted Owl* (Washington, D.C.: Island Press, 1994).

14. Tom Kenworthy, "Lujan to Assemble Panel to Study Spotted Owl–Timber Industry Issue," *Washington Post*, October 2, 1991; Associated Press, "Owl Plan May Be Withdrawn," *Livingston Enterprise*, January 16, 1992.

15. Audubon Society, "Chronology"; NFRC, legal updates; Yaffee, *Wisdom of the Owl.*

16. Ralph Saperstein, Northwest Forest Resource Council, interviews, 1994; Yaffee, *Wisdom of the Owl.*

17. Audubon Society, "Chronology"; NFRC, legal updates.

18. Todd True, Seattle Sierra Club Legal Defense Fund, interview, 1994; U.S. District Court, District of Western Washington, *Seattle Audubon Society et al. v. John L. Evans et al.*, decided January 14, 1994; U.S. District Court, Western District of Washington, order approving settlement of plaintiffs' motion for attorneys' fees, *Northern Spotted Owl v. Manuel Lujan*; U.S. District Court for the District of Oregon, stipulated order, *Lane County Audubon Society v. Michael Dombek et al.*, signed August 4, 1994; U.S. Court of Appeals for the Ninth Circuit, *Portland Audubon Society v. Endangered Species Committee*, certificate of service, filed June 10, 1992 (original amount requested was $319,138.94); U.S. District Court for the District

of Oregon, order for fees and expenses under the Equal Access to Justice Act, *Portland Audubon Society* v. *Manuel Lujan*, October 31, 1994.

19. Ted Rohrlich, "State Drop in Logging Mostly Tied to Owls," *Mendocino Press-Democrat*, January 11, 1993; Paul Ehinger, interviews; Ehinger and Associates, "Lumber Production and Timber Volume under Contract, USFS Regions 2 and 3, 1988–92"; Ehinger and Associates, "Timber Volume under Contract — USFS/BLM Ore., Wash., and Calif.," December 1993; Ehinger and Associates, "Timber Sold USFS/BLM-FY91–93, Avg. Annual Harvest USFS/BLM CY 1991–92," November 1993; Ehinger and Associates, "Plywood/Panel Production, Western U.S.," November 1993; "Lumber Production, Comparison — Coast and Inland, 1984–94," October 1993.

20. Paul F. Ehinger and Associates, "Oregon/Washington/Idaho/California Mill Closures," December 1993; Ehinger and Associates, "Plants in Operation," December 10, 1993.

21. U.S. Court of Appeals, *Sweet Home Chapter of Communities for a Great Oregon et al.* v. *Bruce Babbitt, Secretary of the Interior et al.*, argued February 17, 1993; decided March 11, 1993; Kathie Durbin, "Court Sides with Timber Industry," *The Oregonian*, March 12, 1994.

22. The books that best describe the personal accounts of those who formed the Wise Use Movement are Robert G. Lee, *Broken Trust, Broken Land* (Wilsonville, Ore.: BookPartners, 1994); and William Perry Pendley, *It Takes a Hero* (Bellevue, Wash.: Free Enterprise Press, 1994). For other examples of this backlash, see Dixie Lee Rae with Lee Guzzo, *Trashing the Planet* (Washington, D.C.: Regnery Gateway, 1990); and Ron Arnold and Alan Gottlieb, *Trashing the Economy* (Bellevue, Wash.: Free Enterprise Press, 1993).

23. Tom Hirons, Chuck Cushman, and Dave Howard, interviews; Jackie Land and Judy Marr, "200 Citizens Take to the Hill to Put Faces on Timber Facts, Figures," Northwest Citizens Lobby, September 11, 1990; Northwest Forestry Association, "NW Citizens Lobby Trip a Success," *Forestry Forum*, September 16, 1990; Michael Satchell, "Any Color but Green," *U.S. News and World Report*, October 21, 1991.

24. Wilderness Society, *Report on the Wise Use Movement*, 2d printing, rev., March 1993.

25. Carl Deal, *The Greenpeace Guide to Anti-Environmental Organizations* (Berkeley: Odonian Press, 1993). pp. 7, 11. See also David Helvarg, *The War Against the Greens* (San Francisco: Sierra Club Books, 1994).

26. This account is drawn from Environmental Grantmakers Association, 1992 fall retreat, "North American Forests: Coping with Multiple Use and Abuse," "Media Strategies for Environmental Protection," and "The Wise Use Movement: Threats and Opportunities." Taped by the Conference Recording Service, October 3–5, 1992. In 1991 the reported income of the Oregon Lands Coalition was $107,857.

27. Bill Bertain, interviews.

28. Allan Sloan, "A Shady Bond Proposal That Makes One Pine for the 1980s," *Los Angeles Times*, January 17, 1993; Mike Geniella, "Pacific Lumber Co. Strikes Back at Environmentalists," *Santa Rosa Press-Democrat*, March 5, 1993; Karen Jeffries, "PL Refinancing Told, Company Pays Off Merger Debt," *Eureka Times-Standard*, March 25, 1993.

29. Bertain, interviews.

1. Based in part on Douglas Gantenbein, eyewitness report, *Outside* (April 1993); "Ancient Forest Protection Advocates Announce Summit Rally with Music and Speakers," press release, March 25, 1993; "Spirits Soar as Clinton Visit Nears," *Network News*, March 26, 1993.
2. Gantenbein, report; Douglas Gantenbein with Ned Martel, "Enjoy the Chat, Mr. President. Now What?," *Outside* (June 1993).
3. "Rally for the Real People," *Forestry Forum*, April 8, 1993; Gantenbein, report.
4. John Balzar, "Clinton Acts to Break Logjam over Northwest Timberlands," *Los Angeles Times*, March 11, 1993; "The Birds and the Trees: Clinton Convenes Summit on the Spotted Owl," *Newsweek*, April 5, 1993.
5. Elliot Diringer, "Clinton Announces Summit on Forests of Pacific Northwest," *San Francisco Chronicle*, March 11, 1993; Karen Jeffries, "Guarded Hopes for Summit," *Eureka Times-Standard*, March 11, 1993; Les Blumenthal and Michael Doyle, "Can Forest Foes' Meeting in Portland End Logjam?," *Sacramento Bee*, March 11, 1993; Jeff Pelline, "Timber Summit Promises to Be Hornet's Nest for Clinton," *San Francisco Chronicle*, March 11, 1993; President Bill Clinton to Chadwick Oliver, March 27, 1993.
6. Bill Clinton to United Brotherhood of Carpenters and Joiners of America, August 25, 1992; "Clinton Outlines Transition Process for Pacific Northwest Forest Summit," press release, December 18, 1992.
7. Dennis Jensen, "New Director in Touch with Nature," *Washington Times*, May 27, 1993; Ted Gup, "Beattie's Battle," *Audubon Magazine* (March–April 1994); Department of the Interior, U.S. Fish and Wildlife Service, "Mollie Beattie Sworn in as U.S. Fish and Wildlife Service Director," September 23, 1993.
8. This concern with growing congressional opposition to environmental legislation was articulated in March 1994 by environmental lobbyists, who, borrowing a phrase from Al Gore, blamed this resistance on the "unholy trinity" — concern about property rights, rejection of unfunded mandates, and demands that all environmental legislation be subject to cost-benefit analysis. See memorandum, "Draft Legislation Strategy Paper Developed by Environmental Group Lobbyists," March 4, 1994.
9. Steven Lewis Yaffee, *The Wisdom of the Spotted Owl* (Washington, D.C.: Island Press, 1994), pp. 133ff.; U.S. Department of Agriculture, Forest Service, and U.S. Department of the Interior, Fish and Wildlife Service and National Park Service, *Final Supplemental Environmental Impact Statement on Management Habitat for Late-Successional and Old-Growth Forest Related Species within the Range of the Northern Spotted Owl*, February 1994.
10. The White House, "The Forest Conference," agenda, April 2, 1993; Tom Kenworthy, "The Owl and the Lumberjack: Can Clinton Break the Logjam?," *Washington Post*, April 2, 1993; Don Hamilton and Kathie Durbin, "Diverse Group Due for Forest Meeting, *Oregonian*, March 31, 1993; Associated Press, "Clinton Convenes Forest Summit," *Bozeman Daily Chronicle*, April 2, 1993; Associated Press, "Clinton Arrives in Portland, Ore.," *Livingston Enterprise*, April 2, 1993; "Hope Offered in Forest Fry," *Oregonian*, April 3, 1993; Federal Ecosystem Management Assessment Team (FEMAT), *Forest Ecosystem Management: An Ecological, Economic, and Social Assessment*, July 1993.
11. Transcript of proceedings before the Honorable Thomas P. Jackson, U.S.

District Court, *Northwest Forest Resource Council v. Mike Espy, Secretary of Agriculture,* March 4, 1994.

12. Jack Ward Thomas to Chadwick Oliver, May 14, 1993; Oliver to Thomas, May 19, 1993; Oliver to Thomas, May 25, 1993; Oliver to Thomas, May 27, 1993; Chadwick Oliver, interviews; "An Alternative to the President's Proposal for Managing Pacific Northwest Federal Forest Lands, *Evergreen* (October 1993).

13. Chadwick Oliver to President Bill Clinton, April 19, 1993; Clinton to Oliver, April 26, 1993; Oliver, interviews; "An Alternative to the President's Proposal"; Rob Taylor, "NW Can Have Jobs and Owls, Professor Says," *Seattle Post-Intelligencer,* April 1, 1993.

14. "An Alternative to the President's Proposal."

15. Kathie Durbin, "Report Outrages Environmentalists," *Oregonian,* June 18, 1993; "Outraged Loggers Reject Plan," *Seattle Post Intelligencer,* June 18, 1993.

16. .ent.

17. Memorandum from Lesin England of the Sierra Club to fellow environmentalists, "Forest Update," June 14, 1993; memorandum from Jim Owens to Ancient Forest Activists, "Oppose Number Nine," June 15, 1993.

18. Dana Tims, "Environmentalist, Industry Hit Plan for Restoring Owl Habitat," *Oregonian,* October 14, 1993; "President's (Staff's) Forest Plan," *Forestry Forum,* June 25, 1993; "The Forest Plan," *Forestry Forum,* July 9, 1993; William McKillop, "An Economic Analysis of the FEMAT Report," mimeo., October 26, 1993.

19. *Northwest Forest Resource Council v. Espy;* "Industry Files Flurry of Suits," *Forestry Forum,* August 6, 1993; "Jack Ward Thomas Team Met Illegally," *Forestry Forum,* August 6, 1993.

20. Robert Taylor and Stephen Rosenzweig, interviews.

21. Daniel Botkin, interview; Daniel Botkin et al., *Status and Future of Salmon of Western Oregon and Northern California* (Santa Barbara, Calif.: Center for the Study of the Environment, 1994).

22. "An Alternative to the President's Proposal"; Statement of Chadwick D. Oliver before Subcommittee on Agricultural Research, Conservation, Forestry, and General Legislation, November 9, 1993. See also Chadwick Dearing Oliver, "Comments on 'Draft Supplemental Environmental Impact Statement on Management of Habitat for Late-Successional and Old-Growth Forest Related Species within the Range of the Northern Spotted Owl,'" October 1, 1993.

23. Department of Agriculture et al., *Final Supplemental Environmental Impact Statement.*

24. United Nations Environment Programme (UNEP), Preamble, *Convention on Biological Diversity,* June 5, 1992; William Clinton, *Message from the President of the United States Transmitting the Convention on Biological Diversity, with Annexes, Done at Rio de Janeiro, June 5, 1992, and Signed by the United States in New York on June 4, 1993* (Washington, D.C.: Government Printing Office, 1993). See also introduction, chapter 15, "Conservation of Biological Diversity." As of this writing, nearly two years after President Clinton had signed it, the U.S. Senate had not yet ratified the biodiversity treaty. Yet the administration had already created the infrastructure for carrying it out and continued to shape policies to implement it.

25. Memorandum, via the Internet, from William Pace, Executive Committee of the Citizens' Network for Sustainable Development, to APC Committee, August 3, 1993. The President's Council on Sustainable Development was

established on June 29, 1993, by Executive Order no. 12852. See "President's Council on Sustainable Development Seeks Public Comment on Principles of Sustainable Development for the U.S.," press release, May 16, 1994. Some of the information on implementation of the biodiversity treaty was obtained from various government agencies via the Internet.

26. Earl Baysinger, interviews; memorandum from NBS Implementation Team to NBS Steering Committee, May 18, 1993; Tom Kenworthy, "Reorganizing Science," *Washington Post*, June 13, 1993; U.S. Department of the Interior, "Scientific Research to Be Reorganized under National Biological Survey at Interior Department," press release, April 26, 1993; U.S. Department of the Interior, "The National Biological Survey: Integrating Biological Science at the Department of the Interior," April 26, 1993; Department of the Interior, "Questions on the National Biological Survey," n.d.; National Research Council, "Committee on the Formation of the National Biological Survey," release of report and public briefing, Tuesday, October 5, 1993.

27. Congressmen George Miller, Gerry E. Studds, and George E. Brown, "Vote No on the Taylor Amendment," House of Representatives, n.d.; Department of the Interior, "National Biological Survey, Authorizing Legislation Strategy," July 1, 1993. The Lovejoy quote came from several participants of the plenary session of the conference, "From Rio to the Capital: State Strategies for Sustainable Development," Louisville, May 1993.

28. Congressman Richard Pombo, "The National Biological Survey," press release, October 8, 1993.

29. Ibid.; Department of the Interior, "A Proposal to Establish a National Biological Survey within the Department of the Interior," mimeo., March 17, 1993; House of Representatives, "A Bill to establish the Biological Survey in the Department of the Interior," H.R. 1845, April 22, 1993; Congressmen Don Young et al., "Dissenting Views — H.R. 1845," n.d.; Bruce Babbitt, testimony before the House Merchant Marine and Fisheries Subcommittee on Environment and Natural Resources and the House Natural Resources Subcommittee on National Parks, Forests, and Public Lands on H.R. 1845, the National Biological Survey Act of 1993," July 15, 1993; memorandum from Department of the Interior chief of staff to assistant secretaries, "Implementation Team Proposed for National Biological Survey," March 12, 1993; Department of Interior, "Briefing — National Biological Survey Legislation," draft, July 26, 1993.

30. Department of the Interior, Bureau of Land Management, "Special Issue Briefing Papers Prepared for the BLM Summit," April 30, 1994; Environmental Protection Agency, "Background on NPR Efforts," *Creating a U.S. Environmental Protection Agency That Works Better and Costs Less — Phase II Report, National Performance Review*, December, 1993; memorandum from Robert Perciasepe, David Gardiner, and Jonathan Cannon to Environmental Protection Agency administrator Carol Browner, "Ecosystem Protection," March 15, 1994.

31. Perciasepe et al., memorandum; Environmental Protection Agency, "Toward a Place-Driven Approach: The Edgewater Consensus on an EPA Strategy for Ecosystem Protection," draft, May 15, 1994. The Biological Survey is already making use of the Nature Conservancy's Natural Heritage Program, which was started in 1974. Installed in fifty states, the program is building a database which it operates in cooperation with public agencies. Its purpose is to find threatened and endangered species, as well as to count every creature, no matter how small, down to microscopic diatoms, thus identifying targets for acquisition or regulation. A unit of this system, for example, the

Greater Yellowstone Conservation Data Center in Yellowstone National Park, is cataloguing all plants and animals on public and private lands within the "greater Yellowstone area," which spreads into three states. Although funded by the Conservancy, it is located at park headquarters, where the federal government provides housing, office, and other logistical support at taxpayers' expense.

32. Perciasepe et al., memorandum; Frank Salwerowicz, "Mineral Development and Ecosystem Management: The Role of BLM Minerals Staff," draft, April 12, 1994. U.S. Environmental Protection Agency, "Executive Summary, National Performance Review: Ecosystem Protection," August 6, 1993; Environmental Protection Agency, *Creating a U.S. Environmental Protection Agency That Works Better and Costs Less — Phase I Report,* December 1993, pp. EP4, 11–12.

33. The scheduling of the workshop is explained in the memorandum from Larry Irwin to Chris West, March 3, 1994 and was confirmed by the author with several workshop participants.

34. Memorandum from Barry Mulder to Dave Anderson, "Application of the Demographic Workshop," December 16, 1990.

35. Robert Taylor, interview. See Northwest Forest Resource Council, "Comments Submitted to the U.S. Fish and Wildlife Service Regarding the Status Review Supplement, Revised Finding, and Proposed Rule Determining the Northern Spotted Owl as a Threatened Species," December 20, 1989.

36. Memorandum from Robert Taylor to Demography Workshop participants, "Impressions of the Workshop," December 15, 1993.

37. Memorandum, Irwin to West.

38. Department of the Interior, Fish and Wildlife Service, "Spotted Owl Takings Suit, Washington Version, Northwest Forest Resource Council," legal update no. 155, December 22, 1993.

39. Bill Arsenault and Dan Newton, interviews, March 1994; Jeff Mize, "A Nest Egg Ready to Fall," *Roseburg News-Review,* January 16, 1994; Bill Arsenault, "New Eco-Socialism Hurts Responsible Timber Managers," *Roseburg News-Review,* January 23, 1994. Newton was the 1993 winner of the Douglas Small-Woodland Association's "Tree Farmer of the Year" award.

40. Editorial, "New Rule Would Be Bitter Blow," *Roseburg News-Review,* January 23, 1994; Senator Mark Hatfield et al. to Secretary of the Interior Bruce Babbitt, March 17, 1994; "4(d) Proposal Released," Northwest Forest Resource Council, legal update no. 154, December 1, 1993.

CHAPTER 29. THE INFERNO

1. Larry Robertson, interview, November 17, 1994.

2. Cherie Girod, interview, November 8, 1994.

3. Tom Hirons and Judi Bari, interviews.

4. Kathie Durbin, "Court Sides with Timber Industry," *Oregonian,* March 12, 1994; Brad Knickerbocker, "Dangers to Animals in Wild Need Proof, U.S. Court Says," *Christian Science Monitor,* March 14, 1994; Ike C. Sugg, "Defining 'Harm' to Wildlife," *National Law Journal,* June 20, 1994; Ike C. Sugg, "Worried about That Owl on Your Land? Here's the Good News," *Wall Street Journal,* April 6, 1994; Northwest Forest Resource Council, "NFRC Wins FEMAT Suit!," legal update no. 161, March 21, 1994; NFRC, "Judge Unhappy with Administration," legal update no. 164, March 25, 1994.

5. Salomon Brothers, "The Pacific Lumber Co. — the Standard for Comparison!," *United States Corporate Bond Research, Building/Wood Products,* June 24, 1993, p. 4. Palco's willingness to sell large acreage of Headwaters was a sudden reversal. As late as the fall of 1993, it still opposed the buyout. See John A. Campbell, testimony before U.S. Congress, Subcommittee on Specialty Crops and Natural Resources, October 13, 1994. Information on Hurwitz's meeting with Gore came from confidential sources; see also Allen R. Myerson, "The Investor Charles Hurwitz May Be Clearing Up Some Feuds," *New York Times,* July 14, 1994; Derrick DePledge, "Bid for Early Headwaters Vote Fails," *Santa Rosa Press-Democrat,* August 17, 1994; letter to former Pacific Lumber Company stockholders from attorney Richard M. Burnham, regarding settlement of *Thompson v. Maxxam,* June 13, 1994; David Anderson, "PL, Maxxam Settle Fraud Suit," *Eureka Times-Standard,* May 19, 1994; Agis Salpukas, "Maxxam Reaches Pact in Shareholders' Suits," *New York Times,* May 18, 1994; Mike Geniella, "N. Coast Timber Bill OK Likely," *Santa Rosa Press-Democrat,* August 16, 1994; "Committee Approves Headwaters Legislation," *Humboldt Beacon,* July 21, 1994; Associated Press, "High Court Blocks PL Timber Cut," *Eureka Times-Standard,* July 22, 1994; Marc Selinger, "House Votes to Purchase Headwaters Forest," *Santa Rosa Press-Democrat,* September 22, 1994; Manny Frishberg, "PALCO Agrees to Accept Headwaters Forest Bill," *Redwood Record,* August 23, 1994.
6. John Skow, "Redwoods: The Last Stand," *Time,* June 6, 1994.
7. U.S. Department of Agriculture, Forest Service, U.S. Department of the Interior, Bureau of Land Management, *Record of Decision, for Amendment to Forest Service and Bureau of Land Management Planning Documents within the Range of the Northern Spotted Owl,* April 1994.
8. Memorandum from environmental group lobbyists through Erik Oxson, NRDC, to John Adams et al., "Draft Legislation Strategy Paper Developed by Environmental Group Lobbyists," March 4, 1994.
9. "Endangered Species Blueprint," *NWI Resource* 5, no. 1 (Fall 1994).
10. Charles C. Mann and Mark L. Plummer, *Noah's Choice: The Future of Endangered Species* (New York: Alfred A. Knopf, 1995). See also General Accounting Office, *Endangered Species: Management Improvement Could Enhance Recovery Program,* GAO/RCED-89-5, December 1988; U.S. Department of the Interior, *The Endangered Species Program, U.S. Fish and Wildlife Service,* audit report no. 90-98, September 1990.
11. "Endangered Species Blueprint"; Tom Kenworthy, "Administration Moves to Ease Opposition to Biodiversity Act," *Washington Post,* June 15, 1994. Despite repeated inquiries, neither the Fish and Wildlife Service nor the Congressional Research Service could provide information on either expenditures to date or estimated future costs. These figures, however, are consistent with both the 1990 Interior Department Inspector General audit and with figures supplied by Charles C. Mann and Mark L. Plummer in their January 1992 *Atlantic* article, "The Butterfly Problem," which lists the northern spotted owl as the most expensive creature on the list to date ($9.7 million in direct expenditures).
12. "Endangered Species Blueprint."
13. Interviews with Robert Lee and Jim Cotes of Grays Harbor food bank, December 1994.
14. Paul F. Ehinger, interview, January 24, 1995; American Forest and Paper Association, "The 1995 Outlook for the Lumber and Wood Products Industry," technical bulletin no. 94-5, December 1994.

15. Ehinger, interview, October 5, 1994. Timber sales on Northwest public lands were 7.8 billion board feet in 1988 and 1.2 billion in 1993. See Paul F. Ehinger and Associates, "Forest Products Industry Report on Mill Closures, Operations, and Other Related Information," December 1993. See also William McKillop, "An Economic Analysis of the FEMAT Report," mimeo., October 26, 1993; Forest and Paper Association, "1995 Outlook"; "Federal Volume Continues Decline — States Inch Upward," NFRC Timber Facts (December 1994).

16. "Record High Lumber Prices Hurt Gains in Housing Starts," NFRC Timber Facts (January–February 1994); Ehinger and Associates, "Industry Report, 1993"; Chadwick Oliver to President Bill Clinton, April 19, 1993.

17. B. Lippke and C. Oliver, "An Economic Tradeoff System for Ecosystem Management," in Eastside Forest Ecosystem Health Assessment, U.S. Forest Research, 1993; Roger A. Sedjo, "The Global Environmental Effects of Local Logging Cutbacks," Resources (Fall 1994); John M. Perez-Garcia, "Global Forestry Impacts of Reducing Softwood Supplies from North America," draft, Center for International Trade in Forest Products, University of Washington, May 14, 1993.

18. Associated Press, "Private Timber Sales Increasing, Environmental Dangers Loom, Say the Experts," Bozeman Daily Chronicle, March 28, 1994; Paul F. Ehinger and Associates, "Forest Products Industry Report on Mill Closures, Operations, and Other Related Information," July–August 1994.

19. Tom Kenworthy, "Wilderness Society President Sold Timber Cut on His Montana Ranch," Washington Post, April 17, 1995; David Bond, "Activist Defends Own Log Cuts," Coeur D'Alene Press, December 5, 1993; Livingston Enterprise, March 24, 1994.

20. Forest and Paper Association, "1995 Outlook"; Ehinger and Associates, "Report, July–August 1994."

21. National Commission on Wildfire Disasters, report, 1994.

22. General Accounting Office, Federal Lands: Information on Land Owned and on Acreage with Conservation Restrictions (Washington, D.C.: U.S. Government Printing Office, 1995). Information on amount authorized for the California Desert Wilderness came from House Subcommittee on Parks and Public Lands, January 8, 1995. Department of the Interior, U.S. Fish and Wildlife Service, An Ecosystem Approach to Fish and Wildlife Conservation, March 1994; Department of the Interior, Bureau of Land Management, "Special Issue Briefing Papers Prepared for the BLM Summit," April 30, 1994 (emphasis added).

23. For example, the task of implementing section 10 of the treaty was delegated in part to two staffers of the World Resources Institute. See Kenton Miller and Nels Johnson, "Global Biodiversity Assessment Section 10: Measures for Conservation of Biodiversity and Sustainable Use of Its Components," draft, September 2, 1994.

24. Ibid.

25. Associated Press, "Clinton's Logging Plan for Northwest Upheld," Washington Times, December 27, 1994; Forest Service et al., "Record of Decision," April 14, 1994; Tom Kenworthy, "Northwest Timber Sales Cleared, but Battle Over Owl Continues," Washington Post, June 7, 1994.

26. Forest Service et al., "Record of Decision."

27. Ibid.

28. Jan A. Henderson, "Trends in Amount of Old-Growth Forest for the Last 1,000 Years in Western Oregon and Washington," a peer-reviewed analysis prepared for National Forest Service chief F. Dale Robertson, November 19, 1990.

29. Bob Zybach, "Native Forests of the Douglas-Fir Region: A Brief History of the Forests of Western Washington and Oregon from Prehistoric Times to the Present," mimeo., March 29, 1994; "Voices in the Forest: An Interview with Bob Zybach," *Evergreen* (March–April, 1994). Other documentation strongly supporting Zybach's thesis appears in Peter D. A. Teensma, John R. Rienstra, and Mark A. Yeiter, "Preliminary Reconstruction and Analysis of Change in Forest Stand Age Classes of the Oregon Coast Range from 1850 to 1940," U.S. Department of the Interior, Bureau of Land Management, technical note T/N OR-9, October 1991. See also Russell G. Congalton, Kass Green, and John Teply, "Mapping Old Growth Forests on National Forest and Park Lands in the Pacific Northwest from Remotely Sensed Data," *Photogrammetric Engineering and Remote Sensing* 59, no. 4 (April 1993).

30. "Voices in the Forest." On the Native Americans' lack of interest in preserving forests, see Charles E. Kay, "Aboriginal Overkill and Native Burning: Implications for Modern Ecosystem Management," Eighth George Wright Society Conference on Research and Resource Management on Public Lands, Portland, Oregon, April 17–21, 1995; Charles E. Kay, "Aboriginal Overkill: The Role of Native Americans in Structuring Western Ecosystems," *Human Nature*, in press.

31. Forest Service, "Record of Decision." See also Gregg Easterbrook, "The Birds," *New Republic*, March 28, 1994; Federal Ecosystem Management Assessment Team (FEMAT), *Forest Ecosystem Management: An Ecological, Economic, and Social Assessment*, July 1993.

32. Associated Press, "California Owl Delisting Rejected," *GreenSpeak*, September 12, 1994.

33. Oregon Forest Resources Institute, survey, 1994. See also Oregon Business Council, *Oregon Values and Beliefs*, summary, May 1993.

34. Skow, "Redwoods: The Last Stand"; Associated Press, "Photo Crusade May Save Redwoods," *San Francisco Chronicle*, August 18, 1994.

35. Gerardo Segura, "Dynamics of Old-Growth Forests of *Abies amabilis* Impacted by Tephra from the 1980 Eruption of Mount Saint Helens, Washington" (Ph.D. diss., University of Washington, 1991); James A. Rochelle, "Natural Resource Recovery Following the 1980 Mount St. Helens Eruption: Lessons in Ecological Resilience," *Proceedings of the Fifty-Fifth North American Wildlife and Natural Resources Conference*, Denver, March 16–21, 1990; Weyerhaeuser Company, *Mount St. Helens: Weyerhaeuser's Reforestation*, December 1992.

36. Douglas W. MacCleery, *American Forests: A History of Resiliency and Recovery* (Durham, N.C.: Forest History Society, 1992); Douglas S. Powell et al., *Forest Resources of the United States, 1992*, General Technical Report RM-234 (Fort Collins, Colo.: Rocky Mountain Forest and Range Experiment Station, U.S. Department of Agriculture, Forest Service, 1993); Douglas S. Powell et al., *Forest Statistics of the United States, 1992* (Washington, D.C.: FIERR staff Report, Forest Service, 1993); Bruce R. Lippke, "Overcutting vs. Underutilization: Can We Narrow the Debate?," draft, Center for International Trade in Forest Products, University of Washington, April 1992. Jim Bowyer quoted in James Peterson, "Think Globally, Act Locally," *Evergreen* (Summer 1993).

37. Edwin Kiester, Jr., "A New Park Saves the Tall Trees, but at High Cost to the Community," *Smithsonian* (November 1993).

38. Figures obtained from R. Neil Sampson, executive vice president, American Forests, and member of the National Commission on Wildfire Disasters.

1. Interview with Peter M. Bourque, director, Fisheries and Hatcheries Division, Maine Department of Inland Fisheries and Wildlife, January 1990; portions of this chapter originally appeared in a column by the author, distributed by Universal Press Syndicate.

2. Maine Department of Inland Fisheries, "Pleasant Pond Lake Trout Study," January 8, 1975.

3. James Fenimore Cooper, The Prairie (New York: Holt, Rinehart and Winston, 1962), p. 290.

4. Dante Alighieri, The Divine Comedy, trans. John Ciardi (Oxford: Oxford University Press, 1985).

5. Arthur O. Lovejoy and George Boas, Primitivism and Related Ideas in Antiquity (Baltimore: Johns Hopkins University Press, 1935), pp. 11–12. See also John Passmore, Man's Responsibility for Nature (New York: Charles Scribner's Sons, 1974).

6. National Parks and Conservation Association, Report of the Commission on Research and Resource Management Policy in the National Park System, March 19, 1989, p. 4. William C. Fischer and Stephen F. Arno, Protecting People and Homes from Wildfire in the Interior West, U.S. Department of Agriculture, Forest Service, Intermountain Research Station, Ogden, Utah, General Technical Report no. 251, September 1988.

7. John Stossel, "Are We Scaring Ourselves to Death?," ABC News, April 21, 1994. For a criticism of this show, see "John Stossel's Brand of Libertarian Journalism," Environment Writer 6, no 10 (January 1995).

8. Christopher Lasch, "The Revolt of the Elites," Harper's (November 1994).

9. Isaiah Berlin, Two Concepts of Liberty (Oxford: Oxford University Press, 1958), pp. 7, 16, 52.

10. That is, value is the relative importance we confer on things, usually in contemplation of some action.

11. Lewis and Clark reported finding the Shoshone, who would soon wipe out buffalo on the Snake River plain, to be near starvation. The explorers also noted that most game was found in the areas between warring tribes, to which hunters had little access. These intertribal buffer zones played an important ecological role in pre-Columbian America. See Meriwether Lewis and William Clark, The History of the Lewis and Clark Expedition, ed. Elliot Coues (New York: Dover, 1993), 3:1197; C. M. Gates, ed., Five Fur Traders of the Northwest: Being the Narrative of Peter Pond and the Diaries of John Macdonnell, Archibald N. McLeod, Hugh Aries, and Thomas Conner (Minneapolis: University of Minnesota Press, 1933); G. B. Grinnell, The Fighting Cheyenne (Norman: University of Oklahoma Press, 1956); F. G. Roe, The North American Buffalo: A Critical Study of the Species in Its Wild State (Toronto: University of Toronto Press, 1951); Harold Hickerson, "The Virginia Deer and Intertribal Buffer Zones in the Upper Mississippi Valley," in Man and Culture in America: The Role of Animals in Human Ecological Adjustments, ed. A. Leeds and A. P. Bayda (Washington, D.C.: American Association for the Advancement of Science, 1978).

12. For the dangers of centralized management and the promise that localism holds for preservation, see David Dobbs and Richard Ober, The Northern Forest (White River Junction, Vt.: Chelsea Green, 1995); Alston Chase, "Greater Yellowstone and the Death and Rebirth of the National Parks Ideal," Orion Nature Quarterly (Summer 1989); Alston Chase, "The Janzen Heresy," Conde Nast Traveler (November 1989).

13. Interviews with Bill Coates, Steve Self, Frank Ferguson, Stephen Rosenzweig, and Robert Taylor.
14. The bureaucratic hurdles are not all gone, either. As this book goes to press, the Forest Service is considering seven management alternatives for this region. The Quincy proposal is merely one of these. See U.S. Forest Service, "Draft Environmental Impact Statement: Managing California Spotted Owl Habitat in the Sierra Nevada National Forests of California, An Ecosystem Approach," Pacific Southwest Region, January 1995.
15. Rosenzweig and Taylor, interviews.
16. Self and Rosenzweig, interview. See also Forest Service, "Managing California Spotted Owl Habitat."
17. Interviews with Dennis Martinez, Kenneth M. Margolis, and Jack Shipley. See Michael E. Colby, "An Eco-Accounting System for Willapa and Willapa Ecosystem Human Activities Assessment," December 1991; Spencer B. Beebe and Elliot Marks, "The Willapa Bay, Washington, Ecosystem Restoration and Development Program Case Statement," mimeo., October 30, 1990; Dennis Rogers-Martinez, "The Sinkyone Intertribal Park Project," *Restoration and Management Notes* 10, no. 1 (Summer 1992); Dennis Martinez, "Back to the Future: An Ecological Restoration, The Historical Forest, and Traditional Indian Stewardship," presented at the Watershed Perspective on Native Plants conference, Olympia, Wash., February 26, 1993; Dennis Martinez, "Response to AMS (BLM)," for the Intertribal Sinkyone Wilderness Council, Coyote Valley Reservation, Redwood Valley, California, n.d.; M. Kat Anderson, "At Home in the Wilderness," *Native California* 6, no. 2 (Spring 1992); Jack Shipley et al., prospectus, *Applegate Partnership*, founded October 1992.

INDEX

Coniferous forest biome investigations, xviii, 101, 139, 159
Conning and Company, 213–14
Conrad, Joseph, 58
Conservation
  ecosystem approach to, 312
  vs. preservation, 42
Conservation Council, 359
Conservation Foundation, 355
Conservation movement, 3–4, 42
  confrontational environmentalism as sequel to, 51
  and Endangered Species Act (1966), 85–86
  and Pacific Lumber, 68, 70
  and Save the Redwoods League, 45–51
  vs. stewardship, 112
  upper-class perspectives in, 42, 45–47, 343–44
"Constant change" program, 304
Convention on International Trade in Endangered Species of Wild Fauna and Flora (CITES), 89
Convention on Nature Protection and Wildlife Preservation in the Western Hemisphere (1940), 85, 92
Convention for Protection of Migratory Birds (1916), 84
Convention for the Protection of Migratory Birds and Game Mammals (1936), 85
Cooper, James Fenimore, 410
Coos Bay Wagon Road Reconveyed Lands, 19
Coote Valley Reservation, 420
Copernicus and Copernican Revolution (Kant), 258–59
Coronado, Ron, 236
Corporate raider, Hurwitz as, 204
Council on Environmental Quality, 74
Council on Sustainable Development, 389
Counterculture, 64–65, 142–43, 187–88, 345
  at Breitenbush Springs, 220
  in Foreman's resignation, 342
  guerrilla theater, 65, 182, 183–84, 187
  at Round River Rendezvous, 290, 340–41
  Woodstock, 347
Crimes, environmental, 367–68, 393. See also Moral exclusion
Cunner, 410

Cutting, 15, 16
Cybernetics, and ecology, 99, 102, 103–4, 116, 361, 362

Dante, The Divine Comedy, 411
Darling, Jay Norwood ("Ding"), 42
Darwin, Charles, 27, 46, 96, 117
Dasmann, Raymond, 50
Davis, Margaret Bryan, 157
Davis, Mark, 291, 292
Davis, Pam, 297, 310, 317, 319, 326
Debonis, Jeff, 279–80, 378
Deep ecology, xix, 120, 129, 188–89, 199, 428n.29
  and animal rights, 195
  and Cartesian dualism, 199–201
  Foundation for, 354
Defenders of Wildlife, 256, 288
Dellums, Ronald, 324, 328, 338
Delphi approach, 313
Democracy
  economic defense of, 240
  and ideology during WWII, 59
Demographics, 251, 365, 392
Denevan, William M., 222
Denson, Ed, 326
Department of Defense, 390
Department of Energy, 390
Descartes, René, 57
Desert Wilderness bill, 402
Devall, Bill, xix, 119, 120, 126–27, 129, 188, 189, 197–98, 257, 259, 342, 345, 354
Diamond, Jared, 114, 363
Dickens, Charles, 370
Dingell, John, 79, 80, 81, 87, 90, 104, 115, 150, 265
Dioxin, 265, 304, 362
Dispersed patch clear-cutting, 35–36, 153
Divine Comedy, The (Dante), 411
Don't Make a Wave Committee, 64, 433n.2
Douglas, William O., 44
Douglas fir, 8, 22, 23, 31–32
  in British Columbia, 107
  and clear-cutting, 30–32, 33, 36
  extent of, 71, 224
  and Isaac's analysis, 35–36
  litigation on, 372–73
  and maximum sustained yield, 72, 73
  and old-growth study, 152–55